Documentary Report
of the Ann Arbor Symposium

Contents

x

Session I
OCTOBER 30–NOVEMBER 2, 1978

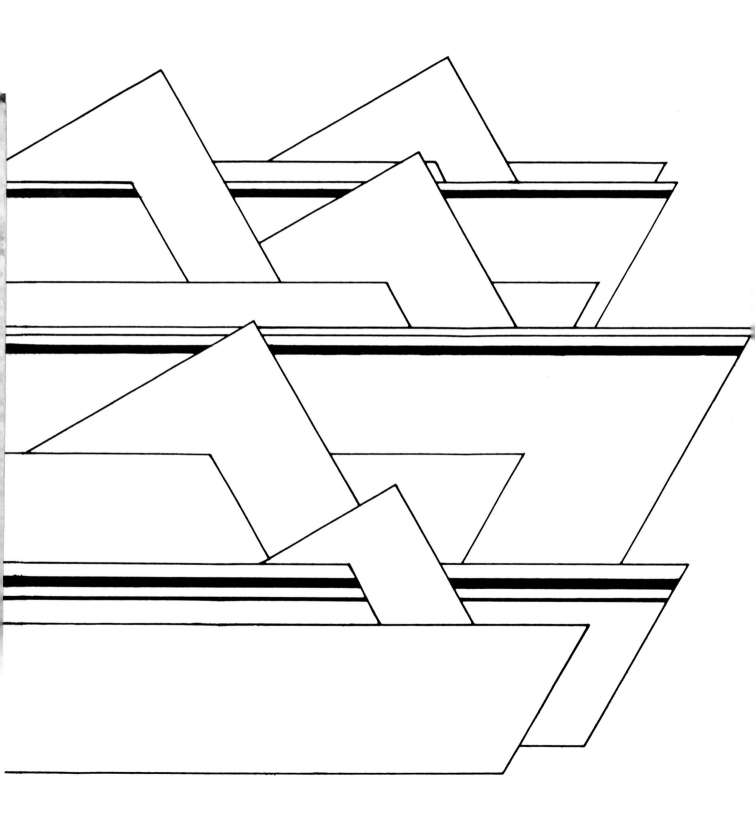

Auditory Perception: Concerns for Musical Learning

James C. Carlsen

What we know, we have learned from information received through our senses. We may be able to imagine, to believe, to speculate, or to predict without direct recourse to sensory modalities, but when we seek confirmation, when we strive to *know*, we depend upon our perception of sensory information.

Perception is the extraction of information contained in the structure of a stimulus in the perceptual field. These stimuli may consist of the time and space boundaries of the perceptual field, the objects that appear in that space, or the events that occur over time. The perceptual field includes objects and events that exist outside of a person (exteroceptive phenomena), but may also involve things and events within the person (interoceptive and proprioceptive phenomena).

Music is a sonic phenomenon and, as such, is a time-dependent event. What we know about music, we know because we can listen and perceive sonic sensations. The perceptual field for music events is both exteroceptive and interoceptive, for not only are we able to hear music from external sources, but we are also able internally to hear music remembered or in the process of creation (Roederer, 1974). The information derived from the stucture of such stimuli is used to discriminate that event from others, to recognize the event if it has been heard before, or to identify the event by naming or describing the critical attributes of the structure.

The initial sensation of the event that attracts our attention is also time-dependent. It may occur as a result of the onset of the music, a structural change during the course of the music event, or termination of the musical sound. The information we extract from the event can be influenced by (1) the transmission medium; (2) the perceptual environment; or (3) the perceiver characteristics: proximity to the event, interest in the event, knowledge and skill with the event, or expectancy patterns for the event.

When we attempt to use auditory perceptual information for discrimination judgments, we utilize some "sound ideal" or

Documentary Report of the Ann Arbor Symposium

*National Symposium on the
Applications of Psychology to the
Teaching and Learning of Music*

MUSIC EDUCATORS NATIONAL CONFERENCE
Reston, Virginia

Copy editing by Rebecca Grier Taylor, MENC;
editorial production by Blue Pencil Group, Reston, Virginia;
cover design by Joseph Scopin.

Music Educators National Conference
1902 Association Drive
Reston, Virginia 22091

**The Ann Arbor Symposium
was sponsored by**

Music Educators National Conference
National Committee on Instruction
Music Education Research Council

The University of Michigan
School of Music
Center for Research on Learning
   and Teaching

Supported by a grant from the
Theodore Presser Foundation
Philadelphia

JAMES A. MASON, *Symposium Chairman*
President, 1978–1980
Music Educators National Conference

PAUL R. LEHMAN, *Project Director*
The University of Michigan

ALLEN P. BRITTON, *Dean, School of Music*
The University of Michigan
(First Symposium Session)

PAUL C. BOYLAN, *Dean, School of Music*
The University of Michigan
(Second Symposium Session)

WILBERT J. MCKEACHIE, *Director*
Center for Research on Learning and Teaching
The University of Michigan

MORRIS DUANE, *President*
Theodore Presser Foundation

Foreword

Interest in the study of the teaching-learning process has increased considerably during the past decade. Much of this activity has not been well publicized, and consequently the results have not become widely known among educators in the various subject-matter fields. Even when teachers have read of such work, they have often found it difficult to translate the abstract writings of psychologists into improved practice in the classroom.

Music educators at all levels have felt a particularly acute need to become aware of the implications of current learning theory for the teaching of their discipline. Because music is a field involving an unusually wide variety of cognitive, affective, and psychomotor learnings, it provides a uniquely useful framework for the study of the teaching-learning process.

The National Symposium on the Applications of Psychology to the Teaching and Learning of Music was sponsored jointly by Music Educators National Conference and The University of Michigan and was made possible by a grant from the Theodore Presser Foundation. It was held on the campus of The University of Michigan in Ann Arbor in two sessions of four days each, October 30 to November 2, 1978, and July 30 to August 2, 1979.

Six priority topics were selected as a means of organizing the presentations and discussion of Session I: (1) auditory perception, (2) motor learning, (3) child development, (4) cognitive skills, (5) memory and information processing, and (6) affect and motivation. For each topic, a team consisting of two music educators and two psychologists was assembled. Thus, the original Symposium panel comprised twenty-four persons (and two of the papers had coauthors as well). By the time of the second session a substitute panelist had been appointed and each psychologist had been assigned a specific, individual topic. A Needs and Issues Team was formed to summarize the major needs identified and the most critical issues raised at Session I. After Session II the Needs and Issues Team identified what remained to be accomplished and made recommendations for the future. A Dissemination Team was also appointed to provide leadership in the effort to acquaint the nation's music teachers with the results of the Symposium.

Each session was based upon a series of generative papers, together with responses and discussion. At Session I the generative papers were presented by musicians and the responses by psychologists. Two papers on each topic were read, followed by two responses that each related to both of the preceding papers. At Session II the generative papers were presented by psychologists and the responses by musicians. This time, each paper was followed immediately by a single response.

The purpose of Session I was to identify the needs, issues, and problems in music education that a clearer understanding of the relevant implications of current learning theory could help to resolve. The emphasis was on acquainting the psychologists with the practice of music education as it currently exists in American schools and on clarifying the needs of the field, as perceived by music educators, with which Session II would be concerned. The purpose of Session II was to summarize and synthesize the insights that psychology can contribute to the teaching and learning of music at all levels. The emphasis was on identifying the implications of current knowledge or theory that can help the practicing music teacher to improve his or her day-to-day instruction. Both sessions were open to the public and provided oppor-

tunities for all persons in attendance to become involved through discussion groups.

A publication summarizing the major ideas presented at the two sessions was issued as an insert in the March 1980 issue of *Music Educators Journal;* entitled "Conflict, Consensus, and Communication," this interpretive report by Judith A. Murphy was also made available separately. The Symposium provided a major focus for the national inservice conference of MENC at Miami Beach in April 1980 and sparked other dialogue as well, including the meeting of The Akron Institute, cosponsored by MENC and The University of Akron at Akron, Ohio, in June 1980. The present publication, a documentary report of both sessions of the Symposium, provides edited versions of all the generative papers and responses, which in some cases were revised by the authors in the light of research that took place between the sessions and of subsequent re-evaluation of the papers and discussions.

It is evident from an examination of the current professional literature in music education that there is an unmistakable awareness of the need for the further study of the learning process as it applies to the teaching and learning of music. Music educators clearly realize the importance of reconciling theory with practice in a mutually supportive relationship for the improvement of music instruction in the nation's schools and colleges. The Ann Arbor Symposium was organized with the intention of making a major contribution in this direction.

James A. Mason
Paul R. Lehman
Wilbert J. McKeachie

standard for comparison, which may be either exteroceptive or interoceptive. This standard may be consensual or quite personal. It may be extrinsic to the event being perceived, or it may be intrinsic to it, generated by the ongoing event itself.

Perceptions are subjective responses to stimuli. As such, we may assume that there are no "misperceptions," only incongruities with consensus. As far as the perceiver is concerned, events are no more than they appear to be; sonic events are what they sound like.

Musicians are interested in auditory perceptual learning because music is an aural art. If we are to develop an effective theory of music instruction we must do so on the basis of data that describe the interactions that take place between the learner and the structure of the event being learned. This paper (1) identifies some of the important auditory perception skills that a musician requires, (2) presents a preliminary overview of research pertinent to these tasks, (3) describes some extrinsic factors that may influence auditory perception, and (4) raises questions intended to identify gaps in our knowledge.

Auditory Perception Skills

A musician must be able to perceive when his instrument is in tune with a standard pitch. Within the normal range of instruments, it is possible to discriminate between frequencies with less than 3 percent differences between them at the 100 Hz level and as narrow as 0.5 percent at the 2000 Hz level (Zwicker, Flottorp, and Stevens, 1957). Investigations of the sort that provide such data typically involve observers comparing two successive pitches or indicating a just noticeable difference (JND) in a frequency sweep. The source of sound is typically an electronic oscillator and not a device that produces complex tones as do orchestral instruments. What influence does a complex wave form have upon the perception of in-tuneness? How accurately can differences be perceived when the perceiver is not simply an observer but is also involved in producing one of the tones being compared?

A musician must be able to perceive when the pitches within a melody are performed in tune. Whereas tuning an instrument involves an extrinsic standard with which the tuning can be compared, playing a melody in tune involves an intrinsic standard generated by the constituent pitches of the melody itself. The direction of the melodic line influences one's perception of in-tuneness, although the data appear to be somewhat contradictory as to directional influence (cf. Madsen, 1966; Edmonson, 1972). Timbre has also been shown to produce differential perceptions (Greer, 1970; Swaffield, 1974), as have tempo, intensity, and direction of required correction (Swaffield, 1974). Numerous other variables of music deserve investigation into their potential perceptual influence upon intonation, such as rhythmic pattern, register of the instrument, other pitches sounding in ensemble, and room acoustics. Again, what differences in perception are a function of being an objective observer as opposed to being a participant in the performance?

A musician must be able to perceive the sequential pattern of a melody. This task requires the perception of pitches and of tone durations in sequence. Evidence suggests that the types of variables that influence the perception of intonation also influence the perception of other structural attributes of melody (Carlsen, 1969; Carlsen, Divenyi, and Taylor, 1970; Dowling, 1973). The role of memory operates in this perceptual task, but it is not completely clear how (Taylor, 1971; Williams, 1973).

A musician must be able to perceive variations on a theme and other melodic transformations. Melody is frequently transformed in music compositions. The perceptual task is to recognize the melody in spite of the distortions of the original. Dowling (1972) demonstrated that inversions of a melody are easier to recognize than retrograde inversion. Distorting the melody by octave generalization of the pitches is a device used by serial composers, but preliminary investigation of the perceptual capabilities with this type of music transformation suggests that the original pattern will not be recognized by many (Deutsch, 1972).

A musician must be able to perceive simultane-

ous melodies in polyphonic settings. The rationale underlying polyphony is the implicit ability of persons to appreciate the separate contributions of each line to the whole. This presumes the perceptual ability to track each part simultaneously. How many simultaneous melodies can a person recognize and identify? What conditions inhibit perception of simultaneous melodies? The recognition of two simultaneous familiar melodies is a difficult task unless they are separated sufficiently in register such that their pitches do not overlap (Dowling, 1973). But is a recognition task an adequate measure of this perceptual ability? Identification would seem more nearly like what is expected of the musician, and this might require notating the melodies heard. Perhaps other potential dependent variables need to be explored.

A musician must be able to perceive chords and their sequence through time. At the simplest level, this task involves discrimination skills comparing two successive chords. Permutations would include spacing of the pitches within or beyond an octave, and inversions of the chords, using a variety of harmonies in addition to tertian, including tone clusters in semitones. A more complex task would be the recognition of a chord sequence, and the most complex, the identification of variance in a prescribed harmony occurring in a music context. Transformation of harmony, similar to that of melody, occurs frequently in music. What extent of harmonic distortion will still permit perceptual recognition?

A musician must be able to perceive the tonal center or key of tonal music. What factors contribute to the establishment of tonal strength in music? It would appear that the frequency of occurrence, centrality in the pitch range, the final pitch of frequent phrases, and the relationship to the dominant harmony are indicators of the pitch of the tonal center. Taylor (1971, 1976) has suggested that certain experiential factors may also be operating. In addition to identifying the perceived tonal center of a music selection, musicians must also recognize when the music modulates to another key and be able to identify the new key. What are the structural attributes that contribute to this perception? How subtle can they be and still be perceived?

A musician must be able to perceive the mode of a composition. The mode refers to the intervallic relationship of pitches in the scale from which a selection of music is derived. These are not limited to the church modes, and may be other than diatonic. I have observed eight- and nine-year-old children in Hungarian schools easily identifying a new song they were learning as Mixolydian in mode. I have also observed university students in sophomore music theory classes discriminate poorly between minor and Dorian modes. Certainly nationality of geographic location is not functional, but experience and training procedures may well influence mode-perception ability. How much and what kind of perceptual information must be extracted to recognize mode and modal shift? What variables serve to inhibit such recognition?

A musician must be able to perceive changes in the tempo of a performance. Kuhn (1974) demonstrated that observers could recognize that a series of pulses were slowing more easily than they could detect an increase of tempo. Interestingly, his observers indicated they detected change even when no objective change was present. This finding may be a function of the experimental design in which observers are to make a signal when detecting a change. Perhaps persons given such instruction develop an expectancy for change that influences their perception of objective phenomena. Swaffield (1974) encountered a similar result in his study of fine-tuning responses. Evidencing perception of tempo by means of performance has also been investigated (Kuhn and Gates, 1975). There is some question whether such procedures measure perception or performance abilities, particularly when the performers are using a clapping task to demonstrate the ability to maintain a steady tempo. Whether the tendency to speed up, which Kuhn observed, was a perceptual function or a kinesthetic characteristic is debatable.

A musician must be able to perceive rhythmic patterns. Petzold (1966) and Thackray (1972) both used performance tasks of tapping to

4

demonstrate primary grade children's perception of rhythmic patterns. The same question of validity raised with the Kuhn and Gates (1975) study is applicable here, particularly since the subjects were musically unskilled young children. What evidence of performance skill is required to provide confidence that data so derived are valid indicators of auditory perceptual ability?

Using a subjective response technique, Divenyi (1971) demonstrated the ability of highly trained observers to detect time increment variances of as little as thirty milliseconds in the second interval of a three-note melody. To what extent this would generalize to perception of time variance in a rhythm performance task, even by highly trained performers, is not known. Rhythm performance involves muscle control. Does kinesthetic activity have an influence upon auditory perception? Because perception of rhythm involves memory for sequence, how long a pattern can be perceived as a single rhythm pattern? To what extent does the addition of another attribute such as melodic pitch contribute to the perceptibility of rhythm?

A musician must be able to perceive a specified instrument or voice and to track its performance in an ensemble. Conductors must be able to follow the melody line of each of a number of given instruments in an ensemble. This task is a form of the "cocktail party effect." To what extent does knowledge of the score aid such tracking? Dowling (1973) indicated that consciously searching for a known melody can aid the discernment of that melody even when it is embedded in a confusing context. To what extent can this expectancy mislead when that melody fails to fulfill the expectancy? What happens to perception when there are multiple melodies and some high degree of overlapping? What strategies can be employed to aid perceptual learning in such circumstances?

A musician must be able to perceive when a vocal ensemble is blending. Conductors must control the quality of the different voices in an ensemble so that no one singer is heard apart from the group. This unified sound is apparently not a function of uniform timbre be-

cause polyphonic choral works use different vowel sounds at the same time with no negative effect upon blend. Certain aspects of vibrato do appear to influence a perception of blend (Trevor, 1977). There may be a complex of factors with possible interactive effects. Little investigation has taken place in this area of music.

A musician must be able to perceive an ensemble balance. Loudness levels within an ensemble must be controlled so that one instrument does not mask the tone of another. Psychoacoustic investigations of loudness discrimination provide evidence of a person's ability to perceive whether one tone is stronger or weaker than a preceding one, but this is not the most important music task related to loudness perception. Investigations that demonstrate a person's perceptual recognition of equality of loudness of two or more coterminous sounds are more pertinent.

Knowledge of a musical score can mislead an observer to believe that a tone or series of tones have been heard because they were expected to occur even though they have been objectively masked by other tones (Warren, Obusek, and Acroff, 1972). Research on contextual masking in music, including forward and backward masking, is needed.

A musician must be able to perceive the metric organization(s) occurring in music. Metric organization refers to the grouping of beats. This grouping is a function of accent and there are at least seven different types of accent: loudness; duration; pitch arrangement; timbre; visual gesture; location of sound in space; subjective accent, which typically results in grouping periodic pulses into twos and threes, when no objective accent is present. Dvořák, for example, in his *Slavonik Dance, No. 1*, employed a combination of loudness, duration, and pitch arrangement to achieve a polymetric effect. He aided the perceiver by introducing each metric organization separately before presenting the two meters (two and three) together. Are there other ways of separation in time to facilitate polymetric perception? What hierarchy of strength of accent may be present in these sources of accent? Which auditory sources contrast most preceptually?

5

A musician must be able to perceive performance departures from the printed score. The preceding perceptual tasks required the comparison of a sonic event with some "sound ideal," either exteroceptive or interoceptive in nature, whereas this perceptual task assumes music literacy to translate a printed music score into an interoceptive sound ideal. Once that is accomplished, the perceptual problems become those of earlier cited skills.

These are some of the music learning tasks that are dependent upon auditory perceptual skills. The problems that have been referred to and the research cited are related, for the most part, to the structure of the sonic event itself and the constraints that the event places upon perception.

Other Factors That May Influence Auditory Perception

Attention. It was said in the preliminary working definition that perception required attention to the sensation evoked by the stimulus in the perceptual field. Within complex music events, numerous coterminous attributes compete for attention. The perceptual environment surrounding the event also possesses potentially competing stimuli. What magnitude of a stimulus is required to attract the attention of a person already attending to other phenomena? Are there known and effective strategies for directing attention to previously unperceived stimuli? Does it make a difference to the ease of attraction whether current attention is to an event other than the sonic one or to an attribute of structure within the sonic event but other than the attribute being examined?

Education. The underlying assumption of perceptual learning is that the ability to extract information from our perceptual field can be improved (Gibson, 1969). Most research on music task performance does not compare musically trained persons with the untrained, but some recent research in hemispheric specialization in music has done so. As expected, trained musicians score better on auditory perception tasks than do non-musicians (Bever and Chiarello, 1974; Reineke, 1978). How do these auditory perceptual abilities distribute themselves across the general population? How are they distributed across musicians? Are there music abilities other than auditory perceptual ones that contribute to perceptual learning?

Perceptual expectancy. Most people have had the experience of perceiving a small portion of an event and then predicting what the continuation of that event will be. We expect certain events to happen because of information we have already extracted. These expectancies, which are a function of our experiences, (1) are capable of influencing our perceptions of melody (Carlsen, 1976), (2) can lead us to "hear" masked tones (Warren, Obusek, and Acroff, 1972), and (3) facilitate the discernment of a melody embedded in a confusing context (Dowling, 1973). Expectancy probably accounts for the difficulty Western musicians have, for example, in hearing the pitches of non-Western musics as other than deviations from equal-tempered scales. It would appear undesirable (if even possible) to develop an expectancy so catholic that nothing is *un*expected. Is it possible to develop categorical expectancies, dependent only on the intrinsic cues of the event and minimizing generalized experience? To some extent, this appears to be what takes place within a music style. This categorical expectancy control would appear to be a useful ability.

Stress/tension/anxiety. Auditory perceptual decisions must occasionally be made under stressful conditions. Performing a solo in front of an audience is a good illustration. Taking an ear-training test in school may be another. What inhibitory effects does stress (tension, anxiety) have upon perceptual accuracy? How can perceivers reduce stress levels in such situations? What aspects of perceptual learning are useful to reduce the inhibitory function of tension upon auditory perception?

Memory. Because music is an event occurring over time, auditory perception is influenced by the limitations of memory. What are the limits on length and complexity that reach Miller's (1956) magic seven plus or minus two? What precision and detail are lost as we involve chunking as a perceptual strategy? If a functional strategy, what perceptual learning steps bring one to this level of skill?

Reprise

Music is a perceptual phenomenon. Its meaning (or purpose) is realized only insofar as its structures are discretely perceived. This is not to say that complex structures of sonic events, which have a logic and which may even constitute change phenomena that in isolation lie within the JND thresholds of humans, cannot be organized; but the musical effectiveness of these structures does not depend upon an intellectual awareness of their existence, but upon their perceptibility as a sonic event in time. If such sonic events are beyond human perception, they can be judged superfluous and nonmusical.

With computers we are now able to generate and control sonic events with a precision of frequency, wave form, intensity, and duration that has not been possible before. We can create some structures that exploit JND thresholds, but the pertinent question is this: Are these finely honed events perceived when they reside in some music context?

We must avoid falling into a trap as we explore this question. It is quite possible that typical research methods will provide a negative answer to this question. We must bear in mind that perceptual ability is learned, and when we introduce a fine discrimination task embedded in a complexity of musical context it is quite possible that the results of tests of perception may indicate the degree of perceptual learning that has taken place and not the perceptibility of the event. For this reason data on the auditory perception of music need to be derived from highly trained musicians as well as from sophomore students enrolled in psychology classes. Such data should demonstrate the within-context JNDs of sonic structures for the persons tested. Presumably these JNDs would represent some distribution in the populations sampled. In correlation with various organismic and demographic data derived from the target populations, such data could be useful to composers, describing reasonable sonic limits within which to operate; to performers, in assessing their potential to perceive ef-

fectively under performance conditions; and to teachers, identifying goals for perceptual learning with music events.

References

Bever, T. G., and R. J. Chiarello. Cerebral dominance in musicians and non-musicians. *Science*, 1974, *158*, 537–539.

Carlsen, J. C. Cross-cultural influences on expectancy in music. *International Society for Music Education Yearbook*, 1976, *3*, 61–65.

———. Developing aural perception of music in context. *Journal of Research in Music Education*, 1969, *17*, 47–50.

Carlsen, J. C., P. L. Divenyi and J. A. Taylor. A preliminary study of perceptual expectancy in melodic configurations. *Bulletin of the Council for Research in Music Education*, 1970, *22*, 4–12.

Deutsch, D. Octave generalization and tune recognition. *Perception and Psychophysics*, 1972, *11*, 411–412.

Divenyi, P. L. The rhythmic perception of micromelodies: Detectability by human observers of a time increment between sinusoidal pulses of two different successive frequencies. *Experimental Research in the Psychology of Music*, 1971, *7*, 41–130.

Dowling, W. J. Recognition of melodic transformations: Inversion, retrograde, and retrograde inversion. *Perception and Psychophysics*, 1972, *12*, 417–421.

———. The perception of interleaved melodies. *Cognitive Psychology*, 1973, *5*, 322–337.

Edmonson, F. A. Effect of interval direction on pitch acuity in solo vocal performance. *Journal of Research in Music Education*, 1972, *20*, 246–254.

Gibson, E. J. *Principles of perceptual learning and development*. New York: Appleton-Century-Crofts, 1969.

Greer, R. D. The effect of timbre on brass-wind intonation. *Experimental Research in the Psychology of Music*, 1970, *6*, 65–94.

Kuhn, T. L. Discrimination of modulated beat tempo by professional musicians. *Journal of Research in Music Education*, 1974, *22*, 270–277.

Kuhn, T. L., and E. E. Gates. Effect of notational values, age, and example length on tempo performance accuracy. *Journal of Research in Music Education*, 1975, *23*, 203–210.

Madsen, C. K. The effect of scale direction on pitch acuity in solo vocal performance. *Journal of Research in Music Education*, 1966, *14*, 266–275.

Miller, G. A. The magic number seven, plus or minus two: Some limits on our capacity for processing information. *Psychological Review*, 1956, 63, 81–97.

Petzold, R. G. *Auditory perception of musical sounds by children in the first six grades.* University of Wisconsin, 1966. (Cooperative Research Project No. 1051, U.S.O.E.)

Reineke, T. R. *Dichotic and monaural perception of music and speech by musicians and nonmusicians.* Unpublished doctoral dissertation, University of Washington, 1978.

Roederer, J. G. *Introduction to the physics and psychophysics of music.* New York: Springer-Verlag, 1974.

Swaffield, W. R. Effect of melodic parameters on ability to make fine-tuning responses in context. *Journal of Research in Music Education*, 1974, 22, 305–312.

Taylor, J. A. *Perception of melodic intervals within melodic context.* Unpublished doctoral dissertation, University of Washington, 1971.

_____. Perception of tonality in short melodies. *Journal of Research in Music Education*, 1976, 24, 197–208.

Thackray, R. *Rhythmic abilities in children.* London: Novello and Co., Ltd., 1972.

Trevor, B. W. *The influence of vibrato upon vocal blend.* Unpublished doctoral dissertation, University of Washington, 1977.

Warren, R. M., C. J. Obusek, and J. M. Acroff. Auditory introduction: Perceptual synthesis of absent sounds. *Science*, 1972, *176*, 1149–1151.

Williams, D. B. *Short-term retention of pitch sequence: Effects of sequence length, serial positions, and delay time before recall.* Unpublished doctoral dissertation, University of Washington, 1973.

Zwicker, E., G. Flottorp, and S. S. Stevens. Critical bandwidth in loudness summation. *Journal of the Acoustical Society of America*, 1957, 29, 548–557.

Auditory Perception in Music Teaching and Learning

Jack J. Heller
Warren C. Campbell

Our charge for the symposium was twofold: (1) to identify the major needs and issues concerning auditory perception with which this symposium should be concerned, and (2) to summarize the kinds of learning that music teachers typically seek to develop and the difficulties they face in accomplishing these goals.

Probably the best rationale for any category or labeling system is the convenience it provides for the users. In view of the wide audience to which this symposium is addressed, we believe it is important to make explicit a point that will be implicit in much of the discussion. A taxonomy that is useful for delimiting a topic area may not be useful, and may even be misleading, if it is thought to specify "real" components of behavior. Peters deals with this issue as it relates to affect and emotion when he points out that

Probably the basic source of confusion (about affect and emotion) is·in the fallacy of reification of concepts. This is the same error which has infested so many of the concepts in psychology, including that of "mind" itself. Specifically, the error consists in assuming that, because we have a single noun-word, "emotion," something in nature must correspond to it, something as independent, as unique and unchanging, and as readily capable of entering subject-predicate relations with other things. (Peters, 1963, p. 437)

With the problem of reification in mind we concern ourselves briefly with the way in which the perception concept has been used by psychologists. Eleanor Gibson provides a tentative definition when she states

> Perception, functionally speaking, is the process by which we obtain firsthand information about the world around us. It has a phenomenal aspect, the awareness of events presently occurring in the organism's immediate surroundings. It also has a responsive aspect; it entails discriminative, selective response to the stimuli in the immediate environment. (Gibson, 1969, p. 3)

Three processes are suggested by Gibson as basic to perceptual learning: abstraction, filtering, and selective attention (Gibson, 1969, p. 117). She concludes

> The mechanism of perceptual learning is not association, but filtering and abstraction. The process is an active one, involving exploration and search. The search is directed by the task and by intrinsic cognitive motives. The need to get information from the environment is as strong as to get food from it, and obviously useful for survival. The search is terminated not by externally provided rewards and punishments, but by internal reduction of uncertainty. The products of the search have the property of reducing the information to be processed. Perception is thus active, adaptive, and self-regulated. (Gibson, 1969, p. 144)

Leonhard and House seem to agree with Gibson when they state that

> Perception is defined as an act by which meaning is gained from the sensory processes while a stimulus is present. Musical perception is the act of gaining meaning in the presence of musical stimuli. . . . Perception results in the formation of concepts. . . . Musical perception results in the formation of musical concepts. (Leonhard and House, 1959, p. 110)

Since our emphasis is on auditory perception in music, we shall focus on the listening process as a covert, but active, task-oriented behavior in music that leads to understanding of concepts used in the communication process. Listening, after all, is ubiquitous activity in all school music programs.

Music teachers typically seek to develop four types of learning, all of which involve processes that can be called auditory perception. These are labeled kinesthetic/motor learning, cognitive learning, notational learning, and aural learning. Except for cognitive learning, they are all nonverbal.

Kinesthetic/motor learning is that behavior that is associated with movement, both large muscle movements and small, finely developed, laryngial, mouth, arm, hand, and finger movements. In preschool and the early grades, teachers seek to develop the larger movements in association with listening to music. Typically, in the fourth or fifth grades, instrumental music programs are offered as electives in which teachers seek to develop very high level motor skills. In some cases these motor skills are developed in much younger children (typical of the Suzuki string instrument programs). While one may isolate kinesthetic/motor learning for discussion or study purposes it is unlikely that this type of learning occurs in isolation from other categories of learning. For example, auditory perception skills related to pitch and timbre provide information for embouchure adjustment and fingering changes on a musical instrument. Nevertheless, the general field of education and the specialty of music education have given a fair amount of discussion to a psychomotor taxonomy in isolation. While this taxonomy in music has been developed in great detail (Simpson, 1966), it is sometimes misconstrued by music teachers. The taxonomy was developed to help organize instructional objectives and evaluation procedures. Whether music learning processes can be predicted with confidence by this taxonomy has yet to be determined.

The second type of learning we label cognitive. Much discussion has taken place in relation to Bloom's taxonomy for the cognitive domain of learning (Bloom, 1956). But it is artificial to assume that cognitive learning

9

takes place in isolation, and it is highly unlikely that cognitive learning takes place in the hierarchy suggested by such a taxonomy. Taxonomies are merely what their definition states—schemes or plans for organizing material. In music education the taxonomy may be useful for organizing instructional objectives and evaluation procedures in the cognitive domain. Methodology may also be organized according to the taxonomy, but research has not demonstrated that more effective learning takes place when a particular hierarchy is followed (Leonhard and Colwell, 1976). The category "cognitive learning" is used to distinguish those demonstrations of "knowledge, comprehension, application, analysis, synthesis, and evaluation" (Bloom, 1956) in music (in the broad sense of music literacy) from other musical behaviors, such as performance, in order to organize and limit our discussion of auditory perception in music.

The third type of learning, notational learning, describes the process of learning to read music. This category includes two subheadings: realization of notation (note to performance) and dictation (performance to notation). The ability to properly associate music pitches and rhythms to the symbol system known as music notation is assumed by many to be developed by a variety of methods. We might argue that this development takes place more or less spontaneously (depending upon a certain environment), and that it is difficult to document that success in reading music can be accomplished by any one method. Some believe they read music when they have learned to manipulate keys or other mechanisms according to the rules of notation. Others would argue that music reading involves much more than this. For example, in sight reading the whole realm of music interpretation begins with the performer's ability to transform the symbols on the page into music imagery. Once again, this type of learning is not usually isolated from other categories such as cognitive or motor learning except for study purposes. We simply mean to point out the possible relationships that may be involved between notational learning and auditory perception.

The fourth type of music learning is called aural learning. This category focuses on the music listening process. The development of perceptive music listeners is an objective that would probably be embraced by all music educators. This is the foundation upon which music performance skills and all aspects of music literacy are based. But, while there may be little disagreement with this overall goal, we believe that wide discrepancy occurs among music educators, general educators, educational administrators, and the public as to what constitutes perceptive music listening.

Is it necessary for a person to have knowledge about a composer, his life, and his times in order to be a perceptive listener? Many (mostly music historians) would argue that this knowledge is important for perceptive listening. Verbalizing about various phenomena has great status in the academic community. But does this mean that the person who is a very experienced, discriminating listener, but who has not had formal training and therefore cannot verbalize about the music, is *not* a perceptive listener? Is the popular music or jazz aficionado who can immediately identify the performer and many subtleties in performance, but who cannot verbally label certain characteristics in the music, *not* a perceptive listener? If this is the case, how do people listen perceptively to traditional folk music or, for that matter, how did Western European listeners fare before the study of music history was fashionable? Johann Sebastian Bach was rather provincial in this regard, but our guess is that he was a very perceptive listener.

What about the effects of explicit knowledge about formal structural elements in music upon a person's level of perceptive listening? Here, the music educator would argue that knowledge of the elements, explicit structure, and form in music heightens the listener's perception. Does this mean that the untutored listener misses much of the communication between performer and listener? People return to the concert hall over and over without "knowing" in verbal terms about such constructs as diminution, augmentation, inversion, or final cadence.

10

Surely it cannot be that knowledge of such items is essential to the listening process. Or is it? It may be that such knowledge is an overlay on a more basic (and critical) communication between performer and listener. The intellectual elite may enjoy playing the game of labeling certain characteristics that appear in music. However, many elements that appear to be active in the music communication process have not been constrained by such labeling schemes.

While we recognize that music listening can encompass a wide range of perceptual and cognitive activities, we have limited our research to an area we call interpretive listening (Heller and Campbell, 1977). These are the processes in musical auditory perception that are not yet well represented by the music theorists, and those processes that are taught (if at all) only incidentally. Some of these processes are the ability to recognize composer style in performance, the ability to recognize performer hallmarks in performance, and the ability to discriminate different interpretive gestures in a performance both within and between instruments. We believe this type of listening is critical to the communication process in music (Campbell and Heller, 1978). While we have provided some data to support our view, there does not seem to be general agreement about the role of music listening to communication and meaning in music.

Since research studies in psychology use the term "musical perception" in many different contexts, it is not surprising to find conflicting results in that literature (Ward, 1970). The wide range of definitions given to a single label has created confusion. As an example, absolute pitch studies define this phenomenon in many ways (Ward, 1963a, 1963b). Furthermore, the tasks required of subjects (dependent measures) are often quite different in studies designed to investigate similar independent variables.

This same confusion can be observed in the research literature and in the practice of music education. A great deal of variability exists in the kinds of listening tasks required of music students that have traditionally been subsumed under the umbrella labeled auditory perception. Nevertheless, one can be relatively safe in stating that, in the practice of music education, there is general agreement that auditory perception in music is concerned with the process of listening to music.

Music listening tasks discussed by music educators fall into at least two categories: (1) those tasks the listener can perform in response to a music stimulus and (2) those tasks the performer carries out in response to the auditory feedback of the music stimulus. Our concern here is with the listener who is not performing rather than with the motor responses guided by the listening process of the performer. Yet, since the field of music education attaches great significance to music performance and its development, we cannot completely ignore the kind of listening (auditory perception) required of the performer.

The listening process of the performer has been addressed by Simpson in her taxonomy of psychomotor objectives (Simpson, 1966). The first level in Simpson's taxonomy is labeled perception; the remainder of the taxonomy categorizes performer tasks. We are concerned with Simpson's first level. As Colwell aptly states

> Professor Simpson's first category in the psychomotor domain is perception, with subdivisions of sensory stimulation, cue selection, and translation. There is some question as to whether cue selection and translation should not be at a higher level, perhaps between guided response and mechanism. Secondly, auditory-perceptual skill, a major part of the musical act, fits only in the perceptual category of the taxonomy and yet seems to encompass a wide range of difficulty. For example, cue selection may include acts as simple as mentally hearing and then reproducing a single tone and acts as highly complex as recognizing registration in organ music or sensing the proper articulation and phrasing from auditory cues. A good case can be made for the need to develop a separate taxonomy in the perceptual domain. (Colwell, 1970, p. 169)

Sidnell (1973) also argues persuasively that since "music is an aural art and calls for highly sophisticated aural perceptive abilities," it may be useful to develop a "separate hierarchical domain of music perceptive behaviors"—that is, a perception taxonomy separated from motor performance. Work by Colwell was begun in this general area several years ago (Colwell, private communication, 1974). Gordon (1976) has completed initial work on the development of a taxonomy of tonal patterns and rhythm patterns based on experimental evidence. He asked fourth, fifth, and sixth grade students to discriminate between a variety of tonal patterns and rhythm patterns in order to determine the difficulty level of these patterns. A hierarchy was then proposed for these patterns based on the responses of over 10,000 subjects. One of the purposes of this research was to "establish the aural perception difficulty level and growth rate of the individual patterns in the taxonomies" (Gordon, 1976, p. 6). Gordon has provided for the first time a paradigm for the development of a taxonomy of specific auditory music patterns. He points out that this research

> bears on only the aural perception of tonal patterns and rhythm patterns and not directly on the ability to perform the patterns or on the music literacy skills of reading and writing the patterns. However, assuming that aural perception is the most basic music readiness skill and therefore it must properly precede oral skills, and music reading and writing skills, the results of this study should provide direction for future study of the sequential development of students' performance and literacy skills. (Gordon, 1976, p. 6)

Our emphasis here, too, is with the aural perception of music rather than with performance or literacy. Gordon, in this study, limited student response to discrimination tasks that are the most basic perceptual tasks. Sidnell (1973, p. 74), however, points out that "multilevel perceptive behaviors" should be developed for a taxonomy to be useful in an educational setting. He states that "identification of perceptual objectives along a simple to sophisticated continuum should be a responsibility of the music

educator." There seems to be some consensus that music education may indeed profit from a task-oriented taxonomy of auditory perception. With this in mind we have examined a variety of music behaviors (tasks) that are limited to some aspect of listening to music. This provides the framework for the questions we pose at the end of the paper. This sample of music behaviors is intended to give the psychologist a flavor of the typical listening tasks encountered in the music teaching literature.

One of the most comprehensive sources of objectives (tasks) for music instruction in the schools appears in the interpretive manuals for Colwell's *Music Achievement Tests* (1969, 1970). He inspected eight published music texts used in grades three through eight in order to develop content validity for his achievement battery. He pointed out that "unless it was possible to find sufficient agreement on the objectives of the various levels of the music program, a standardized achievement test was not feasible" (Colwell, 1969, p. 10). Careful scrutiny of the objectives in these music texts revealed a strong similarity. Verification of this was determined by examining other sources of music education objectives such as curriculum guides and texts used in college music education classes. General agreement was found as to the important goals of the music program. Lack of achievement of many of these goals was attributed by Colwell to the lack of effective evaluation.

Typical objectives that relate to auditory perception extracted from these sources suggest nonspecific tasks, such as recognizing meter, differentiating between melodic patterns, recognizing repetition and contrast, recognizing tonality and key change, recognizing chords, aural discrimination, and identifying style. The basic auditory perception proficiencies required in the final version of Colwell's *Music Achievement Tests* are clearly task oriented. These tasks involve pitch discrimination, interval discrimination, meter discrimination, major/minor mode discrimination, feeling for tonal center, tonal memory, melody recognition, instrument recognition, music style, chord recognition, and cadence recognition. Each of these behaviors is defined by the specific task required in the tests and most of the tasks require verbal labeling.

Gordon's *Music Aptitude Profile* (1965) is another excellent source of auditory perceptual tasks in music. This battery is classified into three main divisions—Tonal Imagery, Rhythm Imagery, and Musical Sensitivity—and the student tasks are "to compare a selection with a musical answer and to decide if the selection and musical answer are alike or different, exactly the same or different, or to decide which is indicative of a more musical performance" (Gordon, 1965, p. 5). These may very well be examples of the kinds of covert tasks the listener performs.

The *Iowa Tests of Musical Literacy* (Gordon, 1970) also require tasks specifically labeled "aural perception." The student is expected to identify tonal and rhythmic characteristics of short, synthesized music examples. These characteristics range from basic to uncommon major, minor, and modal patterns, and from basic to uncommon duple, triple, and unusual rhythm patterns. Verbal labeling is required for all these tasks.

Another source of student listening tasks can be found in the report of the first music assessment carried out by the National Assessment of Educational Progress (NAEP, 1974). The report summarized a panel discussion by leaders in the Music Educators National Conference (MENC) about the implications of the first music assessment. The panel generally agreed that ability to recognize instruments and voice types "helps to increase [musical] sensitivity and to lead students to more mature, more sophisticated materials" (NAEP, 1974, p. 9). While this report limits discussion of auditory tasks to the explicit labeling of instruments and voice types, the original set of music objectives developed for the national assessment program by the Educational Testing Service (NAEP, 1970) outlines a more detailed set of music perceptual tasks under the heading "Listen to Music with Understanding." Such tasks as perceiving various elements (for example, timbre, rhythm, melody, harmony, and textures); perceiving features of rhythm, meter,

and melody; identifying different textures; and perceiving structure in music are stated in general overt behavioral terms.

Finally, a comprehensive listing of music experiences was developed by the MENC National Commission on Instruction in conjunction with the National Council of State Supervisors of Music. The Commission's 1974 publication represents a broad-based position of the music education field, and states that

> Although the experiences comprising the music program are diverse, they tend to cluster under three headings: (1) those having to do with the performance of music, (2) those having to do with the creation and organization of music, and (3) those having to do with the perception, analysis, and description of music. (MENC, 1974)

The point is made that the stated descriptions are "suggested experiences rather than . . . instructional objectives." But study of the third heading labeled "describing" suggests a variety of tasks related to auditory perception that are similar to the tasks identified by the national assessment group and represented by standardized tests in music.

With the exception of standardized tests, the various lists of aural tasks provided by music educators are usually not precise in expressing the response mode or modes appropriate for the task. This is not surprising, if one considers that in a typical listening situation the response is covert. Overt responses are generally inappropriate, since they interrupt the flow of the music. Music teachers must therefore devise overt response modes in order to gain information about their students' abilities as listeners.

Music teachers have two options in gaining information about their students' abilities. They can require some type of music performance that, by inference, indicates ability level in a covert process. Or, they can devise a nonmusic response task that appears to require success in the covert task before it can be performed properly. Most of these tasks require explicit labeling, usually of concepts abstracted from notation by music theorists. In either case, components have been added to the listening task that are not present in the covert process. Skills in music performance must be developed before they can be used to demonstrate correct aural processing. Failure to achieve the performance criterion may indicate a deficit in the perception process or in the motor skills required for performance. Verbal labeling may impose an additional memory load that increases task difficulty. More importantly, verbal labels may distort the task either because of their extra-musical connotations or because the label designates more than one aural process. The terms "higher" and "lower" for pitch relationships are an example of the former. The terms "dynamics," "accent," and "stress" are examples of the latter. A performer can accent or stress a note in a wide variety of ways, and a considerable dynamic range can be imposed on a performance without any change in the sound intensity level (Campbell and Heller, 1978). A student must therefore organize a number of different aural processes as subcategories under one label in order to provide responses that meet the established criterion. In some labeling situations there may be redundancy (i.e., multiple cues) in the stimulus that prevents the student from generalizing the label properly. In each preceding case failure to achieve the task criterion may be diagnosed as a problem in auditory perception when a failure in the response process is the cause.

Some of the learning problems facing the music teacher may be related to the use of verbal labels. Labels may facilitate perceptual learning by "pointing" to previously undifferentiated features in the stimulus. However, the use of a label may also obscure the need for a representative sample of the labeled class to provide perceptual generalization. In order to isolate the pertinent features of a sound complex, the naive listener probably needs a variety of settings and counter examples (examples in which the settings are maintained but from which the distinctive features are missing or replaced by others). For example, some children are able to echo-sing a melody sung by the teacher, but are unable to perform the task if the melody is played on the piano. It might be inferred that in this case the child has not yet abstracted the pitch features from the other attributes of the vocal sound.

One approach to the response problem may be to categorize listening tasks under the headings "discrimination," "recognition," and "identification." Only identification tasks would require an explicit label.

Discrimination tasks would require only a same/different choice in a variety of formats such as ABCX, in which the "odd" item is chosen from a group of four, or a multiple choice format in which the first (model) item is followed by a choice set. The advantage of these formats over the AA and AB (same/different) task is the possibility of providing distractor settings that allow for stimulus generalization. For example, in an ABCX task, the same melody may be played on three different instruments, or with three different starting tones, while the fourth item (randomly ordered) would be a different melody.

Recognition tasks would require a stimulus in which a previously heard item was embedded in a sequence of new items. The student would provide a signal when he heard the familiar feature. For example, a melodic or rhythmic motive would be presented by the teacher, followed by a short composition using the feature. The teacher might employ the recognition format for teaching motivic and interpretive features in music, eliminating the need for explicit labeling.

Tasks under each of these headings preceded any attempt at labeling, and might prevent premature assignment of a label to an undifferentiated stimulus. The rationale for using discrimination and recognition tasks is based on the consideration that listening tasks in music generally are covert and do not depend upon explicit labeling.

In summary, we believe that perception is strongly task oriented and that listeners who do not perform may organize auditory perceptions differently than those who do perform. Because of the problems associated with stimulus generalization, we believe that greater use of discrimination and recognition tasks in the classroom may move important areas of auditory perception from incidental

14

to directed learning. It is likely that many successful music teachers, particularly directors of performance groups, already utilize these techniques.

In conclusion, we propose the following four questions from among the many that might be asked:

(1) Is there any evidence from studies in psychology that the transfer from a covert task to an overt one (particularly labeling) is facilitating only after feature differentiation of a complex stimulus has occurred?

(2) The auditory perceptual skills required for specific tasks in music have at least three possible sources: they may be structurally innate; they may be learned in a nonmusic setting and transferred to music; they may be learned in a specifically musical setting. In addition, there may be developmental or maturational contingencies in any of these cases. What is the evidence for a transfer of auditory perceptual skills from other listening modes to music (or vice versa)?

(3) Perception has been characterized by Gibson and others as "task oriented" rather than (or in addition to) being "stimulus oriented." In terms of perceptual organization, is the performer like the skillful listeners in his audience, or does he have a musical perspective shared only by other performers?

(4) The Leonhard and House statement quoted does not indicate any difference between perception in general and perception in music. However, music is considered by many to lead to unique ways of understanding because it is an "aesthetic experience" and is often judged on the basis of its "aesthetic merit." Is there a difference between "aesthetic perception" and perception in general? Can one model of perception serve both situations?

References

Bloom, B. S., and D. R. Krathwohl. *Taxonomy of educational objectives: Handbook I: Cognitive domain.* New York: Longman, 1956.

Campbell, W., and J. Heller. *Covergence procedures for investigating music listening tasks.* Paper presented at the Seventh International Seminar on Research in Music Education, Bloomington, Indiana, 1978.

Colwell, R. *Music achievement tests, interpretive manuals.* Chicago: Follett Educational Corp., 1969, 1970.

_____. *Evaluation of music teaching.* Englewood Cliffs, New Jersey: Prentice-Hall, 1970.

_____. Personal communication, 1964.

Gibson, E. J. *Principles of perceptual learning and development.* New York: Appleton-Century-Crofts, 1969.

Gordon, E. *Music aptitude profile, manual.* New York: Houghton-Mifflin, 1965.

_____. *Iowa tests of musical literacy, manual.* Bureau of Educational Research & Service, University of Iowa, Iowa City, 1970.

_____. *Tonal and rhythm patterns: An objective analysis.* State University of New York: N.Y. Press, Albany, 1976.

Heller, J., and W. Campbell. The relationship between the interpretive element in music and the acoustic microstructure. *Bulletin of the Council for Research in Music Education*, No. 50, Spring, 1977, 29–33.

Leonhard, C., and R. Colwell. Research in Music Education. *Bulletin of the Council for Research in Music Education*, No. 49, Winter 1976, 1–30.

Leonhard, C., and R. House. *Foundations & principles of music education.* New York: McGraw Hill, 1959.

Music Educators National Conference, National Commission on Instruction, Paul Lehman, Chairman. *The school music program: Description and standards.* Reston, Virginia: Music Educators National Conference, 1974.

National Assessment of Educational Progress. *A perspective on the first music assessment.* Report 03-MU-02, Denver, Colorado, 1974.

Norris, E. L., and J. E. Bowes (Eds.), National Assessment of Educational Progress. *Music objectives.* U.S. Office of Education, 1970.

Peters, H. N. Affect and Emotion. In M. H. Marks (Ed.), *Theories in contemporary psychology.* New York: MacMillan, 1963.

Sidnell, R. *Building instructional programs in music education.* Englewood Cliffs, New Jersey: Prentice-Hall, 1973.

Simpson, E. *The classification of educational objectives, psychomotor domain.* Urbana, Illinois: U.S. Office of Education, 1966.

Ward, W. D. Absolute Pitch, Part I. *Sound*, 1963, 2 (3). 14–21. (a)

_____. Absolute Pitch, Part II. *Sound*, 1963, 2 (4). 33–41. (b)

_____. Musical Perception. In J. V. Tobias (Ed.), *Foundations of modern auditory theory.* London: Academic Press, 1970.

Response

Ruth S. Day

Carlsen and Heller have raised a rich array of questions of central importance in understanding the role of auditory perception and music perception and performance. Unfortunately, the richness of their ideas makes it very difficult to respond to all the issues they have raised in a brief commentary period. So given the somewhat peculiar state of affairs, I think it's only fair that I begin with a very peculiar question. And in so doing I hope to tie together some of the themes that run through both of these presentations. My question is this: Why did Beethoven write Beethoven's Ninth? Why did *Beethoven* write Beethoven's Ninth? Why not John Doe or Mary Roe or someone else? Why don't we have Rachmaninoff's rhapsody on a theme by Doe? Did Beethoven, Paganini, Bach, Stravinsky, and others achieve what they did because of some given talent or because they had some crucial learning experiences?

The discussion thus far suggests that by setting the process of perceptual learning we will be able to determine how best to teach music to the general population. As reasonable as this sounds, I would like to suggest that the ability to perceive music events involves more than perceptual learning. In order to discuss this possibility I'd like to look at two examples of recent auditory perception experiments and I'd like to contrast some in music with some in language.

Let's consider a specific problem in music perception—the perception of major and minor harmonic modes. Let's say we take just two chords, a good major and a good minor, and play them to listeners. And we tell them, "This is a major chord," and we play it. "This is a minor chord," and we play it. And we go over this many, many times. Then we give a test. What we do is simply play one of the chords, then the other, and then maybe that one again, and back and forth, just these two chords over and over in random order. What we find depends on who the people are that we have asked to perform the task. Let us consider first of all professional musicians. The musicians I'm talking about here were graduate student organists in the Yale School of Music. They play the organ twenty-nine to thirty hours a week, on the average.

So what we want to look at now is the percentage of correct identification. And we are going to look at the number of subjects who receive a variety of scores. So we'll start at the low end at say forty-one to fifty percent correct, which would just be a chance fifty percent, all the way up to say ninety-one to 100 percent correct. As you would imagine, professional musicians do just fine here. In fact the mean is about 98 percent correct. They clearly can do the task. Now the question is, what about nonprofessional musicians? Carlsen raised this question. What is the distribution of auditory perceptual skills in the population at large?

We might suppose that we'd get a function where of people in the general population, some would be as good as professional musicians, and some would be very poor, but most would fall in the middle. Actually, something very different occurs.

What you find is that you get a cluster of people in the very poor range. And you get a cluster up with the true, professional musicians. The mean of the lower group is about fifty-four percent correct, and the mean of the others is approximately ninety percent. For the nonprofessional musicians, these subjects were drawn from your typical sophomore psychology pools. Let's consider the nonmusicians.

Some are very good. And their performance in this task and in other tasks that we've studied is often indistinguishable from that of the professional musicians, or very close. Other people have tremendous difficulty with this task. They do no better than chance. The general results hold up no matter whether you need to have labeling or not; so there were some simple discrimination tasks and you get more or less this same kind of result. Now why does this happen? One possibility is that the people who do poorly in this task simply have poor auditory discrimination capabilities. In order to study this possibility, Mark Bleschner did another experiment and in this experiment he got rid of the upper and lower tones of the chord and simply played the middle tone. That was the only way to discriminate between the major and minor modes before. Now he just played the single notes, in isolation. Again, the task was set up; there were many examples of these two notes in random order. Each time the person simply told whether it was a high tone or a low tone.

Everybody did well: ninety-eight percent correct no matter whether the person was a professional musician or a nonmusician of either the good or poor variety that we had seen in perception of the chords. There were no differences across these three distributions of people. So the people who had performed poorly in the perception-of-chords tasks can perceive differences in the central tone pitches; they are not tone deaf. Instead, they have trouble with harmonic relationships. The outer tones of a chord represent some kind of interference for them that masks the change in frequency of the middle tone. But we could still ask why the nonprofessional musicians break into such disparate groups in terms of their ability to perceive tones when they are in the context of the full chord. Another obvious possibility, of course, is that the two groups differ in their past experience—the number of years they studied a music instrument. Perhaps the people who performed well have studied a music instrument and those who performed poorly have not. Well, it turns out that the good subjects often did have some music training, four or five years on a music instrument, but not all. Some had absolutely zero training in this regard. Among the poor people, the people who could not discriminate the chords, most of them did not have much music training, but some of them did; one had as much as five years. So we are faced now with a chicken-and-egg type of problem. We have music training on the one hand, which many of you seem to want to suggest then influences our music ability. We can get better in our music ability if we have this music training. But I would like to suggest that there's a portion that makes it a full circle. That is, some people may come equipped with some kind of music ability to begin with, which then leads them to get training. Who is it that takes music lessons? Perhaps these are the people who already have some kind of talent. Things are not gloomy for the music educators' profession! Perhaps we must have a certain a priori level of talent to begin with. Perhaps, then, the more traditional view of perceptual learning in music achievement needs to be modified. Perhaps there's an interaction between music training and a priori capabilities. But beware! It is easy to proclaim that some people have talent and other people do not. This really doesn't explain anything. Instead, let us ask what it is that these allegedly talented people can do better, and how they differ in general cognitive processes—perception, attention, memory, conception formation—from ordinary people. I am strongly supporting the need for research on accomplished musicians as well as college sophomores, as suggested by Carlsen.

I inadvertently also found big differences in people's abilities to do auditory perception tasks. In this case the stimuli were language materials. In the basic experiment, the person wears earphones and gets a different message in each ear at the same time. The two channels of an auditory tape are played to an individual. The top channel is the utterance "banket" and the bottom channel is the utterance "lanket." Now in this particular example, both of the items begin at the same point in time. But in the experiments that we conduct we time stagger them. On some trials, the items that begin with the stopped consonant, such as the "b" in "banket," begin first, say by fifty milliseconds, or seventy-five, or 100, or 125. The average speech sound takes about seventy milliseconds; so we really pull these quite far apart. And then on another series of trials, the item begins with the liquid consonant, such as the "l" in "lanket," by these same symmetric leads. And then we just randomize all these kinds of items, and conduct a very simple task.

We say to people, "You'll be getting some messages over the earphones. Tell us the first sound that you hear. If the first sound that you hear is "b," as in "banket," write down the letter "b." If the first sound that you hear is "l," as in "lanket," write down the letter "l," and so on. And of course there are lots of items like this one; this is just an example.

The results are that we get two very different patterns of perception. Some people do very well when the stop consonant begins first. However, when the liquid leads, they do very poorly. Now note that in English, we can have a stop followed by a liquid, in initial position, but not vice versa. We cannot have "lbanket," only "blanket." In languages such as Polish, you can. I have come to call these people language-bound when they report what the language allows, not the true stimulus events. The rules of language structure bias their perception.

Other people have a very high percent of correct temporal order judgment no matter which class of speech sounds begins first. I have come to call them language-optional. They can use language rules or set them aside, depending on the nature of the task before them. It turns out that these individual differences are very robust.

We have given a lot of practice to these people. Every day for eleven days, over and over, we have given them feedback on a trial-by-trial basis. Language-bound people get better but they are never as good as the language-optional people. Practice does not make perfect in this situation. Perhaps more important, these two groups show differences in a lot of other perception and memory tasks.

What about memory for brief events, such as digits going by very fast—8, 5, 4, 3, 2, 6, 9, 1, 7—and then you ask people, "What were those digits?" Language-bound people have a lot of trouble. They cannot remember the order in which those things were presented. Language-optional people do just fine. The importance of short-term memory, in a lot of tasks of music ability, is very striking.

Consider long-term memory. In long-term memory, both groups of people do just fine. And, in fact, language-bound people sometimes have more organized forms of memory. So the kind of memory that is involved in the tasks can distinguish these two groups.

So far, I have classified people as language-bound and language-optional and I haven't done much work on music perception, but I have tested a number of musicians. Virtually all of these people have been language-op-

18

tional. I have yet to find a language-bound true musician. Furthermore, I've taken the general population, the college sophomores, classified them as language-bound or language-optional, and then given them standardized tasks of musical ability, such as the Colwell test, Seashore test, and so on. What I find is that the two groups of individuals differ on some tasks but not on others. They differ on the kinds of tasks, such as in the Colwell test where you might have melody one, pause, then melody two, and one of the notes has been changed in its frequency. The language-bound people have a tremendous difficulty in telling which note was changed. And it may be because of the short-term memory component of this task. Language-optional people do just fine.

On other kinds of tests, such as those concerned with music style, language-bound people do just fine. This is a more conceptual task, as opposed to perceptual. Although it's a bit early, in my own work, I hope to be able to pull apart the subtests currently available in tests of music capability into general clusters. And they may well fall out with emphasis on short-term memory, as opposed to those involving more global recognitions with an emphasis on long-term memory. So indeed we may have a contrast between perception and conception.

This relates to an interesting, recent distinction in cognitive psychology made by Don Norman and others, between data-driven tasks and concept-high drive tasks. Perhaps some individuals are more data-driven, and these are the people that I would call language-optional. I bet musicians are more like those. Other individuals may be driven more by higher-level concepts, and these are the people that, in terms of my language studies, I'd call language-bound. So, concerning Heller's question about the role of explicit knowledge in music perception, the answer may depend on what type of individuals we are testing.

I think that the two groups of individuals possess different general patterns of cognition, general patterns of knowing. Let's suppose that these kinds of differences do exist in the population at large. What implications might such a distinction hold for music teaching and music learning? One thing I think we need to do is to study professional and nonprofessional musicians, to select tasks with emphases on subtle acoustic distinctions but also on more global syntheses. And then we should look for patterns of performance across these tasks in the different populations. It may well be that professional musicians are echoed in the population at large, in the people who have some basic capability for doing the tasks that musicians do, whereas others will not benefit from music instruction very much, no matter what you do. So, I'm suggesting that we establish different kinds of goals in music education for different kinds of subjects.

One goal might be Heller's interpretive listening. For some people it may be more appropriate to teach them or to emphasize such things as a composer's style or performance hallmarks. These would be language-bound-type people. For other people, it might be more appropriate to teach them to make fine discriminations in music, and to produce music. And these may be the people whom we traditionally think of as musically talented. In addition to different goals, we might be able to use different teaching techniques in order to achieve the same goal.

In my language studies, I sometimes have people do word-search puzzles. We tell people, "Scan these letters in any direction—right to left, left to right, up and down, down and up, and back and forth along the diagonal—and see if you can find words that fit the category of music instruments. People who are language-bound typically sound out letters; they'll say "bu-u-gle, oh, bugle!"

Language-optional people describe a very different process. You say, "How do you do the task?" They say, "Oh, I just sit back and wait for the words to leap out at me." As a language-bound person, I have tremendous difficulty in understanding what that means. But perhaps we have a parallel here to the learning of music notation. Some people seem to be able to pick up music notation right away and can sight-read almost instantaneously. These may be the language-optional people; they can get these visual images and see the notes going up in certain intervals. Other people may do something very different.

Let me give you one anecdote. I know of at least one language-bound person who learned to read notes in the following way. He sat down at the piano, looked at the score, and sang D, C, F, E; G, F, B; F, E; C, D, E, C; B, C, D, C; and so on. He sang the names of the notes in order to figure out how to use the music notation system. It could be that we could teach both kinds of individuals to read music efficiently by using different teaching techniques—emphasizing the intervals in a visual, musical sense on the page for some people, and for others, attaching the names of the notes may be helpful. I don't know. The idea is to take the natural cognitive tendencies of people as they arise and try to build on those, rather than trying to teach them to do something in a way that does not fit in with their general patterns of cognition.

So perhaps there are two very different, general approaches to teaching music. There have been suggestions that you start with music perception, and you work with people, and that gets them to the formation of music concepts. That may well be so, but only for some people. Perhaps for other people it has to go the other way. Maybe we should teach them the music concepts first, and that will then enable them to dig into the acoustic events and perceive these kinds of things as the music goes by.

To summarize, I am arguing that we may not all arrive at the tabula rasa—that is to say a blank slate on which our sensory experience writes. In music education, perhaps we have to take into account a triple interaction: an interaction among past experience with music, the nature of the task, and general patterns of cognition in the people we're working with. Beethoven may well have had some crucial exposure to music and some crucial learning experiences. But he was probably Beethoven to begin with. And there are probably potential Beethovens lurking in the general population, and others who may never benefit much from music training.

Response

Diana Deutsch

Both Carlsen and Heller have raised the issue of musical capacity and capacity limitation, and I'd like to explore this further. Generally speaking, people vary in their musical capacities, as evidenced by their performance in music situations. But when we try to pinpoint *specific* capacities, by asking, for instance, how much we can attend to at any one time, or how much we can remember following a single presentation, we find ourselves faced with difficulties.

Let me illustrate this with a couple of examples. The first concerns attention. It has been argued that there is a limit to the rate at which we can switch attention from ear to ear in monitoring auditory information. Evidence for such a limitation comes from experiments showing performance decrements in processing streams of speech where rapid switching between ears is involved. So we can ask ourselves whether such a limitation exists in music situations. Is there, for instance, a limit to the rate at which we can switch our attention from ear to ear in identifying melodic patterns?

Figure 1. Two eight-tone musical patterns.

In one experiment I constructed sequences consisting of ten repetitions of a basic eight-tone pattern. Two such patterns were employed (Figure 1) and subjects indicated on forced choice which of these had been presented. The tones occurred at a rate of roughly seven per second. Subjects were selected who had no trouble discriminating patterns A from B when these were presented through a loudspeaker, and they listened to the patterns through earphones under a variety of conditions (Figure 2). In Condition 1, the component tones of the melody were presented binaurally; and, as expected, the error rate was very low. In Condition 2, the component tones of the melody switched in quasi-random fashion from ear to ear, and a severe performance decrement occurred. This is as expected from the speech literature. However, in Condition 3 a drone was added, so that whenever a component of the melody was in the right ear the drone was simultaneously in the left ear, and whenever a component of the melody was in the left ear the drone was simultaneously in the right ear. The drone produced a dramatic improvement in performance even though the melody components were switching from ear to ear exactly as in Condition 2. One might argue here that this improvement was due to perceiving the harmonic relationships between melody and drone. So in Condition 4 a drone was again presented, but this time to the same ear as the ear receiving the melody component, rather than to the opposite ear. Performance in this condition was at chance. So the improvement in performance when the drone was presented to the opposite ear cannot be attributed to perceiving the harmonic relationships between melody and

drone. What would *appear* to be a limitation in our capacity to switch attention from ear to ear can be shown to melt away with a change in the stimulus conditions.

My second example concerns memory. We can ask, for instance, how well tones are recognized in a short-term memory situation. Suppose you use the following paradigm. You present a test tone, and then after a delay of several seconds another test tone, which is neither identical in pitch to the first or a semitone removed. The subject judges whether the test tones are the same or different in pitch. With just a silent interval between the test tones this task is trivially easy. However, if during this interval you interpolate a sequence of extra tones, this produces a large decrement in recognition performance, even when the subject is instructed to ignore the interpolated tones.

This might lead us to hypothesize that pitch information is retained in a store of

Figure 2. Pitch presentation to subjects under four conditions.

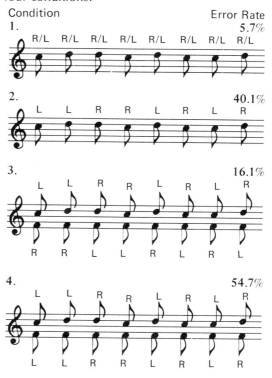

Figure 3. Pitch relationship between a critical tone (CT) and a test tone.

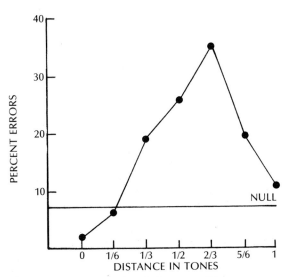

Figure 4. Error rates in pitch recognition.

limited capacity, and that memory impairment results simply from an overload produced by introducing too many tones. But the answer is not that simple. In one experiment I studied the effect on pitch recognition produced by a tone that formed part of an interpolated sequence, as a function of its pitch relationships to the first test tone. This critical tone was always placed in the second serial position of a sequence of six interpolated tones (Figure 3). TT1 is the first test tone and TT2 is the second test tone. G-sharp is the critical interpolated tone. The pitch relationship between this critical tone and the first test tone varied in equal steps of one-sixth of a tone between identity and a whole tone separation (a semitone in this example).

Figure 4 plots error rates in pitch recognition as a function of the relationship between the first test tone and the critical interpolated tone. As shown, the disruptive effect of one tone on memory for another was found to vary systematically as a function of their pitch relationship. When the critical interpolated tone was identical in pitch to the first test tone, memory facilitation was produced. Errors rose progressively as the pitch difference between these tones increased, peaked at a separation of two-thirds of a tone, and then returned to baseline. This experiment shows, therefore, that impairment in pitch memory occurs as a property of a system that is organized in a precise and sys-

tematic manner. The functioning of such a system cannot be explained simply in terms of storage capacity limitation.

I have chosen these two examples from my own work, and there are further examples provided by other symposium participants. But essentially my point is the following: When we ask questions such as "How much can we attend to during a given span of time?" or "How much can we remember following a single presentation?" we find that we end up with very different numbers depending on the exact stimulus configuration used, and this is true even when such configurations are extremely simple. We hope that in the next few years we shall obtain a firmer understanding of the structures underlying the processing of music information, so that questions about ability can be couched in terms of these specific structures.

Psychomotor Skills

Steven K. Hedden

Music educators work diligently to help their students gain all sorts of skills, knowledges, and understandings, for the music education program is a multifaceted one. However, only a part of the program, the part concerned with psychomotor skills, usually is visible to the general public. Parents and other school patrons who attend music programs have observed psychomotor outcomes as they have listened to first graders performing short songs, to fifth graders performing in a band, to seventh graders participating in a swing choir, or to high school students performing in an orchestra.

At first thought, it might seem that a performance by first graders and a performance by high school students would have been approached through vastly different means. This paper argues instead that there are several similarities between the process used to teach psychomotor skills to first graders and the process used to develop the psychomotor skills of high school students.

The teaching and learning of psychomotor skills in music can be conceptualized quite simply: The teacher provides a model or stimulus, the student imitates the model or decodes the stimulus in order to produce a sound, and the student receives feedback regarding the success of his or her efforts. The foregoing model seems to apply to all types of psychomotor outcomes at all grade levels; yet it is a simplistic one and there are other factors that need to be considered. The order in which these factors are discussed here corresponds to the order in which they typically occur in a teaching/learning sequence.

Level of Difficulty

First, the teacher must consider the degree of correspondence between the ability level of the student and the difficulty level of the music. This might take place in several ways. The general music teacher in an elementary school who wishes to teach a song to a class will be concerned with the apparent difficulty level of the song and the ability level of the students. The teacher probably will have made a subjective assessment of the difficulty level of the song, but there have been few formal attempts to construct a difficulty continuum that would tell the teacher whether the tonal and rhythmic aspects of the song are easy, moderate, or difficult for students at a given grade level.

Those who teach private lessons in instrumental music are faced with a similar situation. The teacher makes a diagnosis of the level of the student, determines the student's strengths and weaknesses, establishes a goal for the student, and then constructs a logical sequence of events that will ameliorate the weaknesses and help the student attain the goal established by the teacher. Unfortunately, some evidence suggests that a sequence of events that seems logical to the teacher—one that becomes progressively challenging—may not be perceived by students as proceeding from easy to difficult (Luce, 1965). What makes one rhythm or tonal pattern more difficult to perform than another?

The second factor in the teaching/learning process to be considered here is the presentation of the stimulus. The teacher might provide an aural model for the student to imitate (rote learning) or a visual example (music notation) for the student to read. The use of rote learning typifies the primary-level general music class, where the aural model may be augmented by the teacher's use of visual cues (hand signals). The use of these visual cues is predicated on the notion that learning proceeds more efficiently when two sensory modalities are employed rather than one. These visual cues also are intended to direct students' attention to certain characteristics (usually the melodic contour) of the music stimulus. In addition, a teacher sometimes makes prefatory comments before presenting an aural model; these comments also are intended to focus students' attention. Music education research has not yet completely answered the question: What is the most effective way of directing a student's attention to salient characteristics of an aural stimulus?

Those situations in which a student is asked to read a piece of music also present problems for which there currently are no answers. The student engaged in reading music must consider several aspects of the stimulus: what pitches must be performed, at what times, at what loudness level, with what kind of tone quality, and with what style of articulation? In addition, the instrumental performer must ascertain that he or she recalls the fingerings or positions for the notes in the music. It is expected that the performer at this point will form an aural concept of how the music should sound (Petzold, 1963).

Several questions pertaining to the process described in the previous paragraph need to be resolved. One of these questions concerns the number of music aspects to which performers at various levels of competence can attend. Music educators apparently assume that a concert artist almost simultaneously attends to several features of a notated example of music, while a beginner struggles to attend to more than one feature. Does the literature from other disciplines support this assumption? If so, is there a way to "force" this developmental process so that the beginner can attend to multiple aspects of the stimulus, or must the teacher wait patiently for the student to progress from one developmental stage to another?

Another question pertains to the eye movements that occur as a performer scans a music stimulus. Young (1971), for example, found that better music readers made more fixations while reading music than did the poorer readers; yet studies of the eye movements used in reading verbal materials suggest that better readers make fewer fixations and fewer regressions. Is the number of fixations related, then, to the type of task? Is the strategy of increasing the number of fixations an optimal one in terms of reading music successfully?

Also, one study has concluded that skill in music performance is related to several variables, including certain visual capabilities of the student (Barrett and Barker, 1972). Can more rapid progress in music performance be obtained when the teacher provides instruction in visual scanning? Of course, an answer to this question would have to be based on a knowledge of the eye movement patterns of successful music readers.

Preparation

Preparation—called mental rehearsal by some—receives increasing attention by the teacher as the student becomes a more proficient performer. The student is told to "think through" the music before attempting to perform it; he or she is encouraged to "hear it in your mind before playing it." The value of this practice has been supported by several studies that have shown that pre-

rehearsal seems to reduce the number of trials to criterion. More recently, Holdsworth (1974) found that the period of mental rehearsal is one in which electromyographic activity occurs in the muscles that are later used to perform an excerpt; yet, his subjects were unaware of the activity in the muscles that were supposedly at rest. It seems possible, then, that greater reliance on pre-rehearsal might increase learning efficiency. Is there evidence that supports the idea that mental rehearsal, by eliciting covert electromyographic activity, acts to reduce the number of trials necessary to learn a psycho-motor task to criterion?

Execution

Another part of the teaching/learning process transpires when the student attempts to perform a piece of music. The complexity of this task is staggering; the performer must attempt to produce the right notes (pitches) at the right time (in correct rhythm) at a given loudness level. In addition, appropriate tone quality and articulation will be expected of the player. Furthermore, if the student is performing as part of a group, he or she must consider whether the individual effort blends with that of the group. Finally, a performer may need to follow a conductor and may be asked to move (march or dance) while playing or singing.

Because performance is such a complex task, music educators have adopted various strategies for teaching the requisite skills. The most common strategy seems to be hierarchical: The teacher seeks to identify and rehearse isolated aspects of performance, and then combine these isolated components in an effort to produce the "finished" product. For example, pitch and rhythm aspects may receive attention as a student first encounters a piece of music, while matters related to tone quality or articulation are somewhat ignored until the "notes are learned." Music educators who use this strategy have done so primarily on the basis of informal evidence; apparently no research study in music education has attempted to evaluate a hierarchical strategy for the teaching of performance skills. Is there literature from other disciplines that supports the idea that complex psychomotor skills are learned most efficiently when the teacher uses a "hierarchical" strategy?

Another need pertains to the anatomical and physiological parameters that influence performance. For example, electromyographic activity in trumpeters' embouchure muscles has been monitored in more than one experiment (Basmajian and Newton, 1974). Also, cinefluorographic techniques have been used to examine various changes that occur in the oral cavity as a person prepares to perform and does perform (Anfinson, 1969; DeYoung, 1978). One such study provided tantalizing information that suggested that the tongue placement employed by brass players does not necessarily conform to what those players believed was happening (Haynie, 1969). It is tempting to speculate that the brass players in the latter experiment would be more effective teachers if they were provided with objective evidence regarding tongue placement, for these players then could communicate more accurately with their students. The pertinent question here could be phrased in this manner: Is there research-based evidence that suggests that students can acquire complex psychomotor skills more efficiently when they are provided with objective information that describes the requisite muscular activity?

Feedback

Another part of the process occurs as the student compares an attempt at performance with the aural model or the notated example that served as the stimulus. The internal feedback thus generated is subject to certain limitations; the student can supply reinforcement only for those aspects of the stimulus for which he or she has already developed aural concepts. In other words, efficient practice sessions at home are obtained when the student knows when and how to supply self-reinforcement for a particular attempt at performance. What is the optimal way of developing students' self-reinforcement skill?

Another aspect of self-generated feedback is that which is called kinesthetic. Experienced performers have developed a good

"feel" for kinesthetic feedback as they perform, and they quickly note when certain bodily sensations are "not right." A skilled performer processes this proprioceptive feedback and makes adjustments that may be so rapid that the listener does not become aware of any deviation in performance level. Apparently there are important differences among individuals in their use of kinesthetic feedback. For example, Jacobs (1969) investigated twenty young violinists and found that those classified as having trained music hearing tended to use aural cues to guide performance, while those without training in music hearing seemed to rely on kinesthetic cues. Such a finding implies that teachers may need to make frequent use of methods that emphasize kinesthetic feedback if students do not have well-developed aural concepts. Is there research in other disciplines that supports the use of kinesthetic feedback as an important adjunct to the teaching of psychomotor skills to young learners?

The instances in which external feedback (reinforcement) is provided by the teacher also need research attention. Some teachers prefer to supply positive reinforcement for those aspects of performance that are exemplary, while negatively reinforcing weaker aspects of performance by not mentioning them. Other teachers positively reinforce exemplary aspects while simultaneously providing information about other aspects. ("Your tone quality was very nice. Now, let's get your intonation up to that same level.") Other teachers seem to dwell on the negative aspects of a performance. These differences in the type of feedback teachers provide presently are primarily attributable to differences in philosophy; for example, some teachers believe that only positive statements should be used. It would be valuable for the profession to have objective evidence regarding the effectiveness of the various types of feedback. To be more specific, have the three approaches outlined above been found to have demonstrably different effects on student achievement, attitude, and self-concept?

The intent of the external feedback, of

course, is to enable the student to make modifications so that a second, third, or fourth attempt will conform more closely to what is desired. It is not difficult for teachers to provide feedback; what is difficult is to gauge how much feedback a given student can assimilate at one time. Unfortunately, music education research has not been able to describe what amount of feedback is optimal for a student of a given experience or grade level. Are there research-based guidelines that describe the optimal quantity of feedback for students of various grade levels?

A related problem concerns overlearning. The profession has little research evidence that bears on the positive or negative effects that accrue from the overlearning of psychomotor skills, yet many teachers say to students, "Let's try it once more to make sure you have learned it well." It would be of great value for the profession to be apprised of the results of recent studies on overlearning and its effects on psychomotor skill retention.

Similarly, it would be beneficial to have more information pertaining to student practice sessions when the student is away from the teacher. Students frequently are asked to practice an assignment outside of the lesson or rehearsal. As the students practice, certain movements are being repeated; the goal of this activity is to enable the students to perform certain psychomotor operations in a smooth, consistent manner. Repetition is necessary, of course, to develop desirable playing habits (long-term memory), but self-reinforcement also is required. A student must repeatedly attempt a certain passage, monitor his or her performance, then supply reinforcement according to the goodness of fit between the *a priori* model and the actual attempt. Unfortunately, there seems to be no research that has examined the role of repetition and self-reinforcement in students' practice. What are the contributions of repetition and self-reinforcement to the acquisition of psychomotor skills?

Other Concerns

Finally, there are other specific areas that this symposium should address. One of

these pertains to a student performer's ability to maintain a steady tempo or, alternatively, to coordinate his or her effort with an ongoing tempo. Some students, for example, speed up or slow down as they perform a solo; other students have difficulty as members of a group in coordinating their efforts with those of the group. Research has shown somewhat consistently that performers are less sensitive to increases in tempo than to decreases (Kuhn and Gates, 1975) but research has not yet attempted to determine whether this differential sensitivity should be attributed to neurological or conceptual factors.

A second need pertains to intonation. For example, those music teachers (usually band directors) who administer some sort of music "aptitude" test to prospective students typically use the test results to generate predictions about the likelihood of success for a given student. Many of these tests include a section that asks the testee to indicate which of two successively presented pitches is higher (or lower): yet, the skillful performance of music requires that the musician first discern whether one of two simultaneously produced pitches is higher (or lower), and then make an adjustment. Furthermore, there is tentative evidence that suggests that there is only a moderate relationship between the ability to discriminate between two successively presented tones and the ability to produce a tone that matches a simultaneously presented tone (Pedersen and Pedersen, 1970). Is there literature in other areas that supports the finding that the relationship between perception of stimuli and production of stimuli is only of moderate strength?

A related need is for a theory of intonation. Scattered references in music education literature document how one person evaluated two or three specific "methods" for improving the intonation of students' performances; yet each of these studies generally has been conducted in a theroretical vacuum. The impression one forms after reading these studies is that music educators are interested in specific teaching techniques that offer symptomatic relief for certain intonation prob-

26

lems, but are not interested in investigating the causes of these problems. Such a posture is not in the best interests of the profession, of course; more theory-based work regarding intonation is needed.

Playing or singing in tune requires that psychomotor skills be executed within a narrow tolerance level; for example, a trombonist must have the slide of the instrument in an exact location while supplying an appropriate amount of breath support to the tone. Are there other disciplines where scholars have been able to devise an effective, theory-based method for teaching psychomotor skills when those skills must be demonstrated within a narrow tolerance level?

A third need pertains to the prediction of success in music. Several variables have been used previously as predictors—music "aptitude," prior achievement in music, achievement in other classes, intelligence, performance on tests of specific psychomotor skills—but certain questions remain. Based on the experience of other disciplines, what set of variables accounts for maximal variance when predicting level of psychomotor skill? Also, are measures of psychomotor parameters such as general coordination, reaction time, and level of perceptual-motor development good predictors of success in the learning of psychomotor skills?

A fourth need—for information pertaining to performance anxiety—has been partially met within the profession, in that some music educators have conducted research studies dealing with "stage fright" (Wardle, 1972; Lund, 1972). The extant studies, however, differ so dramatically in terms of the techniques employed, the age or experience levels of the subjects, or the length of the treatment period that it is difficult to draw generalizable conclusions. Music educators would benefit by learning of the results of carefully controlled studies that have examined the effects of various techniques—systematic desensitization, insight, relaxation with applications—on the management of performance anxiety. Is there one technique that is helpful for a majority of students? Do various teaching situations require the use of certain anxiety reduction techniques? What level of

performance anxiety is optimal in terms of maximizing the quality of an ensuing performance?

A fifth need pertains particularly to band instruction. Existing studies have suggested that students should begin band in the seventh grade, but these studies (Pence, 1942; Cramer, 1958) are more than twenty years old; their findings and recommendations may no longer be valid. Based on current evidence pertaining to mental and physical development, dental development, use of out-of-school time, and physical maturation and coordination, what appears to be the optimal grade level to begin the study of instrumental music?

A sixth need is closely related to the preceding one in that it deals with physical maturation. To focus on extremes, it is readily apparent that first-grade students and twelfth-grade students differ in physical maturity and in the rate at which each acquires a given psychomotor skill. What role does physical maturation play in the acquisition of psychomotor skills? Are differences in rate of acquisition attributable more to differences in physical maturation or to differences in mental development?

References

Anfinson, R. E. A cinefluorographic investigation of selected clarinet playing techniques. *Journal of Research in Music Education*, 1969, *17*, 227–239.

Barrett, H. C., and H. R. Barker. Cognitive pattern perception and musical performance. *Perceptual and Motor Skills*, 1973, *36* (3), part 2, 1187–1193.

Basmajian, J. V., and W. J. Newton. Feedback training of parts of buccinator muscle in man. *Psychophysiology*, 1974, *11* (1), 92.

Cramer, W. F. *The relation of maturation and other factors to achievement in beginning instrumental music performance at the fourth through eighth grade levels.* Unpublished doctoral dissertation, Florida State University, 1958.

DeYoung, D. *A videofluorographic analysis of the pharyngeal opening during performance of selected exercises for trombone.* Paper presented at the meeting of the Music Educators National Conference, Chicago, April 1978.

Haynie, J. J. A videofluorographic presentation of the physiological phenomena influencing trumpet performance (pamphlet). North Texas State University, 1969, cited by Rainbow, E. R., Instrumental music: Recent research and considerations for future investigations. *Bulletin of the Council for Research in Music Education* No. 33, 1973, 8–20.

Holdsworth, E. I. *Neuromuscular activity and covert musical psychomotor behavior: An electromyographic study.* Unpublished doctoral dissertation, University of Kansas, 1974.

Jacobs, C. Investigation of kinesthetics in violin playing. *Journal of Research in Music Education,* 1969, *17,* 112–114.

Kuhn, T. L., and E. E. Gates. Effect of notational values, age, and example length on tempo performance accuracy. *Journal of Research in Music Education,* 1975, *23,* 203–210.

Luce, J. R. Sight-reading and ear-playing abilities as related to instrumental music students. *Journal of Research in Music Education,* 1965, *13,* 101–109.

Lund, D. R. *A Comparative study of three therapeutic techniques in the modification of anxiety behavior in instrumental music performance,* Unpublished doctoral dissertation, University of Utah, 1972.

Pedersen, D. M., and N. O. Pedersen. The relationship between pitch recognition and vocal pitch production in sixth-grade students. *Journal of Research in Music Education,* 1970, *18,* 265–272.

Pence, D. P. *A study to determine the optimum grade for beginning class study of wind instruments.* Unpublished master's thesis, University of Kansas, 1942.

Petzold, R. G. The perception of music symbols in music reading by normal children and by children gifted musically. *Bulletin of the Council for Research in Music Education* No. 1, 1963, 62–66.

Wardle, A. *Behavioral modification by reciprocal inhibition of instrumental music performance anxiety.* Unpublished doctoral dissertation, Florida State University, 1969.

White, E. R., and J. V. Basmajian. Electromyographic analysis of embouchure muscle function in trumpet playing. *Journal of Research in Music Education,* 1974, *22,* 292–304.

Motor Learning in Music Education

Robert G. Sidnell

The importance of motor skill development to the practice of music education is enormous when one reflects upon the process of making music. The speed and precision of neural/motor processes necessary for accurate music performance can easily be thought of, along with speech, as some of the most demanding body movements. Furthermore, when one traces the perception and assimilation of visual music symbols, their decoding and processing, and the decision and initiation of appropriate motor responses, all within extremely short time periods, the argument for demanding precision and accuracy grows in weight. Even without the music reading process present, music performances by ear, memory, or improvisation require long chains of precise motor activity, always with constant, sophisticated auditory monitoring.

Music educators have long been aware of the importance of motor learning in music education. This awareness has classically taken the dual view of (1) fundamental large-muscle motor response for basic rhythmic development in small children, and (2) refined, small-muscle motor response necessary for purposes of precise music performance. When one surveys the research literature in music education, the paucity of systematic investigation by music educators of motor learning problems is alarmingly evident. For all our verbal dedication to the importance of motor learning to rhythmic development, for example, neither the lone bibliographer nor Lockheed, BRS, or Datrix can provide much bibliography of significance. On the other hand, the populist literature of all types in music education catalogs extensive opinion supporting the importance of motor learning in the music education process. We have well-accepted teaching strategies that include clearly defined motor activities designed to help children experience music through motion. For example, movement in early music education is based upon:

> the kind of movement children have without any special training. It develops, without help, out of itself. The child likes to run, jump, skip, turn and do many things without any purpose (Klie, 1970).

Music educators believe in motor learning as a means to the end of rhythmic achievement but somehow have avoided any careful inquiry into its nature. We simply know it is important. Any elementary music educator would instantly affirm, without question, a directional hypothesis between increased motor development and increased music achievement; if A, then B—no question. Since the relationship is a foregone conclusion, no real investigation is necessary. I suppose we should savor such a solid, unshakable epistemological viewpoint. My sarcasm is not wholly appropriate, however. There is casual, empirical evidence that supports a strong belief in the relational benefits of motor learning in terms of music achievement. Much of this view is evident in the extensive instructional programs in eurythmics as proposed by Jaques-Dalcroze. While controlled rhythmic learning was only one aspect of the Dalcroze method, the notion of eurythmics seems to have outlived Dal-

croze's well-organized curriculum in solfege and improvisation. Simply stated, Jaques-Dalcroze's model identifies rhythmic feeling and understanding as fundamental to all forms of music achievement. Most currently early childhood music methodology is indebted to his model, but not his practice. This view has been held by music educators for some fifty years. Pennington's first adaptation of the work of Jaques-Dalcroze was published in 1925. Mursell noted that, "Eurythmics is the best known scheme for isolating and training the sense of rhythm" (Mursell, 1927, p. 55). Little systematic research of this model can be found, but music education process materials continue to uphold the theory as fact, by means of the copious number of lines devoted to it in method books. For example, as recently as 1975, MENC indicated the importance of movement in the music education process. This follows a long pattern of endorsement, as in 1946 when MENC said through its elementary curriculum committee that "bodily response to music of simple rhythms" was fundamental to rhythmic learning. The problem is not that we recognize the importance of motor learning but that we tend to treat the subject lightly and without any systematic inquisitiveness. As a beginning, we should take time to research the area carefully in order that we (1) understand motor learning processes better; (2) recognize and study the relationship between motor learning and other kinds of music learning; (3) economize our motor teaching procedures; (4) recognize variables in motor differences in children; and (5) discover optimum motor learning periods in children.

The above can be phrased as questions that we, as music educators, need to think about and refine. But we also have some concerns for the psychologists who have more extensive expertise in the area of motor learning.

Some Psychological Foundations

When one reviews the general literature in motor skill development, motor learning, kinesiology, biomechanics, and psychology of human movement, one finds the antithesis of the extant literature in music education motor learning research. There is much to investigate, all the way from the Ann Arbor Motor Learning Symposium of 1972 to the CIC Conference on Motor Learning in 1968. In fact, there is a one-hundred-year history of motor learning investigation. There are publications from several motor learning research centers around the country, such as those at the University of Wisconsin and Florida State University. Vast international sources are also available. There is much that may have great relevance to our problems in music education. Basic, and perhaps most interesting, are the fundamental theoretical models evident in the literature. Three models for motor learning move to center stage. These are the Closed Loop Theory (Adams, 1971, 1976), the Open Loop Theory or Motor Program (Lashley, 1917, 1951), and the notion of motor schema (Head, 1920; Bartlett, 1932; and Attneave, 1957).

Persuasive arguments may be made for each notion of motor learning. There are conflicting findings in supporting research, or, in some cases, no research of first-rate quality to support the theory. One might well argue that there is a probable similarity in theoretical division among music educators. Without knowing very much about motor learning, music educators oscillate in their support of closed, open, or schema viewpoints. Frankly, I would characterize the music educators' theoretical position as eclectic ignorantism on the issue. For example, there is evidence that some music performance operates (or unwinds) without the benefit of any feedback—the motor program unfolds beginning to end, without interruption. This is the open loop theory. On the other hand, the same music educators might, at other times, advocate the closed loop view stressing feedback error detection, and error correction on a different occasion. Finally, there are those who would support the notion of schema—a kind of motor concept idea in which a generalized class of learned motor responses is called upon to produce certain specified behaviors either old or new, but possibly different from the one or more originally learned. Personally, I have never heard

of a discussion of any fundamental aspect of motor learning in relation to music behavior. It is almost a rule that music educators think in terms of practice rather than underlying theory. Competent researchers in music education could confront some fundamental problems in the application of motor learning models and perhaps provide very interesting data for the motor learning psychologist. After all, one of Lashley's basic arguments for the motor program or open loop theory is the trilling speed of the concert pianist—something no one ever bothered to measure. Essentially, motor program theorists claim that the act of high-speed trilling (16/second) does not leave enough time for proprioceptive feedback. I think most musicians would not agree and could show that feedback is a part of this high-speed rhythmic motor behavior. Incidentally, subsequent research by Chernikoff and Taylor (1952), and more recently Bowman and Combs (1969), supports the possibility of extremely fast feedback—in the range of four to five milliseconds, thus permitting a round trip (with processing) of perhaps ten milliseconds. These findings have not been documented in auditory feedback systems, however.

Music educators not only have to ask questions of others but also must be prepared to undertake organized plans of research on their own. Because of the complexity of auditory processing, aspects of motor performance that rely on aural error detection and correction may call for special adaptations or modifications of motor learning theory.

Music Education Research

As noted earlier, music educators tend to stress the importance of motor learning in the early stages of musical growth and in the development of music performance skills. In the latter instance very precise motor tasks have to be learned primarily through repetition. Of greater interest, though, is the notion that much of this learning takes place without guidance. Singing, keyboard, and instrumental performance skills are perfected (for the most part) during individual practice periods (at least we assume individual practice periods). Individual practice is notably of low efficiency in terms of learning. Generally, young learners are unsure of an ideal outcome, incapable of error detection or correction, and unaware of efficient practice strategies. In a recent monograph, Duerksen (1972) reported scanty research on the topic of individual practice for developing motor skills.

Similarly, there is little of substance to report in the area of motor learning research in early childhood music education. Zimmerman's (1971) review of research concludes that "music with fast tempi should be used first in rhythmic moving experiences. Slower tempi can be gradually inserted as the children become more adept in synchronizing movement with music" (p. 26). Also: "Creative movement should be encouraged and used as a basis for organized dance forms" (p. 29). A later research summary of Klemish (1973) quoted the following: "Rhythmic sensitivity appears to be important for the development of skill in motor activity, reading, organization and recollection of information, and the appreciation of music" (p. 33).

Leonhard and Colwell (1976) listed only four or five titles that might constitute music research in motor learning. Rainbow's (1973) recent research summary included three motor learning studies in the bibliography of research pertinent to instrumental music. Notably, one of these studies is addressed to the investigation of kinesthetics involving violin performance (Jacobs, 1969). The most recent psychology of music teaching volume (Gordon, 1971), while not containing a specific section on motor learning, includes the following kinds of suggestions: "Knowing the fractional value of notes does not necessarily contribute to the kinesthetic interpretation of a rhythm pattern seen in notational form" (p. 79). In a section devoted to the application of current learning theories to music education, Gordon noted: "Because music is an aural art, one must first acquire aural perception and kinesthetic reaction in order to develop musical understanding in a conceptual sense" (p. 60). He further claimed that, "kinesthetic reaction is activated through aural perception" (p. 61). A computer search of various bibliographic retrieval services in

music produced a substantial number of research entries that indicated some interaction of motor and music learning. A number of the entries were studies that used music as background to a motor task. Cross references of terms such as "motor learning," "music education," "child development," "motor development," "psychomotor skills," "perceptual motor learning," and "motor performance" were used. The total output was forty-five citations. Few were theory bound and many were in the area of special education and music education.

Psychological Literature

There is much research in motor learning and behavior—in fact, too much. For example, one can look at a study by Wing (1977) investigating a small muscle rhythmic motor task and effects of imposed perturbance by means of anticipated or delayed feedback. Or one might look at Michon's work on temporal tracking emphasizing the structure of temporal sequences as hierarchies indicating they do not consist of mere successions of events but of rhythms (Michon, 1967, 1972). Or one might go completely physiological and search the literature for works on the kinesthetic or proprioceptive/somasthetic sensory system. According to Higgins (1972), "Kinesthetic sensory information is the result of movement-produced stimulation only" (p. 315). For example, the work of Montcastle (1974) indicates that the proprioceptive system transmits three basic kinds of sensory stimulation: occurrence of mechanical event, absolute detection of a mechanical event, and absolute detection of position. On another tangent, the search might end in the literature of biomechanics, which involves relationships between mechanical and physical principles within the biologic system. Finally, one might choose a review of instructional strategies for psychomotor skills that can be found in *Review of Education Research* (Singer, 1977). His bibliography lists sixty-nine articles on the topic and he adds the following conclusions:

(1) If the purpose of learning a skill is only for the highest level of performance in that skill,

31

then a guided and prompted method of learning would seem to be the appropriate choice, especially if there is concern for economy in training time.

(2) If the purpose of the learning situation is to lead to the application of what has been learned for transfer to other related skills and situations, it would seem that some form of discovery, problem-solving, or trial-and-error strategy should be employed.

(3) Self-paced, closed-loop tasks should be learned primarily through a guided technique, for response consistency.

(4) Externally paced, open-loop tasks should be learned primarily through a discovery technique for familiarity with diverse situations and response adaptions.

(5) The later learning situation should be considered and might determine what the prior learning method should be; e.g., if subsequent experiences are going to occur with the availability of prompts and guides, then it would seem to be a waste of time and effort to conduct the initial learning experience under a discovery method (p. 494).

Some Questions

There is no way for the interested music educator or researcher to stay abreast of all research in motor learning. Rather, we must find those areas of research that hold specific promise for our work. To that end, I submit the following questions for consideration:

What is the relationship between motor learning and other forms of learning in music? Current music education practices place great value in the use of motor activities to develop sensitivity to music stimuli. Is there evidence to warrant belief in such a hypothesis? Does motor ability assist in the perception and subsequent manipulation and recognition of aural events? Can we expect motor performance abilities to enhance or ensure affective and cognitive outcomes?

What application of current motor models should be made to music education? Of the available models of motor learning, which might assist us in understanding motor performance in music? Is there some reason to believe we have different problems in music motor learning? Should we initiate research to test various theories? Should we look for our own model?

What motor skills are important to musical growth? As noted, a large-muscle to small-muscle motor learning program is practiced in music education. There is some current belief and evidence that very refined, small-muscle movement is possible with very young children. Is there objective evidence to explain highly precise, small-muscle capability in four and five year olds? What kinds of generalized motor skills might help to develop sensitivity to music stimuli?

What is the role of proprioception in small-muscle music responses? A large number of correct music performance responses are dependent on precise set prior to the initiation of the response. A thorough understanding of the proprioception/somasthetic phenomenon would help in designing instructional strategies to optimize psychomotor outcomes. We, in music education, have only a generalized knowledge about objectives of this type, and our teaching procedures are, for the most part, chosen without any understanding of this and other important phenomena in motor response.

What about the timing sequence and consideration of motor responses; how are they accomplished? What physiological mechanisms are at work? How do we make so-called automatic patterns from irregular sets? Higgins (1977) has written that coordination is a manifestation of a series of movements that are the result of a complex organization and interactive process. The process involved the integration of experience, central nervous system activity (memory, planning, and information processing), biomechanical factors and conditions of morphology and the environment.

Hence, we are attempting to understand a complex organization of factors that produce a musical response. To this problem of coordination we must add the restraint offered by the fact of rhythm tolerance; we dare not violate by very many milliseconds the timing of either single or multiple music motor responses. In organizing complex sets of motor responses, would it be beneficial to discover how complicated lengthy motor sets develop from diverse types of motor responses?

What can we learn about efficient motor practice? There is much research produced by motor learning specialists on a large variety of motor tasks. What is available in the general area of repetition and practice? Would findings be helpful to us in our attempts to teach accurate motor music performance responses? How can we increase efficiency during nondirected practice? What about overlearning? Does it really ensure retention in a music motor response? What about practice length? Rest between practice? What is the effect of fatigue in motor music learning?

What is the transferability of motor skills in music? What part does cognition play? A prevailing view in music performance training is to develop high levels of technique on the assumption that there will be application to a whole population of motor performance problems. We assume transfer in accurate interval performance in singing, scale passages, arpeggios, and other identifiable pitch and rhythm patterns. Yet one can document countless hours in performance training where lack of pattern recognition retards the accomplishment of an accurate, complete motor response. Hence, this question addresses the problem of transfer of response to supposedly identical patterns of motor response. Are they, in fact, identical or does the ecology of the pattern cause a complete lack of recognition? Is cognition a big factor in this problem? Is there some way to optimize transfer on the basis of more recent research into the problem? According to Lawther (1977), "There is much evidence that individuals do not have a general motor learning ability. Not only do individuals vary greatly in learning rates under comparable conditions, but each individual varies in learning rate from activity to activity."

What are the relationships between motor learning and other types of music learning? This is a key issue for music educators. We are very concerned with efficient learning of pure motor responses for performance, but perhaps more, we want to develop awareness and sensitivity to the aesthetic content of music. For many of us the latter is the primary goal of music education. How, then, does motor learning impact upon such outcomes? Is motor experience and learning really beneficial in producing awareness and sensitivity to

the content of a music event? Can music values be directly influenced through motor experiences and learning?

What about motor learning theory? Is there reason to believe motor patterns in music are different than other motor patterns? The accepted motor learning theories would be a revelation to most music educators. When revealed, however, most music educators would identify elements of several fundamental viewpoints in music motor learning problems. Since the "reals" of music are aural and perhaps less concrete, do feedback loops function differently? If so, is the difference enough to develop different basic models? In order to establish testable hypotheses, should we apply available models or should we theorize differently?

How does motor memory function? The notion of motor memory is very important in music learning. Even the casually questioning music educator is aware of the presence of motor memory in much music performance. There are times when memory for motor activity functions quite apart from any cognitive awareness. On the other hand, certain well-established motor patterns often become jumbled when high-speed recall is necessary; somehow the trace, no matter how well established, will not emerge to produce an action known to be in the vocabulary of the performer.

What about human growth and motor learning? What information might help us understand learner capabilities better in terms of muscle and neural development? Recent developments in music performance indicate that very young children are capable of producing highly refined motor patterns—as in, for example, violin performance. On the other hand, we are reminded of the usual neuromuscular growth program. Are these two phenomena unrelated? Is there evidence that the practice effect has deep consequence in changing motor growth rates? What about optimum music motor growth periods? Are there times when motor learning tasks will show significantly unusual growth? How do carefully programmed drill and overlearning effect normal neural muscular growth?

What aspects of neurophysiology might assist

the music educator in motor learning problems? How about some basic physiological inquiry, particularly as it may relate to some aesthetic activity relatable to aural stimuli and response? How does the feedback system operate when we are dealing with the totally nonverbal sound idea—the sound concept level? Would research on the fundamental aspects of the motor system and processes be helpful to us?

Are there specific types of research paradigms that might prove more efficient in expanding our knowledge of motor learning processes in music?

References

Adams, J. A. A closed loop theory of motor learning, *Journal of Motor Behavior*, 1971, *3*, 111.

————. Issues for a closed loop theory of motor learning. In *Motor Control: Issues and Trends*, G. Stelmach (Ed.), New York: Academic Press, 1976.

Attneave, F. Transfer of experience with a class schema to identification-learning of patterns and shapes. *Journal of Experimental Psychology*, *54*, 81.

Bartlett, F. C. *Remembering: A study in experimental and social psychology*. London: University of Cambridge Press, 1932.

Berel, M., L. Diller, and M. Orgel. Music as a facilitator for visual motor sequencing tasks in children with cerebral palsy. *Developmental Medicine and Child Neurology*, 1971, *13*, 335.

Bond, M. Rhythmic perception and gross motor performance. *Research Quarterly*, 1959, *3*, 259.

Bowman, J. P., and C. M. Combs. Cerebeller responsiveness to stimulation of the lingual spindle afferent fibers in the hypoglossal nerve of the rhesus monkey. *Experimental Neurology*, 1969, *23*, 537.

Boyle, J. D. *The effects of prescribed rhythmical movements on the ability to sight read music.* Unpublished doctoral dissertation, University of Kansas, 1968.

Chernikoff, R., and F. V. Taylor. Reaction time to kinesthetic stimulation resulting from sudden arm displacement. *Journal of Experimental Psychology*, 1952, *43*, 1.

Connolly, K., and J. Elliot. The evolution and ontogeny of hand function. In N. B. Jones (Ed.), *Ethnological studies of child behavior.* Cambridge, England: Cambridge University Press, 1972.

Duerksen, G. L. *Teaching instrumental music.* Washington, D. C.: Music Educators National Conference, 1972.

Elrod, J. M. *The effects of perceptual-motor training and music on perceptual motor development and behavior of educable mentally retarded children* (Doctoral dissertation, 1972). *Dissertation Abstracts International*, 1972, *33*, 2148.

Gates, A., and J. L. Bradshaw. A note on interactions of ears, hands and cerebral hemispheres in a musical performance task requiring bimanual coordination. *British Journal of Psychology*, 1975, *66*, 165.

Gordon, E. *The psychology of music teaching.* Englewood Cliffs, N.J.: Prentice-Hall, 1971.

Groves, W. C. Rhythmic training and its relationship to the synchronization of motor rhythmic responses. *Journal of Research in Music Education*, 1969, *17*, 408–415.

Head, H. *Studies in neurology* (2 Vols). London: Oxford University Press, 1920.

Hickman, A. T. Some preverbal concepts in music. *Journal of Research in Music Education*, 1969, *17*, 70–75.

Higgins, J. R. Movements to match environmental demands. *Research Quarterly*, 1972, *43*, 312.

————. *Human movement: An integrated approach.* St. Louis: C. V. Mosby, 1977.

Il, I., and S. D. Rudneva. The mechanism of musical experience. *Voprosy Psikhologii*, 1971, *17*, 66.

Jacobs, C. Investigation of kinesthetics in violin playing. *Journal of Research in Music Education*, 1969, *17*, 112–114.

Jaques-Dalcroze, E. *Rhythm, music, and education.* New York: G. P. Putnam's Sons, 1921.

Jersild, A., and S. Bienstock. Development of rhythm in young children. *Child Development Monographs.* Teachers College, Columbia University, 1935, *22*, 1.

Jett, A. The analogy of 'learning a language' and 'learning music'. *Modern Language Journal*, 1968, *52*, 436.

Johnson, O., and A. Kozma. Effects of concurrent verbal and musical tasks on a unimanual skill. *Cortex*, 1977, *13*, 11.

Keele, S. W., and J. J. Summers. The structure of motor programs. In George E. Stelmach (Ed.). *Motor control: Issues and trends.* New York: Academic Press, 1976.

Klie, U. Principles of movement in the Orff-Schulwerk. *Musart*, 1970, *22*, 42.

Klemish, J. A review of recent research in elementary music education. *Bulletin of the Council for Research in Music Education*, 1973, *34*, 23.

Kokas, K. Development of interest shown in the process of vocal musical activity. *Magyar Pszichologiai*, 1967, *24*, 187.

Landis, B., and P. Carder. *The eclectic curriculum in American music education: Contributions of Dal-*

croze, Kodály, and Orff. Washington, D. C.: Music Educators National Conference, 1972.

Larsen, R. L., and C. G. Boody. Some implications for music education in the work of Jean Piaget. *Journal of Research in Music Education*, 1971, *19*, 35–50.

Lashley, K. S. *American Journal of Physiology*, 1917, *43*, 169.

———. In L. A. Jeffries, (Ed.). *Cerebral mechanisms in behavior*. New York: Wiley Publishers, 1951.

Lawther, J. D. *The learning and performance of physical skills*. Englewood Cliffs, N.J.: Prentice-Hall, 1977.

Leithwood, K. A., and W. Fowler. Complex motor learning in four year olds. *Child Development*, 1971, *42*, 781.

Leonhard, C., and R. Colwell. Research in music education. *Bulletin of the Council for Research in Music Education*, 1976, *49*, 1.

Mainwaring, J. Kinesthetic factors in the recall of musical experience. *British Journal of Psychology*, 1933, *22*, 284.

Michel, P. The optimum development of musical abilities in the first years of life. *Psychology of Music*, 1973, *1*, 2.

Michon, J. A. *Timing in temporal tracking*. Saesterberg, Institute for Perception RVO-TNO, 1967.

———. Programs and 'programs' for sequential patterns in motor behavior. *Brain Research*, 1974, *71*, 413.

Montcastle, V. B. (Ed.). *Medical physiology* (13th ed.). St. Louis: C. V. Mosby Co., 1974.

Mursell, J. L. *Principles of music education*. New York: MacMillan, 1927.

Pennington, J. *The importance of being rhythmic*. New York: G. P. Putnam's Sons, 1926.

Rainbow, E. Instrumental music: Recent research and considerations for future investigations. *Bulletin of the Council for Research in Music Education*, 1973, *33*, 8.

Reardon, D., and G. Bell. Effects of sedative and stimulative music on activity levels of severely retarded boys. *American Journal of Mental Deficiency*, 1970, *75*, 156.

Reitmeyer, J. W. The application of negative practice to the correction of habitual fingering errors in clarinet performance. *Dissertation Abstracts International*, 1973, *33*, 3403.

Richman, J. S. Background music for repetitive task performance of severely retarded individuals. *American Journal of Mental Deficiency*, 1976, *81*, 251.

Seashore, R. Studies in motor rhythm. *Studies in Child Welfare*, 1926, *2*, 149.

Schmidt, R. A. The schema as a solution to some persistent problems in motor learning theory. In George E. Stelmach (Ed.). *Motor control: Issues and trends*. New York: Academic Press, 1976.

Singer, R. N. Instructional strategies for psycho-motor skills. *Review of Education Research*, 1977, *47*, 479.

Stelmach, G. E. *Motor control: Issues and trends*. New York: Academic Press, 1976.

Taebel, D. K. The effect of various instructional modes on children's performance of music concept tasks. *Journal of Research in Music Education*, 1974, *22*, 170–183.

Thackray, R. Rhythmic abilities and their measurement. *Journal of Research in Music Education*, 1969, *17*, 144–148.

Welford, A. T. *Skilled performance: Perceptual and motor skills*. Glenview, Illinois: Scott, Foresman and Co., 1976.

Wing, A. M. Perturbations of auditory feedback delay and the timing of movement. *Journal of Experimental Psychology: Human Perception and Performance*, 1977, *3*, 175.

Zimmerman, M. P. *Musical characteristics of children*. Washington, D. C.: Music Educators National Conference, 1971.

Response

Frank Restle

Is it possible that music means something and embodies an idea or a concept? If so, the conclusion throws a certain light on the problems of perception, conceptual learning, motor learning, and motor performance.

You can have a child try to perform or reproduce some music by singing it to him and having him try to sing it back. Alternatively, you can show the music to him as a score and have him try to produce the music from its written form. Those two ways of presenting information to the child are obviously quite different, and, it seems to me, both present very difficult problems to a child or musician, and somewhat different problems. When you present the music auditorily, essentially in the form the child is to give it back to you, if there is an idea in the music, then auditory presentation of that idea is presumably appropriate. I am assuming that musical ideas are best expressed through music. So the first thought I have is that if you sing a vocal line to a child, the singing is a good way of presenting it; there is a very high probability of his getting the idea, of extracting the concept you wanted.

Of course, the stimulus is fleeting, and so it can't be studied unless it can be remembered. Now suppose that it is very difficult to remember this auditory stimulus itself. What the listener remembers is whatever information he or she got out of it, which is fine if he gets the information. If he can remember the line, then he can study it. But if the listener did not get any information, he cannot rehearse the melody to himself, and he is in trouble and needs to hear it again.

If the teacher presents a musical line in visual form, the problem is different. Now I am not a great lover of the standard way of writing music, because I find it extremely difficult to decode, but it has an advantage in that some representation of the melodic, harmonic, and rhythmic pattern is there to study. The listener can scan back and forth, see how the melody starts and how it ends, and can compare patterns on the page. In a sense the listener can get out of real time and simultaneously look at two forms or music patterns that do not exist at the same time. There are things you can do with written music in the way of analysis in which the visual presentation itself is superior. Now, written notation is awkward for the beginner, especially rhythm notation. Also, a great deal of detail is missing. The difference between the total musical experience and what can be notated is tremendous. It is almost impossible, I gather, to write down the interpretation. It's understood in written music that the musician is going to have to have some freedom, that written music is merely a sketch of what is contained in performance.

A question that came up, has to do with levels of difficulty. My musical gifts, which are somewhat limited, were inherited by my children, who also have very limited musical skills. The children were all, however, dutifully trained up to a certain point. Despite my other limitations, I am a good father; I sat on the sofa while they practiced so they would be encouraged, so they would have someone there to applaud if they should happen to hit a right note. When Kathy went through the book I found some pieces were easy and others were not so easy; when Phillip went through the book I heard similar difficulties, and it seemed to be with the same pieces. By the time Andrea studied, I would cringe in anticipation; she would play exactly the same wrong notes as the other two. And, simple pieces like the "Little Minuet" by Bach, which has fewer notes at a lower speed and a lower range and simpler fingering than anything else in that book, was by far the most difficult for the children. Later, I tried an analysis of this piece and concluded that Bach just could not be simple and the piece has various sources of difficulty. I suppose that the musical idea is almost a pure example of organization, of how things can fit together, how you can take an abstract idea, vary it, and combine it with other ideas and establish a cognitive process to organize things serially.

In music, very generally, the parts of the work are related to one another in such a way that you have little pieces or phrases that are combined into larger expressions, which in turn are combined into larger expressions, which in turn are combined. You can look at a piece at several different levels and analyze in that way. In my laboratory, over the years, we have done some work on that sort of process that subjects might engage in learning a pattern or a sequence.

Consider a work that takes a simple melody, repeats it, maybe makes a little change in it, repeats it, then goes back to the original form and repeats it. If it gets really exciting, it introduces a related fragment and then goes back into the first melody. Such a work has a structure that is really very simple, and can be described as a central strain with a few repetitions and variations on it. Another work of the same length can have a much deeper structure. For a long time I thought that this sort of conceptual depth of music was the source of difficulty. Our experiments have yielded evidence that more or less disagreed. Perhaps it is not the depth of the music but the complexity of the structure of the sequence that controls how difficult it is. More recently I have come to question my own earlier conclusion, and I now think that the trouble comes from ambiguity. That is, the difficulty of a piece comes about because it has more than one interpretation. Typically, more difficult works do not have a single, simple interpretation, but they offer distinct alternatives. The performing musician has the opportunity of changing his interpretation so as to suggest more than one way of understanding the music.

I come to this hypothesis not only because of my children but because the subjects in our experiments also tend to make exactly the same errors. As we have tried to find out what is characteristic of the points in the music that produce the errors, it always turns out that the subject has one idea of the structure but the task demands a different one. This, if you think of it, means the structure of the music is ambiguous.

I'd like to talk about another related topic, the execution of music, from the experimental psychologist's point of view. Music performance is a task of incredible complexity; you see many variables including the instrument used, the speed in selecting the note to be played, how the pitch is to be achieved correctly, and how the vibrato and loudness are controlled. And as you observe closely it is easy to come to the conclusion, at least from the psychologist's point of view, that the whole performance is quite impossible. I think that's the most sensible conclusion one can draw. The only possibility that I can see is that these many different aspects of this very complex task really must not be that complicated. Because the musician who is doing all these impossible things with his eyes closed and with a very concentrated but somewhat dreamy look on his face is engaged in a dance, is obviously enjoying himself, and is not thinking about any of these competencies or mechanical, technical questions at all. We must suppose that the musician is expressing, dealing with the musical ideas, and that the motions and the sounds are all subordinated to cognitive structures of some sort. Somehow, if we understand this process correctly, the subordination is complete in an accomplished musician so that all those complexities that we talk about will be found to be manifestations of a completely wrong interpretation and analysis of what's going on—completely wrong, at least from a psychological standpoint. A person is not coordinating his intonation with his rhythm, with his accents, and so forth, but is expressing an idea, and all these other characteristics simply follow.

There are a few things I'd like to know more about. To what degree *does* the trombonist have to have the right amount of air, the right tightness of his lips, and the slide in the right place? Or, does he have here a set of variables that can in effect compensate for one another, so that he has many different ways to produce the note he wants and the sound he wants? He might produce it differently sliding into it from above or below, or in different phrases. We see some of that sort of thing in speech perception, in which people make recognizable sounds in different ways, depending on the context. And, of course, most people have no idea how to control their speech gestures. Most people, who can speak the language fluently and have normal hearing, have practically no idea how they speak. The only people who know how to do it, mostly, are deaf people.

From a psychological point of view, the extreme complexity of musical performance may have to be understood in terms of this higher level of organization which is composed of the musical ideas. This makes me want to inquire about the procedure of the child being taught to play something letter-perfect and then go on to something else. In this process, there is little attention to whether students had the right idea. My children played minuets without anyone ever in any way trying to explain to them what in the hell a minuet was. They looked at notes and were required to produce them. When they produced them with the right total time distributed more or less the way the teacher intended, that was it and then we went on to something else. That is, through no fault of the teacher, it was never clear what the idea was. Maybe the teacher knew, but I'm sure some of the students can never find out. And, if that is true, then the child, especially learning the piano at a rather young age, is put in front of an extremely complicated machine which he is expected to learn to operate.

In some of our laboratory experiments, we got students in the university who were musicians. One of the tasks they had to do, was to listen to a melody being played on a little beeper, and, using a keyboard, to play along with it as if they were playing the melody. We found that untrained people with no music training could not learn this task in any reasonable time. Anyone with music training, keyboard or no, learned it, with one exception. We had one piano student who could not do it. I'm not sure this was a student in the music department in piano, but it was a student who had years and years of training in piano. Fortunately, the graduate student who was doing the experiment held a rather lengthy conversation with this subject since her failure was rather puzzling. It turned out that she did play rather well and played very difficult pieces, but she did remark that she had never been able to memorize anything or play anything by ear; if you took the score away, she stopped. Here we had a woman who unfortunately had never improvised, who was almost a pure case of going from eye to the fingers directly, without any involvement in the auditory realm.

One thing I am really interested in and would like to hear discussed by music educators is the art of improvisation. I think that when one learns language, one learns a little bit of vocabulary and then starts to use it. It's remarked sometimes that children don't begin repeating back what their mother says,

but pick up some pieces and then start saying what *they* have to say, and working on ideas. Children do much the same thing with humming, dances, and whistling, but I'm not sure to what extent it is part of the modern music education system. A way to develop a set of musical ideas, of course, is to play with them. And my limited experience suggests that that sounds very much like improvising.

The other comment that I will make using this same theme has to do with over-learning. Over-learning is a funny term in psychology, because the question you're asked is "Over what?" It is training beyond some point. And the point usually is the point at which the subject can just barely struggle through the task. And if he has once made it somehow over a criterion that is often quite imperfect, from then on it's over-training. I suppose that most of the learning of the cognitive structure or the idea in the music really only begins when at least the ordinary, technical difficulties have been mastered. A person cannot just look at a score or listen to music and think deeply about it. People seem to think about it more as they are playing. My suggestion would be that as the learner is coming to understand the structure of the music, which in many cases is very deep, learning would require many repetitions as the child might perceive a small part, then another, and then see the relations between the parts, gradually building up larger and larger relational structures. That is certainly the way people learn the patterns in our lab; they learn low-level pieces first, and then start seeing the relations between them.

Some of the things that we know from psychological experiments suggest that complicated motor performance is difficult unless it is guided by a well-organized cognitive structure. It seems reasonable to me that this would be true of music. What I have tried to do is to frame at least an approach to some of the questions that were brought up with the hypothesis that music might have meaning.

38

Response

David LaBerge

Before we teach any skill we should really understand how it is done. For many hundreds of years, people built bridges without really understanding the underlying principles. They went ahead and built them because they needed them, and they could not wait for science to provide basic principles. The skill was an art and not a science until engineering came along and taught us something about the strength of materials and stress patterns. Today they first teach us engineering from the basic principles of physics, and then the methods of building a particular kind of bridge simply fall out of theory, because it is now understood how the process of supporting a body or a vehicle across a space works. In reading research today we are trying to understand how written language is processed. We do not yet know how we process a work. Surely students cannot wait for us to understand all the basic principles before we try to teach them to read. It may be years before we know how the perceptual and semantic processing in reading works. We teach the best we can with the tools we have available from our present level of understanding.

The related problem in music education as I see it is similar to that of teaching reading. How does the mature performer carry out his skill and how do we get the novice to that stage? I would approach a problem such as this one as I did with reading. I would devise a theory, at least the beginnings of a theoretical framework, to tell me what kinds of experiments I should be doing. Typically a researcher sees many experiments that could be done. The big question is which one to do next. Theory can answer that question. In addition, theory organizes findings and mediates applications. Eventually, theory should give us an understanding of how a skill is performed at each of the stages as it becomes more and more mature and perfected. However, the expectations from a theoretically oriented research program of this kind should be cautiously considered because we are not likely to get quick results from a crash program. Apparently, in scientific problems as complex as education, one cannot throw a lot of money at a problem and expect to come up with an answer. I think that we should expect genuine progress only from long-range research programs.

If one were to outline a theory-based research program, what issues should be central? I believe the most important thing we can say about motor skill is that it is organized in a complex way and that we must get the key to this organization. Often an analogy is drawn between music and language skills. We hear it said that reading is like listening, because perceptual skills are dominant, and that speaking and writing are like singing and instrumental performance, because motor skills are dominant. But in performing, of course, perceptual skills are needed as well. A difference between the two skills is that performance in music repeats patterns and is typically practiced to a point of a predictable perfection in detail, while language production is not. There are exceptions such as in poetry and theatre. But curiously, when sentences become highly repetitive, we often find that they are put to music. For example, the litany in religious services is often sung, and a mother can wake up her child and call the child to dinner with words put to melody.

Consider one of the most critical problems in reading today—namely, the problem of units. I think that the understanding of how units are formed is an appropriate beginning to the understanding of any complex skill, whether it be a perceptual skill, a motor skill, or a combination of the two. We often say that a skill is structured in terms of units, perhaps because they provide a manageable way to approach structure. We usually can point to a unit. For example, a unit may be one finger pressing on a keyboard as an instance of a motor unit, or a letter may be singled out as a perceptual unit. One of the problems with the unit approach today, however, is that it is commonly believed that units are organized and combined hierarchically. Many psychologists take this view of reading. They tell us that we first teach all the subskills, and then put them together to produce an accomplished reader. Hedden points out this problem by observing that the common strategy in music is that of practicing components first and then combining them. First we learn the notes and polish up the tone quality, and then we add phrasing, somewhat like topping to the dessert. I believe that this approach is very suspect in perceiving a word, because a word may very well not be the sum of the letters. Experiments carried out over the past several years seem to be converging on the conclusion that the importance of letters in the recognition of a word has been grossly overrated. Apparently there are other features that we perceive in a word. A trivial example is its length. There seem also to be internal relationships, but these features are very hard to point to, compared to the ease with which we can point to a letter. Likewise, we might find the same thing true for a phrase of music. Suppose we take as an example the first six notes of the familiar F major *Invention* of Bach. An accomplished performer would say that these notes can be regarded as one unit, and if the person wants to put that sequence together with the rest of the phrase and make a good envelope of sound, he or she is certainly not going to think of the first six notes as 1-2-3-4-5-6. There is something different about the combination of the parts that is not in any one of the parts. This is an old problem, first enunciated clearly by the Gestalt psychologists who stated that the whole is different than the sum of the parts.

Now, the very thing that may be most important in performing these notes as one unit is the hardest thing to point to or verbalize, and therefore the hardest thing to teach. We can teach things we can point to because we can draw people's attention to them. But we cannot draw a person's attention very easily to whatever makes these six notes hang together. Rather we must find our own particular ways of interrelating the notes to chunk them into a higher order unit. In the learning of these units, control of attention shifts from smaller units to larger units.

This is related to Sidnell's question about the relationship between motor learning and other forms of learning. I would say that motor learning is close to perceptual learning in many respects. In perceptual learning of letters, for example, we can identify three stages. In the first stage we learn to select the distinctive features by which we tell letters apart. In the second stage we unify the features into a letter unit. In the third stage we do the unitizing automatically; that is, we progressively withdraw our attention from the task. I am suggesting that the same thing happens in the organization of any skill. I would tentatively say that for motor learning we select small movements in the first stage; that is, we select the right notes. In the second phase, we must unify these notes somehow, and that process takes a lot of attention. We use trial and error trying to find the right global relational features. In the third stage, the act becomes relatively automatic.

The process of unitizing in large chunks requires that the performer perceive rather large global relationships, both in the musical sounds and in the kinesthetic feelings. It seems that Hedden's statement about pre-rehearsal fits this notion of perceiving larger global relationships as learning progresses. If we rehearse by imagining a section of music before we play it, we are much more likely to pay attention to the overall shape of the section than when we are actually playing the individual notes. The very act of execution fills attention with detail, so that we are less likely to pick up some new structural type of information. It would be very valuable to know how to explicitly teach a person to perceive the larger global relationships necessary to form larger units. Unfortunately the method of conscientious repetition is used too often for the good of the student. When one is too careful, one focuses on small units and it is easy to get stuck at that level. This seems to happen to students of reading as well. They never risk making an error, so they do not try new ways of looking at words. If the student is to perceive the larger globals, they must look at the word in a new way. And that means taking a risk of making some mistakes.

Discovering global relationships may be considered a creative event and should be encouraged. Each student should do it in his or her own way. We should let students find the way that their hands best put the notes together. Let them discover their own particular kind of kinesthetic feedbacks, and thereby form their own way of unitizing. Once a motor unit is formed, the next goal is automaticity, which frees attention so that one can use it for the purpose of the task at hand—namely, to create the mood or overall shape of the music.

Now we move into another section of motor learning, which involves attention to the structuring of the piece as a whole, especially to its mood and to whatever content it may have, metaphoric or otherwise. I believe we seek to free attention from the fingers and perform in the manner of the best improvisers. We want the music to occur spontaneously, as if it were born at that moment.

We are beginning to see that there are two kinds of patterns in the world. First, there are a few things that we deal with very often. For example, there are only a few letters and relatively few words, but we use them very frequently. Secondly, there are many things that we deal with very seldom. For example, there are a great many sentences that we hear and use, but each one is typically used only once. Likewise in music, there are relatively few individual sounds and small patterns that are used over and over again, but there are a very large number of possible sequences of these units, and the sequences are repeated relatively infrequently. Consider the small patterns that we use over and over again, (for example, scale segments and arpeggios). We want these small patterns to be automatic because we want to free our attention to focus on the larger sections of music, which is what people come to our performances to hear. The life that is in the music stems from patterns of large scope performed in ways that are infrequently repeated. Thus, to put the shapes of long sections of a piece at the focus of our attention, we must develop the smaller component patterns to the level of automaticity.

The goal here is not perfection; perfection is the aim of technique. The goal here is the life in the music.

Child Development

Robert G. Petzold

The most cursory examination of the extensive amount of research and writing available in psychology, educational psychology, developmental psychology, child development, and learning theory is sufficient indication that some clarification is needed to bring these various fields into focus.

Developmental psychology, although frequently classified as a branch of psychology, is not an isolated or independent field any more than psychology and educational psychology are mutually exclusive disciplines. Principles of learning, perception, motivation, social behavior, and the physiological bases of development are as basic to developmental psychology as they are to other branches of psychology. The study of the developmental processes from infancy through adolescence did not emerge as a scientific discipline until the twentieth century. Earlier efforts in the field had emphasized the normative development of the individual and were limited to the discovery and precise description of age trends; to measuring age changes in physical, psychological, and behavioral characteristics. However, this precise description of events and phenomena such as detailed tracings of the sequences of steps in the child's acquisition of behaviors, such as walking, talking, or manipulating objects, or plotting age change curves of intellectual growth failed to produce any satisfactory explanation of these behaviors. The need to examine the antecedent-consequent relationships from which theories of behavior might be generated led to a dramatic shift in the direction of research.

> For the last forty years, researchers in developmental psychology have become increasingly concerned with the processes underlying human growth and development—with a theoretical synthesis of observed phenomena which can provide us with the *how* and *why* of the origins of behavior and changes in behavior (Mussen, Conger, and Kagan, 1974, p. 10).

The earlier distinction between child psychology, with its primary concern for the ways in which children behave and how this behavior differs from that of an adult, and developmental psychology, where maturation is examined, may no longer be tenable.

Child development, regardless of whether or not it is considered a separate discipline, represents a field of research and theory-building that seeks to describe and explain how the motives, beliefs, behaviors, personality, and cognitive-intellectual abilities of the adult are gradually formed over the first twenty years of life. In addition to the efforts of developmental psychologists, educational psychologists and psychologists with interests in specific aspects of child development have made significant contributions to the field. Since the terms appear to be used interchangeably, it is difficult to differentiate between child development and developmental psychology.

Literature in the field of child development shows that substantial research occurs in at least four major areas: (1) physiological development, (2) language development, (3) cognitive development, and (4) socialization and personality development. Each of these, together with their related sub-areas, is of concern to music educators. Although the efforts of developmental psychologists have not usually been directed toward specific subject-matter fields, there is reason to believe that certain of their findings might be generalizable to music learning and development.

Our understanding of the child's psychological world helps us plan and organize instruction so that we are constantly aware of the probable behavioral responses of children. We know that children move from concrete to abstract goals; that younger children are unable to respond to a wide variety of stimuli but focus attention on one stimulus at a time; that they move from responding to objects that are immediately present to objects or goals that are more remote in terms of time (past or future), space (travel distance), logic (planning moves in a checker game), or mediation (how we obtain information about the external world).

Although development is a continuous process, there may be "critical periods" when certain events assume more crucial significance in the individual's life than they do at other times. Although various labels have been attached to these periods, stages, or phases by different theorists, most child development textbooks present them as prenatal, the first two years, the preschool years, middle childhood (ages six to twelve), and adolescence. Mussen, Conger, and Kagan (1963) list five major categories or agents of influence that include (1) genetically determined biological variables, (2) nongenetic biological variables such as the lack of oxygen during the birth process or maternal diseases during pregnancy, (3) the child's past learning, (4) the child's immediate social environment, and (5) the general social-cultural environment in which the child develops. The first two have been called nature forces, while the others are nurture or environmental forces. Although some may take a position as to which, if either, is most important, the matter appears rather academic unless one examines the kind of question that is being asked and why it is even asked in the first place. For example, is it not possible that illiteracy could, under some conditions, be attributed to a lack of educational opportunity in the society while under other conditions to inherited mental deficiency? Or that a fine singer is not necessarily the consequence of the mother's singing to herself and her unborn child during pregnancy? It is more reasonable to accept the position that either heredity or environment, or an interaction involving both, may influence the appearance or development of a certain characteristic, behavior, or ability. Researchers now are directing their attention to how genetic or environmental factors affect behavior and development rather than continuing to pose unanswerable questions of which trait or how much of a given trait is attributed to heredity or to environment. Although the effects of biological variables are irreversible in most cases, we can give meaningful attention to the environmental factors as these influence the child throughout critical developmental periods.

To establish a manageable target area, I have elected to limit the balance of this paper to matters relevant for children of elementary school age, recognizing that infancy, early

43

childhood, and adolescence also are within the domain of child development.

The elementary school music curriculum has been viewed by many American music educators as the only means whereby substantial numbers of children can achieve a minimal level of music literacy. Once the child leaves the elementary school, at approximately twelve years of age, required music classes are replaced by elective, more specialized performance-oriented classes generally involving fewer children. If we agree that the major objective of the music program of the elementary school is to develop music understanding and responsiveness, it would follow that the attention of teachers must be directed toward helping students attain those music concepts that are the substance of a music program at any level of instruction. Because the conceptual structure of music resides within the elements of music, it is possible to group concepts, and principles, into at least five general categories. Selected examples of these would include:

(1) Rhythm: duration, beat, pulse, accent, meter, subdivisions of units (even, uneven, duple, triple), and durative combinations yielding rhythmic patterns.

(2) Melody: tonal movement, tonal patterns, and tonality.

(3) Harmony: multiple sounds, chords, progressions of chords as these relate to melodic material, and texture, as experienced in homophonic and polyphonic music.

(4) Music form: motive, phrase, section, repetition, contrast, variation, and the more complex forms-structures for which we have specific names.

(5) Style: the complex, interrelated concepts or principles used to identify or characterize music of different historical periods, styles, types, genres, and cultures.

This *means* by which this broad array of music concepts can be attained includes the development of skills in listening, performing, and music reading through a variety of class and individual activities.

Most of our music learning depends upon the ways in which we perceive and respond to music. It is interesting to note that al-

though child development literature is replete with studies of visual acuity, perception, and discrimination, there are relatively few studies concerned with aural discrimination except those that utilize language or numbers. Attempts to measure the musical perceptual abilities of children younger than seven or eight have not always been successful because of the inherent difficulty of constructing tasks to which children can make meaningful and understandable responses. For example, most discrimination tasks call for a verbal response such as "up," "down," "higher," "lower," "same," "different," "long," "short," "faster," "slower," "louder," or "softer" for comparing a second sound, or group of sounds, with an initial stimulus or for describing the stimulus itself. These are words that children use in contexts other than music and, until they have actually learned how to apply the word to a music situation, they may be unable to provide adequate discriminatory responses. To illustrate the problem, Andrews and Deihl (1967) found that even fourth-grade children evidenced semantic confusion by interchanging terms such as "high," "loud," and "fast" with "low," "soft," and "slow." Laverty (1969) found similar confusion at both the third- and fifth-grade levels; children frequently used words we normally assign to dynamics in describing changes in pitch or tempo and used words associated with pitch or tempo to describe changes in dynamics. Even the meaning young children give to "same-different" comparisons, as well as their evident failure to understand that they are to compare the second example against the first, has produced confusing and inaccurate data.

Van Zee (1976) found that kindergarten children have no common or characteristic vocabulary in using verbal responses to describe certain kinds of music stimuli, and Hair (1977) recommended that substantial amounts of training were needed before children were capable of using appropriate verbal labels to indicate tonal direction. Taebel (1974) concluded that verbal cues used to call attention to music events are useful only if the child has a stable concept of the phenomenon and that there may well be a critical point in the child's development when verbal cues and labels are most beneficial in concept learning.

In an effort to minimize such data-gathering problems, several researchers, including Andrews and Deihl (1967), Boekelheide (1960), and Jeffrey (1958), developed tasks that required nonverbal or manipulative responses. These included using hand and arm gestures and larger physical movements, pushing one or more colored buttons to correspond to different tones, or duplicating the sounds that were heard on simple instruments. Still another type of nonverbal response is for the child to reproduce the given music stimulus by singing that stimulus. This latter response requires that singing accuracy and adequate vocal control be in evidence if the child's response is to produce accurate data.

Although these data-gathering difficulties tend to disappear as children mature and have had additional instruction in music, it is essential that the problem be resolved in order to conduct meaningful research relating to the development of music awareness and responsiveness. Although many children have had substantial informal contact with music prior to the time they enter school, they do not use music as they do language. Therefore, music researchers cannot necessarily employ the same techniques as child development researchers interested in the development of language.

Boekelheide (1960), studying the perceptual skills of eight- and nine-year-old children, found that only half of the children could accurately identify whether the second phrase was played higher, lower, or at the same pitch level as the initial phrase; and that approximately sixty percent of the children could identify that the second playing of a phrase, using instruments that were in contrast to those employed in the initial performance, was "alike," "not alike," or "almost alike," with the latter differentiation being most difficult. However, almost half of these children could, on the basis of three examples notated in simplified "line notation," identify the six- to fourteen-note melodic

fragment that they heard three times. She also found that more than eighty percent of the children were able to select the stick figure illustration that was most representative of the rhythmic response one might make to a given music excerpt. The options, which presumably had to be learned and experienced first, included walking, swinging, hopping, marching, skipping, jumping, galloping, swaying, and turning.

Piaget and others agree that young children tend to center their perception on the dominant or attractive (to them) aspects of an otherwise diffuse and complex perceptual field. The ability of children to perceive multiple sounds, or to differentiate between several elements present in a given music situation, has been studied by several persons. Although children do not appear to have consistent preferences for "appropriate" harmony (Bridges, 1975) it is clear that simple harmonic accompaniments lead to more accurate melodic responses than when more complex and distracting accompaniments are provided (Petzold, 1963). In studies that have combined the rhythmic and melodic elements into a single perceptual situation there is some evidence that children, because of the mode of response, find it easier to focus on the rhythm (Petzold, 1963). Complex rhythmic discriminations, tonal memory, and judgments as to form and music style are, together with skills in utilizing music notation, dependent upon both maturation and instruction.

Music concepts, however they may be defined, are formed as a consequence of aural perceptions, overt behavioral responses in a variety of music situations, and the concurrent development and application of a meaningful vocabulary. Many researchers have discovered that the child's verbal ability is a more significant factor in certain tasks than is age or maturation, something Piaget already has suggested for tasks at successive developmental levels.

The majority of Piagetian research in music is concerned with applying the principle of conservation to a variety of music tasks. Pflederer (1967), taking her cues from Piaget, has discussed the role of intellectual processes in music learning and suggested that five "conservation-type" laws might be identified in the development of music concepts: identity, metric groupings, augmentation and diminution, transposition, and inversion. Her pioneer work in this field is well known (Pflederer, 1964, 1966, 1967) as is her collaboration with Sechrist (Pflederer and Sechrist, 1968; Zimmerman (née Pflederer) and Sechrist, 1968, 1970). Larsen (1973) utilized a four-part variation task, parts of which involved concrete operations and others of which involved formal operations. He concluded that older subjects were more aware of the permutations than younger ones, which was compatible with Piaget's theory. Taebel (1974) explored the concepts of tempo, volume, pitch, and duration in order to ascertain whether training had a significant influence on the conceptual abilities of children. Jones (1974) attempted to delineate an invariant sequence of stages in the development of a concept (selecting meter as the concept), and had confidence that he had been successful. However, Perney's follow-up to the Jones study (1976) yielded inconclusive results and so the issue of an invariant stage remains somewhat in doubt. Foley (1975) concluded that music conservation of tonal and rhythmic patterns can be improved with training, and that such training need not extend over a long period of time.

Multiple discrimination training, defined by Gagné and others, has served as the theoretical basis for several studies of music-perception skills. Porter (1977) found no evidence that faulty singing is the result of inaccurate pitch perception when she examined the pitch-matching behaviors of uncertain singers, but that training in multiple discrimination increased the probability of transfer to other related tasks more than did the method of successive approximation. The work of Hufstader (1977), Jetter (1978), and Kuhn and Gates (1975), to cite only three studies, all bears upon the highly probable existence of a developmental sequence as this relates to selected perceptual skills.

The development of skill in reading music notation, although never completely eliminated as one of the objectives of the elemen-

tary school music program, has received varying amounts of emphasis from decade to decade. It would appear that this skill depends entirely upon the attainment of those tonal and rhythmic concepts that are represented by music notation. Attainment of both the essential concepts and the skill of reading occurs over time as children engage in meaningful activities that use music notation. Interest in this complex cognitive process, although producing substantial amounts of research, has received relatively little attention in recent years. Without attempting to discuss any of the research, it would appear that the instructional procedures followed in the general music classes of the elementary school are not as efficient and effective as we had hoped them to be in terms of helping children acquire minimal music-reading competence. In addition to the many variables that are not directly under the control of the music teacher, we appear to experience difficulty in identifying an appropriate sequence of tasks and activities that can facilitate this kind of skill development.

There is a substantial body of research literature, spanning several decades, that deals with the development of vocal skills and with motor-rhythmic development. These skills continue to be used by children as they perceive and respond to the several elements of music that they encounter both in and out of class. Much of this information, although readily accessible, has not yet been effectively used in organizing the music learning experiences of children in the elementary school.

For obvious reasons, only limited information is available with respect to the attitudes, interests, motives, and needs and values of children of elementary school age. The difficulty of interpreting children's verbal responses to music, which are highly introspective and unclear, has led researchers to turn their attention to the music preferences and attitudes of adolescents. This is not to suggest that the very strong influences upon children's learning by these factors, together with the implications of their out-of-school environment upon these attitudes and

46

interests, are ignored by teachers. The substantial contributions made by child development specialists to our knowledge about children's motives, needs, and values must become more familiar to music teachers since these variables are as influential in student achievement as are the ways in which we organize learning experiences to facilitate conceptual growth and skill development.

I would like to conclude with what I consider to be issues and concerns related to child development and music learning and teaching:

(1) Anyone who has read Hilgard and Bower's *Theories of Learning* is aware that there is no single, unified, comprehensive theory of learning to which we can refer. Although learning theorists may agree on a definition of learning, they are divided on most of the substantive issues related to the nature of learning and the conditions under which learning occurs. A similar situation exists in child development where, according to Baldwin in his *Theories of Child Development*, theories do not overlap; there are few issues on which any two theories actually confront each other, and generally they talk past each other on the issues. How can music educators and researchers make decisions as to which portions or which theories are most relevant to the field of music? At the present time we appear to be "swept off our feet" by the blandishments of S-R and behaviorists, Piaget, Bruner, and others. We pick and choose, often misinterpret and misapply the research findings and generalizations based on nonmusic data to problems in music. We examine the literature on language development and suggest that there are parallels in music; the literature on cognition, which uses data that are essentially verbal or mathematical, as well as the literature on perception, all tends to hold out the potential for application to the field of music and to music phenomena.

(2) Developmental psychologists have emphasized the need for longitudinal studies as providing more meaningful information than that which normally comes from cross-sectional studies. We are familiar with the techniques, but continue to use the latter as

we attempt to identify developmental sequences or trends in the acquisition of music concepts and skills.

(3) Much has been said about conceptual development. Without falling into the usual trap of listing music learnings in the cognitive, affective, and psychomotor domains—although these categories of objectives have been most useful—can we now begin to establish some kind of logical and reasonable hierarchy of music concepts and principles? From an instructional point of view, will it make a substantial difference if we begin with concepts that are more closely related to the "rhythm of the words" rather than with concepts that emphasize the beat or pulse of the music? Does it make any difference whether we use music materials that are scalar before we involve children in chordal kinds of tonal movement? Or is the reverse order of presentation more effective? Or does the order actually make no difference?

(4) The cognitive development of children has been studied extensively and several theories have been advanced to account for this kind of development. Are the processes and structures that developmental psychologists have identified applicable to music? How can music educators and developmental psychologists use the expertise of both groups in defining the processes and structures of musical thought?

(5) And finally, what techniques that have been successful in helping children acquire concepts in other areas of human learning can be adapted to music learning? If, as Bruner and Piaget both say, the child learns through manipulating real objects in acquiring concepts of length, space, volume, and number, how can we make more "real" the concepts of pitch, duration, and all others with which we now deal from a purely aural approach?

I am convinced that the preschool and middle childhood years are the most crucial in the development of children. It is here that their attitudes toward music, their interest in music, and the foundation for successful musical learning are established. There is scarcely a high school anywhere in the country that does not have an established music program to meet the needs and interests of those adolescents who seek further experiences in music. However, many of these students have developed these interests "in spite of" rather than "because of" their experiences in the elementary school music class. If we are to influence the value system of adults in our society, we must start while they are children—with strong, viable, and extensive elementary school music programs.

References

Andrews, F. M., and N. C. Deihl. *Development of a technique for identifying elementary school children's musical concepts* (Cooperative Research Project 5-0233). Pennsylvania State University, September 1967.

Boekelheide, V. *Some techniques of assessing certain basic music listening skills of eight and nine year olds.* Unpublished doctoral dissertation, Stanford University, 1960.

Bridges, V. *An exploratory study of the harmonic discrimination ability of children in kindergarten through grade three.* Unpublished doctoral dissertation, Ohio State University, 1965.

Foley, E. Effects of training in conservation of tonal and rhythmic patterns of second-grade children. *Journal of Research in Music Education,* 1975, *23,* 240–248.

Hair, H. Discrimination of tonal direction on verbal and nonverbal tasks by first grade children. *Journal of Research in Music Education,* 1977, *25,* 197–210.

Hooper, S. The development of a test battery to measure music reading readiness of children in grades three and four. *Journal of Research in Music Education,* 1966, *14,* 115–125.

Hufstader, R. An investigation of a learning sequence of music listening skills. *Journal of Research in Music Education,* 1977, *25,* 184–196.

Jeffrey, W. Variables in early discrimination learning (pitch). *Child Development,* 1958, *29,* 531–538.

Jetter, J. An instructional model for teaching identification and naming of music phenomena to preschool children. *Journal of Research in Music Education,* 1978, *26,* 97–110.

Jones, R. The development of the child's conception of meter in music. *Journal of Research in Music Education,* 1974, *24,* 142–154.

Kuhn, T., and E. Gates. Effects of notational values, age, and example length on tempo performance accuracy. *Journal of Research in Music Education,* 1975, *23,* 203–210.

Larsen, R. Levels of conceptual development in melodic permutation concepts based on Piaget's theory. *Journal of Research in Music Education,* 1973, *21,* 256–263.

Laverty, G. *The development of children's concepts of pitch, duration, and loudness as a function of grade level.* Unpublished doctoral dissertation, Pennsylvania State University, 1969.

Mussen, P. J., J. J. Conger, and J. Kagan. *Child development and personality.* New York: Harper & Row, 1963.

_____. *Child development and personality* (4th ed.). New York: Harper & Row, 1974.

Perney, J. Musical tasks related to the development of the conservation of metric time. *Journal of Research in Music Education,* 1976, *24,* 159–168.

Petzold, R. The development of auditory perception of music sounds by children in the first six grades. *Journal of Research in Music Education,* 1963, *11,* 21–43.

Pflederer, M. The responses of children to musical tasks embodying Piaget's principle of conservation. *Journal of Research in Music Education,* 1964, *12,* 251–268.

_____. How children conceptually organize musical sounds. *Bulletin of the Council for Research in Music Education,* 1966, *7,* 1–12. (a)

_____. A study of conservation of tonal and rhythmic patterns in elementary school children. *California Journal of Educational Research,* 1966, *17,* 52–62. (b)

_____. Conservation laws applied to the development of musical intelligence. *Journal of Research in Music Education,* 1967, *15,* 215–223.

Pflederer, M., and L. Sechrist. Conservation-type responses of children to musical stimuli. *Bulletin of the Council for Research in Music Education,* 1968, *13,* 19–36.

Porter, S. The effect of multiple discrimination training on pitch-matching behaviors of uncertain singers. *Journal of Research in Music Education,* 1977, *25,* 68–82.

Taebel, D. The effect of various instructional modes on children's performance of music concept tasks. *Journal of Research in Music Education,* 1974, *22,* 170–183.

Van Zee, N. Responses of kindergarten children to musical stimuli and terminology. *Journal of Research in Music Education,* 1976, *24,* 14–21.

Zimmerman, M. P., and L. Sechrist. *How children conceptually organize musical sounds.* (ERIC Documents No. ED 028 200) Northwestern University, 1968.

_____. Brief focused instruction and musical concepts. *Journal of Research in Music Education,* 1970, *18,* 25–36.

Child Development and Music Education

Marilyn P. Zimmerman

One of the major contributions of the present century to our understanding of human development and personality has been the systematic study of child development. This study has encompassed a variety of disciplines, viewpoints, theories, and methods. Each viewpoint recognizes the importance of interactions of intellectual, emotional, physical, and social growth. The theories seem to agree that child development is a process that entails sequential levels, phases, shifts, steps, or stages through which a child passes from infancy to youth.

Developmental theory studies patterns of behavior that emerge as the individual interacts with his environment. It takes into consideration the progressive changes in each individual's adaptive functioning with his or her consequent integration of genetic and learned factors. Research in developmental psychology has provided insight into the developmental patterns of children's cognitive, affective, and psychomotor growth. These insights, in turn, have had an effect on curriculum revision and reform.

A recurrent issue in child development was described by Shakespeare in Scene I and Act IV of *The Tempest.* We hear Prospero as he describes Caliban, a deformed savage and slave:

> A devil, a born devil on whose
> nature
> Nurture can never stick; on whom
> my pains Humanely taken,
> all, all lost, quite lost. . . .

Shakespeare seems not only to have pinpointed the nature/nurture controversy but also to have anteceded humane education. The nature/nurture controversy also appears under headings of environmentalism versus genetic endowment, heredity versus environment, or innate potential versus learning. In music education, questions pertaining to a hereditary or genetic basis of musical talent are often posed. The controversy is evident in the dualistic measures of musicality, music aptitude, and music achievement, rather than in developmental measures.

Some current attention is being given to

ascertaining which children will profit most from music study and what level of factors seems to be critical to this judgment. The factors include music aptitude, intelligence, physical coordination, interest and motivation, parental encouragement, and cultural background. A positive relationship appears to exist between intelligence, music aptitude, and music achievement.

According to Kohlberg (1971), American education in the twentieth century has been shaped by the victory of Thorndike, with his emphasis on achievement, over Dewey, who emphasized development as the aim of education. In a parallel situation, it was forty years ago that Seashore and Mursell posed their differing viewpoints on the psychology of music. Seashore argued for a psycho-acoustical approach, whereas Mursell opted for the psychomusical. We still need developmental studies in music that focus on the sequential changes in the psychological structure of the individual as he interacts with music. These changes, according to the developmental viewpoint, are mediated by quite different processes at various ages. Developmental psychology can and should be the foundation of life-span developmental research in musicality.

Piaget has provided us with a particularly fruitful theory of child development that is based on the continuous process of interaction between an individual and his environment. The adaptive processes of assimilation and accommodation form the opposite poles within which this interaction occurs. These invariant functions continually disrupt the equilibrium of thought and force the individual to revise his thinking as he simultaneously assimilates the environment by taking in new perceptual data and accommodates former ways of thinking to use it. Through assimilation the quantity of perceptual information is increased; accommodation allows for qualitative changes in the information as new schemes of thinking are formed. The critical factor is the child's own activity through which he assimilates novel, external experiences and accommodates himself and his thinking to these new environmental experiences. Child to environment;

environment to child: messages and pressures are exchanged as the child and the setting engage in mutual and reciprocal interaction.

Within this setting Piaget has described an elegant theory of cognitive growth that views human intelligence as moving through successively higher stages from sensorimotor to operational thinking. The order of stages is both organismic and experiential—organismic because they unfold systematically, and experiential because they are dependent upon environment and experience. The age levels vary according to particularities of physical, social, and cultural environments.

In the delineation of his theory Piaget ties thought to action. The level of thought is a direct reflection of the actions an individual is capable of performing, whether crudely and explicitly as in the sensorimotor stage or subtly and implicitly as in operational thinking. Another crucial contribution of Piaget lies in his formulation of tasks and his method of observation and questioning as the child solves these tasks.

To whatever theory we ascribe, we should be cautioned against permitting it to become dogma. We must maintain a sense of proportion in regard to the way theory affects practice in the classroom so that developmental theory does not cause us to overlook developmental facts as exhibited in the behavior of our students.

Several areas of concern confront music educators as they plan a comprehensive music curriculum. One is the increasing importance placed on early childhood education and the implications of this education for music development. Learning in infancy and early childhood is dominated by sensorimotor and perceptual activity. Indeed, music activity begins with a confusion of environment and self-awareness in a universe consisting of aural images and personal activity. The very young child communicates through movements long before his vocabulary develops. Instead of words and concepts he uses percepts and movements organized into action patterns as the basis of his vocabulary.

Michel (1973) has described the first six months of infancy as a period of "learning to hear." Infants learn early to discriminate among sounds according to their timbre and volume. By approximately the age of one month, the infant shows signs of recognizing family members by their voices. As the child learns to hear, he begins to differentiate his vocal sounds from others and is soon imitating the aural images and impressions from his sound environment. The infant derives pleasure from this type of activity and so tends to prolong it. Here is an early example of affect as a source of motivation. Michel has further determined that a child progresses from concrete-descriptive thinking to abstract-logical thinking. He asserts that the ages between three and six are extremely important to musical development and that music activities should be planned to facilitate this development.

Music educators have little direct control over the earliest learning and development. Yet, in order to fill in the gaps in our present knowledge of musical development, parent (adult)-child-music interaction studies are needed. We need to devise techniques and methods for the keen observation of children in their early play activities in order to gain insight into the genetic development of rhythmic movement, vocal range, and chant. What techniques and observational methods can be adapted from child development studies?

In a provocative piece of research, Meltzoff and Moore (1977) reported that infants between twelve and twenty-one days can imitate both facial and manual gestures. Such imitation implies that human neonates can equate their own unseen behaviors with gestures they see others perform and suggests that the ability to use intermodal equivalences is an innate ability of humans. This would make the ability to act on the basis of an abstract representation of a perceptually absent stimulus the starting point for psychological development in infancy rather than its culmination. How should studies using aural stimuli be designed to determine early processing of and response to sound stimuli?

Moog (1976) on the basis of observations, parents' comments, and recordings of 500 in-

fants and preschool-age children has outlined stages in singing, listening, and movement. He also noted the importance of parental influence in initiating these activities by providing models for the children to imitate. We need more complete answers as to the role of the home environment in the musical development of young children.

Although early education is crucial, recent research by Kagan has indicated that early retardation caused by sensory deprivation can be overcome by later experience and environmental change. We have yet to determine the effects of either sensory deprivation or multisensory stimulation on musical development. What kinds of studies will give us this information?

In early music education, chanting, singing, expressive movement, and sound exploration and discovery through creative experiences form the basis of the curriculum. Permeating each experience should be a focus on listening. How can an appropriate mix of aural, visual, and kinesthetic tasks be determined?

There is some evidence to suggest a developmental sequence in sound discrimination from loudness to timbre to pitch. By discriminating among qualities of sounds, a child responds to a cue and so exercises a degree of selective attention. These are learnings with which preschool teachers are concerned. It is difficult to manipulate a music stimulus systematically to vary only one aspect at a time; yet this should be done in perceptual activities.

We need further research in the area of dimensional salience to determine if there is a preference for the selective attention given to one quality of sound over another. Questions to be answered include the following: Is there a change with age or experience? How are cognitive style or conceptual tempo related to the development of selective attention (and the converse)? What learning theory would best facilitate this type of learning?

A second major area of concern for music educators pertains to instructional problems inherent in conceptual development. How can the transition from perceptual exploration to concept development best be ef-

51

fected? It is difficult to draw a strict line of demarcation between perceptual and conceptual learnings in music, for here the interdependence of percept and concept is particularly evident. Music learning begins with perception, and from these perceptions are formed the concepts that underlie musical thinking. In my work I have stressed the dependency relationship between perception and concept formation. In any given perceptual field there must be a selective focus for one's attention. Then internal operations of labeling, categorizing, and organizing follow. It is here that concept formation takes place.

In recent years several research studies concerning the development of music concepts have added to knowledge in this area. Some of the studies followed the Piagetian model in which conservation-type music tasks were designed and administered to children to determine stages of conservation in the development of music concepts (Pflederer, 1963; Zimmerman and Sechrest, 1968; King, 1972; Larsen, 1973; Botvin, 1974; Jones, 1974; Foley, 1975; Serafine, 1975). Others, using a variety of multimodal and instructional techniques to determine concept attainment, were not based on any one theory (Andrews and Deihl, 1967; Laverty, 1969; Taebel, 1971). A developmental sequence pervades the findings in music-concept formation, with concepts appearing to develop in the following order: volume, timbre, tempo, duration, pitch, and harmony.

One difficulty is the differentiation between the existence of the concept and the possession of a vocabulary to express the concept. Teachers experience this difficulty in distinguishing between teaching a concept and teaching the meaning of a term that designates that concept. Woodruff (1970) identified two behavioral manifestations of concepts—symbolic or verbal, and instrumental or manipulative. In several studies, lack of vocabulary was mitigated by the use of multimodal techniques with behavioral measures—that is, the children were asked to produce or reproduce a sound or movement.

Young children simply do not have an adequate vocabulary and appropriate labels to attach to their emerging concepts. At a minimum, school music programs should enable children to talk about their music experiences with the same level of technical vocabulary that is characteristic of other fields. We need further knowledge concerning the role of language development and its interaction with the formation of music concepts. What behavioral responses are more productive in ascertaining concept attainment? What teaching techniques and styles can be used to shape this attainment?

A third area of concern that is especially relevant in cognitive and psychomotor skill development lies in the area of critical periods, readiness, and maturation. Developmental psychology has shown that there are optimal periods in which the child can acquire certain skills and understandings more efficiently than at others. An arbitrary setting of curricular levels according to age quite possibly has a deleterious effect on the musical development of children. For instruction to be effective, the child must be at a level of maturity that allows him to assimilate it. Although instruction cannot transcend maturity, maturity does tend to modify the results of instruction. Hence, instruction may be quite uneconomical before a certain level of maturation is reached. For example, children's abilities to synchronize body movements with a rhythmic stimulus are more dependent upon age and maturation than upon instruction (Groves, 1969).

These statements do not negate the importance of critical periods in the development of specific skill and behavior patterns. When a child reaches a stage of maturation where he can best profit from a certain kind of learning, the withholding of it may cause the behavior pattern in question to remain undeveloped (Zimmerman, 1971). Each critical period in the child's development is also a critical period for the adult, whether parent or teacher, to provide that environmental encounter that will maximize the child's potential, since it is during the critical periods that the environment is most influential.

Studies by Simons (1974) and Taebel (1971) show that ages five to six are a critical period

52

for the acquisition of music concepts and music listening skills. Research by Sergeant and Roche (1973) shows that attention to the absolute pitch of a melody is greatest with three- and four-year-olds and diminishes with five- and six-year-olds. By the time children begin elementary school, it is quite possible that the critical period for the development of absolute pitch has already passed. Petzold (1963) found that the most significant development in auditory perception occurs between ages six and seven.

Maturation is stimulated when a child encounters challenges that are not too difficult. If one takes seriously the view that adaptive achievements are cumulative in development, a maximal rate derives from continuously fostering the new possibilities achieved from each new adaptive modification in music knowledge and skills. It is this view of development that Hunt (1961, 1966) attempted to capsulate conceptually and practically in what he called "the problem of the match."

Piaget seems to minimize maturation and believes that mental development progresses as limited understandings are revised, expanded, and related to each other. The originality of Piaget's developmental method is not so much in his observational and experimental procedures but in his search for affiliations—that is, developmental transitions between different levels of behavior.

Since development is both continuous and discontinuous, optimal periods of growth alternate with plateaus where seemingly little new learning occurs. Petzold (1966) reported a plateau at the third-grade level; Hill (1968) and Zimmerman and Sechrest (1968) found a plateau to exist at the fifth-grade level. Do similar plateaus exist in other learnings? What kinds of music experiences can be used to the best advantage to help students integrate prior learnings into existing thought structures and prepare them for further learning when the plateau is bridged? Can an appropriate balance of perceptual, cognitive, affective, and skill learnings be determined for maximum musical development during periods of optimal growth and learning plateaus?

Skill development is another area of concern. In music study the combined areas of performance, perceptual, and cognitive skills are so closely entwined that it is difficult to ascertain where minimum and maximum learning is occurring. This leaves teachers unsure as to where they are directing, or should be directing, their efforts.

Music reading is also a skill and develops as linkages are formed between the aural, the visual, and the conceptual. In reading music the objective is to "see with the ear" and "hear with the eye." In teaching music reading the visual is used to clarify aural understandings. Is there an interface between language reading and music reading? Where in the developmental sequence can music reading be stressed to best advantage? How can the transition from "rote to note" be effected most easily and efficiently?

A fifth area of concern involves types of instruction best suited to the teaching and learning of music. These might be designated as discovery versus directed learning and responsive environment versus behavior modification. In a perceptual learning experience in which a cue response is desired, directed learning may be the most expeditious, whereas the discovery method can be used to good advantage in learning the principles of major and minor scale construction.

Mainstreamed classrooms will interject yet another variable into the teaching and learning of music. To ensure equality of opportunity we also need early identification of the gifted with special opportunities for them. It seems that so-called "enrichment programs" too often do not provide enough challenge and intellectual stimulation for our gifted children.

In early music learning, children need a rich and responsive music environment to stimulate their creativity and curiosity. As adumbral concepts begin to emerge and skills develop, behavior-shaping through successive approximation and rule instruction may be useful. What types of instruction are best suited to skill learning and to conceptual learning in music? The research literature is replete with studies pitting one method against another; but too often wrong assumptions or questions were raised, controls were inadequate, and findings were inconclusive. What kinds of developmental and pedagogical research would lead to the knowledge music educators need to effect efficient, effective, and affective learning for all students?

A sixth area of concern revolves around problems of measurement. One purpose of research with children is to assess behavior in order to establish norms and standards. It is difficult to discuss an individual child's musical behavior unless some sort of standard has been defined against which his performance can be evaluated. Perceptual studies can require either discrimination or performance tasks. In some instances it is feared that we did not look for the right thing. Some tasks did not measure what they were intended to. Inconsistencies in findings can result because we do not select the proper behavior developmentally to reflect perception.

We need to consider the type of study that will be most advantageous for the music attribute being researched. For example, a longitudinal study will yield the most conclusive evidence concerning the development of various aspects of musicality. With very young children an intensive analysis of certain well-defined aspects of their behavior in natural surroundings, as opposed to artificially controlled ones, is essential to those who desire to investigate the problems of transition between stages and the development of concurrences among different conceptual contents.

Mobility of society and changing school boundaries are not conducive to longitudinal studies. Sometimes it is necessary to conduct a cross-sectional study that will yield information as to what large numbers of children at a specific level, across wider geographical areas, are capable of doing. If it can be determined that nine-year-olds can conceptualize meter, a composite picture of development can be constructed and a type of developmental norm established.

Other types of studies that can be used to good advantage are (1) convergence, in which a series of shorter-term longitudinal studies with overlapping age ranges is used; (2) the clinical approach, in essence a case-history study with or without depth analysis; and (3) scalogram analysis, in which a series of tasks is chosen in order of increasing difficulty and children are ranked according to performance of the tasks.

Ordinal scales provide for assessment of this type. Each step on an ordinal scale represents a developmental advance so that when a child performs a task constituting the criterion for a specific step, it is presumed he has the capability to perform the tasks in each preceding step. The steps on the scale should be nested logically along a developmental line with tasks functioning as hypotheses to be tested as to their sequentiality. If musical achievements are cumulative in development, then the sequencing of a series of tasks should maximize the development of music concepts and skills. This would facilitate that "dynamic match" between innate potential and curriculum.

Traditional measures of cognitive development are based on mental age and intelligence quotient. These measures treat chronological age as the cause of development or the independent variable. Ordinal scale measurement, on the other hand, treats the steps on the scale as the independent variable and the mental age of achieving the criterion behaviors for the steps on the scale as the dependent variable (Hunt, 1975). This subtle shift of emphasis places the focus on the task or curricular experience and its relationship to other tasks or experiences. Thus, the results of the various interventions provided by the curriculum can be viewed in terms of the mean ages at which the children can perform the designated music tasks along the ordinal scale. The classic statement of developmental theory—that response variation is a function of age (Kessen, 1960)—can be rephrased: response variation is a function of developmental level interacting with task. Does this approach to measuring music ability seem logical and feasible? How can it best be implemented?

Wohlwill (1973) has proposed a sequential program of research in child development that uses five methods of study. Such a pro-

54

gram could be applied to the study of musical development, preferably in conjunction with other aspects of development. The five methods are (1) define a set of scales along which consistent developmental changes can be observed and mapped; (2) collect facts to provide a descriptive study of the changes; (3) correlate the developmental changes in music with other behaviors developing simultaneously; (4) study the variables that affect developmental changes; and (5) study individual differences in development. Information from this type of research would lead to a better match between ability levels and curricular levels.

Current research in music learning has focused on how children develop music concepts and skills. Another approach is to consider the nature and origin of musicality. Beament (1977), a biologist, suggested that ear mechanics will define a pitch in direct consequence of the way the ear encodes incoming cues and signals. He further suggests that both inherited factors (a special regularity of firing of aural sensors of certain people) and learning (auditory processing machinery) are involved in musicality. We need basic research by teams representing different fields to arrive at a more complete understanding of human development, including musical development.

I have attempted to outline six areas of concern for music educators: (1) early childhood education; (2) instructional problems inherent in conceptual development; (3) critical periods, readiness, and maturation; (4) skill development; (5) types of instruction best suited to the teaching and learning of music; and (6) problems of measurement. In some instances I have proposed ways of meeting these concerns within a developmental framework; in others I have asked questions as to how these concerns can be met. In addition, Piaget's theory of development was summarized as one particularly useful to music educators. To the extent that we apply ideas from child development in the teaching of music, we will meet the music needs of our students and provide them with the basis for a full and rich musical life.

References

Andrews, F. M., and N. C. Deihl. *Development of a technique for identifying elementary school children's musical concepts* (Cooperative Research Project 5-0233). The Pennsylvania State University, 1967.

Beament, J. The biology of music. *Psychology of Music*, 1977, 5, 3–18.

Botvin, G. J. Acquiring conservation of melody and cross-modal transfer through successive approximation. *Journal of Research in Music Education*, 1974, 22, 226–223.

Foley, E. A. Effects of training in conservation of tonal and rhythmic patterns on second-grade children. *Journal of Research in Music Education*, 1975, 23, 240–248.

Groves, W. C. Rhythmic training and its relationship to the synchronization of motor-rhythmic response. *Journal of Research in Music Education*, 1969, 17, 408–415.

Hill, J. D. The musical achievement of culturally deprived and advantaged children: A comparative study at the elementary level. *Journal of Music Therapy*, 1968, 5, 77–84.

Hunt, J. McV. *Intelligence and experience.* New York: Ronald Press, 1961.

———. Toward a theory of guided learning in development. In R. H. Ojemann and K. Pritchett (Eds.), *Giving emphasis to guided learning.* Cleveland: Educational Research Council. 1966, pp. 98–160.

Hunt, J. McV., K. Mohandessi, M. Ghodssi, and M. Akiyama. Development of orphanage-reared infants (Tehran): Interventions and outcomes. Unpublished manuscript, University of Illinois, 1975.

Jones, R. L. The development of the child's conception of meter in music. *Journal of Research in Music Education*, 1976, 24, 142–154.

Kessen, W. Research design in the study of developmental problems. In P. H. Mussen (Ed.), *Handbook of research methods in child development.* New York: John Wiley & Sons, Inc., 1960. 36–70.

King, C. D. *The conservation of melodic pitch patterns by elementary children as determined by ancient Chinese music.* Unpublished doctoral dissertation, Ohio State University, 1972.

Kohlberg, L., and C. Gilligan. *The adolescent as philosopher: The discovery of the self in a post-conventional world.* Daedalus, 1971, 1051–1086.

Larsen, R. L. Levels of conceptual development in melodic permutation concepts based on Piaget's theory. *Journal of Research in Music Education*, 1973, 21, 256–263.

Laverty, G. E. *The development of children's concepts of pitch, duration and loudness as a function of grade level.* Unpublished doctoral dissertation, Pennsylvania State University, 1969.

Meltzoff, A. N., and M. K. Moore. Imitation of facial and manual gestures by human neonates. *Science Magazine,* 1977, *198* (4312), 75–78.

Michel, P. The optimum development of musical abilities in the first years of life. *Psychology of Music,* 1973, *1* (2), 14–20.

Moog, H. The development of musical experience in children of pre-school age. *Psychology of Music,* 1976, *4* (2), 38–45.

Petzold, R. G. The development of auditory perception of musical sounds by children in the first six grades. *Journal of Research in Music Education,* 1963, *11,* 21–54.

————. *Auditory perception of musical sounds by children in the first six grades.* Cooperative Research Project No. 1051, University of Wisconsin, 1966.

Pflederer, M. The responses of children to musical tasks embodying Piaget's principle of conservation. *Journal of Research in Music Education,* 1964, *12,* 251–268.

Serafine, M. L. *A measure of meter conservation in music, based on Piaget's theory.* Doctoral dissertation, University of Florida, 1975.

Sergeant, D., and S. Roche. Perceptual shifts in the auditory information processing of young children. *Psychology of Music,* 1973, *1,* 39–48.

Simons, G. M. A criterion-referenced test of fundamental music listening skills. *Child Study Journal,* 1976, *6* (4), 223–234.

Taebel, D. K. The effect of various instructional modes on children's performance of music concept tasks. *Journal of Research in Music Education,* 1974, *22,* 170–183.

Wohlwill, J. F. *The study of behavioral development.* New York: Academic Press, 1973.

Woodruff, A. D. How music concepts are developed. *Music Educators Journal,* February 1970, *56,* 51–54.

Zimmerman, M. P. *Musical characteristics of children.* Washington, D.C.: Music Educators National Conference, 1971.

Zimmerman, M. P., and L. Sechrest. *How children conceptually organize musical sounds* (Cooperative Research Project No. 5-0256). Northwestern University, 1968.

Response

Roger Brown

My own music education began where Robert Petzold suggests that it more or less must—specifically, in the fifth grade at Wilkins Elementary School in Detroit when I was identified as the loudest monotone heard at Wilkins School and everything blacked out after that through elementary school. Now one of the very interesting but rather shaky things that reading these papers and being here again at the university have done for me is to give me access to things that were in my long-term memory but that I have not thought about for years and did not really know were there. When I trace the history of my own musical development, I'm impressed with how very little of it was under the control of any educator—psychologist, musicologist, or any other. At certain crucial points, however, it was.

The first thing I remember is in high school. I was running with the intellectual crowd. I don't know exactly why, but I was. And they had some contact with what was generically called "classical music." I had none. My parents didn't play any music and it was the depression in Detroit, and those are all factors that played quite a large part. I was not given music lessons but I developed aspirations of a sort of ferociously competitive or compulsive type; namely, I wanted to know what this group that I ran with knew. They could make references to obscure things like Beethoven's Fifth and so on and I did not know what that was. I thought I had to learn and it was really my peer group at a certain point that motivated me to do something on my own. Now that meant contact with very heavy reading. So I learned that there was a world beyond Detroit; and there was a group out there that I sort of identified with that knew about all kinds of things like chamber music and opera and I wanted to learn about those, too.

Now what were my resources? Well, in Detroit in the late thirties and forties, you had daily from nine to ten the minute parade, which played classical or semiclassical music, rather short pieces between rather long ads. Then there was the New York Philharmonic on Sunday, and the Ford Sunday Evening Hour for quite a while, and the Firestone Hour, which was rather too taken with Eleanor Steber in my opinion.

Now, being compulsive and sort of horrible, in many ways, I got a big shoe box and started to make three-by-five cards for every composition that I heard. I wrote them down and was determined at first simply to recognize; I gave myself a little check if I recognized something before the name was announced. And I began to recognize quite a lot of things. Of course, certain things were never played at all. Most of the things you people like best were never played at all. The first thing that I really liked was the "Toreador Song" played by an orchestra—that was great. The second thing that I really liked was the *Light Cavalry Overture*. I remember them vividly; I have my list still, of course. So preferences began to develop. For a while I dated a girl who was studying the piano, was not very good at it, and decided she would be a coloratura sporano. So she began singing "Caro nome" and things at me, and we started going to the performances of the San Carlo Opera Company.

Then something began to develop that I am inclined to think of as natural affinities. Despite the fact that I cannot play an instrument and cannot read music, you have the odd outcome that music is almost the most important thing in my life, next to psychology and to people. If I were to become deaf and I could become selectively deaf, I think I might choose to lose hearing speech and keep music, which is very odd. So some kind of affinity began to develop and that was a kind of recognition acquaintance and a kind of low-order preferential ranking for quite a large literature, mostly symphonic literature, but not much chamber music because it was not coming my way. I began to discover that certain composers and certain works, for some mysterious reasons, spoke to me with tremendous power at that age. For example, Wagner was one and Mozart was one. Bellini was one, but later.

Probably at one time I could have been reached and improved and caused to develop better affinities, but by this time, which is now late high school, I felt my affinities were me and I would never give them up. I would regard that as a denial of what I had become. So I think natural affinities are a real thing. I don't know how far back in our history they go, our individual histories, and I don't know how changeable they are, and I don't know what determines them.

Then I came to this great university and I got some real music education of a certain kind. People would deprecatingly call it, I think, music appreciation. I would call it learning how to hear certain kinds of music. I didn't take enough courses to learn to hear all kinds. I have never forgotten a course in opera to which the instructor simply brought a kind of catholic enthusiasm that was enormously contagious; he pointed things out. You heard them. He gave you an exposure that made it possible to discover what you resonated to. It would not be everything. There would be some things you were glad you knew; you could see why some people thought they were the greatest things ever. But somewhere along the line there would be other things that really spoke to you. The instructor was a great teacher in that way. I

57

learned something about hearing and psychoacoustics and so on in the psychology department. But still, there was no music education in the proper sense.

You will notice how little of the variance teachers account for and how much of it is accounted for by things like economic conditions, the family you are raised in, your personality, all kinds of things that we do not control. Literacy is, I think, a reasonable goal for everyone. I think the discovery of natural affinities is a more important goal because I find that even thirty-year-old post-doctoral students who have never heard certain music that I know occasionally discover that that's the music for them, and they just had not heard it before or it had been sort of talked down to or dispersed in some way. I think what a terrible deprivation that is.

Now, I do want to respond directly to a few things in the papers. One of these is Petzold's discussion of words like "high" and "low," "loud" and "soft," and so on, which have multiple meanings in English, not just musical meanings. Almost every word, of course, has multiple meanings and that is not confusing for various reasons. Now these particular words are rather like a set of words that we think of as sensory metaphors like "sharp," "dull," "heavy," or "light," which are also used on the social-psychological level where one speaks of a sharp intelligence or a sharp person or a dull person. A little inquiry has been made into those words and they are actually extremely interesting. Solomon Ash, a great Gestalt psychologist, was interested in the degree to which those words bundled together the same sets of qualities in historically unrelated languages; they do so in surprisingly great degree—that is, "high," "loud," "sharp," and so on go together in very many languages. Ash also asked children of various ages if they were aware of the fact they used a word like "warm" for something thermal and also for certain kinds of persons, or if they were not aware of it. The different levels of discourse, to put it in sort of a rough way, keep them apart so well that it is a recognition that the

vocabulary has been extended in this way, and it doesn't confuse. Then they were also asked if they could give an account of how it came to be that a word like "warm" would be applied in this way. And they could not until they were at the stage of formal operations, roughly early adolescence. On the other hand, Howard Gardner and I did a little experiment in which very young children were given tactile and thermal experiences like the feeling of velvet or feeling of ice, or something of that sort. Then they were asked which of the various characters known to them might be said to be like this feeling. In other words, they were asked to sense a common abstract quality. And they recapitulated very easily the history of the language. That is to say, they knew which words belonged to which kinds of people, but they did not know why. So there is a difference between doing and knowing. That is, I think, directly responsive to one aspect of Petzold's paper, but I also feel very strongly with him that there is a great deal outside of our control.

Zimmerman's paper, the science article on imitation, is in one way a little misleading because it describes a very young infant, twenty-one days old, and they saw certain movements; that was the visual modality. Then they imitated them with their fingers or their tongues. But the important thing there is that those responses were in the repertoire of those infants. Probably a little earlier than that the parents were imitating the infants. Imitation is really terribly complicated and this kind of crossmodal possibility does exist early, but more generally, it means making an attempt to approximate a model. It is close enough to be recognized as an attempt and that's a very much more complicated process. Quite clearly I cannot imitate the music that I hear and see. I am still a monotone and a husky one at that!

There also is this whole question of music's connection with language, which I find fascinating and puzzling. I have never been able to understand how the ability to perceive music meaningfully, to understand it, and to produce it could have evolved as a universal characteristic of the human species. And it had to, of course. In view of the doctrine of natural selection, it is a little hard to figure out how understanding music would have improved the species. It's very unlikely, but there it is; it is a human universal. I am inclined to think that it might be genetically similar to the capacities that make language possible. I think that this is because of the utility of language. Since it is communication, it can accomplish things for the individual that will enable him to leave more progeny. The utility of music is not evident. So, although there may be some fairly close connection in terms of basic capacities, that does not mean music and language are very much alike.

The differences between language and music are enormous. The similarities are fairly striking, too. With regard to language, everyone is a competent practitioner, competent producer, and also one who can receive and understand. A select group are also artists in language, and I think also some trained and somewhat select group are artists in response to language. That is, I think it takes training to comprehend a Shakespeare play although not as much talent as to write it.

But now in music, most people are not producers. Or are they? I am not sure. It depends on what improvisation is, how much of it goes on, and how many people sing under their breath. But most people seem not to be practitioners or producers. The main concern is with re-creation of a select group of productions from the past that are regarded as art, and then with the training of reception apprehension so that one can respond to these creations. In that way they are really quite unlike one another.

If music is like a language, how many languages is it? That is, where are the boundaries? Where do you get mutual unintelligibility? Certainly you do between me and rock music, but you did also between me and Tommy Dorsey and Glenn Miller. So I don't quite know what to make of that. There is music around the world to be considered and many different traditions. It is not all Bach,

Beethoven, Brahms, and occasionally Bartok; there are a few other things. To do research on music development, you have to immerse youself in the deepest understanding of music theory that you could get. Similarly, I think that in studying the development of language, the first thing is to understand as much of the theory of linguistics as you can. That is the terminal state. That is what you are aiming at.

I would be interested in such matters as what is happening today to the many young people who are practically bathed in eighteenth-century music. On the other hand, it may be that they are making a dichotomy between music for old people and music for young people. That would sort of close their minds to discovery of what may be the deepest things in their nature.

There are many music traditions or cultures. In the nineteenth century, in a certain number of countries in Europe, there was a rather high consensus in the sense that many people were in on the tradition. What amazes me about this is that if you are really imbued with it, if you know how to read it or hear it or appreciate it, you get a rather substantial consensus on what is a great new instance in that tradition. I find it a very fascinating problem—a social, psychological, and cognitive problem. That is it is different, but different in a way that enables you to understand it as an extension of something that you already understand. There were millions of people waiting to hear Verdi's *Otello*—a display of tremendous excitement and in huge populations, which must have meant a kind of unification of a culture that is musically very fragmented. But I think that this ability is probably true of every music culture, every music tradition. There may also be aesthetic grounds for thinking that some are deeper or higher than others, but that seems to be a secondary and debatable question. The first thing is to plant yourself in the tradition or find your right tradition and your natural affinities so that you are not deprived all your life of one of the biggest things that you can have.

Response

William Kessen

When I first saw the program listing I thought that asking a university professor to talk for fifteen minutes is like asking somebody to stuff a cow into a milk bottle. But when I began to read the papers I realized that I had my story a little wrong. You have in your generative papers, more or less presented to the psychologists a bottle of milk and asked us to build a cow!

I have good news and bad news. And both of them can be represented in a story. You can walk into a laboratory, can do it at home if you want to, and without too much trouble sing or play on a pitch pipe D above middle C to a six-month-old child and he or she will sing it back to you on pitch. That's the good news. The bad news can be represented in a story of an American mother confronted with the difficulties of teaching or helping to teach her child to play the violin in the Suzuki method. Almost in a wail she said, "I can't tell my child to shut up and stand still." We may have more help from our ancestry and less from our culture than we usually expect. Let me talk about each of those briefly.

A jazz pianist, an undergraduate at Yale who is now a jazz pianist in Kansas City, a violinist, also an undergraduate at Yale, who is now a graduate student in psychology at Harvard, the director of the neighborhood music school in New Haven, and I were struck by the fact that children at five or six or seven seem to come to that school in two groups. There are those who would, almost without instruction, sit down and begin to play the piano or the recorder and those for whom it was a constant, never successful, struggle—for whom the piano and the recorder were always enemies. We train a lot of those, don't we? How could it be that some people were ready to learn music and other people were not ready to learn music? Because of my interest in infancy, some five years ago we began a series of studies basically bringing children into the laboratory, more because we could control the recording of their output than for any other reason, and began to sing to them and to ask their mothers to work with them at home. I will not report the details of those studies here, but I can report to you that each of the twenty-four children we observed not only can match pitch but can shift when asked to and will occasionally respond in octaves; and our lead singer will imitate descending minor thirds. Moreover, there seems to be no relation between this ability and the music experience of their parents or the music that's available in their homes. We divided the group in two, and half of them were given very intensive exposure to music over the year. But when they returned at age eighteen months, there still were no differences between the groups and they were still able to imitate. Obviously children at three and four cannot, or will not, or do not perform this task. Does the oncoming of speech, which, at least in English, has so little concern with intonation, either block or supplant that sensitivity to tone, to pitch? Or rather, as Roger Brown has suggested, because music is not for anything, certainly to the young child, it may go away because it is not used. Somehow it may be that those children who can come to a music school at five or six and immediately hear may be the ones who have preserved some primitive, maybe even universal, talents. It is for that reason that I would be concerned if Zimmerman meant literally that music educators have no control over the very earliest learning and development. If that is the case, many of the questions posed for us may not be answerable.

Let me now return to my second story. "I can't tell my child to shut up and stand still." Some five years ago, a group of us went to China and we saw many wonders—well-behaved children, for example. (We all have nightmares about the time when the Chinese will visit our typical junior high school.) What we saw that impressed all of us, particularly those of us who have some interest in music, was the remarkable competence of very young children in song and dance. Four- and five-year-old children in China perform complicated choreographies as they tell about the harvest in Hanon and the capitalist warmongers in Vietnam, and, contrary to some psychological dogma, they sing very well indeed, on key and even, primitively, in harmonies. Why is that?

It may be, and this I guess is the bad news,

that music education is not a fact about children. Music education is not a fact about psychology. Music education is a fact about culture. The Chinese children danced as well as they did because people expected them to dance as well as they did. And they sang as well as they did because people expected them to sing as well as they did. Who, aside from music educators and musicians, expects American children to know anything about music? Listening to some of the productions of adult Chinese culture—for example, Chum Ching's marvelous people's operas, which even if you like repetition get you down after a bit—led Jerry Kagen to say that the Chinese people reach their musical apogee at age four! But all that we want to do with our children is so inextricably linked to economics and tax structure and attitudes about achievement and expectations of parents and sharing of a vision that this colloquy between us is incomplete.

I should also add, in support of what Brown said about his own musical development, I met and began to hear that work that I henceforth will know as Haydn's F minor Mass in a barracks in Litchfield, England, during the war. This is the other side of my emphasis on early attention, early education, and preservation of musical values. Different things happen at different times. And I began listening to Bach because people I respected and admired told me I should. We learn first for somebody and then for something and then for learning.

One last theme: categorization is essential to musical learning; labeling is not. Only physicists *talk* about volume; only grammarians and linguists *talk* about language; only music educators and musicians *talk* about music. Why do we need to teach children the vocabulary and syntax of music? It seems to me that one of our legitimate goals, for people who are going to be citizens and not musicians, is rather to teach them tuned sensitivity, those affinities you have already heard described so well. That seems to be, even in this culture, an achievable goal. Perhaps our first step in this conference is not really an intellectual one but a moral one— what do we want the children to know?

I'd like to close by emphasizing my Suzuki point. Child development theories are not about individual, detached, singular chil- dren. They are about children in society. And both music educators and psychologists need to know a lot more about that.

Music Learning and Learning Theory

Edwin E. Gordon

Music education today is a profession in search of a discipline. The typical program a music education undergraduate follows is a collection of courses that were specifically designed for other, though related, purposes. These are in addition to one or more methods courses, the content of which may have little association with the conditions experienced during the student teaching requirement. At the graduate level, advanced methods courses abound, and in most institutions the more traditional historical, philosophical, and social foundations of education courses adapted to the concerns of musicians are offered in conjunction with those in allied fields. That one profession, self-governed or not, borrows from, and may even be based on aspects of, another is becoming increasingly common. However, the core of any profession must have substance, and that substance must be more than essential to a given profession. It must be unique to that profession.

It would seem that when music education ultimately evolves into a discipline, what are now referred to as methods courses will have undergone a metamorphosis whereby they will form the core of the undergraduate curriculum. Further, research activities that will produce the content of these methods courses will permeate the graduate curriculum. The content of future methods courses must bear on how we learn when we learn music—that is, learning theory in music.

By definition, a method is a procedure for accomplishing something. In music education, a teacher may embrace the objective of teaching children to be musically literate. To accomplish this objective, the teacher becomes concerned, for example, with whether letter names, numbers, or syllables should be used and what literature is appropriate. Clearly, the first concern is techniques and the second is materials; neither can be thought of as method. Method takes on significance when the teacher becomes concerned with how a child educes knowledge from information transmitted in relationship to the sequence of objectives in a course of study. The following illustrative questions are indicative of the need for a sequence of objectives: (1) Should children first learn to hear and perform by rote what they are expected to read and write in music notation? (2) Should children learn to read music notation before they learn to write music notation or should the two be learned concurrently? (3) Should children learn to aurally recognize familiar tonal and rhythm patterns before they attempt to aurally identify unfamiliar tonal and rhythm patterns? (4) Should children learn tonal patterns before rhythm patterns or rhythm patterns before tonal patterns, or should the two be learned concurrently? (5) Should children learn to compose and improvise music, with or without instruments, before they learn to interpret music composed by others? (6) In conformity with phylogenetic, rather than ontogenetic, theory, should children be exposed to pentatonic music before diatonic music? (7) Should music theory be taught as introductory material or culminating material, or not at all in the music curriculum?

Techniques and materials are properly thought of in terms of appropriateness to chronological age, whereas method is properly thought of in terms of appropriateness of sequentiality of objectives regardless of chronological age. The determination of sequence of objectives—that is, method—is based on learning theory. At present, typical methods courses are concerned primarily with techniques and materials, and to a much lesser extent with isolated objectives and haphazardly sequential and incomplete series of objectives. In the future, techniques and materials courses will be supplementary to the methods courses. Once a body of knowledge that pertains to the proper sequencing of objectives is established, this will become the content of methods courses; students will be in a position to select or develop for their own use appropriate methods to accomplish series of objectives; and the emergence of music education as a discipline within a profession will be assured.

Over the years there have been music educators, and there still are some, who were aware of the important role of learning theory in music education. Try as they did to interpret and apply writings of psychologists, for the most part they were dissuaded by the Gestalt/S-R controversies. It would seem that the music educators did not become cynical about the value of learning theory to music but rather that they became skeptical of the isolated principles of learning with which psychologists have been concerned: the isolated principles of learning masqueraded as being contiguous and thus as constituting a learning theory. Cognitive psychologists have done little to remedy the situation. Acousticians occasionally tried to fill the void but it soon became apparent that psychoacoustics, not simply perception or acoustics, was the discipline more relevant to music education. But psychoacoustics, cognitive psychology, and semiotics are relatively young and as yet have not offered much to music educators. Music psychologists, currently called psychomusicologists, have not been inactive during the past seventy odd years. However, they never have collectively faced the issue of learning theory in a continuing scholarly manner; isolated interests predominated.

Needless to say, I am not looking for a Utopian solution as a result of this conference. Solutions, even when forthcoming, interact with changing conditions and become inadequate. My realistic hope is that you, the psychologists, will more than understand and be empathetic. I hope that you will work with us, the music educators, to begin to develop approaches for solving some of our problems. We can learn much from you and, without doubt, you will benefit from observing and generalizing music learning processes. It has been said that music is the only art in which one conceptualizes aurally. To ask you to solve our problems without our help would be absurd, because you are not professional musicians. And history has suggested that we probably cannot solve our problems without your help. Music learning theory questions cannot be neatly separated into learning theory on the one hand and music on the other. We must work together.

When Lowell Mason introduced music into the Boston, Massachusetts, public schools, he set down seven principles of teaching music, based on the philosophy of Pestalozzi, and incorporated them into his *Manual of Instruction*, published in 1834. I quote the first principle: "To teach sounds before signs—to make the child sing before he learns the written notes or their names." And the fifth principle: "To give the principles and theory after practice, as an induction from it." By virtue of these two principles alone, one can say that Mason was probably the first music educator to try to apply learning theory to instruction in music. After almost one hundred fifty years these fundamental principles have not systematically taken root and flourished in the music education profession. Let's examine these principles, derive implications, and propose some questions that require our immediate attention.

Music, like English, has aural, oral, and visual dimensions. One hears English spoken and one hears music performed; one speaks English and one performs (speaks) music vocally and instrumentally; and one reads and writes English and one reads and writes music. Without endeavoring to suggest that music is a language, universal or not, it is useful to parallel the process of learning a language to that of learning music. A child hears speech and imitates speech during the preschool years. That is, the aural and oral dimensions of speech interact at a very early age, up through age three being most crucial. This is very important to know even if we never know whether listening or speaking occurs first. Children enter school with a limited but common aural/oral vocabulary, expand it, and then learn to use that vocabulary as a readiness for learning to read and write. Probably of more significance is that children generalize and create with their aural/oral vocabulary long before they learn to read and write. As the child continues through school, and indeed through life, the aural, oral, and visual dimensions are constantly interacting

and they serve as readinesses for one another.

Should the aural, oral, and visual dimensions be developed in the same way in the language and music learning processes? To the best of my knowledge, they are not. During the preschool years, a typical child rarely performs music (particularly when compared to speech). It is an unusual environment in which systematic singing and eurythmic activities are provided either before or after age three for the child, the occasional nursery songs, patriotic and religious songs, and "Happy Birthday" notwithstanding. Systematic activities would include songs that are appropriate at any given age in terms of at least range, tessitura, and tempo. It can be said with certainty that the preschool child hears more music than he performs. I believe that it can be said with equal certainty that Lowell Mason meant singing as well as listening when he used the word "sound" in his first principle. Indeed, the typical child is not even exposed to listening to music in a systematic way. Yet, music educators espouse and regularly continue to champion music appreciation as the primary goal of music education as if every child has developed or is developing tonal and rhythmic understanding, or as if aesthetic education requires no readiness and one does not need to learn how to listen. That one can "enjoy" the flow of sound of a language that he or she cannot comprehend does not necessarily mean that a similar response should be the goal of listening to music.

Other questions arise: Does the lack of appropriate music performance inhibit a child's ability to understand what he hears?

Does the lack of hearing music in an intimate setting inhibit a child's ability to perform music?

Does the lack of appropriate aural/oral experiences in music inhibit a child's ability to read and write music?

Does the lack of music reading and writing abilities inhibit the continuing development of a child's music performance and listening skills? It should be understood that in the reading and writing of music, one sees with his ears and hears with his eyes. To read and write music with comprehension—that is, to be musically literate—one must hear what he sees.

If there is a proper sequence of learning in terms of the aural, oral, and visual dimensions of music, what is it? Are there more than one?

Do the answers to these questions become dichotomous as they relate to preschool and school-age children?

I am persuaded, and I hope intelligently, that the answers to these questions are largely affirmative. Nonetheless, my further questions are not totally dependent upon positive answers to those already offered. As I speak, it is obvious that I am engaging in the oral process and that you are engaging in the aural process. But am I not listening to myself as I speak and are you not speaking silently as you listen? Of course, what is important is that you naturally understand and give meaning to what I am saying through syntax. Whether you are hearing what I said, are listening to what I am saying, or are anticipating what I will say is irrelevant to our immediate purposes. The phenomenological concerns of Husserl in "presencing" what is heard in terms of retention and "protention," in contrast to recollection, go beyond the scope of this paper. It would be sufficient if music teachers, upon demonstration, would learn not to say to the pupil "see what I mean" but rather, "hear what I mean."

It is reasonable to assume that musicians give intrinsic meaning to music they perform and hear performed by others through music syntax. I am not insisting that one cannot give extrinsic semantic meaning to programmatic music without syntax. I am simply trying to make the point that in order to help a child learn music, we must know what a child attends to when he performs and hears music. He does not memorize individual notes or groups of notes any more than you are memorizing individual words or sentences to derive meaning as you listen to me.

What is music syntax? To answer that music syntax comprises tonal and rhythmic elements is to beg the question. We must distinguish among music elements to answer the question with precision. And we must come to terms with congruent, and possibly more basic, issues that demand consideration.

If you close your eyes, you can form an image of me. Open your eyes and you have a vision of me. If I sing, you can hear me. You may rehear in your mind (the music not being physically present) what I sang, and it is curious to discover that there is no word to describe such behavior. To call it aural imagery is only to create confusion, because you are really not seeing what you hear. To call it aural perception, much of which is actually aural conceptualization, is to make no distinction between hearing music that is physically present and hearing music that is not. Therefore, I have coined the verb "to audiate" as a definition of this process. How audiation is learned probably would be best explained as a correlate to the answers to my earlier questions. When we ask what music syntax is, we should also ask what we audiate. To arrive at satisfactory answers to these questions, I believe that we must distinguish among music elements.

Do we attend differently to key (C, E-flat, A, and so on) and tonality (major, minor, dorian, and so on) as we listen and give meaning to music?

Do we attend differently to tempo and meter as we listen and give meaning to music?

Does melodic rhythm affect our perception of tempo and meter as we listen and give meaning to music?

Is motion a part of time or is time a part of motion? Is the concept of rhythm derived by perceiving accent groupings that fill and divide time or by perceiving time that connects accents into groupings?

Does the mind pair beats subjectively in order to give objective meaning to overall rhythm?

To what extent is the mind capable of attending to both tonal and rhythm dimensions when listening and giving meaning to music? Or must the mind attend to both tonal and rhythm dimensions concurrently in order to give sophisticated meaning to music? Many persons cannot recite the text of a song without stopping, unless it is chanted

65

in the rhythm of the song. Similarly, many persons cannot reproduce the exact tones of a song when it is required that the tones be performed in equal lengths.

I have tried to focus my remarks and questions so that by this time you will be searching for ways of clarifying what to me is a pervading problem. It is true that we are gathered here to discuss learning theory as it applies to music. However, Hilgard and Bower, Gagné, Ausubel, Piaget and Montessori, indirectly, and other psychologists think of learning theory in a general way. What I am suggesting is that there are learning theories specifically in terms of disciplines as well as in terms of individual philosophical preferences. I believe that there are a skills learning theory and a content learning theory for music. Though to say so may be an exaggeration, skills learning theory is common to all disciplines of learning. Regardless of what we are learning, we perceive, discriminate, generalize, conceptualize, create, and memorize. But the content to which we apply these skills is, of course, different for each learning discipline. Furthermore, the content of each learning discipline is multifarious. In music we think in terms of tonic, dominant, major, minor, atonal, duple, triple, binary, ternary, folk, classical, jazz, timbre, keyboard, singing, and dancing to name but a few dimensions.

Therefore: Does content affect the application of a generalized skills learning sequence?

Should content be sequenced in the form of a learning theory?

Should different dimensions of music content be sequenced differently in the form of learning theories?

If both content and skills are sequenced in terms of learning theory, how might the different dimensions of content and skills be coordinated and articulated in the instructional process?

Music aptitude tests possess more content and construct validity, and at least as much predictive and diagnostic validity, as intelligence tests. Because one does not need to be musically literate to take a music aptitude test, as one needs language literacy to take an intelligence test, music aptitude tests are fortunately much less saturated with corresponding achievement factors. Since we are able to diagnose children's musical strengths and weaknesses with a reasonable degree of assurance, we are compelled to be concerned with how children's individual musical differences interact with learning theory.

Should children with high tonal, rhythm, and aesthetic/expressive/interpretive aptitudes be taught differently (that is, should skills or content learning sequences be adapted) from children with correspondingly low aptitudes?

If so, how might this be most appropriately effected? For example, should high aptitude children be, as Bruner might suggest, spiraled into creativity and generalization activities?

Should low aptitude children be expected to engage in some form of creativity and generalization?

Should generalization activities precede creativity activities or vice versa?

Should only high aptitude children be exposed to music theory?

Should creativity and improvisation be thought of as eliciting highly similar behaviors or should they be sequenced?

And I cannot refrain from asking another question for which I do not really expect an answer: Is there really such a thing as creativity or are there only eternal ideas that one rediscovers with assiduous study?

In all learning theories there is a direct or indirect reference to verbal association skill. I think it is important to emphasize that music is primarily an aural rather than a visual art. In language we informally learn to give verbal association to an object we see and to an image. In this way, the object we see becomes the word and vice versa in the learning process. However, in music we can hear a melody or a rhythmic line, but little provision is made in the formative years for giving verbal association to what we hear and audiate. This, if done at all, is done usually through formal instruction at a later, less crucial, time.

Because verbal association is a different but equally important type of learning in music and because in its absence the development of higher levels of learning might be retarded or prevented, should it come at an earlier level in the music learning sequence than in the language learning sequence?

If so, should verbal association learning come directly after aural/oral learning and before symbolic association learning so that what is being read can be given precise verbal association and in turn be directly associated with sound?

Given the aural/oral, verbal association, and symbolic association levels of learning, is the music reading sequence the reverse of the music writing process?

It is common in music education, both vocal and instrumental, for children to be taught the letter names of lines and spaces of the stave, and to be taught the time value names of notes. That is, in reality, children are being taught theory before practice, or sign before sound, because the technique used to attempt to achieve the objective of verbal association is untenable. Other than in a "perfect pitch" or "perfect time" sense, it would seem impossible for the musical mind to verbally associate the sound of an individual pitch or note other than at the symbolic level, and even that is uncertain.

At any level of learning, should a child develop skills with tonal and rhythm patterns (groups of pitches and notes, respectively) rather than with isolated pitches and notes in the same way that the child deals with words rather than with individual letters for comprehension?

Regardless of whether patterns are used, does retroactive or proactive inhibition occur with certain techniques used at the verbal association level of learning more than with other techniques?

Now to the final topic, instrumental music. I do not intend to deal directly with motor skills any more than in the previous discussions I dealt directly with short- or long-term memory. Nor am I concerned with the efficacy of different degrees of overlearning, the beta hypothesis, or the comparative benefits of massed and distributed practice. What I am directly concerned with is how the musical mind "tells" the fingers (and, of course, the arms, hands, tongue, lips, and so on) what to do when one performs on a music instrument, assuming physical coordination is established or forthcoming. The following queries are preliminay.

Is a music instrument an extension of the human voice?

Does the ability to sing in tune affect a child's ability to play an instrument with acceptable intonation? The interest should be in preciseness of pitch and not necessarily melodic direction.

Does muscular ability, in terms of eurythmics, affect a child's ability to play an instrument with good overall rhythm? The interest should be in both large and small muscle movements as they apply to tempo, meter, and melodic rhythm.

Is it possible, as Carl Seashore implied, that the answers to these last two questions must be qualified depending upon instrument type?

Will preference for timbre affect a child's success with a given instrument?

By the previous questions I am assuming that in order to perform on a music instrument consistently with his or her aptitudes, a child must develop a musical mind through a learning theory sequence at least at the time, but preferably before, he begins the study of an instrument. Stated another way, there is an appropriate musical age rather than a chronological age to begin the study of an instrument. Furthermore, we as teachers must distinguish between the techniques used to develop the musical mind at each level of learning and the executive techniques used for manipulating the instrument. It would seem that the richer the experiences—in terms of the development of levels of music skills and content learning, learning theory techniques, and instrumental techniques—the more motivated and successful the beginning instrumentalist will be.

Should the same skills and content learning sequences be followed for instrumental music instruction and general music instruction?

If so, would it necessarily follow that each level of learning is paralleled in general music and instrumental music instruction or that all or some levels of learning are taught contiguously in general music before the first level of learning is introduced in instrumental music? Might the answer be different for skills learning sequence and content learning sequence?

Assume that a child sequentially develops aural/oral, verbal association, and symbolic association skills in general music. When the child begins the study of an instrument, should he or she return to the aural/oral level and play tunes by rote on the instrument before engaging in symbolic association, both reading and writing?

Regardless of the answer to the previous question, should the child be introduced to instrumental sight reading if he or she has not learned vocal sight reading?

Would it be best, if it were possible, for a beginning instrumentalist to begin performing at an inference level of learning, exemplified by creativity and improvisation, and to work backwards, as it were, to symbolic association? Is it possible that one is always sight reading even if the music being read is familiar?

Can a child satisfactorily generalize an understanding in singing, for example, major and minor, to performing in dorian and mixolydian on an instrument?

Regardless of the comparative nature of the sequence of learning for vocal and instrumental music, sooner or later an instrumentalist is usually confronted with the necessity of reading music. This situation raises questions that have more technical ramifications.

When an instrumentalist sees notation (the symbolic association level), does he first relate the symbols back to the verbal association level and second, in a tactile sense, associate names with fingers, and fingerings, on the instrument? Where does and should the aural/oral level of learning enter this sequential process?

Is verbal association at all necessary for instrumental music reading?

What is the role of verbal association in instrumental creativity and improvisation? That is, is some type of verbal association the vehicle by which the musical mind indicates to the fingers what is being created and improvised and how they, the fingers, should move to effect a result?

Is it possible that there is a skills learning sequence, a content learning sequence, and an executive learning sequence, all of which should be coordinated? If the answer to the previous question is positive, we must remember that there are many types of instruments, each requiring at least one unique skill.

I fear that until the questions I have proposed, additional questions they have raised, and many others have been answered, music education will not be a discipline and the teaching of music will continue to be less than satisfactory. Moreover, I have a greater fear. It is for society in general. If the arts are not taught effectively, children may never experience the pleasure of gaining insight into themselves through the arts. Though all children are not created equal in ability, they should be given equal opportunity to develop such insight.

Cognition and Musical Development

Popular journals, television, newspapers, and radio have caused this to be the "age of psychology." Behavior is analyzed, motives are scrutinized, and the popular story of two psychiatrists analyzing the motivational exchange of their social greeting is now part of American culture. We are dedicated to understanding human nature with greater sophistication. More specifically, our interest is in knowing how helpful a knowledge of learning theory can be in the teaching of music. However, the direct application of learning theory to teaching is not an easy task.

Here are some of the problems. The experimental evidence obtained from much of the legitimate research in the field is accepted by all psychologists as valid. However, the interpretation of this information depends upon the set of assumptions that each psychologist believes. There is the oversimplified view that there are three approaches to learning theory—behaviorism, cognitive orientations, and third force—when in fact each of these areas may be extensively subdivided. We also have views that connect two approaches and sometimes attempt to work with all three. Finally, there is a painful gap between the establishment of experimental evidence from the laboratory, its organization into testable theory, and the application of both of these components to the classroom.

If we ask ourselves to identify some of the components of the cognitive processes involved in learning, it is possible to offer the following: perceiving, remembering, differentiating, discriminating, integrating, generalizing, and evaluating. All of these behaviors are related, overlapping, and interactive. In addition, there are other factors that affect cognitive processes, but which some do not consider generic—for example, psychomotor activity, motivation (social, achievement, creative, and so on), school environment, and teacher personality.

This paper makes the assumption that *cognition involves all mental processes concerned with knowing*. It is, therefore, not possible to limit consideration to any single theory of learning. What seems more practical for application to the teaching and learning of music is a composite view that allows us to acknowledge the cognitive, developmental, behavioral, and social influences that impinge upon the reality of learning.

It seems eminently practical to use what I call a clinical approach to teaching and learning. The clinical approach involves knowledge of (1) the cognitive-developmental status of the learner, including the level of social, emotional, and psychomotor mat-uration; (2) a variety of enabling approaches for organizing the instructional event(s); (3) the epistemology of the subject with the appropriate music skill for its artistic delivery; (4) the cultural and subcultural influences that impinge upon the value orientation of the learner; (5) ways in which to structure a positive learning environment; and (6) ways to evaluate cognitive development that contribute to its continued stimulation. These factors go beyond a single theory of learning, yet they are ingredients that affect the cognitive development of music students.

The questions I propose to my colleagues in psychology are: Can we use the contributions of Jerome Bruner, Jean Piaget, Abraham Maslow, and Carl Rogers even though their theories were not intended to be combined? Can we select, as the physician does, a combination of approaches that combines the best insights into the nature of the learner? And, can we combine into the practice of our profession the best we know of the experimental, theoretical, and empirical? As a music educator, I have no difficulty in viewing the compatibility of "habits" versus "cognitive structures" or "trial and error" versus "insight." My analysis suggests that each school of psychology is describing the *same* set of circumstances through a *different* system of knowledge. And while this view may appear to be simplistic to the professional learning theorist, it is useful to be able to use each approach in accordance with the clinical demands of the particular learning environment.

Bruner

Jerome Bruner's impact became apparent during the 1960s when American education undertook what is now referred to as the curriculum reform movement. He has written much on the nature of cognitive development and from this I would like to discuss what he calls "some benchmarks about the nature of intellectual growth. . . ." (pp. 5–6)

(1) *Growth is characterized by increasing independence of response from the immediate nature of the stimulus.* Much of what the young child does is predictable because of our knowledge

of the stimuli that impinge upon him. Furthermore, Bruner feels that a great deal of growth consists of the child's being able to maintain an invariant response in the face of a changing stimulus environment, or being able to alter the response in the presence of an unchanging stimulus environment.

(2) *Growth depends upon internalizing events into a "storage system" that corresponds to the environment.* It is this system that makes possible the child's increasing ability to go beyond the information encountered on a single occasion. This is done by making predictions and extrapolations from a stored model of the world.

(3) *Intellectual growth involves an increasing capacity to say to oneself and others, by means of words or symbols, what one has done or what one will do.* This is the way that Bruner describes the process through which children progress from merely orderly behavior to logical behavior. It is the human capacity that accounts for the analytic mode of the philosophers and takes mankind beyond empirical adaptation.

(4) *Intellectual growth depends upon a systematic and contingent interaction between a tutor and a learner, the tutor already being equipped with a wide range of previously invented techniques that he teaches the child.* Bruner uses this "benchmark" to deal with the cultural basis of the tutor-tutee relationship. This idea also recognizes the wide sources of stimulation coming to children from all out-of-school activities and relationships.

(5) *Teaching is vastly facilitated by the medium of language, which ends by being not only the medium of exchange but the instrument that the learner can then use himself in bringing order into the environment.* Bruner believes that it is the use of language as an instrument of thinking, the use of language for dealing with the possible, the conditional, and the immediate that contributes heavily to congnitive development.

(6) *Intellectual development is marked by increasing capacity to deal with several alternatives simultaneously, to tend to several sequences during the same period of time, and to allocate time and attention in a manner appropriate to these multiple demands.* Bruner, as Mursell before

him, properly notes that developmental growth brings with it the increased capacity for complexity.

It is Bruner's conception that all of these benchmarks are interrelated and overlapping. He is very much concerned with the problem of how the child translates previous experience into a model of the world. Bruner's concern is how the child becomes free of present stimuli, conserves past experience in a model, and stores and retrieves information. He postulates three forms of representation: enactive, iconic, and symbolic. The enactive form deals with nonverbal activities like riding a bike or skiing. Activity is the key and verbal explanations are of minimal value. Iconic representation is governed by principles of perceptual organization—for example, completing, filling in, extrapolation. The symbolic form involves the use of language, or any other symbol system where there are rules established for usage. According to Bruner, intellectual development involves the eventual ability to use all three forms of representation. While he takes the view that there is developmental continuity among all three forms, it is the movement into the symbolic system, particularly through language, that offers the greatest opportunities for growth:

The very young child uses language almost as an extension of pointing. . . . It is only gradually that words are used to stand for objects not present, and it is still a longer time before such remote referring words are manipulated by the transformational apparatus of grammar in a manner designed to aid the solution of mental problems. . . . (Bruner, p. 14)

Yet Bruner is concerned about the gap in his own theoretical model.

How the transitions are effected—from enactive representation to iconic, and from both of these to symbolic—is a moot and troubled question. To put the matter very briefly, it would seem as if some sort of image formation or schema formation—whatever we should call the device that renders a sequence of actions simultaneous, renders it into an immediate representation—comes rather automatically as an accompaniment of response stabilization. But how the nervous system converts a sequence of responses into an image or schema is simply not understood. (Bruner, p. 14)

Bruner's concern with growth is somewhat reminiscent of Mursell's developmental psychology. His concern that students be taught the structure of the subject causes no difficulty with music instruction. The time he spends on discussions of intuitive and analytic thinking are also congruent with the development of the creative and theoretical skills needed by the musician. My analysis of the Brunerian approach to learning and development finds compatibility with the emerging needs of children studying music. It does not solve all of our problems, but he does see the importance of going beyond a single set of guidelines when he says:

> . . . the heart of the educational process consists of providing aids and dialogues for translating experience into more powerful systems of notation and ordering. And it is for this reason that I think that a theory of development must be linked both to a theory of knowledge and to a theory of instruction, or be doomed to triviality. (Bruner, p. 21)

Piaget

Piaget is not a learning theorist. However, he provides a larger context for viewing the acquisition of knowledge as a consequence of growth with full consciousness to both the social and physical environment.

His approach to psychology stems from two sources: an early interest in biology reflected by the publication of his first paper on mollusks at the age of fifteen; and his well-known commitment to genetic epistemology. Although Piaget's view has a biological orientation, he does not try to attach a physiological meaning to psychological behavior. One of the basic problems in biology is adaptiveness and the development of biological structures. For example, the human ear is descended from one of the gill arches of the fish. In the evolutionary setting the gill began with one function and through adaptation it evolved into another function. The biological psychologist asks whether this is intelligent adaptive behavior or just another evolutionary occurence.

Piaget relates two ideas of biological evolution to human development: the continuous fitting of old structures into new functions under changed circumstances. His position is that development is solidly rooted in what already exists and displays a continuity with the past. Adaptations do not develop in isolation; they form a coherent pattern so that the totality of biological life is adapted to its environment. While each organism adapts in its own way, dynamic equilibrium is the process by which Piaget describes the total ecological balance in nature.

We know that epistemology is a branch of philosophy that investigates the origins, nature, methods, and limits of knowledge; it is the study of the theory and structure of knowledge. Piaget's genetic epistemology deals with both the formation and the meaning of knowledge. It is a study of human knowledge through observing the process by which it is acquired in children. He asks, "By what means does the human mind go from a state of less sufficient knowledge to a state of higher knowledge?" Genetic epistemology attempts to explain how the transition is made from a lower level to a higher level of knowledge. The fundamental hypothesis of genetic epistemology is that there is a parallelism between the progress made in the logical and rational organization of knowledge and the corresponding formative psychological processes. It is particularly interesting for us as educators to note the close parallel between John Dewey's educational philosophy and Piaget's genetic epistemology.

According to Piaget, it is the schema that corresponds to the biological structure that changes and adapts. It can be simple or unitary and it can be an entire system. For example, a finger is unitary and the digestive system is distributed throughout the entire body. The schema is an expanding pattern of behavior and consists of a variety of acts not limited to the stimulus. It is mobile, and mobility increases with age and when the action becomes a vehicle for goal-directed behavior. Consider grasping. The child applies this schema to beads, blocks, toys, and particularly to noses. The child soon learns that grasping the nose is an eventful activity since each owner attaches a slightly different response to its gleeful manipulation.

The early schemas usually involve overt behavior and Piaget calls them "sensorimotor schemas." He also describes cognitive schemas as sensorimotor for he believes that they are best conceptualized as actions. He indicates that the cognitive derives from the sensorimotor through a process of internalization. His characterization of the schema includes the following: (1) developmental growth from the neonate to the older child; (2) the ability to merge one schema with another; (3) mobility and the ability to acquire organization; and (4) broadening and differentiating while having unitary qualities. It is a concept that allows for a wide explanation of behaviors accounting for single behaviors and the continuity of many complex behaviors. The schema is the *structure* that adapts.

Piaget uses the terms "assimilation" and "accommodation" to describe the *process* of adaptation. Assimilation describes the capability of the organism to handle new situations and new problems with its present stock of mechanisms. Assimilation means that the organism has adapted. Accommodation describes the process of change through which the organism becomes able to manage situations that are at first too difficult. Thus, accommodation means that the organism must change in order to adapt. The processes are interrelated since an organism must assimilate a new situation before it can adapt to it. For example, an eight-month-old child may be able to pick up certain objects, but not very small ones. The child's grasping schema must accommodate—change. Once the ability has been developed, it can be assimilated into the behavior. In summary, the element of structure that adapts is the schema; assimilation and accommodation describe the process of adaptation.

Piaget is probably best known for his stages of development. He cautions us to remember that all these stages are overlapping and organically related, and that individuals may be in more than one stage at the same time. They represent a developmental sequence through which we all proceed. Birth inaugurates the sensorimotor period. Infant behavior is felt to be intelligent and adaptive and forms the basis for intellectual development. The child learns to coordinate information from the various sense organs and integrates this data, observes the permanence of the world, and learns to take different paths to reach the same destination. The child demonstrates goal-directed behavior and explores the potentials of the objects in his environment.

From about eighteen to twenty-four months, symbolic learning begins to emerge from the sensorimotor schemas. The conceptual schemas become organized into interrelated systems that Piaget calls operational. This kind of transitional stage is not marked by stable equilibrium. The child may be involved in self-contradiction, but the daily behavior is quite stable and integrative as long as it is closely tied to observable behavior. Logical thinking begins to emerge. This is the most confusing stage to evaluate in terms of the developmental level. It is during this stage that the child learns to use language.

At about seven years of age the child's formal thought processes begin to develop more stability as the stage of concrete operations is reached. A more rudimentary conception of time, space, number, and logic is also acquired. The scientific method with its need to control variables is still too difficult; the ability to arrange events in advance is also not yet developed. The child does not yet understand the relationship among the concrete operational groupings that he has already acquired.

The stage of formal operations begins about the age of eleven. At this time, understanding the basis of scientific thinking and causal relationships begins. The child can perform some experiments and deduce their implications. The beginnings of logical thought now emerge.

Piaget's approach to developmental growth appears to be a useful vehicle for the music educator because it provides, again like Mursell did, a foundation upon which the sequence of music experiences can unfold. His

72

attention to perceptual development (sensorimotor schemas) instructs the music educator not to begin with an abstraction. The time-honored principle—*begin with music*—is once again reaffirmed.

Maslow

Maslow was relatively unknown to music educators until 1967 when he participated in the Tanglewood Symposium. His views became immediately appealing because he provided discussions of creativity, values, and education. These factors are of critical moment to educators in the arts and they offer us an approach to the organization of the learning environment that is also in keeping with the current evolution of social and political freedom for the individual.

Maslow was not a learning theorist and has been identified as a third-force or humanistic psychologist. He was a member of a growing movement in psychology that has sought to identify those choices and patterns of living that will contribute to what the poets and prophets celebrate as the best that is human. Humanistic psychology is conceived of as an alternative between the various forms of behaviorism and the wide variety of Freudian styles. Maslow has become associated with terms such as "self-actualization," "peak experiences," and "hierarchy of needs." While it is true that these constructs of behavior are generic to his view of humanity, it is easier and just as accurate to say that his is a growth of psychology, a being psychology, a psychology based primarily on the study of healthy and creative people.

This is what is so seductive about his ideas. He began with the assumption that our natural proclivity is toward becoming fully human. In a study of healthy people he lists their clinically observed characteristics: (1) superior perception of reality; (2) increased acceptance of self, of others, and of nature; (3) increased spontaneity; (4) increased problem-centering; (5) increased detachment and desire for privacy; (6) increased autonomy and resistance to enculturation; (7) greater freshness of appreciation and richness of emotional reaction; (8) higher frequency of peak experiences; (9) increased identification with the human species; (10) changed (the clinician would say improved) interpersonal relations; (11) more democratic character structure; (12) greatly increased creativeness; and (13) certain changes in the value system. Maslow set forth a theory of human motivation that provides a significant rationale for those who believe that the satisfaction of needs is basic for energizing and directing behavior. His Hierarchy of Needs, in order of importance for individuals, is (1) physiological needs, (2) safety needs, (3) love and belonging needs, (4) esteem needs, (5) self-actualization needs, and (6) the desire to know and understand. It was Maslow's position that the order of these needs exists in a prepotent sequence. In other words, the most dominant needs must be satisfied before the next in sequence takes effect.

Maslow did not offer us a learning theory; he proposed an approach to education. He did not offer us a new way to teach; he proposed a pathway to self-actualization. And he did not offer us a great deal of experimental evidence, but he provided analysis of his clinical studies of healthy and creative people. Let me conclude this section on Maslow with some selected citations from his *The Farther Reaches of Human Nature*. He offered the following observations on education and learning theory.

> If one took a course or picked up a book on the psychology of learning, most of it, in my opinion, would be beside the point—that is, beside the "humanistic" point. Most of it would present the acquisition of association, of skills and capacities that are *external* and not *intrinsic* to the human character, to the human personality, to the person himself. Picking up coins or keys or possessions or something of the sort is like picking up reinforcements and conditioned reflexes that are, in a certain, very profound sense expendable. It does not really matter if one has a conditioned reflex; if I salivate to the sound of a buzzer and then this extinguishes, nothing has happened to me; I have lost nothing of any consequence whatever. We might almost say that these extensive books on the psychology of learning are of no consequence, at least to the human center, to the human soul, to the human essence. (p. 168)

73

Generated by this new humanistic philosophy is also a new conception of learning, of teaching, and of education. Stated simply, such a concept holds that the function of education, the goal of education—the human goal, the humanistic goal, the goal so far as human beings are concerned—is ultimately the "self-actualization" of a person, the becoming fully human, the development of the fullest height that the human species can stand up to or that the particular individual can come to. In a less technical way, it is helping the person to become the best that he is able to become. (p. 169)

Maslow also discussed the role of music and the arts:

So far, I have found that these peak experiences are reported from what we might call "classical music." I have not found a peak experience from John Cage or from an Andy Warhol movie, from abstract, expressionistic kind of painting, or the like. I just haven't. The peak experience that has reported the great joy, the ecstasy, the visions of another world, or another level of living has come from classical music—the great classics. (p. 176)

His views on education in music and art leading to peak experiences were summarized in the paper he presented at the Tanglewood Symposium:

Finally, the impression that I want to try to work out—and I would certainly suggest that this is a problem for everyone involved in arts education—is that effective education in music, education in art, education in dancing and rhythm, is intrinsically far closer than the core curriculum to intrinsic education of the kind that I am talking about, of learning one's identity as an essential part of education. If education doesn't do that, it is useless. Education is learning to grow, learning what to grow toward, learning what is good and bad, learning what is desirable and undesirable, learning what to choose and what not to choose. In this realm of intrinsic learning, intrinsic teaching, and intrinsic education, I think that the arts, and especially the ones that I have mentioned, are so close to our psychological and biological core, so close to this identity, this biological identity, that rather than think of these courses as a sort of whipped or luxury cream, they must become basic experiences in education. I mean that this

kind of education can be a glimpse into the infinite, into ultimate values. This intrinsic education may very well have art education, music education, and dancing education at its core. . . . Such experiences could very well serve as the model, the means by which perhaps we could rescue the rest of the school curriculum from the value-free, value-neutral, goal-less meaninglessness into which it has fallen. (pp. 178–179)

Just one comment as a music educator: it seems to me that Maslow was on much safer ground defending music education with this rationale than those of us who would try to have communities and boards of education believe that music education is primarily concerned with improving reading or mathematics.

Rogers

Carl Rogers is also a third-force psychologist who is known for his client-centered or nondirective approach to therapy. Although he has not developed a learning theory per se, he has been among the most sought after speakers and writers on American education. Based on his own theory of personality, his construct of the "fully-functioning person," and his unique clinical experience, he offers ten principles for learning:

(1) *Human beings have a natural potentiality for learning*. Rogers has made this point through illustrations of children's natural curiosity for learning until blunted by formal education.

(2) *Significant learning takes place when the subject matter is perceived by the student as having relevance for his own purposes*. The familiar example is the difference in learning between students when one is taking the course as a degree requirement and the other student is taking the course for skills that will be used to forward a professional career. The point is also made that the speed of learning is directly traceable to student relevance.

(3) *Learning that involves a change in self-organization—in the perception of one's self—is threatening and tends to be resisted*. Rogers made this point by dealing with the issue of conformity and nonconformity. If teachers allow students to subscribe to positions that

contradict their own, they feel endangered. Learning that emerges from a contradiction involves a change in the structure of self.

(4) *Those learnings that are threatening to the self are more easily perceived and assimilated when external threats are at a minimum.* Rogers cited the example of the youngster who is a poor reader, who knows that he is a poor reader, is forced to read before the class, and who is then ridiculed for his efforts. He contrasted this with a supportive, nonthreatening environment in which the student's learning proceeds at an individual pace. The results are predictable.

(5) *When threat to the self is low, experience can be perceived in differentiated fashion and learning can proceed.* This principle is actually an elaboration of the former one. Rogers believes that the absence of humiliation, ridicule, devaluation, scorn, and contempt allows the student to perceive increasing differentiation in the field of experience and the assimilation of the meanings of these differentiations.

(6) *Much significant learning is acquired through doing.* Rogers' view is that experiential confrontation with direct practical problems is one of the best modes for promoting learning. He uses examples of the wide variety of professionals who take short intensive courses.

(7) *Learning is facilitated when the student participates responsibly in the learning process.* Rogers' position is that the more responsibility the student has, the more effective the learning is. From my own experience I have found that increased student freedom leads to greater student responsibility and an improvement in academic standards and morale.

(8) *Self-initiated learning that involves the whole person of the learner—feeling as well as intellect—is the most lasting and pervasive.* Rogers observed this phenomenon in psychotherapy where learning from the "gut level" was the most influential. His examples in education all stem from the arts where he recognizes the interplay of feeling and knowing.

(9) *Independence, creativity, and self-reliance are all facilitated when self-criticism and self-evaluation are basic and evaluation by others is of sec-*

ondary importance. The best research in both the academic and industrial worlds indicates that creativity blossoms in an atmosphere of freedom. There is much confusion about this idea. Those unfamiliar with the research are fearful of the absence of structure, academic discipline, and standards for evaluation. Nothing could be further from the problem. Creative children are often so "driven" that they will ignore standards of health in order to work, they will demand higher levels of excellence of themselves than their teachers, and they will never be satisfied with their efforts. I am pleased to report that there is some of this in all of us.

(10) *The most socially useful learning in the modern world is the learning of the process of learning, a continuing openness to experience and incorporation into oneself of the process of change.* Rogers observed that both the social reality and the psychological reality are changing. Hence, for one to participate in this process, the skill that enables us to be responsive to change is a significant component of the learning process.

Rogers has offered ten guidelines for the facilitation of learning, and has identified a few of the basic qualities of the teacher as facilitator:

> He realizes that he can only grant freedom to his students to the extent that he is comfortable in giving such freedom. He can only be understanding to the extent that he actually desires to enter the inner world of his students. He can only share himself to the degree that he is reasonably comfortable in taking that risk. He can only participate as a member of the group when he actually feels that he and his students have an equality as learners. (p. 216)

Rogers places extraordinary demands on the facilitator. He expects the facilitator to have many of the professional sensitivities that are the usual equipment of the therapist. Yet, it is interesting to note that there is one place where the objectives of therapy and education intersect. The person who has been successfully educated and the client who has had successful therapy both have, to some degree, acquired integrated personalities.

The traditional environment in which

most of us have studied music is autocratic. It is often threatening and it can seldom be characterized as Rogerian. If his style is not appropriate for every teacher, his insight about the psychological environment for learning cannot be dismissed easily. While it is true that we participate in a performance group for aesthetic rather than democratic experience, the challenge is clear: to teach music in an environment that enhances the development of the fully functioning personality.

Bruner, Piaget, Maslow, and Rogers form a quartet whose combined approaches to human behavior can be seen as a powerfully instructive context for teaching and learning music. Guilford, Tolman, Bandura, and Gestalt theory may offer additional exciting possibilities. My study and teaching informs me that there is much for us to derive from psychology. The time is now right for a new form of research in psychology and music education and this is "collaborative research." We can learn from the psychologist, and he needs to know what the operational realities of the classroom, studio, and rehearsal hall are and how these factors will influence or reshape the focus or design of research. While there is much for us to gain in this partnership, he will be richly rewarded with direct access to the affective domain. He will have a nonverbal stimulus (music) whose potential for control and manipulation defy calculation.

We need to broaden our psychological horizons to include more information from personality theory, child psychology, and creativity. For example, unless one has a working knowledge of the way Freud conceived the personality, one can understand the third-force psychology only partially, since their orientation is, in part, a reaction formation to the pathological conception of human behavior that has evolved from the Viennese school.

Our approach to research also needs some reflection. We have often kneeled to the graven image of a tight experimental design with elaborate statistical manipulation only to find that we are testing a hypothesis that is at best pedestrian. We need to study how children learn music and we need to study how teachers teach music. In short, we need to become relevant for our profession. What I am suggesting is risky. What models should we use? How do we interpret human behavior when numbers cannot always be used as symbols? But here is an even more dangerous risk. What happens to our profession if we fail to inquire into our own field?

It has already begun to happen to us philosophically. Since we have referred most of our problems to aestheticians and philosophers, we have not trained ourselves to identify our own fundamental assumptions. This is why we still have hopelessly naive statements about what music can do for developing reading, mathematics, and other basic skills. These statements of panic reveal our intellectual bankruptcy. For documentation, please see the January 1978 issue of *Music Educators Journal* on the arts in general education. It plumbs the depths of superficiality in old ways using new cliches.

To avoid this in psychology, we must accept the responsibility for examination of the process of learning together with the psychologist; and eventually we can as a profession do it independently. Some members of our profession—Zimmerman, Petzold, Gordon—are already distinguishing themselves by such efforts. Ours is an exciting mission. We can no longer blame the community or the administration for our fate. The fate of music education rests with music educators.

References

Bruner, J. S. *Toward a theory of instruction*. Cambridge, Massachusetts: Harvard University Press, 1966.

Maslow, A. H. *Toward a psychology of being*. Princeton, New Jersey: D. Van Nostrand Company, Inc., 1968.

Maslow, B. G. *The farther reaches of human nature*. New York: Viking Press, 1971.

Rogers, C. *Freedom to learn*. Columbus, Ohio: Charles E. Merrill Publishing Company, 1979.

Response

W. Jay Dowling

Experimental psychologists use people like Bruner in books like *Theory of Instruction* and people like Maslow and Rogers in the same way, I think, that music educators would use them. And that is for a kind of inspirational reading that feeds into what we do. But that is not very specific about exactly what to do and does not give you tried and tested results to use in your work. I think they are very useful; one reason is that writers like Maslow and Rogers and Bruner are quite willing, to use Bruner's phrase, to go beyond the information given and extrapolate from their situations. One should always understand that what is being said has not always been tested in all the ways that you might want to check something before you say that is really true. So inspirational psychologists sort of sit a world apart from the world in which we do most of our experiments, in which we do testings in a much dryer, more pedestrian kind of way. Both kinds of things have a very definite use, often the use the experimental psychologist makes of the inspirational theorists is similar to the use music educators and doctors and lawyers make of them.

Several papers have touched on the difference between listeners and performers. Such a definite split between listeners and performers is really a product of peculiar conditions in our society of being urbanized, technologically advanced, cultured. With urbanization and technology comes division of labor, and we extend division of labor so that we have music-making specialists who play or sing for us and then the rest of us who tend to just sit and listen. But this split caused by that division of labor is a peculiarity of technologically advanced, urbanized societies. Most of the cultures of the world, in fact, are cultures where music is far more participatory than in our society. That's a very healthy kind of thing and I think that one of the good things about music education is that it is aimed at making participants out of more and more people. A lot of learning to listen might well go on in learning to play, although in terms of Brown's examples it is not absolutely necessary nor the only understanding of listening.

One other issue is at what age is it best to start children to learn to play musical instruments? My own opinion, which cannot really be based on solid facts, is the younger the better. I think we are beginning to have some evidence that really young children are more adept at auditory information processing than we had thought. I think a lot of experiments were done very clumsily back in the 1930s, for example, and they would find that the children had very little in the way of auditory capabilities. One experiment found that one-year-olds could not distinguish tones a perfect fifth apart, which of course is nonsense. A child of probably a few hours can distinguish far more narrow intervals than that. By one year of age, children are systematically singing intervals. Kessen's experiment gives evidence in the direction of far more sophisticated auditory information processing on the part of children than we ever thought possible. In my own work, with kindergarteners through sixth graders, we found that in auditory information processing, once children started to play strings or piano, after say six months of that, their advancement in being able to remember a temporal order of tones, and so on, is really very rapid. It certainly would be wrong, I think, to say that a kindergartener is not ready to learn to play an instrument because he or she does not have the cognitive capabilities. He very rapidly acquires them. It is probably true that different ages are appropriate for different children or different instruments are appropriate for different children.

A lot of discussion centered around differences between language and music and how it is processed in the brain. We keep observing that musical efficiency or proficiency of auditory information processing seems to split people into two groups. In language you generally have a more smooth continuum of proficiencies. There are very few people who cannot use language at all and there tends not to be some dichotomous play between people who are very proficient at it and people who are not. Part of that is reinforced by our culture. We encourage everyone to be good at using language, and if they are not good at it we put them into remedial reading or other courses that try to bring them up to the average. It is an important thing in our culture to be literate. With music we tend to do the opposite kind of thing, which may feed into the split between groups of people. With music we do not encourage the child who's not very good at music to keep at it and at least get up to some level of proficiency. We tend to encourage those who are very good and to discourage those who are not as good, perhaps because music is more optional in our culture. I don't know what the right answer there is, but I think that it is probably a factor that contributes to the split between populations.

Response

Roger N. Shepard

Before this session, having counted forty-three specific questions raised in Edwin Gordon's provocative paper (in addition to the seven general questions he raised in his introduction), I asked my co-speaker, Jay Dowling, which of these forty-three questions he planned to answer and which he was going to leave for me. I wish he hadn't left quite so many for me.

In fact, in thinking about which of these questions I could answer, I was reminded of the incident, once recounted by the visual and auditory researcher Bela Julesz, of the little boy and his parents at the zoo. They no sooner started their tour of the zoo than little Johnny asked, "Daddy, why does that elephant have such a long nose?" His father replied, "I don't know." A bit further along he asked, "Daddy, why does that giraffe have such a long neck?" And his father replied, "I don't know." Still further he asked, "Daddy, why does that monkey have such a long tail?" And again his father replied, "I don't know." This continued for some time until his exasperated mother finally exclaimed, "Johnny! Please stop pestering your father with stupid questions." At this, however, the father said, "No, no, no! Let him ask all the questions he wants. It's the only way he's going to learn!"

I, too, want to say that even if we are not very successful in answering your questions at this time, they seem to be good questions, and it is by continuing to ask such questions that you (and we) are likely to learn. Cognitive science, like medical science, still has many more unanswered than answered questions.

Sometimes the reason we can't answer what seem to us to be important and practical questions is not so much that we haven't been interested in these questions or that we haven't, in some cases, tried. Sometimes the reason is that the science hasn't yet advanced to the point where we know how to answer those questions, or how to formulate those questions so that they can be answered, or even whether we are really asking the right questions. If scientific understanding has not reached a sufficient level of development, desire for answers and money and effort devoted to the search for answers, no matter how great, may not be able to secure those answers.

Often new understandings come first and, only then, are followed by dramatic increments in our ability to affect the world (for better or worse). True, cognitive scientists do not yet understand much about the mental world. But the impression that physical scientists understand everything about the physical world is partly illusory. One of my mentors during my eight years at the Bell Telephone Laboratories, the noted scientist John R. Pierce, once remarked that if one asks a physicist what will happen if a brick is dropped into a bucket of water, the physicist

may well answer that some water will slop out of the bucket. Pierce noted, however, that the physicist is able to give this answer, not because he derives it from his quantum-mechanical equations, but only because he, just as the rest of us, has previously witnessed the descent of ponderous objects into bodies of liquid.

So too, I can offer at least tentative answers to some of Gordon's questions. But, if I do so, it will for the most part not be on the basis of theoretical models that have so far emerged from my laboratory investigations of the structure underlying perceived relations of musical pitch. It will primarily be on the basis of my own informal experiences—in coming to be deeply moved by certain kinds of music and in observing the very different lines along which an abiding interest in music has developed in each member of my family.

I do not mean to imply that the theoretical principles that emerge from our laboratory investigations are inherently incapable of bearing on the practical concerns of the music educator. On the contrary, I believe that the most radical transformations of the world in which we live, in which we learn, and in which we recreate have had their origin in the new understandings that have emerged from basic research at the most fundamental level (in the case of physical science, understandings of such things as thermodynamics, electromagnetism, relativity, and solid-state physics). Thus the illusion that the physical scientists understand our physical world comes about, as Pierce implies, because they have built so much of it! The steam and internal combustion engines issuing from thermodynamic understandings, the electric devices issuing from electromagnetic understandings, and the portable TVs, radios, record players, and organs, and the low-cost high-capacity computers issuing from understandings of solid-state physics are everywhere about us.

I anticipate similar transformations in the world of music and of music education as an eventual result of new understandings that are just beginning to emerge from investigations into the cognitive-structural bases of the perception, cognition, and production of music. Advances in psychoacoustics, electronics, and computer technology are already providing powerful new tools for the analysis, synthesis, and representation of music sounds; what has been lacking has been a deep understanding of the structural constraints governing the *musical interpretation* of such sounds by the human mind.

Gerard Knieter, in addition to urging us toward a very global and lofty view of the goals and problems of music education, remarks, "We have often kneeled to the graven image of tight experimental design with elaborate statistical manipulations only to find that we are testing a hypothesis that is at best pedestrian." I find myself sympathetic to this sentiment without, however, concurring with the implicit premise of his ensuing question, "How do we interpret behavior when numbers cannot be used as symbols?" I take, rather, the position that deep understandings that have the greatest power to transform our world will come from penetrating into and capturing the structural essence of basic phenomena by tightly formalized and, ideally, quantitative models. I should hasten to add, however, that I regard this as a very different enterprise from the over-elaborate analysis of data from uninspired experiments to which Knieter evidently alludes. But I also regard it as departing just as widely from the merely verbal though, as Jay Dowling noted, "inspirational" contributions of Bruner, Piaget, Maslow, and Rogers.

How might we begin to bridge the gap between the truly significant issues, which we so far apprehend only vaguely in terms of purely verbal generalities, and the precision of formulation and prediction that we strive for in the laboratory but in, at best, a "pedestrian" way in the absence of a sufficiently deep conceptualization of the significant issues? This gap does not, of course, coincide with the boundary between music education and psychological research. In both fields we seem to enjoy an abundance both of grandiose but untestable theories and of quantitative but inconsequential results. The difference between the two fields has, rather, to

do with whether the primary motivation behind the enterprise is the achievement of theoretical understandings or of practical applications. The reason for communication between the two fields is the two-sided one that the potentially most powerful applications are those that arise out of newer and deeper understandings while the most conclusive validation that we can have of a new understanding is its demonstrated effect in the world.

The principal point that I would like to make is that truly profitable interactions between research psychologists and music educators may require that workers on both sides of the boundary between these fields strive for significance and quantifiability. This may mean that psychologists concerned with the psychology of music and music learning will have to look more to musicians and music educators for guidance in deciding what are the significant issues to be addressed. (Psychological work on the perception of perceived pitch and perceived relations of pitch, for example, has until recently been dominated by a psychoacoustic approach that almost totally ignores the musically important questions of the role, in the interpretation of tones, of such internal structures as scale and tonality, which are induced by a preceding musical context.) At the same time, music educators may have to move toward the use of computer-based or microprocessor systems that will permit, for example, the precise control of auditory stimuli and recording the students' responses and reaction times in ear-training courses. For then, when we get together, the music educators will not be confined to asking the psychologists questions about training situations for which the psychologists have neither a precise specification nor any quantitative data. Instead, the music educator will be in a position to specify exactly what conditions of training were tried and exactly what patterns of responses were recorded in individual, and possibly very different, students.

Now, for the immediate purpose of music instruction itself, as distinguished from the purpose of collecting data that may lead to

80

later improvements in music instruction, the proposed greater use of the computer may seem quite antithetical to the humanistic approach to music education eloquently espoused by Knieter. And, certainly, I would not for a moment argue that a computer can substitute for a gifted and inspiring teacher. However, my limited experience with music teachers leads me to suspect that not all teachers are gifted and inspiring "facilitators" in the sense of Carl Rogers. And, as Knieter himself acknowledges, the Rogerian approach "makes extraordinary demands on the facilitator." For a large segment of music instruction, computer control is potentially able to permit increased—not reduced—recognition of each student's individuality. For such control allows each student to proceed at his or her own rate and, more basically, it provides (in each succeeding lesson) for the contingent selection of the type of auditory patterns, motor tasks, or cognitive exercises that is most desired by the individual student or that is most indicated by problems that that particular student encountered in preceding lessons. Finally, any improvements in such a computer-aided instructional system that grow out of an analysis of students' recorded performances can be incorporated into future versions of the system, whereas the unique instructional skills of a gifted teacher too often die with that teacher.

At first, of course, our goals and expectations must necessarily be appropriately modest. There are many and complex aspects of music, including, for example, those of auditory perception (of pitch, scale, tonality, melody, harmony, timbre, rhythm, progressions), of visual perception (of score, keyboard, and so on), of motor performance (sequencing, grouping, coordination), of cognition (of correspondences between auditory, visual, or motor representations, of underlying key or scale structure, of over-all temporal organization, and so on), and, I suspect, marked and enduring differences between individuals with respect to these perceptual, motor, cognitive, and motivational dispositions.

It perhaps is not surprising, then, that of the forty-three specific questions raised in Edwin Gordon's paper, I find only one that is in any direct way addressed by my own laboratory research on the perception of music. This is the question that he formulates as follows: "Do we attend differently to key (C, E-flat, A, and so on) and tonality (major, minor, dorian, and so on) as we listen and give meaning to music?" When I return for the second phase of this symposium, I would like to use my own recent work bearing on this question as a vehicle for illustrating how a quantitative, formal model designed to deal with admittedly limited but, I think, basic phenomena of auditory perception in a music context may have a potentially significant bearing on individual differences in music perception, and on music education. In the meantime, recognizing the very limited scope of what has so far been accomplished along these lines, I have to acknowledge that there are still many important questions that remain unanswered and, perhaps, even unasked.

Children's Processing and Remembering of Music: Some Speculations

Henry L. Cady

School music learning is varied in kinds and modes of operation. In general, there are four categories: (1) information about music—that is, knowledge about the past, particular people, and meaning in music; (2) information in music—that is, its components of time, successive and simultaneous pitches, loudnesses and silences, timbres, and the innumerable combinations of these and their treatments as well; (3) re-creation of existent works, a process that requires an imaginative use of information about music and information in music; and (4) creation of sounds in some kind of order—that is, composing or improvising, both of which require an imaginative use of information about music and in music.

None of these kinds is discrete. For example, information about music is essential in the re-creative process in order to determine proper stylistic treatment of components. It is essential also in the creative process in order to differentiate between newness and imitation.

All of these kinds of music learning are in the objectives for school music education. They are subsumed under the general, large objective of filling existing storage systems—children's minds—with useful information. The vehicles for doing this are symbols, signs, thinking, actions, and sounds. My concern here is not for the first kind of music learning, information about music, because that is learned mostly through verbal symbolic systems, and these are not unique to music learning. Rather, the concern is for the symbols, signs, thinking, actions, and sounds peculiar to the three other categories.

For the child, a learning task in music is a complex operation. There are several kinds of information he must process and use in fractions of a second. (We could say "simultaneously," given the capability of the human nervous system.) In the act of performing with a score, for example, there are several variables the child must cope with. There are symbols that are representations of pitch and duration. There are signs that are directives for the treatment of loudness and tempo, and those directives may indicate stable or variable treatments. There are other signs, also, and all of the signs collectively are directives for converting the symbols into sounds. That conversion process is dependent on human action in the form of specific and refined skills. The result of the conversion is organized sounds or what we call music. Therefore, we can say: performance with a score is the conversion of symbols into meaningfully organized sounds through skillful actions made according to signs. There is

one assumption in that statement and that is the existence of a timbre—instrumental or vocal—to use as a performing medium.

Obviously, memory is crucial in music learning. What is not obvious are the answers to many deceivingly simple questions. For example, is memory in music learning different from memory in learning other school subjects? Is there a difference between conscious, deliberate memorizing of a musical work and the usual remembering of what has been learned in class?

Psychologists categorize memory as short-term and long-term, but how does this apply to the analysis of musical behavior? Because we have so little evidence from research about *musical* memory and how it is developed, perhaps it is best to address the large problem of long-term memory.

We all respond to music stimuli, either overtly or covertly, and we cannot, in the everyday sense of control, prevent that response. Whether the response leads to long-term remembering is an individual matter. For example, one can shop in the supermarket where the ambience is seductive music but only remember the rising cost of orange juice. On the other hand, the school music teacher is concerned with long-term memory, except perhaps the teacher of severely handicapped children in special education classes. Therefore, I am addressing the larger problem—long-term memory in relation to the deliberate acquisiton of information *in* music.

Although we can find many variations in theories about the nature of human memory, they all seem to be reducible to two points of view. One of these assumes that the human brain processes different kinds of information in different ways. There are respected colleagues who have played with the idea of a "musical mind." I hope that they will forgive me if I suggest that the idea has a halo effect on faculty psychology. The other point of view assumes that there is only one way the brain can operate, that all kinds of information are processed in the same way. It assumes that man's many symbolic systems are manifestations of the brain's versatility rather than its part.

I accept the latter viewpoint. There is no anatomical evidence or physiological evidence to justify the former. Also, the idea of a multi-operational brain is an inadequate explanation for how we process information, how we remember it, and how we retrieve it. In brief, there is no musical mind. There is a brain that processes all kinds of information in the same way.

To put this in another context, Bloom's *Taxonomy of Educational Objectives* is a convenient device for focusing on the *facets* of human learning, but compartmentalization of learning as cognitive, affective, and psychomotor is essentially spurious. I personally have never known one of these to be operative without the others, either in myself or in other people. I have used the term "facets" deliberately, and the analogy is the cut diamond. The change in appearance as one moves the diamond does not change the diamond itself. We may find different information from each facet, but that information merely explains or reveals more about the diamond's totality.

The musician either consciously or unconsciously reveals that he or she knows information storage is a complex of thinking, feeling, and doing. It is in his language. "That sign tells us to play slower." "Feel the ritard." "Get the slowing down in your fingers." The flutist slows the movement of the fingers when seeing a sign and feels the proportioning of time per tone accordingly. This is not three operations; it is one with three facets—physical movement, feeling, and sign recognition—all processed in fractions of seconds. Each time the flutist plays a ritard, he expands the spectrum of ritards that he knows and enriches his concept of ritard. He develops an inventory of ritards and a knowing of which to select for a particular event in a succession of events. By the time the young flutist has reached high school with the hope of pursuing excellence, he must have a storehouse well filled with information of several kinds obtained through several senses. Especially, that information must be stored in a readily retrievable form. As Bruner has stated, the problem is not storage; the problem is retrieval.

My argument is this: the musician remembers according to the nature of the information to be remembered. Like the historian, he remembers in visual symbolic forms. Like the athlete, he remembers in motor patterns. Like the actor, he remembers successions of emotional states. The comparisons are many. But such singular comparisons are inadequate, because the musician's memories are complexes of seeing, doing, and feeling. Also, those comparisons do injustice to the historian, the athlete, and the actor—all of whom function in as complex a manner as the musician.

Before proceeding further, it is necessary to place in perspective the growing knowledge about the brain's hemispheres. At best, this knowledge is giving the arts a more "respectable" basis for their place in education. However, there is one important fact to be remembered: the two hemispheres of the brain are connected by a million cells. The arts are neither in one hemisphere nor the other. For musicians, the evidence is found clearly in the musical products of the brain. Teleological sound constructions, especially those that are tonally centered, are constructions using culturally accepted, logical progressions of music events. Perhaps the most convincing argument for the existence of abstract logic in musical design is found in the humor of Peter Schickele.

To put the argument another way, the tonal organism's operations are involved in musical processes. There is no way to exclude any element or function of the human organism while it perceives or makes music. The physiological interconnectedness of the human organism obviates any rational argument to the contrary. Out of his aural experience, mankind has created a symbolic system for communicating ideas that is derived from sounds perceived in the enviroment, the storage of those sounds, the propensity for converting stored sounds into a symbolic system, and each person's need to use that system for sharing inner feelings or finding commonality with others. The nature of music memory and how we deal with it in education, then, is found in the products of the general symbolic system that musicians use as well as in the physiological operations by which we process information and remember.

This argument should not be surprising to anyone. We have developed a symbolic system for each of the senses as well as combinations of them. There are fewer instances of discrete sensory perception than there are of multisensory perception. It is good that the human organism is capable of exceeding the limitations of one of its ingenious creations, the computer, because life is not made of sight *or* hearing *or* taste *or* touch *or* smell. For the musician, it is made of sight *and* hearing *and* touch.

Memory and information processing in music are not essentially unique. Rather, the only unique element is the medium—the symbolic system we call music. Because of our anatomical structure and physiological processes, partial closure contributes to the sense of "more to come" and is realized through skills appropriate to it.

My suspicion is that we know more about memory and information processing in music than we recognize. I suspect also that the problem may not be memory or how we process music information for storage. Rather, the problem may be an inadequate understanding of *what* is processed and remembered.

I intend to suggest problems of information processing and memory by identifying some variables in music and the voids in our knowledge about them. In order to do this, it would be convenient to have a readily available theoretical framework within which to function. Unfortunately, there is none agreed upon by music theorists to justify what is heard by what is seen in the music score—that is, the visual symbols and directive signs from which musicians re-create a work. This is spurious because the musical score is merely a blueprint. What we see in the score and what we hear as music are fundamentally different. They are not even comparable in the sense of musical experience.

Until recent years, music theorists did little to help us. Now we find true theoretical products are beginning to appear from the efforts of our colleagues. For example, "A

Theory of Tonal Music" by Lehrahl and Jackendoff, published in the Spring 1978 issue of the *Journal of Music Theory,* is most welcome. Like all beginnings, it raises many useful questions and provides an approach to the problem.

Music is a time art, and time is assumed to exist by the creator of music. If time did not exist, no successiveness could exist. A music work is a structure comprised of successions of events, both sounds and silences. These events are perceived to be not only contiguous but also logically related. And here we must recognize cultural mores about the contiguity and logical relatedness of sounds and silences resulting in music.

In order to assert that contiguity and relatedness do exist in music, we must be capable of remembering prior events. Is this memory function physiologically different in the perception of music? There is no evidence that it is. However, remembering sounds and silences as music may be a cultural problem—that is, a question of priorities for what is musically significant about a succession of sounds and silences.

As we observe children's use of music, we know that the temporal span of memory appears to expand with age. Children's songs are short, and their listening experiences are also. At least, our pedagogical folklore implies an agreement of the timespan of remembered music works increases with age. This is one premise for curricular design. The difficulty for the music teacher is knowing what kind of events are retained and retrievable by children at different ages so that their perceptions of contiguity and relatedness are assisted. Unfortunately, we do not know with certainty how and what kind of music experiences contribute to the development of children's concepts of music structure. To put this another way, we are uncertain about what sounds and silences are perceived by children as significant in music processes so that contiguity and relatedness yield a segment of time.

The musician uses aural space in many ways. He composes for solo timbres, groups of solo timbres, several timbres reinforced by multiple voices per timbre, and combinations of these. He talks about harmonic density and tessitura, which are not only a matter of the number of events occurring in a segment of time but also the number of simultaneous sounds in a pitch spectrum that comprises each event. Therefore, one is tempted to consider simultaneity of sounds as a "third" dimension and a qualitative use of space.

Another characteristic of aural space is the amount of it used for various kinds of musical experience. For example, chamber music is composed for small groups of timbres. More often than not, chamber works are performed by a group of solo timbres. The word "chamber" suggests that originally the idea was to perform these works in relatively small enclosures, such as a living room or a drawing room, a small aural space. Today, that intention seems to be fading and we have almost lost the idea of music designed for differing sizes of space. We seem to have lost the musical meaning of "chamber" as compared to the concert hall or the Tanglewood Shed. If so, have we lost a sensitivity to a kind of sound and with that loss a kind of musical experience?

Regarding the music education of children, does this loss matter? I think it does. There is a great difference between a Haydn quartet performed in a large concert hall for 2,000 people and an intimate hearing of it in a small room. The "aural space" is the difference—a difference that affects the kind of music information we process. It is interesting to note that we treat this difference with indifference, as being insignificant. I suspect that we do not know how to cope with it in education or whether we should. Our great achievements in electronics may not be a blessing in that regard because subtle differences are blurred by recording engineers and by home-grown volume control tinkerers.

There is another phenomenon in which both time and space are functional. Musical time and space are *created* by the sounding of a composition. For example, a Schubert song creates a temporal and spatial framework that is substantively different from his sixth symphony. The former uses less time than the latter; the former has fewer music events than the latter; the former has a density of simultaneous factors that is far less than the most dense moments in the latter. These differences are functional in the nature of the work and therefore functional in the musical experience they generate.

We have little verified knowledge about the relationship between awareness of aural time and space to children's musical responses. We need knowledge about the kinds of aural space and time that are appropriate to the various stages of developmental growth in music. The processing and storage of information about musical time and space is addressed in our music series but only indirectly and on the basis of respected, educated guesses.

Patterns and Principles

In order to use and create aural time and space, music events must occur. For the most part, these events are patterns produced according to certain principles. Some patterns, such as melodic motives, are organizers of structure; others, such as ostinati, are ambients that provide a setting for the organizing patterns. Both are essential to the creation of structures in time and space.

In his *Explaining Music,* Leonard Meyer has suggested principles of organization by which patterns, both brief and long, are constructed. Not surprisingly, they are familiar concepts and they reinforce the assertion that there is no musical mind, that there is one brain that uses a variety of symbolic systems. Meyer's principles are (1) differentiation, (2) continuation, (3) repetition, (4) closure, and (5) return. My question is this: do children perceive patterns as operating by these principles?

Three of these principles are readily understandable because they appear frequently in the literature about music: repetition, closure, and return. The word "repeat" is used in two ways by the musician, as by the layman. A *repetition* may be an iteration or it may restate the essential meaning again but in different guise. In the one case, the identical tones are performed again; in the other, the patterning is recognized as having been heard before. Structure by repetition is obvious for those who have adequately processed the initial statement. Remembering the initial statement is crucial, but so is the amount of distortion of the initial pattern if a restatement is made in a varied form. We know very little about the cues necessary for the recognition of a varied pattern. And yet, this is perhaps the most elementary method for creating musical structures.

Closure almost speaks for itself, except that the musician uses it in subtle ways to create events and to segment large concepts. Children's songs have phrases that are units but incomplete. One phrase leads to another until a large, complete unit results. These large complete units have many moments of partial closure that contribute to the sense of more to come until complete closure, which signals termination. The remembering of prior events is a requisite in comprehending the whole.

We all know that preschool children respond to the phrasing of works, to partial and complete closure, in many ways. Some are sensitive to the varied tempi, the harmonic cues, and the melodic cues that signal partial closure, while other children seem to be oblivious of those cues and have difficulty in synchronizing their responses to the music. This is a total response phenomenon, and we have little understanding about the developmental differences among children regarding that kind of sensitivity. Is this a function of memory, a function of a facile processing of information, or both?

Return is akin to repetition; a music idea is heard again after other music events have occurred subsequent to the initial statement of the idea. This is a basic music form that we describe as a three-part form and we give it the schematic of ABA. Sometimes the restatement of the original idea is an iteration and sometimes it is a paraphrase. How well children at different ages can recognize returning ideas is still a question, and yet this phenomenon is commonplace in music structures. As in the case of repetition, we do not know what cues are essential, what kinds of patterning are most easily recognizable, so that we can know with reasonable certainty

when the elementary three-part form is appropriate in the gamut of the teaching-learning process.

Meyer's other two principles—differentiation and continuation—present us with greater difficulties. First, let us consider the more puzzling of the two—*continuation*. Perhaps its significance can be best explained by asking a question: what cues in a music process indicate that it is not ended, that it will continue? To put it another way, how do we know that events are contiguous and comprise a unit? Here we are dealing with the phenomenon of expectation, and there are those who find this an intriguing and fruitful area for research.

Continuation is crucial to the structuring of musical time, to the idea that a segment of time has been created by a unitary process in sound. Such a process establishes two attitudinal sets in the perceiver—expectation that the end is not yet and expectation that the end is about to happen. In the former, the cues of continuation are greater than those of closure, and yet the potential for either exists in any music passage. If closure is expected, then closure factors are stronger than those for continuation. Children's perceptions of these cues would seem to be a crucial consideration in curricular design. It follows that what they process is as important as how they process it.

Differentiation is the process by which an element in a pre-existing structure develops or is developed into a new structure: the human embryo develops limbs, the tulip bulb develops leaves and then blooms, a human arm evolves into a shovel and then into a giant mechanized shovel. In music, a pattern becomes a sequence or even an entire development section in the sonata-allegro form or a variation for a theme. Differentiation is the process by which potent patterns become significant structural elements. How and at what age does the child hear and appreciate this clever and subtle process?

Meyer's principles and the ideas of musical space and time are useful devices for identifying the voids in our knowledge about the content of the teaching-learning process in school music. It seems to me that too many music educators have been asking tangential questions, or secondary questions. As I see our state now, the essential question has been this: how can we improve (make more economical and efficient) the teaching-learning process in music? Sometimes we have forgotten that the dependent variable is music. For more than a century, school music in the United States has been confounded by the lack of an adequate definition and explanation of music. The result has been confusion about what children should learn, what and how to teach, and what we should be giving as the highest priority in our investigations.

I have chided music theorists for the lack of a music theory on which to construct our curricula. They could respond perhaps less kindly and accuse me of not dealing with the whole truth. They can assert that music is a psychological phenomenon and it is the psychologists who should analyze so that plau-sible music theory construction is possible. It would be difficult to rebut that rejoinder. E. Thayer Gaston proposed a similar point of view, and it is yet to be understood by too many of us (Gaston, 1964).

My concern is a realistic analysis of music as a product of human behavior and as a form of human behavior. It is possible that the question "what is music?" may be answered by psychologists who are concerned about what we process and store as music. In doing so they will help us know what to teach and at what stage of musical development.

References

Bruner, J. S. *On knowing: Essays for the left hand.* Cambridge, Massachusetts: Harvard University Press, 1966.

Gaston, E. T. The aesthetic experience and biological man. *Journal of Music Therapy,* 1 (March, 1964), 1–7.

Music Information Processing and Memory

David Brian Williams

The contemporary concept of human information processing appears to pervade much of cognitive psychology. Haber (1974) contends that the antecedents for an information processing approach to the study of human cognition are the communications theory of Shannon and Weaver (1949) and the development of digital computers. Music theorists have actively used information theory in their research, musicians have made much use of the computer, but little research in music or music education has used human information processing as a theoretical base for the study of music cognition.

As Massaro explains, the central assumption of an information processing model is that "a number of mental operations, called processing stages, occur between stimulus and response" (1975a, p. 20). Haber (1969) called this a "continuum of cognitive activity." On the simplest level a model of the continuum might consist of input, encoding, storage, decision, decoding, and response stages.

How does learning fit into this concept? A definition for learning that many of us have used is "a change in behavior" (Hall, 1966). Manelis and Redding suggest, however, that a "cognitive definition of learning would state that it is a change in cognitive structure, which must be inferred from overt behavior" (1978, p. 11). When we speak of music learning, per se, we are defining learning as the "end result of the interaction of a number of psychological processes (activity during music information processing) rather than a distinct process in itself" (Massaro, 1975a, p. 583).

Let me place this in a music education perspective. If we envision the cognitive processing of music as a time continuum between when Johnny listens to a melody and when he makes some response (he labels the melody, he recognizes the melody, he sings the melody), we can analyze music learning as several stages of acquisition, storage, and retrieval. We can define an input stage (the sensory reception of sound), an encoding and perception stage, a memory stage, a decision stage, a decoding or retrieval stage, and finally an output stage (some music response is made).

One of the frequently expressed instructional problems in general music education is "why Johnny can't sing." On the surface this would appear to be a performance problem. But, if we consider the simple information processing model just described, research data would suggest the problem is much more complex.

If Johnny does not sing a melody correctly, where has the error occurred? In terms of information processing we would want to locate the source or sources of information loss before we pass judgment on why Johnny has not learned to sing the melody correctly. Starting at the beginning of the continuum, we should consider possible hearing problems. Then, what about perception? We should ask ourselves whether Johnny is really listening to pitch change. Or, is it possible he is listening to the rhythm, to the timbre, or to his friend sitting next to him who cannot sing either? Is he aware that pitch moves up and down? Can he hear pitch motion as

small as a semitone? We should consider memory. There is some evidence that our immediate or short-term memory is limited to about seven "chunks" of information. With young kids it may only be three "chunks." Maybe Johnny just needs a chance to practice hearing the melody a few more times. The type of song you are asking him to sing could make a difference in his memory capacity. Repetitive rhythmic patterns seem to make memory for melody easier. Cultural identity and past experience are factors. When kids do know a pop song they remarkably seem to have not only stored the notes but all of the cultural nuances and gestures as well. What about decision and retrieval? Have we asked Johnny to sing this melody before or only to listen and remember, but not recall the melody by singing? There is evidence to suggest that we store information based on how we have to use it. Recall storage is different and more difficult than recognition storage. To recognize a melody, Johnny has to retrieve a contour or melodic image and decide if it matches. To recall by singing, Johnny must have stored (memorized) sufficient information about the rhythm and pitch of each tone in the melody. All of the stages of information processing (and music learning) are susceptible to information loss.

Music Memory

Given the framework of an information processing model for music learning, we can examine memory as a component in music processing. Ronald Thomas emphasized in his report on the Manhattanville music curriculum project that memory is the *sine qua non* of music learning. Thomas stated that the "basic ingredient of all aural skills is memory. Identification of even the simplest sound depends on the student's ability to remember many factors of articulation, pitch, and volume which characterize sound" (Thomas, 1970). The music education process involves teaching the three musicianly roles of performer, composer, and critic. As performers, children learn skills in singing, playing, moving, and accompanying music. As composers, children learn skills in creating, elaborating, and improvising music—in

88

terms of melody, harmony, rhythm, timbre, form, and style.

We cannot consider any of these skills without implicating the role of music memory and storage of music imagery. When we ask Susie to listen to music, we assume she is acquiring a representative image of the music that is an abstraction of the salient features of the music event: the melody, the texture, the harmony. When we ask Susie to play music, we assume that her stored image of the music is sufficient to permit recall of the pitch sequence, the rhythm and time relationships, the fingering patterns. When we ask Susie to identify a music composition we assume her stored image is sufficient to permit recognition of the melodic features, the harmonic features, the form of the music.

Storage of music experience is a very complex process. Imagine for a moment the experience of browsing through albums in a record shop. For example, imagine the experience of looking at an album with Zubin Mehta conducting the Los Angeles Philharmonic in the *Planets* by Holst. Imagery based on my experience would reflect on the dramatic nature of the music, the compositional style of Holst, his penchant for folk tunes, and the repetitive rhythmic patterns. Also included would be Mehta's conducting style (gesture included), certain musicians who are likely to be in the orchestra (Roger Bobo, William Kraft, Roger Stevens), and the spectacular emotive charge I get whenever I imagine the superb depth of sonority generated by the final chord of the Uranus movement and the accompanying vibrations in the floor of my home whenever I play the recording. All of the senses seem involved in the music experience. For the purpose of this discussion we could define memory as the storage of music information. However, our discussion suggests that music memory is more complex than this notion. We must include in our definition of memory both the *process* of music memory (acquisition and retrieval of information) and the *structure* of music memory (the storage systems).

We must consider that the *process* of music memory, as in all auditory processing, is time dependent. Normal and Rumelhart (1970) appropriately describe information processing as "something of a race between the amount of time needed to acquire a sufficient number of features so that new material may be properly perceived and encoded" (p. 23). Before melody, rhythm, or harmony can be perceived as such, discrete perceptual sound events must be processed and retained in some immediate or working memory buffer until sufficient information is available to permit recognition of music events. Massaro's (1975b) description of what he terms the secondary stage in language processing is analogous to music processing. He theorizes that sound events must be transformed from:

> perceptual information into conceptual information, that is meaningful units in general abstract memory. This conceptual stage of processing involves . . . [the] possible utilization of syntactic rules of language, contextual or situational knowledge, and abstract semantic knowledge. (p. 12)

The music memory process is a critical trade-off between time and conceptualization. It may well be that some music is information saturated. George Pearle (1963) wrote about the problems of conceptualizing *Perriot Lunaire*. He commented, "Presumably, only familiarity is required to make this music sound 'conventional.' This is a dubious thesis. Perriot Lunaire, in any case, is not a work that one ever 'gets used to.' " To interpret, Pearle is saying that the amount of experience necessary to completely process this composition is cognitively impossible. The piece overloads the capability of the music memory process.

We have considered the acquisition of music experience; now consider the retrieval process. There is a distinction between the "availability" of memory information and its "accessibility" (Manelis and Redding, 1978). When we ask children to verbalize their musical experience, it hardly represents a true picture of their nonverbal imagery of that experience. The music task affects the success of retrieval. Whenever we ask a student to sing, play, or notate, we assume he or she has memorized the music information. That may be a different process than asking the student to identify the music. It would be the difference between asking a student to sing or play the first theme from the third movement of the Beethoven "Pastoral Symphony" or to recognize the theme from among a set of alternatives. The latter would be an easier task.

We should assume that the *structure* of music memory has some system, some order. In his article on the philosophy of melody, Hickman (1971) illustrated the complexity of our mental image of music events. Melody, he explained, can be everything from the

> little tune that Pooh-bear hummed to himself, through few seemingly aimless notes forming the subject and answer of the C-sharp minor fugue of the first book of Bach's "Forty-Eight," through the great unsupported arch-like theme of the Romeo and Juliet Overture of Tchaikovsky, through the leit-motifs of Berlioz, Wagner, Franck and others, to the tone-rows of the serialists and even beyond to the "glide" motifs which electronic music makes possible. A thoughtful perambulation through the list will induce the feeling that there must be more than the mere "succession tones." And in speculating about what attributes the "more" may include, we come quickly to structure, order and pattern, and the question which is likely to be the more crucial. (p. 5).

Referring to the writings of Tischler (1956), Cohen (1962) pointed to two relations in the structure of music memory:

> The first class consists of syntactical, or internal, relations, which are unique to the medium of the aesthetic object. In music they include rhythm, melody, harmony, counterpoint, tone color or instrumentation, expression or interpretation, and form or "meaningful contour." The second class consists of nonsyntactical, or external, relations, which affect the arts. They include gesture, programme, "ethics or the expression of the composer's emotions and ideas, and his technical mastery," the drives and motivations of the creator as reflected in his work, intended social functions of the work, historical and social conditions, the place of the work in history and tradition of the art, the personality,

and proficiency of the performers, if any, and the conditions of the performance, if any. (p. 137)

This leads to some general questions. First, what is the nature of the mechanisms in music information processing that establishes and orders a person's experiences with music imagery (that is, how are music experiences acquired)? What are the limitations of these mechanisms? What are the dimensions of music imagery? What dimensions are critical to performing certain music tasks? What are the search strategies used in retrieval of music information? What is the relationship between the *process* of music memory and the process of music learning?

Secondly, what is the multidimensional structure of music memory? What "filing systems" do we use to codify our music experience? Verbal cues? Nonverbal cues? Visual cues? As music educators we specify behavioral objectives that ask children to retrieve music along many nonverbal dimensions: melody, harmony, rhythm. We ask children to retrieve music on labels associated with performers, composers, titles, and styles. We ask children to retrieve music along visual dimensions: the instruments of the orchestra, program music, opera.

These questions have direct parallel to those same questions being asked in cognitive psychology. In their book, *Human Associative Memory*, Anderson and Bower (1973) state:

> The most fundamental problem confronting cognitive psychology today is how to represent theoretically the knowledge that a person has: what are the primitive symbols and concepts, how are they related, how are they to be concatenated and constructed into larger knowledge structures, and how is the "information file" to be accessed, searched, and utilized in [problem] solving. (p. 151)

In music education we should ask: "How do we theoretically represent music knowledge through psychological structure so that we are better able to define and evaluate the music learning process?"

90

Review of Current Research in Music Memory

My objective here is to develop a state-of-the-art perspective based on a brief synthesis of current research in music memory. This perspective is biased, no doubt, by my own involvement in research in this area and will tend to focus on memory for melody (this is where the research emphasis appears to be at this time). The observable result of this review should successfully demonstrate that we are a long way from answering the general questions just presented.

There are three theories that I will use as a framework for reviewing the research: (1) Our ability to acquire, store, and retrieve music is affected by physical limitations in the human information processing system. (2) Music is most often stored as contour or generalized abstract imagery rather than absolute imagery. (3) Acquisition, storage, and retrieval of music is a function of the music task— that is, melody stored for recognition or melody stored for recall and performance.

Physical limitations. Cognitive psychology has proposed memory models that show two stages: a short-term or immediate memory and a long-term or more permanent memory. Information is accumulated in the short-term store waiting to be processed into long-term memory. The research of Massaro (1975) and my own research in music memory (1973, 1978) has supported this two-stage model for melody.

Research has shown that there are physical limitations in short-term memory for music. Short-term memory can hold a limited number of tones at a time. Pollack (1952) and Berg (1975) reported four to seven tones. The more tones in a melody, the harder it is for people to remember all of the melody. Graduate music students had extreme difficulty remembering and singing back tones from the center of a seven-tone melody after one presentation. We appear to remember best the first and last tones (Williams, 1975, 1978) with poor memory for pitch in the middle of the melody.

Time is also critical in short-term memory. Information for pitch decays over the first seven to eight seconds (Williams, 1975). The faster the tempo, the fewer notes we can expect to remember.

There are ways to improve upon these limitations, however. We can slow down the tempo when learning a melody (Dowling, 1973). We can give more time for rehearsal. More importantly, our past experience and training allow us to "chunk" the tones of a melody into larger musical units for storage. Tonal melodies are better remembered than atonal. Long (1977) using Taylor's (1976) technique for computing tonal strength, found melodic memory strength to increase with tonal strength. Dowling (1973) found that people used rhythm to help them "chunk" melody. Students could remember tonal configurations within rhythmic patterns, but could not remember tonal configurations when asked to recognize them from across the rhythmic pattern. Carlsen's (1978) research in music expectancy and melodic dictation suggests that people remember melody best when the tunes conform to expected melodic progressions; the greater the melodic expectancy, the fewer the errors in dictation.

Contour and pitch storage. Dowling (1971, 1972) has attempted to determine whether people remember contour of a melody or each tone and interval. He found that people remember each tone under certain conditions: when the melody is played back untransposed and when the melody is a familiar tune heard many times. When the melody is novel and has been transposed people cannot recognize the difference between a contour where relative interval sizes have been changed and the exact repetition of the melody. In most cases, only a generalized contour is remembered.

Sergeant (1973) has reported that young children remember each pitch in a melody, note-by-note, exactly at the pitch level at which it was learned. These children tended to sing melodies they had learned at the pitch level used during the learning process; in other words they did not transpose it. Older children, would transpose the melody but lost overall accuracy in pitch. This suggests they were generalizing the melodic patterns. This study was successfully replicated by MacDonald and Ramsey (1976).

Recall and recognition. Deutsch (1970) found that pitch interfered with pitch. When students were asked to discriminate between two tones, with random tones inserted in between, discrimination became poorer as the number of tones increased. When she inserted spoken digits instead, there was little error.

In the psychomusicology lab at Illinois State University we set up a task where music students were asked to remember a seven-tone melody (Williams, 1978). Some of the melodies were tonal, some atonal. Between hearing the melody and being tested on memory of each pitch in the melody, twenty random tones were played. They were told to ignore these. Performance was very poor, sixty percent lower than students who did not listen to the random tones. Tonal melodies were no better than atonal melodies. I gave some students ten seconds to rehearse before the random tones were played. Surprisingly, they did no better. The rehearsal time was no help. The twenty tones had a drastic interfering effect on memory for pitch in melody. I speculate that if I were to have also tested their recognition of contour they could have performed this task very well.

Most of the auditory tasks we teach children in general music education (without the aid of visual notation) are recognition tasks (identify a melody; label a melodic shape; discriminate between melodies). Memory of a generalized contour works well for this. We teach few auditory tasks that require children to remember each pitch for recall. When we do so, we have specific names for these tasks: memorization, dictation, improvisation. All these tasks are notoriously difficult to teach and require auditory input and a performance output.

Primary areas of uncertainty. My perception is that there are two primary areas of uncertainty regarding our understanding of music memory and its role in music learning:

(1) There is a need to understand the process of acquisition, storage, search, and retrieval of music information. Research has shown some similarity between general processing models and the processing of music information, but only at a rudimentary level. We must consider processing in terms of the total complexity of the music experience from the roles of music composer, critic, and performer. We should begin to develop theoretical models of memory processing as a means to facilitate research in music and to communicate these results to music education.

(2) A good deal of research effort has been spent on the perception and learning of discrete music events: pitch, intervals, chords, rhythms, and so on. There is a need to understand the more general language structures of music and their role in the music learning process. There is a need to understand the multi-dimensionality of the music experience. It is my contention that children's nonverbal imagery of music is more sophisticated than what we give them credit for. Psycholinguistics is concerned with the structure of language; psychomusicology should be concerned with the psychological structure of music. Research has shown that contour, rhythm, expectancy, and tonality may be organizers for our music experience. Perhaps when we understand the system by which music is stored and retrieved, we will understand a good deal about how people learn music.

I wish to address three generative questions to the psychologists:

(1) What insight and knowledge can cognitive psychology provide toward building theoretical models for the structure and process of music memory?

(2) What correlations might there be between music and language processing and memory? What dangers do you perceive in applying verbal language models to nonverbal language or music models?

(3) What research models would you suggest we use to begin to examine the structure and process of music memory on a level appropriate to the complex nature of the experi-

ence? Are there methods for nonverbal-to-nonverbal research—that is, measuring music with the use of nonmusic mediators?

In closing, let me paraphrase Walter Kintsch (1974) from his book, *The Representation of Meaning in Memory*. Kintsch's remarks were referenced to psycholinguistics. Attempts to study the psychological process of music without inquiring what others have to say about the topic, from their own nonmusic standpoints, are doomed to failure. The constraints that other disciplines may impose on music learning theory should not be viewed as foreign intrusions into music territory. When we know as little about music cognition as we do now, we have every reason to grasp at every straw that is offered (pp. 1–2). The contributions of our psychology colleagues represent much more than a single straw; I have great expectations for the discussions ahead.

References

Anderson, R. J., and G. H. Bower. *Human associative memory*. Washington, D.C.: V. H. Winston & Sons, 1973.

Berg, P. A. *Short-term memory for tone sequences*. Unpublished doctoral dissertation, University of London, 1975.

Carlsen, J. C. *Cross-cultural study of melodic expectancy*. Unpublished manuscript, University of Washington, 1978.

Cohen, J. E. Information theory and music. *Behavioral Science*, 1962, *7*, 137–163.

Deutsch, D. Tones and numbers: Specificity of interference in immediate memory. *Science*, 1970, *168*, 1604–1605.

Dowling, W. J. Recognition of melodic transformations: Inversions, retrograde, and retrograde inversion. *Perception & Psychophysics*, 1972, *12*, 417–421.

_____. Rhythmic groups and subjective chunks in memory for melodies. *Perception & Psychophysics*, 1973, *14*, 37–40.

Dowling, W. J., and D. S. Fugitani. Contour, interval, and pitch recognition in memory for melody. *The Journal of the Acoustical Society of America*, 1971, (2, Part 2), 524–531.

Haber, R. N. (Ed.) *Information-processing approaches to visual perception*. New York: Holt, Rinehart, & Winston, 1969.

_____. Information processing. In E. C. Carterette and M. P. Friedman (Eds.), *Handbook of perception*, Vol. 1. New York: Academic Press, 1974.

Hall, J. F. *The psychology of learning*. Philadelphia: J. B. Lippincott Co., 1966.

Hickman, A. Some philosophical problems of melody. *Psychology of Music*, 1975, 3–11.

Kintsch, W. *The representation of meaning in memory*. New York: John Wiley & Sons, 1974.

Long, P. A. Relationship between pitch memory in short melodies and selected factors. *Journal of Research in Music Education*, 1977, *25*, 272–282.

Manelis, L., and G. Redding. *Memory and learning: Basic frameworks*. Unpublished manuscript, Illinois State University, 1978.

Massaro, D. W. *Experimental psychology and information processing*. Chicago: Rand McNally, 1975. (a)

_____. (Ed.) *Understanding language*. New York: Academic Press, 1975. (b)

MacDonald, D. T., and J. H. Ramsey. *A study of musical auditory information processing of children*. Paper presented at the MENC National Convention, Atlantic City, 1976.

Norman, D. A., and D. E. Rumelhart. A system for perception and memory. In D. Norman (Ed.), *Models of human memory*. New York: Academic Press, 1970.

Pearle, G. *Program notes on Perriot Lunaire*. In the music of Arnold Schoenberg, Vol. 1, Columbia Records, 1963.

Pollack, I. The information of elementary auditory displays. *Journal of the Acoustical Society of America*, 1952, *24*, 745–749.

Sergeant, D., and S. Roche. Perceptual shifts in the auditory information processing of young children. *Psychology of Music*, 1973, *1*, 39–48.

Shannon, C. E., and W. Weaver. *The mathematical theory of communication*. Urbana: University of Illinois Press, 1949.

Taylor, J. A. Perception of tonality in short melodies. *Journal of Research in Music Education*, 1976, *23*, 197–208.

Thomas, R. B. *MMCP synthesis*. Bardonia, New York: Media Materials, Inc., 1970.

Williams, D. B. Short-term retention of pitch sequence. *Journal of Research in Music Education*, 1975, *23*, 53–66.

_____. *A study of tonal strength and its influence on melodic memory*. Unpublished manuscript, Illinois State University, 1978.

Tischler, H. The aesthetic experience. *Music Review*, 1956, *17*, 189.

Response

Jane A. Siegel

Research within the information processing tradition on such problems as language, speech, and reading has been expanding rapidly for the last fifteen to twenty years. However, it is only recently that experimental psychologists with that theoretical orientation have devoted any serious attention to an understanding of the psychology of music. Even now, a relatively small number of people are involved and it may therefore be premature to expect information processing psychology to have a major input into the problems of music education at this time. In particular, I feel that information processing psychology has relatively little to contribute to issues of curriculum development. In fact, I am much more hopeful about the potential contribution of developmental psychologists to this area, primarily because my experience working in the educational system has convinced me that one gains the best insight into children's learning by observing children themselves during the learning process.

Let me illustrate this point by taking reading as an example. There have been hundreds of studies on the psychological processes of skilled readers involved in extracting information from the printed page. The evidence suggests that skilled readers selectively sample text, rather than operating on a letter-by-letter basis (Brown, 1970), and that they use words or perhaps phrases as basic cognitive units. Yet, it is by no means agreed that this is the appropriate strategy to encourage when teaching beginning reading to children. (See Gibson and Levin, 1975.) The same argument may apply to music. The study of music information processing by the skilled performer is certainly worthwhile as many of my colleagues at this conference have already pointed out, but I personally do not believe that such study will in and of itself tell us how or what to teach children.

Although it may be premature to apply current research in information processing directly to music education, the time may be ripe for a comprehensive treatment of the psychology of music within this theoretical framework. Information processing models can provide a structure for understanding music perception and memory and for breaking down and analyzing the subprocesses involved in specific music activities and skills. Moreover it can provide us with a body of factual information, some of which may be applicable to music.

An important distinction that has been made by experimental psychologists in recent years is that between verbal and nonverbal processing of information. This issue has been thought to be fundamental, because of evidence for left-brain dominance for verbal or categorical processing and right-brain dominance for nonverbal processing (Kimura, 1961; Shankweiler and Studdert-Kennedy, 1967). Moreover, it has been argued (Liberman, Cooper, Shankweiler and Studdert-Kennedy, 1967) that this physiological division of labor suggests the existence of radically different theories of how verbal and nonverbal stimuli are processed.

Cady in his paper has alluded to the left-brain/right-brain dichotomy and rejects its applicability to music. He may do so wisely, for psychologists, it seems to me, may initially come down on the wrong side of the issue by labeling music as a right-brain, and therefore a nonsymbolic, analog activity (Kimura, 1964; Shankweiler, 1966) that is quite different from language.

To musicians, this must seem like nonsense, for as both Williams and Cady have pointed out, music is a complex and highly symbolic system. Bright (1963), Nettl (1958), and Seeger (1960) have pointed to the analogy between speech and music, and in fact Helmholtz (1954) pointed out many years ago that music is by its very nature a discrete, categorical system just as language is. Why is it then that many contemporary psychologists have come to just the opposite conclusion? I can think of two major reasons. First of all, few of them are musicians, and therefore their experience with the tonal world is relatively sterile. To them, the imagery and mood feelings and other factors that contribute to the symbolism of music may be nonexistent and so they have tended to ignore the writings of musicians. As a result, in most psychology text books, we find, for example, pitch treated as just one more sensory continuum—lumped together with loudness, the brightness of lights, the length of lines—with no special status, even though it is a primary unit of music.

The second reason for the psychologist's misinterpretation of music is that he typically used nonmusicians as subjects in his research. Witness the now-famous experiment by Kimura (1964), which has given rise to the commonly held view that music perception is a right-brain phenomenon. More recently, Bever and Chiarello (1974) compared musicians and nonmusicians in their ability to recognize melodies. They found that for the nonmusicians, this appeared to be a right-hemisphere task, whereas for musicians, musical processing appeared to be mediated by the left hemisphere. (Follow-up work has cast doubt on the generality of these findings. It would not surprise me if many variables influence the phenomenon, but I think it would be a mistake to underplay the role that musicianship may play in this type of task.)

Let me give you another example of how music can be important in information processing experiments—one which in my mind has been almost totally overlooked by psychologists. One of the basic tenets of information processing theory is the idea of a basic perceptual capacity that limits our ability to identify stimuli varying along a single dimension, such as pitch, loudness, brightness, and so forth. This phenomenon has been referred to in the psychological literature as the so-called "magical number seven problem" in a famous paper by George Miller (1956). A number of perceptual experiments had indicated that the typical listener can identify only four or five pitches without error (Pollack, 1952, 1953) and this was thought to be a basic perceptual capacity.

My interest in the psychology of music began here at the University of Michigan, when I was a graduate teaching assistant in the psychology department. A student pointed out to me that he had a musician friend who could identify all the notes of the piano, and asked "How could I explain that?" in view of the magical number seven.

The question posed by my student triggered a thesis and then a program of research in which I tested a large number of subjects ranging from the "tone-deaf" to the professional musician and everything in between. This research has convinced me that musical experience is one of the single most important factors influencing performance in a variety of information processing tasks involving tonal stimuli, including memory (Siegel, 1972, 1974), identification (Siegel and Siegel, 1977a), and psychophysical scaling (Siegel and Siegel, 1977b).

Well, if psychologists have tended to underestimate the importance of musical experience, so have musicians. However, musicians have erred in the opposite direction. Because they are immersed in musical culture, musicians may tend to assume that everyone else ought to find music as easy as they do. Both Cady and Williams point out that one of the problems facing the information processing approach is to discover how the elements of music structure—pitch, rhythm, tonality, imagery, and so forth—are represented in memory. Here one can adopt one of two viewpoints: that the mnemonic representation of music is simply a reflection of the natural order of things or, conversely, that what we have stored in memory is primarily a reflection of what we happened to have learned. I personally hold the latter view, although I would not want to rule out the role of genetically determined individual differences in ability. Moreover, although Western music theorists often have a fondness for ancient Greek mathematicians, or use other models to justify the naturalness of the Western music scale, findings of ethnomusicology lead us to believe in the cultural relativity of music systems and experience.

Several years ago, I was in Australia, visiting Catherine Ellis, a well known ethnomusicologist at the University of Adelaide. She had spent years using both her ear and acoustic transcription devices to decipher the structure of the Australian aboriginal tonal system. I was fortunate to be visiting her at a time when she had invited several tribal elders from the desert to the university to teach music students there simple children's songs. As I sat there I reflected upon my total

inadequacy to *hearing* the sounds correctly—never mind reproducing them. Lacking aboriginal musical and linguistic categories, I would find both the tones and the speech sounds slipping away from me, a problem that was shared by the other nonaborigines in the group. The tribal elders would alternate between laughter and frustration at the apparent stupidity of these university students in not being able to sing even a simple child's song.

Ellis indicated to me that for a long period of time she immersed herself totally in aboriginal music-making. She then went back to Western music, in which she had been a professional oboist. As a result of her exposure to the music of a different culture, she completely lost her ear for Western music and was unable to identify the standard intervals. Interestingly, she reported that she lost even the octave, an interval that, she has argued (Ellis, 1965), is missing in the music of the group that she had studied, and an interval that many psychologists believe is encoded on an innate basis (e.g., Deutsch, 1969, 1972).

I have stressed the importance of the cultural relativity of music skills and perception, partly because cultural and subcultural differences in music experience do occur among children in our schools, and partly because crosscultural variations in performance are frequently not explicitly recognized by information processing theories. I would like to conclude, however, by pointing out one of the key positions of the information processing approach that is well supported by the type of evidence I have presented: Human perception is as much determined by the perceiver, his experience and expectations, as it is by the stimulus. It is the information stored in memory through culturally defined experiences that lends color and richness to the tonal world of the musician and not to that of the musically naive.

References

Bever, T., and R. J. Chiarello. Cerebral dominance in musicians and nonmusicians. *Science,* 1974, *185*, 537–539.

Bright, W. Language and music: Areas for cooperation. *Ethnomusicology*, 1963, *7*, 26–32.

Brown, R. Psychology and reading. In H. Levin and J. P. Williams (Eds.), *Basic studies on reading*. New York: Basic Books, 1970.

Deutsch, D. Music recognition. *Psychological Review*, 1969, *76*, 300–307.

———. Octave generalization and tune recognition. *Perception and Psychophysics*, 1972, *11* (6), 411–412.

Ellis, C. J. Pre-instrumental scales. *Ethnomusicology*, 1965, *9*, 126–144.

Gibson, E. J., and H. Levin. *The psychology of reading*. Cambridge, Massachusetts: MIT Press, 1975.

Helmholtz, H. *On the sensations of tone*. New York: Dover, 1954.

Kimura, D. Cerebral dominance and the perception of verbal stimuli. *Canadian Journal of Psychology*, 1961, *15*, 166–171.

———. Left-right differences in the perception of melodies. *Quarterly Journal of Experimental Psychology*, 1964, *16*, 355–358.

Liberman, A. M. Some characteristics of perception in the speech mode. In D. A. Hamburg (Ed.), *Perception and its Disorders, Proceedings of Association for Research in Nervous and Mental Diseases*. Baltimore: Williams and Wilkins Co., 1970.

Liberman, A. M., R. S. Cooper, D. S. Shankweiler, and M. Studdert-Kennedy. Perception of the speech code. *Psychological Review*, 1967, *74*, 431–461.

Miller, G. A. The magical number seven, plus or minus two. *Psychological Review*, 1956, *63*, 81–97.

Nettl, B. Some linguistic approaches to musical analysis. *Journal of the International Folk Music Council*, 1958, *10*, 37–41.

Pollack, I. The information of auditory displays. *Journal of the Acoustical Society of America*, 1953, *25*, 765–769.

Seeger, C. On the moods of a music-logic. *Journal of the American Musicological Society*, 1960, *13*, 224–261.

Siegel, J. A. The nature of absolute pitch. In E. Gordon (Ed.) *Research in the psychology of music*. Vol. 8, Iowa City, Iowa: University of Iowa Press, 1972.

———. Sensory and verbal coding strategies in subjects with absolute pitch. *Journal of Experimental Psychology*, 1974, *103*, 37–44.

Siegel, J. A., and W. Siegel. Absolute identification of notes and intervals by musicians. *Perception and Psychophysics*, 1977, *21*, 143–152. (a)

———. Categorical perception of tonal intervals: Musicians can't tell sharp from flat. *Perception and Psychophisics*, 1977, *21*, 399–407. (b)

Shankweiler, D. P. Effects of temporal lobe damage on perception of dichotically presented melodies. *Journal of Comparative and Physiological Psychology*, 1966, *62*, 115–119.

Shankweiler, D. P., and M. Studdert-Kennedy. Identification of consonants and vowels presented to the left and right ears. *Quarterly Journal of Experimental Psychology*, 1967, *19*, 59–63.

Response

Asahel D. Woodruff

One of the interesting things about time is its inevitability! And although things may be off in the future, at one point they finally catch up with you.

Since the Research Training Projects, in which so many of us joined together and had so much fun some years back, activities shifted somewhat from being more of a psychologist to being less of a psychologist into educational program designing and field testing. I had some colleagues and we were involved in projects that made this very possible and very exciting. We developed educational models and procedures that would be regarded, I'm sure, as radical against today's still typical system. We reached out from a single psychological base to other sources of ideas and tried to become conscious of what people could give to us that

97

would be useful. As one of the results of that, I became extremely respectful of subject matter and I have listened with great interest to the various statements, particularly about music, in this conference. And then there came to me what is jokingly referred to as retirement, which simply meant another shift. After four years of diversion into some very different pursuits, I have joined this seminar and found it both familiar and challenging. One thing occurred to me as I listened to all these questions: A teacher really walks on many feet like a centipede, and all of these scores of questions that have been raised are like the many feet of the centipede. Now that your attention has been drawn to them, I hope you can keep on walking in music education while waiting for the answers.

Here are some of the things that I have found as I come back. Number one is a language change in my field of psychology, which, of course, is always going on. Theory was used heavily some time back and then almost disappeared from the inner circles. Theory of learning shifted somewhat to information processing, and even now I think I see another kind of a movement coming back from an old term, "cognition." I can remember living through the period when we almost had to fight the stimulus-response behaviorists to exist, and the word cognition wasn't very respectable. But here it is again as one of the dominant areas of serious, significant, productive research.

Secondly—looking at the brain as if it were a digital computer—we make a computer to do something the brain can do and then if we are not very careful we begin to think the brain is like the computer. And that can color our approach to education problems.

Third, there is the continued request of educators that psychologists supply answers to teaching problems—that is, produce teaching programs. But what about all the other disciplines that have something significant to say? It is interesting that in this seminar the outside people, from the standpoint of music, are all psychologists.

Fourth, there is the assumption by educators that theory is useful in planning educational programs. I've heard some good things said about that while we have been here.

There is a fifth matter: how such terms as "theory" or "information processing" or "storage and retrieval" affect our ideas about music, cognition, and the brain.

I would like to do three things. One is to recognize the total message framework within which we are operating here. The second is to turn to the Cady and Williams papers, which I think lie at the core of this seminar. And the third is to comment on the larger dimension of our efforts.

The focuses of the conference framework are reasonably clear: perception, largely auditory both in input and output activities in music; motor learning, dealing primarily with output skills; development and its effect on response to music, on competence, and on performance; cognition, from perception all the way to performance; information, information processing, input, and retention of the stuff of cognition; and finally, affect, emotion, feeling, a concomitant of cognition. Now that's an interesting range to work with. These aspects of music and these functions are dealt with in schools today mostly in a standard curriculum with the old familiar problems, which are familiar especially when we deal with all aspects of music as a mental exercise (I'm afraid we still do more of that than we should) and with performance as the product of mental activity. It's the teaching of a subject, not a learner. Maybe I am making this generalization a little too strong, but I think I have heard many of you express the same concern. The expressed concerns are largely how to loosen up the links or joints in this academic model rather than with the model itself. That is, how to get students to hear better what we present, to think more about it, to perform better, to feel good about it. And yet I have heard some suggestions that maybe we need to take another look at the model to see if it should be abandoned or seriously operated on. The teacher is the heavy in this job even though music is a performing art. The learner is still too much like a vessel with performance capacities. We are putting information into him, through his senses, into the brain, and from there into performance. Now I don't think we feel this way, but I think I hear us talking this way. There is some discontentment with the way we are presenting subject matter, but the real concern expressed in many of these papers has been with the learner and his systems.

I see two very provocative papers on information processing and memory. Information processing, regarded as a continuum, of cognitive activity, includes all the things I mentioned—motivation, perception, developmental problems, cognition, memory, and motor response. The interplay of these produces learning and a change in behavior. The information processing concept is said to stem from a communications theory and the digital computer. The computer analogy, though I think not necessarily Williams in his discussion of it, implies that our job is to put information into the learner in a prearranged form for useful retrieval. Learning is viewed as a change in behavior. Then there arises, as a change in cognitive structure, that which is in storage. And we get into that interesting problem of where the behavior is—whether it is in the cognitive structure or in the interaction between the person and his environment. I wonder if we still have a little carryover effect of old stimulus-response behaviorism in this way of describing learning—that is, an avoidance effect, the need to infer imaginary overt processes because we could not deal with cognitive activity honestly at one time. To discover where learning fails, we may need to check out each point in the processing chain, times every known sensory property in music, times input load size, and as these are affected by anticipated output behavior. This includes time and sequence elements, as well as structural elements. I would hate to face that job. It seems to me that it is so formidable that it is almost unmanageable, on the basis of a computer model.

An alternative would be to start questioning the usefulness of the computer analogy. What might suggest that we do this? (1) There seems to be a general consensus that the complexity of the processing operation comes from music rather than from the learn-er. (2) The nature of memory, in our case, is found in the nature of sound. (3) A performance is one operation with X facets, rather than X operations assembled from a bank. (4) Taxonomic categories of behavior are artificial. Cady says there is one brain and it is not divided into taxonomies, with which I completely agree, although we know there are functional areas in the brain and we know that the brain has a magnificent capacity to transform those areas into other functions when the need arises. (5) A computer cannot hear music but a person can. So music would have to be translated into a computer language before it could be presented to the receptors of the computer, and the computer would never have a holistic concept. The brain does its own translating. I'm aware of very large concepts, and I'm not aware of a segmented bank from which they are assembled as I try to remember them.

(John Platz has given us a startling description of a brain in an article called "Beauty: Pattern and Change." He said there are 10^8—that means one with eight zeros following it—or 10^9 visual inputs, inputs of all kinds, every millisecond. And there are twenty allocating decisions about each input every second. He said the brain consumes information as a stomach consumes food, only more continuously and with more imperious demands. And he backed that up with some physiological evidence, part of which relates to the consumption of energy within the system. I think we know something of the magnitude of concepts. Where and how an input is stored or becomes related to others in the brain is of no importance to us in teaching, in my opinion. The brain handles it all without our help when we supply whole experiences to be perceived. I would have great fear that if we try to get into that marvelous piece of machinery we might do more damage than good.)

(6) The computer does not think or in any way alter that which is put into it.

(7) As Cady commented, music is behavior and sound is behavior. (8) Restle said that music means something, and performance components fall together to express that meaning. (9) In Dewey's wonderful book

Knowing and the Known, there is the idea that these two things are inseparable. They are the joint property of a mind in contact with a real phenomenon. So you cannot have it stored someplace except through that intimate interaction. (10) Perception is an active transaction in which the person is participating fully. Garner's article, written many years back, "To Perceive Is to Know," gives an excellent description of that thought. Many other perception psychologists say the world is structured, just as we know that music has structure. The perceiver selects the structure that he wishes to react to and perceives it, as contrasted with receiving it, so that there is a back-and-forth action going on.

Now all of those little clues suggest to me that the brain is doing something the computer cannot do. In order to cope with this problem of human beings, in a complex field like music, maybe the computer can get in the way.

Now let me refer to the larger dimensions of our work. First, I am concerned about theory again and I would like to contrast theory with description. Theory is an excellent guide to research but I don't think of it as a plan of program operation. A research scientist is involved in a process of differentiation and analysis, not of program engineering. That's a foreign field to him. To ask him to turn away from that intensive and demanding kind of analysis is to ask him to abandon his field and deal almost exclusively with isolated phenomena, instruments of magnified observation, control of all other variables, description of the observed, isolated characteristics, predictions as to where an observed process might be going, and guesses as to where to look for additional information. When scientists start to make those guesses, they are greatly helped by the formation of a theory that helps them discover when the unfilled cells might be. So it's a research tool in its best and finest and oldest form.

Now on the other hand, productive programs of operation have to correspond to the whole, natural processes we intend to facilitate, to involve their dynamics, and to operate like those processes operate. This in-formation comes from description of the processes, which simply is the musical behavior of people.

Well, how can psychologists help? Let me just speak for myself. I was interested in Brown's statement when he spoke of a great teacher and said psychology can give him no help. That's a very oft-repeated comment by psychologists. The question has been asked, to my knowledge, for forty years (and probably longer by educators to psychologists): "Can you help us learn how to teach?" And the answer has been repeated over those decades—psychology has no answer for you. That's not an evasion. It seems to me that requires that we recognize some realities.

Shephard suggested that we are going at this the wrong way. We are asking for quick answers to practical questions from people involved in long-range research. New understandings come very slowly and often indirectly. The answers you may elicit from psychologists about your operational problems, said Shephard, will not come from formal models, but from the same personal observations teachers have made. So what's the advantage of asking the psychologist since he has to fall back on the same base for responding that the rest of us do? But psychology has a wealth of data on the specific learning actions that are involved in such things as motor learning, memorizing, perceiving, and other aspects of behavior. And this will fit very well into instruction if we get the instructional models set to receive it in the right way. So what must educators do?

I have heard a lot of reaction to Knieter's paper. I think he is an example of an educator transforming psychological information into a learning model. He has laid out one part, or a least has started to lay out one part, of a total learning or teaching model—a climate, a set of relationships between teachers and learners, within which we will operate. I was struck with the appropriateness of one of the responder's comments that Knieter has cited essentially inspirational psychologists, which I suppose is true, because the four of them certainly have played that role very intensively in the field of psychology. But also lurking in the things they have said are some usable ideas about procedure—not as sharply stated perhaps as we would like to have them stated, but they are implied and they can be worked on.

Suppose we begin to visualize a three-layer operational model. One of the layers might be the way people are: this is the way you have to treat each other; this is the way you ought to work together; this is the way you ought to encourage and help, and so on. Then musicians have to build the next layer, which consists of music in good learning paths. Nobody else can do that. People who know music are the experts in that field and must do whatever they have to do in the way of analysis or taking music apart of examining it, breaking down the skills into their units. Then after that, it's necessary to reassess goals. I have heard expressed a lot of discontent with the actual goals of operation. Then, arrange those paths to music accordingly. That becomes your plan of operation. As teachers, we must shape our tactics in dealing with the specifics in those paths to match the wealth of information, in the field of psychology, about how those operations can be facilitated. We may need to do much research in laying out the paths. Now that's not scientific research but operational research. It's descriptive at an organismic or holistic rather than atomistic level—descriptive of a person doing something. And it's not just experimental. Sometimes when those descriptions have been faithfully made you say, "Of course, that's the obvious answer to where we should be going and how we should proceed."

We have had reference made already to the processes of assimilation and adaptation. René DuBose, a biologist, defined four types of adaptation involved in health education, one of which was psychic. Translated into our language, that means cognitive learning and behavior. Out of that I began to fiddle around with model designs and with ideas and came up with what I started to call a "man/environment interaction model," which is based on the principles of assimilation and adaptation. One simple way of presenting this is to draw a circle of a person's universe and put the person inside of that

somewhere; everything else in that circle is subject matter. The interaction that occurs is so close and intimate that you don't want to get anything in the way of it. The individual interacts with that stimulus material that is right around him—his world. Then you start to draw arrows to indicate where the forces are going because the individual is doing something to the environment and the environment is doing something to the individual. It's in that interesting loop that adaptation occurs. And adaptation is a pretty good name for learning of the kind that I think we are interested in. This puts the brain and the world right together. It gets rid of our interferences with perception and interaction. Music is the environment. The interactions are all the human uses of music in its real forms. Such a model has been made operational now, carried through very arduous tasks of development, made operational through preschool levels, and tried out in the field. It is a major reorientation, a somewhat radical one, toward the very long-proven power of in-life learning, but now not left to the exigencies of the individual and his experiences by himself. Rather, it is under the skillful coaching of someone who can watch it, can help direct it, and can move it.

I had heard the statement once—with which I think I still tend to agree—that the best teaching in the university is done in the athletic program by the coach; it represents the most effective alteration of behavior and shaping-up of abilities. This is a man/environment interaction model. It's a strong departure for us. I suppose we'll go on and always be going on in a number of directions in our research. I hope that we might be willing to entertain what may seem to be bizarre explorations at first, in the hope that we can facilitate a better engagement between the learner and music. We must get the teacher off the center of the stage, and put the student on it. I have discovered in some of the schools in which we have tried this kind of thing that teachers didn't like that. And to my surprise, the reason was that they enjoyed lecturing and they didn't want to give it up! They were a little bit ill at ease once the student is turned loose and told "Start doing something. You figure it out and start doing it." You lose control. At least you think you will. Then there comes back that haunting question—suppose he comes up with some questions to which I don't know the answers, or wants some help that I can't give him? What does that do to me? A lot of insecurities begin to develop, but it's delightful to see what happens to the learner when he's put in that situation, made responsible for himself, and placed in direct touch with reality. Then, somebody standing by can coach him and help him do it. This is done in ensemble groups and in all performance activities. We could refine and improve the way we do it in those groups but I'd like to see us use that idea in all aspects of music education and not let the rest of them become excessively academic and accordingly more sterile.

An Operant Approach to Motivation and Affect: Ten Years of Research in Music Learning

R. Douglas Greer

A substantial portion of the music learning research during the last ten years has subscribed to the operant learning paradigm. Most of this research has been concerned with either motivation or affect, and this paper is limited to such research. Other research, not related to operant learning theory, is cited only when it concerns issues that are central to operant theory or when it serves to complete the review of motivation and affect.

Operant learning research in general has burgeoned over the last two decades. Britt (1976) in his bibliography of behavior modification and operant research lists over 6,500 articles between 1924 and 1975. Grossman's (1979) extensive, but not all-inclusive, review of research in special education cites 500 studies, many of which are not found in the Britt reference. Over 100 operant music studies are listed in the annotated bibliography of *Research in Music Behavior* (Madsen, Greer, and Madsen, 1975) and the book itself contains twenty original or reprinted articles. This last publication is a collection of the incipient operant work in music learning.

Much of the recent operant research (applied behavior analysis) is devoted to the analysis of techniques for applying operant learning principles to therapy, medicine, business, and education. This research has also resulted in modification of both the operant principles and their theoretical expansion. Several journals are devoted solely to the operant and related social learning approaches. The parent operant journals are *Behavior Research and Therapy, Journal of Applied*

Behavior Analysis, and *Journal of the Experimental Analysis of Behavior.* More recently, other journals have arisen including *Child Behavior Therapy, Educational Treatment of Children, Behaviorism,* and *Behavior Modification.* Considerable space has been devoted to operant research in music journals including *Journal of Research in Music Education, Journal of Music Therapy,* and *Bulletin of the Council for Research in Music Education.* Incipient summaries of operant research in music have appeared in more general publications in education (Greer, 1975), psychology (Spradlin, 1976), and therapy (Madsen, 1974).

Most, if not all operant research has been concerned with motivation, and more recently in music, much research has been directly concerned with affect. Operant learning research seeks to expand and test a set of fundamental principles. These principles are functional statements regarding the relationship of environmental factors (usually reducible to consequences of behavior) to the acquisition and maintenance of emitted behaviors or related behaviors.

In addition to a set of research derived principles, specialized research methodologies, both for laboratory and applied settings, have accrued (Madsen, 1974; Sidman, 1960). A logically cogent and brief summary of the principles as they are used in this paper is found in Burgess and Akers (1971).

Motivation and Learning

Motivational research concerns two basic sets of behavioral controls or constraints—the biological determinants and the environmental determinants. Operant researchers as well as teachers deal with environmental factors. Both are concerned with that part of the study of learning that is devoted to intervention practices that bring about, increase, or maintain behaviors in a relatively permanent fashion. Briefly, for the operant researcher, learning research has to do with ". . . those *changes in behavior* which are a function of training (experience) and which cannot be attributed to other processes such as maturation and temporary physical changes in the organism" (Moore, Manning and Smith, 1978, p. 2).

Motivation: Music as Reinforcement

The operant study of motivation in music has involved the investigation of music as an independent variable and as a dependent variable. Information derived from such study is also relevant to musical affect. Indeed, the motivational aspects of music are regarded by some as one of music's major affective properties. Several experiments have sought to determine whether music listening will function as reinforcement for other behavior. These studies have helped isolate issues concerned with "intrinsic" reinforcement and have served as the empirical framework for the study of musical affect as reinforcement value.

Music as a natural reinforcer. Forsythe (1977) found that elementary children were more attentive during music classes than during the study of other subject matter. Forsythe's descriptive findings validated the findings of several experiments, beginning with the results of Madsen, Wolfe, and Madsen's (1969) research with sixth graders, in which they found no differences in the reinforcement effects of a vocal-task-only reinforcement and a monetary reinforcement group. Both groups significantly decreased vocal intonation error. Such findings are singularly different from those found in the study of other subject matter.

There were no differences in reinforcement effects on attentive behavior of sixth graders for a preferred music listening contingency, a nonpreferred music contingency, and a monetary reward group (Greer, Randall, and Timberlake, 1971). All three reward groups were significantly different from a no-reward control in attentive behavior; yet, all four groups significantly decreased vocal intonation error without the occurrence of significant differences in the effects of the three reinforcement contingencies on intonation. These findings replicated Madsen, Wolfe, and Madsen (1969) with regard to the apparent reinforcing effect of the vocal performance task per se.

Preferred and nonpreferred music listening contingencies each served as reinforcement in a nondifferential manner for daily mathematical computation with upper elementary EMR children (Miller, 1977). The design employed allowed both a within-subjects test as well as a between-subjects test of the variables. No novelty or satiation effects were found. Similarly, Miller, Dorow, and Greer (1974) compared the reinforcement effects on math computation of preferred and nonpreferred music listening and art activities. Again the reinforcing effect was demonstrated with no significant difference in contingencies.

In the previous studies, group listening was used predominantly, raising the possibility that social reinforcement effects were confounding results. In a test of the socialization influence, Madsen and Forsythe (1973) found no difference in reinforcement effects between a social music listening contingency (party with music) and an individual listening contingency (earphones) in terms of their substantial reinforcement effect on daily math computation of upper elementary age students. Both music contingencies were more effective than a math game and a no-reward group. There were no differences in the latter two groups.

Madsen and Madsen (1972) found that sixth graders who received noncontingent tokens and no other treatment bought more music listening with their tokens than the group who received tokens for attentiveness during vocal training sessions. Students selected miniscule time with music listening, but students were more attentive when involved in singing than when involved in other instructional aspects of the study. Greer, Dorow, and Harrison (1975) also found that when given a choice for spending tokens, students equally chose rock music and narrative listening to Bill Cosby tapes and only one student spent tokens for music classes at one of seven sessions. Madsen and Geringer (1976) found that students chose free play over televised music lessons, although in a forced choice setting televised music lessons served as an effective reinforcer. Apparently, nonpreferred music as well as televised music lessons will function as reinforcement for other behaviors when no choice is involved. When given a choice of how to spend tokens, students overwhelmingly chose the pre-

ferred (rock or soul) music or free play.

A large number of single subject experiments as well as other group studies (Yarborough, Charboneau, and Wapnick, 1977) have shown that music listening can function to increase deficit social and academic behaviors in a substantial manner. Single-subject experimental designs (Glass, Wilson, and Gottman, 1975) have been used extensively by Steele and her colleagues (1968), Jorgenson (1971), Cotter (1971), Barret (1965), Talkington and Hall (1970), and Hanser (1974), to name only a few. In these studies music has been used contingently after behavior to increase that behavior or removal of music has been used to decrease other behavior. In short, the therapeutic use of music as a reinforcer has been extensively documented (see the annotated bibliography in Madsen, Greer, and Madsen, 1975).

In the previous studies, music listening or vocal performances were established as general reinforcers. When compared with monetary, primary, or other secondary reinforcers, music held its own, as was the case both with preferred and nonpreferred music (music classics). However, students did not select music classics when given a choice; indeed avoidance was found to be the rule. These findings provoke numerous questions, not the least of which has to do with determining the nature of music's reinforcement potential.

Music: primary or secondary reinforcement? After locating two primary grade children for whom music was not reinforcing, music was conditioned, by pairing it with primary reinforcement, as a reinforcer for a language task (Greer, Dorow, Hanser, Wilson, and Botvin, 1975). The study pioneered a counterbalanced variant of a multiple baseline, but findings were limited by abbreviated contact with students. Clearly several months were needed to test the durability of the newly conditioned reinforcer.

Dorow (1975), using a similar design, located three severely retarded individuals for whom music was not reinforcing. Using the primary reinforcement pairing paradigm, Dorow was able to condition the combination of music plus approval as a reinforcer for

104

all three individuals such that music plus approval was comparable to that of primary reinforcement. Subsequently, all primary reinforcement was dropped, and the music-plus-approval treatment continued to function as reinforcement without benefit of experimenter manipulated pairings for several months. In a second experiment, Dorow (1974) tested one of the individuals in experiment one to ascertain generalization of the newly conditioned reinforcer. Generalization was demonstrated with a transfer task over an extensive period of time.

In numerous studies involving over 1,500 students in which reinforcement value was assessed (Greer, in press), less than five students clearly did not find music reinforcing to any degree. Apparently, music is reinforcing for most people to some degree, although the evidence with a few students or individuals would indicate that music may not be a primary reinforcer. Music is probably a natural secondary reinforcer in that pairings with other events, activities, or materials is unavoidable in society. There are many secondary reinforcers that motivate much of human behavior, and many of them are not natural reinforcers. Music's quality to naturally acquire reinforcement value is one of its distinctive although not unique motivational properties. More extensive scrutiny of this issue has been raised in research concerned with the reinforcement value of the collative properties of music and the study of musical affect as reinforcement value.

Music instruction as reinforcement. The research cited in the last two sections has considerable practical value for formal education as well as theoretical interest. Continuing the practical concern, some investigations have isolated the reinforcing effects of music instruction. Several studies cited earlier (Greer, Randall, and Timberlake, 1971; Madsen and Madsen, 1972; Madsen, Wolfe, and Madsen, 1969) also pointed to the reinforcement value of performance per se.

Eisenstein (1974) found that tokens exchangeable for guitar instruction acted to substantially raise the language reading performance of several primary grade children. She demonstrated that music instruction

functioned as potent reinforcement and that the reinforcement served an educational function for musical performance simultaneously.

Similarly, Gordon (1979) found that tokens dispensed contingently for beginning band lessons substantially increased the daily reading comprehension and vocabulary skills of upper elementary grade children. The control group received beginning band lessons noncontingently. Comparisons made both within and between groups showed that band lessons acted as substantial reinforcement. The study continued across several weeks during which the lessons continued to function as reinforcement. Pretest and posttest measures of band instrument performance showed no difference. Gordon's findings replicated a pilot study using recorders (Gordon, 1977). Both a behavioral reversal design and a group design were used.

Effects of cognitive-skills instruction in music as reinforcement were tested by Madsen, Dorow, Moore, and Womble (1976). Televised music lessons, modeled after *Sesame Street,* were designed to teach aural music concepts to primary age children. The lessons served as potent reinforcers as demonstrated by a reversal design combined with a group design. In addition, students demonstrated significant gains in scores on a music concepts test. Their findings were replicated in a study by Madsen and Geringer (1977) in which it was also found that if given a choice students would buy free time rather than televised lessons.

Dorow (1976) repeated the Madson *et al.* (1976) study with individuals who were severely retarded. She replicated the reinforcement effect, but failed to replicate the educational gain for the cognitive music skills. The author speculated that given the nature of this population, even with the adapted procedures, an extensive number of trials would be needed to bring about educational gains from the reinforcement used.

The above studies have shown that performance and cognitive instruction could act as reinforcement for elementary age children and additionally provide gains in music learning. Studies cited earlier showed that music listening also served as reinforcement.

105

Miller (1977) tested the effects of the use of music listening as reinforcement in terms of its influence on musical affect (reinforcement value of listening). Her data showed no decrements or increases in reinforcement value as a function of the use of music listening to reinforce other behavior.

The reinforcement attributes of performance, as well as the reinforcement that comes as a natural adjunct to performance (applause, peer and adult approval) have long been recognized implicitly by everyone from the music teacher and parent to the major character in the musical *The Music Man*. Dorow and Greer (1977) found that the reinforcement value of performance per se decreased in a rapid and uniform manner after several instrumental music lessons leading the authors to conclude that the reinforcement was a function of novelty. Surprisingly, the decline was not affected by either of two treatments (structured high approval lessons embodying successive approximation and modeling versus a no-intervention discovery approach). The authors measured reinforcement value in terms of the time children spent watching television or playing the recorder in a free operant setting. All subjects in the intervention group acquired performance skills, while only one student in the discovery group scored greater than zero on a posttest performance examination.

The studies cited thus far demonstrate that music listening, music performance, and instruction in cognitive skills (via television) can be used as motivation when used systematically for a variety of academic skills, concepts, and social behaviors. Cognitive lessons and performance instructions were also shown to lead to secondary learning gains in music. Affective learning did not appear to be positively or adversely affected. It was also found that the initial reinforcement value of instrumental lessons is one of novelty. Other data would indicate that other reinforcement must accrue, since the reinforcement effect on nonmusic behavior was not shown to decline in studies by Eisenstein (1974) and Gordon (1977). These findings, in addition to the obvious theoretical value, provide practical and programmatic procedures for cooperative endeavors between music education and other components of the school curriculum.

Motivation of Psychomotor, Affective, and Cognitive Learnings through Reinforcement Contingencies

Teacher approval and successive approximation strategies. In applied behavior analysis, one of the most important contributions has been the identification of the reinforcing properties of verbal and nonverbal approval dispensed by teachers, peer students, and other adults (see the index to volumes 1–10 of the *Journal of Applied Behavior Analysis* Britt, 1975; Grossman, 1979; Leitenberg, 1976). Although approval is not a primary or at least a universal reinforcer it, like music, is a natural and perhaps necessary reinforcer for normal development (Greer and Dorow, 1976; Hamblin, Buckholdt, Ferritor, Kozloff, and Blackwell, 1971).

In the acquisition of musical skills and other subject matter the accessibility of teacher approval and disapproval makes it the most prevalent and available motivational tool. Even with music's "naturally" reinforcing properties, much of music learning is tedious, difficult, and not intrinsically interesting (Dorow and Greer, 1977). Other contingencies, of which teacher approval is one, are necessary at various points in every student's music education.

One of the basic issues in the study of the motivational properties of teacher interaction with students (approval/disapproval) concerns the question of whether such interaction can function in the basic reinforcement and punishment paradigm. Hanser (1974) isolated peer high school students' approval and disapproval while learning a vocal intonation task in a laboratory setting. Peer confederates were enlisted to train vocal intonation of their peers in small groups using approval and disapproval conditions. Using successive approximation, Hanser cued the confederates to motivate and guide student performance under the following conditions: (1) approval after successive approximations of correct responses (simulation of positive reinforcement), (2) disapproval until the correct response (negative reinforcement), (3) disapproval after incorrect performances (positive punishment), and (4) approval until successive approximations of incorrect performance occurred (negative punishment). Findings showed that both positive and negative reinforcement procedures were more effective than punishment procedures in keeping with the expected effects of the implementation of learning principles. In short, approval/disapproval techniques functioned in the expected manner. Over ten percent of the variability of pitch responses was attributable to approval counts alone.

The operant learning literature has traditionally shown that both positive and negative reinforcement are equally viable to teach a behavior. Operant theorists have advocated positive reinforcement because of the known side effects (escape and avoidance) of the use of aversive stimuli. Such admonitions regarding the avoidance of aversive procedures, including teacher disapproval, seem to be wise advice for music education also since adverse effects on affective learning have been found for music (Dorow, 1974, 1977; Greer, Dorow, Wachhaus, and White, 1973).

Wholesale application of various approval/disapproval ratios to performance groups and general music classes in a manner that does not provide systematic and individual successive approximation procedures have met with mixed results. Murray (1975) found that conductor-generated treatments of high approval versus high disapproval affected verbal attitude toward the music rehearsed in high school choral groups, but did not differentially affect performance or attentiveness scores. High approval had more positive attitude scores. Ceiling effects were apparent for performance and attentiveness measures. Perhaps the reinforcing effects of music performance itself, particularly it would seem with groups that perform well, ameliorate any chances for blanket differences, thus serving to mask approval/disapproval effects on these measures. Dorow (1977) found that individual approval was necessary for affective influence. Wachhaus

and Wachhaus (1976) found that periods of rehearsal in which a college band conductor emitted high rates of approval on cue produced more positive verbal statements than periods in which the conductor did not give high rates of (cued) approval. There were no differences in performance between conditions.

Kuhn (1975) found that fifth graders from general music classes did not score differently on a standardized music achievement test (Elementary Music Achievement Test) as a function of high approval versus high disapproval. Similarly verbal attitude toward the teacher was not affected. Consistent with numerous studies in the general literature, he found that high approval conditions produced greater attentiveness.

Wolpow (1976) found that social and academic approval and disapproval respectively showed independent effects on the attentiveness and musical performance of members of a rhythm band who were institutionalized as severely retarded. When approval rates were contingent and high for attentiveness, attentive behavior increased in a corresponding and substantial manner. When approval was dropped for attentiveness, but raised dramatically for performance, correct performance was increased and attentiveness declined. When high rates of approval were given for both categories of behavior, both rose in a similar manner. During baseline periods performance and attentiveness declined to baseline operant levels.

The following studies have used approval successfully as a reinforcer. However, these studies concentrated on another learning principle—successive approximation. Yank (1975) trained sixth graders who had been screened for uncertain singing (monotones). Using adult approval, she successfully taught simultaneous vocal intonation for trained pitches until students met a criterion of ±10 cents. This criterion approaches the performance scores of professionals (Greer, 1970). The major issue of Yank's study concerned a comparison of the number of trials and transfer effects of two successive approximation strategies—multiple discrimination (conceptual strategy) and "single" discrimination (nonconceptual strategy). There were no differences in the number of trials, but multiple discrimination produced significant and substantially greater transfer effects. Effects of multiple discrimination procedures were particularly effective for below-average subjects. A subsidiary question concerned instrumental versus vocal training, but an effective test of these variables was thwarted to some degree by the nature of the task. Reaching criterion on the intonation tasks did not affect standardized music achievement scores, raising questions regarding the validity of such tests to assess performance achievement and reaffirming the notion that performance learning does not necessarily transfer to the acquisition of aural skills. Successive approximation findings extended those of Cobes (1975).

Greer and Lundquist (1976) similarly compared the effects of multiple discrimination procedures with single discrimination scores. Multiple discrimination did not produce greater transfer as was the case with Porter (née Yank, 1977) but did replicate the decreased number of trials required to reach criterion for below-average students. Training was individualized, employed contingent approval, no disapproval, and provision for repeated hearing of the correct model.

Eisenstein (1976) demonstrated an effective successive approximation procedure for teaching the identification of music notation by primary grade children. Similar individualized successive approximation procedures used in conjunction with adult approval have been shown to effectively teach first graders complex paired associated learning tasks (Greer, Dorow, and Wolpert, 1978) and melodic conservation to previously screened nonconservers (Botvin, 1974).

Several studies have produced significant increases in reinforcement value (affect) for low reinforcement value music presented in the treatment via the use of high approval (Dorow, 1974, 1977; Greer, Dorow, and Hanser, 1973; Greer, Dorow, Wachhaus, and White, 1973; Greer, Dorow, and Wolpert, 1978; Tanner, 1976). Corresponding decreases in reinforcement value as a function

of disapproval were shown in two studies (Dorow, 1977; Greer, Dorow, Wachhaus and White, 1973).

Numerous studies in the general literature of applied behavior analysis have shown the efficacy of the use of teacher approval as a motivational tool. Other studies (Dorow, 1975; Hamblin, Buckholdt, Ferritor, Kozloff, and Blackwell, 1971) have shown that other reinforcers are necessary to change the behavior of some children in some settings. When approval has been successful, the criterion of individualization and adequate successive approximation procedures have been met (Fullard, 1975). More blanket and general classroom applications of approval have met with mixed results, presumably a function of the lack of individualization. For example, Madsen, Moore, Wagner, and Yarbrough (1975) found music reinforcement for math achievement to be more effective than music reinforcement for attentiveness. It would seem that individual shaping or reinforcement is a prerequisite when students do not learn in one or even a few exposures or trials. A multiple discrimination strategy is a more viable successive approximation procedure to use with students suffering difficulty.

Several training paradigms have been developed for teaching teachers to utilize behavioral techniques based on operant learning principles (Greer and Dorow, 1976; Hall, 1971; Madsen and Madsen, 1974). Madsen and Madsen (1974) have most notably emphasized teacher approval training and report findings concerning effective procedures for inservice teacher workshops of varying lengths.

Studies looking at individual teachers in reversal and multiple baseline experimental paradigms have demonstrated that cues given while the teacher is instructing are effective in raising contingent approval and lowering disapproval and noncontingent approval (Greer, Dorow, and Miller, 1976 in the *Journal of Applied Behavior Analysis*). Indeed some studies have involved the use of students to shape teacher behavior (Polirstok and Greer, 1977; Sherman and Cormier, 1974).

108

Henderson (1973) found that music teachers in low SES classrooms spent most of their time disapproving and little time approving. This finding is in keeping with that of Madsen and Madsen (1974). Regardless of subject matter, approval also declines with grade/age levels (White, 1975). Henderson was unable to raise approval of music teachers significantly with ten one and one-half hour inservice workshops although she did lower disapproval.

Moore (1976) used components of Personalized Systematic Instruction (PSI), an approach that implements learning principles with large-sized classes, to train preservice teachers in a methods class for prospective teachers. The methods classes were designed to teach both basic musicianship skills and basic teaching skills. Significant but small differences were found in favor of the PSI approaches. Moore and Kuhn (1975) reported several experiments comparing the effects of teaching operant teaching techniques as well as basic musicianship in elementary music methods for prospective teachers. They reaffirmed the stimulus generalization principle; that is, stimulus generalization needs to be taught. When transfer of skills did occur, it occurred more often when the student teachers selected the music skills to be taught than when the skills were selected for them. Additional tutoring was found to be useful and music skills did not suffer when teaching skills were emphasized. A one-semester course could be designed that would teach students operant and music skills commensurate with a two-semester course.

Other motivational contingencies. Although teacher approval is a major motivational tool, it is but a single potential reinforcer among many categories of reinforcement available to educators. Earlier, I noted some of the distinctive and perhaps naturally reinforcing attributes of music for teaching other behaviors. Similar possibilities exist within music education settings, as, for example, private lessons on a second instrument contingent on achieving a criterion score on an individualized assignment in performance, composition, or analysis. The use of primary reinforcement is also feasible, although the use

of primary reinforcers has been minimal in music learning research.

Botvin (1974) used food treats plus approval in conjunction with multiple discrimination procedures (Greer and Lundquist, 1976; Porter, 1977) to teach melodic conservation to primary age children who had been previously tested as nonconservers of melody, liquid, quantity, shape, and form. A successive-approximation-only group was compared with a successive-approximation-plus-verbal-rule group and a no-contact control. Both experimental groups were successful in learning melodic conservation, but the successive-approximation-only group scored higher on the crossmodal transfer tasks. This was one of the earlier Piagetian-type studies to demonstrate training of conservation and one of the few to show crossmodal transfer.

The importance of modeling, both in systematic instruction and in experience, has been documented extensively by investigators in social learning theory (Bandura, 1976) and has long been an accepted learning principle (Burgess and Akers, 1971). Two studies have dealt with the modeling of music performances by students in terms of performance achievement while two others have included systematic modeling in the total treatment package.

Tapes of model performance were developed and tested by Zurcher (1975) to be used by beginning instrumentalists for home practice during the first six weeks of instruction. Students received verbal prompts as well as exemplar performances of assigned exercises. The model tapes were significantly more effective on four of six weekly performance measures across the entire six weeks.

Netherland (1975) found that peer-modeled performances were no more effective than teacher or tape recorder models for piano students during sight reading or practiced performance. The author suggested that the complexity of the counterbalanced design used may have thwarted implementation of treatment. Replication was suggested with a test for implementation of treatment.

Most of the research in programmed learning has not been included in this review because typically such research has been covered elsewhere or has not been related to the mainstream of operant research. Harrison's (1974) study is included because of the use of individualized programmed and non-programmed units used in the PSI packages to be discussed subsequently. Harrison found that a question-and-answer programmed format was as successful and, in some cases, more successful to teach aural discrimination skills to older elementary children than small step frames. Both types of programming, plus published, teacher-made and student-made programs, are used in total PSI programs discussed by Greer (in press) and used by Zurcher (1976).

Zurcher (1977) has implemented a total PSI program in a junior high school band program and has raised performance skills while simultaneously implementing a comprehensive musicianship program. His PSI program makes use of numerous research-based principles and techniques of applied behavior analysis and much of the research reported in this paper, including systematic peer teaching, continual gathering of data by peers in both the traditional behavioral paradigm and its extension to music by Greer (in press) and awarding of points for individualized learning including composition, improvisation, performance, and peer teaching/learning of social instruments (guitar and recorder), as well as band parts and assignments. Points are redeemable for educational reinforcers including lessons on second instruments given by peers (the most popular option), opportunities to conduct ensembles, use of tape recorders and tape recorded solo accompaniments, membership in ensembles such as the jazz band, and tapes of music for home listening. Data demonstrated greater attentiveness during rehearsals when students awarded themselves points. Students took reliable data, both on themselves and tutees. Tape-recorded models and various individualized programs are a standard part of practice assignments. The program has been in operation for over three years.

Alexander (1979) found that students in a beginning band program who were tutored by their peers performed substantially higher than their controls on a performance post-

test. Peer tutors, who unlike their controls did not receive homogeneous group lessons but received weekly band rehearsals only, performed as well as their controls. The tutor finding is consistent with an abundance of literature on the beneficial effects of peer tutoring for both tutors and tutees (Devin-Sheehan, Feldman, and Allen, 1976). Tutors in the Alexander study were divided into two groups, an approval-trained group and a disapproval group. No differences in the approval and disapproval groups were found, reaffirming the equal effectiveness of positive and negative reinforcement. The disapproval technique used is a more prevalent approach since it involves having the peer teachers point out their tutees' errors while the approval technique consists of approving correct components of performance. No affective measures were taken; hence, no data on the escape and avoidance issue are available.

Holz (1978) applied a PSI approach to the teaching of music appreciation in a college setting. Two experiments demonstrated the greater effectiveness of the PSI approach on five out of seven tests. In addition, Holz compared grades only as reinforcement with grades plus recorder lessons as reinforcement. Grades plus recorder was demonstrated to be a potent reinforcer in one experiment. Part of Holz' findings replicate and extend those summarized by Robin (1976).

Numerous studies have investigated various other behavioral techniques. Lipscomb (1972) successfully used a progress chart as reinforcement for performance improvement with a beginning band class. Salzberg and Greenwald (1977) found that a token system, with a party as the backup reinforcer, was effective in increasing the punctuality and attentiveness of stringed-instrument students. Harner (1973) developed an operant paradigm for teaching all aspects of a beginning stringed instrument. Hair (1973) used "happy face stickers" paired with approval to teach harmonic discrimination to first graders. Guerin (1972) found that three types of feedback systems were effective non-differentially in improving pitch matching. In general, it would appear that for feedback

110

to be an effective reinforcer, obtaining the correct answer would have to be a conditioned reinforcer.

Anxiety as motivation or impediment to performance. It might be presumed that anxiety and the stimuli associated with it could function either as negative reinforcement for excellence in performance or as a form of punishment. In the case of the latter or punitive function, anxiety would by functional definition be detrimental to performance. Two studies using systematic desensitization, an operant technique, have shed some light on the issue.

Wardle (1975) found with college-age trumpeters that in a comparison of a systematic desensitization group versus a "discuss-the-problem" approach that systematic desensitization was more effective in reducing anxiety measure—behavioral observation and physiological measures. However, there were no differences in performance scores after treatment.

Appel (1976) found that group-dispensed systematic desensitization procedures patterned after Paul (1966) were more successful than increased knowledge of music and practice plus nonbehavioral counseling in decreasing the anxiety measures she used—physiological and verbal measurements. Students who participated in the study were graduate-student pianists who had been selected for high-anxiety scores using a verbal measure. The systematic desensitization group performed with fewer errors.

Systematic desensitization has been found to be effective in reducing various physiological and verbal measures of anxiety. The therapeutic and psycho-physiological literature, however, is replete with inconsistencies between verbal and observational or physiological measures (Jellison, 1975).

Regardless of the measurement and operational definition of anxious behavior or anxiety, the importance of reducing anxiety for performers is unsettled. Perhaps for students for whom anxiety is not detrimental to their engaging in performance, the reduction of anxiety may be unrelated or the anxiety may even be beneficial to performance. However, students who find the stimuli associated with performance to function as an impediment to even attempting performance, may be served more effectively when anxious behavioral associations are overcome. Then again, differences in Appel's and Wardle's findings may be a function of the type of music instrument or the use of a screening procedure in one study. If the decision is made to decrease anxiety, systematic desensitization seems to be a viable approach.

Affect and Music Learning

To some, the most difficult issue for both researchers and teachers concerns an operational definition and measurement of the affective (or aesthetic, the two are used synonymously herein) domain of music learning. To theoretical aestheticians and teachers of a more speculative bent, the aesthetic response is often believed to be a phenomenological one that is incapable of systematic empirical measurement. Researchers and teachers of a more operational persuasion believe that the aesthetic response ranges from behaviors that are a manifestation of the visceral event (Berlyne, 1974) to those who believe that the aesthetic response is itself behavioral and that visceral byproducts, although important to the individual, are unreliable when studied via self-report. The unreliability of the visceral response raises the point that such responses have the equal probability of being the byproducts of behavior (Greer, in press; Skinner, 1974).

Affect as Reinforcement Value

Research through the late sixties emphasized the use of verbal preference, or attitude, as a means of assessing affect. Sapnick (1976) has provided a cogent review of that literature. Research in music education throughout the seventies that has had an operant theory orientation has in large part made use of free operant selection behavior as the major and direct measure of musical affect. This measure and similar measures have also been used in Berlyne (1974) in his information theory approach to non-speculative aesthetics.

Free operant instruments have included conjugate devices for comparison of static art stimuli while nonstatic art stimuli such as narrative and music stimuli have necessitated the use of episodic instrumentation (Cotter and Spradlin, 1971; Lovett, 1965). The Operant Music Selection Recorder is an episodic reinforcement device that allows the individual to choose between two or more listening alternatives. The number of seconds spent selecting or attending a particular music stimulus, and indeed any stimulus given biological restraints on the behavior, is then seen as a direct measurement of reinforcement value. For music stimuli and other art, reinforcement value may be defended as either a direct measure of aesthetic value (Greer, in press; Staats, 1975) or as a response indicative of the aesthetic state (Berlyne, 1974).

The theoretical basis of the measurement of reinforcement value as free operant selection has been succinctly stated by Premack (1971):

(1) Organisms order discriminable events of their world on a scale of value. (2) The value that an organism assigns to a stimulus can be measured by the probability that the organism will respond to the stimulus. The probability can be estimated from the duration for which the organism responds. Durations can be compared over all possible stimulus and response dimensions under the constraints which reduce to the requirement that either the rate-time for the several responses be comparable or the probabilities compared be momentary rather than average. (3) Value is a unitary dimension. (4) Motivational phenomena—reinforcement, punishment, contrast, arousal—all result from a common state of affairs: a difference in value (p. 122).

All music stimuli that are discriminable have varying degrees of reinforcement value, presumably based on the environmentally evolved or biological components of human capabilities plus the individual's learning history and constantly evolving learning environment. Attentive, selective, or choice behaviors are a function of the payoff obtained for those behaviors. Attentive, selective, or choice behavior that results in stimuli with aesthetic reinforcement value for the individual holds or commands the attention of the

individual. Longer attention and more frequent selection equals greater reinforcement value for individuals or groups. Choices in music consist of listening or not listening, choosing to use one element of music over another in improvisation or composition, and one interpretation over another, to name only a few possibilities.

Nonverbal measures of affect may or may not be consistent with operant selection behavior. It is entirely possible that verbal behavior is related to verbal reinforcement value and not necessarily to the probability that the individual will attend, select, or choose a given music stimulus in the future. This is not to suggest that verbal behavior is unimportant. Indeed, psychophysiologists are suggesting different and biologically specific systems (Davidson, 1978). Reportedly, social psychology also has recently noted the invalidity of predicting what a person will do on the basis of what he says he will do (*Human Nature*, 1978). Therapists and psychophysiologists confronting differences in verbal and nonverbal behaviors also point to probable differences in derivation (Wolpe, 1978). At any rate, the notion of behaviors being a manifestation of a unitary and hidden phenomenon is questionable. Inconsistencies in, or low correlations between, verbal behavior and music selection behavior have been found by Pantle (1978) and by Morgan and Lindsley (1963).

Instrumentation research for reinforcement value: music listening. Lovitt (1965) as well as Cotter and Spradlin (1971) found reinforcement value to be a relatively stable behavior (reliable) as measured by episodic devices. Greer, Dorow, Wachhaus and White (1973) found an episodic instrumentation novelty effect, but Cotter and Spradlin found the effect to be minimal as did Miller (1977). Dorow (1977) found selection behavior to correlate highly and positively with attentive behavior of children during concert attendance. The age and learning ability range of the students tested with the Operant Music Selection Recorder and similar episodic devices suggest that the instrument has few obstacles preventing the measurement of reinforcement value. Thus, this reinforcement value

112

instrumentation is apparently reliable, positively related to other similar free operant behaviors, easy to use with all ages, but not necessarily related to verbal statements of value.

Instrumentation research in reinforcement value: nonlistening measures. Reinforcement value instrumentation other than listening devices remains a relatively new area of research. Dorow (1977) demonstrated that behavioral observations (duration recording via videotape) of attentiveness may be used to assess reinforcement value. Madsen and Geringer (1977) developed a scale for simultaneous use with sound stimuli to assess the relative reinforcement value that trumpeters held for intonation and tone quality. Geringer (1977) used duration observations of students performing on various instruments as a measure of reinforcement value, as did Dorow and Greer (1977). Geringer (1976) also developed an instrument that allowed musicians to manipulate the key of orchestral compositions, thus providing an instrument for the assessment of the reinforcement value of tunings and keys. Numerous other possibilities exist including observation of selection of music, chords, melodies, dynamics, and tempos by performers.

Environmental effects on reinforcement value. The reinforcement value of specific music selections and general categories of music have been significantly increased by pairing the music taught with frequent adult approvals of the students (Dorow, 1974, 1977; Greer, Dorow, and Hanser, 1973; Greer, Dorow, Wachhaus, and White, 1973). The effect has been demonstrated with children ranging in age from nursery school through the sixth grade. Dorow (1977) also found that posttreatment selection behavior correlated significantly, highly, and positively with the number of approvals received by individual students during the listening/approval treatments. Disapproval paired with repeated listening acted to decrease selection behavior in two studies comparing approval and disapproval effects (Dorow, 1977; Greer, Dorow, Wachhaus, and White, 1973). Significant differences between high approval and high disapproval of students while they heard

music were found with approval producing greater listening periods.

Pairing of approval with listening required an average of twelve five-minute individual sessions with four approvals per minute to change preference drastically for first graders (Greer, Dorow, and Wolpert, 1978). Preference and reinforcement value is more amenable to change with children from two to eight years of age than with children after grade three (Greer, Dorow, and Randall, 1974). The reinforcement value of music classics (traditional genres, jazz, electronic music) decreases with age/grade level. Eisenstein (1978) found that the reinforcement value of newly composed music also decreases with age. Listening attention span (that is, to rock and soul music) increases with age. Presumably, these changes are a function of the educational effectiveness of the mass media.

Randall (1975) found that both elementary and high school students (two experiments and two productions) who participated in operetta productions dramatically increased their reinforcement value of the music in the operetta and related music classics. The more prominent the role held by the individual, the greater was the acquired reinforcement value. However, even stage hands acquired a significant increase over control students.

All studies concerned with approval have paired approval of the students' behavior per se with music listening, with the exception of two experiments by Tanner (1976) and one by Pantle (1978). Tanner, as well as Pantle, paired approval of the music per se with repeated hearings. Pantle found no difference in selection behavior between high disapproval pairings and high approval pairings by college instructors. Differences in verbal behavior were found. Tanner, in one experiment, found significant differences in selection behavior for college students as a function of high-approval versus no-approval treatments dispensed by a disc jockey. Approval produced reinforcement value. Similar effects were found for peer approval in a second experiment. No differences between the peer effect and the disc jockey effect were found. The number of listening and paired approval sessions were more extensive than in the Pantle study. The taught channel and the distraction channel in Tanner's experiments were randomly selected. Operant Music Selection Recorder channels consisted of paired recordings by prominent rock musicians—selections that were relatively obscure compositions by these musicians.

Repeated listenings—that is, listening without any known or systematic simultaneous events—have not acted to change selection behavior or reinforcement value (Miller, 1977; Tanner, 1976). However, repeated listenings have been shown to effect verbal behavior, particularly when a part of classroom instruction (Wapnick, 1976). Possibly, one may truly believe (verbalize) that one likes or should like the music, after a period of class instruction, and yet not have the music itself control attentive, selective, or choice behavior.

Relationships between reinforcement value and discrimination or concept learning. One of the most persistent beliefs in education is that increased knowledge of a subject, more specifically of the arts, will lead to greater aesthetic value, thus increased affect. Traditional verbal measures have found this to be the case in only some experiments (Wapnick, 1976). The following series of experiments were undertaken to ascertain whether discrimination or concept learning of music would lead to an additive reinforcement value above the known approval pairing effect. Since it is impossible to teach discriminations without approval or disapproval, or reinforcement of one kind or another, the discrimination or concept learning effect would be necessarily an additive one.

Several experiments as reported by Greer, Dorow, and Hanser (1973) and Brown (1976) attempted without success to show an additive discrimination effect. Significant and moderate-to-high inverse correlations were found between pretraining reinforcement value and time or trials to criterion when those data were available.

Using techniques known to produce melodic conservation, as used by Botvin (1974), melodic conservation was taught to first-graders using approval (Greer, Dorow, Han-

ser, Wilson, and Botvin, 1975). These students were compared with control approval and equivalent listening groups. Both groups obtained significant and substantial increases in reinforcement value for the variation channel (melodic conservation channel). There was no difference in selection between the concept acquisition group and the control. Again, a high inverse correlation was found between pretraining selection of melodic conservation music and number of trials to achieve melodic conservation.

Randall (1975), in a tangential assessment related to his previously discussed studies, found that the higher students scored in the operetta auditions, the longer they selected to listen to pretraining assessments of the reinforcement value of the operetta music and other related music classics.

Greer, Dorow, and Wolpert (1978) taught an experimental group of first graders to have high reinforcement value for selected orchestral music classic excerpts and subsequently tested experimental and control students on the number of trials it took them to meet a stringent criterion for paired associate learning (PAL) tasks related to the music taught for high reinforcement value and to another set of transfer excerpts. A significant and substantial effect in favor of the experimental group was found. Fewer trials were found to be needed by students in the experimental group, particularly for the PAL tasks with the transfer excerpts. It was proposed by the authors that generalization of learning is influenced substantially by learned reinforcement value.

This series of studies is believed to indicate that the learned reinforcement value for music, occurring either through experience or training, substantially affects the learning ability of students at cognitive music tasks and perhaps for performance tasks as well. If this is indeed the case, the importance of the occurrence of positive reinforcement in music education has not only the known and expected effect on affective learning but an even more profound effect on other learning. It may indeed be that affective learning, or learned reinforcement value, is crucial to other types of learning. Correspondingly, the presence of aversive stimuli could be highly detrimental, particularly at formative stages.

Collative properties of music as constraints on reinforcement value. The preceeding studies have concerned the pairing of teacher, peer, other change agents, and activities with music. Several speculative theorists, notably Meyer (1956), have proposed that the arrangement of intrinsic properties or patterns in music regardless of style or genre determine the aesthetic value of that music. Similarly, Berlyne (1974) has proposed an information theory that posits that the arrangement of redundancy and complexity via collative properties of music (melody, harmony, rhythm, dynamics) is related to the reinforcement value that he based on a hypothesized cognitive center in the brain called the "hedonic pleasure center." Such research, with or without the necessity of appealing to the hedonic center, could point to primary or naturally reinforcing attributes in music. Crozier (1973) found differences in choice with complexity and redundancy regarding pitches, as did McMullen and colleagues (1974, 1976) with both rhythm and pitch using verbal measures.

Hanser (1973) found that when first graders could choose (with the Operant Music Selection Recorder) between selections containing (1) all elements of music, or (2) harmony with fixed rhythm and no melody, or (3) melody with fixed rhythm and no harmony, or (4) rhythm (percussion) only, students did not discriminate. No differences in selection behavior were found but it is not clear whether the finding relates to reinforcement value since it was not known whether students could discriminate.

Eisenstein (1978) compared redundancy, complexity, and combined conditions with four elements of music (melody, form, rhythm, dynamics) using tone rows. She found no differences in complexity and redundancy either with primary or upper grade children. Older children listened to less of the music regardless of conditions.

Reinforcing attributes for the collative properties of music are found for college-age students with pitch and rhythm but not found for any of the elements with elementary-age children. The collative properties may or may not be specific to the apparent potential of music to naturally acquire reinforcement value—that is, the "conditionability" of music. Perhaps, research with other aspects of music will identify the biologically based constraints on music's conditionability qualities.

Contributions of Operant Music Learning Research in Affect and Motivation to Practice

The research discussed appears to offer a surprisingly complete paradigm for the day-to-day functions of the music teacher. The learning principles on which much of the research is based also provide practical techniques for motivating music learning and for increasing musical affect. Translation of these findings to the daily problems that confront the music teacher are obvious in some instances and less obvious in others. It is apparent that merely "knowing" the findings is not sufficient to translate. The appropriate place is in the methodological course work of the preservice and inservice teacher.

To briefly summarize the motivational applications: Procedures based on learning principles and related evaluative procedures (applied behavior analysis) provide the music teacher with empirically based procedures to (1) gain the students' attention, (2) shift the attention in such a way that discriminations and concepts are acquired, (3) teach in such a manner that the probability for raising musical affect is high—that is, teach in such a manner that the reinforcement value of music acquires greater stimulus control for the student, and (4) provide ongoing and *in situ* assessment of learning. The research also spells out how to use various components of a music program to motivate music or nonmusic learning.

Theoretical extensions of the findings and other operant research have been proposed by this author elsewhere that attempt to formulate a method of teaching, based on research, that is applicable to most philosophies provided education is seen as an intentional and rational effort to educate

(Greer, in press). To summarize, the paper provides a position for music teaching that outlines and distinguishes:

> . . . (1) between a learning-principles based method and other methods, (2) an epistemological basis for discriminating between what to teach as values and how to teach as method, (3) between a learning definition and that part of the definition having to do with insuring learning (how to), (4) between learning principles anchored in applied research and other learning theories, (5) between behavioristic and behavioralistic learning theories, (6) between the relevance of learning principles of instruction and the irrelevance of some aspects of learning theory to teaching, (7) the adequacy of learning principles in terms of overt instructional strategies. In short the viability of [operant] learning principles is presented as the content of method courses when those principles have an applied base. (Greer, in press, p. 23 of Chapter II)

Contributions of Music Learning Research to Operant Learning Theory

A few incipient contributions to operant learning theory or the extension of or generation of new learning principles have been suggested by music learning research.

(1) The relativity of reinforcement as found in the Premack Principle may be extended to encompass some very similar behaviors. Some music activities may reinforce others, and learning gains may accrue from the use of related contingencies. Reinforcement value is more accurately assessed through episodic instrumentation than through reinforcement effects alone.

(2) Secondary reinforcement (music) may be conditioned using other secondary reinforcers (approval). Recourse to primary reinforcers is needed only with extremely handicapped individuals.

(3) Some secondary reinforcers may not need repeated pairings with primary reinforcement in order to maintain the stimulus control of the conditioned reinforcer. It is unknown whether this is due to the discovered conditioning properties of secondary reinforcement, the nature of the stimuli conditioned, the nature of the organism, or catalytic or interactive properties.

(4) Reinforcement value measures may be used to assess intrinsic reinforcement. Reinforcement value may or may not differ from verbal statements regarding value.

(5) Group designs may be incorporated with single subject designs. The use of group designs for behavioral analysis has been more extensive in music learning research than in any other operant research. Combined designs are not known by this author to have been used in any other body of literature.

Operant research in musical affect and motivation grew out of and continues its association with operant theory and related research. In a manner of speaking the independent variables (other than music) dealt with in this review are similar to those in the mainstream of applied behavior analysis and other operant research. Operant music learning research has, however, concentrated on music behaviors as dependent variables and music contingencies as independent variables. Both areas of study are derived from and contribute to operant theory. Indeed, it is difficult for me to conceive of doing research without some relationship to learning theory. Research can simultaneously address both applied and theoretical issues. One may study many of the major learning issues associated with conditioned reinforcement and simultaneously use music as the stimulus to be conditioned, thus realizing both a theoretical and an applied benefit. Provided the teacher or researcher concerned with an applied issue is somewhat knowledgeable of operant principles and theory, the relationship between theory and practice is always implicit. Perhaps one of the outcomes of this symposium might be to make those relationships explicit. No conceptually cogent teaching problem is without precedent in learning theory or research and correspondingly, no applied issue is without theoretical import. Those areas of music education not grounded in a theoretically cogent structure ought to work toward doing so, while those areas with a history of theoretical allegiance, such as operant learning in musical affect and motivation, ought to work toward a more explicit relationship.

116

References

Alexander, L. *Peer tutoring effects on performance in a beginning band class.* Unpublished doctoral dissertation, Teachers College, Columbia University, 1979.

Appel, S. S. Modifying solo performance anxiety in adult pianists. *Journal of Music Therapy,* 1976, *14,* 2–16.

Bandura, A. *Social learning theory.* Englewood Cliffs, New Jersey: Prentice-Hall, 1977.

Barret, B. H. Reduction of multiple tics by free operant conditioning. In L. P. Ullman and L. Kransner (Eds.), *Case studies in behavior modification.* New York: Holt, Rinehart, and Winston, 1965.

Berlyne, D. E. (Ed.). *Studies in the new experimental aesthetics: Steps towards an objective psychology of aesthetics appreciation.* Washington, D.C.: Hemisphere, 1974.

Botvin, G. J. The acquisition of conservation of melody and cross-modal transfer through successive approximation. *Journal of Research in Music Education,* 1974, *22,* 226–233.

Britt, M. F. *Bibliography on behavior modification, 1925–1975.* High Point College, High Point, North Carolina, 1976.

Brown, A. *The effect of televised cognitive skills instruction in vocal and instrumental music on student music selection, music skills and attitudes.* Unpublished doctoral dissertation, Teachers College, Columbia University, 1976.

Burgess, R. L., and R. L. Akers. Are operant principles tautological? In W. C. Beeker (Ed.), *An empirical basis for change in education.* Chicago: Science Research Associates, 1971.

Cobes, C. The conditioning of a pitch response using uncertain singers. In C. K. Madsen, R. D. Greer, and C. H. Madsen, Jr. (Eds.), *Research in music behavior: Modifying music behavior in the classroom.* New York: Teachers College Press, 1975.

Cotter, V. W. Effects of music on performance of manual tasks with retarded adolescent females. *American Journal of Mental Deficiency,* 1971, *72,* 242–248.

Cotter, V. W., and J. E. Spradlin. A non-verbal technique for studying music preference. *Journal of Experimental Child Psychology,* 1971, *11,* 357–365.

Crozier, J. B. *Verbal and exploratory responses to sound sequences of varying complexity.* Unpublished doctoral dissertation, University of Toronto, 1973.

Cumulative index for volumes 1–10 (1968–1977), *Journal of Applied Behavior Analysis,* 1977, *10,* (part 2).

Davidson, R. J. Specificity and patterning in bio-behavioral systems: Implications for behavior change. *American Psychologist,* May 1978, 430–436.

Devin-Sheehan, R. S. Feldman, and V. L. Allen. Research on children tutoring children. *Review of Educational Research,* 1976, *46,* 355–385.

Dorow, L. G. *Conditioning music and approval as new reinforcers for imitative behavior with the severely retarded.* Unpublished manuscript, Florida State University, 1974.

————. Conditioning music and approval as new reinforcers for imitative behavior with the severely retarded. *Journal of Music Therapy,* 1975, *12,* 30–39.

————. *The effect of teacher approval/disapproval ratios on student music selection and concert attentiveness.* Doctoral dissertation, Teachers College, Columbia University, 1973.

————. The effect of teacher approval/disapproval ratios on student music selection behavior and concert attentiveness. *Journal of Research in Music Education,* 1977, *25,* 173–179.

————. *Generalization effects of a newly-conditioned reinforcer.* Unpublished paper, Teachers College, Columbia University, 1978.

————. Televised music lessons as educational reinforcement for correct mathematical responses with the educable mentally retarded. *Journal of Music Therapy,* 1976, *13,* 77–86.

Dorow, L. G., and R. D. Greer. The reinforcement value of a music instrument for beginning instrumentalists and the influence of discovery versus teacher approval on achievement. *Journal of Music Therapy,* 1977, *14* (2), 2–16.

Eisenstein, S. R. Effect of contingent guitar lessons on reading behavior. *Journal of Music Therapy,* 1974, *11,* 138–146.

————. *Grade/age levels and free-operant music selection of collative properties of music.* Unpublished doctoral dissertation, Teachers College, Columbia University, 1978.

————. A successive approximation procedure for learning music symbol names. *Journal of Music Therapy,* 1976, *13,* 173–179.

Forsythe, J. L. Elementary attending behavior as a function of classroom activities. *Journal of Research in Music Education,* 1977, *25,* 228–239.

Fullard, W. G., Jr. Pitch discrimination performance in elementary school children as a function of training procedure and age. In C. K. Madsen, R. D. Greer, and C. H. Madsen, Jr., (Eds), *Research in music behavior: Modifying music behavior in the classroom.* New York: Teachers College Press, 1975.

Geringer, J. M. An assessment of children's musical instrument preferences. *Journal of Music Therapy*, 1977, 14, 172–179.

————. Tuning preferences in recorded orchestral music. *Journal of Research in Music Education*, 1976, 24, 169–176.

Glass, G. V., V. L. Wilson, and J. M. Gottman. *Design and analysis of time series experiments*. Boulder, Colorado: University of Colorado Press, 1975.

Gordon, M. V. W. Instrumental music instruction as a contingency for increased reading behavior. *Journal of Research in Music Education*, 1979, 27, 87–102.

————. *The effect of contingent instrumental instruction on the language reading behavior and musical performance ability of middle school students*. Unpublished doctoral dissertation, Teachers College, Columbia University, 1977.

Greer, R. D. Behavioral psychology in first chair. *Teachers College Record*, 1975, 77 (1), 123–128.

————. Contributions of the psychology of music to music education and music therapy. *Journal of Music Therapy*, 1974, 11, 208–219.

————. The effect of timbre on brass-wind intonation. *Experimental Research in the Psychology of Music*, 1970, 6, 65–94.

————. Music instruction as behavior modification. *Journal of Music Therapy*, 1976, 13 (3), 130–141.

————. *A scientific approach to teaching music*. New York: Teachers College Press, in press.

Greer, R. D., and L. G. Dorow. *Specializing education behaviorally*. Dubuque, Iowa: Kendall/Hunt, 1976.

Greer, R. D., L. G. Dorow, and S. Hanser. Music discrimination training and the music selection behavior of nursery and primary level children. *Council for Research in Music Education Bulletin*, 1973, 35, 30–43.

Greer, R. D., L. G. Dorow, S. Hanser, L. P. Wilson, and G. Botvin. *Conditioning music as reinforcement: A series of experiments dealing with theoretical issues, applied issues, and design*. Seminar presented at the Eastern Regional Music Educators National Conference, Philadelphia, 1975.

Greer, R. D., L. G. Dorow, and L. N. Harrison. Aural discrimination instruction and the preferences of sixth graders for music listening, story listening, and candy. In C. K. Madsen, R. D. Greer, and C. H. Madsen, Jr. (Eds.), *Research in Music Behavior: Modifying music behavior in the classroom*. New York: Teachers College Press, 1975.

Greer, R. D., L. G. Dorow, and M. Miller. Student initiated instruction and a college instructor's approval in two graduate courses. In Greer, R. D. and Dorow, L. G., *Specializing Education Behaviorally*. Dubuque, Iowa: Kendall/Hunt, 1976.

Greer, R. D., L. G. Dorow, and A. Randall. Music listening preferences of elementary school children. *Journal of Research in Music Education*, 1974, 22, 284–291.

Greer, R. D., L. G. Dorow, G. Wachhaus, and E. R. White. Adult approval and students' music selection behavior. *Journal of Research in Music Education*, 1973, 21, 345–354.

Greer, R. D., L. G. Dorow, and R. S. Wolpert. *The effect of taught musical affect on the learning ability of young children at cognitive musical tasks*. Paper presented at the Music Educators National Conference, Chicago, 1978.

————. *Generalization of learning as a function of learned reinforcement value*. Manuscript submitted for publication, 1979.

Greer, R. D., and A. Lundquist. The discrimination of musical form through "conceptual" and "non-conceptual" successive approximation strategies. *Bulletin of the Council for Research in Music Education*, 1976, 47, 8–15.

Greer, R. D., A. Randall, and C. Timberlake. The discriminate use of music listening as a contingency for improvement in vocal pitch acuity and attending behavior. *Council for Research in Music Education Bulletin*, 1971, 26, 10–18.

Grossman, J. *An annotated bibliography, summary, review, and retrieval package for research in behavior modification and special education*. Unpublished doctoral dissertation, Teachers College, Columbia University, 1979.

Guerin, C. F. *The effect of three feedback modes on the external intonation of selected grade school instrumental students*. Unpublished doctoral dissertation, Teachers College, Columbia University, 1972.

Hair, H. I. The effect of training on the harmonic discrimination of young children. *Journal of Research in Music Education*, 1973, 21, 85–91.

Hall, R. V. *Managing behavior, behavior modification: The measurement of behavior*. Kansas City, Kansas: H & H Enterprises, 1971.

Hamblin, R. L., D. Buckholdt, D. Ferritor, M. Kozloff, and L. Blackwell. *The humanization process*. New York: Wiley-Interscience, 1971.

Hanser, S. B. *The effect of peer approval and disapproval on pitch matching performance and group behavior*. Unpublished doctoral dissertation, Teachers College, Columbia University, 1974(a).

————. Group contingent music listening with emotionally disturbed boys. *Journal of Music*

Therapy, 1974(b), *11,* 220–225.

_____. *Music selection of the elements of music by first graders.* Unpublished manuscript, Teachers College, Columbia University, 1973.

Harner, M. W. *Principles of learning applied to beginning string instrument instruction.* Unpublished doctoral dissertation, Teachers College, Columbia University, 1973.

Harrison, L. N. *The development and evaluation of supplementary programmed materials for teaching meter and major-minor discriminations to elementary school children.* Unpublished doctoral dissertation, Teachers College, Columbia University, 1974.

Henderson, C. *The effect of in-service training on the contingent approval and disapproval of music teachers.* Unpublished doctoral dissertation, Teachers College, Columbia University, 1973.

Holz, Richard. *The effect of behavioral instruction on musical achievement, attitudes, and music selection behavior in an introductory college music course.* Unpublished doctoral dissertation, Teachers College, Columbia University, 1978.

Human Nature, News and Comments, 1978, *1* (4), 12–16.

Jellison, J. Analyzing the effect of music and white noise on physiographic measurements. In C. K. Madsen, R. D. Greer, and C. H. Madsen, Jr., *Research in Music Behavior: Modifying music behavior in the classroom.* New York: Teachers College Press, 1975.

Johnson, K. R., and R. S. Rushkin. *Behavioral instruction, an evaluative review.* Washington, D.C.: American Psychological Association, 1977.

Jorgenson, H. Effect of contingent preferred music in reducing two sterotyped behaviors of a profoundly retarded child. *Journal of Music Therapy,* 1971, *8,* 139–145.

Kuhn, T. L. The effect of teacher approval, disapproval, and errors on student attentiveness, musical achievement, and attitude of fifth grade students. In C. K. Madsen, R. D. Greer, and C. H. Madsen, Jr. (Eds.), *Research in music behavior: Modifying music behavior in the classroom,* New York: Teachers College Press, 1975.

Leitenberg, H. L. (Ed.). *Handbook of behavior modification and behavior therapy.* Englewood Cliffs, New Jersey: Prentice-Hall, 1976.

Lipscomb, L. *The effect of a progress chart on method book completion in a beginning band class.* Unpublished manuscript, Florida State University, 1972.

Lovitt, T. C. *Narrative rate preferences of normal and retarded males as assessed by conjugate reinforcement.* Unpublished doctoral dissertation, University of Kansas, 1965.

Madsen, C. K. No one knows research but me. *Journal of Music Therapy,* 1974, *11,* 169–180.

Madsen, C. K., L. G. Dorow, R. S. Moore, and J. U. Womble. Effect of music lessons via television as reinforcement for correct mathematical responses. *Journal of Research in Music Education,* 1976, *24,* 50–59.

Madsen, C. K., and J. L. Forsythe. Effect of contingent music listening on increases of mathematical responses. *Journal of Research in Music Education,* 1973, *21,* 176–181.

Madsen, C. K., and J. M. Geringer. Choice of televised music lessons versus free play in relationship to academic improvement. 1977, *13* (4), 154–163.

_____. Preferences for trumpet quality versus intonation. *Bulletin of the Council for Research in Music Education, 46,* 13–22.

Madsen, C. K., R. D. Greer, and C. H. Madsen, Jr. *Research in music behavior: Modifying music behavior in the classroom.* New York: Teachers College Press, 1975.

Madsen, C. K., and C. H. Madsen, Jr. Music as a behavior modification technique with a juvenile delinquent. *Journal of Music Therapy,* 1968, *5,* 72–76.

_____. *Teaching/discipline: A positive approach for educational development, second edition for professional development.* Boston: Allyn and Bacon, 1974.

_____. Selection of music listening or candy as a function of contingent versus noncontingent reinforcement and scale singing. *Journal of Music Therapy,* 1972, *9,* 190–198.

Madsen, C. K., R. S. Moore, M. J. Wagner, and C. A. Yarbrough. Comparison of music as reinforcement for correct mathematical responses versus music as reinforcement for attentiveness. *Journal of Music Therapy,* 1975, *12,* 84–89.

Madsen, C. K., D. Wolfe, and C. H. Madsen, Jr. The effect of reinforcement and directional scalar methodology on intonational improvement. *Bulletin of the Council for Research in Music Education,* 1969, *18,* 22–23.

Madsen, C. K., and C. Yarbrough. The effect of experimental design on the isolation of dependent and independent variables. In C. K. Madsen, R. D. Greer, and C. H. Madsen, Jr. *Research in music behavior: Modifying music behavior in the classroom.* Teachers College Press, 1975.

McGee, C. S., J. M. Kauffman, and J. L. Nussen. Children as therapeutic change agents: Reinforcement intervention paradigms. *Review of Educational Research,* 1977, *47,* 451–478.

119

McMullen, P. T. The influence of complexity in pitch sequences on preference responses of college age subjects. *Journal of Music Therapy*, 1974, *11*, 226–233.

McMullen, P. T., and M. J. Arnold. Preference and interest as functions of distributional redundancy in rhythmic sequences. *Journal of Research in Music Education*, 1976, *24*, 22–31.

Meyer, L. B. *Emotion and meaning in music*. Chicago: The University of Chicago Press, 1956.

Miller, D. M. Effects of music listening contingencies on arithmetic performance and music preference of EMR children, *American Journal of Mental Deficiency*, 1977, *81*, 371–378.

Miller, D. M., L. G. Dorow, and R. D. Greer. The contingent use of music and art for improving arithmetic scores. *Journal of Music Therapy*, 1974, *11*, 57–64.

Moore, J. W. Effect of differential teaching techniques on achievement, attitude, and teaching skills. *Journal of Research in Music Education*, 1976, *24* (3), 129–141.

Moore, J. W., and T. L. Kuhn. The effect of different behavioral techniques on teaching and musicianship skills of prospective elementary school teachers: Six studies. In C. K. Madsen, R. D. Greer, and C. H. Madsen, Jr., *Research in music behavior: Modifying music behavior in the classroom*, New York: Teachers College Press, 1975.

Moore, J. W., S. A. Manning, and W. I. Smith. *Conditioning and instrumental learning*. New York: McGraw Hill, 1978.

Morgan, B. J., and O. R. Lindsley. Operant preference for stereophonic over monophonic music. *Journal of Music Therapy*, 1966, *3*, 135–143.

Murray, K. C. The effect of teacher approval/disapproval on the performance level, attentiveness, and attitude of high school choruses. In C. K. Madsen, R. D. Greer, and C. H. Madsen, Jr., *Research in music behavior: Modifying music behavior in the classroom*. New York: Teachers College Press, 1975.

Netherland, V. R. *The effect of adult, peer, and tape recorded models on piano students' sight reading and practiced performance achievement*. Unpublished doctoral dissertation, Teachers College, Columbia University, 1975.

Pantle, J. E. *The effect of teacher approval of music on music selection and music verbal preference*. Paper presented at the Music Educators National Conference, Chicago, April 1978.

Paul, G. L. *Insight vs. desensitization in psychotherapy: An experiment in anxiety reduction*. Stanford, California: Stanford University Press, 1966.

Polirstok, S. R., and R. D. Greer. Remediation of mutually aversive interaction between a problem student and four teachers by training the student in reinforcement techniques. *Journal of Applied Behavior Analysis*, 1977, *10*, 707–716.

Porter, S. Y. The effect of multiple discrimination training on pitch-matching behaviors of uncertain singers. *Journal of Research in Music Education*, 1977, *25*, 68–82.

Premack, D. Catching up with common sense on two sides of a generalization: Reinforcement and punishment. In R. Glaser (Ed.), *The nature of reinforcement*. New York: Academic Press, 1971, p. 122.

Randall, C. A. *The effect of participation in school music-theater productions on the music selection behavior of elementary and secondary students*. Unpublished doctoral dissertation, Teachers College, Columbia University, 1975.

Robin, A. L. Behavioral instruction in the college classroom. *Review of Educational Research*, 1976, *46*, 313–334.

Salzberg, R. S., and M. A. Greenwald. Effect of a token system on attentiveness and punctuality in two string instrument classes. *Journal of Music Therapy*, 1977, *14* (1), 27–38.

Sherman, T. M., and W. H. Cormier. An investigation of the influence of student behavior on teacher behavior. *Journal of Applied Behavior Analysis*, 1974, *7*, 11–22.

Sidman, M. *Tactics of scientific research: Evaluating experimental data in psychology*. New York: Basic Books, 1960.

Skinner, B. F. *About behaviorism*. New York: Alfred A. Knopf, 1974.

Spradlin, J. E. Music for behavior analysis. *Contemporary Psychology*, 1976, *21* (8), 594–595.

Staats, A. W. *Social behaviorism*. Homewood, Illinois: Dorsey Press, 1975.

Steele, A. L. Programmed use of music to alter uncooperative problem behavior. *Journal of Music Therapy*, 1968, *5*, 103–107.

Talkington, L. W., and S. M. Hall. A musical application of Premack's hypothesis to low verbal retardates. *Journal of Music Therapy*, 1970, *7*, 95–99.

Tanner, F. D. *The effect of disc jockey approval of music and peer approval of music on music selection*. Unpublished doctoral dissertation, Teachers College, Columbia University, 1976.

Thompson, M., W. R. Brassel, S. Persons, R. Tucker, and H. Rollins. Contingency management in schools: How often and how well does it work? *American Educational Research Journal*, 1974, *11* (1), 19–28.

Wachhaus, G. B., and G. E. Wachhaus. *The effect of a music ensemble conductor's verbal behavior on student musicians' attitude.* Paper presented at Music Educators National Conference, Atlantic City, New Jersey, 1976.

Wapnick, J. A review of research on attitude and preference. *Bulletin of the Council for Research in Music Education,* 1976, 48, 1–20.

Wardle, A. Behavior modification by reciprocal inhibition of instrumental performance anxiety. In C. K. Madsen, R. D. Greer, and C. H. Madsen, Jr. *Research in music behavior: Modifying music behavior in the classroom.* New York: Teachers College Press, 1975.

White, M. A. Natural rates of teacher approval and disapproval in the classroom. *Journal of Applied Behavior Analysis,* 1975, 8, 367–372.

Wolpe, J. Cognition and causation in human behavior and its therapy. *American Psychologist,* 1978, May, 437–446.

Wolpow, R. I. The independent effects of contingent social and academic approval upon the musical on-task and performance behaviors of profoundly retarded adults. *Journal of Music Therapy,* 1976, 14, 29–38.

Yank, S. H. *The effect of multiple discrimination training on pitch-matching behaviors of uncertain singers.* Unpublished doctoral dissertation, Teachers College, Columbia University, 1975.

Yarborough, C., M. Charboneau, and J. Wapnick. Music as reinforcement for correct math and attending in ability assigned math classes. *Journal of Music Therapy,* 1977, 14, 77–88.

Zurcher, W. *A total PSI program for a junior high school band.* Paper presented at the Second National Symposium on Research in Music Behavior, Milwaukee, 1977.

———. The effect of model-supportive practice on beginning brass instrumentalists. In C. K. Madsen, R. D. Greer, and C. H. Madsen, Jr. *Research in music behavior: Modifying music behavior in the classroom.* New York: Teachers College Press, 1975.

Motivation and Affect

Malcolm J. Tait

The following assumptions have been made as a basis for the development of this paper:

(1) Thinking music is essentially linear activity in which memory assists the identification and classification of music events.

(2) Feeling music is essentially nonlinear activity in which the senses and the imagination are involved in a process of metaphoric derivation.

(3) Musical meaning represents the marriage of thinking and feeling music.

(4) Metaphor seems to be a more satisfactory term than symbol insofar as metaphor emphasizes similarities between different phenomena while symbol suggests the substitution of one phenomenon for another.

(5) The product of music education is a student and not a music composition or a music performance.

During the last decade, music education literature has reflected a solid demand for increased attention to aesthetic education and aesthetic growth. There has been little systematic research to clarify the best means to this end. Several hypotheses have been suggested but the area is in need of clear principles with practical teaching and learning implications.

While there has been increased pressure to deal with more covert affective aesthetic learnings, there has also been an increased effort to deal more effectively with the overt observable and often nonaesthetic learnings. This phenomenon is perpetuating a false dichotomy between musical thought and musical feeling. Perhaps the basic problem facing us is the separation of man's thinking and feeling processes and, in music, the unfortunate association that classical or serious music is for thinking and popular music is for feeling. Music teachers have been trying for years to develop strategies that might bridge this gap. We have added more types of music—non-Western and electronic, contemporary and youth musics—and our image has become more comprehensive, but have we really been successful in relating the wholeness of music to the wholeness of mankind? Humanistic psychology has taken a Gestalt approach to man and to artistic processes and for this reason is more congruent with the nature of music education.

Music becomes educationally significant when it contributes to human development—that is, when learning takes place. We can say that learning is a process of deriving meaning from experience where meaning represents the marriage of thinking and feeling. In music education, learning takes place when a student relates his or her thoughts and feelings to a series of music events.

I would like to consider motivation and affect in a context that views music as a form of human behavior involving our thinking and feeling, as well as our sharing potential. In this way the interdependence of motivation, music, and feeling are most likely to be realized. Consider first thinking music.

Thinking music is, so far as we can tell, chiefly an activity of the left hemisphere of the brain. Logical, deductive, and analytic processes are brought to bear on the content of music—namely, the elements, forms, styles, instruments, and notation.

The sequence of learning via thinking may be posited as follows: motivation, information, elaboration, manipulation, and confirmation. Motivation represents a student's desire or willingness to become involved with a series of music events. The desire may be casual or intense and it may be intrinsic or extrinsic. If a student can see valuable relationships between himself and what is to be learned, intrinsic motivation is likely to be increased. If he can learn more about himself as a result of learning more about music, then motivation is likely to be maximized. Most people are vitally interested in their own growth and development, and music, because it is patterned on human behavior and involves thinking, feeling, and sharing, is ideally suited to assist self-realization.

Information is a preliminary step in learning. A student will ask, or be told, or he may observe or hear, but regardless of the source of derivation, information of a general nature will be received and identified.

A process of elaboration follows, in which information is compared or related to what is already known; for example, new information might have to do with syncopation, which would then need to be related to pulse or meter. Phrase would need to be related to a larger music section within form. Violin might need to be related to orchestra or quartet, or simply other bowed stringed instruments. A clef in notation might be related to pitch differentiation, and a meter signature to metric organization, and so on.

In the next stage of learning via thinking, there is a process of manipulation. Here information is developed, organized, or rearranged. There will probably be some experimentation or "doing" but in the sense of thinking about what is being done. Experimentation will be orderly, convergent, and rather predictable. If the information has to do with style, for example, manipulation might involve preliminary attempts to employ some particular stylistic characteristics in a simple composition or performance. If the information is derived from a music element such as tone, a student may wish to explore varieties of vocal tone through listening or performing, but obviously in an elementary fashion.

A final stage of learning via thinking involves a process of confirmation; the infor-

122

mation, having been manipulated, is ready for application, for incorporation into original and independent effort. This may take the form of performance, composition, analytic listening, or any other bona fide music experience in which the learner accepts responsibility for demonstrating what has been learned.

Feeling music is, so far as is known, an activity that has its locus in the right hemisphere of the brain. Intuitive, divergent, and creative processes are brought to bear on the music—namely, qualities of feeling, qualities of movement, life processes, and imagery.

The sequence of learning via feeling music parallels that for thinking music. But in terms of motivation, learning via feeling may possibly be more intrinsic than extrinsic. Intrinsic motivation for music learning may be demonstrated by those children who frequently hum, dance, or vocalize, reflecting a lively musical imagination, one in which musical feelings are involved. We do not know the source of this creative power; it lies deep within a person, and yet represents a uniquely individual force of great potential.

The garnering of information through feeling is probably experimental in that it is sensed nonverbally and inferred rather than being told or recognized. We talk about a "sense of rhythm" or a "feeling for phrase" or a "tonal awareness." In short, this form of information through feeling is probably derived from all our senses to coalesce in a general sensitivity to sound qualities and the ways in which they flow together to produce "feelingful" events.

Whereas information for learning via thinking might be recognized in terms of rapid dotted rhythms, for example, in learning by feeling, the same information might be experienced as a "skipping movement." Similarly, a series of fortissimo chords might be felt in terms of anger or frustration, or modulation might be sensed as a quality of instability or of deviation.

In the elaborating stage of learning by feeling, what has been inferred, or sensed, now is imagined more clearly. As with learning by thinking, the process involves some relat-

ing or perhaps clarifying. The image of what was sensed becomes more clear and situated in a context. For example, at a simple level, a rhythm pattern may have been sensed without a clearly defined melodic contour. With elaboration, a melody comes more clearly to mind and the two coalesce. At a more sophisticated level, the initial information may involve the beginnings of a feeling for phrasing in a new work that is being rehearsed. With elaboration, that feeling becomes related to harmonic progressions and the image is clarified.

With the third stage of learning by feeling (manipulation), what has been imagined is now projected in a somewhat tentative fashion. The projected image becomes the subject of playful improvisation. Unlike learning by thinking, where manipulation tends to be fairly orderly, deductive, and convergent, and a rather predictable process, manipulation via feeling tends to be tentative, divergent, exploratory, and somewhat unpredictable. This kind of learning by feeling music is frequently found among amateur musicians who, without knowledge of formal notation, have to "try things out." Young pop musicians often spend many hours manipulating music information they have sensed or felt until they feel happy with their efforts. This is trial-and-error learning based on musical intuition (informal enculturation) rather than musical "know-how" or formal schooling. Jazz is a musical genre that has developed via learning by feeling, and in spite of academic efforts, still largely denies learning by thinking.

Confirmation is but a short step from manipulation. What has been sensed, imagined, and projected is now created. Shapes and forms are stabilized and confirmed by their feeling of rightness and completeness.

According to our original definition of learning—namely, a process of deriving meaning from experiencing a music event, where meaning represents the marriage of thinking and feeling, it must be realized that learning by thinking or learning by feeling in isolation from one another does not assist the development of musical meaning. Meaning is dependent on the two processes being mutually receptive and interactive. This is possible at all stages of music teaching and learning, from motivation to confirmation. Information identified by thinking can be related to information inferred from feeling; elaboration via comparing can be related to elaboration by imagining; manipulation by logical experimentation can be related to manipulation via tentative projection and improvisation; and finally, music events that are created should represent an amalgam of thought and feeling.

The third area for consideration here has to do with sharing music. Sharing creates the most desirable atmosphere for music learning in so far as it maximizes constructive interaction among participants. Sharing is not teacher-dominated, nor is it oriented toward competition; rather, it provides opportunities for music discovery and self-discovery in a supportive educational environment. Too frequently music education students in choir, band, orchestra, or general music have been treated as a whole, and success or failure has become a group phenomenon. Music teachers and directors have been known to shoulder the success or failure of a group, thereby removing responsibility from the students. Students need to invest something of themselves in a musical process in order to derive dividends, and this is not possible without a genuine concern for musical sharing.

Sharing may be considered verbally and nonverbally. Verbal sharing consists of three possibilities: First, there is the discussion of thoughts about a music object—namely, a composition or its performance. The vocabulary for such a discussion tends to be professional/technical insofar as it focuses on what an object is made of or what difficulties may be involved in a performance. This kind of verbal sharing is frequently the language of critics, analysts, or theoreticians whose primary concern is to be articulate about an object or its realization.

The second kind of verbal sharing employs a metaphoric language that attempts to describe a subject's feelings about an object. Phrases such as ''turbulent surging waves of sound'' or ''delicate floating melodies'' are

typical of this approach in which verbal sharing attempts to clarify ways that music events affect or stimulate a subject. Verbal metaphors tell us about a subject's capacity to respond as well as his willingness and ability to employ an imaginative vocabulary. It should be noted that this verbal sharing is not sharing of object characteristics so much as subject capacities.

The third kind of verbal sharing employs a technical/theoretical vocabulary as well as a metaphoric vocabulary. By this means an object and a subject can be related, and thinking and feeling processes can be drawn together so that more meaningful sharing can result.

It is true that in translating nonverbal events into verbal events, detailed and subtle meanings may be lost or distorted, but this is also true for language translations and other human behaviors. What is true and real for one context may not be true and real for another; meanings derived from music events in one time and place may differ from meanings derived from the same events in other times and places. Meanings in a social context as well as in an artistic context are subject to change and reinterpretation. While these conditions are important, they should not negate the significance of learning via verbal sharing in music. Verbal meanings in any art form are approximations but the approximations will be more accurate if well-developed technical and metaphoric vocabularies are employed. Figure 1 represents vocabularies drawn from both technical and metaphoric sources.

Clearly, both of the above vocabularies are desirable, for while we may recognize a metric organization of three quarters, it is the quality of the three quarters—whether it is lively, stately, or peaceful—that is of primary significance.

Nonverbal sharing consists of several possibilities, some of which might be quite general and others more specific. Body language, like metaphoric language, represents an extension of a subject's realization of the object; it is an ''outing'' or ''celebration'' of the ways in which a person may be affected by music events. As such, body language is a

Music Vocabulary		Metaphoric Vocabulary	
Elements:	tone rhythm harmony, etc.	Qualities of Feeling:	peaceful angry gentle, etc.
Form:	symphony binary phrase, etc.	Qualities of Movement:	floating bouncing dramatic, etc.
Style:	baroque pop ethnic, etc.		
Instruments:	piano ensembles voices, etc.	Life processes:	stability growth gravitation, etc.
Notation:	key signature clef allegro, etc.	Imagery:	colorful angular mountainous, etc.

Figure 1

vehicle for accepting or rejecting, and clarifying, structuring, and refining those responses. In this way a subject comes to recognize his potential for experiencing and sharing human feeling.

Because of its generalized and disbursed response, nonverbal sharing via body language may tend toward subject clarification more than object realization. However, in the case of conducting, certain body language has been stylized and gestures have taken on specific patterns, that have as much or more to do with an object as with a subject. The formalized metric patterns of two, three, four, or six, for example, are a case in point. Other conducting body language is less specific although clearly suggestive, as with crescendi and diminuendi, melodic contour, rhythmic accent, and so on.

The personality of the music teacher may also affect his body language. For example, if his personality is somewhat subdued and introspective, he may have difficulty in projecting strong outflowing feelings. Alternatively, an overly confident and self-assured

music teacher may find delicate body language something of a challenge.

Vocalization, another form of nonverbal sharing, employs the voice rather than the whole body, although frequently vocalization and gesture of some kind can be mutually supportive. When a music event is vocalized, a subject is conveying what is for him the essence of that event. This may refer to a quality of tone, the way a phrase is conceived, a rhythmic subtlety, or a dynamic growth. Syllables and expressive vowels represent the vocabulary of vocalized music events and that vocabulary can be as varied and as vivid as a subject's musical imagination and musical perception. Vocalization has the distinct advantage of requiring very minimal technical accomplishment so that instrumental or vocal competence need not be a stumbling block for this form of sharing. In addition, there is a potential precision about vocalization that sharpens a music event so that its impact may be doubled. Learning by sharing gesture and vocalization have not been carefully explored and yet they would seem to offer easily accessible and precise possibilities for music education.

It should be noted here how the expressiveness of a teacher's voice can affect the quality of music teaching. A teaching voice is a musical instrument with characteristics of pitch, tone, tempo, and dynamics that are as vital to teaching as they are to music. Used poorly, and in the wrong combinations, the vocal instrument's characteristics—for example, high pitch, loud dynamics, fast tempo, and thin tone—can be devastating. The teaching voice must be exploited so that its full, expressive potential is realized.

Music listening is perhaps the most widely practiced form of nonverbal sharing. In education, listening should challenge a student's feeling, thinking, and sharing capacities. Listening should not be an excuse to escape from life in a personal kind of self-indulgence, but rather, it should serve as an introduction to life by exploring self in relation to sound. For example, students might be encouraged to bring a recording to class that is intensely rewarding for them. They could share it with the class and then demonstrate the kinds of gestures that might illustrate what one section of the music is about, the kinds of shapes and patterns that are implicit in the sounds. They might also identify qualities of feeling (metaphoric vocabulary) that are stimulated by particular music events. In this way the teacher would employ verbal and nonverbal strategies in learning via sharing.

Instrumental and vocal performance represent other forms of nonverbal musical behavior. Sharing via performance should involve a judicious balance between object and subject. On the one hand, a subject has the responsibility to realize an object to its best and most appropriate potential. This involves careful study and preparation as well as the development of requisite skills necessary for that effective realization. On the other hand, if the sharing process stops there, a performer might just as well be replaced by a nonfeeling computer, which can after all fulfill the requirement of clarity with predict-

able excellence. The other dimension, which is not predictable and rarely excellent, has to do with a subject's capacity and willingness to invest a degree of personal feeling into the realization of the object. The product will increase in meaning as the subject becomes congruent in thought and feeling with the object.

If all other factors were equal, one might assume that congruency would be more attainable in solo than in ensemble situations, but such is not necessarily the case. Indeed, the quality of sharing will either enhance or detract from the realization of the object. If a director or teacher is perceptive and inspirational, he will act as a cathartic force toward a unity of realization, not by demand so much as by the inspirational quality of his sharing.

Sharing nonverbally in an ensemble situation brings with it many social and musical responsibilities. If the sharing is to be part of a democratic rather than an autocratic process, there must be a willingness to exhibit tolerance, patience, and goodwill toward the thoughts and feelings of others in the ensemble. Such willingness is part of the humane behavior that is believed to be a fundamental condition for musical excellence.

A further area for consideration here has to do with improvisation in which sharing assumes a uniquely spontaneous aspect. The interaction between object and subject, and subject and subject, has to be fluid and intimate. The process calls for immediate and continuous action.

The most precise form of nonverbal music behavior is composition. Here an object is conceived with as much specificity as a composer desires. His thinking and feeling are imagined and recorded but not yet realized or shared. His sharing is potentially the greatest or the least; his object may become everyone's object or it may be nothing more than a sterile document. It may have meaning for many or only a few. What are the factors that might influence these alternative consequences?

Certainly an object must be recognizable within existing artistic and cultural traditions and must be accessible. Secondly, it must bring forth in a variety of subjects, as well as a variety of contexts, meanings that are considered substantive and durable. Finally, the organization of an object must be able to withstand repeated exposure and therefore be capable of treatment and realization in subtle and diverse ways.

Sharing is perhaps the most profoundly effective strategy a music teacher has available to him for it influences motivation, planning, teaching, and feeling about music. It is a form of social behavior that is wholly desirable because it recognizes and reinforces the uniqueness of the individual and nourishes and rewards the individual in a social arena. The dignity of humanity is recognized on the basis of the worth of individual thought and feeling and the willingness to share.

It may be a matter of some debate as to how much sharing constitutes a part of the traditional music lesson. The position taken here is that more often than not it is a teacher's meaning that dominates a music class. The authoritarian view of the teacher knowing and the teacher telling is a rather familiar pattern in music education. The master teacher and master class concept have helped reinforce the image of one best way to do things musical. But what of divergent and imaginative thought; what of creativity and artistic sensitivity; what of individual integrity and strength? Even a very young child possesses these to some degree and they may be either nurtured or extinguished.

There is little doubt that authoritarian strategies have produced a record crop of performers whose apex reaches to the international competition circuit. But what of the lesser students who fall by the way, frustrated through their own apparent inadequacies of stylistic authenticity or a limited dedication to unending practice? Do these students gain socially and humanely from their engagement with the music process or has their struggle for success in production (by means of competition) confused means and ends and success and failure? The irony is that a truly great aesthetic experience, one that is full of musical meaning, undoubtedly

involves a sharing of thoughts and feelings in a most finely structured manner.

The starting point for sharing is the belief that music events are not finite. The teacher needs to explore music with his students, to be flexible, and to encourage student input, from planning through the evaluating stages. The heart of the process, the catalyst, is of course interaction with music. This is the real opportunity for shared teaching and learning behaviors.

A teacher who has made a commitment to this mode of behavior will not feel threatened or defensive about accepting suggestions from students. On the contrary, he will seek student input in terms of thinking and feeling. He will develop verbal and nonverbal strategies and incorporate them into lessons so that there is a natural flow rather than a rigid teacher-dominated lesson. In this way a creative and artistic atmosphere will develop in which students can grow in confidence, sharing their feelings, verbally and nonverbally, and their thinking, logical and imaginative, and, as a result become more musically and socially responsible.

If we are to maximize motivation and musical affect, we are going to have to maximize music teaching effectiveness. This will be most likely if our strategies are derived from the fundamental nature of music rather than from the image of a general teaching model. Accordingly, music teaching and learning will involve holistic as well as linear, metaphoric and literal, divergent and convergent, creative and logical thoughts, which will be couched in a vocabulary of meanings related to living processes as well as technical expertise. Feeling music will involve nonverbal communication from generalized body language, refined gestures, and vocalizing to listening, performance, and composition. Sharing music will involve a process of relating human behaviors to music meanings in ways that enhance both aesthetic awareness and human sensitivity.

The following are two suggested questions for psychologists to consider:

(1) How can we lessen extrinsic motivation via competition with all the trappings of re-

wards and successes and big business, and also increase intrinsic motivation based on the worth of shared individual musical thought and feeling.

(2) Since human feeling represents a significant part of musical behavior, would some group counseling techniques make for more effective music teaching strategies?

Response

Edward L. Walker

I believe I have detected in this conference a very unrealistic set of expectations concerning the extent to which learning theory can make a contribution to the solutions of the problems of music education. I am reminded of one of the anthropologists' favorite phenomena, the cargo cults of some remote island peoples. On occasion such a group will develop a fervidly held belief that the white man will soon arrive in a large ship laden with all of the material goodies they can imagine. This belief has serious consequences when it becomes so strong that they cease trying to provide the necessities of life for themselves. As a learning theorist I can assure you that learning theory is not going to solve all of your problems. None of us is going to sail up in a large white, heavily laden ship.

Learning theories were developed to account for limited realms of data, often data collected concerning the behavior of animals. For the most part they developed in a convergent rather than a divergent manner. Thus, they tended to account for progressively narrower ranges of phenomena in greater and greater detail. While competition between learning theories has been referred to in this symposium, these competitions in no way resemble a bout between pugilists in a ring. Because they rarely addressed themselves to the same data realms or even to the same problems, a better image is two pugilists fighting each other while shadow-boxing in different gymnasiums. Because of this highly specific character of learning theories, you should not expect any one theory to provide solutions to the problems of teaching and learning.

Do learning theories have anything to offer the educator? I think the answer must be a limited "yes." I think learning theories should be seen as a source of possibly useful concepts. Concepts are useful if they provide intellectual handles that permit the educator to analyze and understand the problems being faced. They are useful if, and only if, they suggest something useful and effective to do in motivating and guiding the student. To illustrate the point, let me cite an example. The elaborate and complicated theory of Clark Hull became progressively more narrowly focused on the behavior of the rat in the maze and was utterly sterile in its direct applicability to real life problems of learning and motivation. It remained for Joseph Wolpe to borrow the concept of conditioned inhibition and produce the behavior modification technique of desensitization, and for Fred Skinner to borrow the concept of reinforcement and develop the behavior modification techniques such as those applied by Douglas Greer to problems of music learning.

If my thesis is correct, it follows that as music educators, you should not confine your attention to any single theory. Rather you should examine all available theories, including my own, for any concept that fits well into your head, and you should find as many such concepts as possible.

I should also remind you that studies of learning phenomena are not always associated with any particular learning theory, and such studies offer a fertile field of possibly useful principles. One of the most important principles that is often overlooked is that there are enormous individual differences in any aspect of learning and motivation. Any general principle must be differentiated in its application through an assessment of individual differences. We know that in general, spaced practice is most efficacious early in the development of a skill and massed practice is effective when the skill is well developed. We know that some things are much easier to learn than others and that we should therefore begin with what the particular student finds easy. From verbal learning studies we know that the direction of association is important. It is easy to learn an association if the direction is from the unfamiliar to the familiar (autarkic motivation is task motivation), but it is more difficult to learn if the direction is from the familiar to the unfa-

miliar (task motivation is autarkic motivation). Mason's principles of learning mentioned by Edwin Gordon are also in this class. All of these and many other principles could prove to be very useful even though they are not associated with any particular learning theory.

Learning and Teaching

Humans are marvelous learning and teaching machines. Both students and educators are human. Therefore it follows that both students and educators are marvelous learning and teaching machines who perform both functions almost continuously during every waking moment of their lives. Music education along with all other formal education has almost nothing to do with learning or teaching. Individuals learn music from parents, siblings, peers, discos, radio, TV, and other informal institutions. There is very little the music educator can do to influence the major portion of what the individual learns.

If it is true that the music educator has little to do with learning or teaching, what is the educator's role? The music educator can do two things: set goals for the student and try to make the learning process more efficient. The first of these, goal setting, is the matter of curriculum, which is not the subject of the conference. The second, undertaking to make the learning process more efficient, is the application of principles of learning or the psychology of learning, and that is the subject of this conference.

It would be wise for you as music educators to keep in mind the fact that your goals, sphere of influence, and roles are all sharply limited. Otherwise you are in danger of feeling that you have failed, even though you may have done a very good job, simply because you harbor highly unrealistic expectations.

Motivation

Malcolm Tait has given us problems, while Douglas Greer has given us answers. Tait has asked us how to make the ineffable effable and more, while Greer has treated us to an impressive instance of the application of

129

learning principles to some problems of music education.

Greer has given us concepts, intellectual handles, with which to tackle problems of music education. The basic concepts are those of operant conditioning, the most important of which is the concept of reinforcement. In horseman's parlance, this concept of Greer's is out of Fredrick Skinner, out of Clark Hull, out of Edward Thorndike, and Thorndike was Adam. The concept of reinforcement is the only new principle of association to appear since Aristotle.

Greer has given us techniques. You are to identify what you want the student to do, identify and choose something that will serve as an incentive for that student, arrange the situation so that performance must occur before the student receives the reward, and the result will be that the student will perform and learn in the process. He has provided a catalog of empirical results. A variety of situations can serve as incentives. Almost any behavior can be modified in this manner. These techniques can be applied to children, adults, students, and teachers.

These techniques are easy to understand, they are easy to use, and they can therefore be quite valuable.

Tait developed a highly useful anatomy of the texture of music education and then posed two specific questions. One with which I am not prepared to deal concerned the possible efficacy of group counseling techniques as strategies in music education. I must leave that question to others. His other question asked how music educators could lessen extrinsic motivation via competition and increase intrinsic motivation. I can at least begin an answer to that question now and refer to more elaborate answers in a book I have completed entitled *Psychological Complexity and Preference: A Hedgehog Theory of Behavior.*

To begin to answer Tait's question, it is necessary to develop some further specification with respect to intrinsic and extrinsic motivation. Let us distinguish three kinds of motivation rather than two. In essence, we need to distinguish two kinds of intrinsic motivation.

Autarkic motivation. This kind of motivation is sometimes called "task motivation." It is motivation specific to the task at hand. An example is listening to music or performing music for the sheer joy of doing it.

Idiocratic motivation. These motives are those enduring characteristics of the personality that are reliably present in the individual. In dealing with idiocratic motivation, a teacher can use any descriptive set of human motives he or she finds effective and useful. Maslow's hierarchical structure of motives is currently popular even though it emphasizes universality rather than the possibility of individual differences. Perhaps a more useful set are those of need theory and attribution theory as represented by Joel Raynor in this symposium.

Extrinsic Motivation. These are motives that are external to the person. The band uniform is an example. The most important characteristic of external motivation is that it can be expected to be effective only as long as the incentive is present in the environment. One can expect performance to cease when the incentive has been removed. Furthermore, if the techniques of inducing external motivation have been coercive the ultimate effect will be a profound dislike for music performance, for music, or both.

This set of distinctions provides conceptual handles that can be used for guidance in encouraging the learning of music. The first step is to find a music task that is at a suitable difficulty or complexity level to induce autarkic (task) motivation. The second step is to find idiocratic (personal) motives to associate semipermanently with the task at hand. Associate the performance of music with the individual's need for personal achievement or the need to affiliate with other individuals. This kind of association can remain with the task (music) indefinitely. Do not expect either autarkic or idiocratic motives to be the same for all individuals. An individual or clinical approach to guidance is necessary. Finally, employ external motivation sparingly and only when all else fails. When it is necessary to employ it, undertake to phase it out so that you can get along without it as soon as possible.

130

Response

Joel O. Raynor

I want to talk about "theory of motivation" and how it differs from "theory of learning." I will then illustrate how I use theory of motivation to deal with some very different kinds of problems—peak experiences, how to order a sequence of tasks to excite a student to learn, how to understand the effects of the career goals of a music teacher on his or her teaching behavior.

We have to look back historically in the field of psychology to recognize that fifty years ago the problem of learning was the dominant problem faced, particularly in American psychology. And the concept of reinforcement that grew from it emphasized the control of behavior through manipulation of what came to be called rewards and punishment, or to use more contemporary terms, positive and negative reinforcers. Essentially, the problem of motivation was not considered a major one, or an important one, or a primary one. In fact, Clark Hull set out to derive the problem of motivation from the principles of learning. However, there was a shift in thinking at the time that the so-called "latent learning" experiments were done, when a fairly widely accepted distinction was made between learning and its demonstration in a performance. The definition of learning as a relatively permanent change in behavior—to me, a more acceptable definition of learning concerns a change in behavior potential—is pretty much accepted by those who say that you can learn, but in order for learning to be exhibited in performance there has to be a reason for this to occur.

Psychologists now generally accept the distinction between a "learning variable" or a "perceptual variable" or an "affective variable," and a separate kind of question that has come to be called the problem of motivation: How do these variables combine to determine a particular person's behavior at a particular point in time? This requires a functional statement. It says that if we can identify a learning variable, a perceptual variable, a cognitive variable, or an affective variable, we are still left with the problem of specifying how these variables combine to influence what the person is doing now. We are beyond the point of assuming that one

131

variable only is directly related to a performance or behavior. The problem of motivation states: How do these many different variables combine to determine that action?

Now that I have made the distinction between the problem of learning and the problem of motivation, and I want to identify the problem of learning as a developmental issue—it concerns how change in behavior potential takes place over time. When we want to study the problem of motivation, we assess each variable's strength, and then ask: How does it combine contemporaneously with other variables to influence performance?

But there is a way to look at the problems of learning and motivation that only becomes clear after you have separately defined each. It helps to understand and put these two pieces together. I call it the motivational syndrome. A syndrome suggests to me a process that feeds back on itself while going in a certain direction. This is the issue and problem. When we talk about the contemporaneous determinants of action (the problem of motivation), Kurt Lewin taught us that we are not interested in how those contemporaneous determinants developed. Motivation is an ahistorical question. If we are interested in the problem of development, we certainly are "historical," but we are still left with the question: How do these variables function *now*? We have to again turn back to our statement of the problem of motivation.

In trying to study what happens in a person's life over time, it has occurred to me that variables might influence behavior differently in the beginning, in the middle, and in the end of a person's career in an area. And that the difference is not so much related to what is learned per se or what factors combine to influence the behavior per se but to the fact that the person is being changed by what he or she has done previously. For example, I will never forget the "peak experience" of giving my first concert—I was on cloud nine for a week—or of presenting my first APA convention paper, or of completing my first marathon. But since then I have published a few more papers, and I do not seem to get the same feeling again; I have

run several more marathons since then, and I do not seem to get the same kick. What has changed? I think I have. I have introduced this concept of motivational syndrome to refer to how the effects of previous behavior—in these instances, success—have produced a systematic change over time that can be characterized as "a loss of interest." This is surprising to some, and does not follow from the concept of reward as reinforcement, as defined in the empirical sense.

We can try to motivate students by presenting a goal, and we can call this "anticipated success as meeting a criteria of good performance." This is something that has come up time and time again in discussions with regard to music. It is obvious that certain music-related activity inevitably involves this kind of standard. You can try to "get the notes right," and you in fact get the notes right or not, and correct performance can become one of the goals of music-related activity. I have heard this point discussed in regard to listening to music as a passive experience, and other people's exhortation to "become good listeners." There can be a standard involved. But when we refer to that standard, we can talk about success and failure in meeting it. The important point I want to make now is that the effect of that same success can be quite different because something important has changed over time to the person who has had a series of successes.

Many of us in our careers have experienced a similar phenomenon. When we move closer to what we had set out to accomplish—the ultimate goal—we often find that in moving toward it a dynamic change occurs over time where there was an ebb and a flow of interest and excitement in what we are doing now. This becomes very important in looking at music-related activity. It suggests that it becomes important to identify individuals in terms of what stage of career striving they are faced with. At the beginning stage there are certain kinds of factors operating, while at the middle stage a different set of factors, and at the final stage still a third set of factors—or, more accurately, at each stage, the same factors have a quite different influence on behavior. Even if we could identify the types of variables that at the more molecular levels of analysis influence behavior, this still would not be enough to explain the very molar kind of activities that refer to playing a music instrument, practicing for that performance, or listening to music, or a composer struggling to write a composition, *at different stages of career striving.*

I have become interested in applying the concept of motivational syndrome to the analysis of some data that exist concerning change over time in creative contributions. At least consistent with that data, we predict where peak "creative contributions" ought to occur in a lifespan, where the magnitude of what we call "achievement-related motivation" ought to be in the life span, and argue that the latter caused the former. This is a different analysis from the more traditional ways of thinking about the distinction between learning and motivation. I do not want to lose that distinction. If you lose it, you lose something very important. But, given that we can distinguish between these problems, we want to start taking seriously the fact that, yes, as we get older we change, in predictable, systematic ways, and whether these changes are motivational changes or learning changes is less important than being able to predict and understand them.

The second point I want to raise concerns the concept of the perceived importance of activities—psychological importance, and how it influences behavior differently for different kinds of people. The kind of person you are with regard to what we call "achievement-related motives" determines how psychological importance influences action. Some are success-oriented people; when you give them the opportunity to compete successfully with a standard of excellence, it really turns them on. They get very excited, the more so when doing well *now* is seen as important to achieve future success. For some people we get opposite reactions; they become very worried, apprehensive, and inhibited and resist engaging in the activity. If they are constrained to do so by some type of extrinsic reward, they perform, but at a lower level than they would otherwise if that resistance had not been aroused, and they

will pay the penalty in experienced anxiety. For these people, the more important the task, the greater the behavioral resistance and anxiety. They are called failure-threatened individuals.

There is this third group that is relatively indifferent to the opportunity to succeed. They are relatively neutral and unaffected. If you look at the experience behind that, it's affectively neutral. So, at least in our work with skill-demanding activity, we have affectively toned dispositions that are related to different and sometimes opposite effects for the same kind of instructions that emphasize the importance of doing well: "Play that piece right," or "Play that over again; I want to hear it without mistakes." In my research, I systematically take into account the perceived importance of the immediate activity for attaining some long-term future goal, as valued by the subject, either in the laboratory by setting up a sequence of tasks, or in life behavior such as the prediction of grades in courses perceived as important or unimportant to the student. We find that characteristic differences in achievement motivation are accentuated when a student believes that it is important for him to do well *now* so as to achieve his future goals. This is an intuitively obvious finding for one kind of person—the success-oriented person. When it is important, when "all the marbles are on the line," and this person has to do well in order to be able to continue on, earn that chance to move on, that really turns on the success-oriented person. But not everyone. Research evidence shows, in fact, that it accentuates the inhibition, resistance, anxiety, worry, and apprehension of that individual who has this characteristic motive type that we call failure-threatened. The same strategy to motivate all students in introductory psychology—"it's important to do well, so buckle down and work hard"—has the opposite effects for these two different groups of individuals. And we get that third group as well. We get that group for whom grades are the same whether it is very important or unimportant to do well. In addition, we conducted one study where we assessed students' feelings right before their final exam, and obtained similar results as when grades are used to infer aroused motivation.

When we look at the problem of motivation as the specification of the determinants that combine to influence music-related behavior, what does this research imply? These findings might apply to music-related activity, where the same teaching method for music instruction may not work equivalently for all students. Let me illustrate this in a concrete example from some of the laboratory work we have done. Using various skill tasks, such as arithmetic problems or digit-symbol substitution, we set up a circumstance where we tell a person in one condition, "You have to attain a certain criterion of good performance in order to be allowed to move on to the next step." We could vary the length of this *contingent path,* or the difficulty of the items as perceived by the person about to face this path. And we do this: Sometimes we set up a long sequence, sometimes short; sometimes an easy sequence, sometimes a difficult sequence, and so on. Or we change the instructions to "whether or not you obtain this criterion of good performance, you will be allowed to work on the next task," or in fact we could do it less explicitly by just saying that "you will work on this entire series of tasks, no matter how well you do on the earlier ones." The evidence suggests that when we structure this as a long contingent path with a series of easy tasks, we increase the enthusiasm, the interest, the performance level, and the persistence of the success-oriented person.

However, to maximize the performance of the failure-threatened student, we need to set this up as a noncontingent series—when we tell them, "It's not important at all whether you do well or not." Then their performance is as high in the first step of a noncontingent path as the success-oriented student's performance in the first step of a contingent path. And we have that third group, again, whose performance and interest are not influenced by these ways of presenting the sequence of tasks.

I think there is an important lesson here for music education and educational instruction in general. The implication has always

been that feedback is necessary and important for increased performance; after setting goals, we want to give feedback to our students or we want to get feedback in our own professional activities, to indicate how we are doing with regard to reaching these goals. But when the issue of continuing on to the next step is at stake, based on good or bad performance, I would suggest that if this type of research finding were replicated with music-related activity, I would try to have the success-oriented student get the correct notes by telling him, "We have a series of music pages here, and each one has a little song on it; you are to work on the first one, and if you do well I will let you work on the second one, but if not, you will have to go back and do it again; we will repeat this until you get it right." However, I would say to my failure-threatened student, "We are going to go through this book; it does not matter whether you make mistakes or not; we will work on this first page for a certain period of time and then we will go on to the next one, and then to the next one, and to the next one, and so on." That should maximize the performance of this failure-threatened individual because we are not arousing resistance contributed by anticipated future failure. I have no basis for making the generalized statement that the factors operating for these other kinds of skill-related tasks would work for music-related activity. But our findings suggest a program of research in which we would systematically look at the interaction between the nature of the personality variables a student brings to a situation, and the particular structural arrangements made for presenting the material to the individual on his or her learning performance.

I want to close by talking about some other kinds of motivational variables, but this time with regard to teacher-related behavior. One of the things that has somehow been neglected in this symposium so far concerns the determinants of behavior at the molar level of the teacher with regard to the student. This is because (1) we had very specific content-substantive areas, so that concern was not for the person as a whole doing things—there was no chance to—with each discipline dealing with its own particular molecular problems; and (2) this has been a learning-theory symposium, and the question of motivation was not entertained. It may be that the student-becoming-teacher has certain sets of motivational factors—opportunities for challenge, attaining long-term goals—that operate when they teach their first year in elementary school. But what happens after teaching the same material for five years? Or for ten years? Or for fifteen years? Comments were made previously about the enthusiasm of the instructor as seeming to be a critically important factor in effective teaching, and that independent of the specific content of learning, "you do not have to teach this person how to teach—they know how already." I would suggest that this is as much a motivational issue, or a problem about the relative intensity of motivation sustaining that teacher's behavior, at that point in his career, than about his teaching skills. In teacher careers, there are effects of success that are initially unexpected. Many teachers tend to lose interest and become bored as they successfully teach the same material over and over. What happens to the student exposed to a teacher at the middle or end of that career-related activity, rather than at the beginning?

I think this is an important issue that has to be faced because I do not believe that teacher enthusiasm is the same at successive stages of career striving. I have a systematic position that tries to derive what these changes are, and when they will occur, for different kinds of teachers: success-oriented versus failure-threatened teachers. Teacher-related behavior and student-related behavior, according to this conception, are determined by the same kinds of motivational variables. I have no direct evidence to support that contention; it serves as a hypothesis, as a guide to stimulate research.

I regret that I have not presented any data that directly relate motivation to music. I would like to be in a position where it is the data that are important that we deal with, rather than speculation about how things might be. However, I have not done any research in this area. The people who have done research—and I am specifically addressing myself to Greer's program of research, which is the only one I have become acquainted with—have done high-quality work. It tells me a lot that I did not know, and I would encourage those people interested in systematic knowledge to follow through with use of his concepts. But, perhaps, use that type of approach within the context of a *theory* of motivation, which emphasizes that reinforcement value might be different for different people, and that reinforcement value might be different at different stages of striving. A good theory organizes and integrates what is known, and suggests steps for future research. In a sense, I have raised a set of questions, but unfortunately I have not been providing any answers. In the second session of this symposium I will raise those questions more explicitly, but again I will be unable to provide any answers. It is the research enterprise that will provide the answers, and if these ideas would seem good enough to use as a guide to future research, then answers will eventually be forthcoming.

Report of the Needs and Issues Team for Symposium Session I

Edgar M. Turrentine: The dictionary defines a need as a condition in which there is a deficiency of something, and it defines an issue as a point, matter, or question to be decided. This symposium is a response to the recognition that there is a deficiency and that there is much to be decided.

It is our hope that at the next session of this symposium the psychologists will respond to the generative papers, which have been so ably presented. We do not expect universal truths but rather encouragement to pursue together solutions to needs and issues that have been voiced in papers, responses, and discussions. Members of the Needs and Issues Team will summarize these needs and issues for consideration. Specifically, I will address myself to those needs and issues concerning auditory perception raised by Carlsen and Heller.

Heller suggests that there are four types of music learning with which teachers are concerned. They are kinesthetic or motor learning, cognitive learning, notational learning, and oral learning. This fourth type focuses on the music listening process, and he said the development of perceptive music listeners is an objective that would probably be embraced by all music educators. This objective is the foundation upon which music performance skills and music literacy are based. Directly or indirectly Heller poses the question, "What constitutes perceptive listening?" Music listening tasks discussed by music educators, Heller suggests, fall into two categories. These are tasks the listener can perform in response to a music stimulus and tasks the performers carry out in response to the auditory feedback of the music stimulus. Carlsen has been specific in identifying fifteen skills, competencies, or tasks. These tasks group themselves under one or another of the psychological attributes of sound, pitch, loudness, time, and timbre. His listing prompts me to concur in the suggestion that music education may indeed profit from a task-oriented taxonomy of auditory perception. Carlsen cited five factors other than the structure of the event that influence auditory perception. They are attention, education, perceptual expectancy, stress, and memory. Heller suggested at least three possible sources of skills required for auditory perception of a specific task in music. Those sources may be inert, learned in a nonmusic setting, or learned in a specifically musical setting, and may be dependent on developmental or maturational contingencies.

I suggest several questions. First, is there a difference between music perception and

general perception? Second, if so, is there a transfer of auditory perception skills to music from other modes of listening? Third, is there a best learning time developmentally and maturationally for the acquisition of these skills? Both Heller and Carlson cite Gibson who points out that there are three processes basic to perceptual learning. They are abstraction, filtering, and selection. It may be necessary to define these processes basic to perceptual learning. They are abstraction, filtering, and selection. It may be necessary to define these processes within music. Both Carlsen and Heller raise more specific questions concerning auditory perception. To summarize the large issues and needs as I perceive them, they grow out of six questions: (1) What constitutes perceptive music listening? (2) What is a task-oriented or *the* task-oriented taxonomy of auditory perception? (3) Is there a difference between music perception and general perception? (4) If so, is there transfer of auditory perceptual skills to music from other modes of listening? (5) Is there a best learning time developmentally and maturationally for the acquisition of music perceptual skills? (6) Within the musical context, what are the characteristics of the three processes basic to perceptual learning?

Answers to these and other questions will help eliminate some of the deficiencies and decide some of the matters with which our profession is concerned. They may even help give our profession a discipline. In searching for the answers, it might be interesting to note Ward's extreme statement "that what we can find out in the laboratory has no bearing on what music should be." However, Carlsen gave us a more useful guideline when he said that data on auditory perception of music need to be derived from highly trained musicians, as well as from sophomore students enrolled in psychology classes.

Richard Graham: My remarks are addressed to the psychologists in regard to needs and issues in motor learning. Project director Paul Lehman has charged me with the task of summarizing the major needs identified, the most important issues raised, and the major problems that session two should seek to resolve in the area of motor learning in music education. My assignment has been made much easier than it might have been by the two excellent papers presented by Hedden and Sidnell. Initially, I would encourage our colleagues in psychology to look closely at these two papers and to make every effort to respond to the thirteen questions posed by Sidnell, and the seventeen or so asked by Hedden. I have synthesized certain points from the papers into a few brief remarks.

First, as issues, I pose the following questions: (1) Can the field of psychology provide music educators with useful information on motor learning, especially motor learning of music behaviors? (2) Since such a large part of music education in the elementary grades is based upon body movement, is it possible to determine the extent to which such motor activities lead directly or indirectly to music learning? In other words, do activities such as Dalcroze eurythmics and the elementary music activities develop sensitivity to music stimuli?

Under the general heading of "needs," our discussion of the Sidnell and Hedden papers reveals several stated needs that might be met by way of the knowledge and research efforts of psychologists: (1) a need for motor learning theory for music educators, which would reveal information on (a) developmental patterns of music skill acquisition; (b) the relationships between motor learning and other types of music learning; (c) improvement of efficiency and practice of music skills; and (d) the relationship between motor learning and music performance outcomes such as intonation, tone quality, and articulation. (2) Many music educators follow research paths and methodology found in other disciplines. Since our special province is music behavior, we may need to learn of research designs that hold special promise for expanding our knowledge of fundamental motor learning processes in music. Even if there are no such special processes, there is a need for outside evaluation of the current research being published in music education literature.

These statements of needs and issues are but a summary of the information presented to us by Hedden and Sidnell. Those of us who are teachers, those of us who are music educators, and those teachers and students we serve will put considerable value upon any effort to assist in resolving the issues and meeting the needs we have identified.

Eunice Boardman Meske: I would like to balance a need that we have from the researcher, be it the psychologist or the music education researcher, on the one hand, and the issue this raises for those of us who see ourselves more perhaps in the role of translator, the issues that this raises for us in terms of what it does indeed mean in terms of classroom implications and applications. I must admit that as I have listened to the papers and to some of the research that has been referred to, I get both excited and frightened, and maybe threatened, because if what the psychologists are hinting at is really true it may indeed mean a vast change in common music education practices in the elementary grades.

Petzold said when you get into child development there is no way to avoid trespassing into all these other areas because I don't know how else a child develops except in these several areas. The first things that we need are simply intensive descriptive studies. We first identified ages two to five, and then moved it earlier to birth and then to school-entrance age, which of course now might be three. Concerning interaction with music stimuli prior to any kind of formal training, what indeed are the natural responses and performance practices of the young child? Part of this, I think, is simply a matter of pulling together very carefully the existing literature. What forces inhibit that interaction, if indeed they do, or on the other hand what elements can be introduced into the environment to enrich or extend those responses? Subsidiary to this, then, would of course be consideration of the young child's responses in terms of the influence of culture and other environmental factors and how these factors result in differences on the part of the child in kind and degree of response—

137

perhaps motor response and also sequence of response. Once this information is provided, the implications are numerous and refer to specific areas of research.

The first is in the area of psychomotor response—whether or not the young children's motor responses can be trained to be much finer than we have assumed. If this is so, the issue that faces those of us in music education is what this means in terms of the kinds of motor responses that we are trying to develop. Are we holding him or her back by our assumption that what the child can do when he enters kindergarten is make only large motor responses to overall music stimuli? I think the implications here are mind-boggling. The next area is auditory perception and its relationship to concept formation. We desperately need to know what research designs and research tools are available to get at the young child's response prior to the verbalization. But also, is there a way for us to find out from these young children what concepts they have formed and the sequence in which they are formed without the confusion of verbal labels? Along with that comes the crucial question of the relationship of concept formation and, prior to that, perception in terms of the context in the whole process of selective attention. Music teachers have had the experience of putting on a recording, expecting children to respond in a certain way because what we have selectively attended to in that piece of music is a particular thing, and, then having the children's response all wrong because they chose not to select the same response out of that musical totality. Is there some kind of order in that selectivity, in terms of the various elements? One of the things that I found fascinating was the assertion that pitch was the crucial distinguishing factor. If that is true, then I have to say to myself, does that mean that that is where I should start with the students? Book after book makes the assumption that the first things the child responds to are timbre and rhythm, and now we hear that the crucial factor is pitch.

Concerning memory aspect of information processing, what is the sequence of child development in terms of the development of

memory and its influence on information processing? At what stage can we expect children to be able to recall, for example, a simple melody. Our early childhood experiences are based on rote learning, which assumes the ability to internalize recall. If this still doesn't really exist, then what are we doing? Lastly, there is the whole investigation of the nature and nurture of dicotomy; we keep hinting that maybe the responses are determined by something that may be genetic. If it does indeed turn out that there are some people who are musically bound and some who are not, what does this do to the slogan, the philosophy, the firm belief of all of us who are in the field of music that music is for every child and every child for music?

Charles Hoffer: In considering the topics regarding cognition in music instruction, there is a strong possibility of overlap with other areas, especially child development. The most significant areas related to cognition appear to be the sequence of learning activities. We music educators would appreciate any thoughts, extrapolations, hunches, or indications that psychologists have about the sequence of learning in music.

Secondly, there is the area of the relationship of nonverbal, especially music learning to verbal learning. The point under consideration is not whether music is a language, but rather the psychological processes involved in the learning of verbal and nonverbal information. Brown has spoken about the closeness of psycholinguistics to psychoacoustics, and Knieter mentioned Bruner's pointing out the emphasis on language as thinking. Again, any more thoughts, explanations, or clarifications would be welcomed.

Third, there is the matter of individual differences in learning—individual styles. Several persons have referred to the differences among people in terms of perception, cognition, motivation, and so on. What can psychologists indicate to music educators about modes of learning, intelligence, and other differences in terms of their effect on learning in music?

The fourth area, creativity, is a very difficult matter to subject to objective experimentation. Is the extant research literature on creativity (by Jackson, Turrentine, and others) of much value to a field like music? Music educators probably would benefit by knowing more about the views of psychologists on the topic of creativity, as it applies to music instruction.

A fifth area is hemispheric dominance. This is a matter that no one wanted to go into at this symposium, but we did anyway. There is a bandwagon rolling on hemispheric dominance in music education, partly encouraged by an MENC publication. As Lehman and Carlsen have pointed out, the bandwagon was created from some rather naive and misinformed thinking. I think it was Carlsen who said that the bandwagon does not have any wheels. The question of "where music lurks in the mind of man" is not nearly as significant as the fact or need of the presence of music someplace in people's minds.

Sixth is the matter of learning theory and eclecticism and clinical approaches. The basic question of the utility and relevancy of learning theory now and in the future has, in a sense, been implicit in much of this symposium. Is the entire notion of learning theories now somewhat outdated? Is it, to quote a song, an impossible dream? Do we now have only some generalizations about learning? Is this as far as we can take it now? As far as we should take it? Can we pick and choose among theories or generalizations or models? Can we do so without incurring inconsistencies and gaps? How far from traditional learning theory is it feasible to stray in seeking these theories and generalizations?

Bennett Reimer: I have taken a different approach to my assignment than the other team members. Rather than focusing my attention on the two papers on my assigned subject—affect and motivation—neither of which are amenable to the kind of summarization or extrapolation performed by the other members of the team, I have instead aimed my attention at all the papers and replies given at this conference.

I begin with an assumption that, I believe, is held by the vast majority of musicians and music educators in the Western world: Music is first and foremost and essentially an art. To be very explicit, music is a tonal analogue of emotive life; art is the creation of perceptible forms expressive of human feeling. These are definitions of Suzanne Langer. Given the pervasiveness of this assumption in our culture generally, and in aesthetic education particularly, it would seem to follow that the teaching and learning of music, a matter of the theory of learning being applied, must at the least be concerned with the creation of expressive sounds, the response to create expressive sounds, and the fostering of all the skills and understandings attentive upon the development of children's ability to create and enjoy expressive sounds. Sounds that are not expressive, that do not include musical affect as a component of their creation or perception, are nonmusical, and, I will submit, of interest to music educators and aesthetic educators only in very special ways and for very special needs. I have further assumed that auditory perception devoid of affective response as an essential component may well be nonmusical auditory perception or, at best, *pre*musical auditory perception. I have assumed that motor learning devoid of expressive intent may well be nonmusical or at best premusical motor learning. I have assumed that child development and cognitive skills and memory and information processing are topics directly relevant to the teaching and learning of art, or, if not so, are nonaesthetic or preaesthetic and therefore perhaps only of informational interest to those seeking to improve the teaching of art.

Given these assumptions, I listened to the presentations at this symposium with an ear toward what aesthetic educators could learn about better ways to cultivate musical affective sensitivity. Attention to the affective component of learning was rather conspicuous by its absence, except, of course, in those papers specifically on this topic. Now I will briefly comment upon some of the statements that did in fact occur, and I will have to ignore those papers and responses in which affect was ignored or peripheral. Heller, as a very last point, raised the issue of what makes perception aesthetic perception. "Is aesthetic perception," he asks, "different from general perception?" I want to suggest that if the answer is "no," then music educators should not be concerned with musical applications of perception. We should only study and do general perception research. To say this is, I hope, to illustrate fallaciousness. We must ask our psychologist colleagues to help us understand how auditory perception gives rise to affective involvement, and how affective involvement influences auditory perception. Further, at what lower level of perception is affect likely to arise? To what degree is the teaching of aesthetic perception—that is, perception of the intrinsic expressive character of music gestures—a socialization process? What labels or symbols would serve to aid the process of auditory perception of sounds and at the same time encourage a growing responsiveness to their feeling tone component? How can expectation systems be developed so that listeners, when confronted with sounds other than simple diatonicisms, will not be so confounded as to assume it's either diatonic or it isn't music, or, by analogy, it's either a picture of something or it isn't a painting.

Sidnell mentioned aesthetic sensitivity in passing, leaving unanswered how music motor activity can serve to enhance aesthetic expression. Restle and LaBerge hit the nail squarely on the head, reminding us of what James Mursell stated as long as forty years ago—study of the parts can misrepresent the nature of musical phenomena. Affect, they say, is at the center of musical responsiveness and can indeed be recognized as the vital force giving sounds and body meaning or significance. The features of music to which we must attend are global features. That is where the conditions for affect reside. LaBerge's assertion that it is the light in the music that people come to hear is stunning—not because we don't know it, we've been saying it for 150 years—but because it comes in this particular context. The discussions of child development included a few brief mentions of subjective responsiveness, as when Zimmerman told us that affect seems to be a com-

ponent of early identification of sounds. She mentioned affective learning but offered no counsel on how to achieve it. Surely, the psychology of human growth and development can give us some glimmers of how children—and adults—progress in emotional sensitivity in openness to the new and challenging needs for expressive behavior skills, needs for emotional satisfaction of the component of self-acceptance, and empathy and integration of the personality. Have psychologists anything to tell us of such matters? We would welcome such information and we could, I'm sure, offer a great deal in return in ways to study how music sensitivity might contribute to general emotional sensitivity.

Brown told us that he has had no music education and has no musical talent but that he loves music. It's not clear whether his devotion to music is the kind of devotion we wish we knew how to cause everyone to feel, or whether it came about in spite of having no music education or because of it. Think about that one. Kessen suggested that we should teach directly for musical affinities without the use of any technical language or the skill that only specialists need.

The question raised by these psychologists are vital to music educators. We must ask them to help us find answers. How indeed can we influence people to have an affinity for music, or, given the present events in education, to have an affinity for any of the arts? Gordon asserts that insights into self come from art, and ultimately this is why we must become more effective at what we do. Knieter tells us of at least three psychologists—Bruner, Maslow, and Rogers—who would agree and, if nothing else, profoundly touch us by their assurance that what we do is not just important: it is essential. I would argue that psychologists or philosophers who explain why aesthetic education is essential do something for us that is very profound and very practical in the long run, and I believe a study of our history as a field would bear this out.

The remarks of Cady and Woodruff add weight to our assumption that the affective dimension of experience be in the forefront of any topic bearing on music education.

Cady reminded us of the artificiality of separating experience into different domains, and Woodruff called our attention to affect as a concomitant of cognition and to the necessity of recognizing richness and complexity of music interactions when we do research. Yet, because of the constraints of our research methodologies, we have found ourselves dealing with those small parts of behavior capable of fitting our designs. We need to know of molar methodology; of ways to probe and clarify the staggering density of experience when children and art interact authentically; of ways that do not obscure or deaden the experience we are trying to understand. We need in the crucial matter of relevant artistic research modes more than just a little help from psychologists.

Finally, Walker and Raynor reinforced many of the principles of motivation we have for so long espoused—that the intrinsic pleasures of music, private pleasures in addition to social ones, must be the prime motive for involvement, and we must honor the individuality of children's motives to learn. We look forward to the development of these ideas and perhaps even to some advice about ways to keep our own motivation high at those inevitable times when it begins to wane. Now, I'm going to be presumptuous and offer a comment, given that we were supposed to deal with issues as well as needs. I think we would agree that the questions raised at this meeting, and the questions that will be raised at the next session of this symposium, and the implications for research, and the carrying out of such research as might flow from these efforts are of great importance for our profession. This belief, however, is not shared by many, perhaps not by most practicing music educators. There are many reasons for the disaffection with research felt by so many music educators. Most of these reasons are, in my opinion, specious, based on misunderstandings of what research is and does, of what research can and cannot help them with, and on a general mistrust of intellectual endeavors. Yet, I cannot help but feel that a part of their uneasiness comes from their perception that much of our research seems to be unrelated to the art they cherish, and I think they might have a little something there. The problem of research in aesthetic education seems to me that the point of research in aesthetic education is to wed the most rigorous methods of investigation with the peculiar nature of the phenomenon in which we are interested. Sloppy research about music as art will not help us. Precise research about sounds that are not music and behaviors that are not musical, I strongly suspect, will not help us. I am not suggesting that affect as such is the only proper subject for research. Not at all. Research recorded at this conference, work done for and at this conference, is germane and important in as great a variety of ways as the subject with which it deals. I am simply asking both music researchers and scholars and the psychologists to be influenced in their work by that which matters most about music—that it is art. To the extent we are all so influenced and reflect this in our work, those of us who regard themselves as teachers in this art are likely to find their efforts influential.

William English: Cady and Williams reviewed research in the areas of memory and information processing, offering some excellent comments about their own interpretation of the problems and raising questions. Cady asked whether memory in music learning is different from memory in learning other school subjects. There are other questions: Is there a difference between conscious, deliberate memorizing of a musical work and the usual remembering of what is learned in class? How is music as a symbol system different from others? What is processed and remembered as music? What kinds of oral space and time are appropriate to the various stages of developmental growth in music? If music is a product of human behavior as well as a form of human behavior, is it possible that the question "What is music?" may be answered by psychologists who are concerned about what we process and store as music, and in doing so will they help us know what to teach, and at what stage of musical growth, and to whom?

Williams summarized his own extensively

prepared paper by presenting three rather significant questions: What insights and knowledge can cognitive psychology provide toward building theoretical models for the structure and process of musical memory? What correlations might there be between music and language processing and memory? What dangers do you psychologists perceive in applying verbal language models to nonverbal language or music models? What research models might we use to begin to examine the structure and process of music memory on a level appropriate to the complex nature of the experience? Are there methods for measuring music with the use of nonmusic mediators?

Session II
JULY 30–AUGUST 2, 1979

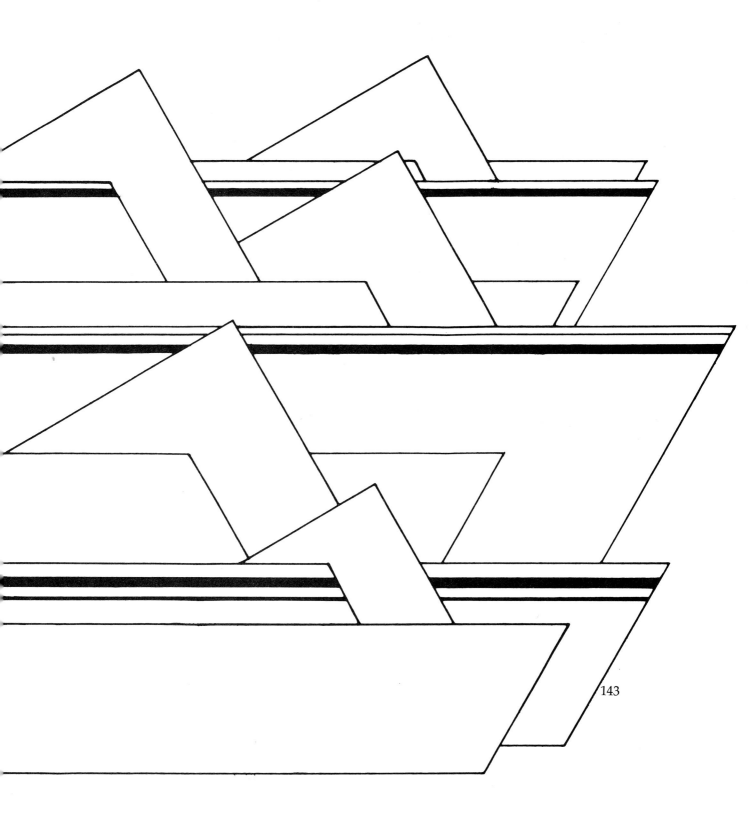

143

Mental Structures Through Which Music Is Perceived

W. Jay Dowling

I will start from the premise, something still debated in philosophical aesthetics, that a person's enjoyment and understanding of a work of art depend upon his ongoing cognitive processing of perceptual information. As William James said:

> The maximum of attention may then be said to be found whenever we have a systematic harmony or unification between the novel and the old. It is an odd circumstance that neither the old nor the new, by itself, is interesting: the absolutely old is insipid; the absolutely new makes no appeal at all. The old *in* the new is what claims our attention—the old with a slightly new turn. (James, 1910, p. 108)

The only way for such a mechanism of attention and interest to work when listening to music is for the person's cognitive information-processing systems to keep track of the old and compare it with the new as the music unfolds. But the listener's mind is not a blank slate upon which the work simply gets written. Both perception and memory are highly selective of what they record, and even what they select is typically abstracted or encoded for storage rather than recorded literally. This paper focuses on those principles of selection, abstraction, and encoding that the mind uses in processing music.

Yet, "the mind" is too sweeping a term here. We need to explore the mental structures used for music with considerable attention to differences among individuals. The mind of the musician, after a lifetime of practice and thought, exhibits a precision and complexity not found in the adult whose experience with music has been more casual. And the child of two who jumps up and down with glee on hearing the "Sesame Street" theme being played on the TV in the next room has a lot of developing to do before becoming an adult who can sing "Happy Birthday" on command. We will see that the way the mind changes with development and training tells us much about the mind itself.

Ultimately we may arrive at a comprehensive theory of the psychology of music, but we are not ready to write that yet. In the meantime we can be guided by a view of cognition inherited from James, Piaget, and Tolman, among others, that sees the person as an active processor of information trying to make sense out of his environment, who brings to that task not a *tabula rasa* but a complex mind and brain replete with strategies for coping with an otherwise overwhelming barrage of stimulation.

We are all born with certain capabilities and structures that shape the way we can hear music and by implication, the way music must be. On the simplest level, our ears are sensitive to tones in the frequency range of roughly 20 to 20,000 Hz. Out of that ten-octave range the four octaves between 100 Hz (about the bottom of the bass staff) and 1600 Hz provide the most useful pitches for music. That is because our pitch perception is best in that range, both for accuracy and precision. Precision declines markedly in the low register, so that down around the C below the bass staff the average listener is barely able to discriminate between tones one semitone apart. Accuracy declines in the upper register, with judgments of the size of the octave becoming more erratic and with the size of the subjective octave becoming more and more stretched with respect to its size in the midrange. The octave itself seems to be built into the human auditory system. Octave equivalence is used by nearly all of the music cultures of the world, including Schönberg's twelve-tone system, and the octave judgments of even nonmusicians are quite precise (Dowling, 1978, in press).

Another universal feature of music systems that Helmholtz (1954) noted over a century ago is that cultures divide the octave into discrete steps, rather than simply use the whole continuum of possible pitches. No one knows why human music should have evolved that way, but it is true that nearly all cutures have five or seven different pitches in the octave. Viewed in terms of humans' categorizing abilities, this seems very natural. George Miller (1956) argued that on any sensory dimension people are able to cope with about seven categories of event, and get confused when asked to sort things more finely. In conjunction with Shepard's model of pitch perception, this suggests that people use one

set of seven or so categories to handle the cyclical pattern of pitches within the octave, and another set of categories to handle octave height within the whole pitch spectrum.

A further aspect of the five-, six-, and seven-note scale systems used by the various cultures is that in all of them there is more than one interval size between notes. No culture uses equal logarithmic intervals, as in our chromatic and whole-tone scales. That all use diatonic scales with more than one size of interval is consonant with the view of variety and interest expressed in the William James quotation at the start of this article. If there is a variety of interval sizes available among the notes in the octave, then you can take the same melody and move it around to create a "tonal answer" that is very similar to the original, yet different from it in detail. This compositional device is characteristic of as diverse music styles as Beethoven piano sonatas and American Indian songs (Dowling, 1978).

Psychologically the seven notes of the scale are not just static categories. They have dynamic tendencies. Francès (1958) tested listeners' ability to notice intonation errors in melodies played on the piano. He had the piano tuned so that A♭ (G♯) was lowered in pitch. Then he played pieces in C minor and E major in which the natural tendency of the note in question would be down or up, respectively. He found that listeners were much better at detecting the flattening in the E major piece. If a pitch is altered in the direction the dynamic music system is pulling it, the alteration is difficult to hear.

Melody Perception and Memory

When notes are combined into melodies the picture becomes much more complicated. We understand a great deal more than we did thirty years ago, but we still don't understand completely how people remember melodies. Perhaps the best way to approach the answer to the question is to start with some plausible but inadequate answers and then refine them, gradually approaching the actual state of affairs. For a start, consider the simplest possible theory, that when we hear a melody we simply re-

145

member the notes—a Literal Copy theory. For example, suppose we have never heard Beethoven's Trio, Opus 97. Someone plays us the phrase Bb-D-A-Bb-F and tells us, "That is called 'Archduke.'" Five minutes later he plays Bb-D-A-Bb-F and we say, "Aha, that's 'Archduke' again." So far so good for the literal copy theory. But suppose he had played A-C♯-G♯-A-E. Unless we were one of the tiny segment of the population with absolute pitch we would have been equally accepting of the new version. So what is stored in memory is more abstract than the notes themselves. You might object that it is still possible that what is stored in memory is a literal representation of Bb-D-A-Bb-F, but that we have available transposition rules that allow us to translate the Archduke theme in any key back to the original and then recognize it. But if that were the case, we should be able to find some evidence for the special status of the original version. People should make fewer errors recognizing the prototype, for example. But no evidence of that sort has been found. So we are led to the conclusion that what people store in memory when they hear a tune is more abstract than a literal copy. The next more abstract candidate for memory representation of tune is the set of intervals from note to note.

For the Interval Set theory it makes no difference formally if we represent the tune as a sequence of intervals in semitones ($+4$, -5, $+1$, -5, in our example) or as abstract pitches in a movable Do system (Do, Mi, Ti, Do, Sol). This sort of representation would explain our ability to sing "Happy Birthday" in any arbitrarily chosen key, even those not on the piano, or transpose the NBC chime pattern anywhere on the scale (Attneave and Olson, 1971). There is considerable evidence that tunes we know well—that we not only recognize but sing—are stored in something like an implicit solfeggio form. We know that because people are not only quite accurate in reproducing the intervals of well-known melodies, but they also notice small changes in interval size in such melodies that they would overlook in novel, unfamiliar tunes

(Bartlett and Dowling, 1979). But let us return to the case of the tune. Though familiar tunes seem to be stored as sets of intervals, novel tunes seem to be remembered at first simply in terms of their contours, or patterns of ups and downs (Dowling, 1978). If we were to wait even ten seconds after presenting Bb-D-A-Bb-F and present Eb-Ab-D-Eb-Bb, the listener (provided he were not a professional musician) would confuse that with an exact transposition.

It is at this point that tonality enters the picture. Brief, novel, atonal melodies are remembered strictly in terms of their contour. That is, transpositions of such melodies are completely confused with same-contour imitations (Dowling and Fujitani, 1971). With tonal melodies confusion depends on tonal relationships. Transpositions of tonal melodies tend to be confused with same-contour "tonal answers" in the same key (C-Eb-Bb-C-G, in our example). Tonal imitations in other keys are confused with transpositions to the degree that their keys are similar to that of the original. The more remote the new key, the less the confusion. That is, F♯-A-E-F♯-C♯ is less likely to be confused with E-G♯-D♯-E-B than F-Ab-Eb-F-C is with Eb-G-D-Eb-Bb (Barlett and Dowling, 1979). Results like these lead me to believe that there are two components of what is stored in memory when we hear a novel tune (Dowling, 1978). We store the melodic contour with some indication of diatonic interval size, and we store a modal diatonic scale. New melodies are confused with the originals if their diatonic intervals are the same, even if they have been shifted to a new rung of the scale. If the scale is changed, the change is effective in eliminating confusion to the degree that the new scale is different from the old. Presumably waiting five minutes would eliminate this key-distance effect, while leaving intact the effectiveness of melodic contour. The key-distance effect is not due solely to the fact that new melodies in nearly related keys share more actual pitches with the originals. When we hear a melody, that seems to invoke in our minds a set of inferred pitches that might occur in that key. Violations in

146

the new melody of that inferred set of pitches make it easier to distinguish from the original (Dowling and Bartlett, 1979).

The picture that emerges of adult melody recognition by nonmusicians is that people remember the contours of melodies they hear without an exact notion of interval sizes between tones. Interval sizes can be reconstructed by comparing the contour to one of the overlearned scale systems the person knows—in our culture, major or minor. But if a novel melody just heard is repeated as a tonal imitation translated along the well-known scale, people are generally not able to detect the change in intervals. People are surprisingly good at remembering melodic contours they have heard. We have found that senior high school girls, after hearing a battery of twenty-five-second excerpts from Beethoven string quartets, were able to recognize same contour excerpts five minutes later with better than chance accuracy. They were unable, however, to discriminate between identical and transformed test items (Dowling and Bartlett, 1978).

Melody Recognition

We can now turn to the development of melody recognition abilities in the life of the individual. One issue that this discussion bears on is the issue of readiness—at what age are children ready to benefit from music training? There are two ways to apply developmental evidence to such an issue. One way is to look for evidence that the child at a given age already has the component skills required for learning an instrument. For example, we might want to know if the child is able to clap his hands in a regular rhythmic pattern. The second way to look for readiness is to see what happens when we begin training at a certain age. Even if the component skills we seek are apparently absent at a given age, it may be that they are very quickly acquired. Were we to find, for example, that a particular skill did not develop naturally until age twelve but nevertheless developed very rapidly with training down to age five, that would be a good reason to start training at five rather than twelve. However, we should always be very cautious in making generalizations about when children are ready to learn this or that skill. Some children are ready much earlier than the norm (for example, Mozart), and it would be doing them a disservice to make them wait for everyone else. Given the nature of our school systems, I suspect we err more often in the direction of unduly delaying the gifted rather than in the opposite direction.

Reading handbook chapters on auditory development from the 1940s and 1950s would lead you to believe that preschool children are abysmal in such skills as pitch discrimination and melody recognition. However, interacting for a while with three-year-olds would convince you that something was wrong with the experiments that led to such negative conclusions. Fortunately, psychologists have recently been doing better and better experiments that disclose the true nature of the child's abilities. A good example is a study by Chang and Trehub (1977a) who worked with five-month-olds, trying to find out if they would notice changes in melodic contour. When a baby is startled by a novel stimulus, its heart rate tends to decelerate. As the baby gets used to the stimulus after several repetitions, the heart rate gradually returns to normal. What Chang and Trehub did was to present a six-note melody over and over again to the babies so they would habituate to it. Then they shifted to either a transposition of that melody to a new key, or to a new arrangement of the notes in the transposition so as to change the contour. That is, in both cases the new stimulus consisted of a new set of pitches, different from those of the original stimulus. But in one case it was a transposition of the same melody and in the other case it was a new melody. The five-month-olds showed deceleration of their heart rate to the new melody, but not to the transposition, demonstrating a sensitivity to change in melodic contour. In a similar study Chang and Trehub (1977b) demonstrated sensitivity of five-month-olds to simple rhythm changes.

Though infants notice changes in melodic contour, the development of the stable pitch relationships of the music scale system takes several years of acculturation. By the age of eight, children are generally able to notice changes in melodies such as switching in midstream from major to minor (Imberty, 1969; Zenatti, 1969). But even by the age of five children discriminate between transpositions to near and remote keys (Bartlett and Dowling, 1979). Kindergarteners did not show an ability to discriminate between "Twinkle, Twinkle" (C-C-G-G-A-A-G) and a tonal imitation (E-E-B-B-C-C-B). But they did show a much greater tendency to reject tonal imitations in distantly related keys (for example, D♯-D♯-A♯-A♯-B-B-A♯) as opposed to nearly related keys (B-B-F♯-F♯-G-G-F♯). This suggests that even for the five-year-old, hearing a melody invokes an implicit set of pitches that might occur in it. The melody and the scale system are not so well learned yet that the child can reliably pick up on small changes of interval size that remain within the tonal system; but the child is able to notice gross changes in the scale system itself. This result is consistent with results that show that six-year-olds are able to use a stable internal pitch framework in other tasks. For example, when asked to remember a pair of pitches, subjects this age perform much better than when asked to remember a pair of loudnesses (Riley, McKee, Bell, and Schwartz, 1967). The dimension of pitch seems to lend itself more naturally to absolute anchor points than the more relative dimensions of loudness. If a person is able to retain stable anchors on the pitch dimension over a period of years we say he has absolute pitch. But even five- and six-year-olds (and nonmusician adults) retain fairly stable anchors over periods of minutes.

First graders are generally quite good at discriminating repetitions of the same, novel five-note melody from different contour melodies, performing at about the seventy-five percent level (where chance would be fifty percent). In such a task the fact that the repetition contains the same pitches as the original helps, especially since the different melodies all contained some different pitches. But even this good performance improves dramatically with music training. First graders who have had seven months of class strings or piano instruction perform almost perfectly on such a task—better than ninety-five percent correct. In the more difficult task of discriminating between repetitions of melodies and permutations of order of the same notes (that is, changes in contour without changes in pitch), first graders also show marked improvement with training, from sixty-five percent to seventy-five percent. Similar gains occur with training for third graders. It is interesting that for neither task is performance by third graders without training better than for first graders with training. That is, music training in the first graders triggered improvements in auditory perceptual abilities that would not occur in normal maturation for at least another two years. And there is every reason to believe that once the first-graders had as memory for a temporal order of events, that those skills would generalize to other areas of the child's cognitive life.

References

Attneave, F., and R. K. Olson. Pitch as medium: A new approach to psychophysical scaling. *American Journal of Psychology*, 1971, *84*, 147–166.

Bartlett, J. C., and W. J. Dowling. The recognition of transposed melodies: A key-distance effect in developmental perspective. Book in preparation, 1979.

Chang, H., and S. E. Trehub. Auditory processing of relational information by young infants. *Journal of Experimental Child Psychology*, 1977, *24*, 324–331. (a)

_____. Infants' perception of temporal grouping in auditory patterns. *Child Development*, 1977, *48*, 1666–1670. (b)

Dowling, W. J. Scale and contour: Two components of a theory of memory for melodies. *Psychological Review*, 1978, *85*, 341–354

_____. Musical scales and psychophysical scales: Their psychological reality. In T. Rich and R. Falck (Eds.), *Cross-cultural approaches to music: Essays in honor of Mieczyslaw Kolinski*, in press.

Dowling, W. J., and J. C. Bartlett. *Memory for Beethoven quartets: Effects of excerpt length and structure.* Paper presented to the Psychonomic Society, San Antonio, November 1978.

_____. *A key-distance effect in melody recognition: Its development and dependence on inferred sets of pitches.* Paper presented to the Psychonomic Society, Phoenix, November 1979.

Dowling, W. J., and D. S. Fujitani. Contour, interval, and pitch recognition in memory for melodies. *Journal of the Acoustical Society of America*, 1971, *49*, 524– 531.

Francès, R. *La perception de la musique* [The perception of music]. Paris: Vrin, 1958.

Helmholtz, H. von. *On the sensations of tone.* New York: Dover, 1954.

Imberty, M. *L'acquisition des structures tonales chez l'enfant* [The acquisition of tonal structures in the child]. Paris: Klincksieck, 1969.

James, W. *Talks to Teachers on Psychology.* New York: Holt, 1910.

Miller, G. A. The magic number seven, plus or minus two. *Psychological Review*, 1956, *63*, 81–97.

Riley, D. A., J. P. McKee, D. D. Bell, and C. R. Schwartz. Auditory discrimination in children: The effect of relative and absolute instructions on retention and transfer. *Journal of Experimental Psychology*, 1967, *73*, 581–588.

Zenatti, A. Le developpement genetique de la perception musicale. [The genetic development of musical perception]. *Monographies Francaises de Psychologie*, 17, 1969.

Response

David Brian Williams

Professor Dowling has provided an excellent overview of the research on melodic memory. He makes valuable references to current research in this area and extends the research I reported at the first meeting of this symposium. I want to make some general comments and then focus on specific points in Dowling's research.

As knowledge seekers we obtain information from our personal experience, authority, and from observation—collecting data. Alice, with her adventures in wonderland, sought knowledge from authority. Her findings touch on what we are about and where we are going from here.

First, the Caterpillar (Lewis Carroll, *Alice's Adventures in Wonderland*). . . . "Who are you," said the Caterpillar. This was not an encouraging opening for a conversation. Alice replied rather shyly. "I—I hardly know sir, just at present—at least I know who I was when I got up this morning, but I think I must have changed several times since then" (p. 59).

And then, the Cat. . . . "Cheshire Puss . . . . Would you tell me, please, which way I ought to walk from here?" "That depends a good deal where you want to get," said the Cat . . . . ". . . so long as I get somewhere," Alice added as an explanation. "Oh, you're sure to do that," said the Cat, "if you only walk long enough" (p. 87).

When I first read Jay Dowling's paper I had sensations of *deja vu*. Where had I heard these theories before? His primary points, it seems to me, are to say that (1) cognitive pro-

149

cessing of music is a necessary component in what we term the music aesthetic experience and (2) that what we process in music is dependent upon learned context, learned music structure—a process which becomes more and more refined as our music experiences expand. Both Dowling and Roger Shepard touch on the notion that critical evaluation of music depends upon a balance between old and new experiences. As Shepard suggests, an "appreciation for the departures in music." As Dowling expanded, this comparative process depends on two factors: memory structure for storing past events or music experiences and memory process for attending, retrieving, selecting, and comparing music events.

What interests me is that these same points have been made, though perhaps in different terms and settings, in music education, in music aesthetics, in music theory. Cognitive criticism is discussed in contemporary music aesthetics.

Music education methodology is oriented more to teaching processes and concepts with less product oriented methodology. Henry Cady made this point well in the recent *MEJ* article on *Seeking a Theory for Music Education*. He speaks of the "recent change in concern for processes rather than products as the basis for music learning . . . our concern has shifted, at least a little, from how to teach products to how to provide students with the knowledge of music elements so they can create their own music" (p. 36). A 1977 article in the *Journal of Music Theory* by Lerdahl and Jackendorf attempted to develop a formal theory of music based on a "description of the musical intuitions of an educated listener." They spoke of music understanding as a listener finding the best coherent structural description that can be associated with the sequence of pitch-time events (p. 115). Above all, both Shepard and Dowling have considerable overtones of Leonard B. Meyer in their papers—his concepts of completion

and closure for example (see *Emotion and Meaning in Music,* 1956).

If I am being interpreted as sounding critical, that is not my intent. My point is that we have "changed since this morning," we are "going somewhere," and we will continue to if we are patient and continue to "walk long enough." The healthy state-of-affairs is that in Dowling's paper alone we have added information in the form of experimental research and systematically obtained data to enhance our perspective of what we as musicians practice and theorize. We must continue to generate such data to enable us to re-examine our theory and to re-examine our practice. We have so little experimental research data upon which to base our pedagogical judgments. Though we still have a lot of walking to do, it impresses me that a new wave of interest has developed in psychomusicology research as the necessary complement to music education.

In his book, *The Body Is the Hero*, Ronald Glasser (1976) makes the point that the rewards of research are slow in coming. The book deals with the history of immunology. The point is appropriate here. "As with any sustained human effort," Glasser writes, "medicine has seen a constant revision of 'knowledge' by facts, the new replacing the old, and the old forever going down hard." Only in the last twenty to thirty years, after centuries of research, can we begin to truly understand the nature of how the body fights disease (p. 29).

If we are to speak of implications for the research reported here—Dowling's research in melodic memory, for example—we need a framework for dissemination and synthesis. Cady's article (1979) focused on one critical element needed before theories of music instruction can be developed. That element is a "hierarchy of concepts and a hierarchy of prior conditions for each concept." Jay Dowling's information concerning melodic memory will perhaps have its most useful imme-

150

diate instructional application in this context, assisting in the ordering of music skills and concepts based on our knowledge of memory processing capabilities.

Now to some specific points of interest that have peaked my curiosity and deserve some discussion:

1. Contour and tonality have been proposed by Dowling as structural factors in music processing. What are the others that make up the multidimensional music event? Can we find a universal set that can be applied to analyzing music response in all cultures? Dowling in other research has suggested rhythm as a structural factor.

2. Shepard noted the wide degree of variability in music response. We will get quite different behavior from a music task depending, in part, on the music experience of a person. However, we frequently stress normative generalization in our research—Dowling's paper did this; I do this in my own research. Shepard's comment that "pooling data from individual listeners prior to analysis is likely to obscure important patterns in the data" has rather potent implications for research methodology in psychomusicology and music education.

3. The predisposition for humans to respond affectively to structured patterns of time and pitch that Roger Shepard mentions in his paper. The psychologist, Robert Bolles speaks of "species specific behaviors." The musicologist, John D. Blacking has suggested, as did Shepard, that music is a species specific behavior of humankind, hence, found in all cultures. If this is an anthropological fact, then why are we having problems selling music education in the United States? I agree, the "evolutionary basis of such predisposition would be a fascinating topic for discussion."

4. Dowling's conclusions regarding contour processing relate to our research in the psychomusicology lab at Illinois State University. He suggests that there are two components to melodic memory for a "novel" tune. We store a melodic contour with some indication of diatonic interval size, and we store a modal diatonic scale. This supports the theory proposed in my paper that most melodic information is stored as contour, not discrete tones or perfect copies.

We have also found in our research that students retain contour for novel patterns (tonal better than atonal) much better than for discrete pitch relationships. In one task, they were to remember seven-tone melodies in the presence of twenty random tones and were then tested on their ability to make pitch matching discriminations about those seven tones. Performance was below chance for all seven tones and for tonal and atonal melodies. Pitch interfered with pitch. The same presentation was used in a subsequent study, but this time students were asked to remember the contour and after the twenty random tones to select the contour that best described the melody. Performance was above chance (sixty to eighty percent) in all conditions and contour for tonal melodies was remembered significantly better than contour for atonal melodies. These data are compatible with Dowling's theory—tonality and contour appear to be significant structural variables in melodic memory.

However, in the first task, we found evidence of rhythm chunking, 3 + 4 and 4 + 3, for the atonal patterns. This suggests that in the absence of scaleness or tonality, other structural determinants take over.

In closing, let me return to the idea that instructional problems in music education, in part, can be approached by an analysis of what happens between the time a music sound is encoded and when some report is finally made—what happens along the continuum of cognitive activity. Within this theoretical framework, research data continue to refine our ability to predict and understand the processing of music along this continuum.

Individual Differences in the Perception of Musical Pitch

Roger N. Shepard

The Problem of Musical Competency

Viewed in the context of human perceptual, cognitive, and productive competencies, our specifically musical competencies seem to present something of a puzzle. Visual-spatial abilities, for example, serve a clear adaptive function, not only for us but for a wide variety of other "higher" organisms as well. One can readily understand how the advantages conferred by such visual-spatial competencies would have been shaped selectively during the eons of biological evolution in a complex three-dimensional world. And even our much more recently developed linguistic competencies, though not so widely shared with other species, can be seen to contribute to the survival of the richly social human species.

It is not surprising then that competencies as valuable to human survival as the visual-spatial and linguistic should by now be essentially fully present in all normal members of all human cultures (except, that is, for those individual members who failed to gain or who lost these normal competencies as a consequence of some specific, usually identifiable abnormality, accident, or disease). True, refined tests of human abilities reveal considerable variations in performance on spatial and verbal subtests even among normal individuals (see Pawlik, 1966). And true, in the recent laboratory studies on such cognitive-spatial operations as "mental rotation," my students and I have typically found that the rate of such mental processes varies over a two-to-one range even in normal college students (Cooper and Shepard, 1973; Metzler and Shepard, 1974). Still, the *qualitative* pattern of the data is strikingly similar for all subjects. And, all such normal individuals are generally successful in finding their ways about, in identifying and manipulating complex three-dimensional objects, and in communicating about situations, events, or intentions.

Musical competence, like linguistic competence, seems to be an almost uniquely human development. However, the evolutionary basis for this development is much less clear than for the development of either the visual-spatial or linguistic competencies.

One can point to various social, motivating, and facilitating functions that music plays in most societies, but it seems difficult to explain how it serves these functions without assuming that the individuals that make up the society already have a predisposition to respond affectively to structured patterns of time and pitch. It is the evolutionary basis of such predispositions that remains to be explicated.

The fact that music in some form is ubiquitous in human culture indicates that these musical predispositions, or at least some more basic rhythmic-auditory predispositions, have contributed to human survival. But the relative difficulty in identifying exactly what their contribution has been suggests that their contribution has not been as essential as have the contributions of spatial and linguistic competencies. If this line of reasoning is correct, then musical competencies might be expected to show more variation from individual to individual than do the more essential spatial and linguistic competencies. In this respect musical predispositions may be like color vision. Although color vision plays an undeniable role in aesthetic experience, it plays an apparently less than crucial role in human survival, and it is known to be subject to wide and indeed genetically determined individual variations (Jaeger, 1972).

Structural Constraints

During the past twenty years, the pendulum of psychological theorizing has swung far away from its extreme behavioristic position, in which the organism was in effect treated as a totally plastic, structureless entity whose eventual predispositions are shaped almost entirely by the contingencies that it encounters in its external environment. Now the emphasis is on inferred internal structure (see Shepard, 1964a) that, following the findings of marked interspecies differences (Bitterman, 1964; Breland and Breland, 1961; Lenneberg, 1967) and the influential arguments of the linguist Noam Chomsky, is often thought to be largely innate. As typically happens, however, changes in thinking originating within a particular discipline are slow to percolate into neighboring disciplines.

For example, many modern composers evidently hold to a view of human cognition that is much more consonant with earlier, behavioristic theories in psychology than with current cognitive-structural theories. Implicit in their efforts, there often seems to be the presupposition that any arbitrary structure can serve as the basis for music composition just as well as the standard Western diatonic system, say. We only need a sufficient amount of exposure to any such new system, they seem to believe, and we will come to appreciate it just as much as the old, diatonic system. Such a view may well be mistaken.

Certainly the visual system seems to have evolved to deal with just the kinds of transformations that occur in a three-dimensional world of rigid and semi-rigid objects (Shepard, 1980). We can still learn to manage if the input is altered in a way that preserves the essential character of these transformations, as in those experiments in which a subject wore a pair of inverting spectacles for several days (Stratton, 1897), but we can never learn to deal with an input that disrupts these regularities, as when we must view the world, instead, through a bundle of scrambled fiber optics.

The diatonic and related systems that have stood the test of time in many different cultures are not arbitrary systems but systems that meet certain basic needs for cognitive processing, such as the requirement that there be fixed and perceptually identifiable reference points with respect to which there can be rest or motion, tension or resolution, and the dynamics that give music its vitality. The structural basis for such systems has deep cognitive and group-theoretic roots (Balzano, 1978; Dowling, 1978; Rothenberg, 1963). It is thus no accident that the diatonic system underlies the great majority of music played and listened to in the Western world today (whether classical, popular, folk, jazz, or rock), and has recently been identified in the earliest archaeological records, dating back some 3000 years (Kilmer, Crocker, and Brown, 1976).

Nor is it an accident that in cultures, such as those of India or Africa, in which structural richness has reached a development in the temporal domain comparable to that achieved in the pitch domain of Western culture, rhythmic constraints are quite analogous to the scale constraints of Western music. Indeed, in certain West African cultures the rhythmic system is, at a deep level, formally isomorphic to our own diatonic system for pitch (Pressing, 1979).

Of course, any rigidly fixed system of constraints eventually becomes too limiting and tiresome. Composers and improvisers thus seek to depart in one way or another from established habits of composition and generation. Such departures are not only refreshing and even exciting, they are essential to the very life of music. I claim, however, that these departures are appreciated because they are perceived *as departures*. Without an implicit underlying scheme, from which to depart, the "departures" would necessarily remain unappreciated and the "music" would fail to rise above a cacophony of random sounds.

Such playing off against an underlying scheme has been regarded as fundamental in cognitive psychology since Bartlett (1932) and Woodworth (1938) wrote about "schema with correction." It can be discerned in all of the arts and, within music, it includes the tension-building delay of return to the tonic, the unexpected shifts of key or rhythmic syncopations of classical music and jazz, the subtle and complex rhythmic variations within a given "tala" of Indian music (Deva, 1973) and many of the more radical experiments of twentieth-century composition. Indeed, a few sophisticated and avant-garde composers can, by playing off of departures from departures from departures, work their irreversible way out onto a very thin limb of the tree of possible musics. It is, I believe, an endeavor that carries with it the seeds of its own eventual collapse (cf., Bennett, 1978). In any case, recent history has shown that few, even among music lovers, are prepared to follow that far from the more sturdy and familiar supporting branches. There may be good reasons for this if, as I conjecture, the

tree of possible musics is rooted in deeply structured grounds of the human mind.

Individual Differences

The extent of the gap that exists between those on the forefront of musical innovation and the listening public was brought home to me during a 1978 concert of the San Francisco Symphony. In the middle of the usual classical fare, Ozawa turned the podium over to a young composer to conduct the performance of one of that composer's recent works. I and a few others I talked with during the intermission found this new work to be sufficiently exciting to have made worthwhile an otherwise uninspiring evening. To our astonishment, however, toward the middle of the performance of that new piece most of the audience grew restless and a few individuals began to boo—a response that became quite general upon the completion of the piece. (How ironic that these same people will happily sit through a Beethoven symphony that was itself booed on the occasion of its first performance!)

The ideas I have tried to sketch in this introduction provide some basis for understanding why this gap between the innovators and the consumers may be even wider in music than in some of the other arts. If there are especially large individual differences in musical predispositions, these differences will only be amplified by processes in which those with the most highly developed musical schemata end up by working their ways further and further out on the branches of departures from departures, while those with the least elaborated schemata hold fast to the security of the main trunk of musical form.

More to the point here, if there are marked individual differences in the predispositions of individuals to appreciate various aspects of rhythm, pitch, melody, harmony, and timbre, then a fuller understanding of these differences should be relevant to music education. Again, I note the swing of the pendulum of psychological thinking. When I was in elementary school the prevailing view seemed to be that all students were equally capable of mastering music as well as any

154

other subject; the fact that there were always some boys who persevered in surreptitiously reading comic books hidden within the music books during the music period was interpreted entirely as an absence of motivation—not of ability. There is, however, accumulating evidence for marked differences not only in the purely sensory discrimination of small differences, for example in pitch, but also in the more cognitive interpretation of music patterns and relations.

Elsewhere (Shepard, 1979), I have argued that, although other music attributes (loudness, tempo, timbre, and texture) clearly play significant roles in the aesthetic appreciation of music, pitch and rhythm are the "indispensable attributes" (see Kubovy, 1980) of music and, alone, afford the structural richness essential to music's power. In this paper I focus primarily on individual differences in the perception of pitch.

Psychoacoustic Versus Cognitive Studies of Pitch

The study of the perception of pitch and of relationships between pitches has generally been approached from one of two quite different traditions: the psychoacoustic or the cognitive-musical. The psychoacoustic approach has typically focused on simple, physically specifiable properties of tones isolated from any musical context—properties of frequency, separation in log frequency, or simplicity of integer ratios of frequencies. The results of such studies have provided some rather precise information about how the ear responds to isolated tones. They have been less informative with regard to how the brain responds to music. Music theory suggests that the perception of music, as opposed to isolated tones, may rely on the listener's sensitivity to different and structurally richer factors determined by tonal and diatonic organization. Such principles are useful in explaining the cognitive phenomena of reference point, motion, tension, and resolution that underlie the dynamic force of virtually all tonal music. They have, however, been subjected to relatively little systematic laboratory investigation or quantitative formulation.

Until very recently most of the studies that were carried out in the laboratory were carried out from a psychoacoustic standpoint. They were therefore dominated by the assumption that pitch is a simply psychological counterpart of the single physical dimension of frequency and, accordingly, varies along a single psychological dimension of what has come to be called pitch "height." The problem of pitch was in this way reduced to the psychophysical one of determining the functional form of the presumably monotonic relationship between physical frequency and psychological pitch (Stevens and Volkmann, 1940; Stevens, Volkmann, and Newmann, 1937).

However, from a musical standpoint, this psychoacoustic approach has been quite unsatisfactory. First, the functional form of the psychophysical relationship obtained from judgments of pure tones without any musical context has led to scales of pitch, such as Stevens' *mel* scale, that do not preserve the musically desirable property of invariance under transposition—a property that is restored in scales that have subsequently been constructed on the basis of judgments in a suitable musical context (Attneave and Olson, 1971). Second, no such unidimensional representation of pitch can itself account for the musically significant fact that within music, tones separated by certain special intervals, especially the octave, perfect fifth, and major third, are perceived to be more closely related than tones at somewhat smaller separations in terms of log frequency (Krumhansl and Shepard, 1979). Third, and most important for my purposes here, the representation of pitch on a simple, linear, one-dimensional scale does not give us the degrees of freedom we need to represent the complexity of the ways in which individuals differ in their perception of pitch (Krumhansl and Shepard, 1979).

Why, one might wonder, has it taken psychologists so long to come around to a musical approach to music? One possible answer is suggested by data reported some sixty years ago by Carl Seashore (1919). Those data, presented in Figure 1, indicate that as a group, psychologists are appreciably less

155

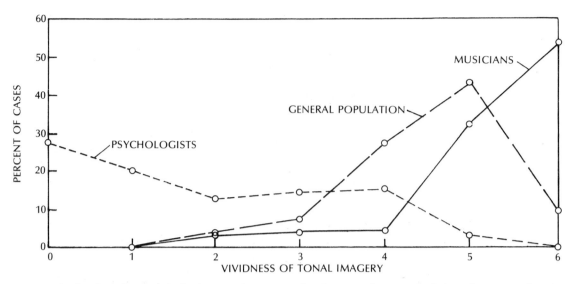

Figure 1. Indication that psychologists as a group tend to be even less musical than the general population. (Redrawn from Seashore, 1919.)

musical than even a random sample of the general population.

Individual Differences in the Perception of Pitch

Evidence on discrimination of pitch height. In his early studies of musical talent, Seashore (1919) had already found that the minimum difference in frequency that can be detected in two successive tones varies as much as 200-fold between different listeners. However, I was unaware of these early results when I first embarked on a study of pitch perception in the early 1960s. As a result, I was astonished when I found that of fifty unselected colleagues and assistants that I tested at the Bell Telephone Laboratories, only sixty-two percent could consistently report whether the second of two sinusoidal tones was higher or lower than the first even when the two tones differed by somewhat more than a semitone (specifically by one-tenth of an octave rather than by one-twelfth). Indeed, the accuracy of several of the listeners with otherwise normal hearing was no better than chance. I had to conclude that "the term 'tone deaf' may well be applicable to an appreciable fraction of the population," but noted, on the basis of information supplied

by these subjects, that those "who expressed an interest in music or who played a musical instrument generally made few, if any, errors" (Shepard, 1964b, p. 2350).

A major purpose of that study was to provide more compelling evidence that pitch cannot be adequately represented by a unidimensional scale of the sort proposed by psychophysicists such as Stevens. Toward this end, I used the general purpose music synthesis program just developed by Mathews (1963) to generate a special set of complex tones with the paradoxical property that when the tones are played over and over in a repeating sequence they are heard as endlessly increasing in pitch (Shepard, 1964b; Shepard and Zajac, 1965; Shepard, 1970). This illusion thus provided a concrete demonstration of the circular component of "tone chroma" that various investigators have suggested must be added to the linear component of pitch height in order to explain the augmented perceptual similarity at the octave (Bachem, 1954; Shepard, 1964b; Deutsch, 1973; Balzano, 1977). These special tones, which suppressed the height component of pitch entirely, could thus be represented as points on a circle in such a way that, for listeners with good pitch discrimi-

156

nation, each clockwise neighbor was heard as higher in pitch. (See the circular representation reconstructed from the actual data in Shepard, 1978.)

However, listeners who confused the nearby pure tones in the already described pretest also tended to confuse the complex tones that were adjacent around the circle. In Figure 2, the results are displayed by the solid circles connected by heavy lines for the twenty-six of the fifty subjects who made no errors with the pure tones (Group 1) and by the open circles connected by light lines for fourteen subjects who made the largest number of errors on that pretest (Group 3). The re-sults for the ten intermediate subjects (Group 2), which are not plotted in the figure, fell between the curves shown for the two extreme groups. The heavy curve shows that all of the twenty-six most accurate subjects always judged the clockwise neighbor of each tone as higher than it in pitch. In contrast, the light curve shows that this direction of the difference in pitch between such neighboring tones was detected only about seventy-three percent of the time by the ten least accurate listeners. Note, however, that their discrimination improved when the tones were farther apart around the circle until, beyond three steps of separation, their per-

Figure 2. Fraction of presentations for which the second tone of a pair was judged higher (or lower) than the first as a function of the number of steps by which the second tone was displaced from the first in a clockwise direction in the circular representation. The heavy and light lines are for the subjects who were previously found to be most or least accurate, respectively, in judging relative pitches of pure tones. (From Shepard, 1964b.)

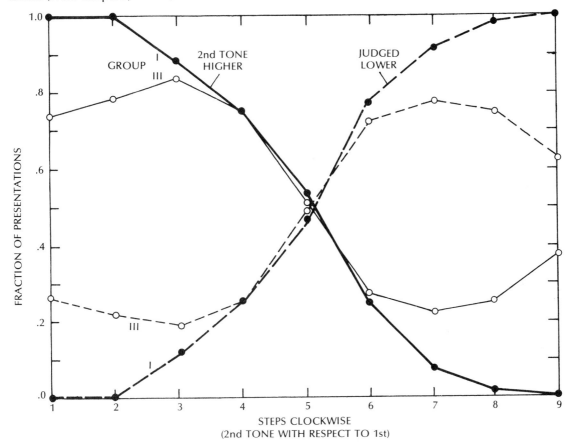

157

formance followed that of the most discriminating subjects in decreasing to chance as the tones (at five steps) were diametrically opposite around the circle and, so, ambiguous as to clockwise or counterclockwise direction of separation.

About twenty percent of the listeners have difficulty in discriminating the direction of pitch difference between tones separated by as much as a semitone, though their accuracy improves with greater separations. These listeners generally report having had little or no background or interest in music. There is also a demonstrable circular component of tone chroma in perceived pitch, which cannot be accommodated within a purely one-dimensional rectilinear representation of pitch and which may go some way toward accommodating the long acknowledged phenomenon of "octave equivalence" (Boring, 1942, pp. 376, 380; Licklider, 1951, pp. 1003–1004; Allen, 1967; Balzano, 1977).

Previous Evidence for
the Influence of Tonality

Gordon asked, "Do we attend differently to key and tonality as we listen and give meaning to music? This question has been almost totally neglected by psychoacoustic research into the perception of musical tones and, specifically, of pitch. It is the kind of question that has recently led a few of us more cognitively oriented psychologists to reopen the question of the perception of pitch, particularly in a musical context—a context that might predispose a musical listener to interpret the presented tones in terms of an underlying "key" and "tonality."

As Krumhansl and I note in a just-completed report (Krumhansl and Shepard, 1979), empirical evidence for the importance of tonality and musical scale can be found in a number of recent studies. Cohen (1978) showed that musical subjects, after hearing a short excerpt from a musical composition, are able to generate the associated diatonic scale with some accuracy. Other investigators (Dewar, 1974; Dewar, Cuddy, and Mewhort, 1977) found that memory is better for tones contained in sequences conforming to diatonic structure than for tones in sequences not conforming to this structure. Dewar (1974) found that changes in musical sequences that took such sequences outside the diatonic scale were more easily detected than changes that left them within the diatonic scale, and Dowling's (1978) subjects had difficulty in distinguishing exact transpositions (a constant shift in log frequencies, but necessarily departing somewhat from the original diatonic scale) from contour-preserving shifts along that same diatonic scale (changing the intervals somewhat, but keeping within the scale). Cohen (1975) and Attneave and Olson (1961) found that subjects are better able to recognize and to produce transpositions of tonal or familiar sequences than other less well-structured sequences. Finally, in a series of experiments undertaken subsequent to the experiments that I am about to review here, Krumhansl (1979) demonstrated that in an explicitly tonal context, the pattern of perceived similarities between tones was highly specific to the tonality of that context and recognition memory was better for diatonic than for nondiatonic tones.

Since tonality and musical scale have been described as constituting the single most fundamental factor in musical organization by music theorists (for example, Piston, 1941; Ratner, 1962), it is not surprising that evidence for the importance of such a factor should emerge from laboratory studies. What is remarkable is that this emergence did not take place until the mid 1970s.

The Tonal Hierarchy

Krumhansl and I undertook our own recent studies of pitch perception motivated by what we perceived as a noticeable gap between the richness and power of the tonal structure implied by music theory, on the one hand, and detailed experimental demonstrations and quantifications of that structure, on the other. Studies of the perception of musical intervals clearly had demonstrated systematic effects of simple separation in log frequency and, in some cases, of octave equivalence, but the hierarchy of tonal functions or stabilities that is so strongly to be expected on the basis of the music-theoretic

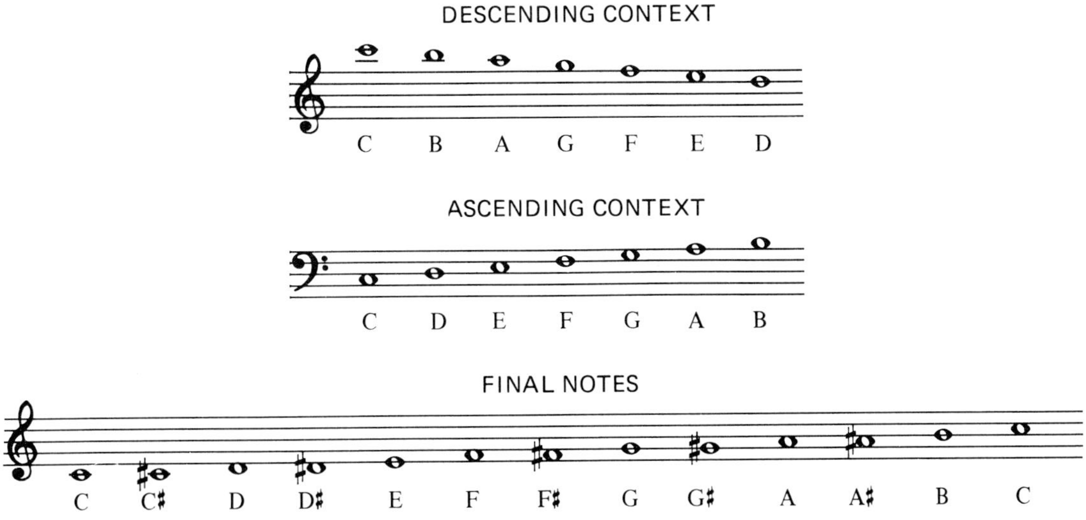

Figure 3. The descending and ascending context sequences of seven tones of the C-major scale, and the thirteen chromatic alternative test tones from the intervening octave that might immediately follow the context sequence. (From Krumhansl and Shepard, 1979.)

notions of tonality and diatonicism had curiously failed to assert itself in laboratory experiments.

Our experiments were based on the conjecture that previous failures to bring out sharply the structure of tonal functions that is expected within the diatonic system might stem from a failure to meet three conditions simultaneously: (1) The tones must be presented within a musical context that strongly and unambiguously establishes the tonal framework with respect to which all test tones are to be interpreted. (2) Detailed quantitative information must be obtained for each of the alternative tones of interest relative to this tonal framework. (3) And, most importantly, the resulting data must be analyzed separately for individual listeners who may differ widely in musical experience, training, or aptitude and, so, vary markedly in their responsiveness to the experimentally introduced musical context.

In our experiments (Krumhansl and Shepard, 1979), we established the tonal context by playing the seven tones of an ascending or descending major scale (omitting the eighth tone an octave from the first that nor-

mally completes the sequence). We then followed this context by a single tone from somewhere in the octave range extending from the omitted tonic tone that would normally have completed the context series to the tone just one octave beyond that tone, as shown in Figure 3. We asked listeners to rate how well each test tone fit in with or completed the preceding context sequence on a scale from 1 for "Very Bad" to 7 for "Very Good." We hoped that the judgments obtained for different tones within the test octave would provide direct, quantitative indication of the stability or tonal function of each tone relative to the tonal framework induced by the preceding context.

Earlier work suggested that a number of factors might influence such judgments of scale completion. First, if pitch height is an important factor, then tones close in frequency to the context tones should be preferred to tones farther from the context tones. Second, if the tones separated by an octave are equivalent or closely related, then tones in this relation at both the high and the low ends of the octave range of test tones should be judged as approximately equally good com-

159

pletions. Third, if the detailed music-theoretic notions concerning a hierarchy of tonal functions within the diatonic system are valid, then the most preferred tones, following the tonic and its octave, should be the other tones of the major triad chord (the third and, especially, the fifth degrees of the scale), followed by the other diatonic tones implied by the scale context and, finally, the nondiatonic.

Krumhansl and I found evidence for the influence of all of these factors. Most significantly, for the more musically sophisticated of our listeners, the tonal hierarchy, which had eluded psychoacoustic investigators for so long, emerged in sharp relief from the judgments obtained within a tonal context. The psychophysical dimension of pitch height had almost no influence on the listeners' judgments of the relations between tones. Instead, the octave and unison were almost equally preferred, followed by the perfect fifth, major third, and other tones within the key defined by the tonal context and, finally, the remaining tones not in that key. But this was true only for the more musical listeners. For, as I shall show in the next section, there were marked individual differences.

In a second experiment we used essentially the same procedure except for two changes: To the thirteen chromatic tones separated by half-tone steps within the octave test range, we added the twelve quarter-tones half way between these to obtain a more finely graded series of twenty-five test tones. And, instead of generating the tones by means of the flute stop on an electronic organ (as in the first experiment), we used a computer to generate pure sinusoids. Now the context, which again consisted of the ascending or descending diatonic scale on each trial, was followed by any one of the twenty-five tones in the octave range falling between middle C (261.6Hz) and C' an octave above (523.2 Hz).

The ratings for the interpolated quarter tones were not lower still than the ratings for the standard half-tone steps. Instead, ratings for these interpolated tones generally were close to the average of the ratings for the two neighboring half tones. This result suggests that the listeners were unable to distinguish clearly between tones differing by no more than a twenty-fourth part of an octave—at least under the conditions of this experiment, in which the tones themselves were free of harmonics, and in which the test tone was presented after the context sequence and within a different octave. As Dowling (1978) suggests, there may be cognitive-psychological reasons why melodies in most human cultures are constructed using a restricted set of discrete pitches. For, as he notes, this set typically contains from five to seven scale-step categories within each octave, as might be expected on the basis of Miller's (1956) well-known generalization concerning the limitation of the human capacity for categorical identification to seven plus-or-minus two categories. Just as the perceptual interpretation of sounds as speech depends on the categorical assimilation of those continuously variable sounds to an underlying discrete set of phonemes (Liberman, Cooper, Shankweiler, and Studdert-Kennedy, 1967), the perceptual interpretation of sounds as music may depend on the categorical assimilation of those continuously variable sounds to an underlying set of tonal steps (Blechner, 1977; Burns and Ward, 1978; Halpern and Zatorre, 1978; Locke and Kellar, 1973; Siegel and Siegel, 1977a, 1977b) arranged, perhaps, in what I am calling the tonal hierarchy.

Otherwise, the rating profiles showed many of the same characteristics as those of the first experiment, indicating again that pitch height, octave equivalence, and the tonal functions of the pitches are important factors underlying the listeners' judgments. Despite the use in this experiment of the relatively less musical sinusoidal tones containing no overtone structure, most listeners showed some degree of octave equivalence and at least some of the listeners provided evidence for the hierarchy of tonal functions, with the tonic the most preferred scale completion, followed by the third and fifth scale degrees, the other scale tones, and finally the nonscale tones. The fact that separation in pitch height was generally stronger while the more structural factors of octave equivalence and tonal hierarchy were weaker in this second experiment is consistent with our gener-

160

al supposition that these structural factors tend to emerge only to the extent that the context is perceived as music. It is also possible that the inclusion of the unconventional quarter tones tended to confuse and hence weaken the listeners' maintenance of an orderly correspondence between the test tones in this experiment and in the listeners' internal tonal system, which presumably makes no provision for such interpolated tones. We tentatively concluded that the harmonics usually contained in musical pitches may contribute to, although are probably not necessary for, the extraction by the listener of the musically important relationship between tones.

Individual Differences in Krumhansl and Shepard's First Experiment

Our first experiment included an original set of twenty-three listeners and a subse-

quently added twenty-fourth listener who was of interest because she had a much more extensive musical background than any of our original listeners and, also, had absolute pitch. In addition to rating the presented tones, all listeners filled out a short questionnaire concerning their musical training and experience.

The ratings of the test tones given by any listener can be presented graphically as a profile plotted over the horizontally arranged sequence of thirteen tones in the octave test range from C to C'. If we exclude for the moment the subsequently added twenty-fourth listener, we can say that twenty-two of the twenty-three original response profiles showed one of the three general patterns displayed in Figures 5, 6, and 7. We computed correlations between the data for each pair of these twenty-three listeners and then analyzed the resulting matrix of correlations by

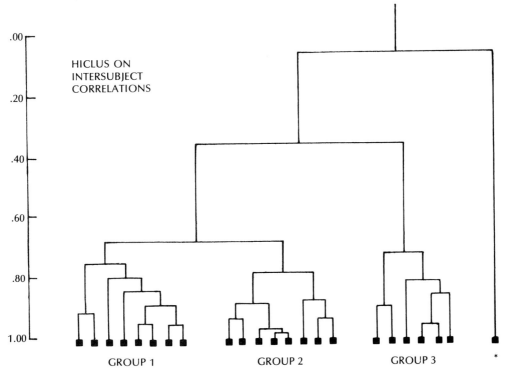

Figure 4. Hierarchical clustering (compactness or complete-link method) of the first 23 listeners in Experiment 1, based on the matrix of correlations between rating profiles for all pairs of listeners. (From Krumhansl and Shepard, 1979.)

means of a hierarchical clustering procedure (Johnson, 1967). The clustering solution yielded three groups of listeners and a single unclassified subject, as shown in Figure 4. These more objective results essentially were in complete agreement with our original classification.

Table 1 summarizes the information that the listeners in these three groups provided in a questionnaire about the extent of their musical experience and training. The differences between the extreme groups (1 and 3) were statistically significant according to *t* tests. As can be seen, there was a close relationship between extent of musical background and pattern of judgment as reflected in group membership.

The average scale completion judgments for the thirteen final tones for Group 1 listeners are plotted for both ascending and descending contexts in Figure 5. These eight listeners manifested a clear preference for the low and high Cs over all other tones. In addition there was a preference for scale tones other than the tonic (D, E, F, G, A, B) over

Table 1. Musical Experience of Subjects

	Number in group	Years instruction	Years performing
Group 1	8	7.4	5.6
Group 2	8	5.5	3.3
Group 3	6	.7	.0

the nonscale tones (C♯, D♯, F♯, G♯, A♯). Among the scale tones, D and B, which are the scale tones adjacent to the tonic C, were judged to be relatively good scale completions, as was the fifth degree of the scale, G. The profiles for ascending and descending scale contexts were similar; the ratings for the tones showed very little dependence on whether the scale context was ascending or descending. In particular, both high and low Cs were judged to be equally good completions of scales.

Group 2 listeners, whose average responses are shown in Figure 6, showed a strong preference for the two Cs over all other eleven tones in the octave range, giving a

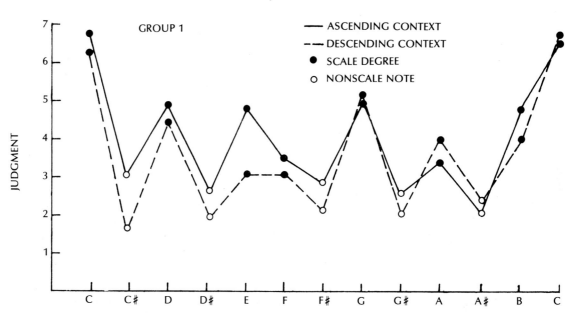

Figure 5. Mean rating profiles for Group 1 listeners. The mean rated goodness of each test note as a completion of the preceding context sequence is plotted separately for ascending and descending contexts. (From Krumhansl and Shepard, 1979.)

162

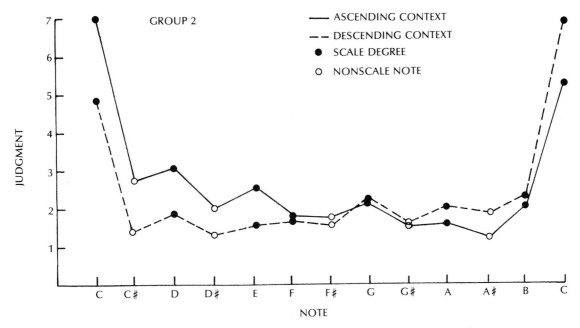

Figure 6. Mean rating profiles for Group 2 listeners. (From Krumhansl and Shepard, 1979.)

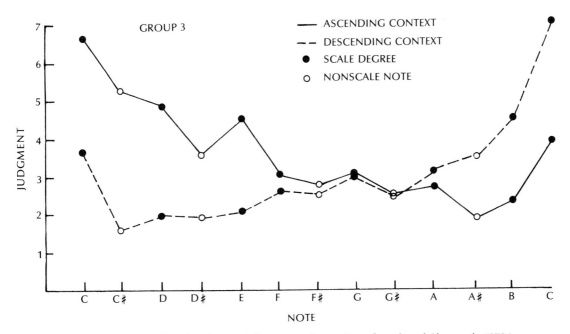

Figure 7. Mean rating profiles for Group 3 listeners. (From Krumhansl and Shepard, 1979.)

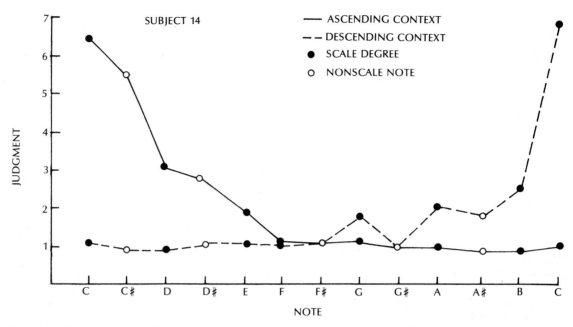

Figure 8. Mean rating profile for the one listener in Group 3 who showed no increase at the octave.

deep U-shaped pattern to the profile. In addition, there was a small, but significant, preference for the scale tones other than the tonic over the nonscale tones. Furthermore, the low tones were judged to be somewhat better completions for the ascending context, and the high tones for the descending context. In particular, every listener in this group preferred the low C on ascending trials and the high C on descending trials.

In the ratings of Group 3 listeners, shown in Figure 7, again there was a preference for the two Cs over other tones in the octave range, although the magnitude of the effect was not as large as in Group 1 and Group 2. Also, there was a small, but significant, preference for the other scale tones over nonscale tones. However, distance from the tones of the preceding scale context accounted for most of the variance in ratings of these listeners. Low tones were judged to be better completions of ascending scales, and high tones were judged to be better completions of descending scales. Indeed one of the listeners in Group 3 exhibited a pure distance effect without even a partial indication of octave equivalence. Each of the two crossing curves,

plotted for this listener in Figure 8, fell off monotonically from the C nearest to the preceding context but without any upswing at the C at the other end of the test range.

The single listener, in this original set of twenty-three, who could not be classified as falling into any one of the three groups, showed a pattern similar to Group 1 listeners for descending contexts, but a virtually flat response profile for ascending contexts.

Figure 9 shows the response profile for the single, subsequently added listener who, in addition to extensive musical training, reported having absolute pitch. As with Group 1, there was little difference between ascending and descending contexts and a general preference for scale over nonscale tones. Within the set of scale tones there was, in addition to the high ratings for the two Cs, a marked preference for the other members of the major triad, namely, the third and fifth degrees of the scale (E and G), over the other scale tones.

Evidently, the relative contributions of the different factors in pitch perception vary markedly with the musical backgrounds of the listeners. The previously well established

164

factor of pitch height emerged once again, with tones close in log frequency to the context tones preferred over tones farther from the context. However, the influence of pitch height was strong only for the least musical listeners, weaker for the intermediate listeners, and virtually absent for the most musical listeners. In fact, the musical listeners gave strikingly similar ratings following both ascending and descending scale sequences, indicating that the context served a very different function for these listeners than for the less musical listeners. For the unmusical Group 3, the context apparently served primarily to define a location on the continuum of pitch height, and so had nearly the opposite effects when the context tones were presented above or below the range of the test octave. In marked contrast, for the musical Group 1, the context evidently defined a tonal structure that, under octave equivalence, applied to tones in any octave according to their individual functions within this invariant structure regardless of their location in pitch height. In particular, the high and low Cs were judged by Group 1 to be equally

good completions of both ascending and descending scales. This octave equivalence was weaker for less musical subjects, with the low C preferred in ascending scale contexts and the high C preferred in descending scale contexts, in agreement with earlier findings (Allen, 1967).

These strong and consistent relationships between the results for individual listeners and their reported amounts of musical interest and training is consistent with similar relationships reported in many earlier studies, including those by Allen (1967), Attneave and Olson (1971), Cohen (1975), Cuddy (1970), Dewar et al. (1977), and Shepard (1964b). Apparently, the kinds of structural relations that are extracted from tonal sequences vary widely depending on the extent of the listener's musical sophistication, whether innate or acquired.

Individual Differences in Krumhansl and Shepard's Second Experiment

In our second experiment (with the interpolated quarter tones) we ran only eight subjects who were, moreover, recruited by post-

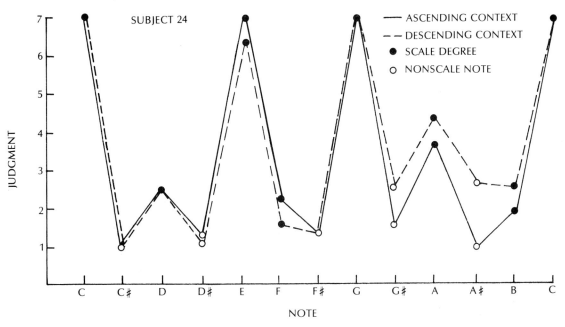

Figure 9. Mean rating profiles for the listener who was subsequently added because of her exceptionally extensive musical training and possession of absolute pitch. (From Krumhansl and Shepard, 1979.)

ing notices in the Stanford department of music. Since all of these listeners had relatively extensive musical backgrounds, we expected to see less marked individual differences than we found in the first experiment. Nevertheless, there still was considerable variation in the rating profiles. Hierarchical clustering analysis of the intersubject correlations again yielded quite distinct groups—this time consisting of one, three, and four subjects. The one subject was the listener with the most extensive musical background who appeared as Subject 24 in the first experiment, and was again the only subject who possessed absolute pitch. As in the first experiment, her profiles were very similar for ascending and descending contexts. There was a strong preference for the tonic C, over all other tones, and relatively high ratings were also given for the third and fifth degrees of the scale, E and G. In addition, there was a hint of a preference for the other scale tones over nonscale tones.

The homogeneous group of four listeners also showed a general preference for the tonic, C, over the other tones. In addition, there were higher ratings for the scale tones than for nonscale tones, with a rise in the ratings for tones near the third and fifth degrees, E and G. The profiles for this group reflected an increase in the effect of separation in pitch height at the expense of octave equivalence.

The ratings of the remaining group of three subjects showed a still stronger effect of pitch height, which held throughout the octave range of test tones, with higher ratings for low tones in ascending contexts and for high tones in descending contexts. For these listeners there was no discernable difference between scale and nonscale tones, but there was some degree of octave equivalence.

Individual Differences in Peynircioğlu and Shepard's Experiment

For her senior honors project at Stanford, Zehra Peynircioğlu (who, incidentally, was the exceptionally musical listener in the two preceding experiments) carried out an experiment that she and I designed in an attempt to extend, in two respects, the paradigm that Krumhansl and I had used. First, we sought to obtain information on the perceived relations between chords, rather than solely between single tones. And second, we wished to extend the range of differences in pitch height beyond a single octave.

The fourteen listeners in this experiment were recruited from both the psychology and music departments and had a wide range of previous music experience or training (from zero to fifteen hours per week for zero to sixteen years). These listeners judged the perceived similarities of major and minor triad chords differing in pitch height from a minor second to two full octaves. In an ancillary experiment they also tried to classify the second of two such chords as "same" or "different" with respect to major or minor structure regardless of separation in pitch height.

There were, again, consistent individual differences in the patterns of judgments produced by different listeners and these differences correlated both with the listener's self-reports of extent of musical background and, also, with the number of errors of identification that they made in the ancillary experiment. (Just as some subjects turned out to be tone deaf in my original experiment on pitch perception (Shepard, 1964b), some of these listeners did not discriminate between major and minor chords with better than chance success.) Consistent with the earlier results that Krumhansl and I obtained for single tones, simple separation in pitch height was the primary determinant of judged similarity for the least musical listeners, while the intrinsic structural differences between major and minor chords, regardless of transpositional shifts in pitch height, prevailed for the more musical listeners. Though reduced somewhat in overall level, the pattern of similarities for the second octave essentially repeated the pattern for the first as would be expected on the basis of the considerations already presented.

Conclusion

Evidently, to the extent that tones are interpreted musically—because they are embedded in a musical context, because they are rich in overtones, and because they are played to musically sophisticated listeners—

166

the simple psychophysical factor of separation in pitch height gives way to structurally more complex and cognitive factors, including octave equivalence or its psychological counterpart, tone chroma, and a hierarchy of tonal functions specific to the tonality induced by the context. Within this hierarchy the tonic is dominant, followed by the fifth and perhaps the third degree of the diatonic scale, followed by the remaining diatonic tones, followed, finally, by the tones that are not in the induced diatonic scale.

Further evidence for the reality of such an underlying hierarchy comes from a subsequent study by Krumhansl (1979), in which listeners judged the similarity between tones in all pairs within a set of tones in a similarly explicit tonal context. Analysis of the results by techniques known as *multidimensional scaling* (see Shepard, Romney, and Nerlove, 1972) yielded a hierarchy in agreement with the hierarchy found here. A tightly organized cluster corresponding to the tones of the major triad was surrounded by a more widely dispersed set corresponding to the remaining diatonic tones, which, in turn,

Figure 10. Projection of the four-dimensional INDSCAL solution onto the plane of Dimensions 1 and 2.

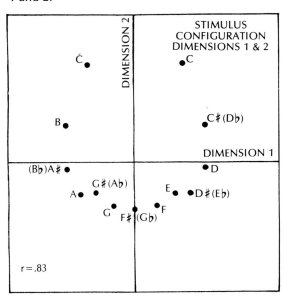

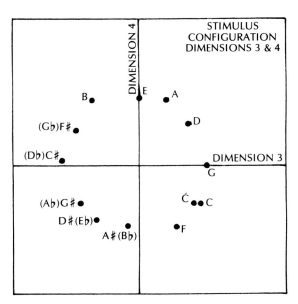

Figure 11. Projection of that same four-dimensional solution onto the plane of Dimensions 3 and 4.

was surrounded by a much more widely dispersed set corresponding to the nondiatonic tones.

That the data from some of the musically sophisticated listeners in the second of the Krumhansl-Shepard experiments provided evidence for such an underlying hierarchy even when the tones were reduced to simple sinusoids argues against theories, widely held since Helmholtz (1863/1954), according to which the perceived relationships between tones is explained principally in terms of coincidences between frequencies of the harmonics (overtones or partials). Further evidence that cognitive factors must be invoked in addition to such physical factors is Krumhansl's (1979) demonstration that the perceived similarities between tones forming an interval of a fixed size depend upon the relation of those tones to the contextually established tonic or tonal center.

Implications of the Marked Individual Differences

These results indicate that individual listeners differ enormously in the extent to which they interpret music tones in terms of an underlying tonal system. This has important implications for research methodology, for theoretical understanding of the internal representation of pitch and, I presume, for practical issues of music education.

It is clear that the indiscriminate pooling of data from individual listeners prior to analysis is likely to obscure important patterns in their data. I suggest, instead, that the systematic pursuit of these individual differences by such data-analytic techniques as hierarchical clustering (already illustrated here) and multidimensional scaling (Shepard, Romney, and Nerlove, 1972) including individual difference scaling (Carroll and Chang, 1970) can help to separate out such underlying perceptual components as pitch height, tone chroma, and tonal function with respect to a musical scale.

As an illustration, Figures 10 and 11 show the four-dimensional solution that I obtained by applying Carroll and Chang's (1970) IND-SCAL analysis to (three-way) matrices of es-

Figure 12. Weights for the listeners on Dimensions 1 and 2.

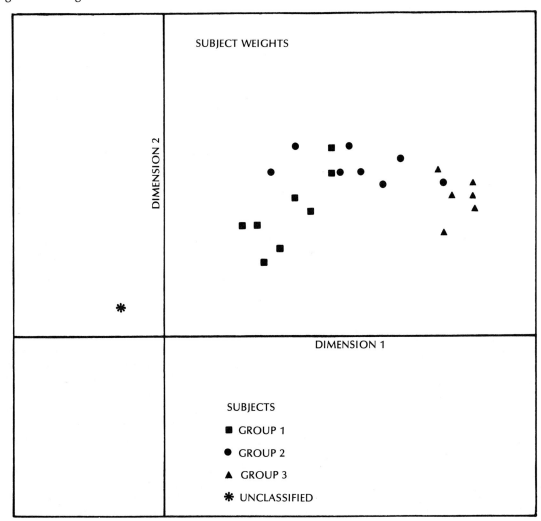

168

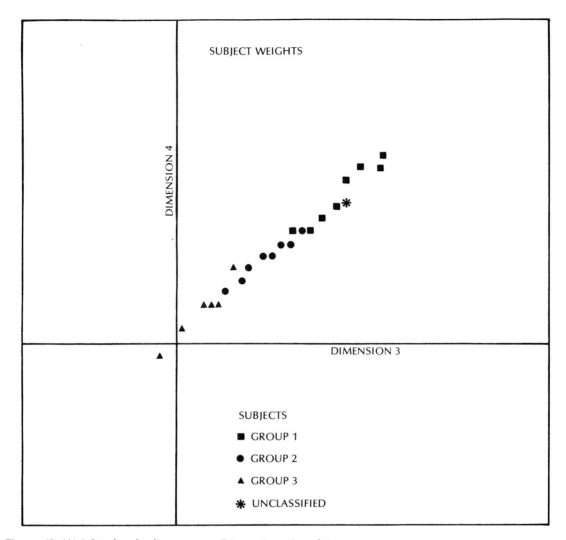

Figure 13. Weights for the listeners on Dimensions 3 and 4.

timates of tonal similarity derived from the data of Krumhansl and Shepard's (1979) first experiment. (The technical details of this analysis are described elsewhere, Shepard, 1979). Figure 10 presents the projection of the four-dimensional solution onto the plane of the first two axes of the solution. Notice that in this plane the thirteen test tones describe an approximate circle. Except for the gap between C and C', it is in fact the chroma circle underlying my earlier demonstration of circularity in judgments of relative pitch (Shepard, 1964). Figure 11, then, presents the pro-

jection of the solution onto the plane of the third and fourth axes. Here again we see that a circular configuration has emerged but, this time, it is the cycle of fifths of music theory.

The INDSCAL analysis also yields a plot of the weights for the individual listeners with respect to these same four axes. The more salient a particular dimension of the tonal relations is for a particular listener, the farther out in the positive direction of that axis the point for that listener will project. Thus Figure 12 shows that the Group 3 listeners, who

169

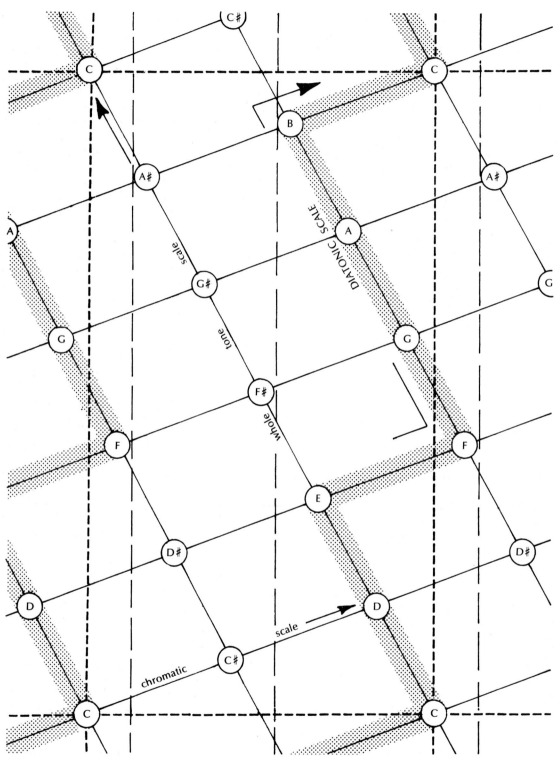

were responding primarily to differences in pitch height, had the heaviest weighting of Dimension 1, which separates the two tones that are farthest apart in pitch height, C and C'. The more musical Group 1 listeners, on the other hand, had the least heavy weighting of that dimension. Figure 13 shows that for these listeners, the most heavily weighted dimensions were Dimensions 3 and 4, which underlie the circle of fifths implied by music theory, while for Group 3 listeners the weights for these two dimensions were close to zero. (The fact that the points for the individual listeners fall on a 45° line in Figure 13 implies that for different listeners the two-dimensional circle of fifths was more or less present or absent, as a coherent unit.)

Analyses of this sort, like that of hierarchical clustering shown earlier in Figure 4, provide a powerful, quantitative, and readily visualized characterization of the kinds of ways in which listeners differ in their perception of music.

Implications for Theory

The four-dimensional structure shown in two of its two-dimensional projections in Figures 10 and 11 is really a double helix wrapped around a torus. This structure was in fact anticipated on the basis of certain theoretical considerations that I have developed elsewhere (Shepard, 1978; 1979). Instead of projecting this toroidal structure, it can be "unwrapped" into the flat topological "map" presented in Figure 14. (If an automobile inner tube is taken as an approximate three-dimensional model of the four-dimensional torus, one can see how the flattened map is obtained: when the inner tube is cut through, it can be straightened out into a cylindrical tube and, when a second cut is then made along the length of that cylinder, it can be further opened out into a flat rectangle.) In Figure 14 the straight lines sloping upward to the left are the representations, in the resulting map, of the two whole tone series making up the two sides of the double helix.

This structure has a number of theoretical-ly significant properties (Shepard, 1979): (1) A plane passed through the axis of the double helix in the four-dimensional embedding space divides tones that are in a given key from those that are not. (2) Rotations of the plane around that axis correspond to changes of key, with smaller rotations corresponding to more closely related keys. (3) Scales and melodies have particularly compact and simple representations in the corresponding two-dimensional map (Figure 14) and, so, this two-dimensional lattice can be thought of as a kind of "melody space." (4) By a simple linear transformation (known, mathematically, as an affine transformation) this same two-dimensional map can also be converted into a kind of "harmony space" in which the most commonly occurring chords have a particularly compact and simple representation.

Actually this four-dimensional representation is itself probably an oversimplification of the true cognitive structure of musical pitch. There are indications that data from experiments including more than a single octave of test tones (such as the Peynirçioğlu-Shepard experiment) require the introduction of a fifth dimension for pitch height. In Figure 10, this fifth dimension could largely be accommodated within the two dimensions for the chroma circle, by forcing a gap between C and C', only because no more than a single octave was included. Whatever dimensions are finally required, they provide for a deeper understanding and a more precise and quantitative representation of the ways listeners differ in their interpretations of musical tones.

An interesting question that remains to be answered concerns the relation of these individual differences to findings of hemispheric lateralization of the processing of music. Early work had indicated that while speech is usually processed in the left hemisphere of the brain, musical stimuli are processed in the right. More recent results, however, have suggested that this may be true only for relatively unmusical listeners and that musically

Figure 14. A proposed "melody space." (A topological map of Shepard's double helix on a torus.)

171

sophisticated listeners may carry out much of their music processing—just as their language processing—in the so-called "dominant" left hemisphere (Bever and Chiarello, 1974). Possibly pitch height (including the closely related "spectral pitch" and timbre) are appreciated primarily in the right hemisphere while interpretation in terms of underlying discrete cognitive structures such as the diatonic system, circle of fifths, and so on is usually carried out in the left hemisphere. However, evidence of such functions is by no means clear at this time. (See the review by Reineke, 1978.)

Another major question that is left unanswered by the findings of enormous individual differences in the perception of relationships of musical pitch is the question of the extent to which these differences are innate (and possibly genetically determined) and to what extent they are learned. Presumably, very careful and extensive studies of patterns of musical abilities in families and, particularly, in monozygotic and dizygotic twins reared together and apart would be needed to probe the genetic basis of musical predispositions. Short of that, one could explore the extent to which subjects such as those in our Group 1 or Group 3 could be trained, within a few experimental sessions, to produce judgments like those of the other group.

In the meantime, there is room for differences of opinion. I suspect that the larger part of the variance is genetic and that the reason that performance correlates so highly with extent of musical background is as much because innately musical people tend to take up music, as because of the training that they then receive. Music educators may prefer the alternative hypothesis (favored, incidentally, by my collaborator Carol Krumhansl) that it is music exposure and training that makes the difference. Note, however, that even if exposure and training are what are most essential, it may be that these must come before some critical time. There is evidence that language competence can only be shifted from one hemisphere to the other if injury to the originally linguistic hemisphere occurs before the age of twelve

or so (Lenneberg, 1967). And it has been proposed that absolute pitch, which evidently cannot normally be acquired by adults, may be learnable only at a very early age—somewhat in the manner of "imprinting" in birds (Hess, 1959; Jeffress, 1962).

Whatever their origin, the enormous individual differences that we do find in adults will have to be understood before we will know how best to deal with them in the classroom—whether by grouping of students or by individualized computer-based instruction. In just the one narrow aspect of musical ability on which I have focused—relative pitch—there appear to be several dimensions along which listeners differ. These differences may or may not be correlated with other differences in absolute pitch, in rhythm, in timbre, in larger-scale structural features of music, and in motor skill. I hope, nevertheless, that some of the experimental and analytical techniques I have illustrated for the study of individual differences in pitch perception may prove useful in the study of these other dimensions of music. Finally, it is just possible that the schemes for representing the structures underlying musical pitch that have emerged from some of this research, such as the melodic and harmonic "maps" mentioned in connection with Figure 14, might offer a helpful heuristic for students in courses of ear training and music theory.

Note. The experiments described in this paper were supported by research grant BNS-75-02806 from the National Science Foundation and by the contributions of Carol Krumhansl, Gerald Balzano, Shelley Hurwitz, and Zehra Peynircioğlu.

References

Allen, D. Octave discriminability of musical and non-musical subjects. *Psychonomic Science*, 1967, *7*, 421–422.

Attneave, F., and R. K. Olson. Pitch as medium: A new approach to psychophysical scaling. *American Journal of Psychology*, 1971, *84*, 147–166.

Bachem, A. Time factors in relative and absolute pitch determination. *Journal of the Acoustical Society of America*, 1954, *26*, 751–753.

Balzano, G. J. *Chronometric studies of the musical in-*

terval sense. Unpublished doctoral dissertation, Stanford University, 1977.

————. The structural uniqueness of the diatonic order. In R. N. Shepard (Chair), *Cognitive structure of musical pitch.* Paper presented at the annual meeting of the Western Psychological Association, San Francisco, April 1978.

Bartlett, F. C. *Remembering: A study in experimental and social psychology.* Cambridge, Massachusetts: Cambridge University Press, 1932.

Bennett, G. Untitled manuscript. Institut de recherche et coordination acoustique/musique, Paris, 1978.

Bever, T. C., and R. J. Chiarello. Cerebral dominance in musicians and nonmusicians. *Science,* 1974, *185,* 537–539.

Bitterman, M. E. Phyletic differences in learning. *American Psychologist,* 1964, *19,* 396–410.

Blechner, M. J. *Musical skill and the categorical perception of harmonic mode.* Haskins Laboratories Status Report on Speech Perception, 1977, SR-51/52, 139–174.

Boring, E. G. *Sensation and perception in the history of experimental psychology.* New York: Appleton-Century, 1942.

Breland, K., and M. Breland. The misbehavior of animals. *American Psychologist,* 1961, *16,* 681–684.

Burns, E. M., and W. I. Ward. Categorical perception—phenomenon or epiphenomenon: Evidence from experiments in the perception of melodic musical intervals. *Journal of the Acoustical Society of America,* 1978, *63,* 456–468.

Carroll, J. D., and J. J. Chang. Analysis of individual differences in multidimensional scaling via an N-way generalization of "Eckart-Young" decomposition. *Psychometrika,* 1970, *35,* 283–319.

Cohen, A. J. *Perception of tone sequences from the Western-European chromatic scale: Tonality, transposition and the pitch set.* Unpublished doctoral dissertation, Queen's University at Kingston, Ontario, Canada, 1975.

Cohen, A. J. Inferred sets of pitches in melodic perception. In R. N. Shepard (Chair), *Cognitive structure of musical pitch.* Paper presented at the annual meeting of the Western Psychological Association, San Francisco, April 1978.

Cuddy, L. L. Training the absolute identification of pitch. *Perception and Psychophysics,* 1970, *8,* 265–269.

Deutsch, D. Octave generalization of specific interference effects in memory for tonal pitch. *Perception and Psychophysics,* 1973, *13,* 271–275.

Deva, B. C. *An introduction to Indian music.* Government of India: Publication Division, Minis-

try of Information and Broadcasting, 1973.

Dewar, K. M. *Context effects in recognition memory for tones.* Unpublished doctoral dissertation, Queen's University at Kingston, Ontario, Canada, 1974.

Dewar, K. M., L. L. Cuddy, and D. J. K. Mewhort. Recognition memory for single tones with and without context. *Journal of Experimental Psychology: Human Learning and Memory,* 1977, *3,* 60–67.

Dewar, K. M. *Context effects in recognition memory for tones.* Unpublished doctoral dissertation, Queen's University of Kingston, Ontario, Canada, 1974.

Dewar, K. M., L. L. Cuddy, and D. J. K. Mewhort. Recognition memory for single tones with and without context. *Journal of Experimental Psychology: Human Learning and Memory,* 1977, *3,* 60–67.

Dowling, W. J. Musical scales as cognitive structures. In R. N. Shepard (Chair), *Cognitive structure of musical pitch.* Paper presented at the annual meeting of the Western Psychological Association, San Francisco, April 1978.

Halpern, A. R., and R. J. Zatorre. *Categorical perception and selective adaptation of simultaneous musical intervals.* Unpublished manuscript, Stanford University and Brown University, 1978.

Helmholtz, H. von. *On the sensations of tone as a physiological basis for the theory of music.* (A. J. Ellis, Ed. and trans.). New York: Dover, 1954. (Original German publication, 1863.)

Hess, E. H. Imprinting. *Science,* 1959, *130,* 133–141.

Jaeger, W. Genetics of congenital colour deficiencies. In D. Jameson and L. M. Hurrich (Eds.), *Handbook of Sensory Physiology,* Vol. VII/4, *Visual Psychophysics.* New York: Springer-Verlag, 1972.

Jeffress, L. A. Absolute pitch. *Journal of the Acoustical Society of America,* 1962, *34,* 1386–1395.

Johnson, S. C. Hierarchical clustering schemes. *Psychometrika,* 1967, *32,* 241–254.

Kilmer, A. D., R. L. Crocker, and R. R. Brown. *Sounds from silence: Recent discoveries in ancient Near Eastern music.* Berkeley: Bit Enki Publications, 1976.

Krumhansl, C. L. The psychological representation of musical pitch in a tonal context. *Cognitive Psychology,* in press.

Krumhansl, C., and R. N. Shepard. Quantification of the hierarchy of tonal functions within a diatonic context. *Journal of Experimental Psychology: Human Perception and Performance,* 1979, *5,* 579–594.

Kubovy, M. Concurrent pitch-segregation and the

theory of indispensable attributes. In M. Kubovy and J. Pomerantz (Eds.), *Perceptual organization*. Hillsdale, New Jersey: Erlbaum, in press.

Lenneberg, E. H. *Biological foundations of language*. New York: Wiley, 1967.

Liberman, A. M., F. S. Cooper, D. Shankweiler, and M. Studdert-Kennedy. Perception of the speech code. *Psychological Review*, 1967, 74, 431–461.

Licklider, J. C. R. Basic correlates of the auditory stimulus. In S. S. Stevens (Ed.), *Handbook of Experimental Psychology*. New York: Wiley, 1951, 985–1039.

Locke, S., and L. Kellar. Categorical perception in a nonlinguistic mode. *Cortex*, 1973, 9, 355–369.

Mathews, M. V. The digital computer as a musical instrument. *Science*, 1963, 142, 553–557.

Miller, G. A. The magic number seven, plus or minus two. *Psychological Review*, 1956, 63, 81–97.

Pawlik, K. Concepts in human cognition and aptitudes. In R. B. Cattell (Ed.), *Handbook of multivariate experimental psychology*. Chicago: Rand McNally, 1966.

Piston, W. *Harmony*. New York: W. W. Norton, 1941.

Pressing, J. Personal communication, May 1979.

Ratner, L. G. *Harmony: Structure and style*. New York: McGraw Hill, 1962.

Reineke, T. *Ear asymmetry of musicians and non-musicians for melodies and digits presented dichotically and monaurally*. Unpublished manuscript, University of Washington, 1978.

Rothenberg, D. *A mathematical model for the perception of redundancy and stability in musical scales*. Paper presented at the annual meeting of the Acoustical Society of America, New York, May 1963.

Seashore, C. E. *The psychology of musical talent*. New York: Silver, Burdett, 1919.

Shepard, R. N. Review of *Computers and thought* by E. Feigenbaum and J. Feldman. *Behavioral Science*, 1964, 9, 57–65. (a)

———. Circularity in judgments of relative pitch. *Journal of the Acoustical Society of America*, 1964, 36, 2346–2353. (b)

———. Shepard's tones. On M. V. Mathews, J. C. Risset et al., *The voice of the computer*. Decca Record DL 710180, 1970.

———. *The double helix of musical pitch*. In R. N. Shepard (Chair), *Cognitive structure of musical pitch*. Paper presented at the annual meeting of the Western Psychological Association, San Francisco, April 1978.

———. Geometrical approximations to the structure of musical pitch. Unpublished manuscript, 1979.

———. Psychophysical complementarity. In M. Kubovy and J. Pomerantz, (Eds.), *Perceptual organization*. Hillsdale, New Jersey: Erlbaum, in press.

Shepard, R. N., A. K. Romney, and S. B. Nerlove, (Eds.), *Multidimensional scaling: Theory and applications in the behavioral sciences*. Vol. I: *Theory*. New York: Seminar Press, 1972.

Shepard, R. N., and Zajac. *A pair of paradoxes*. Murray Hill, New Jersey: Bell Telephone Laboratories, 1965. (A computer-generated 16-mm sound film.)

Siegel, J. A., and W. Siegel. Absolute identification of notes and intervals by musicians. *Perception and Psychophysics*, 1977, 21, 143–152. (a)

———. Categorical perception of tonal intervals: Musicians can't tell sharp from flat. *Perception and Psychophysics*, 1977, 21, 399–407. (b)

Stevens, S. S., and J. Volkmann. The relation of pitch to frequency: A revised scale. *American Journal of Psychology*, 1940, 53, 329–353.

Stevens, S. S., J. Volkmann, and E. B. Newman. A scale for the measurement of the psychological magnitude of pitch. *Journal of the Acoustical Society of America*, 1937, 8, 185–190.

Stratton, G. M. Vision without inversion of the retinal image. *Psychological Review*, 1897, 4, 341–360, 463–481.

Woodworth, R. S. *Experimental psychology*. New York: Henry Holt, 1938.

Response

Robert G. Sidnell

My feelings at this moment are somewhat similar although not precisely the same as Einstein's when asked how he worked. His response was, "I muddle." Similarity stops there. I am further reminded of the King's advice to the White Rabbit, on the occasion of reading the charges against the accused Knave who was on trial for stealing the Queen's tarts, "Begin at the beginning, and go till you come to the end; then stop" (Carroll, 1886, p. 182). I'm not sure where the beginning is right now, and I am truly convinced the end is not in sight. I do, however, plan on stopping.

As I understand my responsibility, I am obligated to discover, enumerate, and emphasize implications of Shepard's contributions. I want to accentuate the notion of emphasis rather than of discovery for I believe he has presented us with some very clear and reasonable implications that do not need discovery on my part. I want to focus, not on the instance of the paper, for I believe it to be the tip of an iceberg, but rather what the larger impact may be for music education. In no way is my response meant to reduce the importance of the event of the paper. Metaphorically, it comes along in time and space to provide a solid base from which new direction for our enterprise can spring. You must read and reread this paper perhaps many times. Please read it without bias or more properly the kind of bias I want you to have—namely, a tabula rasa about what the foundation of music instruction might be.

Several careful readings of Shepard's paper brought me to the issue of a fundamental theory about our work in music instruction. Believing that music education is a study of the nature of, and modification of human music abilities, I am thoroughly convinced that we need to fashion a rational framework upon which a fabric of process can be woven to effect well-directed change in the people we teach. It is all about theory.

We need to talk about theory of music instruction. In my opinion the need is desperate. I refer to theory that can give us direction.

OK, so I'm hooked on systematic inquiry—that is only because my early career in music education as a doer was marked by decisions regarding my teaching behavior based almost entirely upon (1) faith and authority of many former teachers and college methods teachers—not the best of all worlds as most of us could attest; and (2) trial and error—a notably inefficient, but better method of determining action.

I firmly believe that we can do better in music teaching and learning through a pro-

cess of objective verification of a set of reasoned and reasonable beliefs. Our knowledge about process will likely be more generalizable and predictable in results. How do we get there? I think by means of theory. Philosophers of science indicate that theory in the scientific sense begins with facts, and through induction we couch theory from which we deduce predictions that, in turn, can verify facts. Therefore, we move from facts to facts—this is as it should be.

Current theory of music instruction is not well delineated, nor have more than a handful of music educators confronted the issue. I think most music education is based on the house of music knowledge, which has many rooms. We talk about rhythm, melody, harmony, form, and color; but we do so without reference to people. Most views of music education I have read focus on process in relation to musical substance. In many ways that is significantly appropriate, but we have, to a large extent, overlooked the object of our efforts. Many advocate a strong, child-centered emphasis in music education mostly from a humanistic or affective stance. I wouldn't want to change that focus but we must consider the mental capacity of children to deal with the many undiscovered or little understood variables found in the music stimuli we ask children to respond to.

Ed Gordon has been asking for many years, "How do children learn when they learn music?" Not too many years ago there was a study by leading music researchers on how children organize music phenomena and concepts (Andrews and Diehl, 1970, p. 214). In my opinion we need to think very carefully about what music is, how it might best be presented in accordance with our teaching personalities; but most of all, we need to investigate with deliberation, how people of all ages perceive, process, and manipulate musical events. We simply do not know enough about the ways in which available mental musical furnishings interact with new or familiar musical perceptions. Shepard has challenged us with more than one probe in that direction. Others will also. Dowling has written about the perceiving and remembering of music. He states, "the basic questions involve what, out of the wealth of information in the physical sound waves of music, gets attended to, compared with other sounds, and what gets stored in memory by the human listener" (Dowling, 1979).

Clearly, the development of a human-oriented base for an instructional theory in music education is not a simple task. It will not be developed overnight, nor will the first attempts be free from the need for shaping or modification. We cannot go on saying that music education is where we teach music and everyone learns.

Shepard raises a key psychogenetic-anthropological question in his paper regarding the peculiar state of affairs evidenced by the ubiquitousness of music in human culture, human predisposition toward structural patterns of time and pitch (perhaps a definition for music), and some problems in locating adequate variation in human abilities with musical stimuli. On the other hand, the need for music is obscure and would seem to promote the notion that there are genetic determinants that effect musical growth and development. Since free crosscultural attempts at measuring simple music abilities are extant, the effect of acculturation is unknown. He suggests that we reconsider the question of genetic differences in music abilities. Or, more properly, consider the question with greater care and systematic investigation. He makes several suggestions regarding a research strategy for securing more information about innate and acquired music abilities. Few researchers have worked in the measurement area. We need to look deeply into the construct of music aptitude before generating new test materials and exercises. We think of pitch as high and low—but it is more. We think of tones as long and short, but duration is a much more complicated musical dimension. We think of melodic patterns as connected by tonal considerations—but there are other adhesives. We think of pulse as intuitively organized according to certain groupings, which are in truth imaginary.

In the realm of timbre, one can look at the research of Heller and Campbell for a glimpse of the complexity of processing sound quality perceptions. The issue is not one of simplicity but one of complexity in very basic music perceptions. When we have some facts to act upon, I suspect our instructional strategies might differ greatly.

The issues are again raised regarding a fundamental theory of music and music instruction. We are overlooking too much! How can instruction in music be developed without some basic organizing principles that are at least somewhat objectified. I am not here to argue genetic or environmental music ability determination, although I am seriously persuaded by Shepard's view.

What is the immediate application of this notion? I am more than a little concerned with finding instant payoff, when we haven't even reached St. Charles Place, let alone passed GO. I understand the need for "take home" results from this Symposium. But the nature of that idea is more like a yellow flag of caution—we need to investigate before concluding. Be troubled then. I hope methods teachers and those of you who go into America's schools next month will think seriously about the "musical perceptual and processing abilities of school aged youth." Some cannot handle our simplest tasks and cleverly disguise their difficulty behind a cloud of disdain. I am convinced those who can't handle certain music perceptual problems consider themselves subnormal and find solace in peculiar kinds of group behavior. I suspect we skim over or treat with inadequate repetition some very fundamental music experiences. For years we have talked of individualizing instruction. Is there nothing new on this topic? I think there is, but we will need much research to locate differences in perceptual and processing abilities before instructional plans can more properly fit learners who exhibit different capacities. Tasks, musical or otherwise, we think of as simple may not be simple because not all beginners have the mental furniture to perform them.

This brings us to the major thrust of Shepard's paper—the report of studies on the multidimensional nature of pitch. Given the question that there must be more to pitch

176

than highness and lowness, which grew from earlier studies (Attneave and Olson, 1971; Shepard, 1964; Shepard, 1970; Shepard and Zajac, 1965), we have data that confirm an expanded view on pitch perception problems. Shepard was looking for and has documented more hooks upon which to hang variances in pitch perception. He reviewed carefully the psychoacoustic and cognitive approaches to the problem. His report clearly shows some remarkable differences on several dimensions of pitch. I think we may have to broaden our definition of pitch to accommodate the breadth of this idea, particularly as it applies to music teaching and learning.

Two added dimensions for pitch deserve mention. The first is a circular component in perceived pitch known as "tone chroma." Knowledge of the phenomenon was arrived at by producing a sequence of pitches that appeared to increase in pitch height but were, in reality, manipulations of complex tones to give the illusion of ever-increasing height. A visual illustration may help.

The second added dimension of pitch perception is the influence of tonality. Empirical evidence for the power of tonality to affect pitch perception is a relatively recent consid-

Figure 1. Visual illusion of ever-increasing height.

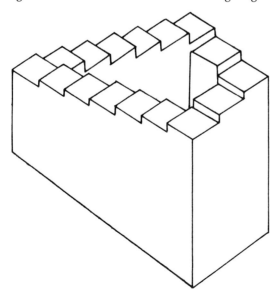

eration among researchers. In the research reported perceived similarities were found to be highly specific to the tonality. In regard to this, I am struck by those data from the musically sophisticated group who find the third-scale degree to be significantly less attractive as a final note in the descending, but not the ascending, context. Interestingly, the same differential appears in the Group 3 (least musically sophisticated) graph. (Figure 2.)

What does this mean? First, as teachers and methods teachers we will need to exercise greater care in presenting pitch perception problems to young music learners. We must be aware that such are multi-dimensional tasks—some learners simply may not be able to process the various competing perceptions regarding pitch. One might even hypothesize that musical growth is a process whereby there is an increasing ability to use all of the keen information contained in tone stimuli. Clearly, it is no longer a question of highness or lowness.

Also, this information should concern researchers in psychomusicology and music education. I can see a dozen studies fundamental to the practice of music education that will assist teachers in determining instructional sequences and strategies. I believe there are teaching procedures we need to use that have not been discovered. Historically, music education research has focused on applied problems without the benefit of strong theoretical bases. Now is the opportunity to expand from an expanding theoretical base. We will get back to the classroom, but it will take some time, and I would like to stress that it is everybody's problem.

I think we should look carefully at the notion of critical times for learning certain music processing skills. This is not a new idea, but the extent of the complexity involved could bring about a worthwhile reexamination of the question. If certain learning gains don't accrue at specific developmental stages, the "catchup" training cycle might be difficult to implement in the ordinary school learning setting.

Researchers, doctoral advisors, and doctoral students should investigate the techniques of data analysis used in this paper. In terms

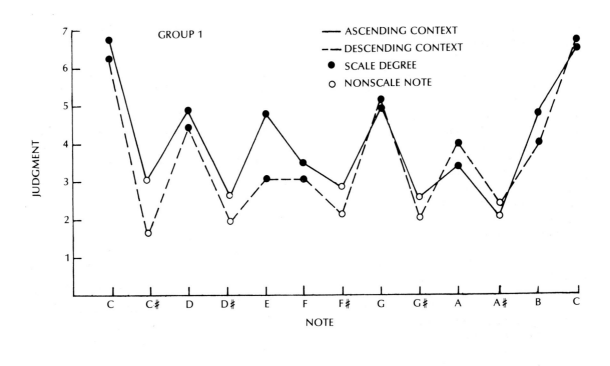

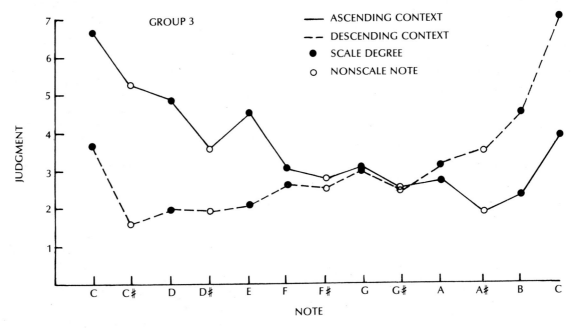

Figure 2. Value judgments for completion notes of tonal set by Group I (Most Sophisticated Music Background) and Group III (Least Sophisticated Music Background). From "Individual Differences in the Perception of Musical Pitch," Roger Shepard, Department of Psychology, Stanford University.

178

of theory generation, I believe the notion of multidimensional scaling has a lot going for it with the kinds of data we often collect in music research. Through the use of the techniques outlined by Shepard, each datum becomes a valued fact. All contribute individually to a deeper understanding of the relationship being studied . . . power to each perception. Normative techniques are set aside in order that instances from each subject may be allowed to make unique contribution. While I suppose it is repetitive to state that no amount of statistical elegance will make up for a poorly designed and executed study, the potential for visualizing constructions derived from reliably obtained data could clarify outcomes so that implications for theory, further research, and practice might gain potency.

It is instructive to follow the directions for dissecting the double helix around the torus. One can grasp a better feel for the display found in Figure 13 of Shepard's paper. The relationships charted confirm much of what we know about the tonal music system. But it is crucial to remember that this projection is based on the pitch perceptions of subjects with varied backgrounds. As Shepard said later, "I was trying to support the cognitive view of the study of pitch as opposed to the psychoacoustic view."

Summary

I would like us to think about Shepard's paper as a guide or foundation for developing programs of research, as well as a basis for practice. It is appropriate to explore the implications for theory section in great detail. But I view the salient points as (1) the genesis of music ability question in the light of this research, (2) the notion that at least pitch has several dimensions that call for cognitive actions, (3) the new data analysis techniques of hierarchical clustering and multidimensional scaling, and (4) the overriding notion of theory development as a fundamental need for our enterprise.

References

Andrews, F. M., and N. C. Diehl. Development of a technique for identifying elementary school children's musical concepts. *Journal of Research in Music Education*, 1970, 28, 214.

Attneave, F. and R. K. Olson. Pitch as medium: A new approach to psychophysical scaling. *American Journal of Psychology*, 1971, 84, 147–166.

Bachem, A. Tone height and tone chroma as two different pitch qualities. *Acta Psychologica*, 1950, 7, 80–88.

Carroll, L. *Alice in Wonderland*. London: Macmillan & Co., Ltd., 1886.

Dowling, W. J. The cognitive psychology of music. *Humanities Association Review*, 1979, 30 (1–2), 58–67.

Kerlinger, F. N. *Foundations of behavioral research* (2nd ed.). New York: Holt, Rinehart & Winston, 1973.

Shepard, R. N. Circularity in judgments of relative pitch. *Journal of the Acoustical Society of America*, 1964, 36, 2346–2353.

Stevens, S. S. and J. Volkmann. The relation of pitch to frequency: A revised scale. *American Journal of Psychology*, 1940, 53, 329–353.

Perceptual and Motor Schemas in the Performance of Musical Pitch

David LaBerge

The array of questions posed by Hedden and Sidnell challenge our basic knowledge of how music performance skills are processed at various stages of proficiency, and test our practical knowledge of how to effectively teach these skills. It is unfortunate that factual answers to their questions are not yet at hand. But houses were built before principles of design and construction were clearly understood, and musicians have been trained regardless of our ignorance of the principles underlying performance skills.

179

Obviously, we cannot wait for basic research to provide final answers before training students. Teaching procedures typically have been based on a combination of available facts plus reasoned inferences. These reasoned inferences are usually based on intuitions that are often vague and difficult to communicate. Those based on theory, however, more often provide a higher degree of clarity and communication. A well structured theory can bring together diverse notions and facts to solve specific problems. But, perhaps more important at the present state of our knowledge, theory can guide our research efforts by organizing findings in illuminating ways and by formulating new questions. These questions, in turn, can help set meaningful priorities for the next steps for research.

This paper is an attempt to contribute both to research and to training in music performance by reviewing current theories of motor skills and by describing a general theoretical framework that hopefully integrates some important aspects of music performance.

It will be assumed here that there is much in common between music skills and other skills that have been studied by psychologists, such as speaking and typing (Shaffer, 1976). On the other hand, it will also be assumed that important differences among these skills exist, just as within the music area there are noteworthy differences between the skills of singing and playing instruments.

The theories treated in this paper will be considered from the point of view of process, as opposed to function or structure (cf. Clark and Clark, 1977). A structural theory of music would describe the formal aspects of a composition, somewhat like a blueprint represents the design of a building. An example of a structural theory is given by the recent article of Lerdahl and Jackendoff (1977) in which the syntactic organization of music is analyzed in a manner reminiscent of Chomsky's (1965) treatment of language. A functional theory might describe the ways in which music is used to modulate moods and personal interactions in social situations. On the other hand, a process theory of music would be likely to describe the cognitive systems and operations used by people when they hear and perform music. Structural theories usually offer representations of what a person *knows* about music, functional theories emphasize what a person *does* with music, while process theories describe how a person *hears* and *produces* music. Theories of one type need not correspond in principle with theories of another type. For example, there is no necessary reason why units in a structural description should be expected to correspond with units in a process description.

The situations in which music is performed range from improvisation, to reading from score, and to performing by memory. These modes of performing may be compared with impromptu speaking, reading aloud, and with reciting lines of poetry or of a play. While theories of speech production deal almost exclusively with impromptu or spontaneous speech (cf. Clark and Clark, 1977, for a review), theories of music production are more likely to be concerned with performing from memory or from a score. As it turns out, the vast majority of research in motor skills investigates skills that are produced from memory (for example, button series and positioning a lever) or from visual prompting (for example, tracking a moving target, and typing).

Review of Theories of Motor Skill

The three main theories of motor skill may offer some insights into the production of music. They are the closed-loop theory, the open-loop theory, and the schema theory. The purpose here is not to determine which theory does the best job of accounting for the available data (cf. Stelmach, 1976) but rather to show how each theory may be used to describe music production at the various achievement levels between the beginner and the advanced musician.

Throughout this review section it will be helpful to keep in mind that there are two general classes of movements that may be addressed by a theory (Keele, 1973). One class is the single movement, which is usually executed with attention and strongly influenced

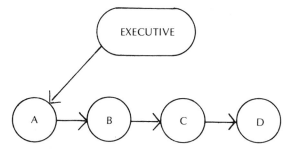

Figure 1. Representation of a closed-loop theory of motor control. Each letter represents an event containing a response and its kinesthetic feedback which initiates the next response. The first response is activated from the executive level.

by feedback from the results of the previous movement. The second class of movements is the movement series, often produced at a fast rate, in which many components are executed with little or no attention and in which successive movements may not be solely influenced by the outcomes of immediately preceding movements.

Closed-loop theory. For this theory, a movement is activated by the sensory feedback from the preceding movement. The processing underlying a series of movements may be represented by a chain shown in Figure 1. Each movement produces a sensory consequence, usually kinesthetic, which acts as a stimulus for the next movement (Greenwald, 1970). Thus the event (A) contains both a movement and its sensory feedback, which is associated to the movement in event (B). The sequence shown here is started by activation from a centrally located executive. Limitations on the speed of sequencing movements appear to depend strongly upon the speed of kinesthetic feedback, which may be as fast as fifty milliseconds (Evarts and Tanji, 1974), and perhaps even as fast as ten milliseconds (Fuchs and Kornhuber, 1969). In view of these results, movements in associated chains could be performed at very fast rates while under peripheral feedback control, a conclusion that weakens the impact of Lashley's (1951) influential criticism. In addition, since the control of each movement after the initial one is determined by

peripheral feedback, the central mechanism could be free to attend to other processes. Thus, the sequence of movements could be performed automatically as well as rapidly, satisfying two general requirements of advanced musical skills. Furthermore, neuroanatomical studies have revealed a very dense array of muscle spindles in the muscles of the tongue (Bowman and Combs, 1968) and in the muscles controlling the hands and arms (Phillips, 1977), which provide a rich source of kinesthetic feedback from the motor organs responsible for the fastest rates of movements performed by humans. For these reasons Sussman (1972) argues in favor of a closed-loop theory of speech control. However, MacNeilage (1970) maintains that the closed-loop issue of speech control has not yet been settled, partly because the muscle movements of the tongue are more complicated than first suspected. For example, the fact that people can communicate effectively when speaking with clenched teeth indicates that speakers can rapidly make a complex overall adjustment of muscle length for vowels. A similar re-adjustment of many movements made simultaneously occurs when one tries to play a piano piece standing up or seated on the floor. Fast adjustments of this sort create difficulties for the closed-loop theory.

However, when relatively simple movements are studied in isolation, one can achieve a rather close connection between theory and data, and this is one of the virtues of Adams' (1971, 1976) closed-loop theory. Another virtue is that this type of task has permitted a close study of the acquisition of a motor skill. The typical task is the positioning of a lever by the hand, which requires learning a movement somewhat like a movement made from a reference point of a slide trombone or on a violin finger board. Errors may be detected by comparing feedback during the movement to an image or perceptual trace of the correct movement. Combining the accuracy of the last movement with the image of past movements leads to an improvement in the next movement. In this way learning takes place.

Thus for simple responses that are similar

181

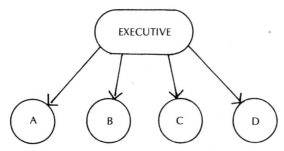

Figure 2. Representation of an open-loop theory of motor control. Each letter represents a response initiated by a motor program at the executive level.

to the positioning response, a closed-loop theory may well provide a useful and objective understanding of the processes involved, especially for initial learning trials. The acquisition of sequences of movements performed in an event-to-event manner perhaps may also be described adequately by this model (Keele and Summers, 1976). But the performance of movement sequences that are characterized by grouping or holistic properties are more adequately described by open-loop or schema theories.

Open-loop theory. This theory has also been labeled the motor program theory, because it assumes a central or executive control of all the movements in a sequence, such that sensory feedbacks from prior movements are not necessary to produce subsequent movements. The common way to represent the organization of a motor program theory is by a hierarchy that contains an executive with control links to each movement in the sequence, as shown in Figure 2. Although this type of theory can be applied to single movements, it usually is intended to describe a movement sequence. This hierarchical structure is also used by coding theories of human memory (Estes, 1972; Johnson, 1972), which describe the learning of sequences of letters or digits more adequately than the traditional associative chain theory. The hierarchy in this theory can easily be expanded to more than two levels by considering each movement element in Figure 2 as a group, and by dropping arrows from each of these groups to component movements. In this way Fig-

182

ure 2 would resemble an inverted tree. Restle and Brown (1970) used this kind of structure to describe the learning of sequences of button responses, in which grouping of movements was generated by sequencing rules. The task required subjects to rest their fingers on six buttons, each located under a light. The lights flashed the sequence that was to be learned, and the subjects followed the series of light flashes with corresponding button presses. The results showed that sequences such as 1 2 3 4 6 6 6 6 2 3 2 3 were segmented into three groups based on rules such as "next in series," "repeat," and "alternate." The authors concluded from a careful analysis of their data that subjects were not learning sequences by simple associative chaining, but rather were grouping sequences into runs by means of these cognitive rules.

Musicians are well aware of other bases for grouping movements, for example, the spacing and stresses in time-driven rhythmic sequences. Martin (1972) analyzed rhythm as symmetrical hierarchical time patterns across equal time intervals, and Michon (1974) also regards temporal sequences as hierarchies driven by programs as opposed to a succession of events. However, Kornhuber (1974) and Vorberg and Hornbuch (1978) favor sequentially organized timekeepers over hierarchical timekeepers.

A variation of the open-loop theory is termed the space-coordinate reference theory, proposed by Lashley (1951). Instead of sequencing movements from a memory store of movements, the person produces movements according to a memory of spatial locations. There is no necessity for kinesthetic feedback because the subject need only know where he intends to move to execute the movement (Festinger and Canon, 1965). Other reference systems that are known to mediate movements in this way are body reference systems and gravity based systems (Attneave and Olson, 1967; Attneave and Reid, 1968; Rieser and Pick, 1976). Indeed, the possibility of producing movements without any kinesthetic feedback at all has been supported by many studies (cf. reviews by Bossom, 1974; and Hinde, 1969).

The open-loop or motor program theory is viewed here as a helpful representation of skill learning at an intermediate stage, at which the movements in a sequence are divided into groups and subgroups. During the practicing of a musical skill, it would seem strategically sound to isolate difficult sections for the purpose of solving technical problems. These sections often correspond to rhythmic groups and melodic phrases. When sections are organized hierarchically, it seems reasonable and strategically appealing to expect that automatic processing of groups can be improved as lower levels become highly practiced. Eventually, groups of groups may become automatized, and ultimately, when the top executive code automatically controls the entire tree, long sections of a piece can be played automatically.

Schema theory. Theories of this type have been gaining favor because they attempt to account for more complex phenomena than the closed-loop and open-loop theories, and because they offer solutions to some of the logistical problems created by these theories. But at the same time, it is more difficult to obtain firm supporting evidence for schema theories because the phenomena they attempt to describe are harder to control by traditional experimental procedures.

The notion of a schema is not new. Neurological studies of motor behavior by Head (1920) gave rise to the concept, and Bartlett (1932) developed the concept both for recall of stories and for describing motor behavior in sports. Bartlett regarded a schema as a small collection of stored movements out of which could be generated a wide variety of movements to meet the demands of novel situations. Thus the tennis player need not store all the movements already made, but only a small set of generalizable movements. Attneave (1957) developed the concept of a schema in pattern recognition as an alternative to the familiar template and feature list models. He regarded the schema as an abstraction that is stored by the perceiver as the result of experiences with a variety of instances of a pattern. Posner and Keele (1968) contributed substantially to this notion by an experiment in which they taught subjects to classify abstract dot patterns generated by slightly distorting three prototypes that subjects never saw. After testing, the subjects classified the prototypes nearly as well as the variations they had seen before. The interpretation given is that during classification training with the patterns, subjects developed three separate "concepts" of the three prototypes that were used to recognize variations as instances of one of the three classes. Applied to motor skills, the schema stores abstract representations of movements and their sensory consequences, and actual movements are produced by an interaction between the schema and the environmental circumstances existing at the moment (Pew, 1974).

Not only does the schema notion offer a solution to the problem of the inevitable novel variations of well learned movements, but it also makes storage of movement traces much less of a problem. The number of movements and sensory consequences that must be stored for the closed- and open-loop theories becomes forbiddingly large, especially when one considers the vast number of vocal and hand movement patterns in the repertoire of the singer and instrumentalist. The schema theory suggests that recently performed individual movements will drop from storage after an interval of time, and that the abstract movement schemas remain as a relatively modest amount of stored information (Schmidt, 1976).

Since few learning studies of movement schemas have been reported, the schema theory has yet to be strongly challenged or supported by evidence (cf. Pew, 1974; and Schmidt, 1975, 1976). The present appeal of schema theory apparently lies in its solution to problems concerned with design and capacity properties of the human processing system, and in its attempt to take on the more complex motor activities. Hopefully, developments of schema theory will suggest experimental procedures that will lead to closer contact between theory and data.

Physiological theory and data. One line of development of motor theory that seems to be related to schema notions is given by physiologists, notably Evarts (1973), Easton (1972),

Phillips (1977), and particularly Bernstein (1967). Bernstein's work, for the most part, analyzes coordinated and automatic motor skills such as walking and writing, but many of his conclusions seem appropriate to the analysis of musical performance.

It is easy to come away from an introductory psychology course with the rather simple notion that choosing to execute a particular movement is equivalent to activating a particular set of neurons in the motor area of the cerebral cortex. Some textbooks show a diagram of the body spread across the motor area of the brain. However, this picture appears to be grossly distorted because a large amount of cortical area is devoted to the mouth and hands, and only very small areas represent muscles of the back and the arms and legs. Since the cortex has been generally assumed to be the locus of voluntary behavior and since surgical stimulation of the cortex surface produces selected muscle movements (Fritsch and Hitzig, 1870), it is an easy step to adopt the metaphor of "a little person in the head" who plays on the surface of the motor area as if it were a keyboard, and thereby produces specific discrete impulses that activate muscles in various parts of the body. There are two notions contained in this metaphor that are particularly erroneous and misleading. One incorrect notion is that the motor area of the cortex is the site of voluntary selection of movements. Brain research (Evarts, 1973) indicates that the cortical motor area functions at a low level of motor control close to the muscular systems themselves, while the higher levels of voluntary control are probably located deep within the brain. Specifically, slow movements may be initiated at the basal ganglia and fast movements at the cerebellum (Kornhuber, 1971).

A second incorrect concept is perhaps more critical to the present level of theorizing, namely that there is a one-to-one correspondence between impulses selected at the higher levels and the selection of specific muscle movements. According to Bernstein (1967) any command from a higher voluntary center enters a "lower coordinational system" that organizes responses by adjusting and balancing information from proprioceptors, external forces, and the inertia of limb movements. The impulse to one muscle simultaneously influences many other muscles, and therefore a coordination system is required to insure that the intended movement selected at higher centers does take place in the desired manner at the muscle level. According to Easton (1972), "Muscles are interrelated so extensively that it would be difficult as well as uneconomical to command them singly."

The new picture that emerges is that the connection between voluntary commands and muscle movements in performance skills is quite remote physiologically. Executive commands are sent to coordination systems or "coordinative structures" (Saltzman, in press; for a related usage of this term see Easton, 1972, and Turvey el al., 1978), which interpret the commands as "advice" rather than as instructions to perform specific movements (Gurfinkel et al., 1971). The coordinative structures appear to "have a life of their own" in which they make adjustments among (1) external forces (e.g., mechanical features of instruments that offer resistance while being played, (2) feedback about muscle length and tension, and (3) the inertia of a moving finger or a moving arm. Even postural states are added to the computations in the coordinative structures.

The concept of a coordinative structure provides a neat solution to what is termed the degrees of freedom problem. The muscles commonly act at joints by bending, straightening, or locking; and when a movement includes several joints (e.g., bowing a string, moving the slide of trombone, or striking a piano key) the number of combinations of muscle settings grows large quickly. For example, consider the number of possible combinations of muscle settings in striking a piano key. If one assumes flexor and extensor muscles controlling movements at three of the joints from the wrist to the finger tip, then there would be 2^3 or 8 combinations. Further, if one takes into consideration the number of velocity settings at each joint, for example, four in each direction, then the number of possible combinations of muscle settings for striking a key becomes 8^3 or 512.

184

With so many muscle settings involved, it would seem unlikely that the higher volitional center could select values for each particular movement (Bernstein, 1967; Phillips, 1977). Fortunately the coordinative structures contain built-in restrictions on the degrees of freedom so that certain combinations of muscle settings are highly likely and others improbable. For example, in flexion of the wrist and arm as in bowing, the ratios between the velocities of the change in joint angles (Kots and Syrovegin, 1966) or muscle forces (Saltzman, in press) may be held approximately constant, whether moving fast or slowly. Similarly, singing the word "we" loudly or softly maintains constant relations between tongue and lip muscles.

Another important role of the coordinative structures is to compute the context in which the intended movement or series of movements takes place (Bernstein, 1967). The problem in pressing a key of an instrument is mainly getting to it from one of many prior hand positions. How the particular pressing movement is made depends upon the position and velocity of other finger movements just preceding it, and the momentary feel of the forces of the instrument on the hand. Apparently the coordinative structures acquire the ability to use context information to adjust or "pretune" the appropriate muscle groups prior to receiving commands from the higher executive centers (Gurfinkel et al., 1971).

Thus, it appears that making a movement or a series of movements is complicated, and it is hardly surprising to find that the voluntary executive center requires a great deal of help from the coordinative structures. For the coordinative structures to function in this complex way from moment to moment, kinesthetic information from the spindle systems must be very rich (Ohman, 1967). Indeed, as was already stated, it is very dense for the hands (Phillips, 1977) and tongue (Bowman and Combs, 1968), where the fastest and most complex movements take place. Bernstein (1967) noted two types of correctional activities that may be produced from kinesthetic feedback: When small obstacles occur, the coordinative structures react by

small accommodating adjustments; but when changes occur that affect the global operation of the system, then the structures may reprogram themselves. Examples of the first type of correction would be increasing the rate of walking, or increasng the tempo of performing a piece of music. Examples of the second type of correction would be walking from smooth terrain to a bumpy one, or encountering excessive and irregular rubato from a conductor. Bernstein regards these adjustments as being carried out automatically by the coordinative systems, although one may be well aware that corrections are being made.

Clearly, coordinative structures typically do not operate without messages from the higher centers. The critical problem here concerns the language in which these messages are cast, and several possibilities have been explored. There is wide agreement that "the executive level does not send messages directly and exclusively to the muscles, playing on them as if they were a keyboard" (Pribram, 1971). Rather, it appears that messages from the executive level activate a center in the coordinative structure. The coordinative structure in turn activates its component muscle actions subject to the current environmental and limb conditions. The commands from the executive levels may therefore be quite crude, needing only to select the type of movement desired (for example, walking, scratching, eating) and to indicate some mode of movement (for example, velocity and force). Presumably, the higher centers store this global information, while the coordinative structures store the operations that translate this global information into finely tuned muscle movements.

The differences in language, which may be used to activate different levels in the motor system, are illustrated by an observation of a patient whose war injuries at the lower levels of the motor system affected his ability to raise his arm (Bernstein, 1947). When asked to "lift your hand as high as possible," the patient moved it to a particular point on a scale (which was out of his sight). Next, he was asked to touch with his finger a highly placed dot on a sheet of paper, and the patient raised his arm 10 to 12 centimeters higher. Then he was asked to "get the object hanging on that hook," and he raised his hand an additional 10 centimeters. These three instructions were apparently delivered to successively higher levels in the motor system, which involved coordinative structures having progressively wider distributions of muscle control, such that the effect of the localized injury had progressively less influence. In this sense, coordinative structures may be nested in each other. For example, three levels of walking across a cluttered room might be activated by the following executive instructions: (1) "raise your feet high as you walk," (2) "don't step on the toys," and (3) "go see who is at the door." For playing a section of a piano piece, three instruction levels might be: (1) "lift each finger high and strike the keys with force," (2) "play loudly," and (3) "give the impression of intensity." In both walking and piano playing, commands at levels (1) and (2) will not typically produce the desired effect at level (3). On the other hand, instructions at level (3) can easily produce the desired effects at levels (1) and (2). Of course, to achieve control at level (3) requires high proficiency in the skill.

The foregoing notions of coordinative structures, levels of controlling units, and the global nature of executive language provide

the basis for an elaboration of schema theory, which may make it more applicable to the performance of music. This application of theory will be attempted in the following section. The reader should keep in mind that these remarks are based on reasoned inferences from theory, on some data from physiology, and from experiments on perceptual skills, such as reading. It is hoped that the field will not have to wait too long before these conjectures are tested by appropriate experiments.

Elaborated Schema Theory

Motor schemas and coordinative structures. A key assumption in the elaborated schema theory is that acquisition of a performance skill involves development of structures at two main levels. At the lower level the automatic reflex-like muscle movements are carried out by acquired coordinative structures. At the higher level, the voluntary motor conceptualizations are organized as motor schemas. These higher level structures process information in a global language. Therefore the motor schemas do not communicate directly to individual muscles; only coordinative structures exercise direct control over muscle movements. In Figure 3 are shown motor schemas and their corresponding coordinative structures for single movements, such as pressing a piano key, and for a movement sequence, such as playing an arpeggio. The coordinative structures are denoted by a circle or oval that represents the network of interconnections controlling the eventual activation of individual muscle's motor neurons. The control centers for individual muscles are represented by the small internal shadings.

The network receives signals from the motor schema in terms of voluntary commands; hence the arrow from the motor schema contacts only the circle or oval. The coordinative structures, in turn, communicate with individual muscles in terms of involuntary reflex-like commands. Thus a particular coordinative structure is selected by global signals from a motor schema, which also "advises" it with respect to force and velocity. The coordinative structure balances this input

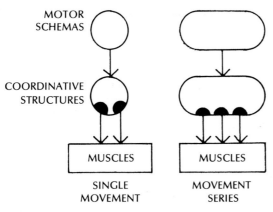

Figure 3. Representation of the elaborated schema theory of motor control for a single movement and for a series of movements.

with ongoing information concerning environmental resistances (for example, characteristics of a keyboard), inertia of moving limbs, and momentary states of muscle length and tension. The observed result of this complex processing is the movement of particular muscles, producing, for example, depression of a single piano key or depression of a series of piano keys in a particular sequence.

The problem of determining what unit is in control at a given instance is a difficult one. However, it may be possible to discover what the performer considers a unit by looking at the types of errors made, as is commonly done in studies of speech production (Clark and Clark, 1977; Fromkin, 1973). When a performer makes an error he or she often begins again at the boundary of a unit. Also a hesitation point in the planning of the next sequence of notes is likely to occur at a unit boundary. It will be tentatively assumed that the desired motor schema unit is a phrase, corresponding to the musical phrase unit. It should be noted, however, that the smallest motor unit, namely the articulation of a single sound, will not correspond to the smallest perceptual unit when this unit is regarded as an interval between two notes (Deutsch, 1969; Dowling, 1978; Jones, 1976).

The role of kinesthetic and auditory feedback in the functioning of motor schemas and coordinative structures will be more easily described if the model of a perceptual schema is briefly sketched. The general framework for perceptual processing is adapted from a recent unpublished manuscript concerned with the perception of words by LaBerge and Lawry (1979).

Perceptual schemas. In Figure 4 is a simplified representation of a short sequence of notes flowing into the auditory receptive area of the brain, along with consequent processing of the information from this receptive area into an organized perceptual schema. The important aspects of this model are the ways of characterizing incoming information and perceptual schemas, and the manner in which information and schemas are interrelated.

The sensory information in a sequence of notes varies from detailed, local features to holistic, global features. Examples of local information are pitch intervals and stress contrasts between adjacent sounds. Global information is regarded here as a relationship that stretches across more than two notes. Of particular importance are those relationships that extend over an entire phrase sequence, assuming it is not too long. A prime example of a global relation is contour (Dowling, 1978; Idson and Massaro, 1976, 1978; Sloboda, 1978). Also, if the listener has a well developed internalized scale (Dowling, 1978) such that each note automatically produces its relationship to the tonal center, then a string of notes produces a corresponding sequence of tonic relationships that may generate global relationships. Sensitivity to where a melody is going may also function as a category that generates global information (Meyer, 1973). Also, rhythm patterns interact with the input to make organizing relationships available to the listener (Dowling, 1973).

It is assumed that, in general, global features activate perceptual schemas, while local features fill in the details after the schema has been activated. This "filling" or "fitting" operation will be described later.

One important reason for the global-local distinction is that local information is typically processed without attention, while global information is at the focus of atten-

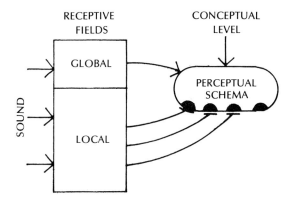

Figure 4. Activation of a perceptual schema from global relationships in a sequence of sounds or from memory. Local, or detailed, features of the sequence fit into the schema.

tion. For example, when we are listening at the level of a phrase, we do not attend to the component pitch and stress details. Instead our attention is given to the broad shape characteristics of the phrase. Of course, we have the option of attending to smaller units than a phrase, but this comes about by shifting our attention to the particular relational features that activate the smaller units.

The global information in a phrase is assumed to activate the phrase unit or schema as the listener follows the music. If the person knows the particular piece of music well enough to anticipate the global information, then the phrase schema will be activated from the executive level. This activation is represented in Figure 4 by an arrow extending from above to the oval line of the schema. For example, the recall of a melody from its name uses this route. This phrase schema is the memory of previously experienced information from this sequence of notes. The local detailed information from the familiar melody "fits into" the details of the schema, represented by the small shadings within the oval. It could be said that the notes fill in the phrase. In a sense, the phrase unit may be regarded as having the property of an expectancy for the reception of local information, such as pitch intervals.

When the local information successfully fits the globally activated phrase schema, the schema's level of activation is raised considerably, and further consolidation of the learned schema is produced. However, it is important to stress that the local information does not activate the schema directly. Only global information is capable of doing this. In order to separate the "fitting" process from the activation process, the lines from the local information in the receptive areas to the components of the schema are tipped with a small arc, while activation lines are tipped with an arrow. One might consider a thin plastic toy analogy, in which the schema is the original mold. If the toy were broken into pieces, these pieces could be fit or matched to the original mold, regardless of what shapes the pieces happened to assume. Thus the largest globals can be regarded as mold-makers, and the locals as mold-fillers.

The relationship between the schema and its component parts follows the gestalt principle that the whole is different than (or other than) the sum of its parts. If instead of being considered a *unit*, the schema were represented as a *group* (as in Figure 2) or a *chain* (as in Figure 1), the whole would be considered as equal to the sum of its parts. This would permit complete reduction of a phrase into component notes or intervals. Indeed, when a sequence of notes is performed as a chain or a group, that is, devoid of large global dynamics, we tend to hear the sequence as "one note after another." These are hardly new ideas. The emphasis on holistic properties as opposed to component parts in music was long ago eloquently expressed by Mursell (1937). What may be new here is the manner in which wholes and parts are considered to interact.

Thus far we have considered perception of phrases in which the local information successfully fits the globally activated phrase schema. If a wrong note is heard, or an unexpected change in rhythm occurs, will this produce a "misfit," and, if so, what are the consequences? The tentative answer is that "misfit" events will indeed occur under these conditions, but the consequences depend upon the type and severity of the mismatch of local information to what is expected on the basis of the schema slots. Consider as a guiding principle the two types of correction described earlier in connection with coordination systems of Bernstein (1967). Small errors such as a wrong note may be accommodated easily by a schema, but larger deviations (for example, when P. D. Q. Bach connects phrases from two different familiar themes) will require resampling at the global level to shift to a different schema.

This model of musical perception may be helpful in understanding how a conductor can attend to the overall shape of a symphony and yet detect a mistake in one of fifteen or more independent parts. If the conductor has acquired schemas that are rich in local detail, then a mistake by any of the instruments will register as a misfit event, and this will subsequently attract the attention of the conductor. Whether or not the conductor can determine where the mistake occurred depends upon the duration of the error and how fast he or she can shift attention to the misfitting event. In view of these considerations it would seem that the well-prepared conductor need not be hindered by the limited capacity of attention, because a schema does not require a division of attention across the many simultaneous lines of music in the way that would be expected from a traditional expectancy theory. A large schema merely requires that the conductor attend to the large global relationships which activate it, while the smaller local details fall into place in the schema automatically.

In summary, this perceptual theory emphasizes two structural aspects and one functional aspect of listening. The two structural aspects are the representation of information in the sensory receptors of the auditory system and the perceptual schemas in the listener's memory. The functional aspect concerns the way that sensory information interacts with perceptual schemas. It is assumed that global sensory information activates perceptual schemas while local information fits the schemas. When local features match up with the detailed characteristics of the schema, they raise the level of activity of the schema, making the sound pattern seem more vivid, and perhaps assisting in the consolidation of the schema memory trace.

Kinesthetic feedback. The sensory information arising from motor activity is assumed to be processed according to the general principles of the perceptual model just described. The two types of information, global and local, correspond to the two general levels in which motor processing is carried out. Global information is produced by the broader relational features of kinesthesis, and speaks both to motor schemas at the voluntary level and to the coordinative structures, which exert direct control over specific muscle movements. Local information is produced by the specific details of muscle and joint sensory receptors and speaks only to the coordinative structures.

The way kinesthetic feedback operates is assumed to be chiefly as a fitting or adjusting

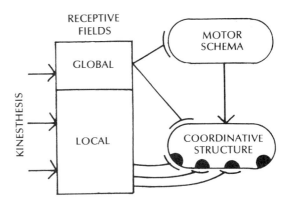

Figure 5. Global kinesthetic inputs "fit" a motor schema and a coordinative structure. Local kinesthetic inputs fit only the coordinative structure.

operation, as shown in Figure 5. When global and local kinesthetic information match the corresponding information in the motor schemas and coordinative structures, there is further consolidation of these networks in memory. If misfits occur, for example, when a pianist plays a piano with an unfamiliar key action or when the person is "out of practice" (which may entail a change in muscle strength and tension), then the kinesthetic feedback will produce misfit events. Following again the guide of the two types of corrections (Bernstein, 1967) discussed before, one would expect the coordinative structures either to accommodate or reprogram, depending on the severity of the misfit events. The person's attention may be drawn to the particular discrepancies at the motor schema level, but the activity directed toward adjusting to the problem may often be done automatically within the coordinative structures. If discrepancies are very severe, the performer might try to shift to smaller motor schemas that command groups of individual notes. But if the person has not practiced the sequence as groups as well as schema units, then the feedback from individual note units would be less familiar, and this could produce a failure in memory.

It should be pointed out that the role of kinesthetic feedback for the playing of instruments may be much richer than is the case for singing. Apparently there is no evidence that muscle spindles exist in the intrinsic muscles controlling the length and tension of the vocal cords (Matthews, 1972; Vennard, 1967) that control pitch. So the singer must rely on his ears for feedback concerning pitch. Moreover, the auditory feedback for timbre is substantially distorted by the conduction characteristics of the internal bone structures of the head. In this case the singer must trust the teacher or resort to extensive use of a tape recorder for feedback. In view of these considerations, the discussions in this paper concerning kinesthetic feedback refer to the playing of instruments, not to singing.

The other major kind of feedback to musical production is sound, which is assumed to influence corrective movements to the motor schemas by way of higher centers. At this level auditory and motor schemas may be closely integrated, somewhat like two sides of the same coin. These schemas in turn may be organized into larger schemas or groups, in various combinations, depending upon the performer. If the person groups small motor schemas, the shapes of melodies may seem lumpy, but if the person groups large motor schemas, a smooth contour may prevail over large sections of music. Long schemas based on conceptual relationships such as implication (Meyer, 1973) and perhaps prolongation (Lerdahl and Jackendorf, 1977), should foster continuity, which in turn could make better contact with ongoing emotional states (Ferguson, 1960, 1969). Indeed, it seems possible that the emotional modulations may help induce the formation of larger schemas. For example, instructing a chorus to express a particular emotional mood often produces a well-shaped section of music when technical instructions about dynamics fail.

One might consider also that practicing long schemas without pause would develop networks at lower automatic levels, which would foster a continuous flow of music. In the discussion of coordinative structures, it was noted that the context of conditions prior to specific response "pretune" the coordinate structures so that very little global information from higher centers is needed to di-

rect the structures. This would imply that the lower level structures may function almost autonomously. Hence, one might expect that it would be difficult to break into the middle of a piece because higher voluntary structures do not exert control over the movements required to begin to play at this point. Thus control of continuous flow may also take place in the coordinative structures, which have become dependent on the prior context of movements and postures.

Learning a performance skill. The course of learning a complex skill such as playing an instrument may be conveniently viewed as progressing through a series of stages. In this paper, major theories of motor skill have been described that could be used to describe particular stages of acquisition of a series of motor movements. In Figure 6 is a representation of these stages within the general framework of the elaborated schema theory. Kinesthetic and auditory feedback loops are omitted here for clarity of exposition. The four stages could represent the development of a three-note sequence on the piano, for example, the first three notes of the C-scale (fingered 123). The remaining five notes of the scale (fingered 12345) could represent another pattern. The performance of the scale could then be treated as a group of two units or schemas. With appropriate practice procedures, this new group should give rise to a new, larger unit, which controls the playing of all eight notes of the scale as a whole. One obvious advantage of forming large units is that more notes can be played while decreasing attention demands.

Motor units may be developed similarly in the learning of melodies, with the ultimate unit determined by the desired musical phrase. If the performer listens only to himself or herself playing repeatedly short sections to solve technical problems, then the auditory guide may shift down to grouping. Hence, it is advisable, according to this framework, to listen occasionally to some other source than one's own playing, even if it be singing or humming the melody, to strengthen perceptual units.

It would be interesting to compare two methods of unitizing a long phrase: One

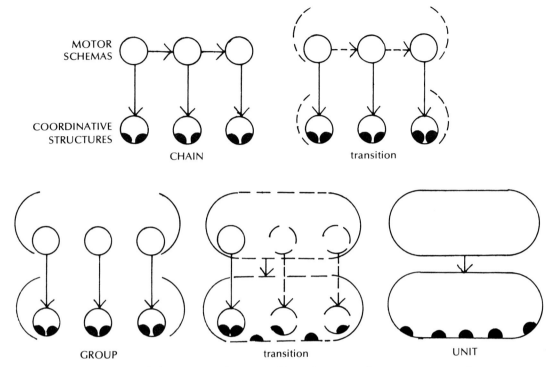

Figure 6. Representation of three general stages of learning to perform a sequence of movements according to the elaborated schema theory.

method would merely group subsections and then unitize the phrase as a whole; the other method would attempt to unitize each subgroup before unitizing the whole phrase. Accomplished performers have many long units in their repertoire that allow them to begin the learning of a new piece by grouping these large units. This procedure resembles the second method just described. The process is represented by entering the sequences of stages of Figure 6 at the group level, but in this case the component units would be much larger than a single response.

The fluency with which a performer articulates a long phrase depends upon how the component movements are coordinated. This coordination typically is made smoother as the performer shifts from a group to a unit. During this transition stage, shown in Figure 6, the performer shifts attention from single movements to relationships between movements. The "width" of the global win-

dow across movements would seem to be critical for developing an easy flow of notes and a smooth melodic contour. Perceiving broadly will permit larger global features to be sampled, resulting in the formation of larger units. Merely repeating a group over and over during practice periods would seem less helpful for unitizing than using successive repetitions as opportunities to try out a variety of larger global "feels," as represented in Figure 5 by the global kinesthetic feedback lines. Bernstein (1967) stated that "practice, when properly undertaken, does not consist in repeating the *means of solution* of a motor problem time after time, but in the *process of solving* this problem again and again by techniques that are changed and perfected from repetition to repetition." The problem here seems to be one of discovering one's own globals from interactions of one's muscles and limbs with the mechanical configurations of the instrument. The global kinesthetic information emerging from these explorations becomes the language, which higher voluntary levels use to modulate the coordinative structures. Of course, one must first make the appropriate movements in order to sense the new kinesthetic feedback. That is, the student must first get the notes into his or her fingers so that the new feedback can begin to emerge. The teacher can suggest, perhaps by metaphor, various changes in the way the notes are played. As the group changes the way of playing the sequence, he or she will feel corresponding changes in the perceived relationships among the movements until an appropriate new global feeling is discovered. This search may produce minor errors at this stage of learning, but this should be tolerated and sometimes encouraged in the interest of moving to a higher unit level. Teachers who overemphasize accuracy can hold back the progress of a student at such transition stages. It would seem to be important to allow considerable freedom to the student to find global kinesthetic "feels," and to learn *when* to signal the appropriate acquired coordinative structures, so that a smooth-flowing musical line can be finally achieved.

Students who differ in learning rates may show important differences in moving from a grouping stage to a unitizing stage. Some move so quickly into larger units that it would seem that they never passed through earlier stages. One suspects that these performers have innate wiring advantages at the coordinative structure level. Others seem to get stuck at a grouping level with rather small component units. Watching a slow student finally move into a larger unit may give the impression that diligent practice in repeating each component somehow builds the larger unit. On the other hand, one sometimes sees an unpredictable jump into the larger unit. The present theory favors the view that one moves from a group to a unit by detecting larger global relationships. Exactly how this shift takes place is not clear. Certainly it helps to have the student sing or even dance the sequence of notes to be sure that the student can perceive the sequence as a unified whole, even if it is being performed

as a group. Currently in the area of reading, reliable teaching procedures have yet to be devised for moving the student from one unit level to another, for example, from seeing a word as component letters or spelling patterns to seeing it as a whole (LaBerge, 1979; LaBerge and Lawry, 1979). Teaching the student to attend to global kinesthetic relationships is an elusive task, perhaps because they cannot easily be pointed to, and because they may vary greatly from person to person.

The transition between a chain and a group would seem to require that the higher, voluntary, level begin to "consider" more responses in the sequence than the one about to be activated. For example, the first four notes of "Frère Jacques" played as a chain requires that each note give rise only to the next note. Played as a group, each note of the melodic segment is emitted in the context of some mild level of activation of the other notes of the group. In particular, before beginning the segment, all the notes should be imaged to some extent. The first and last notes of a group are often most important in initial group images, because these notes constitute boundary information. One way to help to image a group is to play all the notes simultaneously or quickly. For example, the first Prelude of Bach's *Well Tempered Clavier* can be practiced as a series of chords representing the basic group of eight notes. For each piece, and for each performer, some experimentation with the size of groups will be necessary before a large, yet manageable size is decided upon.

Sometimes a sequence of notes requires responding that does not fit naturally into the hand, and the beginning student may be tempted to group movements according to motor predispositions (pre-wired coordinative structures) instead of musical requirements. This state of affairs is quite familiar to music teachers, and the purpose of the present comments is merely to show how the problem could begin to be analyzed within the proposed theoretical framework, and thereby attempt to describe some characteristics of the transition stage from a chain to a group in Figure 6.

192

Seldom does a student learn a work of music by going through all of the stages of Figure 6. Beginning students probably learn a piece by moving from chains to groups, while advanced students learn a piece by unitizing groups of units that are already sizeable. How do students develop large units that transfer from work to work and contribute to the development of proficiency in a skill over a period of years?

This is a difficult question to answer, especially by laboratory evidence collected within the typical subject hour of most experimental studies in our journals. Some studies of the acquisition of automaticity in perceiving novel visual forms (LaBerge, 1973), or automaticity of responses (Logan, 1979), have extended over many days, but few studies systematically follow skill learning over years. Again one must resort to reasoned inferences from theory and from a few pieces of related data for suggestions of answers.

One general trend in the practice of reading is to perceive larger units as the student advances from second grade to college (Samuels et al., 1979). One would expect a similar progressive growth in the size of units in the perception and performance of music. Development of sensitivity to the tonic center in a scale should provide more salient global relationships between heard notes and the inferred tonic center, which should help bind a series of notes together into a strong melodic whole. Development of larger rhythmic groups should potentiate wider melodic and kinesthetic global relationships between stressed events distributed through melodies as well.

There are undoubtedly a vast number of units of moderate size, which are built up over the years, that transfer to new pieces and allow the student to begin at successively higher levels. Arpeggios, scales, trills, and the array of technical figures treated in Chopin's *Etudes* represent well-known examples for the pianist. But it would seem that the skilled performer also has a larger and richer sensitivity to kinesthetic globals, which makes the learning of new pieces relatively easy.

To summarize, as the student moves from a chain to a group, a teacher could ask the student to imagine the next several notes ahead just prior to beginning a section of a piece. In moving from a group to a unit, the task of directing attention seems more difficult, because the student must discover his or her own global motor feelings. Perhaps one could ask the student to look for a *single* feeling that he or she gets while the whole group of notes is played. To do this, the student may direct attention to exaggerated gestures that sweep or curve as the notes are played. In any case, the teacher usually tells the student when it looks and sounds like the student has an appropriate global perception of the unit. It may help teachers to be more patient with students if it is remembered that the student cannot directly command sequences of muscle movements, but must always communicate through the intermediary of a coordinate structure.

The role of exercises in a motor skill could be clarified by considering again the properties of coordinative structures. The factors that adjust these structures include muscle tension and strength, which are affected by use. A performer in top form likely has different muscle and tendon states compared to the performer who is out of practice, and these states produce different kinesthetic feedback patterns to the coordinative structures controlling the performance of pieces. Even exercises performed mechanically (without attention) may suffice to maintain muscle conditions at a stable optimal state.

The elaborated schema theory may offer a framework in which to consider the appropriate attitudes to assume during performance. The attitude of giving satisfactions to others focuses attention on the broader aspects associated with the expressive or architectural form of the music. In contrast, performing as if one is on trial induces fear of making technical errors, so that attention narrows to focus on smaller units to insure accurate performance of details. If the performer has been practicing only the larger units in preparation for a concert, then narrowing of attention at the time of performance to smaller units will produce relatively unfamiliar kinesthetic and perhaps even unfamiliar auditory feedback that does not fit with existing coordinative structures and schemas. The consequence of the influx of new kinesthetic and auditory information may well be a failure of memory retrieval. Apparently high arousal itself also narrows attention (Esterbrook, 1959; Norman, 1976) with similar consequences.

One way to protect oneself from memory failure in performance is to allocate some practicing time to modes that focus attention on smaller unit levels (e.g., slow practice, starting at odd locations, etc.), so that coordination and memory are strengthened here as well as at the larger unit levels. With confidence that memory is secure even if attention is suddenly diverted to smaller units, the performer may be less prone to anxiety. But perhaps the most effective remedy for performance anxiety is to be so immersed in the life of the music at the moment that technical aspects carry little motivational concern, and occasional mistakes are easily accommodated in the schemas that control the performance.

The intent of this paper has been to adapt current physiological knowledge of motor skills and current psychological knowledge of perceptual skills to music performance and learning. This was attempted by incorporating knowledge from these sources into a theoretical framework from which were derived plausible descriptions of some of the basic processes underlying learning and performing. The present theory should in no way be regarded as complete, for many important aspects of performance have not been treated here. Furthermore, even if the framework may help organize existing evidence, and perhaps clarify our thinking about this complex phenomenon, there still remains the task of testing the derived hypotheses by appropriate experiments.

References

Adams, J. A. A closed-loop theory of motor learning. *Journal of Motor Behavior*, 1971, *3*, 111–150.

Adams, S. A. Issues for a closed-loop theory of motor learning. In G. Stelmach (Ed.), *Motor control*. New York: Academic Press, 1976.

Attneave, F. Transfer of experience with a class-schema to identification-learning of patterns and shapes. *Journal of Experimental Psychology*, 1957, *54*, 81–88.

Attneave, F., and R. K. Olson. Discriminability of stimuli varying in physical and retinal orientation. *Journal of Experimental Psychology*, 1967, *74*, 149–157.

Attneave, F., and R. W. Reid. Voluntary control of frame of reference and slope equivalence under head rotation. *Journal of Experimental Psychology*, 1968, *78*, 153–159.

Bartlett, F. C. *Remembering: A study in experimental and social psychology*. London: Cambridge University Press, 1932.

Bernstein, N. *On the structure of movements*. Translated by H. Pick. Moscow: State Publishing House of Medical Literature, 1947.

Bernstein, N. *The co-ordination and regulation of movements*. New York: Pergamon Press, 1967.

Bossom, J. Movement without proprioception. *Brain Research*, 1974, *71*, 285–296.

Bowman, J. P., and C. M. Combs. Discharge patterns of lingual spindle afferent fibers in the hypoglossal nerve of the rhesus monkey. *Experimental Neurology*, 1968, *21*, 105–119.

Chomsky, N. Aspects of the theory of syntax. Cambridge, Massachusetts: MIT Press, 1965.

Clark, H. H., and E. B. Clark. *Psychology and language*. New York: Harcourt Brace Jovanovich, 1977.

Deutsch, D. Music recognition. *Psychological Review*, 1969, *76*, 300–307.

————. The organization of short term memory for a single acoustic attribute. In D. Deutsch and J. S. Deutsch (Eds.), *Short term memory*. New York: Academic Press, 1975.

————. Memory and attention in music. In M. Critchley and R. A. Henson (Eds.), *Music and the brain*. Springfield, Illinois: Charles C Thomas, 1977.

Dowling, W. J. Recognition of melodic transformations: Inversion, retrograde, and retrograde inversion. *Perception and Psychophysics*, 1972, *12*, 417–421.

————. Rhythmic groups and chunks in memory for melodies. *Perception and Psychophysics*, 1973, *14*, 37–40.

————. Scale and contour: Two components of a theory of memory for melodies. *Psychological Review*, 1978, *85*, 341–354.

Dowling, W. J., and D. S. Fujitani. Contour, interval, and pitch recognition in memory for melodies. *Journal of the Acoustical Society of America*, 1971, *49*, 524–531.

Easton, T. A. On the normal use of reflexes. *Amer-*

ican Scientists, 1972, *60,* 591–599.

Esterbrook, J. A. The effect of emotion on the utilization and the organization of behavior. *Psychological Review,* 1959, *66,* 183–201.

Estes, W. K. An associative basis for coding and organization in memory. In A. W. Melton and E. Martin (Eds.), *Coding processes in human memory.* New York: Halsted, 1972.

Evarts, E. V. Brain mechanisms in movement. *Scientific American,* 1973, *229,* 96–103.

Evarts, E. V., and J. Tanji. Gating of motor cortex reflexes by prior instruction. *Brain Research,* 1974, *71,* 479–494.

Ferguson, D. N. *Music as metaphor: The elements of expression.* Minneapolis: University of Minnesota Press, 1960.

————. *The why of music: Dialogues in an unexplored region of appreciation.* Minneapolis: University of Minnesota Press, 1969.

Festinger, L., and L. K. Canon. Information about spatial location based on knowledge about efference. *Psychological Review,* 1965, *72,* 373–384.

Fritsch, G., and E. Hitzig. Uber die elektrische Erreglearkeit des Grosshirns. *Archiv für Anatomie und Physiologie,* 1870, 300–332.

Fromkin, V. (Ed.). *Speech errors as linguistic evidence.* The Hague: Mouton Publishers, 1973.

Fuchs, A. F., and H. H. Kornhuber. Extraocular muscle afferents to the cerebellum of the cat. *Journal of Physiology* (London), 1969, *200,* 713–722.

Greenwald, A. G. On doing two things at once: Time sharing as a function of ideomotor compatibility. *Journal of Experimental Psychology,* 1972, *94,* 52–57.

Gurfinkel, V. S., Ya. M. Kots, V. I. Krinskiy, Ye. I. Pat'tsev, A. G. Fel'dman, M. L. Tsetlin, and M. L. Shik. Concerning tuning before movement. In I. M. Gelfand, V. S. Gurfinkel, S. V. Formin, and M. L. Tsetlin (Eds.), *Models of the structural-functional organization of certain biological systems.* Cambridge, Massachusetts: MIT Press, 1971.

Head, H. *Studies in neurology* (Vols. 1 and 2). London, 1920.

Hinde, R. A. Control of movement patterns in animals. *Quarterly Journal of Experimental Psychology,* 1969, *21,* 105–126.

Idson, W. L., and D. W. Massaro. Cross-octave masking of single tones and musical sequences: The effects of structure on auditory recognition. *Perception and Psychophysics,* 1976, *19,* 155–175.

————. A bidimensional model of pitch in the recognition of melodies. *Perception and Psychophysics,* 1978, *24,* 551–565.

Johnson, N. F. Organization and the concept of a memory code. In A. W. Melton and E. Martin (Eds.), *Coding processes in human memory.* New York: Halsted, 1972.

Jones, M. R. Time, our lost dimension: Toward a new theory of perception, attention, and memory. *Psychological Review,* 1976, *83,* 323–355.

Keele, S. W. *Attention and human performance.* Pacific Palisades, California: Goodyear Publishing Co., 1973.

Keele, S. W., and J. J. Summers. The structure of motor programs. In G. Stelmach (Ed.), *Motor Control: Issues and trends.* New York: Academic Press, 1976.

Kornhuber, H. H. Cerebral cortex, cerebellum, and basal ganglia: An introduction to their motor functions. In F. O. Schmidt and F. G. Worden (Eds.), *The neurosciences: Third study program.* Cambridge MIT Press, 1974.

Kots, Ya. M., and A. V. Syrovegin. Fixed set of variants of interactions of the muscles of two joints in the execution of simple voluntary movements. *Biophysics,* 1966, *11,* 1212–1219.

LaBerge, D. Attention and the measurement of perceptual learning. *Memory and Cognition,* 1973, *1,* 268–276.

————. Perceptual learning and attention. In W. K. Estes (Ed.), *Handbook of Learning and Cognitive Processes* (Vol. 4), Hillsdale, New Jersey: Erlbaum, 1976.

————. The perception of units in beginning reading. In L. Resnick and P. Weaver (Eds.), *Theory and practice of beginning reading instruction.* Hillsdale, New Jersey: Erlbaum, 1979.

LaBerge, D., and J. A. Lawry. *Perceptual and semantic factors in word processing: Theory and data.* Unpublished manuscript. 1979.

LaBerge, D., and S. J. Samuels. Toward a theory of automatic information processing in reading. *Cognitive Psychology,* 1974, *6,* 293–323.

Lashley, K. S. The problem of serial order in behavior. In L. A. Jeffress (Ed.), *Cerebral mechanisms in behavior.* New York: John Wiley & Sons, Inc., 1951.

Lerdahl, F., and R. Jackendorf. Toward a formal theory of tonal music. *Journal of Music Theory,* 1977, *21,* 111–171.

Logan, G. D. On the use of concurrent memory load to measure attention and automaticity. *Journal of Experimental Psychology: Human Perception and Performance,* 1979, *5,* 189–207.

MacNeilage, P. F. Motor control of serial ordering of speech. *Psychological Review,* 1970, *77,* 182–196.

Martin, J. Rhythmic (hierarchical) versus serial structure in speech and other behavior. *Psychological Review,* 1972, *79,* 487–509.

Matthews, P. B. C. *Mammalian muscle receptors and their central actions.* London: Arnold, 1972.

Meyer, L. B. *Explaining Music: Essays and explorations.* Berkeley, California: University of California Press, 1973.

Michon, J. A. Programs and "programs" for sequential patterns in motor behavior. *Brain Research,* 1974, *71,* 413–424.

Mursell, J. L. *The psychology of music.* New York: W. W. Norton, 1937.

Norman, D. A. *Memory and attention.* New York: John Wiley & Sons, Inc., 1976.

Ohman, S. E. G. Peripheral motor commands in labial articulation. Speech Transmission Laboratory, *Quarterly Progress and Status Report,* 1967, No. 4, Stockholm, Sweden: Royal Institute of Technology.

Pew, R. W. Human perceptual-motor performance. In B. H. Kantowitz (Ed.), *Human information processing: Tutorials in performance and cognition.* Hillsdale, New Jersey: Erlbaum, 1974.

Phillips, C. G. Brains and hands. In M. Critchley and R. A. Henson (Eds.) *Music and the brain.* Springfield, Illinois: Charles C Thomas, 1977.

Posner, M. T., and S. W. Keele. On the genesis of abstract ideas. *Journal of Experimental Psychology,* 1968, *77,* 353–363.

Pribram, K. H. *Languages of the brain: Experimental paradoxes and principles in neuropsychology.* Englewood Cliffs, New Jersey: Prentice-Hall, 1971.

Reiser, J. J., and H. L. Pick. Reference systems and the perception of tactual and haptic orientation. *Perception & Psychophysics,* 1976, *19,* 117–121.

Restle, F. Serial patterns: The role of phrasing. *Journal of Experimental Psychology,* 1972, *92,* 385–390.

Restle, F., and E. R. Brown. Serial pattern learning. *Journal of Experimental Psychology,* 1970, *83,* 120–125.

Saltzman, E. Levels of sensorimotor representation. *Journal of Mathematical Psychology,* in press.

Samuels, S. J., D. LaBerge, and C. D. Bremer. Units of word recognition: Evidence for developmental changes. *Journal of Verbal Learning and Verbal Behavior,* 1978, *17,* 715–720.

Schank, R., and R. Abelson. *Scripts, plans, goals, and understanding.* Hillsdale, New Jersey: Erlbaum, 1977.

Schmidt, R. A. A schema theory of discrete motor skill learning. *Psychological Review,* 1975, *82,* 225–260.

———. The schema as a solution to some persistent problems in motor learning theory. In G. E. Stelmach (Ed.), *Motor control.* New York: Academic Press, 1976.

Shaffer, L. H. Intention and performance. *Psychological Review,* 1976, *83,* 375–393.

Sloboda, J. A. Perception of contour in music reading. *Perception,* 1978, *7,* 323–331.

Stelmach, G. E. (Ed.). *Motor control.* New York: Academic Press, 1976.

Sussman, H. M. What the tongue tells the brain. *Psychological Bulletin,* 1972, *77,* 262–272.

Turvey, M. T. Preliminaries to a theory of action with reference to vision. In R. Shaw and J. Bransford (Eds.), *Perceiving, acting, and knowing.* Hillsdale, New Jersey: Erlbaum, 1977.

Turvey, M. T., R. E. Shaw, and W. Mace. Issues in the theory of action: Degrees of freedom, coordinative structures, and coalitions. In J. Requin (Ed.), *Attention and performance, VII.* Hillsdale, New Jersey: Erlbaum, 1978.

Vennard, W. *Singing: The mechanism and the technic.* New York: Carl Fischer, 1967.

Vorberg, D., and R. Hambuch. On the temporal control of rhythmic performance. In J. Requin (Ed.), *Attention and performance, VII.* Hillsdale, New Jersey: Erlbaum, 1978.

Note. This research was supported by grants from the National Science Foundation (NSF/BNS77-22075), the National Institute for Child Health and Human Development (HD 01136), and the Graduate School of the University of Minnesota. The author wishes to thank Paul Fox, Leah Larkey, Janice Lawry, Gerald Siegel, Elliott Saltzman, and Herbert Pick for helpful discussions and comments.

Response

Steven K. Hedden

Let me begin by noting that LaBerge's paper seems to be primarily concerned with psychomotor skill development with intermediate to advanced students. This seems appropriate, for instruction in elementary aspects of instrumental music proceeds in a relatively straightforward and uncomplicated manner. I refer here to how to hold the instrument, how to set the embouchure, how to produce the first tone, and so forth. Music teachers are familiar with the use of aural and visual models and we know how to reinforce certain isolated behaviors with the exceptation that those reinforced behaviors will tend to be repeated. We know how to help a student associate a given visual stimulus with a certain fingering or position, so that the beginning trombonist learns that B♭ below middle C is played in first position. We know that the beginning clarinetist needs to have an aural concept of how a clarinet should sound.

As the student progresses, he or she begins to work on exercises or melodies, which require that several different tones be played in a specified temporal relationship. These exercises might, for example, include the first five notes of a scale, notated in half and quarter notes. Again, the process used to teach these simple exercises and/or melodies is somewhat straightforward and uncomplicated. Any competent band director can help a student progress at this level of skill.

At a later stage of development, however, differences among teachers begin to be manifested. Some teacher's students never seem to progress musically beyond the chaining of notes I have just described. Critics would complain that these students merely play the notes—at the appointed times, to be sure, but the overall impression one gains is of mechanical attempts at music. Other teachers, the more successful ones, produce students whose playing is regarded as highly musical. The notes are played correctly, in tune, with good tone quality, and so forth. What are the differences in teaching strategy that produce such dissimilar results? LaBerge's paper suggests that superior performers may have more highly developed, that is, larger, schema for performance skills. I believe that his paper provides some useful suggestions for helping students develop these larger performance schemas. I should add, however, that the suggestions he has provided have not yet been tested by controlled experiments. As he notes, it is not clear at this point how a student moves or progresses from smaller to larger units. For this reason, the suggestions based on

schema theory will need to be regarded as tentative; we as music educators will have to assume the responsibility for testing them in controlled situations. I believe that my remarks will indicate the types of experiments we will need.

LaBerge indicated near the end of his paper that "beginning students probably learn a piece by moving from chains to groups . . . ." He also suggested that "The transition between a chain and a group would seem to require that the higher, voluntary level begin to 'consider' more responses in the sequence than the one about to be activated." The emphasis here would be placed on helping the student "image" the notes so that he or she comes to regard them as belonging together. This suggests that prerehearsal would be valuable. During this prerehearsal, the teacher would point out how notes could be grouped together. Melodic contour and/or rhythmic flow would be important here.

There also could be an additional benefit that would accrue from prerehearsal. Research by Holdsworth (1974) has shown that covert, electromyographic (EMG) activity occurs while intermediate trumpet students mentally rehearse a music exercise while holding their instruments in playing position. This suggests that motor learning might occur as the student mentally rehearses an exercise, for there was a strong correspondence between the EMG activity emitted while mentally rehearsing and the EMG activity emitted while actually producing the tones. Researchers in other areas have observed a similar phenomenon. Further study of the role of mental prerehearsal in psychomotor learning obviously seems warranted.

Turning to advanced students, LaBerge indicated that they probably learn a piece by "unitizing groups of units that are already sizeable." He also suggested that we could facilitate unitizing by increasing the size of the perceptual unit. A first concern here, then, would be to determine the size of the perceptual unit for the performer. LaBerge has provided at least one clue, which could help music researchers investigate the size of the perceptual unit. He suggests that when an error occurs, the performer frequently

197

starts over at the boundary of what he or she regards as a unit. It would appear that simple monitoring of practice sessions might provide music researchers with information regarding the size of the perceptual unit for students at various levels of development. All that would be necessary would be to note the point in the music where the student resumes practicing. A variant of this idea might also prove helpful, whereby an experimenter would ask a subject to stop playing in mid-stream, so to speak, then start again at a location chosen by the performer. It would be assumed that the student would resume the performance at the boundary of a unit.

The use of either procedure—restarting after an error or after an externally-imposed request to stop—with subjects of varying performance levels could provide some rough, normative data regarding the size of the perceptual unit for students at various levels of skill. Based on previous research, I would expect to find a positive correlation between the size of the perceptual unit and: (1) the age of the performer; (2) the previous playing experience of the performer; (3) the tonal strength of the stimulus; and (4) the rhythmic regularity of the stimulus.

How can we help a student increase the size of the perceptual unit, that is, take in larger chunks of information so that notes will be combined to produce music, not merely chains of successive tones? LaBerge states that students apparently "move to larger units by detecting larger global relationships." He recognizes that how this shift takes place is not clear, but offers some suggestions. One, apprehension of larger units might be facilitated by helping students become more sensitive to tonality; sensitivity to tonality could help bind a series of notes together into a strong melodic whole. Two, it may be possible to help students detect larger global relationships by increasing their awareness of the groupings supplied by the rhythmic line of the music. Both of these suggestions imply that instrumental teachers should devote a significant portion of each rehearsal or lesson to the development of listening skills. During these sessions, the teacher should help students become more

attentive to the overall contour of a phrase, to the departures from the expected, to the way in which the composer has used rhythmic elements to group notes together. Stress here would be placed on directing students' attention to global information, with the hope of building up perceptual schema through successive exposures to sound patterns.

Another important issue that was raised concerns language. The first example cited by LaBerge was the patient whose war injuries at the lower levels of the motor system affected his ability to raise his arm. He was given three different instructions: (1) lift your hand as high as possible, (2) touch the dot on the sheet of paper, and (3) get the object hanging on the hook. Each of the second and third instructions resulted in an increased reach of approximately 10 centimeters. The level of language seemed to affect the performance of the psychomotor task. His second example pertained to piano performance. It was suggested that three levels of instructional language might be used: (1) lift each finger high and strike the keys with force, (2) play loudly, and (3) give the impression of intensity. It was asserted that instructions at levels one and two typically will not produce the desired effect at level three, yet instructions at level three (give the impression of intensity) would easily produce the desired effects at levels one and two, provided that the performer already has proficiency in the skill. In his third example, LaBerge noted that instructing a chorus to express a particular emotion often produces a well-shaped section of music when technical instructions about dynamics fail.

The message seems clear; the level of language employed by the teacher may exert a strong influence on the acquisition of performance skills. Indeed, as LaBerge asserted, emotional modulations may help induce the formation of larger schemas. This seems eminently reasonable, for the elaborated schema theory holds that schemas are concerned with global information, and instructions such as "give the impression of intensity" certainly seem to provide global information.

In any case, what seems to be needed is a series of experiments that would examine the relationship between levels of language and performance skill acquisition. Even an experiment as crude and unrefined as the following one might provide helpful information. Take two randomly-assigned instrumental or choral groups at each of various levels—junior high or high school. Have them rehearse the same compositions for the same length of time. Have the teacher of the two groups in any one school use identical teaching procedures, with one exception. When working with one group, the teacher would be confined to using technical instructions such as "play louder" or "let's take it a little faster." When working with the other group, the teacher would be asked to use imagery, emotional modulations and so forth, such as "make the music sound as if it's coming closer to you." At the end of the treatment period, the performances of the groups could be compared in terms of fluency, musicality, or accuracy. The prediction from schema theory would be that the performance of the second group would be better.

I believe that LaBerge's paper also has some important implications in terms of students' practicing. Of course, we all have our own ideas about frequency of practice and length of practice. These are simple matters to communicate to our students: "I want you to practice 30 minutes daily." What is more difficult to communicate is how to practice. Sometimes that message is never given, possibly because the teacher is uncertain about the answer to the question, why practice?

LaBerge cited Bernstein to the effect that "practice, when properly undertaken, does not consist in repeating the means of solution of a motor problem time after time, but in the process of solving this problem again and again by techniques that are changed and perfected from repetition to repetition." The intent of the practice is to develop a schema, which is abstracted from a variety of instances of a pattern. The student can perform this process of abstraction most efficiently when he or she has the opportunity to investigate what LaBerge calls kinesthetic feels. The student's repeated attempts provide an opportunity to obtain global kinesthetic information; for example, the clarinet

student learns how it feels to go from third-line B to second-space A and back again. The emphasis here is on how does a particular movement from note to note feel; the student needs to try out various solutions in order to develop his or her own globals. As LaBerge notes, "The global kinesthetic information emerging from these explorations becomes the language which higher voluntary levels use to modulate the coordinative structures. One must make the appropriate global movements first in order to create the new kinesthetic feedback." In short, a student should use a practice session to explore different ways of solving a musical problem. I want to add, though, that the student first must have an idea of how the music stimulus should sound when properly executed. Unless the student has this concept of how the music should sound, the explorations during practice sessions will be wandering and nonproductive.

I would like to summarize some of the points I have made. (1) Music educators need to devote attention to efforts designed to determine the size of the perceptual or motor unit for students at various levels of development. If we are to help a student progress from smaller units to larger units, first we must know the size of the unit at the level where the student is currently operating. (2) It appears that we may be able to help a student move from smaller to larger units by using a portion of each rehearsal or lesson for listening activities. In particular, attempts should be made to heighten the student's awareness of the overall contour of a phrase and the rhythmic elements that are used to unify it. We need to help students become more aware of the larger, architectonic aspects of music. (3) We need to embark on a series of studies designed to evaluate the effect that different levels of language have on the development of psychomotor skills. LaBerge's remarks imply that we might better facilitate psychomotor skill development by using higher levels of language, language chosen for its global information. (4) We should provide models for our students to consider or refer to as they practice. They should be encouraged to explore possible solutions to the performance of the music and to investigate the various feels they obtain from these possible solutions, all with the intent of generating global kinesthetic feedback, which will help them form their own schemas.

Reference

Holdsworth, E. I. *Neuromuscular activity and covert musical psychomotor behavior: An electromyographic study.* Unpublished doctoral dissertation, University of Kansas, 1974.

Culturally Defined Learning Experience

Jane A. Siegel

Over the past 10 years, my interest in the psychology of music has brought me into contact with a large number of individuals having a variety of backgrounds—performers, music educators, acousticians, physicists, engineers, anthropologists, and psychologists.

This conference gives me the opportunity to present a point of view that has been rankling in the back of my mind for some time now—that the classic textbook approach to the psychology of music is wrong-headed and destructive to the creation and enjoyment of music.

If one takes the trouble to examine the treatment of music perception by psychologists, one finds that the standard approach is the psychoacoustic one. That is, we are led to believe that musical experience can be explained by analyzing the acoustic waveform into its basic physical dimensions, and by discovering the corresponding psychological dimensions that are mapped onto them. This approach is empiricist, positivist, and reductionist, and leads to a focus on such problem areas as discrimination and scaling of basic sensory dimensions, such as pitch and loudness. Attempts to explain the basic phenomena of music perception have largely been limited to two key areas, the external acoustic stimulus and the sensory transducers in the ear.

When I discuss the psychoacoustic approach with musicians, I usually am left with the impression that it does not address very well their perceptual experience. Musicians are concerned with qualitative aspects of listening—mood, tonality, imagery, rhythm—areas for which traditional sensory psychophysics has little to offer. At the same time, there has been a tendency among musicians to accept the psychophysical approach as correct, even though it contradicts their own experience, perhaps because it represents "real science." Thus, it is worth pointing out to musicians that the psychophysical model has proven inadequate in its ability to account for the phenomena of human perception. The last two decades in psychology have seen the rise of more sophisticated information-processing models of perception, models which have integrated ideas and data from fields as diverse as sensory physiology, mathematics, computer science, cognition, learning, and memory. It is my belief that the information-processing approach is much more compatible with the interests and concerns of music educators than the psychoacoustic model, and hence should give rise to a rapprochement between psychologists and musicians that until now has not been possible.

Perception as an Active Process

Implicit in the psychophysical model is the idea that perception is a passive process, that there is a one-to-one correspondence between the physical and perceptual worlds. Take pitch, for example. Pitch is thought to be the psychological correlate of the fundamental frequency of an acoustic waveform. Similarly, according to the psychophysical model, loudness is the perceptual correlate of amplitude, timbre is explicable by the patter of overtones, and so forth.

Current information-processing theories, on the other hand, view perception as an active process. The sensory systems, according to information-processing theorists, provide us at best with a set of ambiguous cues about objects and events in the outside world. There is no one-to-one correspondence between perceptual experience and the physical stimulus, except in rare instances.

To quote Lindsay and Norman (1973):

> The patterns of energy that strike the sensory organs can be interpreted as meaningful signals only through the combination of sensory analysis, memory processes, and thought.
>
> Analysis by synthesis is a pattern-recognition scheme that works at the task from all pos-

sible angles. It attempts to convert the sensory evidence into an interpretation consistent with our knowledge about the outside world. It is continuously constructing, testing, and revising hypotheses about what is being perceived . . . . It is a complicated mechanism, but so is the human brain. Every bit of its complexity is needed to explain human pattern recognition. (pp. 146–147)

In this paper, I will present evidence that an active information-processing mechanism underlies the perception of music. Here I will deal primarily with pitch perception, since pitch is more usually treated as a simple sensory dimension that is encoded passively. The evidence that I will review supports the position that, for the musical listener, pitch perception is often a highly illusory event, where culturally defined music experience counts more than the external stimulus. To paraphrase Richard Gregory, the well-known British psychologist, musical pitch is less a matter of the ear than the brain.

The Perception of Pitch by Musicians

Eleven years ago, William Siegel and I began a program of research investigating the role that learning and culture play in the perception of pitch. Since then we have tested a large number of individuals with varying degrees of music experience in a variety of information-processing tasks. While most of our respondents have been raised in the Western musical tradition, our research has also brought us into contact with non-Western musicians and enthnomusicologists from such cultures as India, China, Australia, and Indonesia.

One basic fact has emerged from this program of research–that the perception of pitch is strongly colored by culturally-defined music experiences. Musicians do not hear pitch in the same way as non-musicians. Moreover, Western musicians do not hear pitch in the same way as musicians raised in other cultures. For musicians within a given cultural tradition, the perception of elementary auditory events in music is an interpretive process that is influenced as much by their knowledge and expectations as by the acoustic stimulus.

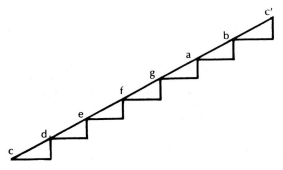

Figure 1. The tonal line and the tonal scale (from Helmholtz, 1877).

Pitch is usually thought of by psychologists as a monotonic continuously increasing function of tone frequency (Stevens and Volkmann, 1940). Yet, as Helmholtz (1887, pp. 250–252) argued:

> . . . alterations of pitch in melodies take place by intervals, and not by continuous transitions. This series of degrees is laid down in the musical scale . . . the musical scale is, as it were, the divided rod by which we measure variation in pitch.

Helmholtz illustrated his point, as shown in Figure 1, by drawing a contrast between the tonal line and the tonal scale. The tonal line represents pitch as a simple sensory continuum, an increasing function of tone frequency. The tonal scale on the other hand is a step-function, with the plateaus representing the notes of the musical scale. Music derives its meaning, according to Helmholtz, from the fact that only a very limited number of pitch values are allowed to occur. It is the discrete nature of music that distinguishes it from the howling of the wind or the shrieking of a siren.

While different music cultures vary in the manner in which they subdivide the continuum of tone frequency, the smallest meaningful unit of pitch for Western music is the semitone. In our culture, the well-tempered scale divides each octave into twelve logarithmically equal steps. Each note in the scale is related to its neighbor by a frequency ratio corresponding to a semitone (1.059:1). Western music fixes not only the step size of music intervals, but also the absolute frequency value of each note. Most Western musicians with formal training have acquired good rel-

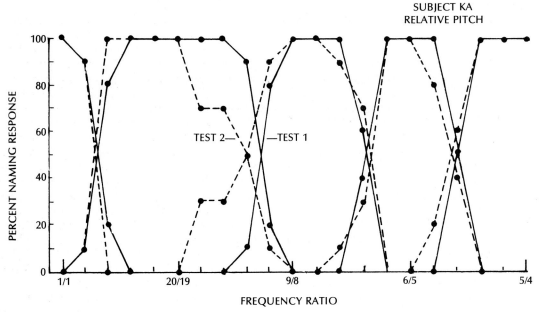

Figure 2. Identification of tonal intervals by a musically trained observer. The dotted line shows the result of a retest over one month.

202

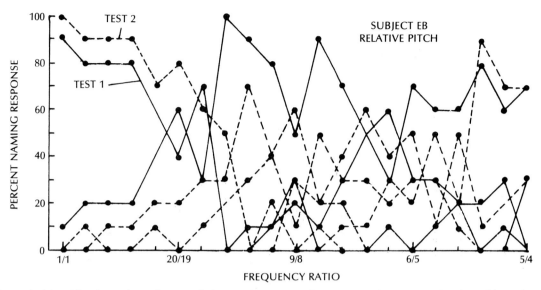

Figure 3. Identification of tonal intervals by an observer without musical training. The dotted line shows the result of a retest over one month.

ative pitch, the ability to recognize and name intervals. Only a very small number of musicians have acquired absolute pitch, the ability to identify single notes without reference to a standard. Because in our society, transposition of melodies is part of the music system, the possession of absolute pitch is a luxury, rather than a necessity.

Identification of Notes and Intervals

Over the years, I have tested a number of individuals with absolute or relative pitch. Figure 2 shows the data of a highly trained musician with relative pitch, who was asked to identify randomly presented tonal intervals ranging over five semitones, from unison to a major third, in twenty-cent steps. The solid line shows the results of a first test session, while the dotted line shows the results of a retest over one month later (Siegel and Siegel, 1972). The data are remarkably consistent and orderly, indicating musicians with relative pitch can be very accurate at identifying tonal intervals.

Contrast these results with those of a nonmusician (Figure 3), and you will see that the accurate and consistent identification of intervals is not an easy task for persons who

have not been trained musically. Yet there may be some music educators who, because good relative pitch seems so natural to them, are not sufficiently appreciative of their novice students' inability to hear musical intervals appropriately.

Figures 4 and 5 present similar identification data for possessors of absolute pitch and nonmusical control subjects. Here the stimuli are single tones varying in frequency over a range of five semitones (C to E), in twenty-cent steps (Siegel and Siegel, 1977a). As you can see, the ability to identify notes accurately and reliably can be acquired, but we have found few individuals who have this ability.

I am making the assumption here that musicians' note and interval categories are acquired through training. There are a number of writers who would disagree with this view, and would argue that the Western musical scale is a "natural" one, on either mathematical or acoustic grounds (e.g., Meyer, 1956). This point of view is contradicted by the inability of nonmusicians to identify notes or intervals with any degree of accuracy. Furthermore, there is a great deal of crosscultural variation in both scale forms and absolute tuning.

203

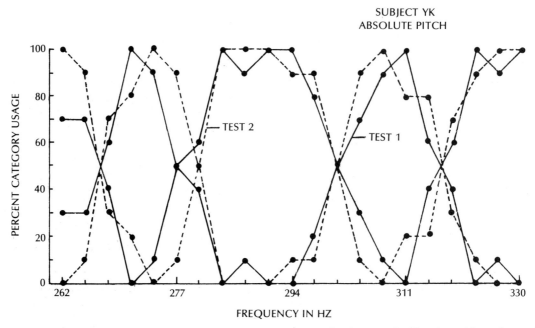

Figure 4. Identification of tone frequency by an observer with absolute pitch. The dotted line shows the result of a retest over one month.

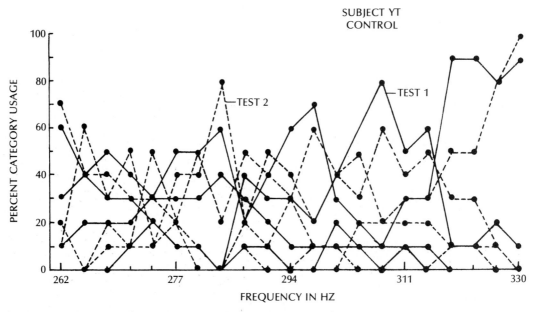

Figure 5. Identification of tone frequency by an observer with no musical training. The dotted line shows the result of a retest over one month.

204

The Perceptual Experience of Musicians

The previous section examined the ability of musicians and nonmusicians to identify or label tonal stimuli. It appears that musicians do acquire as a result of their training and experience a set of internal mnemonic reference points or categories that allow them to perform quite accurately in an absolute identification task. These internal anchors correspond to notes and intervals defined by the Western musical system.

What influence do these acquired mnemonic categories have on the way musicians actually hear pitch? Is the perception of pitch for a musician analogous to the perception of other simple sensory continua, such as brightness, length, or loudness? That is, does a simple psychophysical representation of pitch, such as Stevens' Mel Scale (Stevens and Volkmann, 1940), do justice to the perceptual experience of musicians? The answer is, I believe, a clear-cut "no."

Let me support this view first with the results of a simple experimental study (Siegel, Siegel, Harris, and Sopo, 1974). We set up a task in which subjects judged a set of twenty different tonal intervals spread over a range of five semitones from unison (a frequency ratio of 1:1) to a major third (5:4), in twenty equal steps.

A computer was used to generate the intervals, each of which consisted of two .25-second sinusoids separated by a 1-second silent period. In each of five blocks of trials, the subject first heard a standard interval of 9:8 (a major second) three times, and was asked to assign the standard any value over 100. He then listened to the twenty intervals once each in random order, and was asked to judge how far apart the two tones of the interval were. He was told if, for example, the interval seemed twice as large as the standard, he should assign it a number that is twice as large.

This task is a standard psychophysical paradigm known as *magnitude estimation*. Interestingly, the magnitude estimation task has been used in the past to generate the Mel Scale for pitch (Stevens and Volkmann, 1940), using respondents of indeterminate and likely mixed degrees of musical experi-

ence. The Mel Scale is a continuously increasing function of tone frequency, but unlike Helmholtz's tonal line, it does not have a logarithmic relationship to tone frequency.

Figure 6 shows the results of BF, a musician with excellent relative pitch. Each panel shows data for one block of trials, and each point represents a single, unaveraged judgment. As you can see, in every block BF produced a perfect step function with five steps. Moreover, the steps are centered on the five standard musical intervals covered by the stimulus set.

It is interesting that, although we presented twenty acoustically different intervals, BF used only five different numbers to describe his perceptual experience. Was this simply laziness on his part, was it some sort of response bias, or was it an accurate representation of what BF actually heard?

To answer this question, we conducted an in-depth interview with BF after the experiment. When asked to guess how many physically-different stimuli these were, BF replied, "I guess if there were five stimuli and twenty trials, there must have been four of each." Although fully three quarters of the intervals presented to him were musically inaccurate, BF reported hearing nothing but in-tune intervals.

We then asked BF to describe to us how he actually went about making his numerical estimates during the task. He said that he arbitrarily assigned a value of fifty to each semitone difference. On each trial, he would listen for the unique sound quality that each interval elicited, and then would assign the appropriate number to the interval. When asked to define what these qualities were, he used color or mood imagery. For example, to BF, the minor third sounded "dark, closed, and sad." The tritone was easy to recognize because of "that tinny quality that you sometimes hear in Oriental music."

Further discussion with BF led us to the conclusion that his musical experience had resulted in the transformation of pitch from a simple sensory continuum to a set of discrete qualities. For him, the perception of pitch was analogous to that of color, rather than length. While he was willing to assign num-

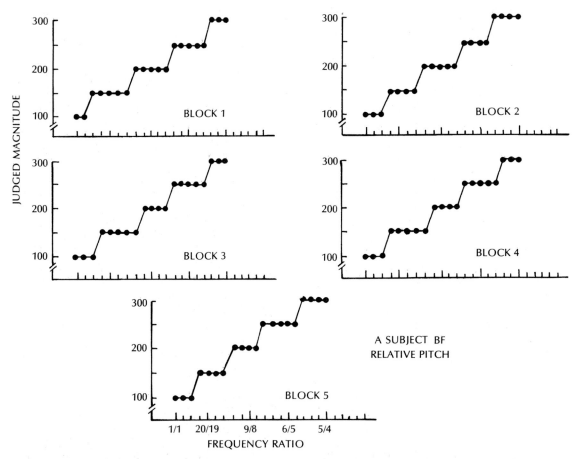

Figure 6. Judgment of tonal intervals by BF, an observer with good relative pitch. The task was to assign each interval a number according to how far apart the two tones of the interval were.

bers to tonal intervals, that assignment was arbitrary (or *nominal*, from a scaling point of view), in the same sense that the numbers on the sweaters of a football team are arbitrary.

We then went on to ask BF what he would do if he heard something exactly halfway between two musical intervals, say a major and minor third. He felt that it was difficult to imagine something halfway between two intervals that sounded to him totally different from one another, and guessed that "our ears would tend to justify them into one category or the other."

Indeed, that was what appeared to happen in the experiment. Figure 7 shows the means and standard deviations of BF's judgments over the five blocks of trials. As you can see, while BF used only five different numbers to describe the twenty tonal intervals, his use of those numbers was inconsistent for those intervals that fell between the standard Western intervals. This gave rise to a "cycling" of the standard deviations, with high variability at the boundaries between interval categories. Subjectively, in-between intervals were not heard as in-between; rather they "popped" into one category or the other.

BF was a highly trained musician with years of experience as a performer and teacher. At the time of the experiment, he reported participating actively in music forty to fifty hours per week. We have observed similar

206

perceptual categorization in a number of other musicians with relative pitch (see Siegel and Siegel, 1977b), and have yet to find a single Western musician who can differentiate accurately between different examples of the same musical interval–that is, who can distinguish between "sharp," "flat," and "in-tune" intervals. A similar conclusion has been reached by Burns and Ward (1978) using somewhat different experimental techniques.

It should be pointed out at this time that the perceptual categorization typified by BF's data represents an auditory illusion. BF and the other musicians with relative pitch do not have a "fine ear," an ability to pick up small acoustic differences between tonal stimuli. On the contrary, they are different from nonmusicians because they tend to listen musically, rather than acoustically. They hear what they ought to hear, according to the expectations generated by their music training, instead of hearing what is presented to them via the acoustic waveform.

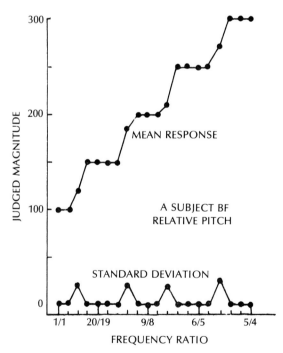

Figure 7. Mean and standard deviation of BF's judgments.

Over the years, we have also tested a number of individuals with absolute pitch, and have observed that they tend to impose culturally defined categories on single notes in much the same way that musicians with relative pitch categorize intervals. For example, Figure 8 shows the results of subject MT, a musician with excellent absolute pitch, in a magnitude estimation experiment (Siegel, Siegel, Harris, and Sopo, 1974).

The task was identical to the relative pitch experiment reported earlier, except that the stimuli were twenty single tones, varying in frequency from C (261.6 Hz) to E (329.6 Hz). The subject's task was to make numerical ratings of the perceived height of each tone relative to a standard, which was presented at the beginning of each block of trials. Like BF, MT produced magnitude estimation functions with five steps, one for each musical note. Like BF, the variability was concentrated at the boundary between two music categories (Figure 9), indicating that she misclassified in-between notes, rather than hearing them as intermediate. Like BF, she reported listening for the unique sound quality inherent in a note, and used color imagery to define what she meant by the qualitative aspect of notes. Like BF, she was unaware that three-quarters of the stimuli were out-of-tune.

I have obtained similar step-like magnitude estimation functions from a number of other musicians with absolute pitch. In one of our experiments (Harris and Siegel, 1975), several subjects chose to use adjacent numbers as responses—that is, they did not even allow for the possibility of having to judge intermediate tones. (When we asked one of these subjects what she would do if she heard something in between two notes, she replied, "I wondered about that, but fortunately, it never happened." In fact, three-quarters of the stimuli were physically in between two notes of the scale but apparently were not perceived as out-of-tune by these subjects.)

For musicians with absolute pitch, then, variations in tone frequency are heard categorically, rather than continuously. This point of view fits in with the reports of pos-

207

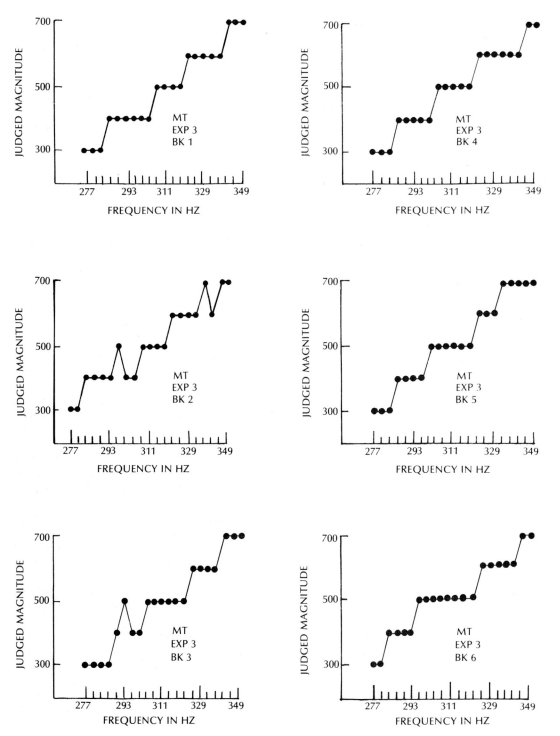

Figure 8. Judgment of tone frequency by MT, an observer with absolute pitch. The task was to judge the *height* of each tone relative to a standard tone presented at the beginning of the experiment.

208

sessors of absolute pitch, such as Bachem (1955) and Revesz (1913), who likened their own experience of pitch to the perception of color, a phenomenon known as synesthesia (see Carroll and Greenberg, 1961).

For musicians, then, the most salient characteristic of tonal stimuli is not their magnitude, but rather the unique sound qualities that differentiate one from another within a music context.

Judgment of Intonation by Musicians

The data presented above suggest a conclusion that totally contradicts a widely held view about musicians, that they have a "good ear," an ability to make fine sensory discriminations along the pitch continuum. Indeed, the step-like magnitude estimation functions shown in Figures 6 and 8 suggest

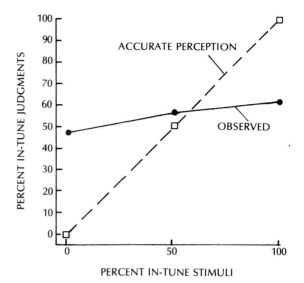

Figure 10. Percentage of in-tune judgments as a function of the percentage of in-tune intervals.

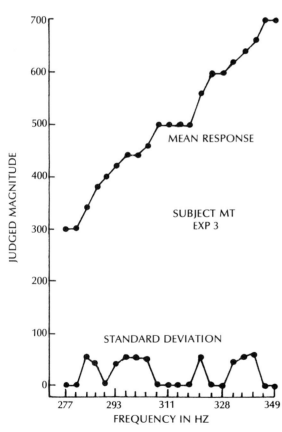

Figure 9. Mean and standard deviation of MT's judgments.

that musicians categorize over a range of an entire semitone, and that they cannot even tell "sharp" from "flat."

I carried out a strong test of this hypothesis (Siegel, 1977) by requiring highly trained musicians to judge randomly presented tonal intervals as "in-tune," "sharp," or "flat." The actual number of in-tune intervals was varied without their knowledge. They were not asked to identify the interval itself—only its intonation.

There were three stimulus sets, differing drastically in their proportion of sharp, in-tune and flat intervals. In one condition, all of the intervals were in-tune. In a second condition, twenty-five percent were flat, fifty percent were in-tune and twenty-five percent were sharp. The third condition contained only musically inaccurate intervals, fifty percent being sharp and fifty percent flat. My purpose was to determine if subjects were sensitive to shifts in the intonation of the stimulus set. Here the subjects were the musicians with the best relative pitch in the immediate area. All could identify accurate tonal intervals virtually without error.

Figure 10 shows the mean percentage of in-tune judgments as a function of the per-

209

centage of musically accurate intervals in each of the three experimental conditions. If the musicians were accurate, their data points should lie on the major diagonal, with the judged percentage of in-tune intervals ranging from zero to one hundred percent. On the other hand, if subjects are poor at distinguishing sharp, in-tune, and flat intervals the response curve should be flat.

The results conform much more closely to the second hypothesis, in that as the percentage of in-tune intervals varied from zero to one hundred percent, the percentage of in-tune judgments increased from forty-seven percent to sixty-two percent. In general, then, the musicians were found to be quite insensitive to drastic alterations in the distribution of in-tune intervals.

These results confirm that even highly-trained musicians are relatively poor at recognizing stimulus variations within a semitone. This was in spite of the fact that they were specifically told to listen for differences in intonation.

Accuracy of Musical Performance

One could argue that musicians would be more accurate if they were dealing with a context with which they were more familiar—tones produced by real instruments within a musical context—rather than stimuli presented in a laboratory. Are we not aware of inaccuracies in musical performance—as, for example, when the chorus goes flat, or the violins play out of tune?

In order to answer this question, it is necessary to find out something about the accuracy with which notes and intervals are produced in real musical performances. A number of years ago, Carl Seashore made acoustic measurements of recorded performances of the leading musicians of his day. He was quite surprised at the "constant and relatively gross deviation" of the frequencies that were produced by musicians in comparison to those that would have been expected on the basis of the music score. This was especially true of singers, perhaps because there are fewer constraints on the voice than on music instruments.

One of the most obvious irregularities was the presence of a constant frequency modulation, or vibrato, of approximately a semitone. This width was constant across a number of singers, but is not usually heard as a fluctuation in pitch. Rather it is heard as a steady-state tone of constant pitch, but having a rich quality. We find this quite interesting, since the semitone is the same interval over which the musicians in our experiments failed to notice acoustic variations in tone frequency. If the vibrato were any larger, our data suggest that it would straddle the boundary between two note categories, and be heard as a distinctive pitch fluctuation, that is, as a trill.

Seashore found that the mean pitch of the vibrato often corresponded reasonably well to the pitch required of the musical score, but even this rule was violated surprisingly often. Short notes in particular, tended to be sung out of tune, while long notes often started flat and then were gradually adjusted to the appropriate pitch—as if the singer were correcting himself through hearing. Overall the pitch fluctuations were so marked that, in many cases, it would have been difficult to tell which note the singer was attempting to produce, if one simply looked at the acoustic measurements of his voice.

Seashore's (1967) conclusion was:

It is shockingly evident that the musical ear which hears the tones indicated in the conventional notes is extremely generous and operates in the interpretive mood. Compare this principle for the various singers, and you will see that the hearing of pitch is largely a matter of conceptual hearing in terms of conventional intervals. (p. 269)

In other words, we are just as likely to ignore pitch variations within the conventional music categories when listening to real music as when judging sinusoids in the laboratory. In fact this seems almost a matter of necessity, rather than choice. If we were perceptually aware of all the acoustic variations that occur, we would find ourselves in the position of being so distracted by them as to be unable to hear the music.

Subcultural and Crosscultural Differences in Pitch Perception

Numerous studies of human pattern recognition confirm that we cannot explain perception solely in terms of the passive analysis of sensory features. Rather, perception is very much an hypothesis-testing process in which expectations about what ought to be there are generated on the basis of information about prior experiences stored in memory. These expectations can be used to evaluate incoming sensory signals, with the result that we are able to perceive or attend to what has been previously found to be important in our environment.

What happens when a perceptual expectation and the pattern of incoming sensory stimulation are incompatible? This depends on the circumstances. Sometimes, especially when our opportunity to examine the sensory signals is limited, our expectations will dominate—and we will experience a perceptual illusion. However, when the incompatibilities are clear and consistent, the expectations themselves can be revised and perceptual learning is said to occur. Thus, if this model of human perception is correct, our current perceptions will be greatly influenced by the kind of environmental stimulation to which we have been exposed in the past.

In our culture, most music conforms to the well-tempered scale, for which the basic unit is the semitone. Variations in pitch of less than a semitone certainly occur in music, as the Seashore data demonstrate, but these microtonal differences are not consistent and are not viewed as musically important in our system. It is not surprising, therefore, that the musicians in our laboratory experiments also found it difficult to differentiate frequency variations of less than a semitone.

Cultures other than our own have different music systems (Hood, 1971; Malm, 1967). For example, ancient Chinese music notation employed a pentatonic (5-tone) scale, while in other cultures—Indian music, for example, microtones are thought to play an important role. Some music systems, such as the Javanese, do not employ fixed tunings, as does Western music (e.g., $a_4 = 440$ Hz.).

If what we hear depends upon our music environment, then it follows that musicians trained in different music cultures will learn to focus only on those variables that have significance for them. Consider, for example, the phenomenon of absolute pitch. The notes of our Western scale are tied down to specific frequencies, though this fact is not particularly important musically, and it is often acceptable to transpose melodies to fit the musical range of a particular performer or instrument. It follows, therefore, that while many musicians have a good sense of relative pitch, only a small number possess a sense of absolute pitch. In fact, the phenomenon is so unusual and so striking when it occurs that some writers have viewed it as an inherited ability. There is some evidence, however, that absolute pitch is a culturally based phenomenon. In Javanese music, for example, there is no standard "correct pitch"; the instruments of a gamelan orchestra are tuned to each other on a relative basis. We have been told by Susilo, an Indonesian ethnomusicologist, that absolute pitch does not exist in Java and that there is no word for absolute pitch in the language. Thus it appears that absolute pitch, rather than depending solely on inheritance, may be a good example of how perception depends on culturally defined learning.

Ethnocentrism in Musical Perception

What happens when a person trained in one musical system attempts to listen to the music of another culture? According to the point of view presented here, he initially should assimilate it to the expectations of his own musical environment, and therefore he misperceives it, misinterprets it, and fails to appreciate it. An interesting example comes from Rao, an Indian musician writing a book on the psychology of music in the early part of this century. The reader may remember that Indian music is a microtonal system—in which pitch variations of less than a semitone are important. Rao (1923) describes a grace called the trill:

When the agitation of the mind increases *en masse* the voice trembles. The trill is then produced. It is the fundamental grace. Western singers seem to be more fond of it . . . . Real trill is correctly produced on the voice, or the violin. Nervousness also begets trills in the voice. (p. 143)

This is a rather curious description of trill as we understand it in Western music, since trills can be played on many instruments, including the piano, and do not usually come about as a result of nervousness. What he seems to be referring to instead is vibrato, which Seashore found to be very prominent among Western singers. Rao, of course, misinterpreted this as a pitch variation, while in Western music, vibrato is meant to provide a rich sound quality to a note of constant pitch.

Remember that Seashore's acoustic measurements indicated that Western operatic singers typically produce a vibrato whose width is just slightly less than a semitone, a variation that according to our perceptual data ought not to be heard as a pitch fluctuation. The fact that Rao, an Indian, misinterpreted Western vibrato as a meaningful variation in pitch is to me a most interesting finding. It is also quite unlikely that I am misinterpreting Rao because he illustrated his point with the following figure (Figure 11), in which he transcribes the "trill" as a series of thirty-second notes.

The Transcription Problem in Ethnomusicology

The problem of how a musician from one culture can misinterpret another culture's music arises not only in listening to the music, but also in describing it, and has come to be known as "the transcription problem." It was initially common practice to transcribe the music of other cultures in terms of the twelve notes of the Western musical scale. This was deemed as unsatisfactory, how-

ever, since it was quickly discovered that intervals and notes other than those of Western music occurred frequently. Another solution has been to describe the music employing a notational system such as cents (100 cents = 1 semitone) which allows for the existence of much finer gradations. A difficulty here, however, is that one is still left with deciding how to represent each of the intervals in the music. The unaided ear is likely to be inaccurate, and to compare each note against some acoustic standard is a tedious and time-consuming process.

This last difficulty could be overcome through the use of an acoustic transcription device, such as Seashore did in the studies cited earlier. In fact, ethnomusicologists have designed such an instrument (called the Melograph) and there was a time when it was hailed as the ultimate solution. However, use of the Melograph has proven to be less than conclusive. For, even if one has an accurate acoustic transcription of the music, one still has to decide which of the acoustic variations are important musically in the system being studied. As Seashore found, the musically important elements for an acoustic signal do not emerge unless one already has an idea of what to look for.

Some societies have formal notational systems and instruments with fixed tunings, and these can provide important clues about the basic structure of the music. However, not all societies have a notational system, and some have very few, if any, instruments. In such cases, the task of the ethnomusicologist is very difficult.

Several years ago, I had the opportunity to discuss this problem with Catherine Ellis, an ethnomusicologist at the University of Adelaide who has made an extensive study of the musical systems of Aboriginal tribes in Australia. Much Aboriginal music consists almost entirely of singing, and there is no system of music notation and very few instruments to provide clues about its basic structure. Yet, making music plays a very important role in Aboriginal culture.

After studying this music for many years as an observer—that is, as a *Western* musician, Ellis came to the realization that her on-

Trill or Shake

Figure 11. Rao's transcription of "trill" (adapted from Rao, 1923).

ly means of understanding it was to, in effect, become an Aboriginal musician—that is, to abandon her role as an observer and to become a participant. This procedure has been advocated by others as well (Hood, 1971).

In Ellis's case, this decision resulted in her inviting a group of Aboriginal elders to come to the University of Adelaide to teach her and her students Aboriginal music making, a difficult task. When one approaches this music from the perspective of a Westerner it is difficult to hear the notes accurately, let alone sing them.

What were the *perceptual* consequences of Ellis's involvement in Aboriginal music? Being immersed in the music of another culture should lead to a substantial alteration in one's perceptual information-processing systems, and this turned out to be the case for Ellis. So different is Aboriginal music from that of our Western culture, that she reported losing her ear entirely for Western intervals—including even her ability to recognize the octave! This is most interesting, since although the octave plays a fundamental role in Western music and its recognition appears to reflect the operation of a built-in feature detection mechanism (Humphreys, 1939), it is apparently of relatively little importance in some Aboriginal tribal cultures. In one group studied intensively by Ellis, men and women seldom sing the same song together and even when they do, they typically sing in unison. Moreover, there are no melodic instruments. The problem of establishing a harmonious relationship between different voices or instruments playing simultaneously in different frequency ranges is, therefore, one which simply does not arise. Man may indeed possess a built in feature detection system for octaves, but if Ellis's observations are correct, they may not be operative in the absence of appropriate perceptual learning experiences.

Catherine Ellis's experience in learning Aboriginal music, is, therefore, consistent with my general thesis. Musicians, apparently, develop skills for recognizing only those acoustic features that are important in their music environment. Variations that do not

occur in the system, or that are unimportant musically, are ignored. As a result, musicians may misperceive or misinterpret those features of other musical systems that do not occur in their own.

Implications for Music Education

The experience of ethnomusicologists has, I think, some interesting implications for music education. The music educator must not only teach students how to produce music, but also how to hear it.

Most music educators have been immersed in music from a very early age and have, perhaps, forgotten what a long and difficult process it is to discern the perceptual structures of music. In fact, many musicians have an ethnocentric bias. Although we now know that different cultures around the world have music systems that are radically different from our own, musicians have traditionally believed that there is something "natural" and inevitable about the particular intervals of the Western musical scale.

Many musicians, therefore, stress the importance of developing a "good ear," of teaching their students to listen carefully to sound, as an important part of music training. Yet the musicians who take such an approach may, in fact, be trying to teach their students the wrong thing. This is because the particular notes and intervals of our scale have acquired their importance, not because of their acoustic properties, but because of the role they play in our music system.

Merely instructing students to listen, therefore, is insufficient. One must also teach them what to listen for.

A good example of what I mean by this is teaching students to recognize intervals by thinking of common melodies in which they occur. One can recognize a major sixth, for example by thinking of "My Bonnie Lies Over the Ocean." Over the years, we have talked with many musicians who have adopted this strategy, although for a number of them, the process eventually has become automatic. At that point, the intervals do indeed seem to develop distinctive qualities that are inherent to their sound. It should be stressed, however, that these qualities are not based on acoustic cues, but on information stored in memory about the way that the intervals ought to sound in music. Thus, for example, there is nothing inherent in the acoustic properties of a minor third that makes it "sad." Rather, its "sad" quality comes from the fact that the minor third occurs frequently in music that has been written for sombre occasions.

Musical versus Acoustic Listening

The acoustic bias of many music educators is reinforced by the common practice of using tests of pitch discrimination as predictors of music aptitude and for assigning children to music classes. Yet data collected in my laboratory over a number of years suggest that musicians are not particularly good at discrimination of fine pitch differences. There are, of course, good reasons why they shouldn't be. Seashore's studies of the acous-

tic structure of real music performances led him to the conclusion that music perception is, of necessity, a striking illusion, rather than an accurate translation of acoustic reality. If we listened acoustically rather than musically, the illusion would be destroyed.

We have observed first hand the systematic, though hopefully temporary, destruction of a number of fine musicians' ability to listen musically by subjecting them to laboratory experiments where we have forced them to listen for fine acoustic differences amongst tonal stimuli. When we have done this we have found that, invariably, our musicians report this to be an extremely unpleasant experience. They complain about "losing their ear," that the music qualities that they normally hear in notes and intervals have disappeared, and that they all have begun to sound the same. Their performance often deteriorates and they assert that they

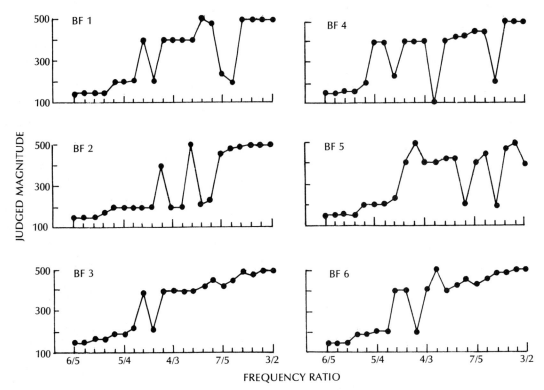

Figure 12. Judgment of tonal intervals by subject BF. These data were collected after he had been informed about the nature of the stimulus set and should be compared with Figure 6.

214

feel they could do much better—if only they could listen to some music for a while.

A good example of this phenomenon is shown in Figure 12. You may recall observer BF from the magnitude estimation study I discussed earlier. After the first experiment was completed, we informed BF about the many musically inaccurate intervals that actually had occurred and asked him if he thought he could estimate pitch intervals any better. Figure 12 shows that he did do somewhat better, in that some of the out-of-tune intervals are accurately ordered in terms of rather small variations in their frequency ratios. However, this accuracy in hearing fine acoustic differences was made at the expense of being able to assign them to the appropriate musical category. Wild errors of more than a semitone now occurred, although previously BF had made these judgments with perfect accuracy.

It has been our experience that musicians who are most aware of acoustic variations, and report hearing many out-of-tune intervals, are relatively inaccurate in assigning them to the appropriate music category. It appears, therefore, that listening acoustically is incompatible with listening musically, and that the ability to discriminate fine acoustic variations may actually be detrimental to the enjoyment of music.

An interesting illustration of this point comes from Seashore's (1938) anecdote of the famous musician whose brother was thought by the family to be nonmusical. Seashore tested the sensory capacities of both brothers, and found that the non-musical brother was ". . . extraordinarily keen, indeed keener than his brother, the famous musician. The interesting confession came out that the reason he was not musical was that practically all the music that he heard seemed to him so bad that it jarred upon him and was intolerable" (Seashore, 1938, p. 4).

To play the role of the critic, therefore, is to destroy the illusion on which the perception of music depends.

On the Contribution of Psychology to an Understanding of Music

I have on several occasions in this paper

commented on the research and insights of Carl Seashore. Seashore was keenly aware of the importance of illusion in music, and of the role of the mind in music perception. It is ironic, therefore, that he is widely known as a reductionist who placed great stress on analyzing music into its components and then studying the perception of those components in the laboratory. This, of course led to an acoustic bias, and in his *Psychology of Music,* Seashore devoted many chapters to a discussion of such variables as tone frequency, intensity, and duration, and their role in music. In his tests of music aptitude, the student's ability to discriminate among these acoustic variables played an important role.

Why did Seashore stress the psychoacoustic approach when, both as a musician and a scholar, he was so keenly aware of the role of illusion in music? I suspect that this was because Seashore was above all a scientific psychologist. Unfortunately the psychological models of his day were reductionist and behaviorist in orientation, and did not have very good explanations for such concepts as mind or illusion. The complex, hypothesis-testing model of human perception outlined earlier in this paper would simply have not been allowable in that time.

This may, in fact, be one reason why Seashore's extensive work in the psychology of music at the Iowa Laboratories has failed to have the impact on psychology that it deserved. The psychology of the 1930s, '40s, and '50s continued in its behaviorist orientation. As we have seen, music was something that could not be easily dealt with using that kind of model—and so it was simply ignored.

The computer revolution of the 1960s and '70s has allowed psychology to entertain the existence of much more complex models of human perception, memory, and learning than had been previously possible. It was now possible to construct and test models of great complexity with precision and objectivity. In fact the views on human perception expressed in this paper have come to be accepted in psychology, at least partially because of the failure of computer-based models of pattern recognition which relied solely on passive analysis of features of the stimulus environment. Although the role of expectancy, hypothesis-testing, and memory had been previously recognized by some theorists (e.g., Bruner, 1957), the failure of machine models of pattern recognition to operate successfully without these properties clearly demonstrated their importance (see Neisser, 1967).

Now that models more appropriate for music exist, it is likely that psychology will make more of a contribution to the understanding of music—and music to the understanding of psychology—than has been the case in the past.

References

Bachem, A. Tone height and tone chroma as two different pitch qualities. *Acta Psychologica*, 1950, 7, 80–88.

Burns, E., and W. D. Ward. Categorical perception. Phenomenon or epiphenomenon. Evidence from experiments in the perception of melodic musical intervals. *Journal of the Acoustical Society of America*, 1978, 63, 456–468.

Bruner, J. S. On perceptual readiness. *Psychological Review*, 1957, 64, 123–152.

Carroll, J. B., and J. H. Greenberg. Two cases of synesthesia for color and musical tonality associated with absolute pitch ability. *Perceptual and Motor Skills*, 1961, 13, 48.

Harris, G., and J. A. Siegel. Absolute pitch: A case of categorical perception? *Research Bulletin #324*. London, Ontario, Canada: Department of Psychology, University of Western Ontario, 1975.

Helmholtz, H. L. F. von. A. J. Ellis (Trans.). *Sensations of tone*. New York: Longmans, 1930.

Hood, M. *The ethnomusicologist*. New York: McGraw-Hill, 1971.

Humphreys, L. G. Generalization as a function of method of reinforcement. *Journal of Experimental Psychology*, 1939, 25, 361–372.

Lindsay, P. H., and D. A. Norman. *Human information processing: An introduction to psychology*. New York: Academic Press, 1973.

Malm, W. P. *Music cultures of the Pacific, the Near East, and Asia*. Englewood Cliffs, New Jersey: Prentice-Hall, 1967.

Meyer, L. B. *Emotional meaning in music*. Chicago: University of Chicago Press, 1956.

Neisser, V. *Cognitive psychology*. New York: Appleton Century Crofts, 1967.

Rao, H. P. K. *The psychology of music*. Bangalore, India: Guruvilas Printing Works, 1923.

Revesz, G. *Zur grundlegung der tonpsychologie*. Leipzig: Weit and Company, 1913.

Seashore, C. E. *Psychology of music*. New York: Dover, 1967.

Siegel, J. A. Judgment of intonation by musicians: Further evidence for categorical perception. *Research Bulletin #375*. London, Ontario, Canada: Department of Psychology, University of Western Ontario, 1976.

Siegel, J. A., and W. Siegel. Absolute identification of notes and intervals by musicians. *Perception and Psychophysics*, 1977, 21, 143–152. (a)

———. Categorical perception of tonal intervals: Musicians can't tell *sharp* from *flat*. *Perception and Psychophysics*, 1977, 21, 399–407. (b)

Siegel, J. A., W. Siegel, G. Harris, and R. Sopo. Categorical perception of pitch by musicians with relative and absolute pitch. *Research Bulletin #303*. London, Ontario, Canada: Department of Psychology, University of Western Ontario, 1974.

Stevens, S. S., and J. Volkmann. The relation of pitch to tone frequency. *American Journal of Psychology*, 1940, 53, 329–353.

Response

James C. Carlsen

Siegel has focused her remarks on data related to pitch perception. She has noted the lack of correspondence between measures of acoustical phenomena and of perceptual response. Her data suggest that, normally, musicians extract only the pitch cues necessary to categorize the sound into semitone units. This she demonstrated for both interval and tone identification. In one kind of task, we learn that musicians don't demonstrate good intonation perception. Finally, interpretations of empirical events suggest the significant role that expectancy plays in influencing our perceptions.

The thesis emerging from her paper is summarized in her words:

> Musicians, apparently, develop skills for recognizing only those acoustic features that are important to their musical environment. Variations that do not occur in the system or that are unimportant musically, are ignored. As a result, musicians may misperceive or misinterpret those features of other musical systems which do not occur in their own. (p. 27)

Let me address my comments first to the implications that these data hold for music teachers and for music researchers. If there is not a one-to-one correspondence between the acoustic measure and the perception of that event (and there is not), then electronic devices that music teachers use that can only measure the acoustic event must be used with understanding and with caution. It was nearly fifty years ago that S. S. Stevens (1935) demonstrated that our perception of pitch could be changed by altering only the intensity of the tone. We have long known the Fletcher-Munson (1933) effect that demonstrates the influence of changing frequency upon our perception of loudness. For this reason, having student instrumentalists use stroboscopic tuners without also controlling for the interactive factors of intensity and frequency can have the effect of training students to perceive acoustically when you may really want them to perceive within a twelve-tone music system.

On the other hand, as we make final preparations to leave the twentieth century for the twenty-first, we find ourselves still struggling to enter the twentieth century musically. We talk about having a twelve-tone system when, practically, many of our students can only function diatonically. *Twelve equal semitones* is still only a transpositional aid for many, and excursions into dodecaphonic music stretches those persons' perception beyond ability. If our expectancies have not been adjusted for twelve-tone music, they certainly lack adjustment to micro-

tone events, as the data Siegel reported indicate. It appears that we need to assist our students in learning to perceive pitch units smaller than semitones inasmuch as these units are functional in our musical repertoire (e.g., Bartok; Elliott Carter) as well as in the music of certain non-Western cultures.

I want to comment upon some possible limitations of Siegel's data that I'm sure she would acknowledge. The data reported were gathered in response to sine tones. Psycho-musicologists have begun to realize the limitations of such data and are beginning more and more to use complex tones as the basis for their data collection. Sergeant (1973) demonstrated that musicians scored significantly better than nonmusicians in a pitch perception task using a sine tone as the perceptual event. Using an electronically generated complex tone, musicians scored even better, but nonmusicians showed no improvement. And with a natural complex tone—a piano specially tuned for the purpose—the musicians did even better still, although the nonmusicians scored no better than they had on the sine tone signal.

The other element that is pertinent when considering the pitch perception task is that of the musical context itself. *Set* is a familiar psychological term to most of us. It refers to our preparedness for an event. Set may be manipulated externally, but may also operate internally as a function of our past experience with events. I wonder to what extent Siegel's data on the tuning of intervals may have been a result of set for semitones because of the sparse context. We do know that in melodic settings involving more than two notes, musicians will make systematic adjustments in tunings as a function of variations in context. As a matter of fact, in the reference to the Seashore study, Siegel says, "long notes often started flat and then were gradually adjusted to the appropriate pitch," indicating that context does influence intonation.

Swaffield (1974) showed that fine-tuning with a multiple-tone melodic context was influenced by several factors. First of all, if given the opportunity to actually do the tuning, musicians do not agree ($p < .001$) on what

217

constitutes being in tune. Second, different instruments require different ($p < .001$) pitch adjustments from a standard to be judged in tune. Third, tuning responses will be different ($p < .001$) as a result of how loudly the instrument is playing. This difference was an intrinsic one, not dependent upon a manipulation of an extrinsic factor. Fourth, the tempo of a melody affects what is accepted as an in-tune pitch ($p < .001$). Finally, whether the note to be tuned is initially sharp, flat, or on standard influences the tuning response ($p < .001$). Flat pitches are tuned to another pitch below the standard, sharp pitches to one above, and those that were already on the equal tempered standard were returned to pitches either below or above, but closer to the standard than tones initially off.

I have to express a strong belief that it would require too many assumptions to conclude from Siegel's data that musicians are unable to tell sharp from flat except for certain tasks that are not very much like those in the musicians' real world. Assigning a name to a pitch or obtaining a magnitude measure of distance is quite likely a different process than tuning a pitch. Researchers would be well advised to continue the testing of refined "in-tune perception" theories using procedures similar to those developed by Siegel, but in contextual frames more nearly like those in which musicians work.

Finally, I was pleased to find considerable emphasis being placed upon the role that expectancies play in the perceptual process. My own research on this theory (1976) has revealed a high correspondence between melodic expectancy profiles and melodic dictation scores. Unfortunately, we still fall into the trap of predicating perceptual theory on

yet another theory. Little data have been derived that establish expectancy patterns, and what data are available speak only to pitch factors and largely melodic ones at that. It would appear fruitful for music teachers to have such expectancy profiles of their students available. Then we might determine the extent to which they are perceptually set. In so doing, we might improve our curricula and individualize our instruction.

Several questions about music perception raised at Symposium I remain unanswered. One in particular is that of perception of music when the observer is also a participant in the performance. This appears to be a critical area for future investigation. One would hope that the information contained in the Symposium II papers would be examined in light of the issues raised in the papers from our musicians' panel. In so doing, we may begin to identify the needed directions that our research should take.

References

Carlsen, J. C. Cross-cultural influences on expectancy in music. *International Society for Music Education Yearbook III,* 1976, 61–65.

Fletcher, H., and W. A. Munson. Loudness in definition, measurement, and calculation. *Journal of the Acoustical Society of America,* 1933, 5, 82–108.

Sergeant, D. Measurement of pitch discrimination. *Journal of Research in Music Education,* 1973, 21, 3–19.

Stevens, S. S. The relation of pitch to intensity. *Journal of the Acoustical Society of America,* 1935, 6, 150–154.

Swaffield, W. R. Effect of melodic parameters on ability to make fine-tuning responses in context. *Journal of Research in Music Education,* 1974, 22, 305–312.

Musical Illusions and Handedness

Diana Deutsch

Ever since the time of the ancient Greeks, writers have commented on the fact that we are subject to perceptual illusions in listening to music. The purpose of this paper is to explicate some of the ways in which these illusions occur.

A central problem in music perception is how the brain sorts and organizes a complex set of tonal stimuli into different configurations. In listening to music, we do not simply hear a set of independent tones; rather we combine tones to form perceptual groupings such as melodies and chords. Some of these groupings come to the foreground of our attention, and others are relegated to the background. This process is similar in many respects to the organization of visual stimuli into figure-ground configurations. The experiments to be described examined the principles whereby we link successively presented tones into sequences. Listeners were presented with two simultaneous tonal sequences, each emanating from a different position in space, and they were asked to report what they heard. This technique led to the uncovering of a series of quite paradoxical musical illusions. Further, the type of illusory percept obtained varied in correlation with the handedness of the listener.

In many of these experiments, a computer was programmed to control two sine-wave generators, so that the tones could be precisely regulated in terms of amplitude and duration, as well as frequency. The technique used was to present sequences to the listener through earphones so that when one ear received one tone, the other ear received a different tone (this is known as dichotic presentation). In other experiments the two sequences were instead presented through loudspeakers, so that both ears received both sequences, though these were emanating from different positions in space. In yet other experiments the sequences were generated on a piano, and timbral and loudness differences were introduced between the stimuli presented through the two speakers. Thus this paper is concerned with investigations both under highly controlled conditions and also in more natural musical situations.

In the first experiment (Deutsch, 1974) listeners were presented with the auditory pattern shown on Figure 1a. It can be seen that this consisted of a sequence of tones that alternated from one octave to the other. The identical sequence was presented to both ears simultaneously; however when the right ear received the high tone, the left ear received the low tone, and vice versa. So in fact

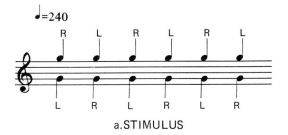

a. STIMULUS

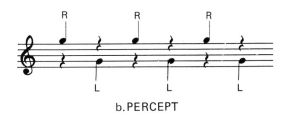

b. PERCEPT

Figure 1. a. Tonal sequence giving rise to the octave illusion. b. Percept most commonly obtained.

the listener was presented with a single, continuous, two-tone chord, but the ear of input for each component switched four times a second. The frequencies employed were 400 Hz and 800 Hz; these are closest in the musical scale to G_4 (392 Hz) and G_5 (784 Hz).

One can easily imagine how this auditory pattern should sound; however, I have come across only one individual out of hundreds who was able to describe it correctly. Instead, a variety of paradoxical illusions was obtained, and these varied from listener to listener. The most common illusion is diagrammed on Figure 1b. It can be seen that this consisted of a single tone that alternated from one octave to the other in synchrony with the localization shift. That is, the listener heard a single high tone in one ear alternating with a single low tone in the other ear. Paradoxically, when the earphones were placed in reverse position, most people heard exactly the same thing; that is, the positions of the high and low tones remained fixed. So it seemed to the listeners that the earphone that had originally been emitting the high tones was now emitting the low tones, and that the earphone that had been

219

emitting the low tones was now emitting the high tones.

This percept presents us with a strange paradox. If we assume that the listener attends to one ear and ignores the other, then we can account for the percept of a single tone which alternates from one octave to the other. However, both of the alternating tones should then appear to be localized in the same ear. Alternatively, if we assume that the listener attends to each ear in turn, then we can account for the percept of a single tone which alternates from ear to ear; however, this tone should not then change in pitch as it shifts its apparent location. The percept of a single tone that alternates simultaneously both in pitch and in localization appears quite nonsensical.

There is a further surprising aspect to this illusion: right-handers and left-handers show different patterns of localization for the two pitches at the two ears. It was found that right-handers tended strongly to hear the high tone on their right and the low tone on their left, and to maintain this percept when the earphones were placed in reverse position. On the other hand, left-handers as a group did not preferentially localize the high and low tones either way. In the overwhelming majority of right-handers the left hemisphere is dominant; that is, they have speech represented in the left cerebral hemisphere. But this is true of only about two-thirds of the left-handed population, the remaining one-third being right hemisphere dominant. So this pattern of results indicates that we tend to perceive the high tones as emanating from the side of auditory space that is contralateral to the dominant hemi-

sphere, and the low tones as from the other side.

Although most listeners showed a preference for one localization pattern rather than for another, and although such a preference could be very strong, it often happened that after continued listening, the high and low tones suddenly reversed position. Such reversals were most likely to occur when the sequence was discontinued and started afresh; but they sometimes occurred in the middle of a sequence. Some listeners experienced very frequent reversals, so that the percepts were as shown in Figure 2. These cases provide us with an auditory analogue of reversal of ambiguous figures in vision. For instance, if you look at a Necker cube, you will perceive it in either of two orientations. As you continue to look at it, your percept will suddenly flip from one orientation to the other, but you never perceive it both ways at the same time. Analogously, some listeners perceived the present sequence either as a high tone to the right alternating with a low tone to the left; or as a high tone to the left alternating with a low tone to the right; but the two percepts did not occur simultaneously.

The illusion so far described was the one most commonly obtained. However, other listeners perceived this sequence quite differently. Some heard a single tone which alternated from ear to ear whose pitch either remained constant or changed only slightly with a change in its apparent location. Others reported complex percepts, such as two low tones alternating from ear to ear, together with an intermittent high tone in one ear, or a sequence where the pitch relationships appeared to change gradually with time.

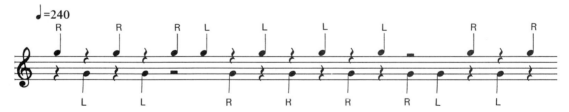

Figure 2. Percept obtained by some listeners. The frequent reversals of the positions of the high and low tones provide an auditory analogue of reversals of ambiguous figures in vision, such as the Necker cube.

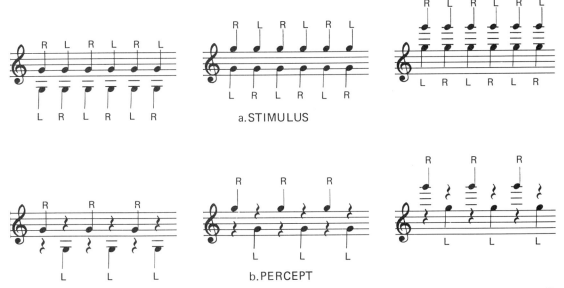

Figure 3. Tonal sequences and percepts obtained in experiment to determine whether the octave illusion is based on absolute pitch levels or relationships between the tones.

Some listeners remarked on striking timbral differences between the tones; for instance, that the low tones had a gong-like quality and the high tones a breathy, flutelike quality. This group of percepts tended to be quite unstable, often changing from one to another within a few seconds. It was found that the proportion of listeners obtaining complex percepts was higher amongst left-handers than amongst right-handers.

Let us now return to the illusion most commonly obtained—that of a single tone that alternated from one octave to the other, and that also alternated simultaneously from one ear to the other. One question which arises is whether this is based on the absolute pitch levels in the stimulus pattern, or on the pitch relationships between the tones. To find out, a group of listeners was selected who had consistently localized the 800 Hz tone in the right ear and the 400 Hz tone in the left ear, showing no tendency to reverse this pattern. These listeners were presented with sequences consisting of tones alternating between 200 and 400 Hz; between 400 and 800 Hz; and between 800 and 1600 Hz, as shown on Figure 3a. The results of this experiment were quite clear. Except for one listener's report on the 200 Hz-400 Hz sequence, the higher of the two tones in each pattern was always localized in the right ear, and the lower in the left. Thus, for instance, the 800 Hz tone was localized in the left ear when it alternated with the 1600 Hz tone, but in the right ear when it alternated with the 400 Hz tone (Figure 3b). This combined set of results can only be explained by assuming that the illusion is based on the pitch relationships between the competing tones, rather than on a differential sensitivity between the ears at absolute pitch levels.

How can we account for this paradoxical illusion? There is clearly no simple explanation, but we may suppose that separate and independent brain mechanisms exist for determining *what* pitch we hear, and for determining *where* the sound appears to be coming from. In an interesting parallel, there appears to be a separation in the visual system between the mechanisms subserving localization and orientation on the one hand, and those subserving pattern discrimination

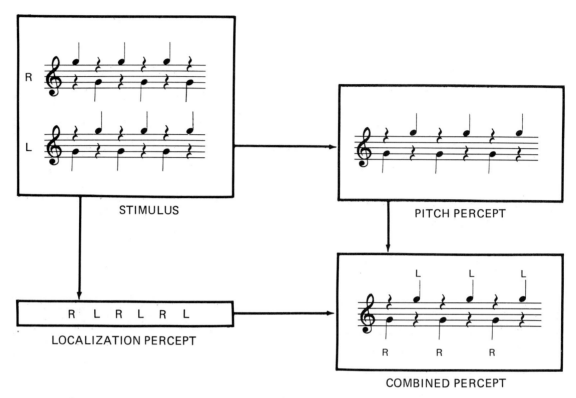

Diagrams showing how two auditory decision mechanisms, one determining what pitch we hear and the other determining where the sound is located, combine to produce the octave illusion.
Figure 4a. Model for the listener who follows the sequence presented to the right.

on the other. For example, Schneider (1967) found that a hamster deprived of its visual cortex shows very poor pattern discrimination, but easily locates objects in space—that is, it can tell *where* an object is, but not *what* it is. On the other hand, if the superior colliculus is removed instead, pattern discrimination remains excellent, but the animal cannot now locate the object—it can tell *what* it is seeing, but not *where* it is! Recently, Evans (1974) has argued for a similar functional separation in the auditory system. He proposed that the early stages of the auditory pathway involves a ventral route, subserving localization functions, and a dorsal route, subserving discriminatory functions. This follows an old suggestion by Poljak (1926).

If we assume, then, that two separate auditory mechanisms exist, one determining

what pitch we hear, and the other determining where the sound appears to be coming from, we are in a position to explain the illusion. We can hypothesize that we perceive the sequence of pitches arriving at one ear and not the other, and more often than not, the sequence arriving at the dominant ear is attended to rather than the nondominant. We can further hypothesize that each tone is localized towards the ear that receives the higher frequency signal, regardless of which ear is followed for pitch, and so regardless of whether the tone is heard as high or low. As shown in Figures 4a and 4b, the combined operation of these two decision mechanisms would produce the illusion of a single tone that alternates simultaneously both in pitch and in localization. First take the case of the listener who follows the sequence of pitches

222

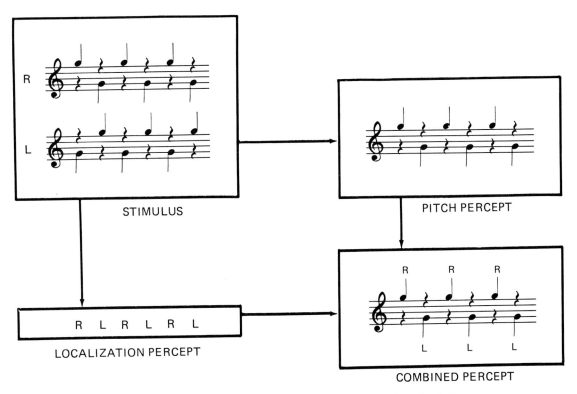

Figure 4b. Model for the listener who follows the sequence presented to the left.

delivered to his right ear (Figure 4a). When the high tone is presented to the right ear and the low tone to the left, this listener hears a high tone, since this tone is presented to his or her right ear; and he also localized the tone correctly, since the right ear is receiving the higher frequency signal. However, when the low tone is presented to the right ear and the high tone to the left, he hears a low tone, since this tone is presented to his right ear; but he localizes it in his left ear instead, since the left ear is receiving the higher frequency signal. So the entire sequence is heard as a high tone to the right alternating with a low tone to the left. It can be seen that reversing the position of the earphones would not alter this basic percept. However, as shown on Figure 4b, if the listener follows the sequence of pitches delivered to his left ear instead, keeping the localization rule constant, the same sequence is now perceived as a high tone to the left alternating with a low tone to the right. The frequent reversals experienced by some listeners, illustrated on Figure 2, would then be due to a reversal of the ear being followed for pitch, leaving the localization rule constant.

In order to test this hypothesis, a new dichotic sequence was devised (Deutsch and Roll, 1976). The basic pattern employed is shown on Figure 5. It can be seen that this consisted of three high (800 Hz) tones followed by two low (400 Hz) tones on one channel, and simultaneously three low (400 Hz) tones followed by two high (800 Hz) tones on the other channel. This pattern was repeated ten times without pause.

The results confirmed the hypothesis. Right-handers tended significantly to report the pattern of pitches delivered to the right ear rather than to the left. That is, with Channel A to the right and Channel B to the left,

223

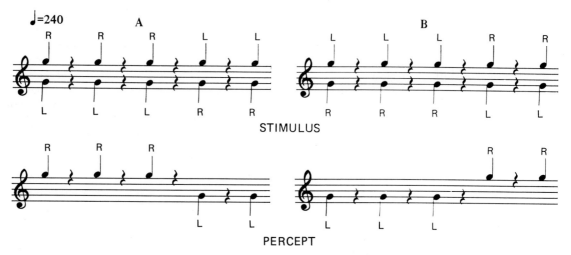

Figure 5. Tonal sequence that presents a different pattern of pitches to each ear, used to investigate the mechanisms determining pitch and localization in the octave illusion.

they tended to report the repetitive presentation of three high tones followed by two low tones. With Channel B to the right and Channel A to the left they tended instead to report the repetitive presentation of three low tones followed by two high tones. However, all listeners localized each tone toward the ear receiving the higher frequency signal, regardless of which ear was followed for pitch and whether the tone was heard as high or low.

The combined operation of these two decision mechanisms gave rise to a percept that was subjectively most paradoxical for listeners who followed the same ear for pitch regardless of earphone position. This percept is illustrated on Figure 5 for the case of the listener who consistently followed the pitch information delivered to his right ear. With Channel A to the right and Channel B to the left he heard the repetitive presentation of three high tones to the right followed by two low tones to the left. When the position of the earphones was reversed, he now heard the identical sequence as the repetitive presentation of *two* high tones to the right followed by *three* low tones to the left! The procedure of reversing earphone position therefore appeared to cause the channel to the right to drop a high tone and the channel to the left to add a low tone!

We can next ask whether the interactions underlying these effects take place between pathways conveying information from the two ears, or whether instead pathways conveying information from different regions of auditory space are involved. To find out, the sequence was presented through two spatially separated loudspeakers rather than earphones. The listener stood in an anechoic chamber, positioned equidistant between two speakers, with one on his left, and the other on his right (Figure 6a). It was found that the analogous illusions were still obtained under these conditions, even though both ears now received the entire stimulus configuration. An intermittent high tone appeared to be emanating from the speaker on the right, and an intermittent low tone from the speaker on the left. When the listener slowly rotated, the locations of the high and low tones appeared to move with him, so that the high tones remained on his right and the low tones on his left. This percept was maintained until he reached the position where he was facing one speaker, with the other speaker directly behind him (Figure 6b). The illusion then abruptly disappeared, and a single complex tone appeared to be emanating simultaneously from both speakers. However, as the listener continued to ro-

224

tate, the original percept abruptly returned, with the high tones still on his right and the low tones on his left. So when he had turned 180° from his original position (Figure 6c), the speaker that had first appeared to be emitting the high tones now appeared to be emitting the low tones, and the speaker that had first appeared to be emitting the low tones now appeared to be emitting the high tones!

This experiment demonstrates that the illusion must have a very complex basis. In order for it to occur with speakers, the listener must first identify, for each pair of simultaneous tones, which speaker is emitting the high tone and which the low. Following such correct assignments, the information must then travel along pathways that are specific to region in auditory space, and the above interactions must take place between such second-order pathways so as to give rise to

the illusory percepts. The mechanism determining what pitch is heard chooses to follow the frequencies that are emanating from one side of auditory space rather than from the other; thus the decision as to *what* is heard is determined by *where* the signals are coming from. However, the localization mechanism chooses instead to follow the higher frequency signal; thus the decision as to *where* the signal is located is determined by *what* the signal frequencies are.

What happens if, instead of two alternating tones, a more elaborate sequence is presented? In a further experiment, the sequence shown on Figure 7a was employed (Deutsch, 1975). It can be seen that this consisted of the C major scale, with successive tones alternating from ear to ear. This scale was presented simultaneously in both ascending and descending form, such that when a component of the ascending scale was in the right ear, a component of the descending scale was in the left ear, and vice versa. Figures 7b and 7c show these ascending and descending scales separately, and it can be seen that the sequence shown in Figure 7a is produced by the superposition of the sequences shown in Figures 7b and 7c. This sequence was played repetitively ten times without pause.

Another set of surprising illusions were here produced. About half of the right-handed listeners obtained the percept illustrated in Figure 7d. They heard the correct sequence of pitches, but as two separate melodies—a higher one and a lower one moving in contrary motion. Further, the higher tones all appeared to be emanating from the right earphone, and the lower tones from the left. When the earphone positions were reversed there was no corresponding change in the percept. So it appeared that the earphone that had been producing the higher tones was now producing the lower tones, and that the earphone that had been producing the lower tones was now producing the higher tones.

Other listeners perceived the sequence differently. A few reported hearing all the higher tones in the left ear, and all the lower tones in the right ear, with earphones positioned

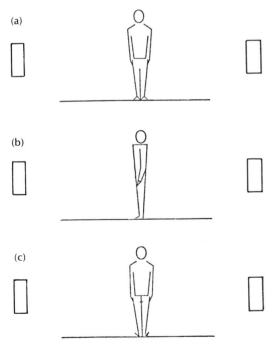

(a)

(b)

(c)

Figure 6. Experimental arrangement for investigating the illusion with sequences presented through loudspeakers.

225

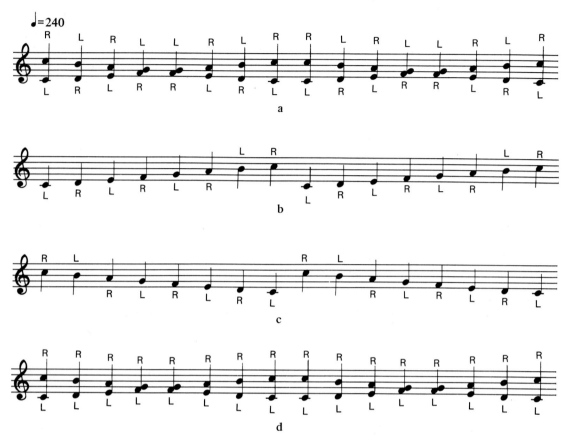

Figure 7. Tonal sequence giving rise to the scale illusion. a. The entire configuration. b. The ascending component separately. c. The descending component separately. d. Percept most commonly obtained.

both ways. For yet other listeners, when the position of the earphones was reversed, the apparent locations of the higher and lower tones reversed also. The two-handedness populations were found to differ in terms of these localization patterns. A strong tendency was found amongst right-handers to hear the higher tones on the right and the lower tones on the left; however, the left-handers showed no such tendency.

A small number of listeners also perceived this sequence as composed of higher and lower melodic lines that moved in contrary motion, but they localized the individual tones in a variety of ways. But so far, I have found only one listener out of over a hundred who localized all the tones correctly.

Finally, a number of listeners reported on-

ly one stream of four tones, which repetitively descended and then ascended. Little or nothing of the other stream was perceived. All these listeners, when asked to sing along with the sequence, sang the higher tones and not the lower. The proportion of listeners reporting a single stream was found to be higher amongst left-handers than right-handers. Interestingly, one-third of the listeners who reported a single stream correctly identified the individual tones as switching from ear to ear. The remainder of these listeners obtained a variety of localization percepts; such as the entire sequence in one ear, or the sequence traveling from left to right as it went from high to low, and then back from right to left as it went from low to high.

It is interesting to note that all listeners, in

226

perceiving this sequence, formed perceptual groupings based on frequency range. That is, they either heard all the tones, but as two simultaneous nonoverlapping pitch streams, or they heard the upper stream but little or nothing of the lower. It is particularly surprising that no listener reported a full ascending or descending scale as a component of the sequence, since the major scale is much more familiar to all listeners in our culture than the patterns actually reported. In order to evaluate the strength of this effect, a group of listeners was presented with the dichotic sequence shown in Figure 7a and then with the ascending scale shown in Figure 7b, and they were asked whether the second sequence had been included in the first. All replied that it had not; so here the principle of grouping tonal stimuli by frequency range is so powerful as to mask the perception of a full scale which is actually present in the sequence.

This returns us to the problem raised at the beginning of the paper. An important part of listening to music involves the linking of tonal stimuli into sequences. When more than one tone is presented at a time, listening involves a constant decision process as to which successive tone to link with which; so a central problem in music perception concerns the rules whereby such linkages are formed. A classical contribution to the general question of how we group stimuli into configuration was made by Max Wertheimer (1923) who proposed the existence of several principles of perceptual organization. One of these is the principle of proximity, which states that nearer elements are grouped together, in preference to elements spaced further apart. An example of this principle is shown on Figure 8a, where the closer dots appear to be grouped together in pairs. Another is the principle of good continuation, which states that elements which follow each other in a given direction are perceived together. For instance, we perceptually group the dots in Figure 8b into the two lines AC and BD. The visual pattern shown on Figure 8c sets these two principles in opposition to each other. Dot 'A' can be perceived either as part of the vertical row, to which it is closest, or as part of the oblique row, with which it is continuous. We opt to perceive it as part of the oblique row, so here the principle of good continuation is stronger than the principle of proximity. Our present musical se-

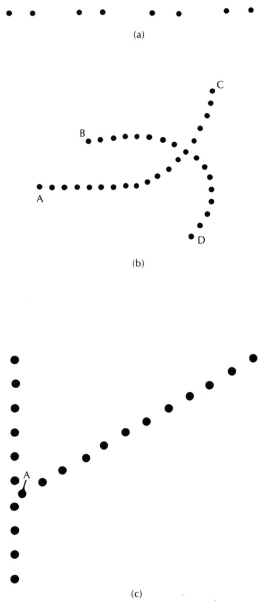

Figure 8. Visual illustrations of the principles of proximity and of good continuation.

quence provides us with a similar choice. We can perceive either a full ascending or descending scale, thus opting for the principle of good continuation, or we can form separate configurations out of the higher tones and the lower tones, thus opting for the principle of proximity. As we have seen, listeners always opt for the principle of proximity.

Butler (1979) has demonstrated that these findings may be extended to a broad range of musical situations. He presented the sequence shown on Figure 7a to music students through spatially separated loudspeakers rather than earphones, and in a free sound-field environment. The listeners notated separately the sequences that were emanating from the speaker on their right and those that were emanating from the speaker on their left. In some conditions the stimuli were generated on a piano. Further, timbral and loudness differences were sometimes introduced between the stimuli presented through the different speakers. Butler found that despite these variations, virtually all responses reflected channeling by frequency proximity, so that higher and lower melodic lines were perceived, apparently emanating from a different speaker. A fur-

ther interesting finding was that when timbral differences were introduced between the tones presented through the two speakers a new tone quality was perceived, but as though emanating simultaneously from both speakers. So not only were the spatial locations of the tones perceptually rearranged in this sequence, but their timbres were also.

To determine whether these findings generalize to other melodic configurations, Butler presented listeners with the two-part contrapuntal patterns shown in Figures 9b and 9d. Virtually all responses again reflected grouping by pitch range. For both configurations a perceptual reorganization occurred, so that a melody corresponding to the higher tones appeared to be emanating from one earphone or speaker, and a melody corresponding to the lower tones from the other. These percepts are shown in Figures 9a and 9c.

Butler's experiments are of importance in that they demonstrate that this illusion, originally discovered in a laboratory with the use of sine wave tones and earphones, and with very simple pitch patterns, can be shown to operate powerfully in a wide range of natural musical situations. The illusion occurs in the

Figure 9. (b and d) Two-part melodic patterns as presented to subjects through left and right earphones or speakers. (a and c) The patterns as most frequently notated by the subjects. From Butler (1979).

228

face of durational inconsistencies, imperfectly timed attacks, differences in timbre and loudness, with different melodic configurations involving relatively complex rhythmic patterns, and in a free sound-field environment.

This tendency to group tonal stimuli by frequency range is commonly made use of in traditional music. When a solo instrument plays a melody and an accompaniment, these are generally in different frequency ranges; more often than not the melody is in the higher range. One interesting musical technique, known as pseudopolyphony, is to present a sequence of tones in rapid succession, which alternate between two different frequency ranges. As a result, the listener perceives two melodic lines in parallel. Following by frequency proximity has been demonstrated in a variety of experimental situations (Miller and Heise, 1950; Heise and Miller, 1951; Shepard, 1964; Dowling, 1967, 1973; Bregman and Campbell, 1971; Van Noorden, 1975; and Bregman, 1978).

But why do many listeners, upon perceiving the sequences we have described, localize all the higher tones to one side of space and all the lower tones to the other side? This illusion does not follow as a simple consequence of perceptual grouping by frequency proximity. It must also have a different basis from the octave illusion, described earlier; since in the present case all the tones are perceived—they are simply localized incorrectly. On the other hand, there are strong cognitive reasons for expecting such an illusion. In everyday life, similar sounds are likely to emanate from the same source, and different sounds from different sources. Our present sequence consists of tones, drawn from overlapping frequency ranges, which are continuously emanating from two specific locations in auditory space. So the best interpretation of this sequence in terms of the real world is that an object that emits sounds in one frequency range is located in one place, and that another object, which emits sounds in a different frequency range, is located in another place. This inference may be so strong as to override our actual localization cues.

The power of unconscious inference as a basis for perceptual illusions has been well documented in the case of vision. One famous example is the "Ames Room," which, when viewed monocularly from a certain position, gives rise to the same visual image as a rectangular room, but which is not in fact rectangular. The image we obtain is consistent with an infinite number of shapes, but we view the room as rectangular, since this is the most probable interpretation. This percept is so strong that people standing in different places in the room appear grossly distorted in size. Another striking example is the fact that a picture of a hollow mask will always appear as a normal face rather hollow. This illusion even holds when the picture is presented stereoscopically. Here we reject true but improbable stereoscopic information, and opt instead for a highly probable, though actually nonveridical, percept.

The present illusions also bear on the question of hemispheric specialization in the processing of musical information. Most neurologists studying deficits in music perception resulting from brain injury (sensory amusia) have concluded that these occur more commonly with damage to the dominant hemisphere (Henschen, 1926; Kleist, 1962; Wertheim, 1963). However, the evidence is much less clear-cut than, for instance, for the case of speech (Luria, 1966; Bogen, 1969). It is likely that there is considerable bilateral representation of musical function. Further there is good evidence from studies both on patients with brain damage and also on normal individuals, that some musical attributes are processed predominately in the dominant hemisphere, and others in the nondominant. For instance, the nondominant hemisphere appears to play a more important role in processing the quality of nonverbal sounds (Vignolo, 1969). Further, dichotic listening studies on normal individuals have found that right-handers process complex sounds better through the left ear than through the right (Kimura, 1964; Chaney and Webster, 1966; Curry, 1967; Gordon, 1970; Knox and Kimura, 1970; and King and Kumura, 1972). On the other hand, the processing of sound

229

sequences appears to occur predominantly in the dominant hemisphere. Patients with damage to this hemisphere show deficits in identifying the temporal order of auditory stimuli, or in processing rhythms (Luria, 1966; Carmon and Nachshon, 1971; and Swisher and Hirsh, 1972). Analogously, dichotic listening studies have found that right-handers show a right-ear advantage in processing sequentially presented sounds (Papcun, Krashen, Terbeek, Remington, and Harshmann, 1974; and Robinson and Solomon, 1974).

Our present finding that right-handers tend to follow the sequence of pitches delivered to the right ear rather than to the left in the octave illusion is another example. Since listening to music involves many functions, including the appreciation of timbral quality and the processing of tonal sequences, it would appear that both hemispheres play important, though different, roles in music perception. The extent of involvement of each hemisphere would depend both on the type of music performed, and also on the perceptual strategy of the listener.

It is clear from the present studies that there are substantial differences between individuals in how even simple tonal sequences are perceived. It is likely that misperceptions of the sort described in this paper occur quite commonly in actual music, but that we are not aware of them. Since these differences correlate with handedness they are likely to be due not only to variations in experience, but also to basic neurological differences existing between individuals. Such misperceptions should not be thought of as failures, but rather as reflecting the operation of mechanisms that generally lead to the right conclusions in interpreting our environment.

References

Bogen, J. E. The other side of the brain II: An appositional mind. *Bulletin of the Los Angeles Neurological Society*, 1969, *34*, 135–162.

Bregman, A. S. The formation of auditory streams. In J. Requin (Ed.), *Attention and per-* formance VII. Hillsdale, New Jersey: Lawrence Erlbaum Associates, 1978.

Bregman, A. S., and J. Campbell. Primary auditory stream segregation and perception of order in rapid sequence of tones. *Journal of Experimental Psychology*, 1971, *89*, 244–249.

Butler, D. A further study of melodic channeling. *Perception and Psychophysics*, 1979, *25*, 264–268.

Carmon, A., and I. Nachshon. Effect of unilateral brain damage on perception of temporal order. *Cortex*, 1971, *7*, 410–418.

Chaney, R. B., and J. C. Webster. Information in certain multidimensional sounds. *Journal of the Acoustical Society of America*, 1966, *40*, 455–477.

Curry, F. K. W. A comparison of left-handed and right-handed subjects in verbal and nonverbal dichotic listening tasks. *Cortex*, 1967, *3*, 343–352.

Deutsch, D. An auditory illusion. *Nature*, 1974, *251*, 307–309.

———. Two-channel listening to musical scales. *Journal of the Acoustical Society of America*, 1975, *57*, 1156–1160.

Deutsch, D., and P. L. Roll. Separate "what" and "where" decision mechanisms in processing a dichotic tonal sequence. *Journal of Experimental Psychology: Human Perception and Performance*, 1976, *2*, 23–29.

Dowling, W. J. *Rhythmic fission and the perceptual organization of tone sequences*. Unpublished doctoral dissertation, Harvard University, 1967.

———. The perception of interleaved melodies. *Cognitive Psychology*, 1973, *5*, 322–337.

Evans, E. F. Neural processes for the detection of acoustic patterns and for sound localization. In F. O. Schmitt and F. T. Worden (Eds.), *The neurosciences: Third study program*. Cambridge, Massachusetts: MIT Press, 1974, 131–147.

Gordon, H. W. Hemispheric asymmetrics in the perception of musical chords. *Cortex*, 1970, *6*, 387–398.

Heise, G. A., and G. A. Miller. An experimental study of auditory patterns. *American Journal of Psychology*, 1951, *64*, 68–77.

Henschen, S. E. On the function of the right hemisphere of the brain in relation to the left in speech, music and calculation. *Brain*, 1926, *49*, 110–123.

Kimura, D. Left-right differences in the perception of melodies. *Quarterly Journal of Experimental Psychology*, 1964, *16*, 355–358.

King, F. L., and D. Kimura. Left-ear superiority in dichotic perception of vocal nonverbal sounds. *Canadian Journal of Psychology*, 1972, *26*, 111–116.

Kleist, K. *Sensory aphasia and amusia. The Myelo-*

Architectomic basis. Oxford: Pergamon Press, 1962.

Knox, C., and D. Kimura. Cerebral processing of nonverbal sounds in boys and girls. *Neuropsychologia*, 1970, *8*, 117–137.

Luria, A. R. *Higher cortical functions in man*. New York: Basic Books, 1966.

Miller, G. A., and G. A. Heise. The trill threshold. *Journal of the Acoustical Society of America*, 1950, *22*, 637–638.

Papcun, G., S. Krashen, D. Terbeek, R. Remington, and R. Harshmann. Is the left hemisphere specialized for speech, language and/or something else? *Journal of the Acoustical Society of America*, 1974, *55*, 319–327.

Poljak, S. The connections of the acoustic nerve. *Journal of Anatomy*, 1926, *60*, 465–469.

Robinson, G. M., and D. J. Solomon. Rhythm is processed by the speech hemisphere. *Journal of Experimental Psychology*, 1974, *102*, 508–511.

Schneider, G. E. Contrasting visuomotor functions of tectum and cortex in the golden hamster. *Psychologische Forschung*, 1967, *31*, 52–62.

Swisher, L., and I. J. Hirsh. Brain damage and the ordering of two temporally successive stimuli. *Neuropsychologia*, 1972, *10*, 137–152.

Van Noorden, L. P. A. S. *Temporal coherence in the perception of tone sequences*. Unpublished doctoral dissertation, Technishe Hogeschool, Eundhoven, Holland, 1975.

Vignolo, L. A. Auditory agnosia: A review and report of recent evidence. In A. L. Benton (Ed.), *Contributions to clinical neuropsychology*. Chicago: Aldine, 1969, 172–231.

Wertheim, N. Disturbances of the musical functions. In L. Halpern (Ed.), *Problems of dynamic neurology*. New York: Grune & Stratton, 1963.

Wertheimer, M. Untersuchungen sur Lehre von der Gestalt, II. *Psychologische Forschung*, 1923, *4*, 301–350.

Response

Edwin E. Gordon

I feel I can best serve the needs of this symposium by offering comments about a few aspects of Diana Deutsch's paper rather than commenting about the paper in general. Thus I choose to focus attention on the problem associated with the research because, in my opinion, it preempts in importance other aspects of the paper.

The overall problem of the studies summarized in the paper was to examine the principles of how we link tonal stimuli into sequences. This is, without question, a very important issue to music educators. In order to be effective educators, we must have some insight into how a listener brings meaning to music and not how a listener tries to take meaning from the music he hears. Without this knowledge, an educator wanders aimlessly. With this knowledge, an educator can guide the learning processes of his or her students.

Deutsch's primary interest appears to be in how the right and left ears psychoacoustically take in different sounds in regard to what is heard and from where the sound is coming. She chose to use an octave dyad in the major portion of her research to gain insight into how we link tonal stimuli into sequences. That Deutsch used only two tones isolated from a musical context to investigate a psychoacoustical question and apply the findings to music perception is disappointing to me. Two tones an octave apart, heard either simultaneously or independently, can suggest only a pitch center and possibly a tonic for a musician with imagination, regardless of the fact that right-handed persons tend to hear the higher tone on their right, but left-handed persons do not. Because the consecutive tones are of the same pitch, and supposedly of the same duration, it would be almost impossible to link the tonal stimuli into sequences *in a musical manner*. Even if it could be demonstrated that we link such stimuli into sequences, it does not follow that we are comprehending the stimuli as musical phenomena. It simply demonstrates that we are comprehending the stimuli acoustically. Certainly, we might explain how we perceive visually but this does not mean that we understand graphic artistic ability. Similarly, because we might explain how the ears interact in the perception of sound, it does not mean that we know any more about the nature and development of musicality. To be fitted with eyeglasses does not make one an artist and to be fitted with a hearing aid does not make one a musician.

In one experiment, ascending and descending diatonic scales were used. Deutsch expresses surprise that not one listener reported hearing a full ascending or descending scale as a component of the sequence because, as she states it, "the major scale is familiar to all listeners in our culture." It is imperative that it be understood by one doing research in music perception that scales are only theoretical models derived from melodies common to a culture. As language precipitates grammar, melodies precipitate scales. When involved in the musical process, musicians hear melody; they do not theorize scales. Moreover, musicians attend to key, mode, form, timbre, and other variables as they bring meaning to the music they hear. And, I must add, that tempo, meter, and rhythm play no small organizational part in the process of comprehending melody. To isolate tones and to ignore interacting musical elements in the study of how we link tonal stimuli into sequences begs for dan-

gerous conclusions and misinterpretations. And, I say this with some knowledge of Wertheimer's contribution to the explanation of how we group visual stimuli into configuration by using dots.

Deutsch states that there are substantial differences between individuals in how even simple tonal sequences are perceived. She also indicates that misperceptions occur quite commonly in music but that we are not aware of them. That is, we are not aware that we do not always hear what is physically present. Good musicians are constantly compensating through normal illusion for the less than perfect performances they participate in and listen to. In this regard, I will conclude my remarks with a reading from *Psychology of Music*.

> . . . it should be made clear that in reality the hearing of tones is rarely an exact copy of these physical characteristics of the sound (frequency, amplitude, duration, and form) because hearing is seldom complete and many principles of distortion operate. We are subject to a great variety of faults and errors in hearing. These are due primarily to five sources: the physical limit of the sense organ, the physiological limitation, inaccurate or inadequate perception, principles of economy in hearing, and principles of artistic hearing. These deviations from direct correspondence to the actual physical sound we call "normal illusion." It is significant that they are not mere errors but may serve in the interests of economy, efficiency, and the feeling of beauty in mental life. And it is particularly significant for us at this stage that all these illusions may themselves be measured in terms of these same four attributes of the sound wave. (Seashore, 1938, p. 17)

As far back as 1919 in *The Psychology of Musical Talent*, Carl E. Seashore suggested the need for psychologists, acousticians, and musicians to cooperate with each other and to be cognizant of each other's research in order to begin to understand the musical process. I cannot help but wonder if today, in spite of technical advances, we are as far apart as were Seashore and his contemporaries. I hope this symposium will prove to be a major factor in bridging such separations.

232

Music and Language

Roger Brown

The subject of this paper, when I first began my research, was to be an informed comparison between music and psycholinguistics. However, I became so interested in one aspect of the subject that the focus of my research changed. What interested me was a certain analogy between the sign languages of the deaf and music. Obsessed with this analogy, I had to begin doing experiments instead of concentrating on books on music theory. This paper is a report on a selection of my research efforts.

A psychology of music would have to be more like a psychology of literature than like psycholinguistics since all musical activities are special skills not even approximately evenly developed in any human community—composition above all, performance also, and even good listening. The acquisition of language is a robust process. It will occur in any human child living with humans old enough and interested enough to keep the child alive, so long as the child is not profoundly deaf or retarded. Even congenital deafness does not prevent the learning or, if necessary, the invention of sign language (Feldman, Goldin-Meadow, and Gleitman, 1977; Goldin-Meadow, 1978). The development of minimal linguistic skills must be robust in the species since such skills are essential to survival. Minimal musical skills are not essential, so far as we know, so it is an interesting question how musical capacities can have evolved.

Of course, linguistic skills are not evenly developed in human beings, and are only minimally developed. There are linguistic giants as there are musical giants, and in both domains there are many intermediate levels of talent and expertise. Psychology has not learned much about linguistic expertise above the minimal level. A start has been made, in research on the understanding of stories, but Shakespeare remains as great a mystery as Mozart. However, Shakespeare worked on his level with the same medium as the average Elizabethan, and Mozart on his level with the same medium as an eighteenth century Salzburger violinist. The media could be interestingly and probably illuminatingly compared.

Whoever starts out from language will look in music for parallels to distinctive features, phonemes, phonotactics, morphology, semantics, syntax, deep and surface structures, presuppositions, implicatures, and even pragmatics. Whoever starts out from music will look for parallels to melody, harmony, rhythm, meter, key, tempo, and tonality. Either enterprise in an early stage is likely to hope for simple parallels: perhaps melody carries the semantic of music, perhaps the musical phrase is a unit comparable in importance to the sentence. Nothing so neat is likely to be true. I do think that music has a semantic level, but I can think of no aspect of music, whether melody, key, meter, rhythm, tempo, tonality, or performance that does not contribute to musical meanings as I experience them.

Language is not specific to one sense modality in the way that music is, and, thanks to recent penetrating linguistic studies (for example, Klima and Bellugi, 1979; Siple, 1978; Wilbur, 1979), it can no longer be doubted that the sign languages of deaf communities are true languages (with semantic, morphological, and syntactic levels) operating in a visual mode. I first thought of comparing sign languages with music when I noticed that the elementary unit in such languages, the sign, is not really built up out of binary, + or −, features in the way that vowels and consonants are. Signs are constructed in systematic ways, different from one sign language to another, but they are not built of present-absent features.

American Sign Language, for example, constitutes its signs from values on four parameters: hand shape or configuration, hand location, hand orientation, and hand movement. The values used on these dimensions in the American Sign Language (ASL) are far more numerous than features—nineteen hand shapes, twenty-four movements—but still are few enough that a descriptive orthography exists (Stokoe, Casterline, and Croneberg, 1965). The important difference between dimensional values and features is that a feature is either present or absent, + or −, but in the case of the four dimensions used to create signs, *some* value of each di-

mension must always be present since a sign without configuration, location, and orientation is inconceivable; movement is a bit different. In this respect, signs seem to be more like musical tones than vowels and consonants are; a tone, if it exists at all, must have some pitch, loudness, timbre, and duration.

Iconicity within Formal Constraint

Another feature of sign languages motivated me to compare them to music. Many signs, probably most, are not arbitrarily linked with their meanings but are, rather, in one way or another, "iconic," by which I mean to say that they represent or suggest their meanings. Nothing of the sort is true of words except for those trifling few that are onomatopoeic. I think that a significant portion of western classical music of the past two centuries is also iconic but that the meanings represented are primarily emotional as they are not in sign languages. It is not iconicity alone that causes sign languages to remind me of music. The iconicity of a sign must be produced within the formal constraints operating in a given language. These constraints are mainly cultural rather than biological; e.g., in ASL a sign may go from head to center chest but not from head to either shoulder. The existence of cultural formal constraints distinguishes the iconic sign from pantomine. The combination of formal constraints and expressive iconicity constitutes an opportunity for the exercise of wit, for creative invention. Signs are recognizably more or less ingenious. Nothing of the sort can be said of words. Something of the sort can be said about music, but before pursuing that possibility, it is necessary to enter a number of disclaimers and qualifications.

One must, first of all, understand that there is no universal sign language; there are about as many different ones as there are different nations. While there are still few comparative studies of sign languages, it is clear that they differ in lexicon and grammar. They also differ quite radically from the languages spoken in coterminous geographic areas. Manual alphabets are not sign languages in the present sense; a manual alphabet is used to fingerspell the spoken language and is no more independent of it than typewriting or telegraphy. Such great linguists of the past as Edward Sapir and Leonard Bloomfield failed to distinguish fingerspelling from signing and so, for a long period, sign languages were considered "derivative systems" and not accorded the status and interest they deserved.

Sophisticated linguistic study of ASL began with a 1960 paper by William Stokoe. I suppose the primary question on the minds of most of us at that time was whether ASL was a language at all, whether it had the powers and complexities of spoken languages. Stokoe's analysis made it apparent that ASL had signing or, as he said, "cherological" parallels for phonemes.

The "cheremes" of Stokoe's analysis were the dimensional values I have mentioned that, themselves meaningless, combined to create a stock of minimal meaningful forms. The printed symbols for the many values adopted by Stokoe are, perhaps, fairly de-

scribed as little squiggles, lines and angles that suggest nothing in particular. The analysis of signs into cheremes had an unsought side effect. When a sign is fractured into the parameters—location, handshape, orientation, and movement—any iconicity that might be seen in the whole is likely to disappear. For example, if I attempt to synthesize the ASL sign for *baby* from the values given in the Gallaudet College Dictionary, I have a hard time putting together certain elbow positions and hand configurations and movements, and the result is awkward, unfamiliar, and hard to reproduce. However, no one is so foolish as to attempt to teach ASL signs from cheremic recipes. Instead, children see them modeled and adults have manuals with photographs illustrating the sign. In such a manual, the elbow positions, movements, and handshapes blend together as "cradling."

However, Fernand de Saussure's (1959) first principle of the nature of the linguistic sign is that it is "arbitrary" or "unmotivated, . . . that it actually has no natural connection

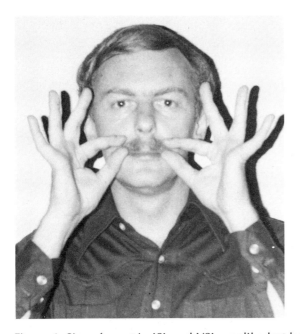 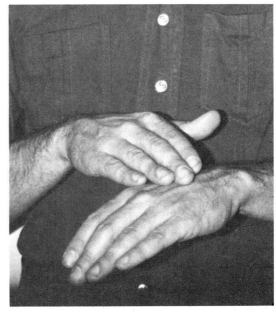

Figure 1. Signs for cat in ISL and VSL—unlike but both iconic.

235

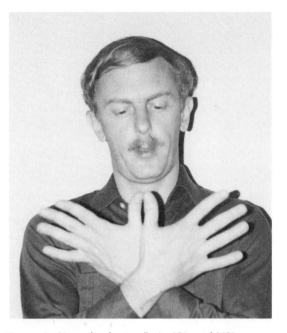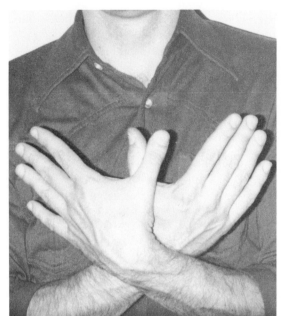

Figure 2. Signs for butterfly in ISL and VSL.

with the signified." So I think that Stokoe's analysis, without aiming at an arbitrary sign, cannot have been unwelcome to the academic friends of ASL who were ambitious for its standing in the semiotic league.

When I first began looking into signed languages, I felt that I had been seriously misled by authorities about the role of iconicity. Each signed language I know something about (only five), though always in part conventional, is also shot through with iconicity. But, of course, *iconic* is a weasel word, and Nelson Goodman (1972) has warned us of its tricky ways; so let me say the little I can that is clear about what *iconic* will mean here. I do not mean to imply that an iconic sign must be any sort of universal; in my sense iconicity is culture-bound, time-bound, and, in general, experience-bound. The Israeli Sign Language (ISL) signifies *cat* by twirling imaginary whiskers whereas the Victorian (Australia) Sign Language (VSL) does so by stroking the imaginary fur of the left hand with the right hand (see Figure 1). There are many grounds of resemblance between refer-

ents and possible hand motions, and only a few are so distinctive as to be found in multiple languages. It does sometimes happen, however. The signs for butterfly in ISL and VSL (see Figure 2) are almost identical.

How do sign languages represent emotions? As with concrete objects and also relations and actions, the signs are usually iconic, but with no visible referent, the best one can do is manifest exaggerated behavioral symptoms of inner states. With emotions, as with visible referents, different languages, once in a long while, hit upon nearly identical signs. See, in Figure 3, the similar " . . . *hab ein Messer in Meiner Brust*" signs for anger in ISL and VSL. More usually, the signs, though iconic, are quite unlike (see Figure 4). In the pictures of Figure 4, a certain difficulty with the visually iconic representation of emotions is evident. While both are translated "love" in the respective manuals, they seem to be quite different varieties. I think we need not ask which is the rapture of the prototypical Italian tenor and which is the love of Elizabeth in *Tannhäuser*.

236

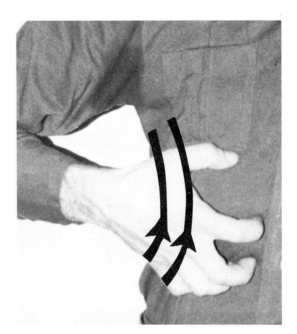

Figure 3. Signs for anger in ISL and VSL.

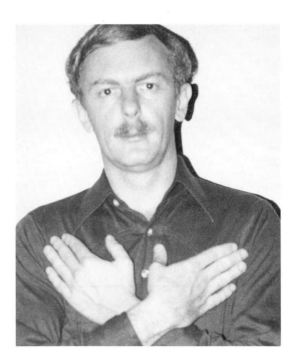

Figure 4. Signs for love in ISL and VSL.

In general, sign language seems to me to be badly suited to the expression of emotions. Iconic representations are not easy to think of, and sign language lexicons in the domain of emotion tend to be impoverished. Of course, this does not mean that the emotional lives of deaf people are comparably impoverished. While they may not be able to sign emotions very eloquently, they are quite able to manifest them in nonlinguistic ways.

In saying that many, probably most, signs are not arbitrary, but rather iconic, I do not mean to make the strong claim that the sign alone is likely to be so powerfully suggestive, so "transparent," as to be translatable on first sight. In controlled research (Bellugi and Klima, 1979), naive hearing subjects have been asked to guess English equivalents from the sight of signs alone, and they have had next to no success. If you glance back at Figures 1, 2, 3, and 4, I think you will agree that you probably could not have decoded the signs without any aid. What you could have done, and by now have done, is recognize the appropriateness or iconicity of the sign—given its linguistic translation. Experiment (Bellugi and Klima, 1979) has shown that when told the meanings of signs, subjects usually can say what it is that makes them suggestive of their sense. Signs are said to be not "transparent," but rather "translucent."

There is one other behavioral effect of the iconicity in signs that has now been richly documented (summarized in Brown, 1978). For both children and adults, it is very much easier to learn the meaning of an iconic sign than of an arbitrary sign. Subjects who are shown the sign and told its English translation learn iconic signs two to three times as easily as arbitrary signs. The link is there, but it has to be pointed out.

The Musical Task

What are some ways in which we might seek to demonstrate an iconicity or expressiveness that is not strong enough to support simple, unprompted translation? Think first of the signs in Figures 1 to 4. One might give the English word that is said to

translate a given sign and ask subjects to explain the appropriateness of the sign. That has been done with signs and is the evidence for "translucence." One might show subjects an array of signs, half of them drawn from one sign language and half from another, with each sign in one language having a synonymous mate in the other, and ask subjects to select out the synonymous pairs. This operation would not be interesting with look-alike pairs, but it would be interesting with perceptually unlike pairs whose only link is in the meaning of which each represents some different facets.

For musical selections, it seemed to me that the translucence task, asking persons to explain what it is that makes a piece of music expressive of a given named emotion, could only have two equally uninteresting outcomes. A subject without technical knowledge would be willing, but incompetent. A subject with a good deal of technical knowledge would be competent, but probably unwilling. Even if the latter were prepared to admit that music had something to do with emotion, he would quite correctly assert that no interesting musical selection could be adequately translated by a single word or cluster of words.

Asking subjects to identify semantically synonymous pairs of musical selections that were, as acoustic objects, very unlike is the operation that appealed to me. Synonymity is a fundamental property of meaning in language, and so if one could find, in music, synonymous pairs that were not "sound-alikes," that would be an argument for the existence in at least some music of a kind of semantic.

I do recognize, of course, that no perfect musical synonymies exist. There are not even two words that are exact synonyms. How much less possible then that there should be synonymous musical compositions? All one can sanely imagine is selections that are near neighbors in a multi-dimensional emotional space. No one will deny that some pairs of compositions are more alike than others. But one is likely to think first of sound-alike pairs, and that is not what I am interested in at all. Everyone

238

has noticed the odd phrase in one composition that is, by accident, quite similar to a phrase in another composition by a different composer, perhaps quite remote from the first both historically and in style and favored genre. These are like the statistically inevitable occasional identities in words from historically unrelated languages. Quaint, but not interesting.

What I have in mind is the occasional intuition that two "stretches" of music, for it is almost never true of complete compositions, express closely similar emotions even though the stretches are quite unlike in most ways. Probably not in all ways. I am sure that someone with technical knowledge of the many dimensions of music could point out similarities as music in any semantic pairs I put forward. Whether these similarities would generally be greater than in random stretches not semantically similar, I have no way of knowing. I am not going to make arrays of military marches, piano sonatas, and soprano arias and ask people to find the synonymous pairs. It will be more subtle than that. Whether it is yet subtle enough to be interesting, you will be in a position to decide for yourselves; I myself am quite uncertain.

There is a major technical problem in asking subjects to pair synonymous musical stretches, which does not arise with photographs of people making signs. The visual materials can be kept before the subject simultaneously, and he can compare and contrast at his leisure. Music has duration and different stretches cannot be simultaneously attended to. I wanted to work with twelve selections (thought to be made up of six synonymous pairs) because I found that they could be heard twice in one hour and carefully attended to, but that one hour was about the limit. However, the selections have to be sequential and even when they are played twice, how can they possibly be held in memory well enough to admit of the possibility of comparing and contrasting meanings? Musicians could do it, but then they would be likely to recognize a good many selections, and all the information attendant on recognition would probably influence their judgments. Persons not knowledgeable about classical music could not, without some aid, hold the twelve selections in memory.

I decided to begin with the not-knowledgeable subjects and provide them with an aid, going on to try the task without an aid and with musicians. The aid may seem presumptuous and may give offense to some music educators.

It probably has occurred to you that someone is going to have to pick the twelve musical stretches thought to be composed of six synonymous pairs. I can think of many persons I should like to have asked to select these pairs, but in the end, whom could I reasonably ask to take so much trouble but myself. Of course, I do not suggest that my pairings and namings were "correct" or even especially well informed. I was simply the starting point, a person with many years of experience of listening with much pleasure to certain kinds of music, but ignorant of many kinds of music and with no performance skills at all.

Once I had settled on a match, I found that I could always think of clusters of two or three words that seemed roughly appropriate to both members. The words always came to mind after the selections had been found, never before. A single word never seemed adequate, of course. Seldom were any words at all frequent. Rather, such clusters used were:

A. Elegiac, gentle sorrow
B. Rapturous, luminous
C. Tender, hushed
D. Rustic, good-humor
E. Spring morning buoyancy
F. Boisterous, rude, heavy

Having "names," as it were, for the pairs solved the memory problem. The first time selections were played, subjects were advised to write down any of the verbal translations that might conceivably apply as well as anything else they chose, including emotion words they found apt, notes on the nature of the selection, etc. The second time they heard the selections, subjects were to force themselves to apply just one letter (corresponding to a set of terms) for each selection and to use each letter exactly twice. In effect, they were told they would be identifying pairs that were maximally similar in meaning. In practice, though, subjects may simply have picked the most apt terms for each selection and created a kind of incidental synonymity. I would have preferred a more direct comparing and contrasting of selections to the method used, which made it possible to go from one selection to its mate by way of a linguistic link supplied by myself. Eventually, I found such a method, but I began by using my own terms, which were terms expressive of emotion, and I gather that this step is in particular need of defense.

Music and Emotion

I suspect that there is an intimate relation between sound and emotion, though this could be an individual matter. Some persons who become deaf as adults have testified that there is a consequent draining of feeling from the world about them.

> In my own case my conception of its effect was literally that of a lost world. The palpable reality of life was suddenly void—its elemental phenomena suspended. Silence fell upon the world like a hush of death and I alone seeemed alive in the midst of it. . . . The impairment of those things most intimately connected with the utilitarian and social relations of life, while an intense source of trouble was never so destructive of the individuality as the loss of beauty and inspiration that went out with certain sounds. . . . There must be something more elemental in the background of these things than was generally understood. . . . sound pure and simple has a specific relation to feelings widely different from that of sight. Its primary effect was that of creating moods. It has been specialized into all kinds of forms that convey facts to the intelligence, but its earliest business was something else, and that business still exists. This being so, the simple fact is that sound has far more to do fundamentally with originating our emotions, or how we feel from day to day, than has what we see. . . . A writer has pointed out that we can see with indifference the writhings of a suffering animal that is silent, but that if there are cries of pain, it produces emotion at once. (Heider and Heider, 1941)

To these striking observations I can only add certain facts so familiar that we may have forgotten to ask why they are as they are. Why was it necessary with the old silent movies to hire a pianist to bang out a crudely appropriate musical background? Why must the movies and TV have musical scores? And if there are more moments of silence in good movies today, that is clearly only because intelligent directors have learned that silence, well used, can become a part of a complete score. Why, when I first saw the Grand Canyon and the Piazza San Marco and the Alps, did I feel that these things had all been more moving in Cinerama? Why? Because both God and man forgot to put in the music.

Some music educators will find these halfplayful remarks offensive and, indeed, will find any suggestion that music embodies emotion both retrogressive and uncongenial. They have had their fill of record dust jackets that "explain" the mood of the music in terms of contemporaneous tragic or rewarding events in the life of the composer. We are all suspicious of any suggestion that one cannot "appreciate" a work like *Mozart's B Flat Major Piano Concerto* unless one can hear in that work the combination of resignation, sorrow, courage, and elegance that the novelist William Styron (1979) hears. A musical composition can be comprehended fully without reference to any nonmusical terms or any terms at all, and it is certain that when we are most fully caught up in a performance, we do not verbalize either aloud or covertly. For performers, it is only beforehand, in rehearsal, that some speaking must be done. For listeners like myself, it is only afterwards that we say anything and then only if there are absent others to whom we seek to convey a great experience or others who were present with whom we attempt to compare what is always ultimately private.

Whether they ought to or not, people will talk about musical experiences. In what language ought they to do so? Some music educators would have them do so only in the technical terms of musical theory. However, these terms are not used with quite the shared precision one might hope for and often leave unexpressed the unique qualities of

240

the experience that most cry out for expression. It may be that music theory, psychological theory, and linguistic theory will some day, in some combination, find a new technical language that does the job. I am sure that it will have little in common with the technical language of contemporary linguistics and that rummaging through the concepts of that field will add nothing to the intellectual stature of music education.

Back then to the fact that people who care about music, musicians or not, insist on talking about their experiences. Musicians among themselves, in rehearsal sessions or outside, can accomplish limited objectives with strictly musical terms. But one cannot say much to nonmusicians in these terms, so critics and conductors and composers and teachers of music appreciation courses have always addresssed nonmusicians in other terms. These terms seem always to have been emotional. Even more embarrassing, conductors, composers, and teachers will use emotional terms, "body English," and anything else they can think of to musicians themselves when they want to elicit something beyond "one note following upon another."

Dmitri Shostakovitch, in the preface to the score of his Fifth Symphony, writes: "The theme of my symphony is the stabilization of a personality. In the center of this composition—conceived lyrically from beginning to end—I saw a man with all his experiences. The finale resolves the tragically tense impulses of the earlier movement into optimism and the joy of living." Poor, misguided genius to have written thus when he ought to have "confined his discourse" to: "1) Moderato; 2) Allegretto; 3) Largo; 4) Allegro non troppo." But, then, it has been ever thus with most of the great composers; they will not learn to eschew the language of the emotions.

Much of the distress felt by some music educators at the suggestion that music expresses emotion is unnecessary and derives from a misconception of the nature of emotion. The fact that the familiar European languages use a certain number of nouns for naming emotions can have the effect of suggesting that emotions are bounded entities, like the referents so many nouns name. And it is perfectly obvious that our experience of music is not a series of such entities, succeeding one another like beads on a string. Emotions are continuous processes: expectations, tensions, surprises, resolutions, climaxes, relaxations, and so on. It is an arbitrary kind of butchery that natural languages commit to cut up these ever-changing continuities into lexical items. But that fact about language should not deceive anyone who is in touch with his or her emotions as to their actual character.

Nor should anyone be so naive as to think that the nonmusician believes there are no more emotional states than there are nouns to name them. To begin with, of course, nouns are not the only lexical items used to characterize emotions; adjectives, for instance, are also commonly used. We have *happiness* and *sorrow* and *serenity* and *joy* and *contentment,* but also *elegiac* and *jubilant* and *buoyant* and *depressed.* But the complete lexicon of emotionally relevant words in any language seems clearly to underdifferentiate the domain in question. One can only approach linguistic expression that is as fine-grained as is the experiential domain by means of linguistic constructions, ultimately poetic.

There is still another confusion that may contribute to the distaste for linking emotion and music. Emotions involve activation of the autonomic nervous system: the heart thumps, one catches one's breath, or breaks out in goose pimples. But surely these and other autonomic responses *can* be evoked by music. It does not follow that they are the only responses music evokes. Contemporary psychology knows rather little about emotion, but it does know that emotion and thought are not absolutely distinct domains, but are impossible to disentangle in the central nervous system. Nevertheless, there is an ancient notion that emotion is, in some way, a lower function than thought, and that unfounded distinction between strata of unequal value may contribute to the belief that linking music to emotion somehow demeans music.

What should we make of the ineradicable

tendency to speak of the musical experience in words and constructions that are also used to speak of emotional experience? I would say that we speak this way, *faute de mieux*. Emotional language comes nearer than other languages to conveying the musical experience. Perhaps technical musical language is more precise, but it is only known to a relatively small community. There must be some affinity linking emotional and musical experience that causes nonmusicians, at least, to use the former as metaphor for the latter. It did not arise from any conspiracy of the enemies of music, if such there be. Eventually, I would guess, we shall find a new sort of terminology that suits both emotional and musical experiences as well as some experiences that are now thought of as "purely intellectual," a terminology far more precise than is now offered by English, French, German, or Italian.

In any event, I had chosen to begin by investigating short-stretch musical synonymities as judged by intelligent adults generally and not as judged by advanced musicians alone. For the larger population, there was no choice as to the kind of words to use. They were accustomed to using the lexicon of mood and emotion in connection with music. They thought they knew how to do it, and I was interested in having them try.

The Selection of Pairs

In candor, I must confess that this task brought me extra-scientific pleasure that played a role in motivating the research. It was not until someone explained to me this summer the aesthetic value of disco that I understood the nature of the pleasure attendant upon the creation of tapes of roughly synonymous musical stretches. In disco, the disc jockey plays a kind of lower-order creative role. The unit of dancer participation is not the individual musical number as in conventional ballroom dancing, but rather the complete set, from beginning to end. The disc jockey creates that set by sequencing recordings, and can build effective climaxes, make jokes with the dancers, introduce new music in a way that makes it welcome. It is not unheard of for all dancers to walk off the floor

when a disc jockey proves artless. In making my tapes, I was a kind of classical disc jockey exercising limited control and judgment, but without doubt enjoying some creative pleasure. Hereafter, I shall refer to myself as the "D.J." and hope that this practice will divest what I did of any pretentiousness.

In selecting synonymous stretches of music, it was my intention never to pair two selections by the same composer and never to pair two selections of the same genre. My initial strategy was to start with something operatic, since the lyrics and my knowledge of the plot would presumably anchor the semantics on one end in something not entirely personal and subjective, and then search for something instrumental but synonymous. I even imagined I might name the emotion expressed by the pair with words from the lyrics on the operatic end. This last notion did not work at all well. The lyrics were never usable because they were always specific to some mad situation whereas what was needed linguistically always turned out to be fairly abstract and general terms.

In general, it was difficult to establish operatic and instrumental matches. For the most part, they seemed to operate in distinct emotional domains. Instrumental works by Mozart, for instance, present a problem. They are always undeniably "elegant" and rather little operatic music, not by Mozart, can be called elegant. I think Bellini's music is elegant, but his idiom is not very well known. I found the matches that suited me primarily in composers who had written both operatic and instrumental music, though generally being best known for the one or the other.

Potential pairs that came to mind for largely verbal reasons almost never worked out when put to the test. The test consisted in first playing the likeliest stretches on my phonograph and if they survived that test, taping them in succession on a Sony TC-158SD cassette recorder.

An example of a verbally mediated match that I thought ought to work, but did not, is the following: Tchaikovsky's instrumental love music from his *Romeo and Juliet* and Puccini's vocal love music from *Madam Butterfly*.

242

Both composers were very romantic, not to say sentimental, chaps who wrote very romantic, but not especially sexual, love music, and both can always be counted on for a good tune. As the musicians probably would guess, even the most closely matched passages in the two compositions inhabit different planets. After a time, I stopped trying to think of pairs that seemed promising for linguistic reasons.

Then, a few pairs began to come directly into memory as music. One of the first, and one that not many subjects agreed with me about, was Bellini's aria *Qui la Voce*, sung by Callas, and Mahler's familiar adagietto from his fifth symphony. Both had registered a powerful and distinctive emotional quality in my memory and I thought, as remote as these composers are, that the quality had been similar in the two cases. I did not have any name for the quality; one does not name the feelings that music creates as they arise. However, the two compositions passed my comparison test and continued to pass it on repeated playings, and there was no difficulty finding apt words: "elegiac, gentle sorrow."

Another odd pair came back together: Berlioz's instrumental love music for his *Romeo and Juliet* and Wagner's vocal and instrumental "Good Friday Spell" from *Parsifal*. Quite a few subjects agreed with me that these two could be called "rapturous, luminous," though, as always, the words occurred to me only after listening again to the music. The fact that the Berlioz is named for a night scene and the Wagner for a spring day only shows the irrelevance of titles. Berlioz was not trying to describe the night nor Wagner the day. Both were, I think, trying to express something in the line of rapture.

The few pairs that had spontaneously come to mind as pairs were, I realized, selections that had had a powerful and distinct emotional effect on me, at least at first, and for that reason, were reasonably accessible. The strategy that I followed from then on was systematically to go through, in memory, works I knew well, searching for marked distinctive emotional reactions that seemed relatively stable for a minute or two. At the

same time, I listened to great quantities of lieder, instrumental solos, and chamber music. I filled many tapes with no-so-bad pairs but kept only the ones that still seemed good after many playings. For an experimental session, I put twelve selections in random order on a tape. The selections varied somewhat in length, but they averaged about two minutes each. In making the breaks, I was ruled by emotional uniformity, the need for clarity and repetition in key phrases, and musical decency.

A Sampling of Research

It will, perhaps, facilitate exposition if I describe first the three kinds of subjects who were involved in one or more study and follow that with a description of the two basic procedures ("With Words" and "Without Words") as well as a sample data sheet. Next will come descriptions of the two principal tapes used (called, respectively, "The Spaced Tape" and "Twelve Variations on Sadness") together with descriptions of principal modes of data analysis. It will then be possible to recount the major results in fairly systematic and succinct form. This style of exposition will leave, as a brief addendum, an experiment with two tapes called, respectively, "Tone Painting" and "Great Texts."

This has been scandalously unsystematic research. Not a "Latin Square Design," but more of a "Yellow Brick Road Design" in which one research foot is planted after another, not because I envisaged a remote goal from the start (unless it be the Land of Oz), but because the results of each single study made it urgent to ask some particular next question. The account given does not conform to the temporal sequence in which studies were done as that would make it almost impossible to make clear what things happened and why I think they happened as they did.

The Three Kinds of Subjects

Nonmusicians. These subjects were recruited by advertisement in Harvard's William James Hall (Behavioral Sciences) for persons not very knowledgeable about classical music. Those chosen for participation were, for

243

the most part, graduate and undergraduate students of psychology. They belong to an exceptionally intelligent population; many of them had had some years of piano lessons as children; their current lack of knowledge of classical music was confirmed by preliminary brief questionnaires and by their failure ever to recognize any of the musical selections played.

Instrumentalists. These subjects were recruited from a conservatory of music. They were all accomplished instrumentalists with many years of training, studying for advanced degrees and aiming at careers as performers or as music educators. Almost every one expressed a preference for early music and contemporary music over the music of the nineteenth century, and most of them disliked operatic music.

Nineteenth Century Knowledgeables. These subjects were recruited by advertisements placed in the classical record departments of the two principal music stores in Harvard Square as well as in the Harvard Music Library. The advertisment asked for persons exceptionally conversant with nineteenth century music in all genres, both instrumental and vocal. Those who responded were asked to answer a set of questions probing familiarity with symphonic music, Italian and German opera, lieder and chamber music. About twenty-five percent of the respondents were not included because they appeared to be insufficiently informed in one respect or another. As it turned out, almost all of the subjects in this group were musicians studying for advanced degrees. Most were skilled instrumentalists or vocalists, but were often specializing in music history or music theory. One young composer and professional harpsichordist took part and also one young professional opera singer. Several subjects had no technical musical training but, as one said, were simply "obsessive listeners." The musical tastes of this group were extremely catholic. "Everything from the fourteenth century to disco," one wrote.

The Two Procedures

With Words. The directions quoted in full here will serve as a generic base, making it possible to describe other sets of directions only insofar as they differ.

You will hear twelve selections corresponding to the numbers on the left margin of the data sheet. The selections are taped from high-quality performances. A few selections will be heard in their entirety, but most of them have only been taped in part. Nothing in the original music has been altered or deleted. Each of the twelve selections seems to me to have an approximately synonymous mate; that is, I think of them as six pairs, such that the members of a pair have about the same meaning. There is a long controversy in the theory of music as to whether anything that can properly be considered semantics or meaning exists at all. If there is a semantic level of response to music, it is surely emotional and, of some music, it does seem correct to say that it expresses one sort of emotion rather than another. This little study assumes that one can reasonably say that the twelve selections to be heard express emotions and that it is possible to identify six pairs expressing similar emotions.

The study further assumes that while there may seldom, or never, be a single English word that exactly names an emotion expressed by any of the twelve selections, it is possible to think of two or three words that are more or less suggestive of the feeling of the piece. On the right-hand side of the data sheet, lettered A, B, C, D, E, and F, are six sets of words. The assumption is that each of the six sets may be judged to be aptly descriptive of just two selections. In short, the word clusters represent attempts to suggest in English the meanings conveyed by the two selections constituting the synonymous pairs. The ultimate aim for you, as a subject, is to place each letter after the two selections that you think express the complex meaning suggested by the words accompanying that letter. Each of the six letters will serve then to mark two selections you find roughly synonymous in the way named.

Many things make this task difficult. To begin with, it may be that the meanings are entirely subjective and that no agreement can be found. If so, that will appear in the data. In the second place, the two selections I think of as expressively similar *will not usually resemble one another at all closely as acoustic objects.* One may be vocal; another instrumental or orchestral. Keys may differ as well as rhythm and tempo. One piece may be short; another long. Composers may be different and may be very far apart historically and in style. Pairs may differ in genre; one may be operatic, another chamber music or symphonic or a simple song. When moving from one style to another, say a richly romantic piece to a spare Baroque piece, it will be very hard not to be swamped by the qualities common to all works of a given style. The situation is a little like what would happen if we were now to have several sentences in Chinese; the Chinese-iness they have in common would drown their uniqueness. Try not to let this happen with the music, none of which is as remote from us as the Chinese language. The thing to remember is to try to penetrate to the emotional essence of each piece, setting aside as far as possible style, composer, artist, tempo, etc.

On the other hand, it should not be assumed that synonymous pairs will be *totally* unlike; music represents emotion, and so there must be some resemblance between matched pairs, however abstract that resemblance is. You must even allow for the possibility that in some cases the resemblance will be quite close. *In general, try to find the resemblance in the expressive qualities named by the word clusters and do not make any assumptions about the degree of superficial similarity to be expected in the selections as sound patterns.*

All twelve selections will be played twice in the same order. The first time through it is not to be expected that you will be able confidently to assign single letters to each selection. One reason why this will not be possible is that you will need to experience the full range of selections before being able to decide which ones are the best *instances* of particular word clusters. Words like "rapturous" and "luminous" might easily seem to be applicable to a number of selections on first hearing. But on second hearing, you may feel that they *best fit* just two selections. The situation is like one in which you would be going to see twelve undisclosed colors and had the word "red" among the verbal possibilities. Until you had seen the full set of colors, you could not possibly know which one was the best, most typical, example of red. The first time through, however, one could, with colors, usefully list "red" opposite each candidate that might conceivably be considered red, whereas the second time through you would try to settle on the two best reds. In similar fashion, you will find it useful, with the twelve musical selections, to list all the letters (representing word clusters) opposite every selection to which it might conceivably apply. This will probably mean many uses of each letter and many letters after each selection on the

first trial. On the second trial, please force yourself to put just one letter opposite each selection and to use each letter just twice. This, possibly uncomfortable, forcing is necessary in order to make the final data comparable across subjects.

On the first trial, please also feel free to make any notes you like. These may be descriptive of physical qualities of the selection to help you remember it, or they may be emotional or expressive terms other than those listed in A to F. You may very possibly hit on terms that you personally find more apt for a selection than any I have listed. Write down anything that seems apt to you on the first trial. On the second trial, use just one letter for each selection and use each letter just twice, thereby indicating your choice of six synonymous pairs.

Minor Points: If you should recognize a selection or its composer, please write in that information. Vocal selections will never be in English, but if you catch a few words of German or French or whatever, you need not note them down. However, you ought not to be strongly influenced by a random word or two or more because my sense of the emotional meaning of a taped section does not follow in any simple way even from the full lyric.

Table 1 is a sample data sheet for the "With Words" procedure used with the tape called "Twelve Variations on Sadness." All other data sheets correspond to this generic type except as I shall indicate.

Without Words. In this procedure I provided no words, but words were used. The difference from the generic directions, quoted in full above, is that subjects were told how to generate their own terms. The following paragraph describes the ways in which the "Without Words" procedure differed from the "With Words" procedure.

The study further assumes that while there may seldom, or never, be a single English word that exactly names an emotion expressed by any of the twelve selections, it is possible to think of sets of words which, in conjunction with one another, are more or less suggestive of the mood or emotion expressed in each piece. On the right-hand side of the data sheet are the letters A, B, C, D, E, and F with good-sized spaces after each. In some versions of this experiment, I have myself put forward words that seemed to me to capture reasonably well emotions expressed by, in each case, a pair of selections. In the present version of the experiment, I would like you to characterize each piece for yourself, in whatever emotionally toned words seem apt. The twelve selections will be played twice. On the first trial, just write down any words at all that seem apt, including, if you like, terms descriptive of the music that will help you to remember it. The ultimate aim of this note-taking and listening is to generate sets of terms to be written alongside the letters A, B, C, D, E, and F. On the second trial, you will be asked to place alongside each selection number just one of the letters and to use each letter just twice. In effect then, you will be identifying six pairs of selections which seem to you to be maximally close in the mood or emotion represented. My principal interest is in the pairs you mark as roughly synonymous. Of course, there is no such thing as complete synonymy. Not even any two words are ever perfectly synonymous. How much less likely is it then that two musical selections should be. All one can possibly say is that of the twelve selections heard, X and Y are most alike in feeling and so have been marked by the same given letter.

The data sheet for the "Without Words" procedure was just like that presented as Table 1 except that the letters A, B, C, D, E, and F had no words following them.

The Major Tapes

The Spaced Tape was the first tape I made, and I christened it only after it was complete and it struck me that the six emotional mean-ings were rather well separated in any presumptive emotional space. The tape I am calling "Twelve Variations on Sadness" was created to push the process of identifying synonymous pairs to a limit of density in emotional spacing and minimal acoustic resemblances. A simple semantic density index that is more objective than my intuition was devised with the aid of the dictionary. I looked up the characterizing terms I had chosen for the two sets of twelve musical stretches to see how often the words utilized for "The Spaced Tape" enlist one another in their dictionary definitions and how often the words used in connection with "Twelve Variations on Sadness" do the same. As you might guess, from the words in Table 1, there is only one such cross-reference for "The Spaced Tape"; the entry for "elegiac" includes sorrow. In the words for "Twelve Variations on Sadness" there were fourteen such cross-references. This is a way of saying that the words in the latter tape, and perhaps the selections they were used to characterize, were close to synonymy in the first place. We shall later see that the data obtained with the two major tapes bear out the supposed difference of density.

Twelve Variations on Sadness. "Sadness" is a misnomer really; "gravity" or "seriousness" would be better. The intention, as I have said, was to create a tape of twelve selections that would be densely packed in semantic space. The judgments were mine alone, and

Table 1. Sample Data Sheet for "The Spaced Tape"

Selection	Trial I	Trial II	Semantic
1			
2			
3			
4			A. Elegiac, gentle sorrow
5			B. Rapturous, luminous
6			C. Tender, hushed
7			D. Rustic, good-humor
8			E. Spring morning buoyancy
9			F. Boisterous, rude, heavy
10			
11			
12			

Table 2. Selections and Intended Answers for "The Spaced Tape"

Selection			Semantic
1	Haydn's "Lark" Quartet, opening phrases. (Cleveland)	E	
2	Schubert's song "Die Forelle." (Fischer-Dieskau)	D	
3	Mahler's Fifth Symphony, Adagietto. (Von Karajan)	A	
4	Leoncavallo's song "Mattinata." (Bjoerling)	E	A. Elegiac, gentle sorrow
5	"Qui la voce" from Bellini's *Puritani*. (Callas)	A	B. Rapturous, luminous
6	Berlioz's *Romeo and Juliet* orchestral music: Love Scene. (Giulini)	B	C. Tender, hushed
7	"Der Vogelfänger bin ich ja" from Mozart's *Magic Flute*. (Berry, Klemperer)	D	D. Rustic, good-humor
8	"Good Friday Spell" from Wagner's *Parsifal*. (Boult)	B	E. Spring morning buoyancy
9	"Steuermann" chorus from Wagner's *Flying Dutchman*, Act III. (Solti)	F	F. Boisterous, rude, heavy
10	"Lullaby" (a song of the Auvergne). (Davrath)	C	
11	Mahler's First Symphony, Second Movement. (Tennstedt)	F	
12	Beethoven Sonata No. 7	C	

they were very difficult to make. Table 3 lists the selections and my (the D.J.'s) intended answers.

Major Modes of Data Analysis

The first two modes of data analysis to be described have something in common that differentiates them from the third. The first two modes use the intentions of the D.J. as a kind of answer sheet. The word clusters (A, B, C, D, E, or F) that the D.J. thought best characterized each of the twelve selections were in "Selection Characterization" analysis treated as the answers for the respective individual selections. Each subject, in following the directions to use just one letter (verbal characterization) for each selection and to use each letter exactly twice, was forced implicitly to match each selection with one another. It is possible to score a subject's data in terms of the number of pairs matching the D.J.'s intended pairings by using the

D.J.'s verbal characterizations. This mode of data analysis uses the D.J.'s verbal characterizations and consequent implicit pairings as a kind of answer sheet or template against which to compare each subject's pattern of responses. Analyses of this sort are called "D.J.'s Intended Pairings." There is a third mode of analysis that substitutes for the D.J.'s intentions a group's own pattern of majority responses, and this third mode will be called "Most Frequent Pairings." It is this last mode that enables us to get beyond the limited perspective of the D.J. (myself) and, in effect, enables a group to define its own "correct" answers. Correct pairings in this third sort of analysis are simply the set made most frequently by the group.

Verbal Characterizations of Individual Selections

The most revealing way in which to report results with this mode of data analysis is also

247

Selection			Semantic
1	End, Act I of Strauss's *Rosenkavalier.* (Schwarzkopf, Von Karajan)	C	
2	Beethoven's Seventh Symphony, Second Movement. (Böhm)	A	
3	Lensky's aria from Tchaikovsky's *Eugene Onegin.* (Bjoerling)	E	A. Funereal, strong but sorrowful
4	Mozart's Piano Concerto KV467. Second Movement. (Eschenbach)	C	B. Sadness tinged with romantic mystery
5	"In mia mano" from Bellini's *Norma,* Act III. (Callas)	A	C. Wistful, delicately regretful
6	Bruch's Violin Concerto No. 1, Adagio. (Stern, Ormandy)	B	
7	"Was duftet doch der Flieder" from Wagner's *Meistersinger,* Act II. (Fischer-Dieskau)	F	D. Depression, the "pits"
8	Tchaikovsky's Sixth Symphony, First Movement. (Abbado)	D	E. Poignant, plaintive
9	Berlioz's song "Spectre de la Rose." (Crespin)	B	F. Relaxed, somber, reflective
10	Mozart's Double Concerto, Andante. (Stern, Trampler)	E	
11	"Ella giammai m'amo" from Verdi's *Don Carlo,* Act III. (Christoff)	D	
12	Brahm's Double Concerto, Andante. (Stern, Rose, Ormandy)	F	

Table 3. Selections and Intended Answers for the Tape "Twelve Variations on Sadness"

the simplest: the percentage of subjects in any group choosing the verbal characterization of any selection intended by the D.J. to be attributed to that selection. There are ways of combining percentages and comparing groups, of course, but in this report limited use is made of this mode of analysis because it is the least interesting. The D.J. initially chose words primarily to give subjects a way to make pairings in a task involving a formidable memory load.

D.J.'s Intended Pairings

In order to form one pair that agreed with the D.J.'s intentions, a subject would have to select the intended words for the intended two selections. The initial probability of choosing the intended words for a given selection by chance is, of course, one in six

(there being six clusters), or .16, and the probability of selecting the intended words for both selections in a pair is only .029. For larger numbers of pairs, matching the D.J.'s pairs by chance, the probabilities are as follows: two pairs, $p = .001$; three pairs, $p = .00007$; four pairs, $p = .000008$; and either five or six pairs, $p = .000003$. The probability for six pairs is the same as for five because once five intended pairs have been selected, the last pairing is fully determined. It is conventional in research employing probability theory to consider a result statistically significant when the probability of its occurring by chance is .05 or less. In short, a subject who matches even one intended verbal pairing has operated at a level above chance. More than one intended pairing is a statistically significant outcome, and matching three or

248

more pairs would happen by chance very rarely indeed. Anyone who has not worked with probability theory is likely to be surprised by the rapid rise in extremes of improbability. What has to be kept in mind is that the probability of *both* "x" and "y" occurring is not the sum of their individual probabilities, but the *product,* and so we are dealing with successive multiplications. We shall see that there are circumstances in which many subjects do not match even one of the intended pairings and other circumstances in which subjects match as many as four, an event that would happen by chance three times in 100,000, or less.

Most Frequent Pairings

This is the method of analysis that enables us to bypass the intentions of the D.J. It is best introduced in connection with the procedure called "Without Words." In this procedure, each subject generates his own set of six verbal characterizations. He is, however, directed to use each one just twice, and since there are always twelve selections, he is forced by the procedure to create six implicit pairings. But pairings linked by terms of his own choice. In the "Without Words" procedure, it is not possible to do the two kinds of analysis that treat the D.J.'s intentions as answers. Nevertheless, each subject in any given group has implicitly created six pairs out of twelve selections. Of course, no two subjects ever generate exactly the same terms. What kind of analysis is possible?

One begins by disregarding the terms, the words that mark out the pairs. One takes the first selection on a given tape for a given group and simply asks how often that selection was paired (in whatever terms) with each of the remaining eleven selections. For the tape "Twelve Variations on Sadness," on which Selection 1 was the *Rosenkavalier* excerpt, nonmusicians matched 1 with 9, the Berlioz song, thirty-six percent of the time; with 5, the Bellini aria, eighteen percent of the time; with 6, the Bruch concerto, eighteen percent of the time; and nine percent each with 12, 3, and 4 (the Brahms, Lensky's aria, and the Mozart concerto respectively). The last of these, be it noted, was the D.J.'s

intended match. The most frequent pairing was: 1 with 9, or *Rosenkavalier* with Berlioz.

In the present example, the most frequent pairing, 1 with 9, was not much more frequent than 1 with 5, and, across all subjects, 1 was sometimes paired with six different selections. I have deliberately chosen this example because it is extreme in its spread and lack of consensus, but even in this case, six possible pairings never occurred. No nonmusician ever matched the mood of the *Rosenkavalier* excerpt with, for instance, the Beethoven Seventh or the Tchaikovsky Sixth.

The important point at present is that 1–9 has been established as the most frequent pairing. One proceeds in exactly the same fashion to find the most frequent pairing for each selection. For Selection 2, the Beethoven Seventh, for instance, fifty-five percent of nonmusicians chose the Tchaikovsky Sixth, and that was the majority pairing. Once again—not the D.J.'s intended pairing. The goal is to determine for any tape and group the six most frequent pairings. As the first example illustrates, the *most frequent* was not always a majority, or even much more frequent than some alternative. In a few cases, a selection might have been matched with either of two other selections because frequencies were tied for these two. In these cases, the rule adopted was to choose the pairing that maximized group frequencies for the full set of six pairs. In just two cases, the solution was still indeterminate, and the final tie was broken by tossing a coin.

What the above procedure yields is the set of answers, or pairings, which the group in question most often agreed upon. This set of six pairings is then treated as a template or answer sheet against which each individual is scored. Individual scores, therefore, indicate the subject's typicality within the group rather than his closeness to the intentions of the D.J. It provides a way of scoring individuals against a set of answers that is directly comparable to scoring individuals against the D.J.'s intentions. However, analysis by most frequent pairing maximizes individual scores. It is possible to obtain scores much higher than the scores obtained by the method of D.J.'s intended pairings, and when this happens, it is reasonable to say that the group has gone beyond the D.J. in that there is more agreement on a set of group responses than on the responses intended by the D.J. It is possible for most frequent pairing to yield exactly the same results as D.J.'s intended pairing. If this happens, it means that the group, insofar as it can agree at all, agrees with the D.J. What is not possible is for the method of most frequent pairing to yield lower individual scores than the method of D.J.'s intended pairings.

The method of most frequent pairing has been introduced in connection with the procedure called "Without Words," but the method is completely general and can also be used to score results when the D.J. did provide words. It occasionally happened that a subject matched the pairs the D.J. intended him to match; e.g., the Bruch and the Bellini selections on "The Spaced Tape," but did not do so by way of the intended words ("A. Elegiac, gentle sorrow"), but by way of another set of available words (e.g., "B. Rapturous, luminous"). In such a case as this, the method of most frequent pairings would credit the subject with one more "correct" pair than would the method of "D.J.'s intended pairings."

Finally, the calculation of chance probabilities yields slightly different values for the present method than for the method of D.J.'s intended pairings. There is a difference because, in the present case, a correct pairing need not involve any particular words, but need only match a most frequent pairing made by the group. There are sixty-six ways of combining twelve objects two-at-a-time,

and just six of these will be correct for a given group and tape. A subject has then six chances in sixty-six of getting one pair right at random. The chance probability of just one pair matching a group favorite is then .09, slightly larger than when it is necessary to select certain words, and not quite statistically significant by conventional criteria. However, the improbabilities mount rapidly, because of the multiplication theorem, as additional pairs are added. For two pairs, p = .010; for three pairs, p = .001; for four pairs, p = .0002; and for either five or six pairs, p = .00007.

Results and Discussion

The results will not be reported as they would be in a research monograph written for psychologists. Instead, I will mention results that seem to me to be of some musicological interest.

"Twelve Variations on Sadness" was not the first tape made nor the first tape for which data were collected; it was created after "The Spaced Tape" for the purpose of providing a set of selections more densely packed in semantic space. However, a report of studies done with this tape provides our best starting point.

Nonmusicians. The tape (Table 3) was first heard by a group of twenty nonmusicians using the generic With Words directions. The degree to which subjects agreed with the D.J. on verbal characterizations or on pairs was slight. Across subjects and selections there was verbal agreement in only 38.3 percent of the time, and the average number of pairings that agreed with those intended was only .55. This last figure reflects the fact that about

---

Table 4. Pairings Made by Nonmusicians for "Twelve Variations on Sadness"

D.J.'s Intended Pairings	Most Frequent Pairings by Groups, Without Words or With Words
1–4 (wistful)	1–9 *Rosenkavalier*—Berlioz (soprano solos)
2–5 (funereal)	2–8 Beethoven Seventh—Tchaikovsky Sixth (symphonies)
3–10 (poignant)	3–7 Lensky—Sachs (male arias)
6–9 (romantic mystery)	4–10 Mozart Concerto—Mozart Sinfonia (Mozart instrumentals)
7–12 (relaxed, somber)	5–11 Bellini aria—Verdi aria (Italian opera)
8–11 (depression)	6–12 Bruch—Brahms (German string concerti)

250

fifty percent of the subjects did not make even one pairing that was the same as the D.J.'s. In short, the two kinds of data analysis that use D.J. intentions as answers yield an unimpressive outcome. To be sure, the results were not entirely random: certain word clusters were never applied to certain selections and certain pairings were never made.

It is the method of most frequent pairings that best reveals what happened in this experiment. Insofar as the subjects were able to agree at all, they matched selections that have obvious surface similarities. For instance the two soprano solos, 1 and 9, and the two symphonies 2 and 8. The full set of most frequent pairings and the superficial similarities between the members of each pair appear in Table 4.

In fact, one does not know that these twenty nonmusicians formed their pairs on the basis of the similarities listed in Table 4. Not one said that he had done so. All had used the emotional language provided by the experimenter, and all clearly understood the directions. Furthermore, it must not be supposed that all, or even a majority, of the twenty nonmusicians made the matches that appear in Table 4. In fact, the most popular pairing (1-9) was made by only forty-two percent, and one (3-7) was made by only seventeen percent. The point is, however, that these pairs were the six on which agreement was the highest. Insofar as the group approached any sort of consensus, it was on pairs that as musical forms were most like one another. The consistency of the principle in accounting for the pairs and the difficulty one has in improving on this "solution" convinces me that the similarities described in Table 4 in fact afforded the bases for the pairings. Everything else in the results was variable and subjective even though the directions were followed and emotion terms used.

I thought it quite possible that the twenty nonmusicians fell back upon surface musical forms because the characterizing words I provided were simply not apt enough and, on that account, devised the Without Words procedure, which told subjects how to make pairs using their own terms. Only the method of most frequent pairings could be used with the data collected this time (from twelve nonmusicians). Of course, none of the subjects involved in the With Words condition was involved in the Without Words condition; they were simply all drawn from the same population. In fact, in every experiment conducted this was the case: different subjects for each session, described by the population from which they came.

As Table 4 shows, the procedure Without Words made absolutely no difference. None of the D.J.'s pairs was among the most frequent set, and that set was, as in the first experiment, just the set of pairs you would put together if your matches were governed by superficial types of musical selection. These results were very discouraging for any notion that there is a deeper semantic level to music that is accessible to intelligent listeners, even when these listeners are nonmusicians. If such a level existed, it appeared to be largely idiosyncratic, which means there is not much real communication at all. But then, perhaps these nonmusicians were just too nonmusical for a semantic level to be discovered. Perhaps they simply had no idea how to "read" the musical surfaces in order

Table 5. Pairings Made by Instrumentalists for Twelve Variations on Sadness

Most Frequent Pairings by Groups	
Without Words (N = 12)	With Words (N = 10)
1–9 Rosenkavalier—Berlioz (soprano solos)	1–4 (wistful)
2–8 Beethoven Seventh—Tchaikovsky Sixth (symphonies)	2–5 (funereal)
3–7 Lensky-Sachs (male arias)	3–10 (poignant)
4–10 Mozart Concerto—Mozart Sinfonia (Mozart instrumentals)	6–9 (romantic mystery)
5–11 Bellini aria—Verdi aria (Italian opera)	7–12 (relaxed, somber)
6–12 Bruch—Brahms (German string concerti)	8–11 (depression)

		Mean No. Matching Group	Mean No. Matching D.J.
Nonmusicians	Without Words (N = 12)	1.2	.55
	With Words (N = 20)	1.6	.58
Instrumentalists	Without Words (N = 12)	1.33	.42
	With Words (N = 10)	1.3	

Table 6. Mean Numbers of Pairs Matching Group Favorites and D.J. Intentions

to discover meanings. Let us, therefore, see what instrumentalists did with the same tape and the same two conditions: Without Words (*n* = 12) and With Words (*n* = 10).

Instrumentalists. The outcome Without Words, displayed in Table 5, is startling. Highly trained musicians taking advanced degrees at a conservatory, insofar as they agreed at all, did the same thing as nonmusicians: they fell back upon superficial musical forms as a basis for matching and, in fact, produced precisely the same most frequent pairs. Most surprising—at least to me.

The results, for instrumentalists, With Words surprised me once again. When the D.J.'s words were provided, the most frequent pairings were not those based on surface musical form, but corresponded exactly with D.J. intentions. It is important to note, however, that the form in which Table 5 presents the results has the effect of suggesting a more powerful effect than was actually obtained. This is because the amount of agreement on the pairings With Words was low, never higher than thirty percent for any pairing, and that is just three subjects out of ten. Still, I believe that Table 5 represents the essence of what happened. Without Words, the instrumentalists performed like the nonmusicians. With the D.J.'s words, the instrumentalists, insofar as they agreed at all, and they agreed very little, made pairings that coincided with the D.J.'s intentions. Recall that it made no difference to nonmusicians whether words were provided or whether they hit upon their own terms. To instrumentalists, it did make a difference. Why should that be so?

Before attempting to answer the question above, let us see how many pairs, on the average, subjects matched with their group template (most frequent pairs) and with the D.J. template. Nonmusicians, With or Without Words, averaged only about one-half of one pair that agreed with the D.J., which meant that about half the nonmusicians matched none and half matched one. These results are not significantly better than chance. And the results of instrumentalists, Without Words, were even a bit lower. The average numbers of pairs created by individuals that matched the respective group favorites are, by operational definition, bound to be at least as large as those matching the D.J., and probably larger. They are, in fact, larger, but not much so, and that simply means that there was not a high level of agreement within any group ever. Among the groups, there are no significant differences in this column.

Only one value in Table 6 is significantly distinctive. Recall from Table 5 that when the instrumentalists were given words, their most frequent pairings matched the D.J.'s intentions. Consequently, the two columns in Table 6 converge on the same value for instrumentalists; With Words, an average of 1.3 pairs matched both the group favorites and the D.J.'s intentions. This value of 1.3 is significantly larger than the three values in the right column (by the Mann-Whitney test $p < .05$ in all cases). What this means is that instrumentalists when they had the D.J.'s words made pairs corresponding to his intentions more often than nonmusicians ever did and more often than instrumentalists did when they used their own terms. Why should these things fall out as they do?

Notation Strategies

One's first thought might be the facile notion that nonmusician psychologists are, in some sense, more verbal than conservatory-trained instrumentalists. It is not immediately obvious what kind of verbal ability would account for the interaction obtained between procedures and subject populations. There are possibilities, however. Suppose the words used by the D.J. were, in fact, fairly apt verbal characterizations of the selections. Many of these words are also infrequent in English and not invariably present, perhaps, in the passive vocabularies of even highly educated adults. Perhaps nonmusicians, in taking notes and generating their own terms in the Without Words procedure, more often thought of the D.J.'s words than did instrumentalists. In such a case, it might make no difference to the nonmusicians whether the D.J.'s words were provided or not since such subjects would, in any case, think of them themselves. The instrumentalists, failing themselves to hit upon the D.J.'s words, might, when the words were provided, find them fairly apt and agree more closely with the D.J.'s intentions than they did in the Without Words procedure. This is a hypothesis that I could test quantitatively by studying the notes taken by both kinds of subject and searching for the words of the D.J. There is no significant difference of this kind.

It is also my impression that in the Without Words procedure there is no difference in the colorfulness or imaginativeness or complexity of the notes made by nonmusicians and instrumentalists. All subjects in both groups clearly understood the intent of the directions and in both groups there were instances of strikingly apt verbal characterizations, amusingly irreverent characterizations, and dreamily poetic characterizations. These notes did not, in the Without Words procedure, lead to a high degree of agreement on most frequent pairings, but they are so interesting that one wishes there were an easy objective way of scoring them directly. The samples in Table 7 give a qualitative "feel" of the verbal terms subjects hit on for themselves.

I made a careful study of all the notes taken by nonmusicians and by instrumentalists on the first trial in the Without Words procedure and in the With Words procedure and was rewarded for doing so. For instrumentalists there was a large and obvious difference in the notes taken the first time the twelve selections were played between the Without Words and the With Words procedures. For nonmusicians there was no difference of the kind found for instrumentalists. The difference found was not foreseen and yet it offers a plausible explanation for the interaction found. In exploratory work of this kind, it is important to have close first-hand knowledge of the data. If they had been prematurely thrown into the computer, nothing would have been found.

The reason for taking notes on the selections the first time they were played was to help hold them in mind for the pairing operation required on second hearing. On the With Words procedure, the directions suggested listing all the letters corresponding to verbal characterizations that might conceivably apply to each selection. Both kinds of subjects did that. About half (forty-five percent) of the nonmusicians did only that, but the majority (seventy percent) of the instrumentalists also did something else. When the D.J.'s words were provided, seventy percent of the instrumentalists made technical musical notes on each selection (together with possible verbal clusters). No nonmusician ever did that.

In the Without Words procedure, both kinds of subjects had no choice but to write

Table 7. Five Characterizations of the *Rosenkavalier* Excerpt

1. "Gentle, resigning, sad yet desperate, heart-wrenching, emotion-packed, loving." [Nonmusician]
2. "Sensuous recollection but not too poignant . . . still caught in the present." [Instrumentalist]
3. "Hopeful, wishful, the way it might have been." [Nonmusician]
4. "Operatic, Hollywood movie prelude, syrupy, 1930-ish." [Nonmusician]
5. "Constant feeling of forward motion heading for a resolution but never getting there, with lots of arches on the way with the resolution being the end. Very similar to sex." [Instrumentalist]

down the kinds of things we have seen in Table 7—emotion words, mood words, and many objective correlatives. By "objective correlative," I mean the description of a situation likely to arouse a complex emotion for which one can think of no name. Subjects had to do it because in the Without Words procedure, it was necessary to generate emotion terms that could be collapsed, on second hearing, to just six sets. With that necessity clearly set before them, instrumentalists, with one exception, made no technical musical notes. In the With Words procedure a majority of instrumentalists took technical musical notes, wrote down letters corresponding to acceptable characterizations, and almost entirely eschewed the business of writing down their emotional impressions.

The facts described above are all set down in Table 8. In that table, I have classified the various note-taking procedures into three types and called them "strategies." The three strategies are so obviously distinct in the data that they may be considered almost "objective" facts, and reliability checks seem to me to be superfluous. The question is how could the distinctive strategy of the instrumentalists on the With Words procedure, the use of technical musical notation, account for that group's distinctive degree of agreement with the D.J.'s intended pairings?

I do not have a fully explicit theory as to how the music notation might mediate be-tween the music itself and the words of the D.J. It seems reasonable to me to suppose that the music notation comes closer than a subject's impressionistic musings to preserving the selection itself; that the musical description is a less ambiguous record of the selection than the average set of emotion terms. Every subject in either procedure has the problem of holding twelve complex stretches of music in mind from a first hearing to a second, and since no nonmusicians and only a small minority of instrumentalists ever recognized any selections on this tape, the problem of finding some sort of notation to "stand in" for that first hearing is not a light one. Essentially, if one is going to compare selections directly, it can only be done by comparing the notation records from the first hearing with the experiences of the second. When instrumentalists were given the Without Words procedure and the necessity of generating their own terms, they used the language of emotional impression, but, provided with words, they restricted their note-taking time to musical terms. My guess is that these latter terms simply make a less ambiguous record of the first hearings and, therefore, a better basis for comparing pairs either directly or with the D.J.'s words.

The Nineteenth Century Knowledgeables

At best, the instrumentalists did not agree very well either with the D.J. or among them-

Table 8. Strategies Used on Trial I by Nonmusicians and Instrumentalists, With and Without Words

	12 Variations Without Words		12 Variations with Words	
	Nonmusicians (12)	Instrumentalists (12)	Nonmusicians (20)	Instrumentalists (10)
Predominantly own words for emotions, moods, objective correlatives, etc.	100%	92%	55%	10%
Predominantly musical terms (portamento, appogiatura, tremolo, ppp, allegretto, tonic minor, etc.) and musical notation.	0%	8%	0%	70%
Only letters for D.J.'s terms.	0%	0%	45%	20%

selves. From their questionnaire, I discovered that the instrumentalists did not, in general, like nineteenth century music. As a group, they strongly disliked operatic music, and half of the selections were operatic or quasi-operatic vocals. These facts taken together suggest that the instrumentalists were not a population likely to agree closely with the D.J. nor likely to agree closely on this task among themselves (because they found the matching of operatic and instrumental pieces in semantic terms unnatural and difficult). Reasoning by analogy with language, it seemed to me that the nineteenth century knowledgeables who were conversant with all genres of nineteenth century music and who liked these several musical traditions ought to agree more closely among themselves and, perhaps, more closely with me. If music traditions are something like either languages or dialects, it should be necessary to be acquainted with the conventions involved in order to make semantic matches across traditions with any high degree of agreement. And so it turned out.

The procedure used was With Words since this had already been shown to maximize agreement for instrumentalists, and the majority of the nineteenth century knowledgeables were also trained musicians. The tape was, as before, "Twelve Variations," and in the notes taken, the strategy of musical notation appeared spontaneously in seventy-one percent of the protocols. The results appear in Table 9. A most frequent pairings analysis now yielded an average of 2.5 pairs per subject agreeing with the group favorite. This is now far above chance levels, which are .001 for two pairs and .00007 for three pairs. However, the D.J. does not fare so well, and I have ruefully considered entitling Table 9 "On Beyond Brown." Agreement with my verbal characterizations of individual selections is only up to an average of 51 percent over the 38.3 percent of the instrumentalists, and agreement with the D.J.'s intended pairings only rises from an average of 1.3 pairs to 1.4 pairs; these are not significant increases.

Table 9 seems to show that a sample of listeners highly conversant with a set of musical genres and style can show substantial

Most Frequent Pairings (With Words: N = 14)

1–4	(wistful)*
2–10	Beethoven Seventh—Mozart Sinfonia
3–5	Lensky—Norma
6–12	Bruch—Brahms
7–9	Sachs—Berlioz
8–11	(depression)*

Mean No. Pairs Matching Group Favorites: 2.5
Mean No. Pairs Matching D.J. Intentions: 1.4
Mean No. Pairs Matching Nonmusician
  Favorites: .93

*Agree with D.J.'s Pairings

Table 9. Pairings Made by Nineteenth Century Knowledgeables for Twelve Variations

agreement among themselves on the underlying meanings expressed in emotional terms of selections drawn from the genres in question. When the selections are semantically close, as they are in the "Twelve Variations" tape, it is evidently necessary for the listeners to be "literate" in the genres involved, to be able to comprehend the various styles, since nonmusicians and instrumentalists, either not well acquainted with or else unsympathetic to the styles, agreed much less well among themselves. The pairs in Table 7 clearly are not based on superficial musical forms. Two of the six matches put operatic and instrumental selections together. Two pairings agree with mine, and those that do not now sound better to me than those with which I started. Notice that the mean number of pairs per subject matching my intentions falls between the mean number matching the nonmusicians and the mean number matching the group favorites. That probably places the D.J. in question about where he belongs: more able to listen comprehendingly to nineteenth century music than nonmusicians who are uninterested in classical music, but less able to listen comprehendingly than the expert nineteenth century knowledgeables. Note that the fundamental evidence for the conclusions is the creation of approximately synonymous pairs; the words used are only a nontechnical language that makes pairing possible. We cannot, from such data, say just what the

Group	Selections Recognized (Twelve Variations)
Nonmusicians	0%
Instrumentalists	17%
Nineteenth Century Knowledgeables	34%
Pairings of Nineteenth Century Knowledgeables	
Pairings matching group favorite or D.J. intentions	24%
Unshared individual pairings	24%

Table 10. Selection Recognition and Selection Pairings

meanings of the Beethoven Seventh excerpt and the Mozart Sinfonia may be, but the two are closer to one another, in this set of twelve selections, than either is to any other.

Table 10 shows that shared pairings could not have depended upon selection recognitions since such recognitions were no more strongly associated with shared pairings than with idiosyncratic pairings. The questions asked with regard to each pairing and each subject were: (1) Was either selection recognized? (2) Was the pairing one that corresponded with the most frequent pairings of the group or one that corresponded with the D.J.'s intended pairings or one that corresponded with neither? The hypothesis to be tested was whether the recognitions were associated with pairings that were shared in one way or another. Several tests are relevant: one can count as "recognitions" only pairings in which both selections were recognized, and one can count as such pairings in which just one selection was recognized. Group sharing can be tested independently of D.J. sharing. I made all of these tests and found no evidence that selection recognition was associated with agreement on a pairing. The percentages listed in Table 10 summarize the most comprehensive test, a recognition was scored if either selection *or* both were recognized and the two kinds of shar-

ing combined. As it happened, the percentages of recognition were exactly the same (twenty-four percent), whether the pair was shared or unshared, and so the competing hypothesis that agreement depends upon a network of associative knowledge may be considered disconfirmed.

I was surprised to find no dependence at all upon recognitions and you may be also, having the *Pathétique-Don Carlo* example in mind. For this reason, I examined each individual case to try to see what had prevented such a plausible possibility from being realized. In some cases, such as the funeral march movement from the Beethoven Seventh, the "funereal" character of the music was evident to almost all nineteenth century knowledgeables whether they recognized the selection or not. In some cases, no subject at all recognized the selection (this was true of the *Don Carlo*), and so all subjects had to rely on the expressive value of the music. In some cases, nonrecognition seemed to favor a shared pairing; for example all those who paired Lensky's aria and the Mozart Sinfonia (the D.J.'s intended pairing) failed to recognize either. The only shared pairing that did seem to depend upon recognition and, presumably, associations was that of the *Rosenkavalier* excerpt and the Mozart *Twenty-first Concerto*. Not improbably, because the prevailing mood of the famous opera could be called "wistful" and the Mozart concerto is also sometimes identified as the "Elvira Madigan" theme, from the wistful movie of that title. In general, however, one can see that the possibilities of associative connection are so varied as not consistently to operate so as to facilitate the adoption of shared pairings.

The Spaced Tape
"Twelve Variations on Sadness" set a difficult music-comprehension task in that the selections were close together in meaning. On this difficult task, "comprehension," defined now simply as a high degree of agreement on synonymous pairs that are not alike in superficial ways but only in some deeper semantic sense, proved to depend upon very high levels of familiarity with the musical genres and

styles involved. The question that can be asked with The Spaced Tape is whether a less difficult synonymity task might enable listeners with less expert knowledge to agree well among themselves. The question was first asked with respect to the nonmusicians.

I am sure that this population is not the least knowledgeable my advertisements might have recruited. The majority of the nonmusicians had had several years of lessons playing an instrument, and many had had a single college music appreciation course. They had, after all, enough interest in classical music to participate in the experiments, and my impression from talking with them is that many privately suspected they were quite responsive to classical music, though having no expert knowledge. A minority, I think, were looking for the answer to the interesting question: "Why had their exposure to classical music affected their lives as little as it had?" The truly indifferent and least knowledgeable students who read the advertisements probably selected themselves out of the experiments altogether.

Nonmusicians

A glance back at Table 2 will refresh your memory for The Spaced Tape, reminding you of the important fact that the intended pairings were far from obvious on grounds of superficial resemblance as acoustic objects or musical forms. The nonmusicians ($n = 13$), operating on the generic directions, agreed very well both among themselves and with the D.J. on the task posed by The Spaced Tape. Analysis of the verbal characterization of individual selections revealed that for nine of the twelve selections, the ma-

jority verbal characterizations agreed with the D.J. and the average size of the majority was seventy percent. For two selections—the Haydn and the Wagner—agreement with the D.J. was 100 percent. Analysis by the method of D.J.'s intended pairings revealed that individual subjects, on the average, selected 2.1 pairings that agreed with the D.J. This is a statistically significant result ($p < .001$).

Analysis by most frequent pairings yielded the pairs displayed in Table 11. Some of these cannot possibly be said to be based on likeness in the superficial musical forms, and no selection at all was ever recognized by these subjects. The most striking of the group's favorite pairs is 1–4, the opening measures of Haydn's "Lark" Quartet and the Leoncavallo song "Mattinata," sung by Jussi Bjoerling. The pair is, from my point of view, an exceptionally good one. The musical idioms could scarcely be farther apart, but the "buoyant" feeling of the two musical stretches is difficult to deny. Of course, the particular performance is always a factor that contributes to meaning in music, and that is nowhere more evident than in this pair. Bjoerling's clear, true voice, devoid of egregious Italianate sentiment, gives the song a simplicity that makes a match with Haydn's inspired melody possible. The pairing of 9 and 11 (Wagner and Mahler) also links a vocal selection and an instrumental selection, but the acoustic and musical similarities (both were loud and strongly rhythmic) are too great to persuade us that the pairing is a semantic one.

The nonmusicians gave consistent strong evidence of a significant ability to "comprehend" the selections on The Spaced Tape. I

Table 11. Pairings Made by Nonmusicians for "The Spaced Tape"

Most Frequent for Nonmusicians (N = 13)		D.J.'s Intended Pairings	
*1–4	Lark—Mattinata (buoyancy)	*1–4	Lark—Mattinata (buoyancy)
*2–7	Forelle—Papageno (good humor)	*2–7	Forelle—Papageno (good humor)
3–8	Adagietto—*Parsifal* (elegiac or rapturous)	3–5	Adagietto—*Puritani* (elegiac)
5–10	*Puritani*—Auvergne (tender)	6–8	*Romeo and Juliet*—Parsifal (rapturous)
6–12	*Romeo and Juliet*—Beethoven (elegiac)	10–12	Auvergne—Beethoven (tender)
*9–11	Steuermann—Titan (boisterous)	*9–11	Steuermann—Titan (boisterous)

*Group and D.J. Pairings the Same

Most Frequent for Nineteenth Century
Knowledgeables

1–7   Lark—Papageno (good humor)
2–4   Forelle—Mattinata (buoyancy)
3–12   Adagietto—Beethoven (tender or elegiac)
5–10   *Puritani*—Auvergne (tender or elegiac)
*6–8   *Romeo and Juliet*—*Parsifal* (rapturous)
*9–11 Steuermann—Titan (boisterous)

*Group Pairing Agrees with D.J.'s Intended Pairing

Table 12. Pairings Made by Nineteenth Century Knowledgeables for The Spaced Tape

decided not to use the tape with instrumentalists but was curious to see whether the greater "literacy" of the nineteenth century knowledgeables would be apparent with this comparatively easy task.

The Nineteenth Century Knowledgeables

A majority of the nineteenth century knowledgeables ($n = 16$), using an analysis of the verbal characterization of individual selections, agreed with the D.J. on nine of the twelve selections, and the average size of the majorities is sixty-eight percent. The result is almost identical with the comparable results for nonmusicians, though the pairs on which the majority agreed with the D.J. were not exactly identical in the two groups of subjects. Analysis by most frequent pairing yields the pairs listed in Table 12. These pairs are extremely interesting to compare, both with those of the D.J. and those of the nonmusicians. About forty percent of the expert panel paired the "Lark" quartet with "Mattinata," as had the D.J. and the nonmusicians. However, slightly larger percentages (fifty-six and sixty-three percent) preferred to pair the "Lark" with Papageno's aria and "Mattinata" with Schubert's song "Die Forelle." Not because of recognitions, an incidental analysis shows, but surely because all four of these selections are close together semantically. My own guess is that the nineteenth century knowledgeables heard more buoyancy in "Die Forelle" than did the D.J. or the nonmusicians because they were far better acquainted with the "language" of Schubert lieder.

258

The pairings in Table 12 all seem to me very penetrating, remote from superficial musical characteristics. I am especially interested that these subjects matched the love music from Berlioz's *Romeo and Juliet* and the "Good Friday Spell" from Wagner's *Parsifal* because this is one of the matches I find most lastingly convincing, though very far from obvious. Table 13 puts together the results obtained for both nonmusicians and nineteenth century knowledgeables using the methods of D.J.'s intended pairings and most frequent pairings. The results seem to me to be both consistent with all that has gone before and impressive in the evidence they provide for the existence of an underlying semantic level in music.

One should note in Table 13 that with this easier task nonmusicians agree very well among themselves. The individual subject averages 2.7 pairings for synonymy that agree with those most frequent in his group, and this is an outcome that is *entirely independent of particular verbal characterizations*. Using the method of most frequent pairings, words serve only to provide a mechanism by which to make judgments of synonymy. The figure 2.7 directly reflects the pairing of selections, regardless of the words used, and it is a result that would occur by chance only a little more than once in a thousand times. For the nineteenth century knowledgeables, this most penetrating mode of analysis yields a

Table 13. Pairs Made Matching the Group's Favorites and Pairs Matching D.J. Intentions for The Spaced Tape

	Mean Number Matching Group	Mean Number Matching D.J.
Nonmusicians (N = 13)	2.7	2.0
Nineteenth Century Knowledgeables (N = 16)	2.9†	2.2*

†Six subjects in this group matched four of the group's Most Frequent Pairings.
*Five subjects in this group matched ten of twelve of the D.J.'s verbal characterizations as well as four of six pairs.

figure that is still larger (2.9), though not significantly so. What it means is that the individual subject agreed with his group's favorite pairings almost half the time, and six subjects agreed with the group on four pairs. This is unquestionably a group of listeners to whom the set of twelve musical stretches *communicates* much the same meanings. The table also shows that, for these selections, the D.J. is also communicating fairly well, indirectly, but through music, with the group.

I lay so much stress on Table 13 because it brings forward a point of similarity between music and language that many assume exists, but which has not been easy to demonstrate. With respect to language, in those Dark Ages when behaviorism was dominant in psychology, most of us uncritically assumed that the ability to talk played an essential role in language learning. It is never as easy to obtain evidence of skilled comprehension as it is of skilled performance. Eventually, however, the late Eric Lenneberg (1962) found a way to show that high levels of linguistic comprehension were possible in the absence of any ability at all to speak. It was done with a single subject who is representative of a sizable group. Lenneberg studied an eight-year-old boy with a congenital inability to articulate (anarthria) arising from low-level organic defects and not involving either cortical injury or psychiatric disease. The boy lived at home with his mother and was seen more than twenty times by Lenneberg between the ages of four and eight years. Lenneberg was able to show that this child had learned implicitly a substantial portion of English grammar as well as the meanings of many words. Lenneberg did this to the satisfaction of neurologists, speech therapists, and other specialists and made a completely convincing film when the boy was eight years old. The evidence is straightforward. The boy is asked to obey commands, both simple and complex (e.g., "Take the block and put it in the bottle."). He is told a short story and then asked to answer questions about it by nodding. The questions were sometimes couched in complex grammatical forms (e.g., the passive voice). The situation was so designed as to exclude

nonverbal cues, and the boy almost always responded correctly. There is no way that he could have responded as he did without extensive knowledge of English grammar and semantics. We know now that a language can be comprehended by those who cannot "perform" in it at all. It now appears that something comparable is possible with music.

The nonmusicians, the D.J., and four of the nineteenth century knowledgeables were not able to perform music. In the case of the D.J., not even able to sing in tune. However, the D.J. and four of the nineteenth century knowledgeables were obsessive listeners to classical music. The nonmusicians were not, of course, but in their lifetimes they must necessarily have listened to quite a lot. Had these nonperformers learned to comprehend anything? Apparently they had since they were able to make judgments of approximate synonymy that agreed with judgments made by skilled musicians. Of course, listening alone did not result in any ability to answer questions about the explicit theory of music, questions of the sort that musicians can answer. However, it was similarly the case that Lenneberg's anarthric boy could answer no questions about the explicit structure of English. Nor can any preschool child. Explicit knowledge requires explicit "schooling." Implicit knowledge, manifest as comprehension, seemingly does not.

The comprehension performances of nonmusicians are, however, much more important than the "drop-the-needle" recognitions that music appreciation courses sometimes use as tests of learning. Comprehension is also vastly more important than any statements of facts about composers' lives or works or testimony as to the relative aesthetic merits of musical compositions. Evidence of comprehension, of the sort presented in Table 13, is singularly important because it is behavior that could not be learned by rote. And it is almost axiomatic in developmental psycholinguistics that one can only be sure that the child has begun the process of implicitly learning a system when he does something recognized as correct by the community but which he has had no possibility of learning by imitation.

259

Tone Painting and Great Texts

This last section employs the familiar synonymy task in a different sort of inquiry. Instead of comparing performances of different sorts of subjects on one tape, it compares different tapes with subjects of the same kind; nonmusicians, as it happens. An effort is made to answer questions about the efficacy of certain kinds of music. In a fundamental sense, the effort cannot succeed because one works with tapes that are samples of certain kinds of music but there is no way of ensuring that the samples are fair and representative and so no way to justify generalizing conclusions to the kinds of music in question. All that can be done is to proceed in good faith, attempting to be fair, because one wants to learn what can be learned.

Tone Painting

At the very beginning of this work, I made an unreflecting, automatic decision to exclude selections with explicit programs committing the composer to represent through music nonmusical phenomena in nature such as the sea, the forest, the seasons, and so on. I thought of that sort of thing as the business of words and signs whereas music seemed to me to be the medium specially adapted to emotion. However, as I worked, I began to have second thoughts about such music. Were even the most brilliant and evocative examples such as Wagner's "Forest Murmurs," Britten's "Sea Interludes," Beethoven's "Pastorale" calm after the storm, and Rossini's calm in the "William Tell Overture" really simply imitative? The more I thought, without relistening, the more it seemed to me that they did not simply represent the sea or the forest, but rather represented an emotion that might be evoked by the natural phenomena. And in each case, only one particular emotion among a number of potential emotions. It might even be especially difficult, I persuaded myself, to link selections with the names of natural phenomena because one would most directly receive an emotion and then have to judge whether it was among the evocative potentialities of the sea or forest or whatever.

In this instance, I wrote my directions before finding and listening to my musical pairs. The directions below differed markedly from the generic directions and reflected the notions I had just formed about so-called Tone Painting.

All of the selections to be played belong to the category of program music; i.e., the composer provided an explanation in words of what he intended to express. In the present case, each selection was explicitly said to have been inspired by some aspect of nature; e.g., the sea, the forest, springtime, etc. However, the selections are not simply imitative of sounds in nature. One should rather think of them as expressing some feeling or emotion inspired by the natural phenomenon. Now it is clear that anything as complex as the sea or the forest or springtime can give rise to a variety of moods; e.g., the sparkling blue sea on a sunny day in June is a different thing entirely from the grey winter Atlantic. The selections you will hear were not selected because they seemed to be emotionally synonymous, but only because those who composed them named some aspect of nature as the inspiration. The very difficult task in this session is, as before, to penetrate the musical style, genre, composer, key, rhythm, tempo and now even the mood itself, and ask yourself instead this question: "Can I imagine myself feeling this way in response to the sea (or the forest or spring or whatever)? Which of the listed sources of inspiration is most credible for this piece of music?"

On the right-hand side of the data sheet, lettered A, B, C, D, E, and F are six names of phenomena in nature. The assumption is that each of the six natural phenomena may be judged to be maximally credible as a source of inspiration of just two musical selections. The ultimate aim for you, as a subject, is to place each letter after the two selections that you think are most likely to have been inspired by the aspect of nature in question.

The search for compositions to use in creating a Tone Painting tape was easy. I went by title and program and, in most cases, long familiarity. Then I played the records and made the tape. The music almost immediately convinced me that I had been wrong in anticipating that this task would be difficult. Table 14 names the selections and gives the intended answers.

To be sure, the Britten "Interludes" reflected different aspects of the sea, but each is also so brilliantly imitative as practically to project pictures on the wall. In the first "Interlude," no one would miss the high thin calls of the gulls and then their graceful swoops through the air, the gentle swells, the almost embarrassing imitation of the sound of whitecaps on a fair June day. Or, in the second "Interlude," how could one fail to hear the groaning grey Atlantic and then the dragging, rattling undertow. As for "Forest Murmurs," it has rustling leaves, suggesting shifting patterns of sunlight, and bird calls galore. In the Beethoven and Rossini Calms, we hear, in Rossini, the plink! plink! of a few last raindrops and then the shepherd's pipe whereas Beethoven gives several receding rumbles of thunder and then a seraphic calm.

Vivaldi's second movement of "Winter" has those brilliant scratchy strings that are snow on the ground and then the swirling violin that is snow caught up in a sudden gust. At this point, I thought hardly any subject would miss any questions except perhaps the not very descriptive Shostakovich piece. Nevertheless, I played fair and taped just those stretches that seemed most unmistakable. The order of selections even turned out to be such that Beethoven's Calm immediately followed Rossini's. At the experimental session itself, I was embarrassed to have set eighteen intelligent and sensitive adults so obvious a task—even if they happened to be nonmusicians.

I was right the first time. When I tabulated the results, I could scarcely believe them. Only two selections of twelve were "cor-

Table 14. Selections and Intended Answers for the Tape "Tone Painting"

Selection			Semantic
1	First Sea Interlude from Britten's *Peter Grimes*. (Bernstein)	F	
2	"Ging heut morgens übers Feld," a song by Mahler. (Fischer-Dieskau)	B	
3	Glazunov: "The Seasons. Winter." (Svetlanov)	E	
4	Beethoven's Sixth (Pastorale) Symphony, First Movement. (Von Karajan)	B	
5	Third Sea Interlude from Britten's *Peter Grimes*. (Bernstein)	F	A. Calm after a storm
6	"Forest Murmurs" from Wagner's *Siegfried*, Act II. (Boult)	D	B. Sunny summer meadow
7	Vivaldi: "The Four Seasons. Winter." (Stern)	E	C. Autumn
8	Overture to Rossini's *William Tell*. (Gardelli)	A	D. The forest
9	Beethoven's Sixth (Pastorale) Symphony, Fifth Movement (Von Karajan)	A	E. Winter
10	Glazunov: "The Seasons. Autumn." (Svetlanov)	C	F. The sea
11	Shostakovich: "Song of the Forests." (Yurlov)	D	
12	Vivaldi: "The Four Seasons. Autumn." (Stern)	C	

rectly" linked with aspects of nature by a majority of subjects (I dare to say "correct" this time since the answer is the composer's, not mine). The majorities in these two cases were just fifty percent. Hardly any pairs were linked in a fashion congruent with the programs of the composers. Exactly two subjects of eighteen chose to match the successive calms of Rossini and Beethoven. The data are more nearly random than with the "Twelve Variations on Sadness." How could such a thing be?

Essentially, I think the reasoning I did before relistening to the music was correct. None of these works is a simple exercise in onomatopoeia. What each of them represents is a mood or emotion that can be evoked by the sea, the forest, or a season. But, as subjects pointed out to me afterwards, it is quite possible to hear the high spirits of "Ging heut morgens übers feld" as exactly expressing the way some people feel dashing through the snow. Had I named the feelings represented, say "intoxicating high spirits," both winter-lovers and winter-haters would have answered it correctly. The name of the season actually adds a degree of difficulty interposing itself between the music and the emotions it represents. There is considerable variation across persons in the mood that is first brought to mind by the name of an aspect of nature.

But what about the imitative things in the music? They seem so unmistakable when you listen, knowing the title. It turns out, upon inquiry, that Britten's seagulls strike some people as brilliant evocations of icicles and that the repetitive groaning Atlantic *can* suggest waves—of storm clouds. As for Wagner's "Forest Murmurs," what better imitation could one imagine of a calm after a storm—with its rustling leaves and tentative birdcalls? These acoustic signs are simply not "transparent" though my subjects could, given the titles, see their appropriateness.

Great Texts

Tone painting, I had concluded, is not transparent because there is no possibility of representing nature, as such, in music but only nature as apprehended, nature as experienced, usually nature in some sort of mood. However, composers sometimes have attempted to express not phenomena with psychology left out but, rather, psychological states as initially expressed in linguistic form, to express musically what an author has already expressed effectively in words. Should not such music which aims to represent mood, emotion, and thought be more transparent, even to nonmusicians, than attempts to convey phenomena of nature? The rest of the argument is incorporated in the directions given to nonmusicians ($n = 13$) for a new tape called Great Texts. What is novel in the directions appears below.

Certain great texts have inspired a number of composers, for example, Goethe's *Faust*; Shakespeare's *Hamlet, Othello, Romeo and Juliet, Midsummer Night's Dream*, etc.; *The Lord's Prayer, The Twenty-third Psalm*, the *Missa Solemnis*, and so on. In some cases, a composer has set the actual text or an adaptation of it as a song, an opera, or an oratorio. More often, composers have been inspired to write incidental music, ballet music, "symphonic poems," or something else— in a completely instrumental, nonvocal form. In the present session, we shall be concerned with just three great texts: *The Mass for the Dead*, Shakespeare's *Romeo and Juliet*, and Shakespeare's *Midsummer Night's Dream*. Each of these has given rise to nearly half-a-dozen fairly well known musical compositions in a great variety of forms.

Each of the three texts is, of course, very long, and so I have selected from each one just two relatively brief episodes. For example, from *Romeo and Juliet*:
a. Love music from the balcony scene.
b. Conflict between the Montagues and the Capulets.
In similar fashion, two episodes have been selected from *Midsummer Night's Dream* and the *Mass for the Dead*. Capsule descriptions of these episodes appear on the data sheet under "Semantic" as "A, B, C, D, E, and F." These episodes, as they are described on the data sheet, are the "meanings" (moods, emotions, or feelings) expressed by the music to be played. There are, then, six "meanings" (two each from three texts). For each meaning, I have selected two musical "expressions" and so there are twelve "stretches" of music on the tape. The twelve are recorded in a random order, and the

Selection		Semantic
1	Love music from Prokofiev's ballet *Romeo and Juliet*. (Previn)	C
2	Overture to Mendelssohn's *Incidental Music to Midsummer Night's Dream*. (Haitink)	E
3	"Lacrymosa" from Berlioz's *Requiem*. (Davis)	B
4	"Conflict between the Montagues and the Capulets" from Prokofiev's ballet *Romeo and Juliet*. (Previn)	D
5	Finale to Mendelssohn's *Incidental Music to Midsummer Night's Dream*. (Haitink)	F
6	Love music from Berlioz's *Romeo and Juliet*. (Giulini)	C
7	"Lacrymosa" from Verdi's *Requiem*. (Reiner)	B
8	Overture to Britten's opera *Midsummer Night's Dream*.	E
9	Opening section of Berlioz's *Requiem*. (Davis)	A
10	"Conflict between the Montagues and Capulets" from Berlioz's *Romeo and Juliet*. (Giulini)	D
11	Finale to Britten's opera *Midsummer Night's Dream*.	F
12	Opening section of Verdi's *Requiem*. (Reiner)	A

The semantic options:

A. *Mass for the Dead:* "Grant them eternal peace, O Lord."

B. *Mass for the Dead:* "Mournful the day when the dust shall rise, guilty man to be judged."

C. *Romeo and Juliet:* Love music from the balcony scene.

D. *Romeo and Juliet:* Conflict between the Montagues and the Capulets.

E. *Midsummer Night's Dream:* Elves and fairies in the enchanted forest.

F. *Midsummer Night's Dream:* Closing scene: Blessings on this house and marriage.

Table 15. Selections and Intended Answers for the Tape "Great Texts"

basic task is to match each selection number with the meaning you think it expresses (A, B, C, D, E, or F).

Aware of the fact I was on very slippery ground in trying to generalize about two kinds of music from two small samples of each, I took pains to be fair in making the tape called "Great Texts." It was necessary to pick up stretches of vocal music at points such that no word could be recognized that might serve as a clue. This was possible partly because words in song (even the English in Britten's opera) are notoriously difficult to make out and, in fact, no subject did recognize a single word. It was necessary to bypass such old friends as Tchaikovsky's love

music from *Romeo and Juliet* since it is too well known; no subject did recognize any selection. I found the comparison of Mendelssohn's and Britten's settings of *Midsummer Night's Dream* especially interesting. The two compositions, almost two centuries apart, both struck me as brilliantly expressive, though very unlike. Table 15 lists the selections and the intended answers.

The results were not at all decisive, and I will not trouble you with a full report. A majority of the nonmusicians agreed with my verbal characterizations for only three selections. The average number of pairs agreeing with the D.J.'s intended pairings was only 1.15. While this value is absolutely larger than that obtained for Tone Painting, it is not

263

significantly larger, and I think we would be right in refusing to take a comparison of this kind seriously unless the difference obtained was very large indeed.

It is not possible, in principle, to prove anything about tone painting in general and music setting great texts in general by this method. There is evidence in the data that Prokofiev's idiom was not comprehensible to these listeners and Britten's only slightly more so. Does one include such music or does one not in a tape sampling Great Texts? Or consider the problem posed by the *Requiems*. Should one include the *Requiem* section and the *Dies Irae*, which are remote in mood, or the *Requiem* and the *Lacrymosa*, which are not so very remote and which I, wishing to be fair to the hypothesis, used? On the other hand, if I wanted to be really fair, ought I not to have used the Mozart *Requiem* with the Verdi, rather than the Berlioz? Or suppose I were prejudiced against the hypothesis, I could have done it in by using the Berlioz *Hostias* (an awe-struck, hushed tenor solo) with the Verdi *Hostias* (a rather noisy fugue). Of course, the correct conclusion from this study, as musicians knew all along, is that composers do not simply set out to represent nature or to express the meanings of great texts; they set out to write musical compositions. These compositions derive inspiration from nature or a text, but they have, as music, aims and requirements of their own that render them only intermittently translatable one to another.

Conclusion

The major conclusions that may be drawn from the research are: (1) Some substantial portion of classical music may be said to have meanings underlying the musical surfaces. (2) Meanings that approach synonymy may be identified with a substantial amount of agreement, if the meanings are not too similar, even by persons not highly knowledgeable about the kinds of classical music in question. (3) If the meanings are very close together, then agreement on synonymous pairs can only be achieved by listeners highly conversant with the traditions involved. (4) Recognition of specific selections is not

necessarily the factor mediating agreed-upon judgments; something more general that may be characterized as "literacy" is involved. (5) It is possible to attain to high levels of musical comprehension without being able to perform music. (6) It is possible to use a nontechnical language of emotional impressions to express musical meanings that listeners will agree upon, and this same nontechnical language can serve to mediate judgments of synonymy that listeners can agree upon. (7) The language of emotional impressions provides a nontechnical general metaphorical medium in which talk about music achieves substantial success in communication.

There is another conclusion that does not follow from the results but from my experience in making the tapes and studying the results. I was always surprised by one outcome in each experiment and always surprised in the same way. Subjects always were less "successful" in the sense of agreeing either with me or with the composer than I expected them to be. What that means, of course, is that I always had information that subjects lacked, information that somehow made the answers seem obvious. That information was, in a word, context. If you know the scene in which the aria is sung or know the words of a great text or know that an interlude is a sea interlude, if, in short, you know the answers, the meaning of the music seems unmistakable. This is much the same conclusion as has been drawn with regard to the iconic quality of signs. If you know that the man is supposed to be signing "cat," then the movements he makes seem unmistakable in their sense and one can give an explanation of why they mean what they do and cannot imagine that anyone could fail to get the message. But if you do not know what his signing is intended to convey, you usually cannot guess. Both music and sign language are, at best, translucent. The two are seldom transparent.

However, translucent meanings are not arbitrary meanings. The sign is in some respects suited to the sense. Not so unambiguously as to render the sign exactly comprehensible in isolation, but with enough iconicity so that one can judge it as more or less apt or inspired within the conventions of the idiom. Here music is different from the sign languages of deaf communities. The conventions of musical communities are enormously complex, and there is much more that must be learned—implicitly—before musical selections become translucent.

References

Bellugi, U., and E. S. Klima. Two faces of sign: Iconic and abstract. In E. S. Klima and U. Bellugi (Eds.), *The signs of language*. Cambridge, Massachusetts: Harvard University Press, 1979.

Berry, W. *Structural functions in music*. Englewood Cliffs, New Jersey: Prentice-Hall, 1976.

Brown, R. Why are signed languages easier to learn than spoken languages? Part Two. *Bulletin of the American Academy of Arts and Sciences*, 1978, 32(3), 25–44.

Cogan, R., and P. Escot. *Sonic design*. Englewood Cliffs, New Jersey: Prentice-Hall, 1976.

Feldman, H., S. Goldin-Meadow, and L. Gleitman. Beyond Herodotus: The creation of language by linguistically deprived deaf children. In A. Lock (Ed.), *Action, gesture and symbol: The emergence of language*. New York: Academic Press, 1977.

Forte, A. *Tonal harmony in concept and practice* (3rd ed.). New York: Holt, Rinehart & Winston, 1979.

Goldin-Meadow, S. Structure in a manual communication system developed without a conventional language model: Language without a helping hand. In H. Whitaker and H. A. Whitaker (Eds.), *Studies in neurolinguistics*, (Vol. 4). New York: Academic Press, 1977.

Goodman, N. Seven strictures on similarity. In N. Goodman, Problems and projects. New York: Bobbs-Merrill, 1972, 437–447.

Heider, F., and G. M. Heider. Studies in the psychology of the deaf. *Psychological Monographs*, 1941, 53(2), 1–158.

Klima, E. S., and U. Bellugi (Eds.). *The signs of language*. Cambridge, Massachusetts: Harvard Univesity Press, 1979.

Lenneberg, E. H. Understanding language without ability to speak: A case report. *Journal of Abnormal and Social Psychology*, 1962, 65, 419–425.

Ratner, L. G. *Harmony*. New York: McGraw-Hill, 1962.

Saussure, F. de. *Course in general linguistics*. New York: Philosophical Library, 1959.

Siple, P. (Ed.). *Understanding language through sign language research*. New York: Academic Press, 1978.

Stokoe, W., D. Casterline, and C. Croneberg. *Dictionary of American sign language*. Washington, D.C.: Gallaudet College, 1965.

Styron, W. *Sophie's choice*. New York: Random House, 1979.

Wilbur, R. B. *American sign language and sign systems*. Baltimore: University Park Press, 1979.

Response

Jack J. Heller

The material presented by Roger Brown to which our original response was directed has undergone considerable post-conference revision. Our original response is printed here with only minor editorial changes. We have, however, appended a few introductory remarks prompted by Brown's revision.

Introductory Remarks

It would be presumptuous for us to predict the value that any new line of research might eventually provide. However, there is a long history of music research in which the stimulus is an extended musical passage, and the response is based upon the subject's feeling for, or characterization of the music. In what way can another study in this genre provide answers to the questions raised by music educators?

Roger Brown does not address this question regarding *his* presented research, but provides us with an opinion regarding *another* research genre. He has no doubt about the value for music education of research based on the concepts now current in linguistics.

> I am sure that it ("a new technical language that does the job") will have little in common with the technical language of contemporary linguistics and that rummaging through the concepts of that field will add nothing to the intellectual stature of music education.

In view of the expected influence of this symposium on the allocation of resources by funding agencies and the choice of directions by researchers in the field we believe that this pronouncement should not go unchallenged.

In defense of music's "language connection" it should be pointed out that the lists of linguistic and musical concepts provided by Brown (see pages 234–235) are not complete. Aspects that we consider to be essential elements in a language/music comparison have been excluded from both lists. Concepts relating to music as performance rather than as text have not been considered. Certainly timbre, accent, vibrato, rubato, attack and legato transients (among others) should be in the list. Important linguistic concepts relating to interpretation, for example, suprasegmental and prosodic features (Lehiste, 1970; Ladefoged, 1971), have also been omitted by Brown.

For many theorists, the interpretive dimension appears to be of minor importance relative to the notated dimensions of music and speech. However, we contend that the speech/music analogy will be productive only when they are compared in *performance*.

One argument for this point of view is implicit in the premise that, with respect to the interpretive and notated dimensions, the acoustic signal available to the listener is undifferentiated. Cues to the notated and interpretive information are co-articulated. Based upon a knowledge of the conventions active in the culture, the *listener* partitions the signal into components that correspond approximately to the notated and to the interpretive

information. An implicit knowledge of the conventions applying to *both* domains is required before the partitioning can be accomplished. Failure to comprehend the nuances of the interpretive gestures could, under this premise, prevent the listener from gaining access to the notated information.

We think it reasonable to propose that the process of partitioning and categorizing components of the stimulus precedes any reliable listener response to music, and that an understanding of this process will provide answers to many of the questions raised by music educators at this symposium.

Response

Emotion, either expressed or evoked, has been a primary focus for discussions about music from antiquity to the present. Research in the past sixty years has produced hundreds of studies dealing with the emotional or affective response to music (see Lundin, 1967; Farnsworth, 1969; Davies, 1978, for extensive bibliographies).

The statement is often made that music is the ideal sound medium for expressing emotional nuance, apparently with the implication that the spoken word in poetry, rhetoric, or drama is somehow less effective. We believe this point of view is a caricature that has limited the range of research in music, and perhaps even in linguistics.

The ability to function linguistically is usu-

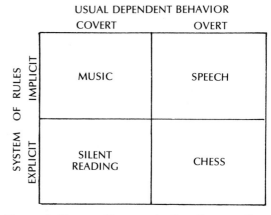

Figure 1. Human Communication Process Categories.

266

ally attributed to the acquisition of a set of implicit language rules. These rules cannot be explicated by means of introspection, but because of the referential component of language, and because each listener is also a skilled performer, many of these rules may be inferred by studying normal speech. Theories of the language process are therefore relatively easy to test, as compared to process theories in music.

An initial emphasis upon emotion was perhaps inevitable in the absence of specific overt responses to the structure of music. In conversational speech, overt responses to the structural relations are quite specific. One can usually tell immediately if the intended communication has taken place.

The predominant conditions of rule-governed behavior may be roughly classified in terms of two characteristics: the rules may be explicit or implicit, and the behavior dependent upon those rules may be covert or overt (see Figure 1).

As an example, the rules of chess are explicit, and the behavior resulting from an application of the rules is usually overt. The rules of language are, for native speakers, implicit. In application, these language rules are repeatedly being tested in overt actions and in the performance of speech. Music is here considered as a rule governed activity. The most common situation is that of the general listener, who uses a set of implicit rules, which, like the rules of language, the listener is not aware of possessing. The application of these implicit rules to the musical stimulus is covert behavior. While the affective end-product may be subject to introspection, the process of applying implicit rules is not introspectively available to the listener. It is no wonder that the caricature of music as a direct route to the emotions has held sway for so long.

Of course music produces an affective response, just as any other art form does when skillfully presented. However, it appears to us that the music research that has focused on the emotional end-product has ignored the *process* of communication. This process is a prerequisite to any reliable evocation of affective response. Subjects must be able to differentiate the musical stimulus before reliable differences in affective response can occur. We believe this differentiation process is, for the listener, both implicit and covert. Yet, as Meyer points out, it should be considered a high order mental activity (Meyer, 1956, p. 30).

It is the study of the pattern recognition required of the music listener during the communication process that we would emphasize in seeking music/language analogies. The music educator should be concerned with the process of musical digestion rather than the gas released at the end of the process. It is through a better understanding of the communication process that instructional innovation can take place.

Language/music comparisons must begin with situational similarity: conversational speech cannot be productively compared with concert music. In our research, the situation considered for the comparison is a concert hall in which a play or a musical performance is presented to an audience. The performer (actor or musician) reads from (or has memorized) previously prepared notation.

The model applied to this restricted range of music and speech activity separates the information contributed by the notation from that provided by the performer, and emphasizes the role of the performer as interpreter (Figure 2). Using a specific set of notational conventions, the composer/author provides the performer with a "script" that constrains the sequence produced by the performer (musician/actor). We call the constraints provided by the notation the "organizational information."

Within the constraints imposed by the notation the performer has considerable latitude in making interpretive decisions. In most performance contexts, the performer is expected to exploit the variability allowed to him. We label the reliable variation imposed by the performer the "interpretive information." For example, in dramatic speech, the same text may be delivered with intended sincerity, sarcasm or humor. Listeners will agree that the same words have been spoken, but with different interpretations. Different

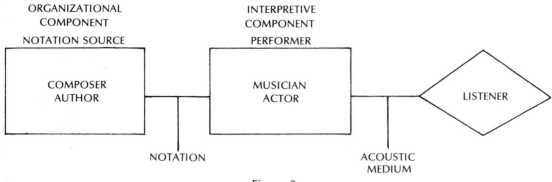

ORGANIZATIONAL
COMPONENT

INTERPRETIVE
COMPONENT

NOTATION SOURCE

PERFORMER

COMPOSER
AUTHOR

MUSICIAN
ACTOR

LISTENER

NOTATION

ACOUSTIC
MEDIUM

Figure 2.

musical interpretations may not be so conveniently labeled, but we have demonstrated experimentally that they can be reliably reproduced by performers and are distinguishable by experienced listeners (Campbell and Heller, 1979).

No communication takes place between the composer/author and the performer unless the performer knows the rules for decoding the notation. These rules (both explicit and implicit) allow the performer to produce a sequence consistent with the intent of the composer/author. The competent performer either says the intended words or plays the intended sequence of notes. The rules are a set of conventions, mutually shared by the performer and the composer/author, which specify the boundaries imposed on specific aspects of performance. Because of the many steps of inference and decision involved in transforming notation into a performance sequence, it may be advantageous to consider that the notation *evokes* the performer's response, rather than *transmitting* the organizational information to a passive receiver.

This same idea is applied to the communication *between performer and listener*. Listener response is only partly determined by the signal transmitted by the acoustic medium. The overall pattern of response can best be accounted for in terms of a shared social/cultural contract (Saussure, 1966) that provides the context in which the acoustic signal is decoded. From this point of view, the performance provides cues that evoke a construct in the listener that approximates the construct

originating in the performer. Communication thus depends upon the extent to which performer and listener share a common social/cultural contract, i.e., an implicit rule structure for relating the gestures of performance.

The auditory stimulus provides the listener with cues to both the organizational (composer/author originated) and the interpretive (performer originated) information. It is up to the listener to construct (perceptually) the intended performance on the basis of his or her knowledge (usually implicit) of the traditions and conventions of the communication process. As Bronowski states " . . . the appreciation of art or mathematics or any creative act is an act of re-creation; . . . You relive the act of creation, and that is why in my opinion appreciation is not passive" (Bronowski, 1977, p. 70). Furthermore, rather than being redundant, each new performance of a musical composition (or play) communicates a different set of interpretive cues for the listener to deal with as an active recreation.

The main premises of this point of view are borrowed from linguistics, but can be applied to speech and music. We postulate (1) a set of culturally determined implicit rules governing the communication process between performer and listener; (2) the participation of the listener in an active, hypothesis testing process, which is normally covert and not directly introspective; (3) the importance of studying both the inter-

268

pretive and organizational components in the communication process; and
(4) the necessity for situational similarity in any comparison of music and speech.

The primary difference between language and music can be stated in terms of what is communicated. To use Meyer's terms, both music and speech communicate "embodied" meaning; only speech regularly communicates "designative" meaning—music usually does not. (Meyer (1956, p. 35) defines embodied meaning in terms of a stimulus that "indicate[s] or imply[ies] events or consequences that are of the same kind as the stimulus itself" and designative meaning in terms of a stimulus that "indicate[s] events or consequences which are different from itself in kind.")

If the premises given are provisionally accepted then two kinds of language/music analogies may be of importance to music educators. One analogy applies at the level of theory and relates the implicit rule system in music to that operating in speech communication. The usefulness of most of the existing structural comparisons is severely limited, because theories dealing with music notation are compared to theories dealing with language notation. These may provide some insight into composer/performer communication, but they do not address the central problem of performer/listener communication. We have found comparisons to be more useful when they cut across the syntactic, phonetic, and suprasegmental components of language, and include both the contextual and interpretive dimensions.

The second analogy relates to research methodology. Even if the implicit rule systems for speech and music appear too dissimilar to support useful theoretical analogies, analogies taken from the research techniques and methodology of linguistics may still be important to music education. For example, linguistic taxonomies defining task complexity have been important in establishing developmental hierarchies and in providing measures of language maturity for children.

If the theoretical and methodological analogies between music and speech continue to be supported by the research results, the following suggestions for music education may be warranted. The music teacher should provide emphasis on the interpretive musical elements rather than on traditional theory based on notation in order to enhance the student's musical competence. Music classes should emphasize comparisons of different performances (interpretations) of the same tunes. We don't mean to suggest that verbal labels should be used. Rather, an ABA form discrimination game, or experiences in imitating various interpretations through singing or playing should be emphasized in the classroom or private lesson.

When the language/music analogy is extended to developmental considerations, it seems plausible that early experiences that reinforce the social/cultural conventions of music may be critical to later perceptivity. This analogy implies that music educators and parents should provide musical experiences that demonstrate musical conventions in the preschool years. We have postulated a

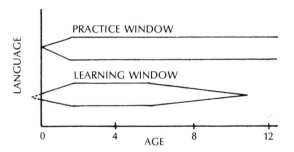

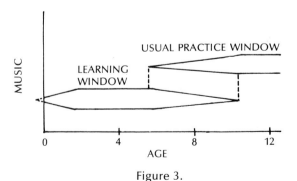

Figure 3.

269

learning window for music (see Figure 3) based on an analogy to language (Heller and Campbell, 1972).

In language the learning window opens at birth (or before) and begins to close between ages six and ten. The concomitant practice window also opens at birth. In music the learning window opens at birth (or before) and begins to close before ages six to ten as in language. The practice window for music may not open during this critical period. As suggested by Lenneberg (1967) language development has a strong correlation with physical maturation particularly in terms of the interpretive nuance. If experiences with music are not provided before the learning window begins to close, the repertoire of usable listening skills may be limited.

Of course, the evidence is not in. Until that time, the music teacher must continue the important job of providing high level education programs. The psychology of music will probably not provide much help for the successful teacher. He or she has already established an appropriate balance between the formal and the interpretive components in the teaching process. However, research in psychomusicology may provide the profession of music education with principles about human musical communication and development can then be incorporated into curricula for the benefit of *all* concerned.

References

Bronowski, J. *A sense of the future*. Cambridge, Massachusetts: MIT Press, 1977.

Campbell, W. C., and J. J. Heller. *Judgements of interpretation in string performance*. Proceedings of the Research Symposium on the Psychology and Acoustics of Music, Lawrence, Kansas, 1979.

Davies, J. B. *The psychology of music*. Stanford, California: Stanford University Press, 1978.

Farnsworth, P. *The social psychology of music*. Iowa State University Press, 1969.

Heller, J. J., and W. C. Campbell. *Computer analysis of the auditory characteristics of musical performance*. U.S. Dept. of HEW, Office of Education, Bureau of Research, Project No. 9-0546A, 1972.

Ladefoged, P. *Preliminaries to linguistic phonetics*. Chicago, Illinois: University of Chicago Press, 1971.

Lehiste, I. *Suprasegmentals*. Cambridge, Massachusetts: MIT Press, 1970.

Lenneberg, E. *Biological foundations of language*. New York: John Wiley & Sons, Inc., 1967.

Lundin, R. *An objective psychology of music*. New York: Ronald Press, 1967.

Meyer, L. *Emotion and meaning in music*. Chicago, Illinois: University of Chicago Press, 1956.

Saussure, F. de. *Course in general linguistics*. New York: McGraw-Hill, 1966.

Music Ability and Patterns of Cognition

Ruth S. Day

One night, a twelve-year old girl happened to hear Beethoven's Third Symphony for the first time. It was a radio broadcast wafting through the windows of a house as she sat alone outside. When it was over, the night was quiet and there was only the smell of warm cedars. And then it happened:

> She was not trying to think of the music at all when it came back to her. The first part happened in her mind as it had been played. She listened in a quiet, slow way and thought the notes out like a problem in geometry so she would remember. She could see the shape of the sounds very clear and she would not forget them.

Although this event took place in a novel, it is a semiautobiographical account (McCullers, 1940) and is similar to experiences described by many people. They find themselves drawn to music, often at an early age; they perceive intricacies of melody, rhythm, and harmony, and can sit down at a piano and duplicate remembered patterns or create new ones.

For other people, this type of music involvement is virtually alien. They often proclaim such things as, "I can't carry a tune to save my life," or "I just don't have any musical talent at all." Such individuals may enjoy listening to music, but do not appear to be aware of its nuances and cannot play known melodies or create new ones.

What accounts for such wide variations in music competence? One possibility is that music training is the critical factor, as illustrated by the filled circles in Figure 1. Thus, people with many years of music lessons demonstrate good music ability, while those with few or no lessons have poor music ability. The problem with this explanation is that there happen to be many people in the "off" cells, as shown by the open squares in Figure 1. Some individuals (including many famous musicians) demonstrate keen musical competence without any training whatsoever. Others are a part of what might be called the "music horror story." These are the people whose parents forced them to take years of music lessons, yet never achieved a high level of competence; furthermore, many of them hated every minute of their training.

Why does music training fail to predict music competence for so many people? Perhaps nature has doled out an entity called "musical talent" with generosity to some individuals but has withheld it from others. Although such an explanation is certainly plausible, this paper takes a different approach. It observes that individuals differ in their general patterns of cognition and suggests that it may be these patterns—not "musical talent" *per se*—that predispose them to have good or poor musical competence. It also examines the effectiveness of music training for individuals with different patterns of cognition.

Patterns of Cognition

People differ in the ways they perform a wide variety of cognitive functions, including perception, memory, and concept formation. My own research (Day, 1977) has shown that some people are language-bound (LB) since they apparently perceive and remember events primarily in language terms. Often this approach helps, but in many cases it leads LBs into misperceptions and mismemories. Other individuals are language-optional (LO), since they can use language or set it aside depending on the nature of the task at hand.

The distinction between LBs and LOs first emerged in studies of speech perception (Day, 1969; for an overview, see Day, 1977). Briefly, different messages are presented to each ear over earphones, with one of them beginning slightly before the other begins.

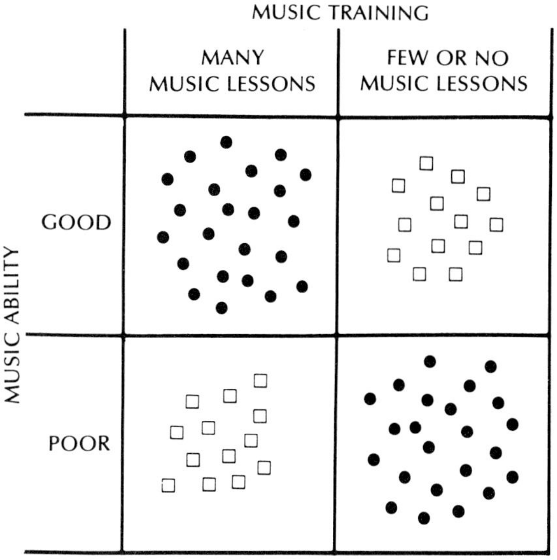

Figure 1. Schematic diagram of the relationship between music training and music ability. The filled circles represent individuals whose music ability can be predicted by their training. The existence of individuals whose ability cannot be predicted in this way, as represented by the open squares, demonstrates that another factor must be involved. Sufficient data are not currently available to determine the relative proportion of individuals in the various cells.

271

For example, the item RACKER might begin 75 milliseconds before the onset of KACKER. When asked to report which speech sound began first, LBs usually report the K, even when the R led by a considerable interval. Thus they report what their language allows (KR-----) rather than the true stimulus events (RK-----). In contrast, LOs are highly accurate in reporting the leading speech sound no matter which one happens to lead.

To date, we have tested over 1,300 people in variants of this experiment and most show either the LB or LO pattern. Furthermore individuals in these two groups perform in characteristically different ways in a wide variety of cognitive tasks. Most important for the present discussion is their performance on short-term memory tasks. For example, when a list of nine digits is read aloud at a relatively fast rate, LOs are clearly superior in their ability to remember the items in their correct order. LOs may have a larger short-term memory capacity or one that enables information to stay "clear" for a longer time; in either case they do not need to spend much time or energy coding the information into linguistic form as it arrives. LBs, on the other hand, need to perform such coding and this apparently puts them at a disadvantage when they try to remember rapidly presented digits. In other situations, however, such coding enables them to achieve higher scores than LOs; for example, LBs show more organized forms of long-term memory.

Major Questions

Three major questions guided the present research. (1) Does music experience, in terms of music lessons, affect performance on a typical test of music ability? (2) Does cognitive pattern, in terms of the LB/LO distinction, affect such performance? (3) If so, do music experience and cognitive pattern affect performance in the same ways?

We began studying these questions by testing college students unselected for music ability and later compared their performance to that of professional musicians. The nonmusicians were undergraduates from psychology classes at Duke University and were

selected on the basis of two criteria. They were classified as LB or LO on the basis of the speech perception experiment described previously and they had either had many years of formal music lessons (mean = 10.7 years, standard deviation = 4.3) or few if any lessons (mean = 1.5 years, standard deviation = 1.8). There were twenty-six subjects in all: ten LBs (five with many lessons and five with few) and sixteen LOs (nine with many lessons and seven with few).

Pitch Change Experiment

General approach. One popular approach in studying music ability is to have listeners compare two brief musical passages. A typical trial is shown at the top of Figure 2. Two melodies are played, separated by a brief pause, and then the listener reports whether they are the same or different. In our experiment, "different" trials were produced by changing the pitch of one note in the second melody (by either a half or whole step), while keeping all other aspects of the first melody constant.

Construction of melodies. The melodies were played on a hand-held electronic device called Merlin (manufactured by Parker Brothers) and recorded onto audio tape. Each note lasted approximately 130 milliseconds, the pause between melodies was 1 1/4 seconds, and the interval between trials was four seconds. While Merlin enabled us to achieve control over the timing of these events, it set limits on the types of melodies we could produce since it only has ten notes; thus all melodies were constructed from the eight notes of the A major scale (beginning on the A below middle C) plus the E a fourth below the scale and the B a ninth above it.

The melodies varied in the extent to which they were melodic. For convenience, they are called "melodic" and "unmelodic," even though they represent only two of many possible degrees along a melodic continuum. As illustrated in Figure 2, the melodic passages had smaller intervals between successive notes than did the unmelodic passages (an average of 3.2 half-steps vs. 5.4 half-steps, respectively) and reversed directions in pitch less often fifty-two percent of all shifts between successive notes vs. sixty-four percent for unmelodic passages). Furthermore the melodic sequences could be supported by the I, IV, and V chords while the unmelodic sequences did not fit into such standard patterns of harmonization. The length of the melodies was also varied in order to place different loads on the listeners' memory; the load was relatively light when both sequences in a trial contained seven notes and

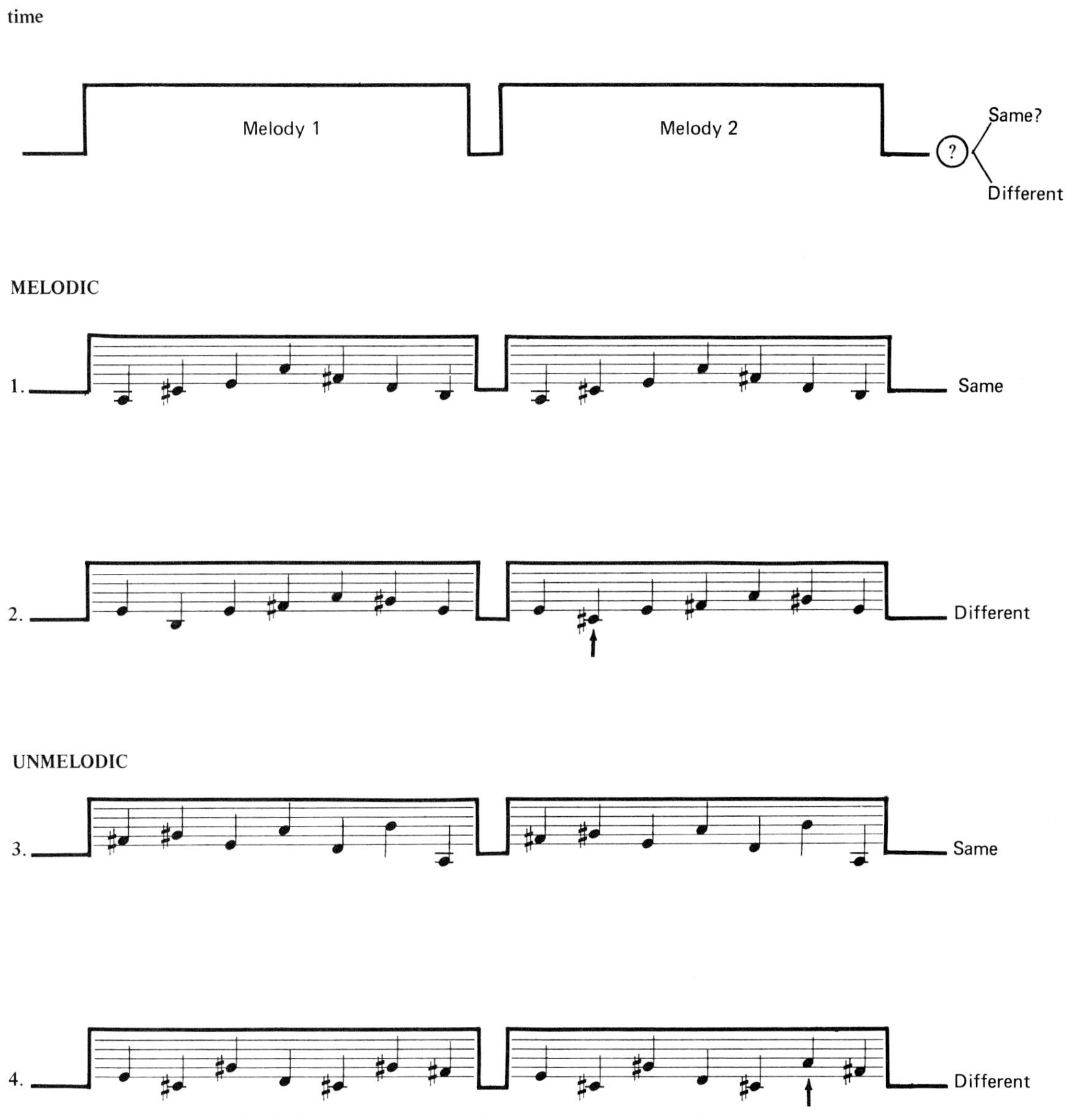

Figure 2. Basic approach of the present pitch-change experiment. The top panel shows the time-course for each trial, while the remaining displays show details for representative trials. The arrows identify which note has been changed for cases where the two melodies are different. See the text for a definition of melodic and unmelodic sequences.

273

relatively heavy when both contained nine.

Overall design. To summarize, there were three stimulus factors in the experiment: musical structure (melodic vs. unmelodic), length (seven vs. nine notes), and type of comparison between the two melodies of a given trial (same vs. different). These factors were varied systematically in order to produce eight types of trials as shown in Figure 3. Six trials were constructed to represent each condition, yielding forty-eight trials in all. Two blocks of twenty-four randomly ordered trials were recorded, one with seven-note melodies and the other with nine-note melodies.

Procedure. After hearing sample melodies and working on two practice trials, subjects listened to the entire block of seven-note tri-

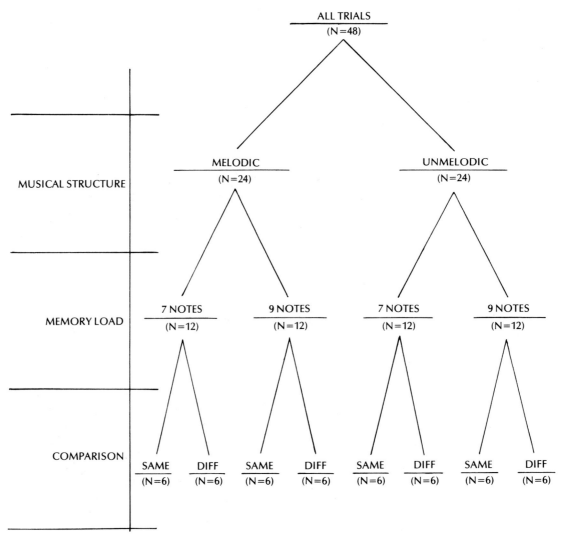

Figure 3. Overall design of the experiment in terms of the three stimulus factors examined. N signifies the number of trials for each subset of factors.

274

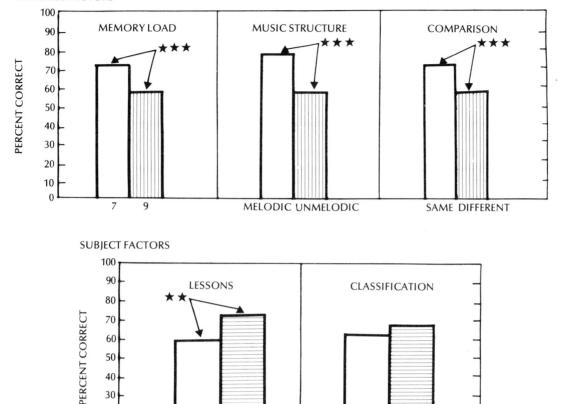

Figure 4. The effect of each stimulus factor and subject factor on overall percent correct. The arrows identify statistically reliable effects, with more stars indicating greater reliability. See the appendix for additional statistical details.

als. After each trial, they put a check-mark in one of two boxes to indicate whether the two melodies were the same or different. Then they followed the same procedure for the block of nine-note melodies. This progression from easier to harder sequences duplicates the usual procedure of standardized music tests.

Results

Responses were scored in terms of percentage correct for each stimulus factor, as shown at the top of Figure 4. For details concerning

the statistical analyses and results, see the appendix; superscripts in the remaining text identify specific entries in the appendix. The results were straightforward; performance was better for trials involving melodic sequences,[1] seven notes,[2] and same comparisons.[3] The arrows pointing to the bars in Figure 4 identify statistically significant differences; stars indicate the magnitude of this statistical reliability, with more stars repre-

NOTE: Superscripts refer to appendix on statistical analyses, pages 283–284.

senting greater reliability.[4] The results shown in Figure 4 are not surprising nor particularly interesting; they simply demonstrate that the distinctions we built into the research design did affect the performance of the listeners.

We begin to see something more interesting when we look at the subject factors, as shown at the bottom of Figure 4. Music experience had a clear effect on performance; those who had many years of music lessons did better than those who had few or none.[5] However, the outcome was quite different when these same subjects were partitioned in terms of their classification as LB or LO. LOs had a slight numerical advantage, but it was not statistically reliable.[6]

The most interesting findings in the experiment are based on combinations of stimulus and subject factors. For each combination, it is useful to examine a given stimulus factor first in terms of the music training of the subjects and then in terms of their classification as LB or LO. The top panel in Figure 5 shows performance on melodic and unmelodic sequences for these alternative groupings of subjects. Music training changed the *level* of the performance lines but did not alter their slopes.[7] That is, subjects with considerable musical training did better overall than those with little or no training, but both groups responded to the melodic-unmelodic distinction in the same way. A different set of relationships occurs when we examine these same data in terms of the LB-LO distinction. All subjects achieved the same performance level for unmelodic sequences, but the LOs were better able to take advantage of the structure provided in the melodic passages; thus the effect of classification was to change the *slope* of the performance lines.[8]

When both musical structure and memory load are considered, a similar pattern of results occurs, as shown in the middle panel of Figure 5. The lines for subjects grouped by music training are parallel, demonstrating that all subjects were affected by music structure and memory load in the same way,[9] even though those subjects with many years of lessons did do better overall. When these data are regrouped by classification, both LBs and LOs showed comparable performance under light memory load; however, under heavy memory load, LOs were better able to take advantage of the melodic-unmelodic distinction.[10]

The same general results occur again when the melodic and unmelodic sequences are subdivided into same and different trials, as shown in the bottom panel of Figure 5. In statistical terms, all the lines are parallel in the breakdown by musical experience.[11] However, LOs were better able to take advantage of the melodic-unmelodic distinction on trials where the second melody was different.[12, 13]

Summary

The displays in Figure 5 can be summarized by two principles: (1) The overall effect of having music training was to improve performance across the board—independent of the particular stimulus factors involved. Thus, in statistical terms, there was no interaction of the stimulus factor(s) with music training. (2) The overall effect of classification was to change the slope of the performance lines as a function of various combinations of stimulus factors. LOs took better advantage of the melodic-unmelodic distinction in general, and especially for cases involving either heavy memory load or two different melodies. Thus, in statistical terms, there was a reliable interaction of classification with each combination of stimulus factors shown in Figure 5. The major conclusion of this experiment, then, is that music training and cognitive pattern affect music performance in different ways. All people can apparently benefit from music training, but LOs do so more fully in terms of various distinctions important to music.

Figure 5. The effect of music training (many vs. few or no years of lessons) and cognitive pattern (language-bound vs. language-optional) on combinations of stimulus factors. Note the changes in overall *levels* of lines on the left side of the display and changes in *slopes* on the right side.

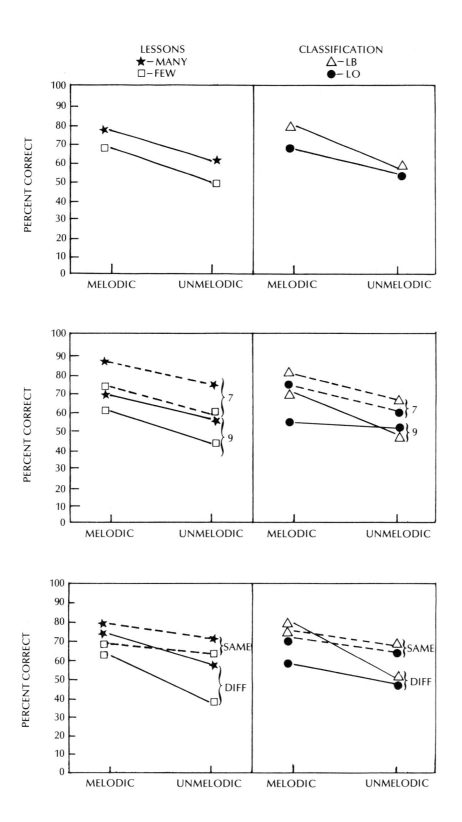

"True" Musicians

Although there are many ways to define "true" musicians they are usually easy to spot using even very gross criteria. Typically they spend a major portion of most days producing music by rehearsing or performing. Most of the true musicians we have tested to date have shown the LO pattern in the basic speech perception experiment. Perhaps, then, general cognitive pattern predisposes an individual to become—or not become—a musician. However, we need to look more carefully at different kinds of musicians. For example, singers might differ from instrumentalists since their music involves a heavy language component as well as general music competence.

Recently we had the opportunity to test principal singers from the National Opera Company. These individuals have all had vast amounts of music training through years of daily lessons and practice and have given many public performances. Although we were able to test only seven opera singers, their results were sufficiently stable and interesting to warrant at least a preliminary discussion here.

Our first observation was that there were indeed some LBs in this group of singers (forty-three percent). Of course a larger sample is needed to confirm this preliminary trend. Nevertheless the possibility that there are more LBs among singers than among instrumentalists is an intriguing one.

Our second observation involved a comparison between the performance of the opera singers in the pitch-change experiment with that of the musically unselected college students described above. It seems reasonable to expect that the vast musical training of the professional singers would be reflected by large increases over the student scores. However the results were not very convincing since the singers were correct on sixty-nine percent of all trials while the college students were correct on sixty-five percent. Since only six opera singers were able to participate in this experiment (three LBs and three LOs), sufficient data are not available for formal statistical comparisons with the college students. Nevertheless, informal

comparisons between these two samples of subjects in terms of the LB-LO distinction yield some interesting trends. The LO opera singers showed a six percent improvement over the LO college students, while the LB opera singers showed only a two percent improvement over their college counterparts. Other breakdowns of the data suggest that the LO opera singers may have been more sensitive to the melodic-unmelodic distinction and suffered less from the effect of heavy memory loads.

If these preliminary results hold up as we test more opera singers, an additional statement could be made concerning music ability and training: that we can provide extensive music training yet performance on tests such as the one used here will continue to show a superiority of LOs over LBs. At first glance, such a statement seems to paint a gloomy picture for LBs. It suggests that they could take lessons and rehearse for years, yet fail to show substantial improvement. But "improvement" on what? The answer is improvement on a short-term memory task. As mentioned above, LOs outperform LBs in memory for digits; the present experiment also emphasizes short-term memory, but just happens to use music instead of language. Therefore we might wonder whether music tests measure "music ability" *per se* or instead more general cognitive processes that cut across different stimulus domains. In order to study this question more fully, we are currently examining various subtests of standardized music tests; preliminary results suggest that although these tests may predict eventual music achievement, they may be better mirrors of general cognitive processes rather than extractors of some entity called "music ability." Our studies also suggest that the design of these tests may reduce our ability to observe differences between individuals with different patterns of cognition.

A Standardized Music Test

Perhaps the most widely known test of music ability is the Seashore Measures of Musical Talents (Seashore, Lewis, and Saetveit, 1960). It contains a subtest called the Tonal Memory Test which is similar to our pitch-change experiment, although it is simpler in several respects, as illustrated in Figure 6. First, musical structure is not varied; all melodies are quite unmelodic. Therefore, the test is unable to demonstrate the robust differences we have already observed between LBs and LOs in terms of this important factor. Second, the number of notes per melody is only three, four, or five. Such light memory loads are appropriate for the youngest students in the Seashore norms (grades four and five), but seem less appropriate for

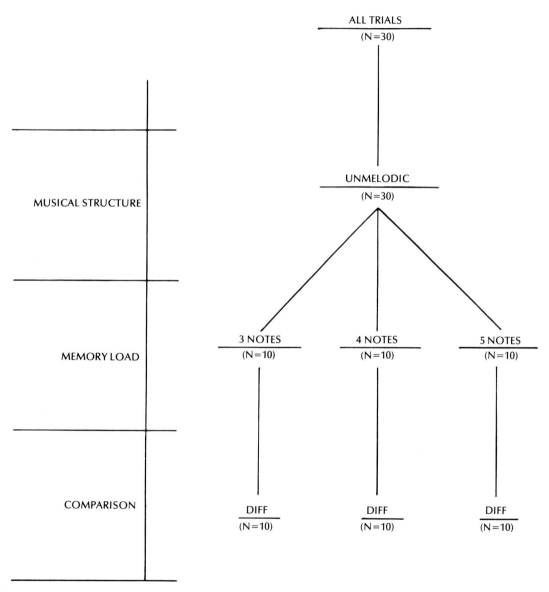

Figure 6. Overall design of the Seashore Tonal Memory Test. Note the simplicity of this design relative to that of our experiment as shown in Figure 3.

279

college students. Finally, the second melody of each pair is always different from the first in terms of the pitch of one note. This feature has both advantages and disadvantages. One disadvantage is that we cannot compare performance between same and different trials for a given individual. Thus if someone performs poorly, we cannot tell whether the person was simply inattentive or whether other conditions were responsible for the poor showing. It helps to observe performance on "same" trials in order to interpret performance on "different" trials. An advantage of this approach, however, is that the listener is asked a more subtle question; instead of "same or different," the subject is asked, "*Which* note is different?" Overall the status of these three stimulus factors in the Seashore subtest reduces our ability to detect whatever differences may actually exist between LBs and LOs. In addition, it has fewer trials than ours, which further limits the range of scores that can occur. Despite these various limitations, we gave the Seashore Tonal Memory Test to the same college students who took our pitch-change experiment[14] in order to compare the relative effect of music training and cognitive pattern on this well-known test of music ability.

Results

Overall performance. As expected, the Seashore subtest was very easy for Duke undergraduates. They were correct on eighty-nine percent of all trials, which was substantially higher than their performance in our experiment (sixty-five percent).[15] It is difficult to compare their performance directly to that reported in the Seashore norms since the norms lump together both high school and college students. However, since students in the norms were correct on eighty-three percent of all trials, and since it is reasonable to assume that college students contributed higher scores to the norm average, the Duke performance is probably comparable to that of the Seashore college students. This level is so high, though, that the test may not detect all the differences that actually exist among the individuals tested. When a task approaches the "ceiling" of 100 percent correct, our ability to observe such differences is reduced. Nevertheless, the same people did well (or poorly) in both our experiment and the Seashore subtest.[16]

Stimulus Factor. The top panel in Figure 7 shows that memory load was so light on trials with three-note sequences that performance was virtually perfect. However, it did drop as memory load increased.[17]

Subject Factors. The same pattern of results occurred for the subject factors here as in our experiment, as shown in the middle of Figure 7. People with many years of music lessons did better than those with few or no lessons,[18] but LBs and LOs achieved comparable performance levels.[19]

Combination of Stimulus and Subject Factors. The most interesting aspect of the Seashore data involves a breakdown of results by both training and cognitive pattern for each memory load, as illustrated at the bottom of Figure 7. LOs with many years of music lessons showed virtually no effect of increased memory load, while the performance of all other groups of subjects did drop. Overall this interaction did not reach conventional levels of statistical reliability,[20] which could reflect the fact that there were so few observations per point in this breakdown and that ceiling effects were present. Since these preliminary trends have great potential value for music education, we have designed an expanded version of this subtest in order to resolve its present short-comings. If the results clearly demonstrate the trends observed here, we would be able to say that music training is more beneficial to LOs than to LBs.

Limitations

The present paper contains several inherent limitations. Most reflect the fact that it

Figure 7. Basic results of the Seashore Tonal Memory Test for the one stimulus factor and two subject factors. The display of the interaction shown at the bottom should be viewed with caution since it did not achieve statistical reliability.

STIMULUS FACTOR

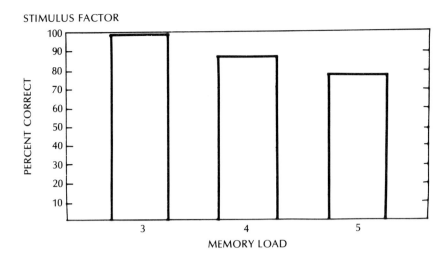

SUBJECT FACTORS

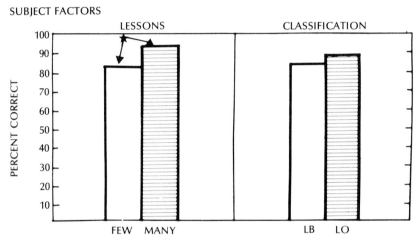

INTERACTION

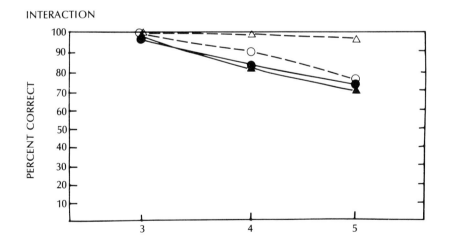

281

represents only a small portion of the work in a fairly comprehensive project on the roles of experience and cognitive pattern in music competence. In principle, such problems should be largely resolved by the time the project is completed. Nevertheless, it is useful to make them explicit.

Only one type of music test has been discussed here. Obviously, music "ability" involves more than being able to determine which note (if any) has been changed in the second playing of a brief passage. Therefore we are studying other types of music tests to determine the generality of our findings. Some of these tests stay within the same general paradigm involving a comparison of two melodies, but make changes in other dimensions such as rhythm. The findings obtained so far demonstrate again that music training and cognitive pattern affect performance in different ways. Other tests examine relationships between perception and production. Other tests emphasize more "holistic" aspects of music perception and memory, such as being able to classify new passages in terms of general musical styles. We are especially interested to know whether LBs will do better on such tasks than on more "analytic" tasks such as the one examined here.

When possible, we try to take two different approaches in studying all of these tasks. On the one hand, we devise an experiment to examine a distinction that is likely to be important (for example, melodic/unmelodic) and supply both variation and control in relevant stimulus factors in order to observe more fully how the distinction works. In addition, we examine whatever related approaches exist in standard music tests, both in terms of their internal designs and in terms of how our subjects perform them. As a by-product of these complementary approaches, we may be able to provide an evaluation of present music tests in terms of the cognitive processes they require and perhaps make some suggestions for the next generation of music tests.

Definition of Music Experience

For convenience, we have taken number of years of formal music lessons as the measure of music "experience." However, many people have been heavily exposed to music through listening and have learned much about it even though they have had no formal lessons. Some of them have even taught themselves to sing or play a musical instrument and have achieved a high level of expertise.

This is especially noticeable in people who play various folk forms such as "back porch" music, but can be observed for other types of music as well.

Music courses also contribute to an individual's music experience. Courses on music theory and music appreciation, however, may make different types of contributions. Once we have tested enough people who have taken such courses, we will be able to assess the effect that they have on music tests.

Even if music lessons are indeed a good measure of music experience, we are at present lumping different types of lessons together—from weekly one-hour lessons when one person was in elementary school to several lessons per week plus many hours of practice when another is in college. And how do we assess the contribution of such experiences as church choirs and high school bands? In some cases formal music training takes place while in others little is provided.

It may be that some of these background factors contribute to music experience more than others, and that we could weight them differentially to obtain a more comprehensive measure of music experience. In order to assess this possibility, we regularly give our subjects an extensive questionnaire concerning their music background. We also have them give a subjective estimate of their "overall music ability," since such self-perceptions can influence whether they pursue music training. However, there is a perennial chicken-egg problem here: (1) Who is most likely to take music lessons? Those who are predisposed to be successful in them. (2) Who does best on music tests? Those who have had formal music training. It is not clear whether we will be able to break into this circularity, but by collecting a variety of background information from people and relating it to both their general pattern of cognition and to their performance on music tests, we may be able to make some progress.

Data Base

Sufficient data are available in our own pitch-change experiment to warrant making several conclusions with considerable confidence. However more subjects are needed to study the breakdown of results by both training and cognitive pattern in a careful way. The presence of fewer trials, fewer stimulus distinctions, and ceiling effects in the Seashore Tonal Memory Test limit the number of conclusions that can be made from that study. Breakdowns of results from both experiments that are based on a limited number of observations must be viewed with caution until experiments that overcome such difficulties have been conducted.

Results from the "true" musicians must be viewed as preliminary. A large number of both singers and instrumentalists must be classified as LB or LO and examined in various music tests before any general conclusions can be made. It may also be useful to contrast different types of singers (for example, opera vs. jazz) as well as persons who play different types of instruments (instruments based on discrete pitch values such as the piano vs. those that permit continuous pitch values such as the cello).

Conclusions

Despite the limitations discussed above, some fairly strong conclusions can be made based on the work presented here.

(1) Formal music training and general cognitive pattern exert different effects on performance in a typical music test. Training raises overall performance levels, while LOs are better able than LBs to take advantage of certain distinctions important to music.

(2) Music tests may be better mirrors of general cognitive pattern than of music "talent" *per se*. In fact, although it would be a strange thing to try, certain language tests (especially those emphasizing short-term memory) may also predict music achievement.

(3) Standardized music tests are good as far as they go, but perhaps they do not go far enough. They need to include important comparisons, such as melodic/unmelodic distinction at a sufficiently difficult level, in order to observe differences that actually exist among individuals.

What implications do these conclusions hold for the music teacher? It is not yet possible to screen a large number of young children in a quick and reliable way to determine whether they are LB or LO. Even if we could, it is not clear what to do with such information in the classroom. If indeed LOs benefit more from musical training, a teacher might decide to concentrate efforts on them and not "waste time" on LBs. However, the general music appreciation of LBs might suffer substantially under such conditions, as well as their basic music competence. After all, we do not need to have formal knowledge about music for it to play an important and enriching role in our lives. Furthermore, it is possible that LBs may be able to achieve music competence similar to that of LOs *if* different teaching methods are used. For example, LBs might benefit from learning to read music by saying the names of the notes to themselves and then playing them, while LOs might benefit from emphasizing the size and direction of intervals between successive notes. There are always many ways to teach the same material. How is a teacher to decide among them? The present work suggests that it may be useful to vary the extent to which language plays a role in the teaching of music.

Note. This research was supported primarily by the Office of Naval Research (N00014-77-G-0079, NR 154-378) and also by the Spencer Foundation. The assistance of Alice K. Finger in preparing the stimulus materials and in collecting and analyzing the data is gratefully acknowledged.

Appendix
Details of Statistical Analyses

Pitch-change experiment. The pitch-change experiment was examined in terms of a five-way analysis of variance, using music structure (melodic vs.

283

unmelodic), memory load (seven-note vs. nine-note sequences), and type of contrast (same vs. different) as within-subject factors, and music training (many vs. few or no years of lessons) and cognitive pattern (LB vs. LO) as within-subject factors. Entries below give details for corresponding points in the text.

[1]$F(1,22) = 45.73, p < .001$
[2]$F(1,22) = 23.53, p < .001$
[3]$F(1,22) = 17.81, p < .001$
[4]$* = p < .05, ** = p < .01, *** = p < .001$
[5]$F(1,22) = 7.82, p < .05$
[6]$F(1,22) = 2.12, p > .10$
[7]$F(1,22) = 0.75, p > .10$
[8]$F(1,22) = 4.35, p < .05$
[9]$F(1,22) = 0.03, p > .10$
[10]$F(1,22) = 4.78, p < .05$
[11]$F(1,22) = 1.03, p > .10$
[12]$F(1,22) = 5.27, p < .05$

[13]No other interactions of any stimulus factor(s) with either subject factor was statistically reliable.

Seashore Tonal Memory Test. The Seashore subtest was examined in terms of a three-way analysis of variance, using memory load (three-, four-, or five-note sequences) as the stimulus factor and music training and cognitive pattern as within-subject factors.

[14]Two of the original LOs were unable to partic-ipate in this experiment; both had many years of music lessons. Thus there were fourteen LOs (seven with many years of lessons and seven with few).

[15]$F(1,22) = 202.10, p < .001$

[16]There was a strong correlation between per-formance on the two tasks: $r = .71, p < .001$.

[17]$F(2,40) = 22.15, p < .001$.
[18]$F(1,20) = 7.10, p < .05$
[19]$F(1,20) = 1.01, p > .10$
[20]$F(2,40) = 1.83, p > .10$

References

Day, R. S. *Temporal order judgments in speech: Are individuals language-bound or stimulus-bound?* Paper presented at the meeting of the Psychonomic Society, St. Louis, November 1969. (Also in Haskins Laboratories *Status Report,* 1970, SR-21/22, 71–87.)

Day, R. S. Systematic individual differences in information processing. In P. G. Zimbardo and F. L. Ruch, *Psychology and life.* Glenview, Illinois: Scott, Foresman, 1977.

McCullers, C. *The heart is a lonely hunter.* New York: Houghton Mifflin, 1940.

Seashore, C. E., D. Lewis, and J. G. Saetveit. *Seashore measures of musical talents.* New York: The Psychological Corporation, 1960.

Response

Henry L. Cady

Both Ruth Day and Roger Brown took seriously the problem of the similarity between language and music. What I didn't expect were the diverse approaches to the problem that they have taken. My concern and that of others here can be summed up in a question: Is language an adequate analog for music? We use language that way rather indiscriminately at times. There are other questions, of course. When we use words to describe music or to represent music, are we doing so correctly or spuriously? We are not certain; we do not know or have no secure basis for knowing. In what ways are language and music comparable linguistically, grammatically, or rhetorically? Our two psychologists found other questions of more interest to them than the questions I have asked.

Day and I have talked about the small number of subjects in her study of opera singers. She was hesitant about discussing the data that they provided, but I believe that there are generative ideas in that data. I find it interesting because the data about those seven people is relatively consistent. What she is trying to do, if I understand correctly, is to analyze the nature of language and music as communicative systems that arise out of human abilities, and she tried to probe into those abilities.

One prior condition to human communication is an internal organization, a symbolic system that will carry a message from a transmitter to a receiver. Thereby, one becomes involved in communication theory. It follows that Day must analyze the sources of transmission and reception, both of which are independent, organizing agents. The results about the receivers—her study of the general college students—indicate that language and music, as abilities, are not on the same continuum for them. On the other hand, her analysis of seven opera singers is a teaser. Do professional singers tend toward a cluster of expressive abilities because they have learned to become transmitters? Is there a catalyst of interest and concern that binds these abilities together?

We should also note that language-bound and language-optional people also generate some interesting ideas. They are compelled to use language as they learn it. They are compelled to use the rules. But there is no difference between the two kinds of people in their SAT scores. There is a resistance to change by language-bound people. They are inclined to impose what they think ought to be there on what they heard. They are better at more organized tasks in terms of long-term memory. They are able to take ideas and process them, and then over a long span of time impose rules on these ideas and organize them.

This information intrigues me, and I wonder: Are there music-bound or music-optional people? My answer at the moment is: Yes, I think so. However, we do not have a means for measuring such a continuum. Is this the difference between the composer and the performer, the jazz musician and the member of the symphony orchestra, the academic musician and the marketplace musician, the temperament of the classicist and the romanticist? And for us as music teachers, this idea

leads to another question: Is the back-to-basics movement dominated by rule-loving, language-bound people?

However, there is a caveat that we ought to keep in mind. The stimuli used by Day, for the most part, have led her to an analysis of short-term memory. She knows that there is much more to be done before she can produce results that are convincing to her. She shares with us a methodological problem because there is little music that fits into the realm of short-term memory in the sense of psychological testing. In that sense we use a series of five, six, seven, eight, nine, etc. stimuli. There are not many melodies of that brevity. I realize that someone will want to point out the motif in Beethoven's Fifth Symphony, but even then we wouldn't accept that as a *musical* term in a testing situation if we did not know it in its original context and if we did not know what Beethoven did with that little figure.

For the present, Day reinforces our desire to prove to the world that there is an interesting phenomenon known as the musical something-or-other in people that is measurable only through the use of music stimuli. We know that there are several continua that run through us and each of us reflect those continua somewhere—musical abilities, language-bound to language-optional, other verbal abilities, the use of numbers, perception of color and mass, and many others. Among all those abilities, which converge in each of us, we have our own way of patterning. Unfortunately, musical abilities are still to be understood essentially because we inevitably communicate about them with words and numbers.

Before closing, I have some thoughts to share regarding fair and unfair comparisons between music and language. During the last few months I had the pleasure of entering an area of knowledge in which I had never been before. That was the field of linguistics. When I read the following in Brown's paper, I read it with sympathy:

Whoever starts out from language will look in music for parallels to distinctive features, phonemes, phonotactics, morphology, semantics, syntax, deep and surface structures, presuppositions, implicatures, and even pragmatics. Whoever, starts out from music will look for parallels to melody, harmony, rhythm, meter, key, tempo, and tonality. Either enterprise in an early stage is likely to hope for simple parallels: perhaps melody carries the semantic of music, perhaps the phrase is the unit comparable in importance to the sentence. Nothing so neat is likely to be true. . . .

After a few months of study, I have come to a conclusion, which may be premature. I believe that there is no comparison whatsoever between language and music. I cannot find a noun; I cannot find a verb or an equivalent. If you tell me that a V7 or a II chord is a verb, you have a problem. I cannot find any way of taking the knowledge in the field of linguistics and applying it to music, in either the scores I read or the music I hear.

There is a reason why I found the task impossible, and it is a surprising one: we do not know much about language. In linguistics, there is not even an agreed upon definition for language.

The most difficult problem seems to be the meaning in language. Perhaps a little information will help you feel better about the communication problems in this symposium. I am told, and I understand that these are vague percentages, that when we become involved in dialogues like this, only about ten percent of what we communicate is found in the dictionary; about thirty-five percent of it is due to conceptual usages that we have become used to in our own lives; and fifty-five percent of it is completely contextual. So, when we search for musical meaning, perhaps we should expect that the only significant meaning is that which we hear in a particular concert hall at a particular time by a particular performer who is playing a particular composer's work on a particular instrument.

Toward a Linkage System Between Psychology and Music Education

Asahel D. Woodruff

This paper is not addressed to ideas that can be put to immediate use in teaching. Rather it is addressed to the process of generating or gathering such ideas. It is my deep conviction, and a matter of some concern, that the need for such ideas is so great that we can do an injustice to those we serve by going at the task somewhat haphazardly. A more systematic approach can yield much greater dividends.

I agreed to address myself to a linking system between psychology and music education. In the planning sessions last October, I also spoke of the powerful in-life form of learning that shapes our behavior, and that could be put to use in formal education.

In the process of working out a pattern for this paper, I came to feel that five tasks could be outlined, to lead us to strong working relationships, and then to greatly improved education programs. The linking system, and the in-life learning pattern, will show up in those tasks.

I think one reason for my presence in this exciting set of seminars is that I have been around for a fairly long time and have enjoyed several years of similar efforts with many of the music educators in this program, as well as with friends in several other fields. A lot of interesting and constructive things have happened over those years in the field of education and in its relationship to its background fields. Having lived through them, I come to this conference bearing their imprint in some ways. What I am going to say reflects my impressions of the best things that have happened, with my own flavor imposed upon them. For that reason it might not be inappropriate to make my biases and limitations visible to you.

I am an old educational psychologist of an earlier generation with a Chicago background. That was soon tarnished by extensive exposure to multi-disciplinary teams of people interested in education who were lured from clean research into meddling in messy education problems. Music education is one of those messy education problems, and it is, and should be, a user of contributions from several fields. I have spent considerable time and effort trying to translate good psychological and biological ideas about behavior into education programs in art, music, health, physical education, home economics, industrial education, and engineering, and in teacher education in most of those fields. During those years we have been bombarded with a parade of educational ideas such as team-teaching, nongrading, self-selection, integration of subject matter, behavioral objectives, behavior modification, competency- and performance-based processes, and others. I have also watched educators reach for theories of learning, one after another, in the hope of solving education problems, only to keep shifting and looking. I well remember a span of years in which educators repeatedly asked psychologists for solutions to teaching and motivation problems, until finally men like Ernest Hilgard began to say openly that psychology had no real use to educators. That was true in one sense, because what psychologists had was research information and theories of behavior, and what educators needed were operational descriptions of learning, upon which to pattern instructional programs. No real linkage had occurred between the two groups, and the missing elements can be traced to both groups.

In what might appear to be a wasteland of derelict ideas, I am now convinced we have a wealth of useful material, but until it is put together in some organismic fashion, it will not run. Out of those experiences I have become convinced that we need a linkage system, and within it we need to redefine behavior, learning, and teaching, and the nature of subject matter. There are respectable sources for all these, both old and recent.

Before addressing the five tasks I should also tell you of a few rather simpleminded rules and guidelines I have imposed on myself in this effort, and which I believe should be observed in trying to put our resources together into a working relationship.

(1) The first is fundamental in all behavior. We should remember that we are trying to educate a whole person, and all aspects of his behavior with music. Therefore there are levels of action from simple recognitions at the level of Gagné's signal responses, through simple motor acts, and on up to complex cognitive-affective decisions, which include creativity. These levels of action deal not with music alone, but with music in a matrix of personal and family life, and beyond that into social relationships. The immediate concern is that behavior varies over a continuum from global to atomistic, and there is no reason for assuming that a description of behavior at one level is valid at another level. We will see that some elements of behavior are present at all levels, but the differences are as important as the common elements.

(2) The next, and those that follow, are fundamental in educational planning. The psychological or other information used as a basis for operating an education program, should be descriptive, rather than theoretical. That is, it should describe a person doing something, rather than explain what makes him do it that way. From this kind of information an educator can construct an educational process. The information is operationally useful, rather than useful for research.

(3) The information used for any level on the continuum from global to atomistic should come from people who study behavior at that level, whether in music or in psychology or any other science.

(4) The rules of behaving/learning/teaching vary along that continuum.

(5) An education program should be designed to match the descriptions of behavior at the various levels on the continuum.

(6) A program that is to affect total musical behavior must consist of an orchestration of processes from all the levels.

The last five guidelines have been demonstrated to some degree in some excellent work of the past several years. I think of Arno Bellack's studies of verbal behavior in the classroom, and several extensions in the work of Bunny Smith and others, and I suppose the building of a successful atomic reactor is based on the same kind of information. A landmark step in this direction was taken by Gagné and Bolles in their review of training problems in the military.

With that preliminary statement, I will turn to the five tasks.

Task One: To identify the major molar-molecular levels of behavior we must consider in education, their unique operational rules, and the way they affect each other.

Here I want to remind us of some things we know, but have not put to use very well in education.

In our study of the human organism and its behavior for a few thousand years, we have moved from the notion that it was a simple isomorphic thing to the recognition that it is the most complex phenomenon in the universe. Now we know that behavior has many facets. Therefore it follows that it expresses many sets of underlying dynamics and processes. A person is both a whole person, and a set of parts, at the same time. Therefore his or her actions are both holistic and atomistic at the same time. The hands or the voice cannot say to the mind or the feelings, we have no need of thee.

Since educators deal with this complex person and all of his inseparable parts, we have to ask what kind of educational arrangement has the capacity for handling

both ends of the continuum from holism to atomism? Where do we find it?

In experimental psychology we have not strayed far from the early focus on single functions. At this point there are many competent specialists in limited functions, and there is a wealth of valid information about those functions.

Most of the psychological rules in education today are variants of the rules of atomistic behavior processes. We have not changed the breadth of our educational rules to keep up with our recognition of the more holistic qualities of learners. There are of course some fine exceptions to this.

If a psychological scientist were to move in the direction of holistic studies, he would be moving out of what we generally regard as basic psychology, toward something like social psychology, or sociology, or biology. But we can do that by means of multi-discipline teams without diluting the special strength of their members.

It was through participating in such a team with René Dubos that I first became conscious of the biological concept of adaptation, in a conference on health education. Although he spoke in the idioms of biology, it was clear to me that he was reflecting behavior concepts of great significance to psychologists who are interested in total behavior, and to educators in all areas.

The adaptation concept is one of the central keys to an effective linkage system. It has the capacity to bring all of the different concepts of learning developed by psychologists into a complete picture. It also infers a three-layer view of the human being, which translates usefully into a three-layer educational program. This appears to me to be what we need to handle the scope of our problem.

I am going to suggest that arrangement now in Figure 1 before stopping to describe the adaptation concept and its relation to educational programs. With that figure in mind, a discussion of adaptation might be more meaningful.

Figure 1 presents three elements of behavior that are important in education. Element one is the most holistic and is the area of interest to the humanistic psychologists. It is

288

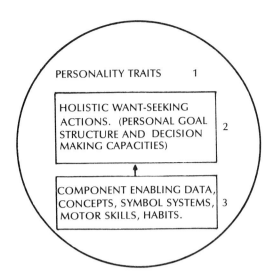

PERSONALITY TRAITS   1

HOLISTIC WANT-SEEKING
ACTIONS. (PERSONAL GOAL
STRUCTURE AND DECISION
MAKING CAPACITIES)   2

COMPONENT ENABLING DATA,
CONCEPTS, SYMBOL SYSTEMS,
MOTOR SKILLS, HABITS.   3

Figure 1. Three elements of behavior.

really a pattern of personal traits that permeates levels two and three. The totality of these traits is the personality of a person.

Element two is also holistic in that it represents a whole person *using* his entire repertoire of facilities and his personal traits in a steady stream of transactions with his real environment. This is the level of activity of which we are most conscious as persons, in which we are most absorbed in the pursuit of our own satisfactions, in which we employ the special talents, knowledge, and skills we possess, which constitute element three. This is the level of behavior that makes us or breaks us in life. It is at this level that our value systems operate most completely. What we do at this level determines our personality, through the shaping force of the consequences of our transactions with life. This is the root of self-evaluation, based on success and failure experiences, and it provides us with practice in self-direction. We are sensitive to the causes of our successes and failures at this level, to the way others treat us, and so on.

Motivation probably operates most basically in element two, so that an activity that is enjoyed at this level tends to infuse its motivational power into any element three actions which are needed for its completion.

Conversely, element three activities have little innate attractiveness of their own, a fact that is of critical importance in education.

Element two actions are also mediated largely by concepts and feelings about the holistic things in our environment. Those actions tend to start and stop through voluntary decision-making processes. They would therefore be affected directly by conceptual learning of the kind which grows out of hands-on experiences.

Element two actions are the ones in which a true cybernetic cycle operates most fully. This makes it the level that corresponds to the adaptation concept. If we define learning in terms of adaptation at level two, then we can find a good relationship between that, and the several psychological concepts of behaving and learning at level three.

Level three actions include a wide array of small habit responses, motor skills, verbalized learnings, and so on, which have well-known learning processes, including perceiving the parts of a whole object, developing concrete concepts, practice, repetition, conditioning, and so on. All of these component actions serve the holistic behaviors at level two, and are useful only as they do this. There is much evidence that they are learned better when they are learned within level two activities.

Level one characteristics are largely self-evaluative by-products of experiences at the other two levels. Success and failure are powerful shapers of the larger traits.

All of these observations have direct relevance for the nature of learning and teaching, and the way they should vary along the continuum.

For some time now a popular and useful description of learning has been the statement that "Behavior is shaped by its consequences." An expansion of that statement might be, learning is a change in behavior that occurs while the real behavior is going on in its natural setting, as a direct result of the consequences of the behavior that impinge upon the person. The consequences may change habits, motor skills, verbal patterns, concepts, values, and several other factors in total behavior. This is a cybernetic

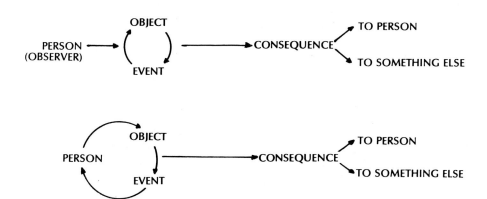

Figure 2. Two common forms of person-environment interaction.

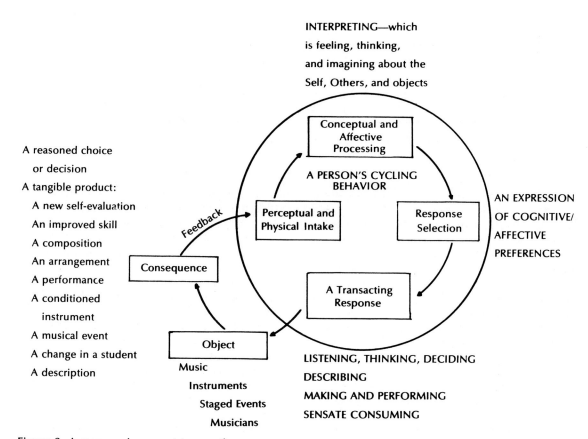

Figure 3. A man-environment transaction.

290

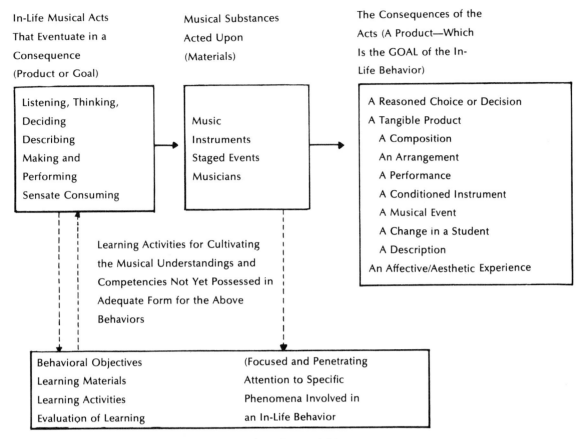

In-Life Musical Acts That Eventuate in a Consequence (Product or Goal)	Musical Substances Acted Upon (Materials)	The Consequences of the Acts (A Product—Which Is the GOAL of the In-Life Behavior)
Listening, Thinking, Deciding Describing Making and Performing Sensate Consuming	Music Instruments Staged Events Musicians	A Reasoned Choice or Decision A Tangible Product A Composition An Arrangement A Performance A Conditioned Instrument A Musical Event A Change in a Student A Description An Affective/Aesthetic Experience

Learning Activities for Cultivating the Musical Understandings and Competencies Not Yet Possessed in Adequate Form for the Above Behaviors

Behavioral Objectives Learning Materials Learning Activities Evaluation of Learning	(Focused and Penetrating Attention to Specific Phenomena Involved in an In-Life Behavior

Figure 4. Musical behavior and supporting learning activities.

concept, and leads us to a description of the adaptation concept. That concept must not be confused with the more limited concept of behavior modification.

Dubos presented adaptation as a person and his environment acting on each other, and changing each other in the direction of a more agreeable relationship. You will recognize this as a biological version of Dewey's concept of man/environment transactions. Dubos speaks of four levels of change:

(1) Genotypic—changes in genetic patterns or genoplasm

(2) Phenotypic—changes in morphology

(3) Psychic—changes in cognitive and affective patterns

(4) Social—changes in social structure

In education we are concerned with the last three, and psychologists with the third.

Adaptation is obviously a cybernetic process, a very important fact for education, since the change in the person is produced by feedback. This kind of feedback is not to be confused with test results or other educational evaluation and reporting. They sometimes mean enough to a student to produce some change in him, but lack the inescapable force of direct behavioral consequences.

Figure 2 is a simple way of depicting a man/environment interaction, or a person involved in an event with an object. The consequences of the event impinge on the person and change him. This goes on without end.

Figure 3 expands the relationship to include perception, conception, the choice of a

291

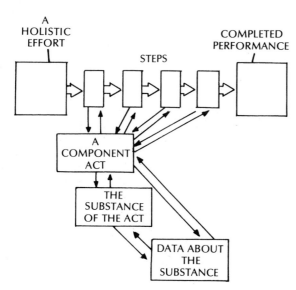

Figure 5. Analysis of a holistic musical act to assist accomplishment.

response, and the action that follows the choice. The action is shown as involving an object in the environment, producing a consequence and having an impact on the person, which he perceives and which is then fed into his system. Music can be substituted for the object.

Figure 4 goes further in identifying a musical behavior within that cycle. A musical act (one of four general kinds) is performed on a musical substance (one of four kinds), using one or more subordinate competencies, and resulting in one of several consequences.

Figure 5 relates the subordinate competencies to the whole musical act.

Finally, the comment should be made that the adaptation process is an excellent basic matrix with two values. It characterizes all behavior with its pervasive principles, and it provides a central frame, or description of a whole organism, within which all psychological positions find a place as specialized functions of the organism. Education needs both of these values.

It is also worth noting that the adaptation concept reveals and illustrates both operational description and theory. The interactions of a person and his environment are described, and can be seen and replicated in school. The concept of feedback is composed of the observable fact that behavior changes concomitantly with the interactions, but the idea that the feedback is causing the change is theoretical. We can't manipulate it or use it. As long as the direct interaction continues, feedback continues also quite out of our reach to manage. It is an explanation, but not a process we can set up ourselves.

Task Two: To get education properly related to the major molar-molecular levels of behavior, as to subject matter content, learning processes, and teaching requirements.

Figure 6 is a transformation of Figure 1 into three layers to permit including more information relevant to each element of behavior. We can begin with the relationship between music and the three levels of behavior. See the bracketed material with the comments on either side of it. Figures 2 through 5 developed the learning process implied in Figure 1. To relate this arrangement to education I would like to turn our attention back to two ancient and well-established models of instruction. I believe the choice of an educational model lies basically between these two. One is the very respectable model, which is traditional in schools today, of a teacher dispensing verbal information to rather passive students who are expected to use it productively at a later time. The other is the rather burly model of an active person doing practical things with his environmental substances right now, and learning in the process. They are represented by Figures 7 and 8.

Figure 7 represents the traditional relationship between a teacher and a learner, in which knowledge is offered in verbal form to the learner for remembering. Figure 8 relates the learner directly to a life task or interaction with a holistic instance of music. Sustaining information, or any other subordinate com-

Figure 6. Some links between psychology and music education.

	Music Panel	Psychology Panel

1 — HUMANISTIC LEVEL

The more humanizing the operations at all levels, the more rewarding the outcomes for both individual and society

The assets and rules for living and working together:
- Confidence
- Self-respect
- Commitment to ideals and major values
- Orderly and responsible participation
- Competence in: Self-management: Decision-making, Decision-execution
- Learnability

PERSONALITY TRAITS

Progressive humanizing or dehumanizing of the person

Guidelines:
Freedom and stimulation for:
1. Imaginative production
2. Originality
3. Synthesizing
4. Generalizing
5. Value formation
6. Making commitments

Music Panel: Knieter, Tait
Psychology Panel: Raynor

2 — LIFE-ACTION LEVEL

The exercising of the whole person including his value system and choices

Competence in the major activities of life at the holistic level, as both producer and consumer, and with enjoyment

Evolution and continued use or disuse in life of one's major activities

THE TOTAL MUSICIAN

The level of greatest cybernetic impact; the organismic adaptation level

Guidelines:
Present music in a form that:
1. matches the rules and assets above
2. maximizes contact with it in its intrinsically interesting forms
3. maintains a progressive pressure on the learner for greater mastery at the wholistic level

Music Panel: Knieter, Tait, Greer, Zimmerman, Petzold, Cady, Williams, Gordon, Hedden, Heller
Psychology Panel: *Siegel, *Dowling, *Gardner, Walker, Kessen

3 — COMPETENCE LEVEL

The more clearly we tie this level to levels (1) and (2) the greater the continuing effect on life

The deliberate and planned improvement in the component skills directly involved in the holistic activities in level (2)

Competence in the sub-functions of major activities, including:
- Cognitive processes
- Affective processes
- Verbal processes
- Manipulative actions

The rise or fall of competence in level (2) activities

THE MECHANICAL ABILITIES

Guidelines:

The Specific Component	*The Type of Shaping*
1. A Signal response	Conditioning through concomitant association with a reinforced event.
2. A habit	Conditioning through affective consequences of the response.
3. A level of motor skill	Improved coordination from knowledge of results.
4. Verbal reiteration	Association of symbol to concept.
5. Conceptual actions	Organizing perceptions continuously.
6. Value preferences	Affect related to experiences.
7. Conceptual communication	Association of words with concepts and their properties.

Music Panel: Williams, Heller, Sidnell, Carlson
Psychology Panel: *Siegel, *Dowling, *Gardner, Brown, *LaBerge, Day, (A submusic level), Deutsch, Shepard, *LaBerge

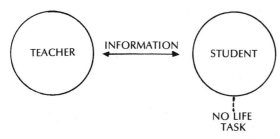

Figure 7. Traditional teacher-learner relationship.

ponent, becomes involved in a natural way. The teacher keeps out of this interaction to avoid interrupting it and breaking the cybernetic loop. He therefore must influence it in certain appropriate ways from the sidelines.

Figure 9 suggests those appropriate ways of influencing the activity, at each of the stages in the learner's cyclic response. This is basically a high level form of coaching, including the most skillful use of all the musician-teacher's own abilities, and the learning materials at his command.

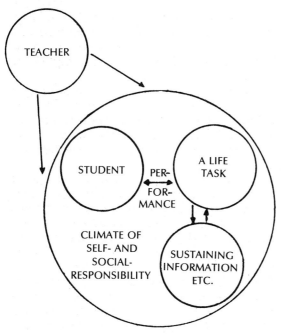

Figure 8. The learner directly involved in in-life learning.

294

Both of these models are old, and both have become laden with biases, as suggested by the heat that still flares when someone speaks disrespectfully of education as training. I am convinced that the layman who does this is more right than the educator who corrects him.

In my opinion, the rejection of the training concept as a vehicle for what we call education is based on a false belief that such fields as philosophy, literature, the fine arts, and general education are not behavioral fields. They are called intellectual, humane, or aesthetic, which seems to imply that they exercise only the mind or the feelings. This is obviously not so, for these fields consist just as much of action patterns as any of the trades. It is enlightening to describe a philosopher behaviorally, and then imagine the power of using the adaptation process to produce another one.

Surely none of us have the biases we are talking about, so I would like to suggest a few of the comparative features of the two approaches as we look at figures 7 and 8.

In the Traditional Model:	*In the Adaptation Model:*
The teacher is a dispenser of information.	The teacher is a coach and a guide to information when it is needed.
The information is learned first; its use in life postponed.	The life function is started first, and information is introduced as it can be related to the function and help it proceed.
The subject matter is organized in logical academic outlines.	The subject matter is organized around its uses.
There is little opportunity for developing self-management.	Self-management is required and practiced in every task.
Academic motivation is low.	The motivation inherent in life tasks is higher and increases with progress.

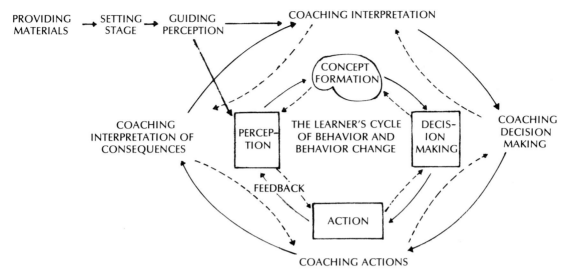

Figure 9. Teaching viewed as facilitation of behavior and behavior change in a student.

The preparation of a performing musician is much more like the adaptation model than the traditional model, but for the non-professional the opposite is true. I think we all know which programs are the most successful in reaching their objectives.

This task might be left now, with these suggestions as to the demonstrated strengths of the adaptation model. They lie in these characteristics:

(1) It is cybernetic; it contains genuine feedback and does change the person.

(2) The feedback is usually prompt and permits readjustments in midstream.

(3) Motivation tends to be high because of direct involvement with the realities of life.

(4) Perception deals directly with the actual and tends to be more varied than in contrived or verbalistic situations.

(5) Transfer is high because of the identity between the learning situation and the using situation.

(6) The person learns how to learn as part of the regular flow of life.

Task Three: To identify a workable division of tasks between educators and specialists in supporting fields.

Thus far I have talked of a learning model but have not related it to the foundation dis-ciplines of education nor dealt with the relationship in it between whole music and its subordinate elements and competencies.

In describing the background from which I approach our work now, I mentioned the long efforts of educators to get help from psychologists and the response of Hilgard and others. It is important that we recognize the sources of that failure and correct them. Here is my version of the problem.

Psychologists have not been interested in developing complete descriptions of human behavior in its full context. Research goes toward the limited and controlled event, not the broad one. Dewey and a few others are exceptions to this.

In psychology we have had a long parade of schools of thought, each focused on some selected aspect of behavior, and each offered vigorously as the real story about behavior. Let me remind you of McDougall's instincts, Watson's behaviorism, Skinner's determinism, Koehler and Koffka's gestalt, Olsen's child-as-a-whole, Thorndike's connectionism, Guthrie's associationism, and of habit strength, meaningful verbal learning, behavior modification, cognitive theory, and problem-solving. These were offered largely in theoretical formulations, dealing with the internal machinery rather than providing step-by-step descriptions of what the person is doing when he is learning.

At one time I formulated what I called the sequential steps in learning. They were common to nearly all theories. A few writers have pointed out that there is nearly complete agreement among psychologists on the observed phenomenal facts. The diversity appears when explanations of theories are offered.

In spite of this, the diverse theories have been effective in identifying numerous subfunctions in behavior, all of which are involved in the undissected student with whom education struggles.

For this whole student, who exhibits all of these processes, educators need an equally whole description of the interwoven motions he goes through in behaving and learning when those natural processes are operating most effectively. This is the pattern they must use either in situ, or by transporting it intact into the school, if they want the same powerful effect we see in the shaping processes of life.

The need implied here is for a parent concept of a total organism in his environmental arena, with all of the kinds of things he does in his transactions with all of the elements of his environment.

An excellent candidate for that parent concept is the biological concept of adaptation. To supply its subfunctions, there are the many kinds of things a person does, which are pretty well described by psychologists.

Theory is a temptress that makes us forget the reality of life in the school and turn to speculation about still more remote internal functions that have little use to educational program planners. Conversely, educators have done about the same thing, by dissecting the learner into speech, motor acts, verbal memory, spatial orientation, mathematical aptitude, and so on, and by working on these dissected functions independently. Emerson, in his essay on "The American Scholar," seems to have been talking of this when he said, "The state of society is one in which the members have suffered amputa-

tion from the trunk, and strut about so many walking monsters—a good finger, a neck, a stomach, an elbow, but never a man." In education we have also set up processes in which information is mistaken for knowledge, memorization is mistaken for behavioral change, and exhortation and test performance are mistaken for conversion.

Implicit in the plea from educators over the years has been the expectation that psychologists would somehow become well enough informed about education to see what was psychologically wrong with it, and then supply the productive practices, which their insights should make possible. It is not in the nature of a dedicated psychologist to spend the necessary time and effort in that kind of deviation from his real interests to be helpful to educators in a conference now and then. The counterpart of this expectation might well be that the educator would similarly leave his major work to become a psychologist, and then answer his own questions. We need not expect a psychologist to assume the educator's role, nor the educator to assume the psychologist's role as a basis for working together. Rather we need to create a useful meeting ground for the two.

I believe this can be accomplished when the educator asks the right questions. Those questions are not for solutions to educational tasks, but for information about behavior that enables the educator to solve educational problems. It was this wrong kind of question that left the psychologist with nothing for educators. Much help is available from psychologists, and similarly from other disciplines, when we in education lay out a topography of musical or other behaviors that we wish to cultivate. Then we must identify in that topography the component elements of behavior, such as perception of various kinds of referents, reaching a comprehension of objects or processes, affect and the ensuing value formation that occurs in these settings, the learning of verbal materials, the acquisition of motor skills, the simultaneous use of several of these processes, and so on. At that point a psychologist can supply the facts about those learning processes and help

296

the educator build them into his program.

Some of the papers presented last October did this rather well, as for example Carlsen's questions about specific forms of learning. They tended to be in the motor skills area, which is only one part of the spectrum.

A beginning, or rather the further development of beginnings already underway, can be made by recognizing more fully the three layers of human behavior of Figure 1: the total personality of a person, including his self-concept, self-direction, and the coordinated use of his capacities; his patterns of engagement in his major pursuits, including his larger competencies and his major values; and his specific competencies or skills and knowledge, which he uses in various patterns to serve his major pursuits.

Then I think music educators must separate music into at least two of the three levels, music in molar or holistic form, and components of music in molecular or atomistic form. This separation, if done incorrectly, leads to one of our sources of difficulty in learning today, namely, a set of courses limited to atomistic elements of music that are dull, hard to learn in that isolated form, and difficult to integrate back into the world of whole music.

A more viable alternative is to plan a curriculum sequence in holistic music, from simple to complex instances, taking full advantage of the innate attractiveness of whole music at all levels. This is for sequence, not scope. The learner is to move along this sequence as he now moves through a set of grades of academic material. A learner would then enter into every experience he or she has with music, on this level of wholeness, with some specific piece of music.

Of course one cannot master any piece of music by dealing with it only as a whole. He must get into its component elements. So each instance of whole music must be supplemented with ready access to its component elements, and the mastery of them is part of mastering the whole. I am well aware of what this will do to our neat curriculum, but that is another problem for which there are workable solutions.

When the climate or level one questions are identified, and when the holistic or level two tasks are identified, and when the component elements of whole music are identified, we will be in a good position to ask psychologists for the rules that govern the learning of those tasks.

At level one, the work of the psychologists is to help identify the working conditions that lead to success, positive self-image, and so on. At level two it is to identify the kinds of learning involved in recognizing, comprehending, enjoying, and performing at the holistic level. At level three it is to supply the technical solutions to those more atomistic learning processes.

I know that psychologists are often broader in their personal interests and experiences than the foregoing discussion might imply, which is fortunate, but I still believe the best meeting ground lies at the point where educators have done their analytical work well, and psychologists can either supply available technical answers to specific needs or put the identified processes into research to find the answers.

Task Four: To get other disciplines related to their appropriate aspects of the educational program.

This task, while an important part of a total working pattern, can be touched very lightly today with this observation. Looking back to Figure 1, and noting the nature of behavior at each of the three levels, I should think people in other disciplines would have something quite significant to say to educators in an arrangement such as this:

Political theory	at Level 1
Cultural biology	at Level 2
Cultural anthropology	at Levels 1 and 2
Sociology	at Levels 1 and 2
Philosophy	at Levels 1 and 2
Psychology	at Levels 1, 2, and 3, depending on the person's specialty

Task Five: To get the right psychologists working on different parts of the educational problem.

Psychology has long since ceased to have a unified subject matter such as the study of learning and forgetting of verbal materials. It is now a multiple-discipline area in itself as broad as the social sciences. A mismatch between any aspect of psychology and any aspect of education can only hinder progress.

In terms of APA divisions, it would seem that the following relationships might be productive.

		Divisions
At Level 1 in Figure 6	8	Personality and social
	9	PSSI
	10	Aesthetics
	16	School psychologists
	20	Maturity and old age
	24	Philosophical psychology
At Level 2 in Figure 6	3	Evaluation and measurement
	7	Developmental
	8	Personality and social
	10	Aesthetics 15 Educational
	16	School psychologists
At Level 3 in Figure 6	3	Experimental
	5	Evaluation and measurement
	6	Physiological and comparative
	7	Developmental
	15	Educational

Levels one and two in Figure 6 seem rather clearly to call for psychologists who are devoted to humanistic and personality problems and who can describe the kinds of influences needed for developing self-confidence, initiative and imagination, consideration, moral and ethical character, and productive patterns of living. I thought Knieter's paper made a strong start on that task, and I was most interested in some reactions that followed it, indicating that it was at least initially seen as being directed to level two or level three forms of learning and therefore challenged as to its relevance. It was partly that reaction that stimulated me to look for the linking system.

One last observation is offered. In October I had these impressions:

(1) That the psychologists generally did not know what to expect from the musicians and did not have time to become involved in the thinking of the musicians before responding. Hence the responses tended to evade the questions raised, and to turn to personal ideas about music, and to descriptions of their own research interests.

(2) In the planning meeting for this session, linkages began to be found, and the psychologists started to sort themselves out into the areas of concern of the music educators in a way that would eventually lead to a layered matrix.

(3) The result even now may not consist of direct help with all the questions asked, but it will start the development of a useful long-range partnership.

It is my hope that that partnership can be broadened to cover all the aspects of music education and open the way to greater power than we have ever known in educational programs.

References

Dewey, J., and A. F. Bentley. *Knowing and the known.* Boston: Beacon Press, 1949.

Dubos, R. *Man adapting.* New Haven, Connecticut: Yale University Press, 1965.

Gagné, R. M. *The conditions of learning.* New York: Holt, Rinehart & Winston, Inc., 1965.

Gagné, R. M., and R. C. Bolles. A review of factors in learning efficiency. In E. Galanter, (Ed.), *Automatic teaching: The state of the art.* New York: John Wiley & Sons, Inc., 1959.

Response

Gerard L. Knieter

I would like to introduce a construct that forms part of the basis of my response to Asahel Woodruff. It is called "meddling." To illustrate, two of the best meddlers this planet has produced were Sigmund Freud and Albert Einstein. The basis of their meddling involved bringing together hitherto unrelated ideas, constructs, and hypotheses, forming them into new syntheses that led to deeper understanding of the phenomena each held as significant for study. One was human behavior and the other dealt with the relationships among time, light, energy, and mass.

In this same time-honored tradition, Woodruff attempts to bring the molar and molecular aspects of human activity, or what in my paper I call a clinical approach, under closer scrutiny. He proposes a linkage system between psychology and music education so that much more than a dialogue between the various enterprises can develop. He takes the same risks that other creative people have taken. It is simply not possible to document a creative idea.

First, I will comment on the guidelines. In my view, they are basically reasonable and workable for music education. Not only are they realistic from a wide variety of psychological orientations, but they provide the reader with a context for the rest of the paper. It is noteworthy that Woodruff has avoided the use of psychological terminology that imposes a particular school of thought on the reader. Hence, one is prepared to deal with his rationale on its own merits.

Next, we will consider the five tasks he proposes. The first task: *To identify the major molar-molecular levels of behavior we must consider in education, their unique operational rules, and the way they affect each other.* In the first task, a team of professionals would be most desirable since what we know about human behavior is housed in a variety of fields and guided by the diverse assumptions that are

299

basic to each discipline. Further, Woodruff exhibits insightful analysis when he observes that "element three activities have little innate attractiveness of their own, a fact that is of critical importance in education." He properly recognizes that these operations exist for their ultimate use as musical creation, performance, and appreciation.

The second task: *To get education properly related to the major molar-molecular levels of behavior, as to subject matter content, learning processes, and teaching processes.* In this section, Woodruff offers a way to conceptualize a cohesive relationship among the several approaches to music education. His three-layered analysis is valid for me, not only because it makes sense psychologically, but because it provides a philosophical basis for the successful interaction among the operational belief systems of music educators.

Woodruff feels that it is desirable to describe philosophy in behavioral terms since the logical sequence of this thinking leads us to recognize that all forms of human activity are human behavior. These judgments by Woodruff are not meant to be merely semantic. The point is that both psychology and music education have now reached a level of intellectual sophistication that requires us to recognize that the several approaches that guide our thinking are based upon assumptions about behavior. When we acknowledge these assumptions, we become more responsive to the notion that experiments that are both reliable and valid can yield insights into the human condition that are relevant only within the universe of discourse out of which the assumptions are stated. Hence, what we know about the reality or truth of our own observations is limited not only by the particular population, the experimental design, or the treatment of the data; it is limited by the assumptions that describe the nature of reality.

The third task: *To identify a workable division of tasks between educators and specialists in supporting fields.* In this case, Woodruff has given us the assignment. It is clear to him that we must ask the right question and we must structure our own environment. It is not appropriate to blame another profession for what we perceive to be their lack of concern for us. My agreement with Woodruff stems from my study of the value derived from anthropology, philosophy, and psychology. Such study contributes immeasurably to one's professional growth. Task three is homework for our profession. Certainly, it provides a number of opportunities for doctoral study in theoretical, experimental, and empirical projects.

The fourth task: *To get other disciplines related to their appropriate aspects of the educational program.* Again I agree with Woodruff, probably because I am a student of other disciplines. The complexity of education demands a wide variety of expertise, and all of us need to expand our areas of competence. Yet, I have heard some teachers complain, "How can I learn all this new information?" What would our reaction be to a physician who raised the same question? It is critical for us to recognize that Woodruff is not asking our profession to learn all these fields, and his remarks should not be misconstrued to this end. He is suggesting the beginning of a dialogue between music educators and a wide variety of other professionals.

The fifth task: *To get the right psychologists working on the different parts of the educational program.* Here Woodruff's analysis of my own paper is most perceptive. Through what I call the "clinical approach," I was suggesting the potential for the several orientations to psychology and music education to form a partnership to serve the entire population.

Finally, Woodruff would be the last person to claim that his plan should be adopted specifically for music education. Yet, his plan deserves serious consideration from music educators because it provides a systematic way of conceptualizing a range of views, which provide a comprehensive approach to music education. At the present time we need to identify some fundamental assumptions that can serve as the basis for theory building and informed debate. Now is not the time for each of us to neglect his own research, but it is the time to go beyond our own interests in order to establish insights to clarify the common relationships and bodies of experiences that bring us all together.

The Acquisition of Song: A Developmental Approach

Lyle Davidson
Patricia McKernon
Howard Gardner

In recent years, many psychologists have become enthusiastic about an orientation within their discipline called cognitive-developmental, structural-developmental, or, simply, developmental. In part this enthusiasm reflects the increasing importance attributed to the work of Jean Piaget and his followers: a search for qualitatively different stages, which all normal individuals pass through in a prescribed order, has become nearly endemic among investigators who work with children. Also reflected in this excitement are larger-scale trends within psychology: a growing dissatisfaction with atomistic, behavioristic, and purely quantitative approaches; an increasing interest in events that unfold over a considerable period of time; and considerable curiosity about the ontogenetic relations among different populations, including normal individuals, gifted persons, brain-damaged patients, those with learning disabilities and the like.

From our point of view, the embracing of the developmental approach has been salutary. It has highlighted many phenomena that were previously ignored; it has facilitated the grouping together of disparate findings into a more coherent view of individual functioning: it has invigorated research in a range of subdisciplines, from social psychology to neuropsychology. Moreover, the general approach has already affected current thinking about pedagogical issues.

But in the wake of enthusiasm, particularly its unbridled variety, some reaction is inevitable; and when expectations are excessive, they are destined to be disappointed. Within psychology, reservations are being voiced about specific claims of the Piagetian program: and within education, the lack of clear-cut classroom payoffs from the Piagetian-developmental approach has also been a source of disappointment.

In these pages we intend neither to dismiss the developmental perspective nor to label it as beyond criticism. Our goal is more modest. We will consider the developmental approach as it bears upon selected issues in the psychology of music. We seek to sift from the developmental approach that which seems most germane to the understanding of

301

musical competence while modifying that approach in ways which promise to inform certain psychological and educational issues. In particular, we concern ourselves here with two issues central to developmental study. The first is the increasingly debated assumption that all cognition is of a piece—that the kinds of general intellectual structures and cognitive operations described by Piaget are manifest with equal strength and regularity across a range of materials and subject matter. We will take seriously a contrasting point of view—that various symbol systems with which humans are engaged may include features special to each; features not adequately considered in a generalized cognitive-structural picture. Thus, in place of a wholesale importation into the psychology of music of the framework devised by Piaget, we will consider *which* aspects of development may be particular to the realm of music, which relate as well to specified other domains, which seem pervasive across the range of cognitive activities.

Our second issue concerns the way in which individuals acquire competence within specific domains of expertise. According to a central tenet of the developmental approach, the acquisition of knowledge should occur in qualitatively different ways, depending upon the level of understanding—otherwise put, the operational intelligence—of the particular individual. Faced with the same task, an individual in the pre-operational period will approach it in a fundamentally different way from an individual at the concrete or formal operational level. Again, while not minimizing the power of this insight, we will entertain here a contrasting possibility: that certain aspects of learning or development occur in much the same way, independent of the age (and sophistication) of the learner. According to this account, mastery of a domain may occur in a similar way, whether the student be six or sixty, naive or knowledgeable.

Beyond doubt, we need an example that can aid our evaluation of these competing perspectives. Our vehicle here will be the processes whereby individuals acquire skill in the production of song. We will consider

three moments in the process of song acquisition: (1) the earliest attempts at song, found among children in the first three years of life; (2) the period between the ages of four-and-a-half and five-and-a-half when children begin to exhibit some facility at learning a new song; and (3) kinds of performances found among music students, who are about to embark upon a professional career.

As we review these points, we will consider the reasonable goals for each population under consideration, the progress each makes in realizing these goals, and the gaps that remain outstanding. We will then review our descriptive account in light of the two theoretical issues raised above: (1) the extent to which the acquisition of song reflects general developmental trends, as opposed to aspects particular to music; and (2) the extent to which song acquisition occurs similarly across populations that differ widely in age and sophistication.

First Steps in Song Acquisition: The Outline Form

During the first three years of life, children engage in a great deal of vocalization, some of which seems to be nondescript noise-making, some of which appears to be linguistic (or pre-linguistic) in nature, but much of which seems related to the subsequent acquisition of music competence. However one wishes to describe this sound production formally—and we are far from able to accomplish this—one fact seems clear: all normal children progress from a period of indistinct babbling to the point where they can produce a recognizable tune. Any developmental analysis of song must describe the steps whereby such initial facility is acquired.

Our means for accomplishing such a description has been a longitudinal study of early symbolic development in which nine first-born middle-class children have been followed for a period of up to five years. As part of this study, we have identified and examined milestones in seven different symbolic media ranging from dance to drawing. Within the symbol system of music, we have looked at both spontaneous song production and the beginnings of the ability to produce songs from the culture, referred to as standard songs. Here, in brief, is what we have found. (For a detailed account, see McKernon, 1979; cf. also Bentley, 1966; Moog, 1976.)

Between the ages of twelve and eighteen months, children engage in considerable experimentation with pitch variations. Typically, they sing in continuous voice, making a glissando over several pitches: at this point no pitch can be clearly differentiated from any other. By nineteen months, however, a qualitative change has occurred: children now begin to produce distinct pitches and can then embark on acquiring the two major components of singing in Western culture, rhythm patterning and melody organization.

For the next several months, children concentrate their energies chiefly on producing what we have come to call spontaneous songs. Relying heavily on major seconds, major and minor thirds, as well as occasional fourths and fifths, the children emit songs with undulating contours and occasional, if irregular, rhythm patterns. As Moorhead and Pond (1941) reported, "The rhythm is free and flexible . . . the melodies are not necessarily diatonic and most seem not to relate to any observable tone center or not to a tonal center found in Western music." As a consequence, these early spontaneous tunes are unpredictable and unmemorable. It is difficult for a listener to repeat them even immediately afterward, to remember them at a later time, and, as we have had all too frequent opportunities to discover, to notate them exactly.

Piaget speaks in many contexts of the operation of assimilation: the process which occurs when some event in the environment is so transformed as to fit into a scheme that the child has already developed. The approach to standard songs at this point is a process of almost pure assimilation. Irrespective of what melodic pattern is actually modeled, the child sings the "target" song—if he attempts it at all—in the way that he spontaneously produces all other songs.

The major agenda for the second year of

ABC at 1:7

ABC at 1:10

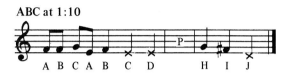

ABC at 1:11

ABC at 2:4

Figure 1.

life, accordingly, is to go beyond the simple production of spontaneous melodies and to attend instead to the individuating properties of songs produced by others in the culture. To adopt Piaget's terminology once more, the child must *accommodate* to the defining properties of culturally-endorsed songs: only by this route will his or her own versions prove discriminable from one another and recognizable by the listeners.

By examining the efforts of a single child, whom we shall call Kathy, as she attempts to learn the familiar ABC melody (Figure 1), we can observe this shift from pure assimilation to increasing accommodation. The first attempt by Kathy, at age nineteen months, strongly resembles her spontaneous tunes: the pitch range is restricted and the contour undulations occur in small groups of two and three notes. She also incorporates the words

303

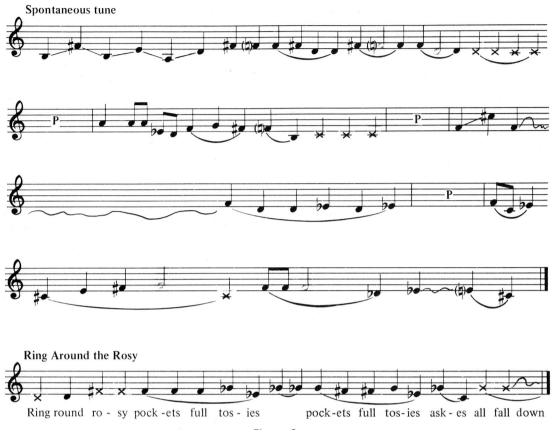

Spontaneous tune

Ring Around the Rosy

Ring round ro - sy pock -ets full tos - ies   pock-ets full tos- ies ask - es all fall down

Figure 2.

of the song into whatever tune repertoire already exists. Thus to the extent that the tune exists at all as a recognizable entity, it does so on the basis of its lyrics, not its tonal or rhythm structure. (This behavior stands in marked contrast to the process in adults, who can readily substitute any set of lyrics without destroying the musical identity of a tune.)

Kathy's next few attempts chronicle distinct progress. By twenty-two months, she can sustain some regularity over the first two groups of notes. By twenty-three months, she has grasped something fundamental to the rhythm of the song: the sustained note at the end of each phrase and the fact that some notes (LMNO) are sung more rapidly. By

twenty-eight months, in addition to having mastered the words in correct sequence, she can produce the appropriate rhythm structure, synchronized to the words.

This child's learning of the ABC tune illustrates some ways in which music resembles other cognitive domains, as well as some of the organizational problems particular to the realm of the music. On the one hand, one is struck by the role played by a dawning understanding of number concepts. At about this age, children become able to imitate drum beats grouped into units of two and three. This same knowledge seems to be exploited as the child systematically organizes notes into precise groups. Other aspects of song mastery, however—for instance, the

304

coordination of words, rhythm values, and pitch intervals—do not have close analogues in other symbolic domains. By the end of this period of music development, the production of standard tunes has diverged markedly from the production of spontaneous songs.

Consider the following two songs (Figure 2) sung on the same day by a child of two years, five months. Though portions of the spontaneous tune are flat in contour, overall it contains considerably more variation than her rendition of *Ring Around the Rosy*, including, for example, larger leaps as well as ascending phrases. Indeed, an examination of songs at about this time indicates that children are beginning to acquire some notion of what a standard tune should sound like.

They seem to be developing a set of song-related expectations, a kind of "song frame," which structures their performance of standard tunes.

Yet, it would be excessive to contend that children can produce the entire span of a song. We have found it more accurate to speak of the mastery of "characteristic bits"—brief melodic structures consisting of a handful of notes. These little patterns, seemingly of independent origin, often unrelated to the contour of the model, are idiosyncratic fragments that the child sings over and over again. Clearly, the child who sings characteristic bits must, at some level, know their structure. He or she has thus achieved a significant milestone on the road to melodic organization and can now recall discrete me-

Figure 3.

Child 1:
Spontaneous tune

march march march march march... etc.

Standard tune

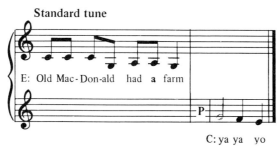

E: Old Mac-Don-ald   had   a   farm

P.

C: ya ya   yo

Child 2:
Spontaneous tune

Nan-no na Nan-no Nan-no na   nan-no.

Standard tune

Ring   a-round the ros - y   pock-ets full   of pose ash-es ash-es every-body fall down!

305

lodic sequences. These bits are the embryonic versions of what become longer sequences of pitches arranged in specific structures—standard tunes.

The question arises as to how children move from rough-and-ready song contours to increasingly correct melodic structures. One interesting fact presents itself: in many child-versions of standard songs, those bits that most closely approximate the model appear at the same time as identical melodic structures in the child's spontaneous repertoire. For instance, one child produces a marching fragment in a spontaneous tune that doubles as the refrain from *Old MacDonald*. A second child's spontaneous chant is similar to the melodic and rhythmic structure of *Ring Around the Rosy* and contributes to the recognizability of her version. (See Figure 3.)

What is new here is the ability to place a musical unit in its appropriate context. Earlier, the child selected any one of his spontaneous bits as he assimilated the standard songs to his current schemes; or he simply repeated a characteristic bit over and over again. Now the child can pick and choose from among his repertoire of fragments and bits those most appropriate to a certain spot in a certain song. This ability to handle one's own repertoire with increasing flexibility so that it can lead to the production of a number of standard tunes, leads us to characterize the child's competence—by the age of three or so—as the mastery of the *outline* of a song.

The capacity to master a number of basic fragments, and then to compose them into a reasonable approximation of a target model, is by no means restricted to the child's progress in the musical sphere. Indeed, this kind of "outline knowledge" of a symbolic domain seems quite characteristic of the child around the age of three. At just about this time, the child can proceed beyond the production of isolated sentences to produce a series of sentences that bear at least a superficial resemblance to a canonical story: an opening line, a series of events (and crises), and an acceptable closing. By the same token, the child is now producing linear representations that exhibit an outline resemblance to objects in the world. The tadpole

man—a circle with radiating rays—serves as an indication that the child can draw upon his arsenal of isolated graphic schemas to produce an acceptable likeness, or indeed, a number of likenesses. Some other cross-media parallels are suggested in Table 1.

We may therefore pose a more general question: to what extent do events in the symbolic domain of music resemble those we have uncovered in other facets of early symbolic development? As the above remarks suggest, some unquestionable parallels exist between events in the realm of music and those in other symbolic spheres. But other lines of musical development seem less tightly related to general symbolic growth. For example, we find at the age of eighteen months the emergence of a skill that we have entitled event-structuring: the capacity to appreciate the roles played by different agents and objects in a sequence of meaningful action (cf. Gardner and Wolf, 1979). This first wave of symbolization has important consequences in the realm of symbolic play and in language, as well as interesting spillovers in more remote domains like drawing and movement. So far as we can see, however, there are no interesting manifestations of event-structuring skills in the realm of music.

Our analyses have suggested the emergence of a second wave of symbolization around the ages of two-and-a-half or three. This wave, which we have termed topological mapping, has its most central manifestation in drawing. At this point the child becomes able to combine his individual graphic schemas and produce a recognizable representation of a person (or some other entity) in the world. What is crucial about this form of mapping is that the individual captures the most general kinds of relationships: enclosingness, proximity, relative size and proportionality, direction, force, motion, and the like. Such topological sensitivity is manifest not only in the plastic arts, such as drawing or modeling with clay, but also in more remote domains. For instance, in the area of language, the child becomes able to produce perceptual metaphors. Noting the topological relationship between two ele-

306

ments, he can capture these in a verbal phrase, for example, terming a barber pole a lollipop, or a spreading tree, a fan.

This second wave of symbolization seems to have reverberations in the musical realm. Those properties of standard songs that the child captures in his own renditions seem aptly captured by the descriptive term *topological*. While the child rarely produces pitch values with total accuracy, the topological properties of the model are captured accurately: particularly in songs with great pitch contrast, the child begins to be able to indicate when the song goes up and when it goes down; when it features a group of notes at a fast pace, as opposed to times when the pace is more desultory; when there is a large gap in the contour line, as against the times when the pitches are closely huddled together. And, even as a more accurate form of mapping awaits the quantitative sensitivity of age four, so, too, a more accurate learning of song requires further development.

Further Steps in Song Development: From First Draft to Mastery

The mastery of a culturally evolved song is an intricate and complex process. The singer

Table 1. Events in Other Media Coincident with the Emergence of Musical Skills

Age	Musical Achievement	Other Domain	Achievement
1:6	First discrete pitches	Symbolic play	Child can sustain two different roles.
		Movement	Child can perform two different movements.
		Language	Child produces first two-word utterances.
		Number	Child can distinguish between big and little seriated pieces.
2:0–2:6	Repeatable "characteristic bits"	Movement	Very short but repeatable movement sequences appear.
		Storytelling	Child reproduces events of two to three elements.
	Child recaptures rhythm of standard songs	Number	Ability to repeat drum beats of two and three even beats emerges.
	First approximations of pitch contour in songs with great contrast	Drawing	Child can recognize patterns in random markings.
		Language	Child produces first metaphors.
3:0	Ability to reproduce a number of basic fragments	Language	Child produces first schematic canonical story.
		Drawing	Child produces first representations of simple objects.
4:0–4:6	Tonality within-phrase, but no cross-phrase key stability	Storytelling	"And then" allows child to string together a series of otherwise unrelated events.
		Movement	Asked to dance, child can generate a series of acrobatic stunts, unrelated in any internal way (i.e., similarity, part of a general theme).
5:6	Emergence of key stability and scale	Blocks	Child reliably produces a number of blocks in a column, and respects an operation such as "plus" one in building a staircase.

Char - lie o-ver the o - cean, Char - lie o-ver the sea, Char-lie caught a black-bird, Might have been me!

Figure 4.

must grasp the pace of the song; the underlying pulse; the movement between registers; specific pitch values and rhythmic patterns must be appreciated and then integrated into phrases; these phrases, in turn, must be combined in proper order into a coherent whole. Throughout, the individual must adhere to a fixed key center—that single pitch that will coordinate the relations among all the notes of the song.

To observe the processes whereby such songs are mastered, it is desirable to present to subjects a song having two characteristics: (1) the song should be unfamiliar in order to control for effects of familiarity; (2) the song should follow the general canons of Western music (otherwise its overall strangeness may yield idiosyncratic effects). It is necessary to have a song that is sufficiently complex to allow for errors of various sorts—given a perfect performance, nothing can be learned about the process of acquisition. On the other hand, the song should not be so idiosyncratic or so challenging as to preclude any learning.

We presented such a melody, a folk song, named here the *Charlie Song* (Figure 4). While a complete analysis of this song goes far beyond the confines of this paper, it is relevant to point out at least three competing ways in which the song might be apprehended and organized:

(1) *Text* (A B X): The first two phrases (first and second lines) are reasonably similar, the third and fourth lines are different and form a unit.

(2) *Rhythm* (AB AB): By this interpretation the song consists of four phrases: the second two phrases basically repeat the rhythmic patterns of the first two phrases. (Considering the text or the rhythm separately from the other elements yields a symmetrical structure of four bars plus four bars.)

(3) *Contour* (ABAC): In this case the con-

tour of the first and third phrases (a rising shape) is contrasted with the falling contour of the second phrase (B) and the essentially flat contour of the concluding phrase (C).

An analysis of the ways in which children's versions of this song epitomize one or more of these rival organizations can yield valuable information concerning their (mental) representations of this song. Moreover, by observing the way in which the organization of the song shifts following repeated rehearsals, one monitors changing organizations over time due to practice or development.

We had the opportunity to teach the *Charlie Song* to two distinct groups: five children, ages four to five who learned the song over a period of a year; a group of college music students, who were presented with the song several times at one sitting and then given an opportunity to rehearse it over the next several weeks. By comparing performances we gained information not only on two widely dispersed points in the process of song acquisition, but also on the relative plausibilities of the rival hypotheses—the developmental and the learning accounts—sketched above.

Song Acquisition at Age Four-and-a-Half: The First Draft

The four-year-old child has advanced far beyond his two-year-old counterpart. Children of this age are able to master all the words of a song quite readily, as compared to a two-and-a-half-year-old, who primarily learns phrases. The boundaries of the phrases, the surface rhythms and the continuity of the pulse are all present and are carried by the delivery of the words of the song.

The feature next most likely to be grasped (after pulse, surface rhythm, and phrase boundaries) is the contour of the song. The basic direction of each phrase is understood,

308

Table 2. Phases of Song Acquisition in Five Year Olds

Phase	Achievements
One: Topology	• Words of whole song, or most distinctive phrases • Phrases, phrase boundaries, lengths, number and order of phrases all present. These are supported largely by the framework of the words. • Underlying pulse present in children's singing • Pace of delivery established
Two: Rhythmic Surface	• Child can extract the surface rhythm of the song (i.e., can play it note-for-note on a drum) synchronized with the underlying pulse. • Child sings an approximation of the pitch contours of the most distinctive phrases, but maintains no key stability across phrases, and sings varied intervals from one rendition to another.
Three: Pitch Contour	• Child attempts to match pitch contour for each phrase, but cross-phrase key stability is still absent, and intervals still vary across renditions.
Four: Key Stability	• Stages 1–3 stabilized • Clear projection of key center across all phrases, though intervals not always correct • Child can extract underlying pulse from surface rhythms. • New ability to perform expressive transformations (e.g., slower pace for sad version)

and the contour can be repeated. In contrast, the child's sense of key has not yet become stable. Each phrase may be sung in a different key; that is, one key will not be honored across phrases. Accurate interval mapping, necessary for contour matching, is also not yet stable. At most, children tend to return to a general location, rather than a precise pitch. Children are able to sing a variety of intervals (seconds through fifths) but only in the context of specific songs. Isolated intervals may not be available to children at this age.

Armed with this background knowledge about children's abilities, we taught the *Charlie Song* to five children participating in our ongoing longitudinal study of early symbolic development. Initially the song was tape-recorded and presented to the child. Thereafter it was presented at least once more during each quarter of the year, either played on the tape recorder or sung by the examiner. The children were coached to sing along with the tape, to echo phrases, and to sing the phrase following the one sung by

the examiner. Once learned, the song served as a "finding clue" in a hide-and-seek game. In addition the children were asked simply to recall the song, and to play the song on a drum or a xylophone. As a result, considerable information was collected on the child's knowledge (representation) of the song.

While the patterns of song acquisition varied to some extent across children, a number of regularities could be seen across the subjects. As shown in Table 2, children passed through four principal phrases in the acquisition of the song. These can be viewed as a sequence of serial acquisitions: mastery of the topology of the song, achieved by phase 1, was supplemented, in turn, by mastery of the rhythmic surface (phase 2), mastery of the contour of the song (phase 3), and acquisition of key stability (phase 4). Viewed more schematically, we found that the child's initial grasp of the song consisted of the words, the rhythms, phrases, contour, but never accurate pitch values. The major progress during the year of song practice occurred on two

309

fronts. First, when asked to sing and play the song, children became able to extract the underlying pulse from the surface rhythm; that is, they stopped playing the rhythm of the words and began playing the underlying dotted quarter pulse. Second, an impressive degree of key stability emerged, bringing in its wake an increase in the accuracy of intervalic and contour reproduction.

Viewed from the perspective of symbolic development, the children were exemplifying in their learning a shift in symbolic processing that also characterizes other domains. At the beginning of the period, the child's approach typified the initial relations that we have termed topological mapping. The children could attend to the global properties of the song and recapture them in their own efforts. The most general aspects of contour (rising or falling), rhythm (long vs. short), and to a lesser extent, pitch values (large vs. small intervals) were respected. The primary shift during the course of the year occurred with the mastery of specific pitch relations, the ability to map precise pitch intervals. While children never achieved full mastery, the shift from topological to intervalic or digital relations was unmistakable. Children were thus embracing the second form of mapping, one that we have termed digital mapping, where quantitative values and metrical distances are respected. Just as in his block play, a child can now reliably reproduce the number of elements in a column, or respect an operation of "plus one" in building a staircase, so, too, the singer at this level will begin to respect the precise intervals presented in a song or a scale.

But if there are overarching parallels between song acquisition and other symbolic landmarks, there are, conversely, a number of features that seem particular to the realm of music. The kinds of competing structural organizations outlined above have no close parallels in other media: the arduous trek toward the achievement of key stability is likewise peculiar to the music domain; and the kinds of relations between surface rhythm patterns and underlying organizational pulses also pose problems remote from those in

other domains of information processing. Even more so than at earlier stages of development, those properties that figure crucially in musical mastery have come to the fore.

What differentiates the child of five from the two-and-a-half-year-old is the degree of accuracy with which he has mastered the song. Whereas, at two, there is still strong competition between the child's spontaneous songs and those modeled after the culture, a clear differentiation between the two song types has taken place by the close of the preschool period. The child's attempts to model the song of the culture are clear: the interference from his own spontaneous melodies, or from other songs that he has mastered, proves modest at best. Moreover, by the end of the period, even the efforts of the less competent children are quite recognizable. Perhaps more to the point, the child is beginning to form a schema of what songs should be like. We may speak, then, of a "first draft" knowledge of songs, one akin to those of "senses" of a story or of a drawing which are coalescing at about this time in other realms of symbolic expression. And, indeed, among gifted youngsters, one may even point to an intuitive sense of what makes a balanced drawing, a well-composed story, or a good song.

Charlie at Eighteen: Mastery of the Song

First-year students in an ear training class at the New England Conservatory of Music participated in a study designed to explore song acquisition among a sophisticated group of musicians. They were presented with the *Charlie Song* as part of an exercise in which they were asked to memorize pieces on the spot and then recall them during later class meetings. The song was first presented in its entirety, and then phrase-by-phrase. The whole class then rehearsed the song until each member could sing each phrase. After this initial learning, the students were asked to recall it on four subsequent occasions (two days later, another two days later, one week later, and another two weeks later). Performances were recorded for later transcription. In the event recall was incorrect, the students were presented with the song

310

Figure 5.

once again, so that they might recall it accurately. The one substantial difference in presentation between the two populations involved the lyrics of the song: to make this exercise comparable to others being taught in the class, the song was presented without words. While this difference precludes certain comparisons, the fact that even four-year-olds learn the lyrics with little difficulty makes it unlikely that this factor significantly affects song acquisition in more sophisticated subjects.

The results of this experiment revealed both interesting similarities and instructive differences between the two groups. In addition, the study yielded a scale of error sources and types that could be reliably related to the age and sophistication of the subjects. Finally, the yoking of the students provided an opportunity to gain some information on a question that motivated the study: the relative tenability of the developmental and learning accounts of skill acquisition.

A first point that needs to be made is that the conservatory students performed well on the task. In fact, 66 percent recalled the song perfectly, another 28 percent had mistakes in only one phrase; thus 94 percent of the first recalls were perfect or nearly perfect.

Despite this vast difference in overall competence, comparison is still worthwhile. In a number of ways, the two groups of subjects resembled one another. One line of similarity centered about the kinds of modifications that occurred when the structure of the model (ABAC) was not realized. Both the younger and the older subjects tended toward symmetrical versions of the structure (ABAB).

A second shared aspect of performance involved individual pitch mistakes. Whether younger or older, subjects tended to make the kind of errors shown in Figure 5.

Some differences between the older and younger subjects were readily predictable. As already noted, the speed of acquisition was virtually incomparable: older subjects with a musical bent are able to acquire in a few repetitions what younger children often take a year or more to master in even a preliminary way. Similarly, the amount of material that can be handled at one time is also incommensurate. Older subjects are able to assimilate several phrases at one time and manipulate them appropriately into position, while younger subjects can often hold only the most distinctive phrases in mind.

More revealing differences, however, center about the general understanding of songs, and song schemata, and conventions of Western musical structure, specifically key stability. Whereas the acquisition of a sense of key stability and the establishment of tonal center is a major challenge confronting the younger subjects, it has long since been mastered by musically inclined adolescents. Older subjects not only have an established tonal memory but they simply assume that a folk song will remain in a single key and exploit familiar and expected tonal relationships. Equipped with these powerful structuring assumptions, they are able to hear and organize materials in a much more efficient way, and to make predictable substitutions and supplements (in the appropriate key) when memory lapses. (See Figure 6.) Lacking this ability, the young children must necessarily

Figure 6.

Figure 7.

inch from note to note, approximating the intervals and pitches by relating them to one another on a local level. (See Figure 7.)

The second qualitative difference among subjects, one related to a sense of key stability, entails the possession of a variety of song schemata. While four-year-olds are merely in the process of learning—or, to use the developmental metaphor, constructing—"song" in the Western tradition, the talented adolescent has already assimilated a family of song types. Just as he knows a variety of story forms, ranging from fairy tales to mysteries, he has also mastered a range of musical schemata. As a result, instead of having to learn each song as a new set of pitch and rhythmic relations, or erroneously assimilating the song to a pattern that is wholly inappropriate, he can search among his arsenal of schemata for the one most intimately related to the target song. Moreover, this ability allows the older subjects to improvise material "in the style of the song," should the actual melody be forgotten; supplementations that happen to be inappropriate can also be integrated into the song without upsetting its fundamental structure, as in Figure 8.

In contrast, the younger subjects, lacking these schemata, must either recall the entire phrases, or contrive a substitution that may

bear little resemblance to the model. (See Figure 9.)

It is worth noting, parenthetically, that this possession of numerous song schemata could conceivably have negative consequences. It may make it difficult to learn songs that depart in a significant way from the arsenal of schemata already developed; or it may induce perseveration of the same error, an error based on the inappropriate importation to the song of features from another song that happens to be highly overlearned. In these senses, there may be a point in development, or a situation in learning, where it is preferable to have a smaller or less well elaborated set of song schemata. However, these observations are only speculative: data from the present study do not address this possibility.

In light of these and other observations in the two groups, we have drawn up the following taxonomy of dimensions of song learning.

Elements mastered by both younger and older subjects. The pace of the song, the existence of phrase boundaries (articulated by pitch or agogic change), and the basic shape of the contour of the piece pose little problem.

Elements that the older subjects could handle but that pose difficulties for the younger subjects. The younger subjects have difficulty in re-

rhythmically incorrect

Figure 8.

Figure 9.

membering pitches and returning to them reliably, even as they exhibit problems in finding and adhering to a tonal center. They lack that pitch template that helps the older subjects grasp the song.

Elements that pose difficulties for both groups. Both older and younger subjects have difficulty recalling the ABAC structure exactly. Of those adults who make formal errors, 96 percent regularized the structure into a symmetrical ABAB shape. Similarly, 47 percent of the children's formal errors are of the same pattern. Thus, both adults and children who err in song recall appear to possess a similar internal representation of the overall form of the song.

Conclusion: Revisiting the Guiding Questions

Our endeavor here has been to sketch some highlights in the developmental process of song acquisition. To be sure, our account contains many gaps, and, based as it is on a small group of subjects and a single tune, it should at most be regarded as tentative. We have traced some developmental trends in specific aspects of song—pitch, contour, rhythm—and have suggested as well some properties of the individuals' grasp of the overall form of the song. Our review has suggested three distinct levels of mastery: a grasp of the basic *outlines* of song by the age of three; a *first-draft mastery* of the schema of a song by the age of five; and, at least with gifted individuals, a virtual mastery of the processes of acquisition of a Western tune by late adolescence.

While our findings will not resolve the vexed issues in developmental theory noted above, they may at least contribute to current debate. Turning first to the question of "universal" vs. "special patterns" of developmental growth, we have provided examples of both perspectives. Clearly it is excessive to claim that differences among media and symbol systems are inconsequential: a number of specific elements in music (e.g., pitch), relations among groups of elements (e.g., rival structures organized around rhythm or text), and features of overall organization (the kinds of previously elaborated schemata that

regulate song) prove particular to the domain under consideration and cannot be mastered simply by a transfer of knowledge or skill gained from practice with other symbol systems. But, by the same token, it is fallacious to consider music a domain apart from all others. The process of musical acquisition reverberates with our emerging view of waves of symbolic development (e.g., the two forms of mapping).

Possibly the most important lesson from such an inquiry is its challenge to the notions that symbolic systems are a single domain, or, alternatively, a collection of only loosely connected domains. Rather, the thrust of our work on overall symbolic development has suggested a more complex picture (cf. Gardner and Wolf, 1979; Wolf, 1979). It makes sense to think of families of symbol systems: symbolic components drawn from different domains that nonetheless bear strong structural parallels to one another. More precisely, it seems to be the case that aspects of one symbol system (S_1) can resonate with aspects of another symbol system (S_2), while other aspects of the former symbol system (S_1) may relate to aspects of yet other symbol systems (S_3, S_6). Thus, the processes of schema acquisition are reminiscent of story learning; elements of rhythmic mastery relate to numerical mastery; and mastery of topological elements like song contour bears a significant relation to early steps in representational drawing. As we more closely examine the similarities and differences among symbol systems, we may in fact find that the whole notion of individual symbolic domains, each exclusive to itself, proves unilluminating. Instead it may be more profitable to envision families of symbol systems, and clusters of capacities, which can be combined with one another in numerous ways, for various representational and expressive purposes. Music can be seen as bearing affinities of different sorts with a range of symbol systems (e.g., literary, gestural, numerical), even as each of the other systems will also, in turn, partake of features drawn from the remaining symbol systems.

A similar pluralism may well mark our second developmental issue. While we sought

313

evidence favoring either the developmental stage or the general learning position, our data prove difficult to harness within either of these competing accounts. In the mastery of the *Charlie Song*, for example, we have found some features—e.g., the symmetrization which occurs between the first pair and second pair of lines—that characterize two groups differing widely in sophistication. Such "Gestalt principles"—leveling, sharpening, simplification, symmetrization—may be intrinsic to general learning strategies, manifest irrespective of the age or sophistication of the learning subject.

In contrast, other aspects of song acquisition seem quite different across our two populations. More so than the simple differences in speed and efficiency of learning, prior knowledge bases of the two populations engender fundamentally different approaches. The two-year-old, equipped primarily with a few spontaneous songs, either assimilates the traditional song to that type of production, or does not attempt it at all. The four- or five-year-old, just beginning to construct a general sense of song, will make some general modifications in light of this schematic knowledge but generally acquires the song in a piecemeal and error-laden way. The adolescent, on the other hand, has already evolved a rich set of song schemata. His task is to choose from amongst a broad collection of possible song types the one which the particular target happens to instantiate. His structural knowledge, as Lévi-Strauss (1966) puts it, dominates the particular event, even as, for younger subjects, the particular event overwhelms the meager structural sense. Indeed, he cannot learn the song afresh—and this may eventually entail its own limitations. For, just as the fluent individual must translate new languages into ones already mastered, so, too, the accomplished singer of songs has difficulty approaching new songs in a totally fresh way.

We cannot, then, declare the developmental view totally vindicated, or wholly undermined. Rather, one's view of it depends upon the aspects of skill acquisition on which one is focusing, the scale of analysis in which one is engaged, and the kinds of error patterns and strategies that are at issue. Final products may look similar but in many cases, the processes by which they are achieved seem to have been quite different. Accordingly, to prove that developmental processes play little role becomes a difficult challenge, but to argue that they are all-determining is equally wrong-headed.

All this cannot prove great solace for the educator, whether he represents the area of music or some other symbolic domain. The terrain of developmental psychology turns out to be rather messy, not yet well worked out, still choked with controversy. Nonetheless, at least some useful hints of a pedagogical sort can be gleaned. For one thing, the purely descriptive efforts in which we (and others) have been involved can provide some orientation about what skills are reasonable to expect at different ages, what skills can be readily acquired, and which ones seem to require more effort. In addition, some of the tasks that we have used, and certain modes of analysis that we have devised may prove useful within the classroom.

While firm conclusions are still premature, our findings suggest that the music educator should hold in mind three balances. To begin with, there is the balance between skills intrinsic to (and exclusive within) music, and skills that cut across a range of intellectual spheres: these latter prove of particular moment at a time when each of us is being held accountable for the intrinsic worth *and* the transfer value of what he is training. A second balance should obtain between principles of learning, that operate across a wide range of ages and personality types, and principles of development, which are much more closely tied to the age and sophistication of the subject. And finally there is a third balance—difficult to achieve but of great consequence. There is, on the one side, the necessity for structured schemata—into which new works of music can be assimilated; and, on the other side, the risk of structures so firmly consolidated that the individual becomes inured to interesting and significant departures from them. As Arnold Schoenberg once noted, it is crucial to appreciate the *style* of work—that language that cuts across a range of instances and composers—but it is also vital to hold in mind the *idea*—that individuating impulse which distinguishes composers, works, and even performances of the same work from one another. As music educators help their students to discover those structures and styles, it is crucial that they engender sensitivity to those individuating nuances that transcend, and sometimes even undermine, the more general schemata that characterize a range of musical instances.

Whatever the ultimate judgment on this proposed balanced sheet, it is our hope that the issues with which we have wrestled here will prove of great importance to individuals concerned with education. After all, whether a skill proves peculiar to one domain, or part of our general intellectual heritage, and whether the process of learning occurs in the same way, independent of the sophistication and knowledge of the subject, are scarcely items of idle intellectual curiosity; they are questions central to pedagogy. By posing these questions in a sharp way, and by devising means whereby they can be resolved,

or at least better understood, developmental psychologists may well make their most pertinent contributions to classrooms of musical education.

The research described in this paper was supported by the Spencer Foundation and the National Institute of Education (G-78-0031).

References

Bentley, A. *Music ability in children and its measurement.* New York: October House, 1966.

Gardner, H., and D. Wolf. *Waves of symbolization.* Paper presented at the Conference of Early Language Interaction, Sturbridge, Massachusetts, May 1979.

Lévi-Strauss, C. *The savage mind.* Chicago: University of Chicago Press, 1966.

McKernon, P. The development of first songs in young children. In D. Wolf (Ed.), *Early symbolization. New Directions for Child Development,* 1979, 3, 43–58.

Moog, H. *The musical experience of the pre-school child.* London: Schott, 1976.

Moorhead, G. E., and D. Pond. The music of young children. *Pillsbury Foundation Study,* 1941.

Wolf, D. (Ed.), *Early symbolization. New Directions for Child Development,* 1979, 3.

Response

Marilyn P. Zimmerman

Gardner's paper provides a descriptive study of certain changes in the musical behavior of children and places these changes within a developmental context that includes other domains of learning, including those aspects of Piagetian theory relevant to music education.

Gardner begins by reminding us that any theory or approach needs to be considered in terms of what is most applicable to a particular pedagogical problem or issue. No one theory can provide us with all the answers. The results of the psychological research presented to us here, including (1) evidence of some developmental trends in song acquisition and also (2) evidence of certain gestalt principles, such as symmetrization, operating in all age groups should fit in well with the eclectic approach to music education. We should be cautioned against allowing any one theory to bias our teaching so that we fail to notice and consider what is really happening to our students.

Gardner has provided us with additional material to the existing research on song acquisition. I think it would be fruitful to pursue research in the area of spontaneous song production and music improvisation with children. Following the models of Werner, the Pillsbury studies, and Gardner, we should be able to speak more definitively about the way in which the music environment is assimilated by plotting changes in the motifs, ranges, rhythms, and so on, that children of various ages use. Then the song repertoire for children could be analyzed according to these spontaneous characteristics, thus enabling us to find a better match between the assimilation and accommodation processes as these operate in vocal production and the learning of new songs. I would like to reiterate the need for a rich and stimulating musical environment and for individual and group experiences in music from a very early age.

The stages Gardner identifies in the acquisition of "standard songs" are quite similar to those found by Bentley (1966). Bentley sees the child as approximating the tonal configuration (Gardner's outline stage) and then moving toward the correct coincidence of pitch. In other words, the child moves from a coalescing or growing together of his pitch with the actual pitch to a coinciding or falling together of his pitch and the actual pitch of the song. Bentley also found that rhythm perception precedes concern for tonality.

Dowling's research in perception noted a sequence in apprehending melodic change moving from contour to transposition to interval. Similar developmental patterns are confirmed by a variety of research findings.

There are two factors to consider in teaching a song: (1) memory, both tonal and verbal, and (2) singing skill necessary to indicate that the song has been learned. Here a consideration of the developing singing range of the child is crucial. Research has shown that the early singing range centers around D-F♯, then middle C-A and finally the C octave (Smith, 1963). Children learn most easily those songs presented within their vocal ranges (Vance, 1914; Bentley, 1966).

If the "Charlie Song" were taught as notated in the key of C, it would have been outside the singing range of the young children and, hence, presented a difficulty that could have been mitigated by transposing the song to the key of F or G. The second example indicates that the children did transpose the piece in reproducing it. (Gardner indicated that the key of C notation was used for convenience.)

We have already been reminded of the copy theory of processing sensory information. Sergeant and Roche (1973) have found that if a song is repeatedly presented to children as young as age three in the same key and within their singing range, they will tend to reproduce the pitches in the same key in which the song was initially learned. Was the "Charlie Song" presented each time in the same key?

Further research as to the role of memory in song acquisition in various performing media is needed. How did performance of the song on the xylophone compare with that of singing it? Were the children able to play it correctly but unable to sing it correctly, or conversely? (Gardner answered that the children had more difficulty learning to play it.)

Gardner has analyzed the "Charlie Song" according to three methods of organization: text, rhythm, and melodic contour. Let us also consider its harmonic organization. The melody is primarily based on the $\frac{6}{4}$ position of the C major triad with perhaps an implied V at the end of the first phrase. There is no strong final cadence since the last phrase is essentially tonic. It would be interesting to determine whether or not a song based on more than a single chord would be easier or more difficult for children to learn and also if the same strategies would be used in its acquisition.

The findings pertaining to the older subjects indicate the importance of one's expectations in learning. If one's memory fails, an individual simply draws upon his experiential bank for information that will "fit" or is congruent with what is needed; and, in

316

the examples cited, the errors added more harmonic implications to the melody.

Applied teachers often stress improvising in the style of one's memorized repertoire. This is speculation, but does the "tyranny of the schemata" developed through such practice help to alleviate anxiety concerning memory lapses for an experienced performer?

Gardner's Table 1, page 307, presents information that can be of great benefit to teachers for it places the emergence of certain musical skills within a more comprehensive developmental framework. For example, our elementary music textbooks suggest that children be encouraged to sing one-sentence stories. This can be done with children as young as two-and-a-half to three. In early childhood music experiences children are encouraged to improvise melodic and rhythmic fragments.

Current research in our field and elementary music books stresses the importance of developmental sequence and of teaching sequence. Gardner's Table 2, page 309, presents practical information that could be reworked into a lesson plan for the sequential teaching of a song.

Gardner's research has shown us once again that a thorough observation of a specific phenomenon will improve our teaching procedures and lend vitality and psychological validity to our pedagogy.

References

Bentley, A. *Musical ability in children.* New York: October House, 1966.
Sergeant, D. and S. Roche. Perceptual shifts in the auditory information processing of young children. *Psychology of Music*, 1973, *1*, 39–48.
Smith, R. B. The effect of group vocal training on the singing ability of nursery school children. *Journal of Research in Music Education*, 1963, *11* (2), 137–141.
Vance, T. F. Variations in pitch discrimination within the tonal range. *Psychological Monographs*, 1914, *16* (69), 115–149.

Hedgehog Theory and Music Education

Edward L. Walker

The Hedgehog is a theory of learning and motivation. It has another name—*psychological complexity and preference theory*.[1] It is a very general theory that I believe to be applicable to most aspects of psychology, and I believe it to be seminal in the practice of music education. I hope you find you have already been using it often without thinking of the problems as I shall suggest you think about them.

I call the theory a Hedgehog because it is a very simple theory, and in some sense a hedgehog is a very simple animal. There is a saying attributed to Archilocus, a Greek poet of about 700 B.C., which can be stated thusly:

A fox has many tricks,
The hedgehog has but one,
But that is the best of all.

[1]The material in this paper draws heavily from Walker, E. L. *Psychological Complexity and Preference: A Hedgehog Theory of Behavior*, Monterey, California: Brooks/Cole Publishing Company, 1980.

ASLEEP AND OTHERWISE   AWAKE

Figure 1. Hypothetical hedgehog performing his one trick.

A fox, whose behavior is unpredictable, has more solutions than he has problems. The hedgehog, on the other hand, has only one trick. Whatever happens, this spiny little animal rolls up into a ball. This single defensive trick (he has no offensive ones) has proved sufficient to permit him to survive over a great span of earthly time.

Psychological complexity and preference theory is extremely simple. It has only one trick to be used on all occasions. It has only two variables, psychological complexity and preference. It has only two major dynamic principles. One principle says that *learning consists of the progressive simplification of material.* The other principle states that for each individual with respect to each dimension of psychological complexity *there is an optimum level of complexity that will be sought and enjoyed.*

The learning principle indicates that while practice may not make perfect, at least if you stick with it the complex will come to be simple. The most basic human motivation is manifest in the quest for optimal complexity level: the effort to move from a nonpreferred state to a preferred one. If you are at or near your optimum complexity level, the experience is pleasant and interesting. If you are some distance from your optimum complexity level, the experience is unpleasant and either boring or frustrating. The sudden shift or movement from nonoptimum to optimum complexity levels produces an aesthetic experience or response.

In the remainder of this paper, I shall try to elaborate the theory, provide some documentation as to its soundness in musical affairs, and suggest some of the implications of the theory for the music educator.

A Word About Theory

The Hedgehog is a theory. No theory is ever complete and consistent. Therefore, the Hedgehog is incomplete and sometimes inconsistent. Gödel's Theorem is thought to prove that no mathematical system can be complete and consistent (see Hofstadter, 1979). If a complete and consistent mathematical system cannot be developed, then no complete and consistent theory of learning and motivation can be developed.

A theory is an abstraction induced from a large body of highly selected data. For you, as music educators, a theory is a good theory if it provides concepts that you can understand and use to solve problems that are important to you. A theory is good if it provides intellectual handles that permit you to think creatively about issues that concern you. It follows that one need not be devoted to a single theory. It is reasonable to employ as many theories as one finds useful. The Hedgehog is offered as a theory of learning and motivation that may help you think about problems of music education and suggest ways of solving them. If it is successful in doing that, it is a successful theory. If it does not, then it will curl up in a ball, wait until you are out of sight, and it will then walk sadly away.

Hedgehog Theory

Psychological complexity and preference theory has a simple structure in which the interrelations of the parts can be stated without taking into account changes that occur in time. This static form is loosely analogous to harmonic structure in music. Each variable in the theory undergoes changes in predict-

318

able patterns with experience or practice. These changes in time are dynamic properties of the theory that are in some limited sense analogous to melodic movement in music. We shall discuss first the static (harmonic) and then the dynamic (melodic) properties.

The Static (Harmonic) Properties of the Hedgehog—Psychological Complexity

This concept (see Figure 2) refers to the complexity of a psychological event. A psychological event is something occurring within the person; it is a characteristic of an internal process. Under many circumstances psychological complexity will correspond to the physical properties of the stimulus that initiated the psychological process. Visual stimuli, such as paintings, can be ordered from simple to complex. Auditory stimuli can range from the simplicity of a pure tone to the complexity of a symphony orchestra in full voice at a particular moment. Intellectual problems can have the appearance of being very easy or very difficult. Physical movements can range from something as simple as the raising of a finger to the complexity of the fingering of a violin in a rapid musical passage.

However, the dimension of psychological complexity shown in Figure 2 refers to the complexity or difficulty in the psychological processes involved. There are a number of reasons why the complexity of the psychological reaction to a stimulus does not always agree perfectly with the group consensus concerning the complexity of the physical stimulus. The failure of the individual to agree with the group can reflect either deficient or superior capacity. Partial deafness simplifies sounds. Acute hearing maximizes complexity. Differences in experience with the particular dimension or parts of it can lead to large deviations from the average or group reaction. Most individuals simply do not hear the inherent complexities of the music of J. S. Bach. Psychological complexity and preference theory is concerned with the behavior of individuals, and only when it can be reasonably assumed that the individuals of a group are very similar in their ca-

pacities and experiences will the theory be applicable to the behavior of groups.

There are three different ways of constructing useful scales of psychological complexity. (1) Many musical stimuli have physical properties that would allow their relative placement on the scale. High tones are more complex than low tones. Loud tones are more complex than soft tones. Some chords have more complex frequency structures than others. Such elements would be ordered from simple stimuli on the left to complex stimuli on the right. (2) A second procedure involves asking a number of people to rate stimuli or tasks for complexity or difficulty and, since they will not necessarily agree, averaging the ratings and placing the items on the scale in accordance with these averages. For many purposes either of these procedures will work even though the scales will not be representative of the complexities of the psychological reactions of many individuals. (3) The third procedure simply involves the determination of the order of complexity for the

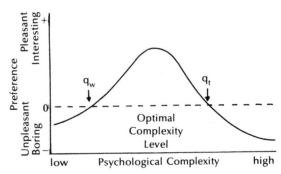

Figure 2. Psychological complexity and preference theory. (Static structure.) The horizontal dimension represents a wide range of psychological complexity or difficulty. The vertical dimension represents preference shown here to be related to judgments of relative pleasantness or interestingness. Optimal complexity level is that point on the psychological complexity dimension at which preference is at a maximum. The point indicated as q_w (quit working) is the level of psychological complexity below which the task is too simple to sustain participation. The q_t point (quit trying) is the level of difficulty above which the task is too difficult to make participation possible.

single individual involved. A teacher teaching an individual or a small group should never depend on the first two procedures but should make direct (and periodic) assessments of the relative complexities of the items of the material being taught. As we shall see, doing so permits maximum learning efficiency and failure to do so leads to unfortunate consequences.

The scale of psychological complexity in Figure 2 is assumed to represent items that have been precisely ordered with respect to their relative complexities for a single individual at a particular moment.

Optimal Complexity Level and Preference

It is a postulate of the theory that there will be a point on the scale of pyschological complexity that will be preferred by the individual. This point (indicated in Figure 2) is called the *optimal complexity level*. Psychological events that are either simpler or more complex will be less preferred, and the degree of preference will decline as the distance from optimum increases in either direction.

The shape of the curve in Figure 2 is somewhat arbitrary and only its most general characteristics have meaning. It is patterned after the curve of hedonic tone suggested by Wundt (1874) to represent the relative pleasantness or unpleasantness of stimuli according to their intensities. Berlyne (1971) has suggested that the underlying hypothesis can be traced back to Aristippus, a Cyrenaic philosopher of the fourth century B.C. He identified pleasure with "gentle motions" set up within the perceiving subject and pain with "violent motions."

Two major sources of problems in documenting the merits of the curve in Figure 2 arise from the enormous fund of words in English to describe the preference dimension and a number of experimental results yielding somewhat different curve forms.

I have used the word "preference" as a theoretical term to represent all of the affective adjectives such as bad-good, ugly-beautiful, boring-interesting, dislike-like, unpleasant-pleasant, and so on, that express an affective reaction to some stimulus object. In Figure 2, I have labeled the vertical axis with two such pairs, unpleasant-pleasant and boring-interesting, because I believe them to be more or less fundamental. They also serve to illustrate a point. The most interesting task is often higher on the psychological complexity scale than the most pleasant task. While this state is little more than a curiosity within the static structure of the theory, it can have practical consequences when we consider problems of motivation within the dynamic aspects of the theory.

The problem of the form of the hedonic curve is illustrated in Figures 3 and 4. The first of these by Heyduk (1972, 1975) involved ratings of four short musical compositions. The pieces differed from each other in the complexities of their chord structures and whether or not there was syncopation.

As Figure 3 shows, they were rated for complexity in the order A, B, C, and D. The

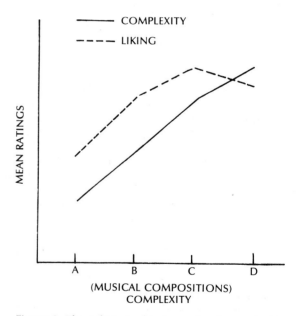

Figure 3. The relation of judgments of complexity to judgments of liking. The stimuli were four short musical compositions played on a piano. Complexity was increased from composition A through D by increasing the number of different chords, the number of minor chords, and the presence of syncopation. Compositions were rated both for complexity and how well each was liked. (Heyduk, 1972, 1975)

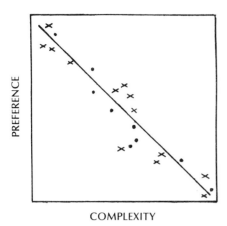

COMPLEXITY

Figure 4. Relation of judgments of complexity to measures of preference in two studies employing laboratory generated dichords. Aeschbach (dots) used a sine wave generator to produce all major intervals from the second through the eleventh. Intervals were judged for complexity and pleasingness. Ayres (Xs) employed a synthesizer and permitted subjects to make preferential choices among the thirteen intervals in a single octave. (Ayres, 1974, 1975; Aeschbach, 1975)

curve showing the mean ratings of how much the subjects like the four compositions shows a group preference for Composition C, less for D, still less for B, and still less for A, the simplest composition of the set. This curve could be thought of as representing the very top of the curve in Figure 2.

A different result is shown in Figure 4. It shows data from a study of Aeschbach (1975) and one by Ayres (1974, 1975). Aeschbach obtained judgments of ten major intervals from the second through the eleventh. The tones were generated by a sine wave generator and recorded on tape. Ayres employed a synthesizer set up to produce each of the thirteen intervals of a single octave with each interval based on middle C. He had people judge the intervals for complexity and allowed them to play the set freely. He counted the number of times each interval was played and took that frequency as the measure of the relative preference for the intervals.

In both of these studies the interval rated as the least complex was also the most pre-

ferred, while the interval rated as the most complex was the least preferred. If one considers that these results were obtained with strange sounding laboratory generated stimuli, it seems possible that the psychological complexities of all of them were above optimal complexity level and the curve in Figure 4 represents a piece of the right side of the curve in Figure 2.

The Hedgehog theory assumes that the curve in Figure 2 is the correct one. If some other curve form is obtained, it can usually be attributed to one of two conditions: either the items being judged are improperly positioned on the scale of psychological complexity, or the range of psychological complexity induced by the material is narrow and thus reflects only a small part of the range drawn in Figure 2.

The Dynamic (Melodic) Properties of the Hedgehog

As is true of music, most of the interesting aspects of the theory of psychological complexity and preference arise from changes that occur in time. Of these I shall discuss motivation, habituation, learning, and some aspects of aesthetic responses.

Motivation

The concept of motivation includes two ideas. They are an account of the sufficient conditions of action or movement, whether mental or physical, and the identification of incentives to give direction to that movement. I think it might be useful to music educators to think in terms of three kinds or sources of motive. I shall suggest extrinsic motivation and two forms of intrinsic motivation, autarchic and idiocratic.

Autarchic motivation. The word 'autarchy' means self-sufficient. Autarchic motivation is intrinsic to the activity being performed. The human organism behaves continuously, even when no greater purposes and therefore when no idiocratic or extrinsic motives are apparent. When one does things simply because they are pleasant or are interesting, one is autarchically motivated. If one were to record all of the elements of the stream of behavior, one would find a surprisingly high

321

proportion of elements that serve no purpose beyond themselves. Autarchically motivated activities represent a narrow range of psychological complexities. One automatically chooses that activity nearest to one's optimal complexity level and follows that with successive choices of activities as close as possible to one's own optimal complexity level. Playing or listening to music for the sheer joy of doing it represents autarchically motivated activity.

What is optimal (and therefore autarchically motivated) will depend to some extent on the set or mood of the individual. I mentioned previously that within any relatively homogeneous set of activities, that which is most interesting is likely to be more complex than that which is most pleasant. Thus at one time an individual might choose to listen to music that yielded the maximum of pleasure. At another time one might choose to listen to music that was somewhat more interesting even though less pleasant. Referring back to Figure 2, one has a limited capacity to slide the psychological complexity scale a little to the right to maximize pleasure and a little to the left to maximize interest and challenge.

In music what is autarchically motivated either in terms of pleasure or interest is subject to enormous individual differences. Efficient and effective teaching requires knowledge of the details of these individual differences in each student.

Idiocratic motivation. These motives have been described and named in a large variety of ways by psychologists. Essentially, they constitute the motives that characterize the individual person and are therefore enduring characteristics of the personality. Examples might be Maslow's hierarchy of needs or such motives as those that are of the particular concern of Raynor: need for achievement, need for affiliation, need for power, and so on. The essential quality of idiocratic motives is that they be enduring characteristics of the person. In this they are in contrast to extrinsic motives.

Extrinsic motivation. These motives are characterized as being external to the person. They are external in the sense that they will be operative only so long as the external circumstances impose them on the person and the task. Extrinsic motives are eminently removable.

When any two sources of motivation are simultaneously operative, the effect is to raise the height of the curve in Figure 2. There are a number of effects of raising the height of the curve. The height of curve reflects the degree or intensity of arousal. The higher the arousal, the more efficient the behavior and the greater the learning. When the curve is raised, the q_w point is moved farther to the left and the q_t point is moved farther to the right. The result is that the person will be willing to spend more time working on dull material when highly aroused than when the arousal level is low. The person will also be willing to try to work on more complex material than would be true if only autarchic motivation were in effect.

For the music educator there are practical consequences of the distinctions I have tried to make. It is possible that autarchic motivation is sufficient for the genius: Bach, Edison, Einstein. It is usually not sufficient for mere mortals. Autarchic motivation must be augmented by motivation from another source. One can undertake to associate musical activity with idiocratic or extrinsic motives. Either will work effectively at the time. However, if one undertakes to engage personal motives and if one is successful, efficient performance and learning will occur and endure. If one engages extrinsic motives, the effect may be equally efficient at the time, but practice and performance will simply stop when the band uniform is removed.

Habituation

This is a fancy word closely related to the common word "tired." Habituation is produced by closely spaced repetitions: practice. Practice has short-term effects, habituation; and it has long-term effects, learning. Habituation is temporary; learning is permanent.

Repetitive practice has two immediate effects. As practice proceeds the material becomes progressively simple and at the same time it becomes progressively dull, less interesting, and even unpleasant. Actually, the progression is a little more complicated (Figure 2). Suppose one chose to practice an interesting exercise somewhat above one's optimal complexity level for pleasantness. Continued, uninterrupted practice will have the effect of moving the exercise down the complexity scale. As it moves downward, the first effect is for the exercise to become somewhat more pleasant as optimal complexity level is reached and then to become progressively less pleasant until finally, if practice is continued, the q_w point will be reached and further practice would become unpleasant and aversive. Fortunately, the effects of habituation are temporary. When one comes back to that same exercise at a later time, one may find that it has rebounded back up the psychological complexity scale. It now may occupy a place that makes it pleasant indeed, but it may not be as interesting as it once was.

Learning

That the exercise did not rebound all the way to its former position is the essence of learning. Learning is a progressive, long-term, semipermanent or permanent simplification of the material practiced. Perhaps one can distinguish two kinds of learning. One kind consists of the acquisition of more and more knowledge at the same level of difficulty or complexity. The kind of learning I am talking about is the development of cognitive and physical skills. In this latter kind of learning, that which is too complex to contemplate today becomes a challenge tomorrow, is optimal the day after, becomes dull the day after that, and intolerable soon after. In music most of us fail to get past day number one. In Figure 2, learning on any given dimension consists of a progressive shifting of the complexity scale to the left. Note that the position of the curve and the position of optimal complexity level remain the same for the individual. After substantial learning has occurred, that which once seemed psychologically complex comes to seem far more simple.

This kind of learning is probably evident in your own experience. Many individuals proceed through a predictable sequence of periods. They may like successively children's songs, light composers, Tchaikovsky perhaps, Bach, Beethoven, an advanced Russian composer, maybe Bach again, and then to modern atonal music. As one passes from one level of complexity to the next, music once liked comes to seem dull or even unpleasant.

An experimental demonstration of the learning effect may be illustrated in Figure 5. These are additional data from the study reflected in Figure 3. The people who participated in this experiment rated each of the four simple piano compositions for complexity and liking. Then each listened to a single composition sixteen times, rating

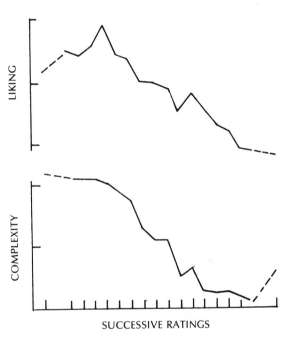

Figure 5. Effect of repeated experience on the complexity and preference for musical compositions. Four short musical compositions that varied in complexity (see Figure 3) were rated for complexity and liking. Then each person heard a single composition sixteen additional times in quick succession providing ratings at each hearing. Finally all four compositions were rated again. The curves show the course of changes in ratings of complexity and liking for a single composition over the course of the experiences. (Heyduk, 1972, 1975)

323

them for complexity and liking each time. Finally, all four compositions were rated again. The lower curve shows that with repeated experience the piece was rated as being less and less complex. After a small delay and with the additional time required to rate four compositions, the complexity curve shows a slight increase. The ratings of liking show a rise and then a fall during this procedure. It is probable that the effects shown in Figure 5 are the result of the temporary effects of habituation as well as the long-term effects of learning.

It may be possible to demonstrate the long-term learning effects within the context of the relative consonance and dissonance of musical intervals. Pythagoras ordered intervals on the basis of the relative simplicity or mathematical beauty of the frequency ratios involved. Two vibrating strings of equal length would constitute unison and the ratio would be 1:1. An interval of an octave is produced by two strings standing in a ratio of 2:1. The 'perfect' fifth has a ratio of 3:2, and so on. Consonant intervals are those with simple ratios, while dissonant intervals are those with complex ratios. The thirteen intervals of the octave could be ordered from the most consonant to the most dissonant in this manner. This problem has received considerable attention from physicists, psychologists, and musicians (see Ayres, 1974, 1975; Aeschbach, 1975). Different orderings of consonant and dissonant intervals have been obtained through both physical analysis and psychological judgments, using various means of generating musical tones.

One of these efforts of pertinent interest was an effort on the part of Moore (1914) to account for consonance and disssonance on the basis of experience or learning. It was Moore's thesis that the more often one experienced an interval, the more consonant or pleasant it would sound. He then undertook to trace the frequency with which musical intervals must have been heard by examining musical scores over the centuries. He argued that in Western music the early Greek choruses were composed of men who sang in unison. When young boys were added to the choruses, of necessity they sang in intervals

of an octave. First the major fifth came into prominence, then the major fourth, followed by major and minor thirds and sixths, more or less at the same time. Later the minor seventh came into use followed by the other four intervals as a group. Moore's thesis, of course, requires that the intervals be represented in these relative frequencies in the music people were hearing in 1914. If there has been a major change in the frequencies with which we hear intervals, then there should be a change in the order in which the intervals are judged to be consonant or dissonant. It is to be noted that the order of the thirteen intervals achieved by Moore through this analysis did not disagree with Pythagoras, and regardless of its merits, his thesis won him a Ph.D. at Harvard.

There is a somewhat more modern study that may have a bearing on the differential consonance of intervals attributable to the differential experience of hearing them. Actually, there were five studies, four by Tom Ayres (1974, 1975) and one by Susan Aeschbach (1975). Different intervals were used in different studies and some involved quarter-

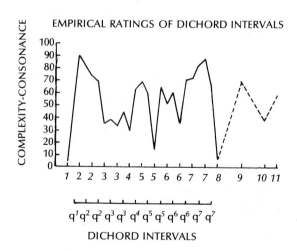

Figure 6. Relative complexity-consonance of various musical intervals. Different musical intervals were rated for consonance in four studies by Ayres and one by Aeschbach. Where more than one estimate for a given interval was available, the results were averaged. Complexity and consonance ratings did not differ.

324

tones. All intervals were rated for relative consonance and some were rated for complexity. Since these two ratings did not differ, they are referred to as complexity-consonance. Some intervals were rated only in a single study, some in three, some in four, and some in all five studies. Where multiple values were available, they were averaged to provide a single 'best estimate' of the complexity-consonance of the interval as shown in Figure 6. The task is to determine whether there is a set of reasonable factors that can account for the perturbations of Figure 6, and whether one of them could involve differential experience with certain intervals.

The first step is to invoke the idea that pitch is best represented by a helix and that tonality can be represented by a circle. I first heard of this idea from Roger Shepard (1964) who attributes it to Drobisch (1846).[2]

While we ordinarily think of pitch as forming a continuously rising or continuously falling dimension between the lower and upper limits of hearing, there are other possible conceptions. If one asks people to judge how far apart two tones are and they judge such distances for tones spanning at least an octave, then it will usually be found that two tones that are an octave apart are judged to be closer together than two tones half an octave apart. If one draws a figure to represent such distances, it is likely to approximate a helix. Figure 7 is such a helix in idealized form. This is the structure within which to search for sources of dissonance.

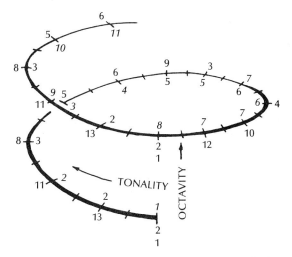

Figure 7. Pitch represented as a helix as might be obtained from an analysis of judgments of relative similarity of tones. The numbers inside the helix identify the intervals with major intervals distinguished by underlining: e.g., 5 is the major fifth. The numbers outside the helix represent the relative ranking of the interval when judged for consonance. Thus unison is judged to be the most consonant, the octave second, and the minor second the most dissonant of the thirteen intervals of the full octave.

First it must be noted that there appears to be no effect of the octave as a contributor to consonance/dissonance. This is true in a comparison of the unison with the octave, and no differences were found in comparing the major second with the major ninth, the major third with the major tenth, or between the major fourth and the major eleventh.

It is obvious in Figure 6 that there is substantial dissonance near the fundamental, and it is mirrored near the octave. I have called this the proximity effect. The proximity effect stands in some degree of correspondence with critical band width, the frequency range over which two tones appear to interact by augmenting each other's apparent loudnesses (Zwicker, Flottorp, and Stevens, 1957). The phenomenon is thought to be attributable to the interaction of the effects of the two tones on the basilar membrane in the inner ear. The dissonance labeled as attribut-

[2]Roger Shepard produced a sequence of tones which can give the illusion of either ascending endlessly or descending endlessly even though the tape is a closed loop returning always to the same starting place. In one version, the tape is coordinated with an Escher visual illusion appropriately entitled *Ascending and Descending* since it portrays monks who appear to be ascending and descending endlessly in a closed loop. Hofstadter, *op cit.*, p. 10, points out that in Bach's *Canon per Tonos*, the lowest of the three voices sings its theme in C minor but modulates to D minor at the end. If repeated again beginning in this new key and the process is continued through six modulations, it will arrive back at the original key of C minor, but an octave higher. He also says (p. 717) that had Bach used Shepard tones, the canon would have been truly 'endlessly rising,' arriving precisely back at its starting point.

325

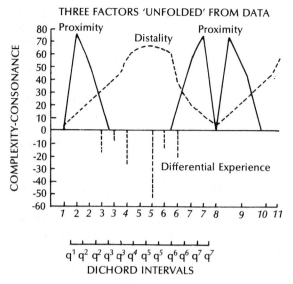

Figure 8. Estimates of sources of dissonance associated with certain musical intervals.

able to proximity could be a product of that interaction. Critical band width varies in extent depending on the frequency. It is approximately half an octave at 100 Hz. and about .13 of an octave at 15,000 Hz. For the frequency ranges used in the Ayres and Aeschbach studies, a range of twenty-eight percent seems reasonable. From the data on critical band width, I have estimated the amount and distribution of dissonance which might be attributed to this source. I have plotted these estimates in Figure 8 where they are labeled 'proximity.'

There is considerable dissonance that remains after the proximity effect is removed. I have labeled a large portion of it as the distality effect because it is concentrated on the distal side of the tonality circle. An auditory phenomenon that might possibly be related to the distality effect is a temporary hearing loss found in both humans (Davis, Morgan, Hawkins, Galambos, and Smith, 1943) and monkeys (Stebbins, Clark, Pearson, and Weiland, 1973) after exposure to intense stimuli. Although the extent of the effect over the frequency range as well as the rate of recovery from loss is reported to be related to

intensity and duration of the stimulus and to be subject to great inter- and intra-individual differences, the greatest loss is located about one-half an octave above the exposure frequency. The discoverers of this effect attributed it to events within the central nervous system and referred to it as 'nerve deafness.' It seems possible that there is a relation between nerve deafness half an octave above the stimulating frequency and the dissonance that seems centered on the distal side of the circle of tonality. Figure 8 shows an attempt to estimate the amount and location of such an effect.

When the estimates of the proximity effect and the distality effect are subtracted from the empirical data in Figure 6, certain major discrepancies remain. The six intervals given the label 'differential experience' in Figure 8 are all rated as more consonant than they should be by the amounts indicated by the downward projections. This rather tortuous analysis carried out at a rather low level of rigor does little more than generate a hypothesis. The hypothesis is that other than the unison and the octave, the interval heard most frequently by undergraduates of Amherst College and the University of Michigan in the early and mid-seventies was the major fifth. Other frequently heard intervals would have been the major fourth, the minor third, the major sixth, the minor sixth, and the minor third.

Despite the limitations of these empirical demonstrations, they do seem to support the intuitively reasonable and popular belief that learning involves the progressive simplification of the complex. Intervals that once sounded dissonant come to sound consonant. Musical compositions that once sounded complex come to sound simple. Physical tasks that once seemed impossible come to flow smoothly and effortlessly. Progress requires practice. Practice produces temporary simplification and unpleasantness. Rest between practices produces permanent simplification and progress.

Aesthetic Responses

Attempts to analyze the nature of aesthetic responses are probably futile. The ineffable

326

cannot be made effable. It might be possible, however, to suggest conditions under which one would expect aesthetic responses to occur. In the Hedgehog there are several general conditions that should produce aesthetic responses.

An event that is precisely at one's optimal complexity level should produce a positive aesthetic experience. The quality of this basic experience depends on the nearness of this experience to optimal complexity level. Such experiences are so common as possibly to go unrecognized. They are simply momentary pleasures. They are the least intense of all aesthetic experiences but they share their momentary character with aesthetic experiences from all other sources. Habituation produces simplification with the result that no aesthetic experience can be sustained for very long. No matter how pleasurable an activity, its optimal character cannot be prolonged.

More intense and interesting aesthetic responses occur when there is a sharp and sudden contrast in complexity. Music is the ideal medium for the temporal manipulation of aesthetic experiences. It is much more difficult to avoid hearing sounds than to avoid seeing pictorial material. In music the composer or performer has control of the temporal sequence of events whereas the painter must leave that sequence to the whims of the viewer. A sequence of psychological events that is below optimal complexity level followed by an event that suddenly increases in complexity to an appropriate level produces an intense aesthetic experience. Likewise, a sequence of psychological events that is significantly too complex for the listener that is suddenly resolved into an event at or near optimal produces an aesthetic reaction.

Habituation can also be used as a mechanism in the manipulation of the aesthetic response. If an event that is initially optimal is prolonged or repeated, the effect is to induce a state of boredom. Boredom is a suboptimal state that can serve as a platform from which one can then restore optimality with a consequent pleasurable reaction. The degree of pleasure can be controlled by the amount of habituation produced before optimality is restored. Since an aesthetic response is, of necessity, brief, an aesthetically pleasing musical composition or performance is one in which the composer or performer has arranged a significant number of momentary aesthetic responses.

While the Hedgehog provides intellectual handles that can be used in the manipulation of aesthetic responses, they do not constitute a panacea. One must have manipulative command of the theory and a thorough understanding of music. One must be able to translate characteristics of music into psychological complexity level for the individual or group. Most difficult of all, one must find means of assessing individual differences among the many developmental dimensions relevant to the experience of music.

Implications for Music Education

The Hedgehog can be applied in a high proportion of the problems that arise in the learning and teaching of music. A few gross examples may serve to illustrate.

The Hedgehog is a theory of individual behavior. Learning on many dimensions occurs as the opportunities for interaction vary in frequency and duration. Without any appeal to differences in capacity, one can expect such large individual differences in progress that it is likely to be true that no two individuals are likely to have attained exactly the same level of development in all relevant aspects of either understanding of music or performance. From this it follows that from the standpoint of the learner, learning efficiency will decline as the size of the student group is increased beyond one. It also follows that because of his great and extensive experience with music, a composer who composes music that is pleasant or interesting to his own ears will have composed for a very small audience.

The role of psychological complexity as the foundation for significant learning implies the necessity to look at musical character and musical performance tasks primarily in terms of their relative complexities or difficulties. Thus the work of those music educators who have attempted to produce scales of difficulty and prescribed learning sequences in terms of the relative difficulty of the material, for example, that of Gordon (1976, 1977), is of primary importance. However, one must be prepared to find that the difficulty scale derived from the physical properties of the music or the experience of groups of individuals will not fit precisely with the psychological complexity scale of any individual.

The division of human motives into the tripartite set of autarchic, idiocratic, and extrinsic has implications for the practice of music education. Listening, learning, or performing music for the sheer joy of doing it, thus under autarchic motivation alone, will produce major musical development in very few individuals. The linking of idiocratic motives, motives that are an enduring part of the personality of the individual, to the autarchic motive to learn and perform music will produce self-sustaining development far beyond the purview of the instructor. Extrinsic motivation, for example the band uniform, can be used with discretion as a seductive device. However, since its effects will not endure beyond its presence, it should be replaced as quickly as possible by more enduring personal motives.

The emphasis in this paper has been largely on the pupil, but the Hedgehog has implications for the teacher. A teacher will function most effectively when operating at or near the teacher's own optimal complexity level. As a set of intellectual handles, the Hedgehog permits one to see the task of teaching in ever-changing lights. It can permit the teacher to modify teaching behavior in continuously progressive ways while simultaneously becoming increasingly effective in terms of the progress of the pupils.

To me, one of the most engaging characteristics of the Hedgehog is that it is a happy little beast. When pleasure and interestingness are at a maximum, learning efficiency is also at a maximum. Effective teachers are also happy. The moral is quite clear—if either learning or teaching is dull or frustrating, somebody is doing it wrong.

References

Aeschbach, S. *Ratings of dichords along the continua of complexity-simplicity, consonance-dissonance, and pleasing-displeasing.* Honors dissertation, University of Michigan, 1975.

Ayres, T. *Exploratory behavior with musical intervals as related to measures of consonance and dissonance.* Research paper, Amherst College, 1974.

————. *Psychological and physiological factors in the consonance of musical intervals.* Honors dissertation, Amherst College, 1975.

Berlyne, D. E. *Aesthetics and psychobiology.* New York: Appleton-Century-Crofts, 1971.

Davis, H., C. T. Morgan, J. E. Hawkins, Jr., R. Galambos, and F. W. Smith. Temporary deafness following exposure to loud tones and noises. *Acta Oto-laryngologica,* Supplement LXXXVIII, Final report, 9-30-43.

Drobisch, M. W. Über die mathematische Bestimmung der Musikalischen Intervalle. In Fürstliche, *Jablonowskischen Gesellschaft der Wissenschaften.* Leipzig: Weidmann'sche Buchlandlung, 1846.

Gordon, E. E. *Learning sequence and patterns in music.* Chicago: G.I.A. Publications, Inc., 1976–1977.

Heyduk, R. G. *Static and dynamic aspects of rated and exploratory preference for musical compositions.* Unpublished doctoral dissertation, University of Michigan, Ann Arbor, Michigan, 1972.

————. Rated preference of musical compositions as it relates to complexity and exposure frequency. *Perception and Psychophysics,* 1975, *17,* 84–91.

Hofstadter, D. R. *Gödel, Escher, Bach: An eternal golden braid.* New York: Basic Books, 1979.

Moore, H. T. The genetic aspects of consonance and dissonance. *Psychological Monographs,* 1914, *17* (2), 1–68.

Shepard, R. N. Circularity in judgments of relative pitch. *Journal of the Acoustical Society of America,* 1964, *36,* 2346–2353.

Stebbins, W. C., W. W. Clark, R. D. Pearson, and N. G. Weiland. Noise-and-drug-induced hearing loss in monkeys. *Advances in Oto-Rhino-Laryngology,* 1973, *20,* 42–63.

Wundt, W. M. *Grundzüge der physiologischen Psychologie.* Leipzig: Engelmann, 1874.

Zwicher, E., G. Flottorp, and S. S. Stevens. Critical band width in loudness summation. *Journal of the Acoustical Society of America,* 1957, *29* (5).

Response

R. Douglas Greer

As a behaviorist and educator, I occasionally hear some of the exotic terms that have been used throughout the symposium. But here, these terms have been used frequently and openly. Initially, I was puzzled as to their meaning, but I now think that I know what these terms mean. They are new forms of an old animal! Here are just a few of them that I have collected from the presentations: mental furnishings, mental structures, plastic brains, echoic memories, memory storages (both long-legged ones and short-legged ones), mental processes, rule users, mental organs, and mental executives, to name only a few. Of course, these are not real animals; they are mythical animals descended from the old mentalistic psychological animal termed the "woozle," which also is related apparently to another mythical figure called inner man. I don't know anything about these animals. I have never seen one or a photograph of one. From time to time, I have seen impressionistic drawings of these animals complete with input and output antennae, but these representations seem unreal to me.

Given my ignorance, you can appreciate my anxiety after having received advance notice of the title of Walker's paper. The hedgehog, indeed! However, after reading Walker's paper, I found the hedgehog to be a real animal. As a theory, it promised to go away if not useful and if it proved not to be consistent with future data. I think it is a good theory and that it can be a useful domestic animal for music education. It will not, unlike many theories, bite the hand that feeds it.

Rather than react only to Walker's theory, I am going to discuss, from an operant psychologist's point of view, some of the central issues raised by all of us. I think this point of view needs representation since I appear to be the only behaviorist on the panel.

Theories have been a major concern for many of the panelists and I think that is an accurate reflection of the thrust of cognitive psychology. However, there is another world of psychology and the psychology of music: this world is concerned with the experimental and applied analysis of behavior. As I noted in my review of the programmatic research in an operant psychology of music, the operant approach has a major impact on educational and therapeutic practice in many fields. Operant or even more generally behavioristic theories differ from cognitive or perceptual theories in that behavioristic theories are drawn almost exclusively from the data and seek to identify classes of lawful relationships between the environment and behavior. We are not concerned with building a brain-behavior interface since we see such efforts as leading only to a new set of adjectives for behavior. We are, however, concerned with all of the important issues in life. For example, we also deal with language, but from the point of view of verbal behavior as it is developed in terms of functional or environmental control of behavior. We avoid issues concerning cognitive structures because we believe that they have little explanatory power for behavior. If we can produce and modify behavior in predictable manners and if those behaviors are indicative of cognitive structures as the cognitive psychologists believe, then obviously cognitive development too must be a concomitant of behavior change.

There is no real need for cognitive psychologists and those of us who are behaviorists to engage in adversarial debates, especially since the issue is no longer what should psychology be. Each group has its own special concerns, journals, and internal organizations. However, from time to time, we do need to listen to each other. If both camps carefully, simply, and operationally describe their independent and dependent variables, we will be able to profit from each other's work. It is important for all of us to be reminded that intensive research, particularly with children, seldom results in findings that are the predictable or logical. Theory is cheaper than data and the data often survive the theory by many years.

One point of agreement in all of the data summarized here has been the emphasis on individual differences. There is no learning or behavior change that is not a function of individual learning. Teaching always is reducible to the shaping of one individual at a time, otherwise each student learns only that which is already discriminated, resulting in the confounding of individual errors with new aspects of the task at hand. It is important for the teacher or psychologist to allow the student's behavior to determine what to do next. The student's behavior will tell the teacher when to increase the complexity of the task and shift the reinforcement schedule as well as when to fade reinforcers other than the task. Those of us in behavior analysis have found it essential to keep simple, accurate records of behavior change and the reinforcement used; otherwise, the teacher will forget or be distracted. To teach in such a systematic manner requires, in addition to appropriate training, careful planning and skilled use of positive reinforcement. Without the planning and positive reinforcement, teachers will resort to aversive techniques unwittingly, such as the inevitable catalogue of don'ts or other forms of disapproval. Metaphors are better than disapprovals. It is better to provide actual models of the music when the student is focused on the relevant properties of the model.

Behaviorists have done research using the single subject or small groups of subjects over a long period of time. There is some evidence that other psychologists are considering the validity of this approach. What you should find out is that some subjects will take longer to learn than others but like children learning to ride a bicycle, you can't compare them to norms but must teach them until learning has occurred. The solution to variability is not a simple diagnosis but the provision of enough learning trials or opportunities to shape each student's behavior. Perhaps a comparison of trials to learn at different age levels would begin to give us a more valid developmental psychology.

The most effective approach to individualization for the harassed music teacher is to systematically use students as peer tutors. The data are clear on this issue, the tutee will benefit as will the teacher and we are finding positive multiple effects including generalization when tutors are reinforced.

Intrinsic motivation, and by this I mean embedded and learned reinforcement for the task not the individual, is the goal of music instruction. Few, if any, have done more research on the issue with children than my colleagues and I, and our research provides tools for the teacher to realize this goal. However, we all need to be reminded that it is most fortunate that intrinsic motivation is not the only motivation or reinforcement that is effective. Indeed, the fact that an irrelevant reinforcer can motivate a behavior unrelated to the reinforcing consequence is one of the reasons civilization has survived. Our data have shown that many educational reinforcers can be used in music programs often with multiple positive effects and no known detrimental effects.

If one is looking inside music for the intrinsic reinforcers one needs not use complexity only as a construct, for as Walker has noted, complexity is an individual matter. Perhaps there are more and less reinforcing musical events for each individual. The more reinforcing ones pull the individual through less reinforcing moments. I would suggest that the schedule of the occurrence of these reinforcing events in a work of music for an individual might tell us much.

I am delighted to see that the cognitive psychologists are moving toward the use of actual music stimuli rather than acoustical components, as behaviorists have been doing since the late sixties. We have been cavalier, if anything, about the acoustical components of our music stimuli. It is the psychoacousticians who have been reductionists, not the behaviorists of the sixties and seventies. For the behaviorists, it is the student who decides on the effective stimulus since to us the real issue is the consequence of the behavior, not a prod-like notion of the stimulus. It is likely that different acoustic components of music produce similar reinforcement or stimulus discriminative effects for different individuals. Perhaps that is why Roger Brown's two very different

groups of subjects can be similarly reinforced by the same music.

The psychoacoustic data are helpful on several counts, for example, simultaneous pitch matching requires fine-honed ($\pm$ cents for the professionals) discriminations.

Research that employs verbal responses to music stimuli should be interpreted in light of the increasing evidence from physiological psychology, social psychology, and behavior therapy that the verbal repertoire is often not related to other behaviors such as performing, listening, and selecting. The student who has been taught about the value of art music in a good music literature class may truly come to believe, verbalize, that value since that is the verbal behavior that has been modelled and reinforced. The actual listening or choice behavior may have no relationship with the verbal behavior. Differences between response repertoires to the same stimuli do not raise issues of integrity but truly raise increasing doubts about hypothetical constructs such as musicality, preference, creativity, and intelligence. Verbal behavior is important, but is usually not the most important behavior for music education and cannot be believed as a reliable predictor of other behavior.

Cognitive and psychoacoustical research may eventually contribute to an empirically-based theory of music. Subsequently, musicians and composers can be taught empirically-based rules of composition. Such a body of music theory might eventually have something to do with music instruction. But then again it may not. Cognitive and psychoacoustical research apparently should not be held accountable for such practical benefits. However, you *should* make such demands on those of us in operant psychology.

None of the data presented here has raised any hard evidence about the role of heredity or nature in music learning. Conclusions based on correlational concommittant variance are suspect even for "laboratory" theory, much less practice. As educators we should be morally bound to deal with instructing those who have not learned, not with selecting those who already have. To make an absurd comparison between music and language, teachers do not select only those children who have language reading ability to teach reading, while relegating all others to classes of reading appreciation. This is not to imply that everyone can or ought to be taught everything.

I hope I have made my point about the existence of a large and flourishing world of psychology that is eminently applicable to teaching. Perhaps the greatest tribute to music is the growing interest in the scientific study of the acquisition of music behaviors and music reinforcers.

Motivational Determinants of Music-Related Behavior: Psychological Careers of Student, Teacher, Performer, and Listener

Joel O. Raynor

My goal in this paper is to provide a theoretical orientation that can be used to view some of the issues involved in trying to understand the motivational determinants of music-related behavior as a specific instance of life activity. This theory has been proposed as a theory of personality functioning and change. Its major assumptions include the integration of the behavioral and self-systems as sources of expected value that determine action, the use of time-linked sources of value to conceptualize the effects of the anticipated future, retrospected past, and the evaluated present as sources of expected value for action, the specification of five substantive sources of value (intrinsic, difficulty, instrumental, extrinsic, and cultural), and the application of these concepts to substantive areas of activity than can provide means of self-identification and that are referred to as "psychological careers." The theory has evolved in systematic research on human motivation, particularly achievement motivation, and has been applied to the understanding of the factors involved in motivational changes over time in psychological careers. The implications of these ideas have direct relevance to substantive music-related careers—that of the music teacher, music student, music performer, and music listener.

For those who would prefer an empirical summary of research findings concerning music-related activity for which new theoretical insights might be proposed, the present paper will be a disappointment. My defense of the strategy I have selected is basic for an understanding of what I hope to accomplish here. I am not a music researcher or music educator. I do not know either literature very well. However, as a student of the psychology of motivation, involved in both systematic research on "important" human behaviors, and involved in attempts to build successively better theoretical understanding of such behaviors, I have some confidence that individuals involved in music-related behavior share most of the properties of individuals involved in other substantive careers, so that insights concerning their behavior may be inferred from a theory built to explain research data in other areas of human activity.

We are concerned with the molar aspects of behavior—music as an activity in a person's life. The problem of motivation, as defined by the psychologist, concerns the direction, vigor, and persistence of action, and most fundamentally, the change of activity, from one to another—or the other side of the coin, the recurrent patterns of activity in a person's life.

Motivation and Action

The present analysis of the motivational determinants of any human activity is exceedingly complex. There is no "one" reason or cause that can account for all of the phenomena that can be identified in the behavioral aspects of human activity. This is particularly so when we try to explain "important human action"—"important" as seen by the individual engaging in that activity. Thus many assumptions are needed to build a sufficiently complex theoretical orientation to deal with life activity of adults engaged in, for example, the teaching of music.

However, in building the present conception I have been extremely systematic; I have started with a particular orientation, called Expectancy × Value Theory of Action, and extended it so that the exceedingly complex analysis that is required is accomplished in terms of only two general conceptual variables—expectancy and value.

An individual is assumed to be motivated to obtain and maximize positive value, and to avoid and minimize negative value. There are several different dimensions or sources of positive and negative value. We distinguish between affective and information value; between intrinsic, difficulty, instrumental, extrinsic, and cultural value; and between different time-linked sources of value; past, present, and future. We also distinguish between the external and internal points of view in analyzing sources of value, different kinds of paths that provide sources of value, and value from the behavioral versus the self-system.

Activity as steps in a path. In this theory, sources of value result from the outcomes of activity. A positive outcome is called a goal and a negative outcome a threat. We conceptualize action as consisting of activity and its positive and negative outcomes; an activity and its outcomes are termed a step. Steps are represented in sequence to form a path. From the external view, this corresponds to a film record taken of an individual as he moves from one activity to another, as coded by the observer, and the outcomes of each activity. From the internal point of view, this corresponds to the anticipated *future* steps that an individual believes he might take, the remembered *past* steps, and the immediate *present* steps.

We conceptualize four different kinds of paths: contingent, noncontingent, partial contingent, and one-step; all but the last having both a future and a past time orientation. A future contingent path consists of a series of steps where an immediate positive outcome is believed necessary by the individual to earn the opportunity to try for additional positive outcomes along that path, while a past contingent path is one where some positive outcome of past activity is believed by the individual to have led to the opportunity to try for some number of subsequent positive outcomes, and for each contingent path, an immediate negative outcome is believed to lead to the loss of the opportunity to continue along that path. A partial contingent path is one where an immediate positive outcome guarantees the opportunity to continue, but an immediate negative outcome has no bearing on future striving. A noncontingent path is one where immediate outcomes, both positive and negative, have no bearing on earning the opportunity to continue along the path. A one-step path consists of a single activity and its positive or negative outcomes.

A path may be open or closed. In a closed path, the original final goal of the path remains fixed so that as the individual successively moves through the path to the final step there are fewer and fewer steps remaining as potential sources of positive or negative value. In an open path, the original final goal of the path is continually revised as the individual successively moves through the path, so that the number of steps in the path remains the same or even increases and therefore there is no decrease in potential sources of positive or negative value.

The concepts of open and closed contingent paths are crucial for the theory, for in these paths it is assumed that all future steps and all past steps of the path contribute motivation sustaining the immediate activity along that path.

The Behavioral and Self-Systems

We assume that each outcome of action has the potential for serving as a means of self-identity. This self-image, defined by the outcome of a past, present, or future action, can then provide its own source of positive and negative value to influence the motivation of activity. Activity and outcomes per se are referred to as the behavioral system, and value in the behavioral system is referred to as attractiveness (positive) and repulsiveness (negative)—corresponding to the term valence. Activity and outcomes that in addition define a self-image that serves as a means of self-identity are referred to as the self-system, and value in the self-system is referred to as positive and negative self-esteem or esteem-income as referred to by self-theorists.

There are two important consequences of the emergence of the self-system in a substantive area of activity: (1) the individual's self-identity and self-worth are perceived by him to be evaluated by the outcomes of activity in that area, and (2) there is greater motivation (positive or negative) sustaining immediate activity in that area.

Immediate action is assumed to be determined by the product of each source of positive value and its expectancy or subjective probability of attainment summed over all sources of positive value, minus the product

of each source of negative value and its expectancy of subjective probability of attainment. When action implicates the self-system, as when outcomes of action define "Who am I?", then net esteem-income (the differences between positive and negative self-esteem) determines the individual's psychological morale for that psychological career defined by the substantive activity in question, and the self-image that can be attained, assessed, maintained by that action.

Psychological Careers

The concept of "psychological career" is used to relate the time-linked senses of self to action. A psychological career is conceived as a joint function of the individual's sense of self or self-image and a particular opportunity for action. In this theory, "career" is a general term that is not limited to occupational pursuits, but rather reflects any substantive self-image that is related to action opportunities that are seen as contingently related to attainment, assessment, or maintenance of that self-image. Thus "career" is the psychological variable that links the internal view of self and the external view of role (as seen by others) so that "careers" are behavioral opportunities for self-identity.

Most individuals in our culture usually pursue at least three simultaneous senses of self—careers in the "occupational" area related to earning a living, careers in the sexual area related to masculinity/femininity and sexual functioning, and careers related to their family identity as spouse or parent. In addition, leisure and avocational careers are becoming increasingly important as means of obtaining positive value.

Intrinsic, Difficulty, Instrumental, Extrinsic, and Cultural Values

Intrinsic value refers to the value of an activity or outcome that is aroused by its inherent properties. When an individual reports that he or she "likes music" or "sex makes me feel very good," or he or she acts in a way consistent with these kinds of statements, the concept of intrinsic value seems appropriate as a conceptual means of representing this attractiveness/repulsiveness. Intrinsic value seems like a necessary concept in a complete theory of action, to account for individual taste preferences and the fact that some activities seem inherently pleasurable for almost all individuals, while others, like getting an electric shock, seem inherently unpleasant. Note, however, that intrinsic value to the individual allows for the possibility that what is positive for almost all individuals might be more or less negatively valued for a particular individual.

The *difficulty value* of an outcome refers to the attractiveness or repulsiveness that derives from the individual's perceived chances of attaining that outcome. Difficulty value is similar to the concept of incentive value in theory of achievement motivation; the easier the task, the higher the subjective probability of success and the lower the difficulty value of the outcome of that task, while the harder the task, the lower the subjective probability of success and the higher the difficulty value of the outcome of that task. However, we wish to use this concept in a more general way. For example, we assume that the greater the scarcity of occurrence of certain attributes of individuals, the greater the positive/negative difficulty value they are perceived to have.

Instrumental value refers to the number of opportunities for subsequent action that the attainment of an outcome, or possession of some competence, is believed to guarantee or to have guaranteed. Future instrumental value refers to behavior in contingent paths where immediate success is believed to earn the opportunity to try for some number of future successes, and immediate failure is believed to guarantee future failure through loss of the opportunity to try for future successes. Thus the instrumental value of immediate success is greater the greater the number of steps in a path to the final goal of a contingent path. It follows that single outcomes not related to other activities usually have no future instrumental value to the individual faced with that activity. Similarly, the final goal of a contingent path has no instrumental value for activity in that path since no further action is contemplated along it. It also follows that as the number of steps

in a contingent path decreases as an individual moves through the path, the future instrumental value of the immediate step also decreases. However, the instrumental value of a past success correspondingly increases as a function of success along the path when an individual perceives that some past success has guaranteed an increasingly greater number of later opportunities for success.

The third source of value comes from what is termed *extrinsic value,* or the "extrinsic incentives." These are sources of value that derive from rewards that are contingent upon goal attainment, but do not relate to the difficulty value or to the intrinsic value of the task per se. Money, approval, power, or security are common sources of extrinsic value, and are assumed to function to provide positive value contingent upon immediate success when they are perceived to be appropriate or usual outcomes of that activity. Extrinsic value may also be negative.

Finally, the individual *cultural value* of an outcome refers to the extent to which an individual has acquired the belief that attainment of that outcome is good/bad or right/wrong or proper/improper. It implicates a moral-evaluative source of value. The consensual cultural value associated with success is most often positive in our culture, and for many individuals in our culture their individual culture valuation of success is also positive. A "successful person" is believed to be a "good" person; so is an "intelligent" person. Most professional/occupational outcomes are highly positively valued along this good/bad dimension in our culture. Individual cultural value may also be negative, as might be the case for "failure," and "alcoholic." Individual cultural value refers to a source of esteem-income that, while not uniquely tied to the self-system, is most often potently aroused when an individual is involved in pursuit of a time-linked self-image. The cultural value of a self-image indicates how good or bad a person I am when I see myself in terms of that self-image. We derive that senses of self, which come to be used as primary means of self-identity, are those that provide substantial (cultural) value to the individual.

Note that these five sources of value can provide esteem-income for each of the three time-linked senses of self, and for each substantively different "career." Thus there are in this theory at least $5 \times 3 \times 3 = 45$ potential, additive sources of positive esteem-income for the individual, and an equal number of sources of negative esteem-income. These can *simultaneously* provide esteem-income for individuals having clear-cut occupational, sexual, and family careers that have future, past, and present senses of self. Of course, the individual may have fewer, or more, simultaneous careers, or the individual may have only one or two time-linked senses of self for any of these, and any of the five sources of positive (or negative) value may provide a large or small quantity of that particular value. Or the individual may have no clear-cut sense of self, so that no value is derived from the self-system. Thus the theory can represent extremely varied sources and amounts of value that a particular individual might experience at any particular time, and that influence motivation of immediate activity.

In the above analysis it is assumed that all sources of value represent the interaction of two factors: something about the person that is brought by him to the particular situation that colors or weights a particular source of value, and that may be relatively stable and characteristic of that person, and something about the particular sources of value that impinges on the individuals faced with that situation and that may have similar effects on many different individuals. Thus the notion of value as a motivational variable assumes that both individual differences in people and differences in situations faced by people, interact to determine value to influence action.

Stages of Career Striving

The concept of time-linked sources of value allows us to derive significant differences in the quantity of motivation at different stages of striving along a psychological career path that is both *contingent* and *closed*. To illustrate these points, we represent the individual as a point on a time line, with the anticipated future steps of the path indicated by positive numbers, the retrospected past steps of the path indicated by negative numbers, and the present by zero (Figure 1). When an individual is faced with the first step of an anticipated contingent path, he is represented as facing a series of possible sources of value in the anticipated future, and in the immediate present, but sources of value do not exist in this psychological career for the retrospected past (see Figure 2). This is the initial or early stage of career striving and is termed "becoming." If and when the individual successfully moves through the entire series of steps of this contingent path, and the initial final goal has remained fixed so that the path is considered closed, the person is represented as recalling a series of past sources of value in the retrospected past, and in the immediate future, but sources of value do not exist in this psychological career for the anticipated future. This final or last step of career striving is termed "having been" (see Figure 3). Some intermediate point in striving along the closed contingent path allows for the retrospected past, the anticipated future, and the immediate present to provide possible sources of value (as in Figure 1). Thus the attainment of goals along a contingent path inevitably produces a change in the time-linked sources of value in that career, from anticipated future, initially, to retrospected past, terminally, so long as the initial final goal of the path remains un-

Figure 1. Middle stage.

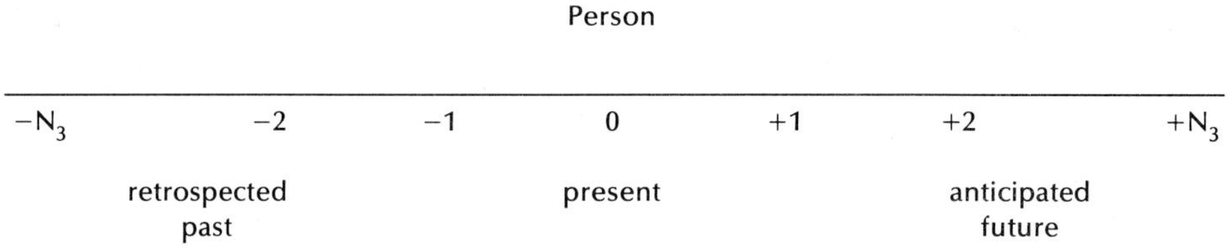

Person

$-N_3$	-2	-1	0	$+1$	$+2$	$+N_3$
	retrospected past		present		anticipated future	

336

Person

| 0 | +1 | +2 | +3 | +4 | +5 | $+N_6$ |

present   anticipated
                                                                          future

Figure 2. Early stage.

changed. This inevitable consequence of successful striving has important implications for understanding differences in motivation between those termed "becoming," who are considered to be "psychologically young," those who are "having been," who are considered to be "psychologically old," and those who are in the middle stage of career striving. One can expect a rough correlation between psychological age in a career and chronological age—younger people tend to be "becoming" while older people tend to be "having been"—although exceptions to this rule are to be expected and are of great interest in understanding such issues as mid-life crisis, second careers, and retirement careers. That is, it is possible for a sixty-year-old to face the initial stages of a psychological career and therefore to be considered "psychologically young" with reference to that career, just as it is possible for a twenty-year-old to face the final stages of a career and therefore to be considered "psychologically old."

The Self-System as a Source of Value

In this theory we assume that an individual comes to use a particular self-image as a means of self-identity if that self-image provides substantial positive value, and such value in the self-system is called self-esteem or esteem-income. Self-images can be de-fined in terms of the outcomes of actions, and therefore, from the internal point of view, we see that some individuals come to see themselves in terms of time-linked senses of self that are defined by anticipated attainment of future goals, or retrospected remembering of past accomplishment, or assessment of possessed prerequisite competences. Thus self-identity is seen as time-related in a psychological career, with the future sense of self tied to "becoming" and initial states of striving, the past sense of self tied to "having been" and late stages of striving, and the present sense of self tied to the evaluation of prerequisite competences, skills, and abilities that are believed to have produced past success and needed to attain future success.

The cognitive capacity to meaningfully ask the question "Who am I?" is assumed to be a necessary prerequisite for value in the self-system to emerge. In addition, an outcome of activity that defines a self-image must provide substantial value (feelings of self-worth) before such outcomes of action can serve as sources of self-identity. Taken together, these assumptions lead to the implication that the self-system may be a factor in contributing motivation sustaining immediate activity for adults, but not for young children, and that the emergence of the self-system in a substantive area of activity to define

Figure 3. "Having been."

Person

| $-N_6$ | −5 | −4 | −3 | −2 | −1 | N_0 |

retrospected   present
       past

what we mean by a "psychological career" is an important factor in the increased motivational impetus thought to sustain "important" life behaviors. While it is possible for a young student to see himself as "becoming a musician," in general, for a very large group of grade school children, the self-system is not a factor. This limited scope for motivational determinants of action is reflected in the inability to motivate children for long periods of time.

Once the self-system becomes part of striving in a given area, it is assumed that the self-images to be attained, maintained, or assessed (for the future, past, and present senses of self, respectively) can contribute value in and of themselves. "Striving to become a musician" is seen as providing sources of value in addition to the concrete goal of "striving to graduate from music school." It follows that individuals who perceive themselves faced with a contingent path linking immediate action to attainment of the concrete goal and the future self-image will be more motivated in that immediate activity than an individual merely striving to attain the concrete future goal. Thus we posit a two-step process: (1) when a goal provides a substantial source of positive value, it becomes a source of self-identity, and (2) the source of self-identity then provides additional amounts of positive value to strive to attain it and the goal that defines the self-image. Thus, when an individual is pursuing a psychological career, where by definition both the behavioral and self-systems contribute value to immediate activity, we expect greater motivational effects of the anticipated future, retrospected past, and evaluated present, than when only the behavioral system is aroused.

Career Striving in an Open Contingent Path

An important distinction is made between a closed and an open career path. The closed path is one where the individual has an ultimate goal $(+N)$ whose attainment will mark the end of striving along the path, because the last goal of the career is fixed at the outset and remains unchanged as a function of success in moving toward it. On the other hand, an open path is one where the individual may initially have a final or ultimate goal, but an immediate success suggests one or more new goals that add on to the end of the path so that the initial "final goal" becomes just another goal along the path whose length has now remained the same or even increased. The implications of this open path for esteem-income are seen in Figures 1 through 4, which show the closed career path in the early stage (Figure 2), and then after several successes have moved the individual to the middle stage of the closed career (Figure 1) and the open career (Figure 4). Note that as in the closed path, both the retrospected past and the anticipated future can contribute to esteem-income in the open path. But there has been no decrease in "becoming" for the open path as "having been" increases, as is the case with the closed path. In the open path the individual can build up a source of positive esteem-income as a function of past successes along the path while still retaining the initial impetus for "becoming" as a consequence of new additional goals that continually become apparent as a function of successful immediate striving. In fact, so long as the path remains open—that is, so long as new goals become apparent as a function of continued immediate success—there will be no "late" or "final" stage of the career because the individual does not ap-

Figure 4. Open career.

Open Path

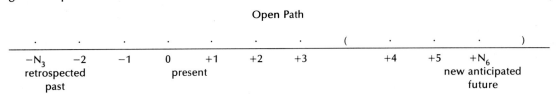

$-N_3$ -2 -1 0 $+1$ $+2$ $+3$ $+4$ $+5$ $+N_6$

retrospected past   present   new anticipated future

proach an ultimate or final goal. In an open path the "final" goal does not exist as a fixed target, whose attainment would signal the end of "becoming" in this career. Thus the open path has extremely important implications for life striving because it provides a means of understanding the difference between individuals who remain psychologically young through continued "becoming" and those who become psychologically old through exclusive dependence upon "having been" to feel good about themselves.

The distinction between open and closed careers provides a powerful tool for the analysis of the apparently paradoxical situation where relatively successful individuals, who would be expected to be satisfied and "fulfilled" as a function of their success, are in fact restless, bored, uninterested, and "lost" at the pinnacle of their careers. First, esteem-income from "becoming" is lost as a function of success in the closed career. In fact, the future sense of self is lost upon attainment of the final goal of the closed career path. The individual no longer knows "who I am becoming." This precipitates an "identity-crisis" (Erickson, 1963) since the individual has previously (in this career path) seen himself primarily as "becoming." We expect that the individual who has been striving successfully along a closed contingent path begins to notice the loss of attractiveness of the final goal only gradually, as each success slightly diminishes its anticipated esteem-income. But the impact of this loss becomes strikingly apparent after successful attainment of the final goal itself, for now there is literally "nothing to look forward to" in the career, and while the loss of value is a gradual process, no longer having a future goal at all is seen and experienced as qualitatively different. The individual wakes up one morning to find he has no reason to continue to pursue the career.

On the other hand, the individual faced with the open path never loses the anticipation of "becoming" because there is always a new sense of self to be attained as a function of the ever-changing final goal of the career. Renewed esteem-income can come to be anticipated and loss of the future sense of self

avoided, while at the same time the backlog of past successes builds a source of positive "having been" and a positive sense of "being" as is the case for the closed career. If the "cake" is "becoming" and the attainment of those goals the "eating," then the person in an open career path "can have his cake and eat it, too," whereas the person in a closed career path cannot. For in closed careers, becoming turns to having been, whereas in the open path becoming produces having been, while still remaining becoming.

Note also that success in a closed path increasingly ties the individual to his past as a summary means of self-identity and feeling good about himself, whereas success in an open path provides a continued link between the individual's past, present, and future senses of self as the means for self-identity and esteem-income.

Interaction of Open and Closed Careers

In the real world it is rare to find an individual whose entire life is characterized as career striving along an open path in any of the substantive identities people usually have. More often we expect to find a path remaining open for some period of time, after which either a change in the impact of some dominant situational (path) feature of their career or the impact of some internal change, usually the failure to use success as a signal for continued upward evaluation of competences, produces a change in the effect of success on the perceived new opportunities for continued striving along that career path. That is, sooner or later, we expect open paths to become closed paths, either because the world imposes some final or ultimate goal that was not initially perceived at which time the new final goal of the previously open path becomes the actual final goal of the now closed contingent path. When immediate success fails to provide for the usual new possibilities, the open path becomes closed and a reduction in "becoming" sets in.

It is also possible that a closed path can become open. Thus, while early successes might not suggest new possibilities to add on to the path, later successes might begin to, so that the closed path becomes open. Again, the apparent length of path will interact with the perception of a final goal of the path to determine whether the path will function as open or closed.

The implications of the above are that the distinction between open and closed paths, while critical for an understanding of adult personality functioning, should not be taken as fixed for a given individual since an open path can become closed and a closed path can become open. However, if and when these changes occur we can predict their effects. Such changes are believed to be critically important in adult personality functioning.

Maintaining vs. Attaining as Determinants of Immediate Action

One of the important new orientations to grow out of the extension of theory presented here is the re-emphasis on the inter-relationship between action in the real world to attain future success, and reorganization of the cognitive field, the maintenance of the values of past success (cf. Lewin, 1938), as alternative means of insuring continued esteem-income. These provide for different purposes in adult life. At the beginning of career striving, attainment of goals through action perceived to be instrumental to their attainment will be seen by the individual as the primary means of obtaining esteem-income. Expectancy × Value Theory of Action as previously defined, will predict best. At the end of career striving, with becoming no longer a possibility, and being limited to evaluation of abilities that cannot be further utilized because there are no future accomplishments to which they can be applied, the individual is left with retrospection about past successes and maintaining their value as the primary means of obtaining esteem-income. Theories addressed to such cognitive work will predict best, and Expectancy × Value Theory needs to be extended to take such factors into account. In middle career striving, anticipation of future goal attainment, retrospection about past goal attainment, and evaluation of present levels of prerequisite abilities (respectively, becoming, having been, and being) will all be seen as contributing to feeling good about oneself in this career. Theory concerned with both *attaining* and *maintaining*, as well as *evaluating* competence through seeking information and making attributions to various causes of success, will be relevant, but if used alone each will be limited in its success because all three kinds of theory are necessary since all three time-linked processes are expected to be occurring at once. In fact, we need theory that considers the interrelationships between orientations toward the future (attaining), the past (maintaining), and the present (evaluating), something that until now has been missing because of the failure to recognize that the dominant theories of motivation/action in psychology have dealt with different aspects of the time-linked behavioral situation. Expectancy-value theory has been primarily concerned with "becoming." Cognitive consistency theory and theories of psychological defenses have been concerned primarily with "having been." Trait theories of personality, self-attribution theory, and information-seeking theory are concerned primarily with "being."

We expect that time-linked sources of esteem-income will produce quite different reactions to a situation where the individual is challenged to justify feeling good about himself as a function of a particular career, either by himself or by others. We expect that in the beginning of striving the individual will take the attitude that, "if I work hard to fulfill those prerequisites that will allow me to move on toward the next steps of the career path, I can justifiably feel good about myself because I will be becoming who I want to become." There is little concern for psychological defensiveness that might involve cognitive distortion in order to maintain esteem-income from past successes because there are none to "defend." The individual is open to information concerning "How I am doing" to meet the stated prerequisites, and is open to both positive and negative feedback that might be useful in attainment of immediate success and therefore earning the opportunity to continue to "become." However, the individual at the end of striving in a closed contingent path is predicted, in comparison to the individual at the beginning of striving in a closed contingent path, to be more motivated to use psychological defenses and cognitive work to insure continued positive valuation of his past successes in order to feel good about himself. This individual will be more likely to "defend his record of past accomplishments." At this time this is the only way the individual can continue to feel good about himself. There is no possibility for further accomplishment, so the individual believes, because all goals have been attained. Now the task is maintenance of the "historical record," the set of accomplishments, particularly if others were to attack that record. Such an "attack" might try to belittle the record by indicating that past successes were trivially easy (reducing difficulty value if believed); that past successes had little to do with later opportunities—the person would have gotten the chance even if they had failed (reducing instrumental value); or that times have changed and the current generation does not value such kinds of accomplishment (reducing cultural value). Such defensive reactions that are expected will be to protect past success from losing its ability to provide esteem-income. The primary goal is to feel good about oneself, however that can be brought about.

As Lewin (1938) implied with regard to the issue of locomotion versus cognitive reorganization, both attaining goals that have value, or maintaining the values of previously attained goals, can function for the individual to provide esteem-income. We explicitly predict that action will be preferred to cognitive work so long as further action is possible, so that the possibility of a defensive reaction will be smallest in early careers, moderate in middle careers, and greatest in late careers, when these careers are perceived as closed. It follows that if a closed career becomes an open one, defensiveness should decrease, and the decrease should be proportionate to the extent of increase in "becoming."

For individuals in the middle of careers of a closed contingent path, we expect some defensiveness, but since the past record can be justified by immediate success and the use of already-acquired skills, we expect this to be limited. The individual can act to attain future success. Since in our society the cultural value of "becoming" is expected to be greater for the majority of individuals than that for "having been," striving to attain valued future goals is expected to provide greater esteem-income. Put another way, in Western culture most individuals learn that others value the forward-looking, open stance with its prospects for continued advancement more than the closed stance, with its necessity for argumentation to defend the status quo. Various measures of openness versus closedness to new information, negative information, and use of psychological strategies of defense to distort reality should yield a consistent picture indicating greater openness for new information, negative information, and lack of defensiveness, for the individual who is primarily "becoming" as described here. Change from the end of a closed contingent path to a new contingent path, or change of a closed to an open contingent path, should produce greater openness for new information, for negative information, and less defensive reaction to maintain values of past successes.

General Implications

(1) Children are less motivated than adults. Because the self-system has not as yet emerged for substantive activity in the majority of children, there is less total motivation sustaining activity. This means that positively motivated children are, in general, less willing to engage in music-related activity, engage in it with less enthusiasm, and persist for a shorter time before going on to something else, than a person for whom the self-system has emerged for music-related activity, and for a child who had a self-identity tied to music and therefore is said to be engaged in a psychological career involving music.

(2) Younger people tend to be future-oriented; older people tend to be past-oriented. Because there are no past steps in the initial stages of striving, there is little or no value to be obtained from the past. Younger people tend more often to be starting out on contin-

341

gent paths involving music-related activity. They are primarily oriented to obtaining positive value from long-term future goals rather than maintaining the value of long-term past goals. On the other hand, older people are more likely to have reached the final stages of striving along a closed contingent path, and are more likely to face a closed than open contingent path. They are primarily oriented to obtaining positive value from the long-term past goals than attaining the values associated with long-term future goal attainment.

(3) Negatively motivated individuals are, paradoxically, less inhibited with self-identity not at stake and with value associated only with the immediate present. Because the self-system increases total motivation, and because motivation increases are negative for an individual who has the motive not to engage in the substantive activity in question stronger than the motive to engage in that activity, additional sources of motivation from the self-system tend to increase total inhibition, even if they also add positive motivation as well. Thus there is greater resistance to engaging in that activity, less vigorous action if the resistance is overcome and the activity is engaged in, and it is easier to interrupt with an attractive alternative activity; while engaging in the activity, there is greater anxiety, worry, apprehension, and dread of negative consequences that might result when the self-system is aroused.

(4) Open career paths arouse more motivation than closed career paths. Because new, additional sources of motivation are continually anticipated in an open contingent path, greater positive and negative motivation influence immediate activity in the open path. Difficulty and instrumental value decrease as one approaches the final goal of a closed contingent path. Because there are fewer steps, there are fewer opportunities to strive for, as the individual successfully moves through a contingent path. And because there are fewer "gates" to negotiate, total probability of attaining the final goal decreases. Thus continued success reduces both instrumental and difficulty value in a closed contingent path.

342

(5) Identity-crises are more likely when the following conditions are met: (a) an individual is positively motivated for the activity in question, (b) initially, they believe themselves faced with a closed contingent path having a clear-cut final goal, (c) the path arouses the self-system, so that striving to attain the final goal involves "becoming" the kind of person defined by the self-image associated with attainment of the final goal, (d) the individual succeeds at each step along the contingent path so that they move closer and closer to the final goal, until the final goal is attained. At this point the individual no longer knows who he or she is striving to become and experiences a loss of future sense of self and an identity-crisis.

(6) Identity-crises are avoided and positive motivation sustained for an open contingent career, where new possibilities for future accomplishment are anticipated or discovered as a function of more immediate successful goal attainment. Here the individual continues to build a backlog of past sources of positive value without losing future sources of positive value. Esteem-income and psychological morale, as well as enthusiasm, interest, immediate intensity, and long-term accomplishment, are expected to be greatest for positively motivated individuals faced with open contingent psychological careers, where both the behavioral and self-systems continue to provide renewed sources of anticipated positive self-esteem.

**Implications of the
Theory for Music-Related Careers**
Since one of the important implications of the present theory is that different kinds of individuals will act quite differently when faced with different stages of career striving, we cannot make general statements about all music-related careers. However, there are particular kinds of individual/career interactions that are of great interest.

Of greatest interest because of its non-intuitiveness concerns the positively motivated individual who has attained his initial career goals so that he or she no longer perceives himself faced with a contingent occupational/educational career path in music. He has attained a position as a teacher, has been granted tenure or perceives other guaranteed job security, and has no further professional goals concerning advancement and promotion. For this individual, in particular, sources of positive instrumental value no longer exist from the anticipated future. We strongly suspect that this individual is going through or has already faced an identity-crisis caused by the lack of motivational impetus from the future, which previously provided interest and excitement in anticipation of attaining distant future goals and a sense of self but which now no longer exist because no future goals are perceived as relevant to immediate activity. This individual experiences a net drop in positive impetus for immediate activity, and a net loss of esteem-income, when he thinks about the future. He is indifferent to this present teaching activity. While he is "turned on" by intrinsic and difficulty value of immediate activity, and can get excited and interested in such activity, the general feeling is that "something is missing" from the activities routinely engaged in on a day-to-day basis that used to be there, and both intensity and duration of career-related activity has dropped substantially.

We believe that this is a common motivational problem faced by teachers in general, and therefore by music teachers, once they perceive that contingent future striving is ended and that future advancement is limited. However, since the *intrinsic value* of music-related activity is probably higher than many other kinds of education-related activity, we suspect that the total drop in interest and enthusiasm may be much less than in other fields. This becomes an interesting question for research. Clearly, for those music educators who are able to obtain substantial intrinsic and difficulty value from their daily teaching activities, the effects of closed path striving will be minimized and there will be less chance of apathy, indifference, and an identity-crisis. But the question must be raised; does the environment of the music educator provide the opportunity to obtain intrinsic and difficulty value? What

are the opportunities to get "turned on by music?" What are the challenges of teaching that are provided by the curriculum or the students? If the interaction with teaching is seen as "easy as pie" so that the chances of success are virtually assured, then little difficulty value and positive motivation can be obtained from these activities. Put another way, can the teacher set challenging personal goals that will produce a source of difficulty value and therefore heighten interest and enthusiasm in immediate activity that no longer has long-term future implications for that teacher's career? If he or she cannot, we find the individual confronted with a job situation where "the love of music" is the only positive feature of immediate activity, assuming the relatively small impact of extrinsic and cultural value in music education. While the reader might say "that is great—only the relevant factor is contributing to why I do what I do"—the implication is that such a person will personally experience a drop in perceived self-worth in comparison to when they were striving to attain their career goals and being turned on by the challenge of teaching.

We do not want to judge whether it is good or bad for individuals to be motivated only by intrinsic factors associated with their professional activity. However, if we are correct in our analysis, the effect of professional goal attainment on the individual music teacher's drop in psychological morale is one that is probably not anticipated by this person, nor understood in terms of its causes, and hence when the individual is faced with it there is often the feeling of "aloneness in crisis" that compounds what is often experienced as a profound career disappointment.

For the positively motivated individual, career goals that are kept open rather than fixed, and contingent steps that are imposed on career striving, are one way to provide for continued motivational impetus from "becoming." Promotions, advancements, new education for continued certification—all of these newer professional hurdles—can be used to prevent this loss of positive motivation and esteem-income, provided that the individual is positively motivated with re-

343

gard to the nature of the activity in question and is success-oriented. These newer contingent steps are not perceived as threats to job security by these individuals but as opportunities for personal and professional advancement. If we define psychological health as a maximization of positive esteem-income through an integrated psychological career, then such newer hurdles serve to increase psychological health for the positively motivated individual.

If the reader is a positively motivated individual, his intuitive reaction to the above will be "knowing agreement." However, if the reader is not, or is a negatively motivated individual, his intuitive reaction will be "but how about the job pressures that such new goals create? You suggest a new rat race." Of course, this is correct. Our reactions to contingent and noncontingent careers, to open and closed careers, are determined by our resultant motivational disposition, which in turn influences our experiences with the educational process, which influence our current attitudes when trying to determine educational and professional practice as "professionals." Unanimity of experience is not to be expected, and agreement based on experience is a pipe dream that will never be attained—unless individuals of like personality make up the "panel" assessing such proposed changes. The point is that as soon as suggestions for change are made, their impact on individuals who have gone through similar "systems" will differentially influence the attractiveness/repulsiveness of such changes.

The insight to be had from the above analysis is that while the positively motivated individual would welcome a renewal of career striving, the negatively motivated individual will not. For him since these sources of value other than "the love of music" are predominantly negative, his experience has been a lessening of negative motivation upon final attainment of career goals, and to reinstitute new career goals would be equivalent to reinstituting the worry, apprehension, and sometimes dread that were all too real for this person during his earlier career striving. Of course, the individual knows

what is best for himself. He does not want these hurdles, which function as sources of inhibition of immediate activity and feelings of anxiety and negative self-esteem.

When we turn to the impact of the retrospected past on present career behavior, we again find some important differences between positively and negatively motivated individuals. As a function of success, the impact of past outcomes along the career path increases for both individuals. There is an inevitably greater impact of the psychological past as we move from early to middle to late stages of career striving. For the positively motivated individual, retrospection about past successes provides positive esteem-income and a feeling of positive self-worth and identity. As the positive value of the psychological past continues to increase, the sense of self defined in terms of those past successes becomes increasingly important to the individual.

Past vs. Future Values, Attitudes, and Teaching

The analysis in this section goes beyond theory of motivation, beyond available research findings, and beyond previous analyses of motivation and behavior within the context of this theoretical orientation. It is based on the additional assumption that attitudes that people have, and attitudinal behavior or the verbal expression of attitudes, are determined by the value of the source of the attitude in question. Thus a person who derives positive value from anticipated future goal attainment along an open contingent path of their career will have a favorable attitude toward strict standards of good performance and enforcement of prerequisites for promotion and advancement, while an individual who derives negative value from the anticipated future will have a negative attitude toward such practices. In fact, in one unpublished study I conducted, we found that positively motivated students favored "other-evaluation" while negatively motivated students favored "self-evaluation." Also, the implications of this assumption concerning the determinants of "attitudes" are consistent with other implications of this theoretical orientation, and suggest some very important insights about teachers and teacher-behavior based on the notion that attitudes of teachers influence the behavior of their students.

If we assume that attitudes are verbal behaviors that express the sources of expected-value referred to in the theory, then as positively motivated individuals move from early to middle to late stages of successful career striving, they come to be more and more favorably disposed to those procedures, practices, and outcomes that they associate with their own past successes. They are more likely to verbally favor such past practices, defend their functional utility, and act to insure that such practices are maintained for the next generation of individuals who aspire to become professional in that substantive area. So long as the individual is also obtaining anticipated value from future expected sources, the defense of past practice is shared with valuation of future practices that the individual must successfully negotiate, so that exclusive defense of the "status quo" is tempered by the unknown experimentally but cognitively anticipated "curriculum" or "set of opportunities" that are programmed by the individual to lead to his eventual own future success. However, when future goals are attained, and future possibilities become past practice, the weight of favorable attitudes shifts to exclusive valuation of "the way things were for me."

To me the implications of the above analysis of attitudinal responding, coupled with the motivational analysis of career striving, offer a profound insight into the continued discrepancy between successive generations of individuals, and provide a framework for understanding some of the problems inevitably generated between teacher and student.

If the above analysis is correct, we end up deriving that "students" will value practices and procedures that are seen to be consistent with attainment of maximum positive value in the anticipated future—to attainment of the student's own important positively valued future goals. Note that these practices not only have to provide the ground rules

for, and ways to strive to attain, future goals, but they must maximize their positive value and minimize their negative value. On the other hand, teachers will value practices and procedures that are seen to be consistent with maintenance of maximum positive value in their retrospected past—to maintenance of the teacher's own important positively valued past goals.

While the above predictions are clear, they are limited if left unqualified. They refer to students as individuals in the initial stage of career striving, and they refer to teachers as individuals in the final stage of career striving, and would be appropriately modified if a student were in the late stage of career striving and the teacher in the early stage of career striving. Put another way, student becomes teacher and a teacher can again become a student. If the correlation between teacher and late career striving and that between student and early career striving represent the majority case, we can make some general statements about student/teacher attitudes.

Those who bemoan the "deadweight" of tradition in human affairs fail to recognize the inevitability of positive value and favorable attitudes that accrue to one's own successful past. To the extent that older people hold positions of power where they can influence the practices that are to be followed by the next generation, and these individuals are no longer engaged in career striving, we can predict the attitude of "what was good for us is good for them." How many times does the new Ph.D. (i.e., the old student) modify the existing program he has just entered to make it fit the program he or she just successfully completed? While this tendency will be prevalent once an individual goes beyond initial career stages, it will predominate once the individual has successfully completed that career.

Notice that an individual can free himself from the effect of his past successful behavior by conceptualizing present activity as the beginning of a new psychological career; then past activity is seen as irrelevant, and the anticipated future rather than the retrospected past will influence attitudes and behavior.

345

Motivation and Teaching

Usually, when teachers talk about "motivating students," they are referring to the question of how to motivate their students to do what the teacher wants them to do. They do not consider that the scientific problem, "motivation," refers to the reasons why the student acts the way he does, or alternatively, that it refers to the reasons why the teacher acts the way he or she does. In either case, as conceptualized here, the teacher and the student each act to maximize positive expected value or positive esteem-income. Neither acts to maximize the positive expected value of the other, necessarily. If the teacher wishes to create a particular kind of behavior in the student, he or she must recognize that the motivating conditions and the personality dispositions of the student interact to determine whether that act will follow, because its motivational impetus is stronger than any other act in that situation.

When we take the interval viewpoint, we see that the teacher's valuation of a particular outcome is irrelevant to the determinants of student behavior. It is the student's perceived valuation of outcomes of that action, and the probability of attainment of these outcomes, that conceptually induces motivation for action. "Reinforcement value" is a personal construct. Only if we refer to an attempt to change the magnitudes and sources of value of the student, or attempt to turn negative value of the student into positive value, can we hope to induce the teacher-desired action. But change in value is a relatively long process, about which relatively little is understood, much less so than the role of value in inducing action. Thus for the teacher to understand student behavior, and provide conditions that elicit behaviors from the student that are desired by the teacher, the teacher must perceive the relevant sources of value present for the student—the teacher must view the world from the interval point of view of the student. That is, the opportunities for action, their possible outcomes, and the potential for the emergence of a psychological career as (music) student must be understood by the teacher before the teacher can hope to bring about certain desired mo-

346

lar behaviors of the student.

The values of the teacher and the values of the student have no relationship one to another. What provides positive value to the teacher may provide positive or negative value to the student, and vice versa. In order to understand student behavior, we must understand the determinants of behavior as they exist for the student at that time, not as the teacher thinks they should exist.

Values of the Past vs. the Present for Student-Teacher Interactions

If teachers tend to value what they have learned in their evolving careers, while students place little positive value on such learning because of a lack of experience of success with this activity/outcome, then we can expect a relatively permanent discrepancy between student and teacher in their enthusiasm, interest, and willingness to work hard to deal with that particular activity in question. We must recognize that such differences are an inevitable consequence of the differences in stages of career striving between teacher and student when the teacher, in the middle or late stages of striving, presents material that represents activity in the initial stage of student striving. Cultural values and instrumental values are usually positive and strong for the history of a field because its mastery represents past successful activity for the teacher, who in the middle-late stages of a career assumes that everyone shares his or her enthusiasm and appreciation of what, to the student, is material devoid of positive sources of value. If teachers attempt to increase appreciation of such material, they must recognize that only after valuation has increased due to mastery will students' interest increase. If they assume that exposure to that material will inevitably lead to a positive valuation of it, they fail to recognize that magnitudes of values in their own lives changed slowly, as a function of successful movement along a career path involving many years of successful striving. No wonder that there is often a communication gap between teacher and student, a lack of mutual interest in commonly shared activity, even though the intrinsic values of the activity for the student and teacher may be equivalent and positive, and perhaps even strongly positive.

For a teacher to devalue those substantive contents of past activity along their own career by recognizing them as irrelevant for a current generation of students, is for the teacher to be faced with the possible loss of self-esteem and self-identity. It follows that, in general, teachers will act to maintain the values of their past successes, including communication of what they have mastered as having great value for others, and in doing so they act to preserve their own feelings of self-worth and ideas about who they are. This presents a strong resistance to attempts to substitute, modify, or share other, newer music-related activity in the curriculum.

Note that this teacher reaction is predicted only for those who have perceived that they face a closed contingent career path, or who have already attained the final step of their previously perceived closed contingent career path. Thus one of the critical factors in predicting resistance to curriculum change concerns the extent to which the individual teacher perceives himself or herself faced with an open contingent path in his or her career as teacher. If opportunities for new activity are seen to be present, attaining immediate goals is seen as necessary to continue along this path, and one's future self-image is seen as tied to attainment of the future goals of that path. In this way the individual is both motivated to attain the values of future success as well as to maintain the values of past success, and is motivated as much with regard to the future as to the past. New and innovative approaches to be mastered are seen as valuable sources of (future) positive self-esteem, so that a more balanced valuation of both past and "on the frontier" material results.

Cultural Value and Music-Related Activity

There is something different, perhaps even unique, concerning "classical" music-related activity/psychological careers/self-images as opposed to other kinds of careers pursued by individuals today. This concerns the link between the differences in kinds of music and the clear-cut cultural values/self-images that these define for individuals engaged in that activity. Classical, as opposed to jazz, pop, avant-garde, contemporary, electric, computer, twelve-tone, or country-and-western, are but a few of the various terms that evoke widely different amounts of cultural value for a given individual, and for a group of individuals faced with any one of these, and the corresponding self-images that often are tied to these cultural values. Rarely is the impact of the past, for example, so ever-present as when playing and listening to music composed 150 years ago, venerated as being the most positively-valued activity, where entire systems of education are geared to the cultural transmission of positive value of activity completed by individuals having lived five, ten, or twenty generations ago. Rarely are there such widely disparate positive and negative cultural values anticipated concerning products of contemporary music activity. The effects of these differing values, which are often tied to age and aging, potentially provide the greatest single source of difference between student and teacher.

Performance from a Score

Musical performance is one activity where the arousal of difficulty value is an inevitable possibility. The need to reproduce the "correct notes" places musical performance from a score in the arena of achievement-oriented activity. The notions of "good, better, best" apply automatically concerning the reproduction of the correct notes, at the minimum, and often also as applied in terms of more subjective standards of artistic performance. However, even if we leave aside the latter, we are left at the minimum with a circumstance where the music performer is confronted with the achievement-oriented activity of "getting the correct notes," and the arousal of positive and negative achievement motivation would appear to follow in ways analogous to that involving other skill-demanding activity. This has important consequences for the relationship between motivation and music performance, including the role of anxiety, in such situations.

Research on achievement motivation sug-

347

gests that certain individuals are more predisposed than others to become excited and enthusiastic when the prospect of doing well in terms of a standard of good performance is presented to them. Such a success-oriented music student is attracted to and most motivated to learn, when such clear-cut standards of good performance are explicit. We suppose that such students look forward to practicing and performing when they know they will be evaluated according to explicit performance standards; that contingent path arrangements where they know that mastering a technique, section, or score is necessary before moving on to other material further motivates such individuals; and that seeing himself as "becoming a musician" or "good piano player" further motivates that student to practice, mastery, and further accomplishment. For this student, the research evidence clearly suggests that the role of clear-cut standards, contingent path hierarchies, and "becoming a future sense of self" all produce heightened positive involvement, excitement, and interest in the performance, and, if the tasks presented to the learner are sufficiently simple, will produce faster learning, more skillful performance, greater persistence, and greater overall accomplishment. An important qualification here is that the learning tasks be kept relatively simple for each step. When made very complex, positive motivation produces "trying too hard," which interferes with recall, retention, and reproduction of the correct notes, and produces a substantially lowered evaluative performance than would have been attained if less positive motivation were aroused. The prescription for maximally motivating this success-oriented student is: (1) make the standards explicit, (2) set up a contingent path, (3) define the future kind of person successful performance can make him, and then (4) keep each learning task simple. Additional research suggests that help to maximize this positive motivation also includes having the maximum number of achievement steps in the minimum time periods, and having each achievement task be not only simple in construction, but one that the student can see as "easy to accomplish" within that time.

Unfortunately, the research evidence suggests that all of the conditions that produce maximum positive motivation for the success-oriented learner produce maximum inhibition, and the accompanying anxiety for the failure-threatened student. Thus we produce the exact opposite effects if we arrange conditions as above for the student who is predisposed to be more concerned about failing to get the notes right than getting them correct. This is a negatively motivated person in the achievement domain, called the failure-threatened individual. When the prospect of success or failure to "get it right" are aroused, this person focuses on not failing, rather than succeeding. This produces resistance to engaging in such activity. For the negatively motivated student, the prospect of evaluation of performance is presumed to arouse a tendency not to engage in that activity, be it practice, taking the lesson, or performance, and feelings of apprehension are presumed directly proportionate to the magnitude of this behavioral resistance aroused by the prospect of failing to get it right. We presume that all individuals have some predisposition to be "turned on" by the prospect of success and that all individuals have some predisposition to be "turned off" by the prospect of failure, and that the relative strengths of these two dispositions determine the resultant disposition of the individual. The empirical evidence shows that these dispositions, as currently measured, are uncorrelated, so that there are in the general population about twenty-five percent who are clearly "success oriented," dominated by the motive to achieve relative to the motive to avoid failure, about twenty-five percent who are clearly "failure-threatened," dominated by the motive to avoid failure, and a middle fifty percent for whom the two dispositions are about equal so that neither predominates. When the student is failure-threatened, then the optimal strategy to minimize negative motivation is to minimize evaluation eliminate contingent steps, fail to emphasize future self-identity tied to the activity in question, and to emphasize extrinsic and cultural positive values as means of feeling good about performance.

348

The question is always asked, "Can't we turn failure-threatened students into success-oriented ones?" For extreme cases, my answer would be "no," and that it would be much better to arrange the conditions of learning to either maximize positive motivation of the success-oriented student, or minimize negative motivation of the failure-threatened student.

How can these observations be translated into action by the music teacher not wishing to become a psychological testing service for her students? Our research shows that affective reactions of interest, excitement, and enthusiasm on the positive side, and worry, uptightness, nervousness, and anxiety, on the negative side, when they predominate in a particular "important" skill-demanding situation, give a very good clue as to the extreme cases of "success-oriented" and "failure-threatened" personality dispositions. Armed with this information, the teacher can modify his manner of presentation of materials when one or the other reaction predominates in his student. For example, a student who shows enthusiasm in just "pittering around" the notes, playing the melody of a song, apparently unconcerned about "whether the particular notes are correct," but who, when confronted with the demand "to get the notes right so we can move on to the next lesson," loses enthusiasm and suddenly appears quite inhibited and anxious, should be on subsequent occasions treated just as initially—as though "getting the right notes" is unimportant. The failure-threatened student *can* perform well, in fact as well or better than his or her success-oriented counterpart, according to our research on other skill-demanding activity, and can learn to the same criterion in the same amount of time—but not when the same conditions of explicit evaluation are imposed on the learning/performance situation. And he or she pays the personal price of negative emotional reaction, and tends to drop out at the earliest possible time, if continually exposed to such evaluative standards.

It should be obvious that the failure-threatened student will be at a distinct disadvantage if and when public performance that demands "getting the right notes" becomes a requirement in his or her training. This is the student who experiences the amount of "stage fright" that is sometimes observed in otherwise talented performers. While even the most positively motivated individual becomes more nervous for an important performance than in practice, the effect for the failure-threatened individual expected to give a solo performance is devastating—lapses of memory, weakness of limbs, incorrect notes, paralysis of movement. In our conception these are not caused by being afraid, but rather both fear and poor performance result from the behavior resistance aroused by this person's automatic predisposition to be more concerned about failure than about success. Such an extreme reaction should be a good indication for counselling against a solo performance career; group performance is probably much less inhibiting.

Listening to Music

The musicologist, music critic, and concert-goer are several of the self-images/activities that characterize the psychological careers of music listener. Conceptualized this way, listening to music is an activity like any other human activity. When large sources of positive motivation are aroused for it, and self-images defined by the outcomes of the activity, then music listening becomes a psychological career, whether it be a leisure career or professional career. More frequently, however, the self-system is not involved since for the average music listener large extrinsic and cultural values are not seen as resulting from listening to music. The pleasure associated with listening to music for these individuals is here conceptualized as "intrinsic" value and, by itself, is rarely large enough to provide a valuable means of self-identity—although this certainly can be the case for a musician or conscientious concert-goer. Thus while listening to music as background to many other activities is a very common activity, it is sustained by relatively small amounts of positive motivation. As the number and magnitude of sources of value increase, involvement in music listening is

349

predicted to increase, so that, like other human activity, persistence of music listening is expected to be greatest for individuals positively motivated by the substantive music in question who see themselves defined in terms of the outcomes of their music listening activity.

Imposition of standards of good, better, and best music listening behavior, including discrimination of the instruments of the orchestra, the ability to follow polyphonic music lines, etc., define degrees of difficulty value for the music listener. Individual cultural values concerning the kind of music that is most appreciated are sometimes exceedingly strong.

Note that the imposition of criteria having nothing to do with the way the notes sound (music structure, ensemble composition, and so on) often take on important roles in defining individual cultural value for music listening and appreciation. Often it is the case that reading the musical score and the musicologist's notes can provide almost as much positive value as the additional component of hearing the sounds produced. I think this more than anything else separates the formally trained musician from his lay counterpart; these additional academic and intellectual criteria define additional sources of value. Again, I do not wish to impose my own cultural valuation upon this; I merely wish to note it, particularly in light of the fact that in such cases, intrinsic value plays a relatively small role in contributing value. I think professional musicians and music educators, musicologists and music critics, tend to not realize the relatively large contribution of sources of motivation for their music-related activities that are not derived from intrinsic value, but rather are derivable from their formal training and its associated sources of value for music. This tends to sometimes create a gulf between the professionally trained musician and his lay counterpart concerning listening to music, particularly when standards of composition are relevant to the musician but not the lay listener. The two activities are experienced quite differently, if I am correct; for the professional, many sources of value are aroused,

often involving self-identity, so that the intensity and positive affect of the activity of listening to music is quite substantial, while for the casual lay music listener, it is rarer for such enthusiasm and interest to reach such magnitudes. I suspect that part of the goal of music educators and teachers is to impose/teach their own sources of value on the young music listener so that he or she will come to appreciate the particular musical performance form.

Concluding Remarks

Motivational factors defined as the source of positive and negative value are not the only factors determining worth to the individual of an activity and its outcome: sometimes they are not even the most important factors. However, the systematic conceptualization of sources of value as presented here allows for insights into human activity in addition to, or sometimes instead of, other ways of defining worth in human activity. In particular, time-linked sources of value that change as a function of stages of career striving due to success in attaining goals and self-linked sources of value that define "who I am" in terms of the outcomes of activity, are useful ways to view some of the determinants and consequences of the fact that some activity is perceived by the individuals engaged in it to be much more "important" than others. We believe that the greater the value involved in the outcomes of activity, the greater its perceived importance to the actor. Thus we have the conceptual tools to understand the reason why activity/outcomes are seen as important as sources and magnitudes of value increase. My assumption has been that the importance of music-related activity to the individual can be conceptualized as being influenced by the same sources of value that influence any other human activity. If this assumption is correct, then my goal of providing insights into the motivational determinants of music-related activity will have been attained.

Note. For the sake of continuity of exposition I have omitted most of the usual internal references. However, I would like here to indicate that many of the ideas that are integrated into the theory of adult personality functioning and change that is presented have been adapted from the work of others: information value (Feather, 1967); intrinsic value (Deci, 1975); difficulty value (Atkinson, 1957); extrinsic value (Atkinson and Feather, 1966); self-esteem (Rogers, 1959; Maslow, 1954). Other concepts, such as contingent paths, open and closed paths, instrumental value as earning the opportunity to continue, the psychological career as opportunities for self-identity, time-linked sources of value, the distinction between the self- and behavioral systems, and consideration of stages of career striving, are based on earlier work of the author (Raynor, 1969, 1974a, 1974b, 1978, in press). A fuller treatment of this theory, its development and implications, can be found in Raynor and Entin (in press).

References

Atkinson, J. W. Motivational determinants of risk-taking behavior. *Psychological Review*, 1957, *64*, 359–372.

Atkinson, J. W., and N. T. Feather. *A theory of achievement motivation*. New York: John Wiley & Sons, 1966.

Deci, E. L. *Intrinsic motivation*. New York: Plenum Press, 1975.

Erickson, E. *Childhood and society*. New York: Norton, 1963.

Feather, N. T. An expectancy-value model of information-seeking behavior. *Psychological Review*, 1967, *74*, 342–360.

Lewin, K. *Conceptual representation and measurement of psychological forces*. Durham, North Carolina: Duke University Press, 1938.

Maslow, A. H. *Motivation and personality*. New York: Harper and Row, 1954.

Raynor, J. O. Future orientation and motivation of immediate activity: An elaboration of the theory of achievment motivation. *Psychological Review*, 1969, 76, 606–610.

_____. Future orientation in the study of achievement motivation. In J. W. Atkinson and J. O. Raynor (Eds.), *Motivation and achievement*. Washington, D.C.: Hemisphere Publishing Corp., 1974. (a)

_____. Motivation and career striving. In J. W. Atkinson and J. O. Raynor (Eds.), *Motivation and achievement*. Washington, D.C.: Hemisphere Publishing Corp., 1974. (b)

_____. Addenda. In J. W. Atkinson and J. O. Raynor (Eds.), *Personality, motivation, and achievement*. Washington, D.C.: Hemisphere Publishing Corp., 1978.

_____. Motivation and aging: A theory of adult personality functioning and change. In J. O. Raynor and E. E. Entin (Eds.), *Motivation, career striving, and aging*. Washington, D.C.: Hemisphere Publishing Corp., in press.

Raynor, J. O., and E. E. Entin. *Motivation, career striving, and aging*. Washington, D.C.: Hemisphere Publishing Corp., in press.

Rogers, C. R. A theory of therapy, personality and interpersonal relationships, as developed in the client-centered framework. In S. Koch (Ed.), *Psychology: A study of a science, Vol. 3*. New York: McGraw-Hill, 1959.

Response

Malcolm J. Tait

When I first began to read Joel Raynor's paper, I felt a twinge of not knowing what he was saying, and of not being sure of what I might say as a result. I suppose my response was typically "failure-threatened," but then I read near the bottom of the first page, "individuals involved in music-related behaviors share most of the properties of individuals involved in other substantive careers." This made me feel better! I was one of the gang; I guess I felt I could cope and I was also fascinated to know how a psychologist would describe behaviors that have been intimate to me for many years. I need not have worried. The paper has proved delightful with significant insights not only into music behaviors, but also into mid-life crises—an unexpected bonus! I was looking for some juicy case histories predicated on the lives of Beethoven or Wagner or even Mrs. Tempo, the piano teacher, but this was all left to my imagination.

In any event it is good to know we are not appreciably different from other career-oriented individuals. We are influenced by expectancies of positive outcomes or goals as well as negative outcomes or threats. We move along our career paths in a closed or open fashion and regardless of open or closed paths, we expect the resulting behaviors to shape our self-image. Indeed, it is suggested that our self-images are shaped into possibly four career paths, namely, earning a living, sex role, family role, and vocational role.

A number of values may impinge and influence the career direction; these values are characterized as intrinsic, difficulty, instrumental, extrinsic, and cultural. A striving factor moves us toward a sense of accomplishment in a chosen path. That striving factor is directly related to our individual perception of self in relation to the tasks and to the degrees of success or failure we anticipate in those tasks. Furthermore, our track record has a profound influence on immediate and future striving.

An open path career is characterized by a capacity for new goal generation and an expanding self-identify, whereas a closed career path is represented by a paucity of goals and a confining or static image of self. It is reasonable to assume that most careers consist of both closed and open paths from time to time. We need a theory or model to bring together the career striving paths in ways which attempt to balance the present self-identity with the past and with the future images.

Career striving in children tends to be minimal because, says Raynor, the self-image is as yet ill-defined; motivation is consequently low level and of short duration. Self-image is likely to develop where open career paths are encouraged. This will assist motivational thrust. I wonder if too open a path too soon might inhibit a failure-threatened student. On the other hand a young

success-oriented student may be turned off if the path is too closed. One wonders again if there are "critical times" here.

In terms of a teacher, there sometimes seems to be a point of depletion in his or her psychological career path when past activities, values, or experiences have a negative outcome on a contingent and closed path; that awful feeling we have all had from time to time when we imagine we are sacrificing our art for the sake of the kids, which might be termed the "pearls-before-swine" syndrome. At these times how pleasant it would be to experience a class of junior high school students who are in Raynor's terms psychologically old or at least middle-aged.

Raynor makes the important point that our attitudes as teachers are influenced by those values that have assisted in the growth of our own self-esteem. This, he argues, can be quite limiting to our students who must themselves be sufficiently exposed or free to find their own identities. In Raynor's words, "The teacher must view the world from the internal point of view of the student." The teacher has to understand the behavioral determinants of the student if he wishes to influence the student's motivation. In order for this to happen, it is clear the teacher must continue to grow with his students. The role function must be flexible and developmental.

The closed/open concept is also used by Carl Rogers (1969) in a similar context.

> When teacher behaviors tend to be open; clarifying, stimulating, accepting, facilitating, the student responses tend to be productive, discovering, exploring, experimenting, synthesizing and deriving implications. When teacher behaviors tend to be closed; judging, directing, reproving, ignoring, probing, or priming, the student responses tend to be reproductive, parroting, guessing, acquiescing, reproducing facts and reasoning from given or remembered data.

The combination of so-called closed teaching behaviors and failure-threatened students is not difficult to imagine and, I suspect, not difficult to document. Can we just as readily imagine and document open

352

teacher behaviors and success-oriented students? I think if we can, we certainly should for these are the models are we urgently need. A bank of protocols illustrating a variety of teaching styles to meet the variety of teaching goals with a variety of students is, I believe, a major priority for our profession.

It would be most helpful to know how the educative and aesthetic process is influenced when a primarily affective strategy is applied to a psychomotor skill, or how a thinking strategy is applied to an affective response, but we do not have this kind of information. More frequently it seems a teacher will, for one reason or another, adopt a particular series of strategies within a style and then maybe reinforce the learning with strategies in another style. So that if the focus is on psychomotor skill development, modelling may be involved in which the teacher actually demonstrates, but this may also be reinforced by verbal questioning and statements, metaphoric imagery and nonverbal gesture and these styles will also, it is hoped, assist cognitive and affective growth.

Raynor forces us to ask this question: How can be build self-esteem through music education? A question that is implicit in the writings of Gaston and Maslow but has somehow been lost in the whirl and swirl of curriculum reform in the last decade. I believe the answer must have something to do with increasing opportunities for self-investment along with opportunities for success. And this must surely be of crucial importance in early life. We might examine the nature of this self-investment and the rewards it might carry. It could be argued, for instance, that composition requires a greater degree of self-investment than performance, and performance requires more than listening. If so, the approach advocated by Schaefer, Self, Aston and Paynter, and others is likely to lead to more self-investment than imitative performance or analytic listening. I am assuming rightly or wrongly that the growth of self-identity is likely to be encouraged rather than impeded by self-investment.

Finally, in music education we have three enormously complex and interrelated variables; namely, the music, the student, and the teacher. Other psychologists and musicians have focused on the music, the phenomena. Clearly there is unlimited scope for generative ideas whether they be in the form of speculation or developed to the point of systematic and refined research. Raynor's paper is full of generative ideas and I am confident we will all take from it food for thought and action. In closing, I would like to ask Professor Raynor if he feels the concept of self-investment is viable within his terms of reference and could it assist in the development of musical self-esteem?

References

Bronowski, J. *The visionary eye.* Cambridge, Massachusetts: MIT Press, 1978.

Rogers, C. R. *Freedom to learn.* Columbus, Ohio: Charles E. Merrill Publishing Co., 1969.

Encounters: The American Child's Meeting with Music

William Kessen

And therefore our fathers admitted music into education, not on the ground either of its necessity or utility, for it is not necessary, nor indeed useful in the same manner as reading and writing, which are useful in money-making . . ., nor like drawing, useful for a more correct judgment of the works of artists, nor again like gymnastic, which gives health and strength; for neither of these is to be gained from music. (Aristotle, *Politics*)

As neither the enjoyment nor the capacity of producing musical notes are faculties of the

353

least use to man in reference to his daily habits of life, they must be ranked among the most mysterious with which he is endowed. (Darwin, *The Descent of Man . . .*)

Few human activities have provoked both Aristotle and Darwin to puzzlement; music may be alone in having called forth nonsense from two of mankind's finest minds. Aristotle, after weighing the possibility that music makes "care to cease," like sleep and drinking, decided that music was worth teaching young men because it would provide for them, in their later years, "intellectual enjoyment in leisure." Darwin, with less hesitation, assigned music to primordial rutting rituals.

> The impassioned orator, bard, or musician, when with his varied tones and cadences he excites the strongest emotions in his hearers, little suspects that he uses the same means by which his half-human ancestors long ago aroused each other's ardent passions, during their courtship and rivalry. (Darwin)

I remind you of our forebears' opinions of music for two practical reasons—first, the mystery that Aristotle and Darwin saw persists to our time and it is the continuing mystery that justifies our attempt to understand the connections between psychology and music; second, their headshaking represents the most lasting single statement of the puzzle, a question that can be heard from the Academy to Board of Education debates about the budget: "What is music for?"

The question is arrogantly grand and not likely, after two millenia of debate, to find its answer on a summer afternoon in Ann Arbor. But I claim the rights and irresponsibilities of the last in a line of twelve—whether as Judas or as John, I leave to you—to continue our conversation by suggesting three new chapters for our book on psychology and music education, chapters that have more to do with context and culture than with the elegant queries and clean observations that you have grown used to during the Symposium. First, I will jog through the history of Western musical education in search of evidence for the answer American culture has given to

our conundrum about the utility and necessity of music; as tail to that very small and under-nourished dog, I will mention the contribution of technical psychology to the larger cultural evaluation. The second chapter that I will point to, in the hope of its future completion, has as hero James Mark Baldwin. In his cumbersome way, Baldwin answered the questions of Aristotle and Darwin with a proposal that has profound implications for the psychology of music and for music education. Finally, I will try to wed culture and Baldwin in several rudimentary accounts of the American child's encounters with music—those moments or, more often, those epochs in which the child is informed about the values of music by his social and cultural surround.

The Relocation of Music

Musicians and music educators have long recognized several major simplicities in the history of music instruction that we psychologists need to be told about. For all his doubts, Aristotle finally decided that only the flute and professional competence were fatal to serious education, and throughout Athenian history the citharist remained on an equal basis with the grammarian and the paedotribe. Also, music instruction remained essential to the education of the Roman wellborn and, when formal studies were revived in medieval times, music, in its full proper seventh, was still a required course. Later on, the same forces of religious reform that produced a saltatory shift in literacy seem also to have extended musical competence; the church hymn came into a prominence that it maintained, especially for Americans, until the day before yesterday. The classical and the Christian justifications for musical instruction brought forth, in turn, a prepared and participating audience for the gradual emergence of secular art music. Ariès gives my almost parodic summary a vivid particularity.

> We no longer have any idea of the place which music, singing and dancing used to occupy in everyday life. [Thomas Morley describes, in 1597, his discomfiture when dining out.] 'But

supper being ended, and music books, according to custom, being brought to the table, the mistress of the house presented me with a part, earnestly requesting me to sing: but when, after many excuses, I protested unfeignedly that I could not, everyone began to wonder; yes, some whispered to others, demanding how I was brought up! (Ariès, 1962, p. 79)

The abstract statement and the specific anecdote, taken as representative of a rich literature on the cultural history of music, serve our present interests in understanding the relation between music education and psychology by revealing some continuities with our experience of music today and, more significant for my later arguments, two major discontinuities. Among the continuities, one deserves far more attention from our Symposium than we can provide—the apparently persistent tripartite diversion into people who perform folk or street or work music, people who perform music "professionally," and the elite, the dilettanti, the "musically literate" who know and appreciate art music. The historical uniformity warrants close attention on a number of counts, the most important is the ambiguity both psychologists and music educators display about which of the three groups we take as our reference when we talk about the psychology of music.

But let me speak briefly of the major discontinuities across time that bears on our joint task—the apparent changes in the cultural location of music and in the more narrowly defined social location of music. The Athenian scholar may not have liked playing the flute and Thomas Morley's entrance into a singing career may have been painful for all, but there was an explicit and widely shared notion in the society about where and when and by whom music would be performed and about how and when and to whom musical education would be delivered. I do not refer here to stability of teaching procedures or musical materials across cultures; rather, I call your attention to the principle that, whatever the variation in particular musical practices of a culture, those practices are governed by a set of expectations, rewards, and sanctions that are communicated to all members of the group. In short, music has a cultural place, a location, in every society. The burden on my present argument, familiar enough to the music educators who fight for another trombone, is that the cultural location of music in American culture has changed drastically over the last century and in an accelerated fashion over the last fifty years. We will not understand what American children learn about music in the classroom or in the conservatory until we have a better hold on the nature and direction of these larger changes in the society they inhabit.

Because the older traditions look simpler and clearer, at least in hindsight, and because so many expectations and sanctions in modern society are not fully explicit, it is tempting to conclude that music and music education have no specific location in American society, that we are in disarray. This conclusion seems to me unwarranted; the full story of the cultural relocation of music can only be told after close empirical study but some rough markers exist. Music is no longer, or is less often, an essential participatory aspect of religious occasions. Music is no longer a usual part of work rhythms. How many secretaries, assembly-line workers, and corporate executives sing on the job? Perhaps closest to the core of American life is the fact that music is not part of the educational gate-keeping system. You cannot be kept back in school for flunking third-grade music and you can top the SATs without knowing *do*, Donovan, or Debussy. And, withal, more music of more variety is played in the United States with more technical competence for more people than ever before in history. Steiner (1971) has remarked,

If we so choose, we can put on Opus 131 while eating the breakfast cereal. We can play the *St. Matthew Passion* any hour or day of the week. Again, the effects are ambiguous: there can be an unprecedented intimacy, but also a devaluation (*désacralization*). A Muzak of the sublime envelops us.

It is not my intention, nor is it within my ability, to examine closely the many aspects of the changing cultural location of music in American life; I want to assert, without proper defense, only that cultural expectations and sanctions may be of limited consequence to the child's musical *competence*, but that they are of paramount importance to his *performance*.

One narrower aspect of cultural change bears intimately on the developmental psychology of music—what I called earlier the social location of music. Before the twentieth century (and in many settings still) music was both active and interactive. Singing, picking, blowing, or hitting, music usually was defined by doing something and doing the something with other people. Music was a participatory social action. As Steiner, among others, has noted, only in our own time has it become possible to encounter all human music alone with radio or phonograph; only now is it possible, thanks to headphones, to use music to shut out other human beings; only nowadays does music appear (in elevators, restaurants, dentists' offices) with no contingent relation to anything we do. We cannot yet assess the persistent effects of music received in isolation, but developmental theories without exception require that inactive and nonsocial experience have consequences different from active and interactive experience, particularly in the first years of life. It is a measure of our ignorance that we do not know what secular changes are occurring in the musical exchanges between parents and young children; we do not even know how the character of such exchanges influences the musical future of children.

Developmental psychologists have participated in the general failure to examine social and larger cultural influences on the musical lives of children. The traditions of the field have put consideration of perceptual and cognitive development in first place and, with rare exception (Farnsworth, 1958, 1969, for example), musical development has not been seen as a social construction. Earlier work on auditory discrimination in children (Jeffrey, 1958) has been followed, more recently, with attempts to cast Piaget's epistemological net over the unsteady facts of mu-

sical development (Zimmerman, 1971; Serafine, 1979). A resurgence of interest in the study of memory for complicated musical materials in adults (Deutsch, 1978; Dowling, 1978) has led to a retrospective examination of the earlier work of the French group (Francés, 1958; Child, 1972; Zennatti, 1976; Teplov, 1966 [cited in Davies, 1978]) on memory for melody in children. The long-lasting gap in our information about musical development in children under six years of age (Petzold, at the first Symposium session, properly pointed out the technical difficulty of asking critical questions about musical concepts even of elementary school children) is slowly being closed (Kessen, Levine, and Wendrich, 1978), especially by the unique work of Gardner and his colleagues at Project Zero.

You have heard a splendid series of statements about how psychologists see the psychology of music in children and adults. In the display of results, social influences have been the unseen visitors. Children possess remarkable discriminatory abilities as early as the first year of life; for auditory, as for visual events, the receptive capacity of the infant seems in good working order. We need not teach the child how to see and to hear. But, while we rejoice in the headstart Providence has given us, we should attend to remarkable changes that take place over the first years of life—the emerging organization of tonal systems, the separation of continuous distributions (of frequency, for instance) into a limited number of categories, the role of familiarity in musical memory, and the changing information-processing abilities of human beings—to begin our research shopping list for the future. Somehow, by mechanisms we do not fully understand, but surely involving critical encounters with music, the receptive child becomes the organizing child.

James Mark Baldwin and the Evolution of Art

Baldwin was one of the founders of American psychology and a mover in the development of the field until his exile from Johns Hopkins in the first years of our century.

Partly because he spent his last twenty-five years abroad, partly because his ideas were washed over by the rising behavioristic tide, and partly because his prose is tough and demanding, Baldwin's direct influence on American psychology after 1910 was slight. However, Piaget read Baldwin's *Thought and Things* during his French tour just after World War I and took much of his basic theory back to Geneva for exploration in brilliant observations of children. It was Baldwin who invented the notion of genetic epistemology, who emphasized the central place of assimilation and accommodation, who speculated about the curious relation of play and imitation, who recognized that many of the classical problems of the philosophy of knowledge have empirical implications and empirical tests, and who saw the essential relation among evolution, development, and art. I will draw chiefly from his *Genetic Theory of Reality* to present several propositions that should counsel and guide us.

Constructivism and originality. Baldwin argued the principle that Piaget so persuasively illustrated for us later on—that the child at any moment is the result of an adaptation between the cognitive abilities he possesses and the problems that are posed by his environment. In a continual dialog, the child reaches out into the ambiguity of his surroundings with his present "theory of the world" and he is changed (he learns) according to the match between his theory and the way the world is. Thus, development is a continuous construction; each encounter the child has with the world is a new occasion for growth and, through such encounters, the child's knowledge develops, the mind constantly under revision.

> The child's originalities are in great part the new ways in which he finds his knowledge falling together in consequence of his attempts to act to advantage on what he already knows. (Baldwin, 1897, p. 99)

In a sense, the child can only learn to do what he is almost ready to do; he can only get to the next construction of mind by taking a short step from where he already is. The no-

tion of construction by adaptation has several more recent forms—the educational notion of "optimal lead," for example, or the attempts to understand figural and musical preference from an examination of stimulus-contained information. The task of the teacher, then, is to present the child with occasions that will pull him a small distance from where he currently is. Baldwin, incidentally, far more than Piaget, stresses the importance of imitation in providing the child with new modes of trying out his theories of the world. It should also be remarked, particularly as we think about the construction and organization of music, that the "reaching out" or "attempts to act" need not be, even in the first years of life, altogether motor or overt. The child almost certainly begins to organize the tonal sound that he encounters without necessarily performing any visible actions.

Accommodation and interest. Piaget follows Baldwin in asserting that no specific tuition or conditioning is necessary for the child to develop; the world contains enough properly graded problems, especially early on, for the child to develop without systematic social intervention. However, Piaget has put aside Baldwin's strong assertion that knowledge is only a part of the story of children's growth. Paired with knowledge there is always interest and the emergence of the child's patterns of interests is almost invariably the consequence of social interactions.

> Not only is [the child's] perception of the given data of sense subject to obscure influences of social suggestion and habit, but the body of meaning given to the data, indicating the direction of his interest, is shaped by social molds. (Baldwin, 1915, p. 36)

There are several elemental messages for developmental psychologists and music educators in Baldwin's commentary. First, the child's adaptation to the world is a socially guided adaptation; there are many courses along which the human mind can develop and the selection of developmental paths is a complexly determined cultural and social event. A purely cognitive theory, such as Piaget is sometimes accused of presenting,

357

will find Mozart in all of us. Baldwin believes that Mozart, like the rest of us, was a social construction as well as a cognitive one. He realizes that, even within the narrow realm of perception and cognition, direction and further development are biassed by the fact that the child tries out those cognitive moves "which he feels justified in expecting to hold for others to act on also" (Baldwin, 1897, p. 99). Second, development requires the evolution of interest and value as well as the evolution of knowledge. From birth on, interest and knowledge develop in parallel and they are united in two defining ways—in social exchange with valued humans and in art.

Logic and hyperlogic. Remember that Baldwin's proposals for genetic epistemology were resisted not only by his psychological colleagues (often because he was moving toward mind when they were moving toward behavior) but also by the contemporary community of philosophers. Baldwin was audacious enough to propose an empirical, a testable, theory of the origins of human knowledge; in short, he held that one could be toughminded and scientific about one of philosophy's favorite domains. Piaget has made the proposal commonplace and I remind you of Baldwin's scholarly credentials because he made another set of assertions about development that Piaget and, as far as I know, all subsequent commentators have ignored (perhaps because Baldwin was moving toward aesthetics while most of us were moving toward cognition).

He argues the case for the child developing through a period of prelogic to a period of logic, a story that Piaget has refined and documented. Baldwin, however, maintains that there is not only the critical step from prelogic to logic ("freedom *of* thought") that opens up vast new possibilities; there is another and further step from prelogic to hyperlogic ("freedom *from* thought") in which a new *informed intuition* is used to understand the world. For Baldwin, the reunion of cognition and intuition, of knowledge and interest, is best represented in works of art. In hyperlogicality, the self "reads its presence into the experience which is already enriched by the accretions of mediate process [here, Baldwin refers to all prior cognitive development], claiming to secure, by direct contemplation or intuition, the full realisation of the subjective meaning" (1915, p. 24).

> The synthesis we seek is not one to be welcomed as fulfilling the exigencies of logical and formal construction, but one to be recognized as bringing to light, in actual experience, a motive of reconciliation. (Baldwin, 1915, p. 210)

Baldwin was at pains to underscore two governing principles. First, he was not suggesting a developmental regression into some sort of mindless communication with nature or with art; he was pressed to avoid both "the abstract indefinite" and "the mystic immediate." The reconciliation of which he wrote always required the undergirdings of cognition, the structures of knowledge. But he was quick to add that a pure cognitive psychology was limited and limiting too, that some return must be made from the "formal and universal" to the "empirical and concrete"; science and practice must be joined in aesthetic interest.

Baldwin was constrained in defending his propositions about hyperlogicality because he had no sound evidence on the development of interest or informed aesthetic intuition comparable to the evidence he had gathered on cognitive development in children. The lack of empirical findings has hardly lessened over the intervening sixty years and Baldwin's proposals, right or wrong, are worth our trying to do for aesthetic development what he did for cognitive development—to find the settings and occasions in which we can begin to understand the child's construction of beauty.

For Baldwin, the prelogical-logical-hyperlogical pattern was a developmental one with each position requiring the foregoing one. I would like to propose that, perhaps for all education but surely for music education, the union of cognition and intuition that Baldwin describes can take place at any point in development. The components of interest and knowledge can be brought together in the infant's hearing of nursery songs or in the adolescent's jazz improvisations or in the

358

"middle-ager's" attempts to try the piano again. But Baldwin's requirements for such a comprehensible aesthetic event are strict; the appropriate level of the learner's knowledge must be joined with the appropriate level of the learner's interest in a setting that has, one way or another, cultural value. It seems to me that the happiest opportunity for cooperation between psychologists and music educators lies in the invention and study of such critical musical encounters.

The Child's Encounters with Music

The relocation of American music and Baldwin's speculations about the development of cognition and aesthetic interest join in pointing toward several occasions in the life of the child where we may gainfully combine skills and information to help Darwin with his problems about music. Throughout my summary statement of likely settings, I am guided by three propositions: The child brings cognitive competence and a pattern of interest to each encounter. He meets, in the encounter, a new problem to be solved. There is, in each encounter, an implicit or explicit cultural evaluation that will be communicated to the child.

The early social encounters. The musical exchange between parent and young child may be the model encounter for our consideration. The intonations of ordinary baby-talk aside, the melodic curve of conventional childish tunes is repetitious and short, the rhythmic patterns are vivid, and the interest and enthusiasm of the child in the social interaction cannot be doubted. (Our observations of the enthusiasm with which four- and five-month-old infants join a pitch-matching game with adults are persuasive evidence that knowledge and interest can meet at an early age.) I will not here argue that the nursery tune fulfills Baldwin's desire for "a motive of reconciliation;" he would surely say not. But the infantile conversation begins the process of music education—the child hears some of the customary tonal intervals and rhythms of the culture and he does so in a setting where high valuation of music is clearly shown. It is an old wise saw that children learn first for someone, then for some-

thing, then for themselves; the first musical encounters are opportunities for babies to see that the people they care about care about the special sounds of music.

Gardner has begun to reveal to us some of the complexities of music education in the child of two and three and four; he is working in a gold mine of opportunity and a desert of data. My guess is that by school age, most American children have formed perceptual schemata for the conventional intervals of Western music; they probably recognize a battery of rhythmic phrasings; they certainly have a storehouse of short tunes. What we need are observations on the circumstances under which the organization takes place, on the involvements of the child's interest that are relevant to his constructions, and in the ways in which he begins to evaluate music as a way of being with other people. In the absence of data, I assert my theoretical prejudice in proposing that the years before school are times of significant musical development and that the best present procedures to broaden musical experience are participation in sound production, a reflective and playful teacher, parallel-peer musical activity, and voice.

Encounters with the surrounding flood. American children are enwrapped by musical sound. From television set and sister's records, the child today hears more music in a year than most people heard in a lifetime before the 1920s. What does he thereby learn of music? We certainly do not know and it would seem to me in the best interests of musicians and music educators to find out. Is the repertory of melodic curves increased? Almost without doubt; toddlers sing television commercials. Is something learned about the dramatic "meaning" of musical phrases? Sure; all of us, including the children, recognize chase music, killer music, and kissing music. What it would be valuable to know as well is the degree to which personally noncontingent television and recording music separates the child from his own participation in music, makes music both external and out of his influence. What does it mean, cognitively, aesthetically, and evaluatively for a child to be taught, in his

359

first school encounters, music discernably less complicated than what he has heard for years on *The Rockford Files* or *Battlestar Galactica* or even the advertisements for beer? We would all guess that children listening to television, like most young people listening to fine rock, have not learned much about music at all; they have, at best, acquired a sense of "melody curve." But, television music has become today's Tafelmusik. We ignore it at the peril of our understanding.

The encounters with teachers of music. Here, whether in public schools or in the neighborhood music school, we meet the accumulated wisdom of devoted and skillful teachers and, in their presence, I should be silent. But let me presume to pose several questions that derive from my reading of Baldwin and Piaget. What is the theory or strategy of the child's *interest* that governs early school education in music? To what degree does music teaching demand the explication of verbal concepts that can be postponed and that interrupt the conversation between teacher and student or between student and student? To what degree are music lessons designed to represent comprehensible aesthetic events where knowledge, interest, and value come together?

Of course, even before school but unmistakably then, the culture's evaluation of music takes its toll. There is little hope that the teacher, in an hour or so a week, can persuade children that music is as important to the culture as reading (or recess, for that matter). And the burden is made heavier by the knowledge that, if the interest in music has not moved from its basis in respect and affection for the teacher to some internal personal reason by the third or fourth or fifth grade, the child will flee further formal music education. The culture lays a stiff tax on music educators.

The social evaluation of music. During the years that music teachers are trying to enlist the child's commitment to formed sounds, the child is busy working on who he is. A host of questions arise about the place of music in the definition of the child's sense of self. What are the gender markings of music, such as the earlier departure of males from formal music education and the infrequency of females in jazz and rock performance, or the continuing predominance of males in elite art-music ensembles? To what degree is music education, beyond what is required by the school, seen as a marker of social class or ethnic origin, with the implication for some children that music instruction is not for them. How do critically important friends communicate their valuation of music and its appropriate use, particularly in the years between twelve and eighteen when the resources of energy and cognitive development would plead for a concentration on aesthetic themes? To what degree do teachers of music subtly turn away the child of insufficient musical skill or duty? How do parents let children know their valuation of music?

Endings and Beginnings

At the first sessions, the music educators among us presented a long list of questions to the psychologists; for one, I have answered them by presenting a different list. Perhaps the recognition that will comfort us all is that becoming a musician is a textured process that brings together the biologically obligatory (for example, the universal imitation of tuned sounds) with the culturally elective (for example, the low demand in schools for musical competence). The music educator and the psychologist of music must be sensitive to the entire range that is contained between the biological and the cultural brackets; all children will recognize a tune, some children will code and remember harmonic variations, few children will listen to the insides of complicated music, and a precious fraction will achieve Baldwin's hyperlogic in music.

But take heart. Our ignorance is a measure of our concern and a measure of the importance of our shared task. Vygotsky, under the eye of Pavlov, as Baldwin was under the eye of Watson, escaped his usual restraint to tell us why we are here.

> Art is the organization of our future behavior. It is a requirement that may never be fulfilled but that forces us to strive beyond our life toward all that lies beyond it.

References

Aries, P. *Centuries of childhood: A social history of family life*. London: Cape, 1962.

Aristotle. *Politics*. B. Jowett (Trans.). Oxford: Clarendon, 1905.

Ayres, B. Effects of infants carrying practices on rhythm in music. *Ethos*, 1973, *1*, 387–404.

Baldwin, J. M. *Social and ethical interpretation in mental development: A study in social psychology*. New York: Macmillan, 1897.

_____. *Thought and things, or genetic logic* (3 vols.). New York: Macmillan, 1906, 1908, 1911.

_____. *Genetic theory of reality, being the outcome of genetic logic as issuing in the aesthetic theory of reality called pancalism*. New York: Putnam, 1915.

Berger, P. L., and T. Luckmann. *The social construction of reality*. New York: Doubleday, 1966.

Brubacher, J. S. *A history of the problems of education*. New York: McGraw-Hill, 1947.

Butts, R. F. *A cultural history of Western education*. New York: McGraw-Hill, 1955.

Child, I. L. Esthetics. *Annual Review of Psychology*, 1972, *23*, 669–694.

Darwin, C. *The expression of the emotions in man and animals*. New York: Appleton, 1896.

_____. *The descent of man and selection in relation to sex*. New York: Modern Library, 1936.

Davies, J. B. *The psychology of music*. London: Hutchinson, 1978.

Deutsch, D. The psychology of music. *Handbook of perception*, Vol. 10. New York: Academic, 1978.

Dowling, W. J. Scale and contour: Two components of a theory of memory for melodies. *Psychological Review*, 1978, *85*, 341–354.

Farnsworth, P. R. *The social psychology of music*. Ames: Iowa State University Press, 1969.

Galton, F. *Hereditary genius, an inquiry into its laws and consequences*. London: Macmillan, 1869.

Gardner, H. E., L. Davidson, and P. McKernon. *The acquisition of song: A developmental approach*. Paper presented at the Ann Arbor Symposium, August 1979.

Hall, G. S. *Adolescence*. New York: Appleton, 1904.

Kessen, W. The American child and other cultural inventions. *American Psychologist*, in press.

Kessen, W., J. Levine, and K. A. Wendrich. The imitation of pitch in infants. *Infant Behavior and Development*, 1979, *2*, 93–99.

Kreitler, H., and S. Kreitler. *The psychology of art*. Durham, North Carolina: Duke University Press, 1972.

Mann, T. *Doctor Faustus: The life of the German composer Adrian Leverkuhn as told by a friend*. H. T. Lowe-Porter (Trans.). New York: Knopf, 1948.

Mencken, H. L. *A Mencken hrestomathy*. New York: Knopf, 1949.

Petzold, R. G. *Child development*. Paper presented at the Ann Arbor Symposium, October 1978.

Pflederer, M. Conservation laws applied to the development of musical intelligence. *Journal of Research in Music Education*, 1967, *15*, 215–223.

Serafine, M. L. A measure of meter conservation in music, based on Piaget's theory. *Genetic Psychology Monographs*, 1979, *99*, 185–229

Steiner, G. *In Bluebeard's castle: Some notes towards the redefinition of culture*. New Haven, Connecticut: Yale University Press, 1971.

Vygotsky, L. S. *The psychology of art* (Scripta Technica, Inc., trans.). Cambridge, Massachusetts: M.I.T. Press, 1971. (Originally published, 1925).

Zimmerman, M. P. *Musical characteristics of children*. Washington, D.C.: Music Educators National Conference, 1971.

Response

Robert G. Petzold

Over the years, either as observers or participants, we have become familiar with a variety of events that appear to share at least two common characteristics. These events range from convention or symposium programs through awards ceremonies and concert programs to races of humans, horses, or Hondas. First, each of these events has an ending that occurs either sooner or later than we had anticipated, or possibly at just the right time. Secondly, some thing or some person occupies the position of providing that ending. Occasionally the program is carefully planned so a variety of trivial events leads into the climax. Since this symposium program was not "orchestrated" so as to build toward any major climax, my position is much like that of the horse that finished last in a field of twenty-four! After three full days and nights of information receiving, processing, and sharing, the least that I can do is keep my response as brief as possible.

William Kessen began his paper with a quote from Aristotle and then briefly considered certain antecedents leading to continuities and discontinuities with respect to the utility and necessity of music in contemporary American culture. Historical evidence, from ancient times to the present century, supports the notion that members of a society (whether the political institutions of that society were aristocratic, autocratic, democratic, or theocratic) were somehow divided into at least two general classes; those in positions of power and authority (the "haves") and those who enjoyed only the privilege of tending to the wants and needs of the leaders (the "have-nots"). At certain times, a middle group of "almost-haves" emerged as a necessary bridging between the top and the bottom.

You will also recall that Plato's influence upon Western thought and ideals was powerful even through the eighteenth and nineteenth centuries, especially in certain positions he took with respect to education in general and music in particular. In his *Republic* he devised an ideal state, essentially aristocratic, in which all individuals were subordinated to the state. Reflecting the reality of his times, he divided people into three classes: the masses who did the work, the courageous and physically fit who did the fighting, and the most intellectually capable who ruled as philosopher-kings. His differentiated educational plans were devised only for the warriors and the ruling class, and his views on music were given within that context. The theoretical study of music as an intellectual discipline in the preparation of the philosopher-kings strongly influenced the thinking of educational theorists and practitioners for centuries.

Historical evidence also points to fairly early beginnings of the tripartite division of music consumers/producers mentioned by Kessen, suggesting that there is a close relationship between the kinds of music and the nature of musical involvement and the social/economic/political class of members of society. Wiley Hitchcock in his *Music in the United States: A Historical Introduction* discards the familiar colloquialisms of classical, popular, and folk in favor of the *cultivated* and *vernacular* traditions of music. At various points in history, these two traditions almost merge. At other times, they appear to diverge sharply, giving rise to numerous educational and musical problems. This discontinuity does exist today and it is important that we, as music educators, recognize the impact this has upon the child's musical "vocabulary." There is evidence that music teachers are modifying both the content of music programs and their teaching strategies to better accommodate the kinds of information and music skills children are bringing to the classroom from their everyday encounters with music. The problem is that we are not always able to identify precisely the nature of the information and skills possessed by the children. Perhaps this is because we have become accustomed to thinking like adults and professional musicians and encounter difficulty as we try to modify our expectations, thus all too often erring on the side of failing to expect enough.

Throughout this symposium we have heard frequent reference to the conventional intervals of Western music or to the dependence upon our traditional diatonic system for developing test stimuli to examine some aspect of pitch perception, musical perception, musical expectation, musical or cognitive structures, and so on, as though there might be something wrong with research findings that are based upon our system of tonality. From time to time we have also heard from individuals who appear to favor deemphasizing this Western European musical tradition in order that children have an opportunity to experience ethnic music that may use some other kind of tonal system. In light of Kessen's observations, it seems that this is an issue in need of further discussion and clarification. The all-pervasive influence of the Western European musical tradition upon cultures all over the world has so diluted and polluted the indigenous music of a particular culture that it has reached the point where this "original" music has all but disappeared. What remains are the archaeological artifacts of that ethnic music, carefully protected and nurtured by a dedicated few who are kept busy "fanning the coals of a dying flame." There are, of course, those examples of the classical musical traditions of India, Indonesia, and elsewhere that appear to be alive and flourishing and consequently are an integral part of those cultures. However, I join with Kessen in cautiously suggesting that American music educators may wish to give more attention to the kinds of music representative of the various subcultures of American society that may help us deal more effectively with the culturally different children and young people in our classrooms. It might be wise to postpone exposure to the classical musical traditions of other cultures until young people have acquired a better understanding of the traditions of our own culture.

A final observation. Kessen raises the issues of the place of music in the definition of the child's sense of self, as well as the difficulty encountered when busy and beleaguered music teachers try to convince children that music is important. There is, fortunately for all of us, no time to discuss the interrelationships of motivation, attitudes, and value structures as these have implications for music teaching and learning. Many music educators have conducted research relating to the musical attitudes, preferences, and tastes of children and adolescents. When this literature is examined, it seems clear that young people have strong, positive attitudes toward music and view it as significant in their lives. The difficulty, as expressed by certain music educators, appears to be with the *kinds* of music children value at a particular stage of development. We may even be concerned with their apparent "lack of taste," with their changing attitudes toward school music, and with the observable decline of the boys' interest in music that seems

to occur at an alarmingly early age, as well as a variety of other concerns that emerge when we begin to consider the goals and purposes of music education. This is not to suggest that you are not already aware of the situation and, as professionals, involved in doing something to effect a change.

We know that attitudes are learned, emotionally toned predispositions to act in a consistent way toward persons, objects, ideas, and situations. We also know that groups and individuals with whom students interact influence their attitude development. Every individual in society is a member of a small, face-to-face *primary group* having a core of common attitudes that hold the members of that group together. This begins with the family, but later changes to a peer group where conformity as a condition of belonging may necessitate attitude change or modification. An individual also has *reference groups*, or individuals, with which he or she identifies and which the individual uses as a standard to judge the adequacy of his or her performance. The music teacher can, and must, serve as a reference person for the student if we hope to counter, at least in part, the very strong influence of peer groups. Precisely how this is to be accomplished is, as you might have guessed, not entirely clear but does warrant our consideration. Many speakers have already suggested that the distinction between "their music" and "our music" may be creating in the minds of many students an idea of school music as something unrelated to their needs and interests. However, no one has recommended (nor should they) abdicating our responsibility toward maintaining the integrity of music within the curriculum in order to provide the learners with experiences that are restricted to "their music."

I would like to close with this observation. You may recall that Roger Shepard, as he wondered why it has taken psychologists so long to come around to a musical approach to music, referred to data collected over sixty years ago by Seashore that showed psychologists to be appreciably less musical than even a random sample of the general population. The data cited dealt *only* with "vividness of

363

tonal imagery," leading Shepard to speculate, facetiously of course, that a profession
tending to select for verbal fluency tends to
select against musical sophistication. Our experience over the two sessions of this sym-

posium clearly shows that *our* psychologists
exhibited not only a high level of verbal fluency, but also a high level of musical sophistication.

Report of the
Needs and Issues Team
for Symposium Session II

Edgar M. Turrentine

In November of 1978 Edwin Gordon described music education as a profession in
search of a discipline. And during this symposium, Asahel Woodruff described music
education as one of those messy educational
problems. They were being dramatic but
they were pointing out that music education,
as any profession, constantly needs to examine and update the foundations on which its
discipline is based and to face its problems
with enthusiasm and all the resources it can
muster. This symposium has reinforced the
need for doing so continuously and using
any and all contributions from other disciplines.

Music education cannot function in isolation; it must establish linkage with other disciplines. Communication is the key, and this
symposium emphasizes what can be accomplished with intensive communication between disciplines. These are the two overriding needs and issues: ongoing activity
and dissemination of its results.

At this point it would seem appropriate to
review specific issues or at least some of
them raised by the psychologists. Dowling
asked at what age are children ready to benefit from musical training? Several of the psychologists hinted at an answer, but the question should be dealt with head-on. In his research he pointed out that musical training
in the first graders triggered improvements
in auditory perceptual abilities that would
not occur in normal maturation for at least
another two years, and there is every reason
to believe that once the first graders had
learned the cognitive skills, those skills
would generalize to other areas of the child's
formative life. This suggests the importance
of determining critical learning periods and
was seconded by Woodruff's suggestion of
sequencing.

Shepard pointed out that the range of individual differences, especially in pitch perception, is a dynamic factor and demands the concern of the music educator. If it is important to individualize instruction, then it is particularly important to be aware of perceptual differences. The utilization of musical tasks in cyclical music investigations is the only way we will determine how the mind responds to music. Whether the extreme variances in pitch perception as reported by Shepard are genetic or acquired, they exist and must be dealt with in instructional models.

LaBerge posed several questions: What is the optimal size of the perceptual unit for the learner? What is the effect of different instructional strategies on the learner's ability to grasp larger and larger units? What is the effect of different levels of language and instructional strategies based on these levels on the acquisition of motor skill and on expressive performers?

Siegel pointed out that music educators must not only teach students how to produce music, but also how to hear it, in other words, what to listen for. This suggests that an identification of those attributes is in order. This also implies that an information-processing approach is more compatible to the interests and concerns of music educators than the psychoacoustic approach. Thus, an identification of that information to be processed is necessary before we determine how it is processed. Theory or theories then can be developed which psychologists and musicians can study cooperatively.

Deutsch presented interesting research data regarding differences between actual and perceived pitch patterns. The studies confirmed the notion that separate brain mechanisms determine what pitch we hear and where the sound appears to be coming from. The studies also seem to support the principles of proximity and good continuation espoused by Max Wertheimer. In addition to stressing the existence of substantial differences in how simple tonal sequences are perceived, Deutsch states that it would appear that both hemispheres of the brain play important though different roles in music perception.

Walker provided the model of the hedgehog with which to examine music teaching. The hedgehog has inspired what Walker refers to as the psychological complexity and preference theory. This theory postulates that for each person there is a level of optimal complexity, at which psychological events that are either simpler or more complex will be less preferred. The hedgehog also has implications for motivation in what Walker termed habituation. The hedgehog view of learning is: After substantial learning has occurred that which once seemed psychologically complex seems much simpler. The hedgehog view of education is that if either learning or teaching is either dull or frustrating somebody is doing it wrong. How can we keep music education interesting?

Dr. Brown has proposed an alternative set of value claims to those currently embraced by music educators for what music consists of and what music learning consists of, which raises issues at every level of the curriculum from the philosophical to the operational. Several of these issues have to do with the fit or lack of fit of linguistics structures and musical structures. Other issues raise the question of what instruction would entail, how an evaluation might be carried out, and who would be most qualified to teach music. No matter which set of value claims are embraced, the issue of how music works, its affective power, and how education can enhance this power in the student's experience is central.

One striking issue, arising from Day's report, has to do with the differences in retention according to shallow or deep teaching cues. Careful study of the affects on learning of verbal or other cues that emphasize more local or more global features of music may well be the most productive that researchers could engage in.

Day's conclusions that relate directly to music testing should be explored very carefully. She suggests that a person's self-rated ability affects performance on music tests in quantitative ways, while his or her assumed cognitive pattern has qualitative effects on performance. Further, a person's cognitive pattern is a good predictor of whether or not long-term music training is likely to result in improved test performance. "What exactly do standardized aptitude tests measure," she asks, "level of innate musical talent, or general patterns of cognitive structure?" If an individual does poorly on such a test it may have as much or more to do with the test design or the person's cognitive pattern as with music ability. As to achievement, different children may require different pathways to reach the same level. Some require more linguistic representations, while others thrive on non-linguistic styles of learning. These notions deserve serious considerations as efforts are made to create tests and use tests in ways that reflect more sophisticated knowledge about this mode of instruction.

Woodruff pointed out that learning is doing and that we ought to describe specifically what the student is doing. In other words we need to identify psychologically, physiologically, and musicologically what one does when behaving musically. He further suggested that we ought to plan a curriculum sequence in holistic music from simple instances to complex instances, taking advantage of the innate attractiveness of whole music at all levels. This, in contrast to our present-day set of courses limited to atomistic elements of music, which are dull, hard to learn in that isolated form, and difficult to integrate into the world of whole music.

Gardner pointed out that all cognition is of a piece, a cross range of materials and subject matter with equal strength and regularity and that various symbol systems may include features special to each. Given this, three questions can be postulated: Which aspects of development are particular to music; which aspects relate to other domains; and which aspects seem intrinsic to the range of cognitive activities? He raised another intriguing question: To what extent does the acquisition of a song reflect general development?

Raynor's multidimensional theory of motivation is many faceted in its implications.

Some of the more intriguing possibilities for consideration are: Recognition of the distance between teacher and student values requires the teacher at every level, elementary through college, to reexamine course content and instructional objectives to try to narrow the distance between past and present values. Awareness of some possible lessons may be reason for the identity crisis and consequent malaise that seem to be affecting teachers in midcareer these days and suggests that MENC investigate ways teachers within our profession can find new goals based on values that are different from those they have been building or that no longer provide an adequate sense of self. Additional research into the relationship between the negative and positive motivation and students' willingness to engage in music-related activities and into applications of understanding of motivating conditions and personality dispositions in organizing the learning environment are needed.

Kessen pointed out the great change in the social and cultural location of music. Because of this change two questions are pertinent: How does one get children on the path of musical development, and after getting the child on the path, what should he acquire?

Woodruff's five-point linkage system seems to serve as a summation and generalization of these issues. The five points are: (1) to identify the major molar-molecular levels of behavior we must consider in education, their unique operational rules, and the way they affect each other; (2) to get education properly related to the major molar-molecular levels of behavior as to subject matter of content, learning processes, and teaching processes; (3) to identify a workable division of tasks between educators and specialists in supporting fields; (4) to get other disciplines related to their appropriate aspects of the additional program; and (5) to get the right psychologists working on the different parts of the educational program.

We recognize that this symposium has been a process of bringing the tip of the iceberg into view. Therefore, we recommend that Music Educators National Conference lend all its resources to addressing the whole concern of the applications of psychology to the teaching and learning of music. We urge the president of MENC to establish a task force for developing a formal agenda for a detailed identification, clarification, and delimiting of the needs in developing theories of teaching and learning.

Summary

Wilbert J. McKeachie

We talked several times about the linkages between psychology and music education, and I think one thing that psychologists have been impressed with is that you have come a long way in bridging that gap. We were very impressed with the sophistication of music researchers; there is no doubt that you are able to keep up with what we are doing. I think you have seen that at least a few psychologists have at least a reasonable cultural awareness and understanding of music, but they may not be as familiar with what teachers are actually doing in teaching music. To be productive in applying psychological concepts to music education, we probably need to get a better understanding of what actually goes on. We have a lot of concepts in psychology, but we may be throwing out some of the wrong ones.

Related to this linkage between psychology and music education there is perhaps some thought on the part of both sides that the growth should be from psychology research to music education. I think one of the things that the conference has demonstrated is that it is a two-way process and that music education has a good deal to contribute to psychology. What we saw happen between the two sessions indicates that you are able to stimulate psychologists and pose problems that cause them to do things that they wouldn't have thought of doing otherwise and that do have significance for psychology.

It is no news to you that it is important to individualize, but one of the things we have been getting an increasing awareness of is that while it may not be possible to completely individualize instruction in some situations, we can make some improvements by thinking about different groups of learners. We have talked about left-handers, about language-bound, about left-brained people, and so forth, and I think these kinds of conceptions of looking at differences in groups of learners can be helpful if they encourage you to think about how to reach this other group of learners. But be cautious. Ever since people have started thinking about human nature they have been trying to dichotomize people into extroverts, introverts, bright, stupid, what have you. No system that puts people into two camps works well. Typically, these dichotomies may have some truths—we still use the concept of introversion and extroversion—but people are simply much more complicated than that. To a degree that a grouping concept gives you the sense you have the answer, you are going to look at left-brained people versus right-brained people, for example, and that is going to be too simple. It is probably going to get you into more trouble than good. So I think the important thing is to recognize that these groupings indicate that there is no one best way to teach. Whatever way you teach, you are probably going to reach some students better than you get through to other students, and that is an important thing to realize. For one thing, it cuts down on your sense of failure because you aren't getting through to everyone. It is also important because it suggests that you need to have a repertoire of skills and alternative strategies for coping with these differences and being more effective with larger numbers of students.

One of the things that comes through as you look at teaching from a cognitive psychology point of view is that we are always teaching at several levels. I think that is important in any field. At the same time that you are teaching students how to read music, how to produce certain pictures or certain rhythms, you also are teaching schema or structures. These structures are very important in determining what is interesting to students and also important in determining how well they retain the individual elements of the schemas. We are also teaching in a third level; we are teaching something about music as it relates to the person, to the student's relationship to the teacher, and to other students in the classroom. Now this kind of multilevel approach to teaching does not mean that we should neglect the basic elements. It is still important that people be drilled on certain things, but it is important in thinking about the function of drill—not looking just at its function in teaching pitch, but thinking about what this does to the student's motivation and sense of competence. It is related to the concept that Day introduced of deep versus surface processing. At the same time that you are drilling on something, are you also getting the student to analyze some of the characteristics of the music so that they relate to the larger whole?

Since we are building schemes whenever we teach, sequencing is probably important, and as you can not build a new structure from nothing—people are not simply blank slates—you are always building from existing structures. Developmental research suggests that different structures can emerge at different stages; to some extent this may be simply a function of growth and maturation, but it also is a function of the way previous structures are formed. We saw that in Shepard's look at the dimensions of pitch perception and we also saw it in Gardner's paper. But I think one of the things that you may feel, if you get strongly oriented toward a sequential approach, is the notion that if we did not get it done by age eight or age twelve or something, it is too late, and we should give up. I think that cognitive theory would say that it is never too late. There probably are periods when things go more easily or faster, but one of the really exciting things about the revolution in psychology, which we have learned from education research, is that good teachers in any field are already fairly close to being as effective as it is possible to be. We have a long tradition of education and there has been cultural transmission from one generation to another so that the best teachers are, we are quite sure, very close to doing the best that anybody can do, no matter how good our science of education gets. Then what we need to do is learn something about how these good teachers are performing, and what science can do is give us better ways of analyzing and understanding some of the things that good teachers probably did intuitively. My hope would be that as we become better at identifying some of the basic processes that it is not so much that we are going to improve those good teachers as that we can move the level of the average teacher closer to that of the good teacher.

Finally, I would like to stress that we have here an important developmental step in building long-term relationships between psychology and music. I am impressed by the new journal *Psychomusicology*, which is an important marker as well. What I believe has happened for us, at least in psychology and I hope from the other side, is that we have made some friendships that will improve the ease of communication, because people will no longer be just names in the journals. I think we have developed here a sense of mutual respect and support for efforts in this area.

Official Participants

Panel (Psychologists)

ROGER BROWN, John Lindsley Professor of Psychology in Memory of William James, Harvard University, Cambridge, Massachusetts

RUTH S. DAY, Associate Professor, Department of Psychology, Duke University, Durham, North Carolina

DIANA DEUTSCH, Associate Research Psychologist, Center for Human Information Processing, Department of Psychology, University of California, San Diego, La Jolla

W. JAY DOWLING, Associate Professor, Program in Psychology and Human Development, University of Texas at Dallas, Richardson

HOWARD E. GARDNER, Senior Research Associate and Co-Director of Harvard Project Zero, School of Education, Harvard University, Cambridge, Massachusetts (Session II)

WILLIAM KESSEN, Eugene Higgins Professor and Chairman, Department of Psychology, and Professor of Pediatrics, Yale University, New Haven, Connecticut

DAVID LABERGE, Professor, Department of Psychology, University of Minnesota, Minneapolis

JOEL O. RAYNOR, Associate Professor, Department of Psychology, State University of New York at Buffalo

FRANK RESTLE, Professor, Department of Psychology, Indiana University, Bloomington (Session I)

ROGER N. SHEPARD, Professor, Department of Psychology, Stanford University, Stanford, California

JANE A. SIEGEL, Psychologist, Toronto Board of Education, Ontario, Canada

EDWARD L. WALKER, Professor of Psychology (retired), University of Michigan, Ann Arbor

ASAHEL D. WOODRUFF, Emeritus Professor of Educational Psychology, University of Utah, Salt Lake City

370

Panel (Music Educators)

HENRY L. CADY, Professor and Chairperson, Department of Music, University of Delaware, Newark

JAMES C. CARLSEN, Professor, School of Music, University of Washington, Seattle

EDWIN E. GORDON, Professor of Music (holds Carl E. Seashore chair for research in music education), Temple University, Philadelphia

R. DOUGLAS GREER, Associate Professor of Education, Departments of Music Education, Special Education, and Psychology, Teachers College, Columbia University, New York City

STEVEN K. HEDDEN, Associate Professor of Music Education, School of Music, University of Iowa, Iowa City

JACK J. HELLER, Professor, Music Department, University of Connecticut, Storrs

GERARD L. KNIETER, Professor of Music and Dean of the College of Fine and Applied Arts, University of Akron, Ohio

ROBERT G. PETZOLD, Professor of Music and Education, School of Education, University of Wisconsin-Madison

ROBERT G. SIDNELL, Dean, Division of Fine Arts, Stephen F. Austin State University, Nacogdoches, Texas

MALCOLM J. TAIT, Kulas Professor of Music and Director of Music Education, Department of Music, Case Western Reserve University, Cleveland

DAVID BRIAN WILLIAMS, Associate Professor, Music Department, Illinois State University, Normal

MARILYN P. ZIMMERMAN, Visiting Professor of Music Education, College of Music, Temple University, Philadelphia

Needs and Issues Team

WILLIAM S. ENGLISH, Professor and Chairman, Division of Music Education/Therapy, Arizona State University, Tempe

RICHARD M. GRAHAM, Professor and Director of Music Therapy Programs, Department of Music, University of Georgia, Athens

CHARLES R. HOFFER, Professor, School of Music, Indiana University, Bloomington

MARY E. HOFFMAN, Associate Professor of Music Education, School of Music, University of Illinois, Urbana

EUNICE BOARDMAN MESKE, Professor of Music Education, School of Music, University of Wisconsin-Madison

BENNETT REIMER, John W. Beattie Professor and Chairman of Music Education, Northwestern University, Evanston, Illinois

EDGAR M. TURRENTINE, Professor of Music Education, Departments of Music and Music Education, University of Minnesota, Minneapolis

Dissemination Team

BARBARA ANDRESS, Professor, Department of Music, Arizona State University, Tempe

WARREN BENSON, Professor of Composition, Eastman School of Music, University of Rochester, New York (Session I)

VICTOR BORDO, Coordinator of Music, Ann Arbor Public Schools, Michigan

MERRILL K. BRADSHAW, Composer-in-Residence, Brigham Young University, Provo, Utah

WARRICK L. CARTER, Coordinator, Music Program, College of Cultural Studies, Governors State University, Park Forest South, Illinois

DON CORBETT, Associate Professor, Department of Music Education, Wichita State University, Kansas

MICHAEL GEORGE, Music Supervisor, Wisconsin Department of Public Instruction, Madison

EDWIN E. HEILAKKA, Director, Division of Music Education, School District of Philadelphia

371

NATALIE HINDERAS, Professor, College of Music, Temple University, Philadelphia

SALLY MONSOUR, Professor, Department of Music, Georgia State University, Atlanta

MARY C. REED, Office of the Chief Deputy Superintendent, Los Angeles County Superintendent of Schools, Downey, California

CARROLL A. RINEHART, Coordinator, Elementary Music, Tucson Unified School District, Arizona

JAMES A. STANDIFER, Professor and Chairman of the Department of Music Education, School of Music, University of Michigan, Ann Arbor

LOUIS G. WERSEN, Director (retired), Division of Music Education, School District of Philadelphia

Administration and Staff

BARBARA J. ALVAREZ, Graduate Student Assistant, School of Music, University of Michigan, Ann Arbor

JOHN AQUINO, Director of Publications, MENC, Reston, Virginia (Session I)

DALE E. BAER, Graduate Student Assistant, School of Music, University of Michigan, Ann Arbor

MALCOLM E. BESSOM, Director of Publications, MENC, Reston, Virginia (Session II)

ALVIN C. EURICH (special consultant), President, Academy for Educational Development, New York City

VICTOR E. HEBERT, Graduate Student Assistant, School of Music, University of Michigan, Ann Arbor (Session II)

PAUL R. LEHMAN (project director), Associate Dean, School of Music, University of Michigan, Ann Arbor

JAMES A. MASON (chairman of the symposium), MENC President, Professor of Music, Brigham Young University, Provo, Utah

WILBERT J. MCKEACHIE (special consultant), Professor of Psychology and Director, Center for Research on Learning and Teaching, University of Michigan, Ann Arbor

CHARLES O. MOODY, Director of Development, MENC, Reston, Virginia

JUDITH MURPHY (writer of the interpretive report on the symposium), New York City

EVELYN SPERRY, Graduate Student Assistant, School of Music, University of Michigan, Ann Arbor (Session II)

JOHN SPERRY, Graduate Student Assistant, School of Music, University of Michigan, Ann Arbor (Session II)

DAVID G. TOVEY, Graduate Student Assistant, School of Music, University of Michigan, Ann Arbor (Session I)

372